Introduction
to the Mystery of
the Church

THOMISTIC RESSOURCEMENT SERIES

Volume 3

SERIES EDITORS

Matthew Levering, *Mundelein Seminary*

Thomas Joseph White, OP, *Dominican House of Studies*

EDITORIAL BOARD

Serge-Thomas Bonino, OP, *Institut Catholique de Toulouse*

Lawrence Dewan, OP, *Dominican College of Ottawa*

Gilles Emery, OP, *University of Fribourg*

Reinhard Hütter, *Duke University*

Bruce Marshall, *Southern Methodist University*

Emanuel Perrier, OP, *Dominican Studium, Toulouse*

Richard Schenk, OP, *Katholische Universität Eichstätt-Ingolstadt*

Kevin White, *The Catholic University of America*

Introduction to the Mystery of the Church

BENOÎT-DOMINIQUE DE LA SOUJEOLE, OP

Translated by Michael J. Miller

The Catholic University of America Press
Washington, D.C.

Original French edition: *Introduction au mystère de l'Église*
(copyright © Parole et Silence, 2006), in the series Bibliothèque
de la Revue thomiste, edited by Fr. Serge-Thomas Bonino, OP.

Copyright © 2014
The Catholic University of America Press
All rights reserved
The paper used in this publication meets the minimum requirements
of American National Standards for Information Science—
Permanence of Paper for Printed Library Materials,
ANSI Z39.48-1984.
∞
Library of Congress Cataloging-in-Publication Data
La Soujeole, Benoît-Dominique de, 1955–
 [Introduction au mystère de l'Église. English]
Introduction to the mystery of the Church / Fr. Benoît-Dominique
de La Soujeole, OP ; translated by Michael J. Miller.
 pages cm. — (Thomistic ressourcement series ; Volume 3)
 Includes bibliographical references and index.
 ISBN 978-0-8132-2960-7 (pbk : alk. paper) 1. Church.
 2. Catholic Church—Doctrines. I. Title.
 BX1746.L2313 2014
 262'.7—dc23   2014005419

Contents

Abbreviations   xix
Preface to the English Edition   xxiii
Preface to the Original Edition   xxv

General Introduction   1

Part One: Theology of Sources: Description of the Church

Chapter 1: Images of the Church and the Kingdom of God   45
  I. Images of the Church   45
    a. Symbolic language   45
    b. Biblical images of the Church   47
      1. Rural images   47
        The flock and the shepherd (or pastor) / 47
        God's field / 47
      2. Social images   47
        The building / 47
        Family life / 48
  II. The kingdom of God (*Lumen gentium* 5)   49
    a. The image of the kingdom of God   49
      1. The basis for the image   49
      2. The content of the image   50
      3. The data of biblical theology   51
        The two major currents of the Old Testament / 51
        The synoptics / 52

4. The data of Vatican II	53
b. The current problem resulting from religious pluralism	54
1. Summary of the moderate position	54
2. The most recent magisterial formulations	55
Conclusion	58
Bibliography	59

Chapter 2: The Church Is the Body of Christ — 61

The order in which to study the three themes	61
"Body of Christ," "Mystical Body of Christ"	64
I. The Pauline data	65
a. The theology of salvation according to St. Paul	65
b. The theology of the Church, the Body of Christ	67
1. The major letters	67
The First Letter to the Corinthians / 67	
The Letter to the Romans / 70	
2. The captivity letters	71
The Letter to the Colossians / 71	
The Letter to the Ephesians / 72	
3. Two complementary clarifications	73
The "plērōma" / 74	
The Church as Bride of Christ / 75	
c. Conclusion concerning the Pauline data	77
II. The data of Tradition	78
a. The Fathers	78
1. The apostolic Fathers	80
2. The Alexandrians	81
3. The beginnings of Greek patristic literature	82
St. Irenaeus / 82	
St. Athanasius / 84	
4. The beginnings of Latin patristic literature	86
St. Cyprian / 86	
5. The beginnings of Greek High Patristic literature	87
St. Hilary / 87	
St. John Chrysostom / 89	
6. The Greek Nicene and post-Nicene period	90
St. Cyril of Alexandria / 90	

Contents

7. The Latin post-Nicene period	92
St. Augustine / 92	
8. Summary of the patristic data	95
b. The medieval data: St. Thomas Aquinas	96
1. Overall explanation	98
The mystery of the Savior: The hypostatic union / 98	
The first consequence for the assumed humanity / 98	
The second consequence for the assumed humanity / 98	
2. Particular points	99
The metaphor of the Head (*ST* III, q. 8, art. 1) / 99	
The efficiency of grace (*ST* III, q. 8, art. 5) / 99	
The question of the members of the Church (*ST* III, q. 8, art. 3) / 102	
3. Particular observations	103
The instrumental causality of Christ's humanity / 103	
The complexity of the Mystical Body / 105	
The twofold influence of the Head (*ST* III, q. 8, art. 6) / 106	
4. Conclusion on St. Thomas	107
c. The modern rediscovery of the Mystical Body	111
1. The schema *De Ecclesia* of Vatican I	112
The overall structure of the document / 113	
Some observations / 117	
2. The Encyclical *Mystici Corporis Christi*	118
The elaboration of the notion of Mystical Body / 118	
The complexity of the ecclesial being / 120	
d. The outcome at Vatican II	122
1. *Lumen gentium* 7: Biblical theology	122
2. *Lumen gentium* 8: Speculative precisions	122
Lumen gentium 8, §1: The unity of the ecclesial being / 122	
Lumen gentium 8, §2: The unicity of the ecclesial being / 123	
3. *Lumen gentium* 8, §3: The moral aspect	130
Conclusion	131
Bibliography	133
Chapter 3: The Church Is the Temple of the Spirit	**140**
Holy Spirit or Spirit of Christ?	140
The doctrine of the different ages of salvation	143

The explicit proclamation of the divinity of the Holy Spirit	145
I. The Church, Temple of the Holy Spirit, in Scripture	146
a. The image of the Temple in Scripture	146
b. The Church, Temple of the Holy Spirit	149
The Holy Spirit raises up ministers / 156	
The Holy Spirit pours out his gifts / 156	
The Holy Spirit, baptism, and Eucharist / 156	
c. Conclusion of this scriptural section	156
II. The Church, Temple of the Spirit, in Tradition	157
a. The patristic data	157
1. Before the fourth century: The Holy Spirit *in and through* the Church	158
2. After the fourth century: The Holy Spirit *and* the Church	165
3. Note concerning the anthropological basis	171
b. Tradition after the patristic era	175
1. St. Thomas Aquinas	175
The Holy Spirit, principle of life and movement / 176	
The Holy Spirit, principle of unity / 177	
Conclusion concerning St. Thomas / 181	
2. The Counter-Reformation	184
3. The contemporary ecclesiological renewal	185
4. The teaching of Vatican II (*Lumen gentium*)	187
The Trinitarian presentation of the Church / 187	
The Spirit of unity / 189	
The life-giving Spirit / 190	
Conclusion	191
Bibliography	194
Chapter 4: The Church Is the People of God	**199**
A note on biblical vocabulary	201
I. The People of God in Scripture	204
a. The People of Israel	204
1. Similarities and specific features of Israel	204
2. Basis for the similarities and the specific characteristics	206
Election / 207	

Contents

ix

      Vocation / 207
      Covenant / 207
   3. Three fundamental titles   208
      The individual as priest, prophet, and king / 208
      The community as priest, prophet, and king / 209
      A plan of communal salvation / 210
      Equality and inequality in the People of God / 210
      The universality of the promised salvation / 210
  b. The Church, the new People of God   211
   1. The continuities and discontinuities with Israel   212
   2. The radical novelty of the Church   213
   3. Priest, prophet, and king in the New Testament   214
      The meaning of the OT and its fulfillment by
      the NT / 216
      Similarities and dissimilarities between Israel
      and the Church / 216
      The social structure of salvation / 216
      The title "citizen" of this People / 217
II. The data of Tradition   217
  a. Tradition in biblical theology   217
   1. The Church Fathers   217
   2. Tradition after the patristic era   222
      St. Thomas Aquinas / 222
  b. Tradition in dogmatic theology   224
   1. The Fathers of the Church   224
   2. St. Thomas Aquinas   225
   3. Modern developments   227
      The classical analysis of society and ecclesiology / 227
      Summary definition of society / 233
      Trends in modern social thought / 235
      The principal social data of Vatican II / 240
      Conclusion concerning these modern
      developments / 241
  c. The teaching of Vatican II   242
   1. General presentation of the Tradition   242
   2. A new question: Israel, a present sign   243
   3. Developments of the theme   246
      Citizenship in this People (*LG* 10–12) / 246
      The extent of the People of God (*LG* 13–17) / 247

Conclusion	253
Two questions by way of recapitulation	253
a. The saying "No salvation outside the Church"	254
1. The scriptural foundation	254
2. Development by Tradition	255
The patristic contribution / 255	
The supplementary system of salvation / 256	
The medieval period / 257	
The modern period / 259	
The state of the question before Vatican II / 262	
Doctrinal recapitulation of Vatican II / 266	
b. The order and the distinction between clergy, laity, and consecrated religious	268
1. The classification "clergy vs. laity"	268
2. The distinction between cleric and layman	272
3. The situation of the consecrated religious	275
Bibliography	278
Chapter 5: Recapitulation: The Church Is a Mystery	**290**
I. The mystery-truth	292
a. The biblical data	292
b. The data of Tradition	294
1. The Fathers of the Church	294
2. Subsequent Tradition	295
c. The Church is a mystery	295
1. The Church as a whole is mysterious, an object of faith	295
2. The three levels of intelligibility of the Church	301
II. The mystery-reality	304
a. The origins of this term	305
b. The patristic tradition	307
c. The medieval period: St. Thomas Aquinas	309
d. Between the end of the Middle Ages and the modern renewal	311
e. The modern rediscovery of sacramentality	312
1. The return to the sacramental idea starting in the nineteenth century	313
2. Recent development of the sacramental idea	316

  f. The teaching of Vatican II   319
  g. The unity of the mystery-sacrament: Modern difficulties   327
 Bibliography   330

PART TWO: SPECULATIVE THEOLOGY: DEFINITION OF THE CHURCH

Introduction   339
 I. Speculative theology: Necessity and possibility   339
 II. Presuppositions of speculative theology   342

SECTION I: THE DEFINITION OF THE CHURCH

Subsection 1: The nominal definition   347

Chapter 6: *Ekklēsia* in Scripture   349
 I. The meaning of the word *Ekklēsia*   349
  a. The secular meaning   349
  b. The religious meaning   350
 II. The theological development of the Pauline *corpus*   352
  a. The data in the letters   352
  b. The primary sense of *Ekklēsia*   353
 III. The major teachings about the name *Ekklēsia*   354
  a. Local assemblies and universal assembly   354
  b. The Church and her communal nature   355
 Bibliography   355

Subsection 2: The real definition of the Church   357

Chapter 7: History of the Question   359
 I. The terms of the debate   359
  a. The statements of the Reformers   359
  b. The response of Catholic theology   361
   1. The contribution of St. Robert Bellarmine   361
   2. Comparison with Reformation theology   363
  c. The patristic and Thomistic antecedents   364
 II. The consequences in Catholic theology   370
 III. The contemporary ecclesiological renewal   372

a. The critique of the Bellarminian tradition	372
b. The theology of the Mystical Body	374
c. Other distinctions in the renewal	376
IV. The situation of ecclesiology after Vatican II	376
a. General situation	376
b. The general structure of "binomial thinking"	378
V. Magisterial judgments	379
a. On the distinction between body and soul in the Church	380
b. On the theology of the Mystical Body	381
c. On the distinction between society and community	382
d. On sacramentality	383
e. The question of membership in the Church	384
Conclusion	384
Bibliography	386

Chapter 8: General Critique — 390
- I. The question of ecclesial visibility — 390
  - a. Notes from Vatican II — 391
  - b. The whole extent of the visible aspect of the Church — 392
  - c. Notes from anthropology — 400
  - d. Christological foundations — 401
- II. Modern objections — 402
  - a. The theme of *Ecclesia ab Abel* — 403
  - b. The transitory character of the economy of salvation — 404
- Conclusion — 405
- Bibliography — 408

Chapter 9: The Intellectual Method — 409
- I. The common binomial method of exposition — 410
  - a. The example of Fr. Congar — 410
  - b. The historical and philosophical presuppositions — 411
    1. The historical reasons — 411
    2. The philosophical reasons — 414
       The birth of the "sense of history" / 414

A philosophy of "life" / 414
Philosophy of knowledge, philosophy of the real / 420
II. Conciliar data for a discernment ... 422
  a. Indications from the vocabulary of Vatican II ... 423
  b. The relationship between nature and grace ... 424
III. Proposed clarifications ... 425
  a. Philosophical clarifications ... 425
    1. Dialectic of knowledge, dialectic of the real ... 426
    2. Integrating the moral dimension of the subject ... 428
    3. The shortcomings of conceptualism ... 429
  b. Clarifications of vocabulary and concepts ... 432
Conclusion ... 434
Bibliography ... 435

Chapter 10: Proposed Definition ... 438

I. The sacramentality of the Church ... 438
  a. At the source of the Church: The Eucharist ... 440
    1. The peculiarity of the Eucharistic sacrament ... 440
    2. The Eucharist in classical sacramental theology ... 441
  b. The sacramentality of the Church in Eucharistic terms ... 442
    1. The ecclesial *res tantum* ... 442
    2. The ecclesial *sacramentum tantum* ... 443
    3. The ecclesial *res et sacramentum* ... 445
  c. Conclusion on sacramentality ... 449
II. Ecclesial communion ... 451
  a. The use of the word *koinōnia* in the sources ... 452
    1. The New Testament ... 452
    2. The patristic data ... 455
    3. The statements of Vatican II ... 460
      The Church comes from the Trinitarian *koinōnia* / 460
      The Church journeys toward the Trinitarian *koinōnia* / 461
      The Church lives by the Trinitarian *koinōnia* / 461
      The Church is a *koinōnia* / 461
  b. The notion of *koinōnia-communio* ... 462
    1. The elements of the notion ... 462

2. The notion properly speaking	463
3. The Church—charity	464
Charity according to St. Thomas Aquinas / 464	
The contemporary development / 465	
III. The sacramentality of the ecclesial communion	468
a. The reality of grace: The communion of the theological virtues	469
1. The genesis of the communion of the theological virtues	469
2. The life of the communion of the theological virtues	471
b. The economy of the reality of grace	473
1. The social communion	474
The divine communication / 474	
Man's partaking / 475	
The social communion that is thus engendered / 476	
2. The diaconal communion	482
The divine communication / 483	
Apostolic mediation / 484	
The life of the diaconal communion / 485	
The diaconal communion in history / 488	
The common good of the diaconal communion / 489	
Conclusion	490
a. The rejection of a dialectical presentation	490
b. The essential visibility of the Church	491
c. The twofold perspective: Essential and historical	491
Bibliography	492

Section 2: The Personality of the Church

Chapter 11: Some Philosophical Ideas Recalled	**497**
I. The metaphysics of being or substance	497
II. The idea of person	499
a. The three senses of the word "person"	500
1. The moral sense	500
2. The psychological sense	500
3. The metaphysical sense	500
b. The person in the metaphysical sense	501
1. Vocabulary	501

2. The person in himself ... 502
   Individuality / 502
   Substance / 502
   Rationality / 503

Chapter 12: The Question about the Personality of the Church ... 504
  I. Elements of social metaphysics ... 504
   a. The criterion of substance ... 504
   b. The criterion of individuality ... 505
   c. The criterion of a rational nature ... 506
  II. The personality of the Church ... 507
   a. The question as to the subsistence of the Church ... 507
   b. Consequences at the level of acts placed by the Church ... 508
  Conclusion ... 509
  Bibliography ... 510

PART THREE: THE PROPERTIES OF THE CHURCH

Introduction ... 515

Chapter 13: The Church Is One ... 518
  I. Different ecumenical attitudes ... 518
   a. The Roman Catholic Church ... 519
    1. The Apostolic See ... 520
    2. Work for the reunion of Christians ... 521
   b. The Orthodox Churches ... 522
   c. The world resulting from the Reformation ... 524
    1. The three major groupings ... 524
    2. Ecumenical work ... 526
  II. The ecumenical situation since Vatican II ... 530
  III. The Catholic principles of ecumenism ... 532
   a. The fundamental notions ... 533
    1. Heresy ... 533
    2. Schism ... 534
      Brief note on excommunication / 536
    3. Dissidence ... 536

      b. Catholic fullness   538
         1. The key statement of *Lumen gentium* 8   538
         2. Evaluating the rise of a dissident movement   539
      c. Important ideas in ecumenical dialogue   541
         1. The *vestigia Ecclesiae*   541
         2. The hierarchy of truths (*UR* 11)   542
      d. The methods of ecumenism   548
         1. Ecumenism from a historical perspective   548
            Judgment / 548
            Controversy / 549
            Dialogue / 549
         2. Ecumenism and the development of dogma   550
   Conclusion   551
   Bibliography   552

Chapter 14: The Church Is Holy   555
   I. The Communion of Saints   556
      a. The *"sancta"* and the *"sancti"*   556
      b. The *communio*   557
   II. The problem of faults and reforms in the Church   559
      a. The nature of an ecclesial reform   559
      b. The object of an ecclesial reform   559
   III. Resolution of the speculative difficulty   560
   Conclusion   561
   Bibliography   562

Chapter 15: The Church Is Catholic   563
   I. The two fundamental meanings of "catholic"   564
      a. The qualitative meaning, or *intensive* catholicity   564
         1. Doctrinal catholicity   564
         2. Sacramental catholicity   564
      b. The quantitative sense, or *extensive* catholicity   565
         1. Geographical catholicity   565
         2. "Human" catholicity   565
         3. Temporal catholicity   566
         4. Catholicity according to state in life   566

II. Connection between intensive and extensive catholicity	566
a. The problem	567
1. The analogous relation: Nature and culture	567
2. Application to the ecclesial situation	569
b. The beginning of a solution	571
1. Starting from the observation of the Church's life	571
2. The question of the historicity of Christianity	573
c. Conclusion	575
III. The universal Church and the local churches	575
a. Statement of the question	575
b. Several proposed solutions	576
1. The "federal" paradigm	576
2. The simultaneity of the universal and the local	577
3. The mutual inclusion of the universal and the local	578
c. Magisterial directions	579
1. The Address to the Roman Curia	579
2. The Letter of the Congregation for the Doctrine of the Faith	580
d. Proposed solution	582
1. Clarification through ecclesial sacramentality	582
2. Genetic-historical observation	583
3. Understanding the diaconal communion	584
Conclusion	587
Bibliography	588
Chapter 16: The Church Is Apostolic	**590**
I. Apostolicity	591
a. The adjective "apostolic"	591
1. The apostolic Traditions	591
2. The apostolic churches	591
b. The apostles	591
c. The idea of apostolicity	593
d. The notion of succession	594
II. The succession of the apostles	596
a. The notion of collegiality	596

      b. Manifestations of collegiality   598
  III. St. Peter and his successors   599
      a. The apostle St. Peter   599
      b. The succession of St. Peter in Tradition   602
  IV. The Catholic doctrine of the Roman primacy   605
      a. The theological justification   605
      b. The dogmatic formulation of the Roman primacy   608
        1. The teaching of Vatican I   608
          The prologue of *Pastor aeternus* / 609
          Chapter one: The primacy of St. Peter the apostle / 609
          Chapter two: The transmission of this primacy / 610
          Chapter three: The primacy *of jurisdiction* / 610
        2. The teaching of Vatican II   613
        3. Proposal   614
      c. The dogma of the personal infallibility of the pope   615
        1. The dogmatic definition   616
        2. The teaching of Vatican II   618
          The immediate context / 618
          The broader context / 619
      d. The question of the supreme authority in the Church   620
  Conclusion   621
  Bibliography   621

Chapter 17: The Question of the Church's Indefectibility   625

General Conclusion   627

  General Bibliography   629
  Index of Names   633
  Subject Index   637

Abbreviations

The abbreviations used to designate scholarly journals that are cited consist of the two or three initials of their title (*RSPT: Revue des sciences philosophique et théologique; RT: Revue thomiste*, etc.). Moreover, we refer to the usage followed by the *Ephemerides theologicae lovanienses* (index periodicum). Note also the following abbreviations:

AAS	*Acta Apostolicae Sedis*
ACW	*Ancient Christian Writers* series (Westminster, Md.: Newman Press, 1946–); series continued by Paulist Press
ANF	*Ante-Nicene Fathers*, ed. Alexander Roberts and James Donaldson, revised by A. Cleveland Coxe (repr.; Peabody, Mass.: Hendrickson, 1994)
AG	Vatican II: *Ad gentes*
AS	*Acta Synodalia Sacrosancti Concilii Oecumenici Vaticani II* (Vatican City: Typis Polyglottis Vaticanis, 1970–2000)
CCC	*Catechism of the Catholic Church*
CCSG	*Corpus christianorum, series graeca* (Turnhout, Belgium: Brepols, 1953–)
CCSL	*Corpus christianorum, series latina* (Turnhout, Belgium: Brepols, 1977–)
CD	Vatican II: *Christus Dominus*
CSEL	*Corpus scriptorum ecclesiasticorum latinorum* (Vienna: Hoelder-Pichler-Tempsky, 1866–)

DC	*La Documentation Catholique* (journal)
DH	Vatican II: *Dignitatis humanae*
DI	Congregation for the Doctrine of the Faith: *Dominus Iesus*
DS	Denzinger-Schönmetzer, *Enchiridion symbolorum, definitionum et declarationum de rebus fidei et morum* (1965)
FC	*La Foi Catholique*, by G. Dumeige, 3rd ed. (Paris: Éditions de l'Orante, 1978)
FEF	*The Faith of the Early Fathers*, trans., ed. W. A. Jurgens (Collegeville, Minn.: Liturgical Press, 1970–1979)
FOC	The Fathers of the Church (Washington, D.C.: The Catholic University of America Press, 1947–)
GS	Vatican II: *Gaudium et spes*
LG	Vatican II: *Lumen gentium*
NPNF	*The Nicene and Post-Nicene Fathers*, ed. Philip Schaff, 1st and 2nd series (repr.; Peabody, Mass.: Hendrickson, 1994)
OE	Vatican II: *Orientalium Ecclesiarum*
PG	*Patrologiae cursus completus: Series graeca*, ed. J. P. Migne (Paris: 1857–1866)
PL	*Patrologiae cursus completus: Series latina*, ed. J. P. Migne (Paris: 1844–1864)
RM	*Redemptoris missio* (John Paul II)
SC	Collection "Sources Chrétiennes" (Paris: Cerf, 1942–)
SC	Vatican II: *Sacrosanctum Concilium*
UR	Vatican II: *Unitatis redintegratio*
US	Collection "Unam Sanctam" (Paris: Cerf, 1937–1970)

Conciliar documents are cited using the initials of the first two or three Latin words, with the number of the paragraph (*LG: Lumen gentium; GS: Gaudium et spes*; etc.). Citations in English are generally taken from *Documents of Vatican II*, ed. Austin P. Flannery (Grand Rapids, Mich.: Eerdmans, 1975).

Abbreviations xxi

The translations for recent papal documents and other documents of the Roman curia normally come from the Vatican website.

Biblical Citations

Unless otherwise noted, biblical citations are from the *Revised Standard Version, Second Catholic Edition* (2006).

Patristic Citations

The Fathers of the Church are cited at times according to the numbering system of the edition consulted (Migne Patrology, Corpus christianorum, Ancient Christian Writers), but often in the more compact format recommended by *The Chicago Manual of Style* (e.g., PG 26.398).

Citations from St. Thomas Aquinas

We list here the main editions used for citations from the works of St. Thomas and the abbreviations that we use:

Scriptum super libros Sententiarum, ed. Pierre Mandonnet (Paris: Lethielleux, 1929), continued by Marie-Fabien Moos (1949 and 1956) (= *Sent.*).

Summa contra Gentiles, 4 vols. (Paris: Lethielleux, 1951–1961), reproducing the text of the Leonine edition, *Opera omnia*, vol. 13–15 (Rome: 1918, 1926, 1930) (= *SG*).

Summa theologiae (Rome: Edizioni Paoline, 1962), reproducing the text of the Leonine edition, *Opera omnia*, vol. 4–12 (Rome: 1888–1905) (= *ST*); cited in English from *The "Summa theologica" of St. Thomas Aquinas*, 22 vols. (New York: Benziger Brothers, 1912–1925).

In Psalmos Davidis expositio, in *Opera omnia*, vol. 14 (Parma: Typis Petri Fiaccadori, 1863) (= *in Ps.*).

In Symbolum Apostolorum, scilicet "Credo in Deum" expositio, in *Opuscula theologica*, vol. 2 (Rome: Marietti, 1954) (= *In Symb.*). "Exposition of the Apostles' Creed," in *Basic Writings of Saint Thomas Aquinas*, edited by Anton C. Pegis (New York: Random House, 1945).

Super Epistolas S. Pauli, 2 vols. (Rome: Marietti, 1953) (= Marietti + paragraph #). English translations by Fabian Larcher, O.P., of many of these commentaries can be found online at http://dhspriory.org/thomas/.

Preface to the English Edition

Having first appeared in French in 2006, this *Introduction to the Mystery of the Church* sought to fill a hole in ecclesiology studies since Vatican II. Within the truly vast quantity of theological literature that has followed the Council, typically one sees either specialized studies on one or other point of doctrine or historical studies on the development of one or other doctrinal affirmation. Such analyses are, of course, invaluable. Nonetheless, there is room to add another instrument for receiving the Council's teaching and the Magisterium's preaching that transmits that teaching to us today: namely, an articulation that presents the doctrine on the Church in a synthesis and that places this synthesis in the continuity of the entire Tradition. Such is the principal goal of this book. More than the detailed presentation of any precise point, this organic exposition of ecclesiological dogma possesses a particular value through its comprehensive perspective, one employing a certain theological method. On the one hand, we must receive the defining principles from the very source of all theology: the Scriptures transmitted to us by an uninterrupted, divinely assisted, interpretive Tradition. On the other hand, it is necessary to grasp the unity of the subject in order to situate each element in its rightful place and so that the work as a whole supplies a superior understanding.

Compared to the French edition, select additional material has been incorporated into this English translation. In chapter 2 an ecumenical development of a formula of *Lumen gentium* 8 ("Haec unica Ecclesia ... subsistit in ...") allows for a more dynamic way of thinking about the march toward unity among all the Churches and Christian communities. In chapter 4 an addition concerning the relationship between the baptismal priesthood and the ministerial priesthood allows one to read *Lumen gentium* 10 as also enlightening the relationships between baptismal and ministerial prophetic activity and between baptismal and ministerial kingship. Finally, in chapter 5, the act of faith that includes the Church ("Credo Ecclesiam") has been rendered more explicit in its relation to the Holy Spirit. Besides these items, enhancements to the bibliographies have been made.

Cultural diversity is, in itself, a treasure. It is such, however, only if it permits us, through communication between the cultures, to better see and to better live that which unites us in the same human condition, in the same salvation history, in the same grace of Christ. The reader will easily discern in this book the stamp of French culture, as well as of the Dominican culture that owes so much to St. Thomas Aquinas. Through this translation that the Catholic University of America Press has graciously accepted for publication, my original efforts will now go forth to meet other cultures. This book is thus fundamentally an invitation to dialogue.

I heartily thank this book's American translator, Michael J. Miller, for his diligent professional efforts, providing a careful but lucid rendition of the original French. For the notes and bibliographies, he has performed a great service in tracking down and incorporating (when available) published English editions of my sources. Additionally, I would like to express my gratitude to Fr. Dominic M. Langevin, OP, of the Dominican Province of St. Joseph (New York), assistant to the chair of dogmatic theology for ecclesiology and the sacraments at the University of Fribourg (Switzerland), who has reviewed the translation for me and who is responsible for the final proofs and indices. Without his competence and dedication, this translation would not have been able to appear.

Fr. Benoît-Dominique de La Soujeole, OP
Fribourg, Switzerland
Easter 2013
In homage and with gratitude to Benedict XVI

Preface to the Original Edition

The present volume is a course in ecclesiology that has been taught regularly at the Dominican House of Studies in Toulouse, and then in the theology department at the University of Fribourg (Switzerland) for around fifteen years.

The title states our purpose well: *Introduction to the Mystery of the Church*. This book is first of all an introduction—that is to say that our primary intention is to instruct. This perspective has several consequences. In the first place, we have taken care to be as accessible as possible, using simple vocabulary whenever we could instead of specialized terminology that might be perplexing. When it seemed necessary, we have explained the more "technical" terms of philosophical or theological language before using them. In the second place, this introduction hopes to be an initiation into the subject matter as a whole, so as to allow those who wish to study one particular topic or another in greater depth to do so without breaking up the unity of the subject matter. This explains our perspective, which aims at a synthesis. A preliminary understanding of the general structure of the subject is necessary in order to situate particular questions in each case within the overall design that supports them and that they in turn clarify.

This presentation of an ecclesiological synthesis is based on more than mere pedagogical demands. At a deeper level it is founded on a certain way of comprehending the science of theology. Without embarking here on a "methodological treatise" on this subject, we must nevertheless state our convictions, which are inspired by the wisdom of the great Masters who went before us, and by what the Second Vatican Council recalled concerning the formation of men who aspire to the ministerial priesthood in the Decree *Optatam totius* 16:

> The following order should be observed in the treatment of dogmatic theology: biblical themes should have first place; then students should be shown what the Fathers of the Church, both of the East and West, have contributed towards the faithful transmission and elucidation of each of the revealed truths; then the later history of dogma, including its relation to the general history of the Church; lastly, in order to throw as full a light as possible on the mysteries of salvation, the students should learn to examine more deeply, with the help of speculation and with St. Thomas as teacher, all aspects of these mysteries, and to perceive their interconnection.

This document makes two principal recommendations that have guided our approach. The first is to base our theological endeavor on a wide sampling of sources from Scripture and Tradition, following a sequence of progressive discovery that is connected with the history of the Church. This is what we call the *theology of sources*,[1] which provides us with the first object of our study: what has been revealed to us—which we therefore believe—and what are we seeking to understand? The major characteristic of this doctrinal history is that it has a unity, a coherence, a continuity. Consequently our endeavor today must begin by entering into this movement so that our present-day theological thinking remains within this essential continuity.[2] The second recommendation by the conciliar document is in reference to speculative theology, which follows after the theology of sources. Theologians these days propose a great variety of speculative endeavors because of the many philosophical choices that necessarily undergird their elaboration. If this is understood properly and one heeds the "specifications" provided by an adequate theology of sources, then this diversity that is found throughout history is part of the Church's wealth. Catholic theology has no lack of Masters, some of them particularly great, and the dialogue among the different Schools that arose from their teachings

---

1. The classic term for this is *positive theology*.
2. As Henri de Lubac recalled, "When it is a question of first truths ... one can never be too classical: insisting on new insights would then be a form of infidelity"; *Les Églises particulières dans l'Église universelle* (Paris: Aubier Montaigne, 1971), 23–24. Generally, except for titles that are quoted incidentally, complete references for the studies cited are given in the bibliography compiled at the end of the chapter or in the general bibliography at the end of the volume.

has always been a source of growth for them all and ultimately has enriched the common doctrinal heritage of the Church. In this respect St. Thomas Aquinas is a reliable instructor, and he is the one that we had as a member of the Dominican Order. But there is another reason, which is alluded to in the passage from the Decree *Optatam totius*, that St. Thomas is commended to every student of theology. We will not expatiate on this point so as not to repeat what has been said on the subject elsewhere. We will only emphasize the fact that citing St. Thomas does not necessarily lead to being locked into the past of a particular School, however venerable it may be. Indeed, it is important to distinguish two ways of belonging to a current of thought. It is intellectually more comfortable to hark back to a tradition—to use a partisan logic—than to ask that acknowledged School to lead us to the truth and consequently to put it to the test (a logic of truth). The danger of remaining in a "partisan" past, moreover, is much less formidable for the disciple of St. Thomas in the field of ecclesiology, because St. Thomas, who in this regard still belonged to the patristic era, left us no unified treatise on the mystery of the Church and was unacquainted with the dogmatic questions that gave rise to the ecclesiology beginning in the sixteenth century. As for affiliation with a particular School: to each his own, according to his preferences. St. Thomas, however, is not only the founder of a School, he is the Doctor whose theology has been most fully taken up into the doctrine of the Church, so that in order to grasp one or another doctrinal point correctly it is important to have a theological education that includes an adequate knowledge of the Dominican Master.

The present course is an introduction to the ecclesial *mystery*. Our scientific perspective in no way diminishes the priority given to the life of faith. The two demands, rational and theological, do not conflict at all; rather, since faith has the primacy, it is at the beginning of any sustained effort of reason, just as it is the end of that endeavor. In order to show clearly this constant alliance of faith and reason, we have capitalized important words (Sacred Scripture, Revelation, Tradition), and likewise we duly refer to a canonized author as "St. N." We do not think that one has to ignore what faith says to the reasoning intellect in order to be truly scientific in theology; quite the contrary.

The published textbook of a course—on any subject whatsoever, but particularly in theology, especially dogmatic theology—can have a checkered career, like the course itself when it is taught *viva voce*. The book can become a manual, for better but also for worse. In the best-case scenario, this present offering will be welcomed and used for what it intends to be: an ecclesiological introduction. It is not a question of accumulating information, as is too often the case nowadays, but rather of forming the mind, of giving it the solid clarity of principles and the flexibility required to apply them in various situations. The mind is thus rendered capable of entertaining new facts and of solving problems that arise. This instruction, therefore, is meant to be assimilated and then surpassed by subsequent reflection with the help of other materials (books, lectures ...), or even references from other theological Schools. In the worst-case scenario, the book may be taken as an account of "what you need to know" and thus become not an entryway into theological wisdom, but a barrier that marks the completion of the intellectual effort, a sort of "toolbox" containing answers to all future questions without any investigation of deeper reasons or more far-reaching consequences. Each reader is responsible for the future of his reading of our presentation, which is intended, we repeat, only as an introduction.

In conclusion we would like to express our thanks to Cardinal Journet and Fathers Marie-Michel Labourdette, Marie-Vincent Leroy, and Jean-Pierre Torrell, these latter all of the Order of Preachers, who were and still are our Masters. We hope that this publication will be a tribute to the wisdom that they were able to receive and willing to hand on, augmented by the value of their patient and humble work. We wish also to express our sincere gratitude to Fr. Piotr Napiwodzki, OP, S.T.D., assistant to the chair of dogmatic theology for ecclesiology and the sacraments at the University of Fribourg, and to our Sisters at the monastery in Estavayer (Switzerland) for their invaluable collaboration in preparing the manuscript.

Introduction to the Mystery of the Church

General Introduction

The course on ecclesiology is one of the four major dogmatic treatises in the theology curriculum.[1] The subject matter is vast and sometimes complex. The purpose of this general introduction is to state precisely the spirit in which we are teaching this course, and at the same time to specify the initial major distinctions that will make it possible to comprehend the subsequent plan of studies that we will follow. We will also address some historical facts that provide an important context for our subject matter.

1. The purpose of the course

A course in ecclesiology introduces the student to a specifically *theological* knowledge of this particular and complex reality that we call "Church." A proper theological understanding of the Church is particularly important for all who are baptized. Not uncommonly today one hears people say, "I believe in Christ, but I really don't see any point in having a Church." Now believing in Christ yet not living in the Church whole-heartedly, fully and resolutely is, to tell the truth, utterly self-contradictory. The response should not be exclusively "functional," asserting that no one can come to Christ except by way of the preaching and the sacraments of the Church; this is true, with a few qualifications that we will examine later on, but insufficient. Not only *by* the Church but also and above all *in* the Church does one go to Christ

---

1. The four-year course in theology is traditionally devoted to the four major parts of Christian dogma, which are the treatises on God, Christ, the Church, and the sacraments.

and remain—as St. Paul says more than one hundred sixty times—"in Christ." To reject the Church knowingly is to reject Christ, by reason of the profound unity that connects these two mysteries. The fundamental intention of this course is to demonstrate as much as we can this coherence of the mysteries of salvation. Rather than go as far as possible in presenting any one part, we prefer to introduce the reader to the connections that allow us to bring to light the unity of the Christian mystery.

2. Ecclesiology, a "sensitive" subject

Today ecclesiology is a potentially "subversive" topic. It is in fact an area of dogmatic theology that stirs up passions. In reference to statements about the Church and ways of behaving within or with regard to the Church, many people sort baptized Catholics into well-defined, competing categories.[2] This is a veritable cancer in the life of the community. The faithful, the clergy, and religious communities thus run the risk of being sorely divided. Nowadays people readily excommunicate each other over this subject.... The dynamism of the Church is sometimes very seriously compromised thereby. As we will see, behind this vocabulary, which is at the same time improper and superficial, important ecclesiological errors may be lurking.

For our part, we intend to take an approach that is above all peaceable and reasonable. We will study carefully and without *a priori* notions Catholic doctrine for its own sake, so as to know it as it is and not as we would like it to be. As we proceed in this way, we will see that many oppositions collapse by themselves like houses of cards. We will go to the sources. The virtue of docility will allow us to enter into an understanding of the mystery. Once we have become sufficiently competent, we will be able to avoid overemphasizing one point of view or another, and we will be able to see what is correct or debatable in a particular teaching of a writer. It is rare that a writer is wrong through and through, and so we must learn to discern so as to accept any bit of truth, wherever it may come from, and not to consider in the first place *who* is speaking but rather *what* is being said. Theology must not get bogged down in questions of personality; it is addressing real-life questions.

2. Supposedly, for instance, there are "conservatives" and "progressives."

3. The place of an ecclesiology course in the curriculum

This course aims to initiate the student into an understanding of the mystery. It does not claim, however, to be exhaustive. It does not intend to be the supposedly perfect manual that one consults the moment a troublesome question arises, which is a rather basic reflex. How then does this course fit into the process of acquiring knowledge?

Learning is a lifelong activity; we develop our knowledge with the help of reading, personal research, lectures.... It is essential for the intellect to remain ever alert, and nothing is more contrary to its nature than to stop in its quest. But this ceaselessly growing knowledge about the Church will not be possible and fruitful unless—from the outset—we possess a basic and truly theological knowledge of the Church. A tree grows starting from a root. The purpose of a course is to give the first preliminary impetus that is necessary for all further study. This course in ecclesiology has no other ambitions: helping students to acquire the basic concepts, showing the structure of the subject matter, in short, serving as a guide so that students can *enter into* ecclesiology and then be able to make progress alone or with others. Therefore this course does not aim to be complete, nor even an exhaustive treatment of the questions that will be addressed. It intends to be, in terms of its subject matter as well as its teaching method, an *introduction*, and it is in this sense that it could be consequential if it is done well: as it helps the student take the first, decisive steps, it ought to make all the later developments possible.

4. One's personal theological thinking

This course must also help the student to develop personally a way of thinking theologically. Not necessarily *original* thought, but more than mere knowledge—genuine *thinking*. Not following the last person who spoke, not getting upset about statements—if they happen to be traditional—not getting all fired up about the latest slogan.... Thinking is analyzing, reasoning, evaluating, judging. One has to have and cultivate a critical mind and not a spirit of criticizing. One has to know in particular how to detect the partial character of a statement. Theological errors nowadays are not so much well-defined heresies as unbalanced or warped thinking that errs by excess or defect. It is more a question of distorted, one-sided truths than of "massive" errors. For example, the infatuation after the Council with the theme of *the People of God* in ecclesiology led many authors and preachers to present the Church *as a whole* in terms of that one theme. This theme is correct, profound, and important, but if one makes that the whole of ecclesiology, one is left with a discourse that is partial (incomplete), if not showing partiality as well, and in any case always unbalanced. Therefore it is necessary to know that this theme is one of the themes in ecclesiology and not *the* theme. Therefore it is not enough to have a personal theological way of thinking; it also has to be balanced. It is the job of a course to provide the major elements in this theological equilibrium.

5. A course that must stay in its place

This course will be profitable only if it is and remains in its place. Since it is about theology, and consequently about understanding the faith, its first task is to cultivate the connection between what is theological in the scientific sense (*le théologique*) and what pertains to the practice of the theological virtues (*le théologal*). Faith is the first prerequisite for our work, since we want to develop its intelligibility. In other words, this course presupposes the life of faith in us. Likewise, the many-faceted preaching of the Magisterium must be indispensable for us. Our theology, like our faith, is ecclesial. And in making sure that this is so, the advances that we make in our theological understanding will help us to advance in faith. The whole human being is the one who believes, who adheres to the faith, and when his highest faculties—intellect and will—develop, the whole subject grows toward the very thing that he knows and desires. Whereas faith is the initial prerequisite for theology and the criterion for judging theological research, the suitable development of theology fosters the development of faith.

It goes without saying—but perhaps it is better to say it—that this connection between theological science and theological virtues should first be found in the instructor. Although the student must first be docile so as to receive this initial impetus that the course provides, docility—a virtue of the intellect—cannot be commanded; one must reasonably consent to it. This will happen if the person who presents himself as an instructor deserves confidence. This confidence must be objectively merited; it is not owed to someone unthinkingly just because he appears with a diploma to teach. What is the basis for placing or withholding this trust? Certainly not the professor's competence, because, by definition, the student has not yet reached the level of education that would allow him to appreciate it. In theology a professor will be able to win his students' confidence if he is intellectually honest and gives proof that he is a "normal" functioning member of the Church. To do that the instructor must carefully identify his sources, justify his statements, specify when he is presenting common doctrine and when he is presenting the viewpoint of a particular school; not everything is on the same level. Furthermore, the instructor must give evidence of an ecclesial sense: can one put one's trust in an academic with a degree who puts his personal research on the same level, if not higher, than a magisterial teaching?

We will make considerable use of the ancillary disciplines of theology: in the first place philosophy, but also history and the human sciences, particularly the social sciences. These are only servants, but necessary servants. They perceive, each according to its own formal object, one aspect of the reality that theology must take into account.

In short, this course will have done its job if it enables the student to acquire and develop the *sensus Ecclesiae*, the *sentire cum Ecclesia* (the "sense of the Church," the habit of "thinking with the Church"): we could say, the supernatural, filial bond that makes us men and women of the Church, not apparatchiks but rather faithful and far-sighted stewards of the treasures that God wants to give to us and, through us, to all mankind.

6. The method

It is a good idea to recall here, if only briefly, what makes a course in ecclesiology theological in nature. These are very general reminders, but they must be kept in mind; they govern, in a sense, one's overall understanding of the course, particularly in explaining the general plan that we will follow.

Theology

Etymologically the word "theology" means *talk about God* or *science of God*. It deals not with God as discovered by the metaphysical approach (*theodicy*, which is part of philosophy) but with God *as he has revealed himself*. For St. Augustine theology is the *"intelligentia"* (from *"intus legere"* the "inner perusal") of the faith. For St. Anselm it is *fides quaerens intellectum* ["faith seeking understanding"]. These are equivalent expressions. They express the normal and natural endeavor of the intellect that aims to deepen and comprehend what it initially believes.

Faith, in its cognitive aspect, will attain its fulfillment in the beatific vision. Although faith is the highest knowledge that a human mind can have on earth, it is nevertheless an imperfect state: its perfection is *vision* (cf. 1 Jn 3:2, "We shall see [God] as he is").

Our understanding of what we still only believe comes about by way of *science*. What does this mean? At the level of method, it denotes in the first place *rigor*. We take the assertions, the affirmations that we believe, for example the one divine essence in three Persons, as the object of investigation and analysis. We scrutinize their intelligible contents so as to distinguish what comes first in explanatory importance from what comes second (which is by no means secondary), to differentiate what is a real cause from what is an effect. This rigor in our intellectual procedure is, at the methodological level, what we call science in the first place. This sense is common to all disciplines that are said to be scientific. At the level of the subject matter, we must beware of a potential misunderstanding. In the language commonly used today, we describe as "scientific" a certitude that can be proved by experiment or mathematically. This is a reductive sense of the term. A science, whatever its object may be, pursues certain knowledge, but not exclusively by using mathematics or the experimental method. One can also arrive at sure knowledge by logic, and in theology it results ultimately from the authority of the Revelation of which the Church is the guardian. Consequently, at the level of subject matter, the definition that fits these various fields in which the intellect exerts itself for the purpose of acquiring the truth is this: *certain knowledge of a thing by its causes*.

Theology is therefore a science, not only insofar as the truth of its statements and of their developments is concerned, but just as much with respect to the seriousness and the rigor of its method, which makes it possible to organize the knowledge. Yet theology is a science in a unique way because it presupposes a *faith*. From that *supernatural* faith it receives its principles and its data, the very subject matter that it treats. To abolish faith is to put an end to theology as such; this deprives the science of its soul and furthermore robs it of its very object. Theology then becomes merely an endeavor to understand a foreign system of thought, as though one were studying the doctrine of Hinduism. Theology only exists thanks to Revelation and in the documents that transmit it—a Revelation that faith alone makes us accept as true. Faith, however, is not just the point of departure for theology; it is also its constant light, its indispensable life principle, the decisive criterion for verifying its conclusions.

The two main functions of theology

Every science has two types of work. On the one hand it must verify (i.e., establish the objective realities of) its specific subject matter, and on the other hand it must render this matter clear.

Verifying the subject matter

This is the first stage, both chronologically and in importance. It is a question of taking possession of the object [of the science], in other words, grasping and taking hold of the truth contained in its texts. There are the fundamental texts of Sacred Scripture. They come down to us through the interpretive transmission of the Church: Tradition. There are not two sources of Revelation, but *only one source*, which is Scripture received in Tradition. To put it another way, there is one *fons essendi* [source of being], Revelation (God speaks), and there are two *fontes inveniendi* [sources of discovery], if we distinguish them from the material perspective, because Scripture and a conciliar declaration, for example, are two distinct sorts of texts. But from the formal perspective, there is only one source: Scripture received in Tradition.[3]

Be that as it may, the theologian receives his subject matter and examines it in multiple texts and through them. Gathering and studying these documents is the first task of theology; this is called the theology of sources (or positive theology). This kind of theology utilizes the

---

3. We have alluded here to the famous, so-called "two sources" debate that perturbed the Fathers of Vatican II during their discussion of the schema that was to become the Constitution *Dei Verbum* (no. 9). Further information on that debate can be found in the course on fundamental theology by Gilbert Narcisse, *Premiers Pas en théologie* (Paris: Parole et Silence, 2005), 340.

resources of the critical methods (historical and philological criticism, exegesis). It is a question of knowing who is speaking, in what context, with what intention, what is really being said and what is not being said.... Take, for example, the dogmatic definition of the Assumption by Pope Pius XII in 1950. The definition strictly speaking consists of this sentence: "the Immaculate Mother of God, the ever Virgin Mary, after completing her course of life upon earth, was assumed to the glory of heaven both in body and soul." Who is speaking? The pope by virtue of his authority as supreme pontiff. In what context? This is a dogmatic declaration, in other words, an irrevocable decision in which the pope enlists his authority as Vicar of Christ and implements his particular charism of infallibility. For what intention? So as to give one more light to the faith of believers. What is being said? We must read the dogmatic formula closely. It can be summarized as follows: Mary is actually present, body and soul, in the glory of her risen Son. What is not being said? Here, essentially, the "moment when" (after the death of Mary, or was she preserved from death?), and the "how" (did Mary experience an ascension similar to Christ's?). Nothing was defined by the pope with regard to those subjects, which therefore remain matters for theological debate.[4]

This first stage of theological work, the positive phase, is of absolutely capital importance. Without it theology is quite impossible because it would be deprived of its object: Revelation. If it is carried out incorrectly, the ensuing theological study is doomed to go astray. One can make a "massive" error ("Jesus is not God"), but more often the error is by excess or defect. For example, by emphasizing the humanity of Christ excessively and consequently neglecting his divinity, one runs the risk of distorting ecclesiology, the sacraments, morality ..., everything that has its source in the divine person of Christ, who through his humanity communicates to us the very life of God. Conversely, underestimating the importance of Christ's humanity leads to minimizing the entire economy of salvation, all the means of grace that Christ has given us.

Positive theology is the art of surveying [*la mesure*] and the art of

---

4. On this specific example, see René Laurentin, *Court Traité sur la Vierge Marie*, 5th ed. (Paris: Lethielleux, 1967), 149ff.; English edition, *A Short Treatise on the Virgin Mary*, trans. Charles Neumann (Washington, N.J.: AMI Press, 1991), 248ff.

being thorough, the art of reading well and correctly understanding the *true sense* of the documents that convey Revelation to us. Positive theology is a fully qualified form of theology. It presupposes the faith that is its light, while the critical methods that it makes use of are at its service. Definitively, positive theology *examines* the revealed *datum*, and in order to do that it determines whether such and such a statement is revealed or not (for example, Abraham had two sons: revealed or not?). If there is a revealed truth, in what sense should we understand what is said? To sum up, positive theology is interested in understanding texts correctly and evaluating their authority (a text is authoritative if it applies to the *faith*). This study follows the order of the texts and their history. It does not lend itself to a scientific synthesis; this is not the study that separates out what is first from what is second. That synthesis, that organic presentation of the entirety of the intelligible content of our faith, can be constructed in a second phase of theological study, thanks to what we call *speculative* theology. This latter sort of theology will be interested in clarifying, explaining, and arranging the matter that is grasped in the sources.

Clarifying and arranging the matter

This is the "fine point" of theology, but once again it depends entirely on the correctness and the rigor of the first positive stage.

What is speculative theology? We have to realize that we cannot limit ourselves to asking: is this truth revealed? What does it mean in a specific context, in the writings of this particular author? We have to go further and ask ourselves: according to everything that God has told us, by many paths and in different eras, what are the divine realities *in themselves*? In other words, no longer according to the historical, linguistic, sociological, and cultural context in which they were revealed, but in themselves, as they are, and according to the real relations that we can discover among them by analyzing them. What is the first truth, really and in its explanatory force, that is central to the other truths and explains the rest? This is the task of speculative theology.[5]

Its characteristic method will be that of rational analysis and proof.

---

5. To understand this correctly one must recall the important distinction between *reality* and *truth*: to say that God is one and that God is triune is indeed to speak about the same *reality*, but it does not state the same *truth*.

It will often—if not constantly—be based on the analogy with natural realities that God himself employed so as to express himself in human language and thereby to reveal himself. For example, the second Person of the Trinity is known to us as "Son." What is this generation? Speculative theology will have its historical part, not the history of the texts (positive theology), but the history of this reality, the history of this communication of divine life to human beings according to various systems of salvation that, taken together, form a divinely guided history (the age of nature, the age of the promise, the age of the Law, the age of the Church). Thus it is a whole vision of the world, of mankind and of history that speculative theology will strive to organize, starting from first causes. Here too reason, with all its flexibility, with the help of all the sciences and of their methods, will place itself at the service of faith and will be measured and verified by faith. Finally, like any science of the real, speculative theology seeks the highest understanding of *what is* and *how it is*. It is a question of discovering the intelligibility of what is real, assimilating it, and giving an account of it.

Like any science about reality, speculative theology tends toward *synthesis,* a scientific synthesis in which the partial and derived truths are reconnected with those that explain them (first truths or sources), and all together these truths make up the *supreme truth.* This order of knowledge is a *scientific order* in the sense already defined: knowledge of a thing by its causes. It is not the order that Revelation itself followed, much less the often quite accidental order that was followed by the development of dogma; it is an order of science, or rather of *wisdom.*

The example of the Thomistic synthesis

In his masterpiece, the *Summa theologiae,* St. Thomas orders his synthesis in an extremely simple manner:

- The first and central object of theology, as of faith, is God, God in himself, in his mystery that the beatific vision will unveil to us face to face. God, in the mystery of one essence and Trinity of Persons, is the center and the summit of all theological synthesis, the object of its essential endeavor.

- After God, we consider everything else, but always in its relation with God as Revelation has made it known to us, beyond what metaphysical reasoning could grasp by itself. This relation of everything else in the Christian mystery with God is twofold:
    - God is the *principle* of all creatures, of everything that is not he; in other words, all creatures come from him and have in him their Creator and sustainer.
    - God is the *end* of all creatures; in other words, they are all made for him, so as to return to him.

This twofold movement of creatures—they come from God and return to God—is traditionally called *exitus/redditus*. Consequently, we have the following overall schema of the synthesis:

* God in himself,

* God in relation to his creatures ⟶ as principle
⟶ as final end

In the *Summa theologiae* this division of the whole work is made as follows:
- *Prima pars* [Part I]
    * God in his mystery (qq. 2–43)
    * God, the principle of created things and of their order (qq. 44–119).

- *Secunda pars et Tertia pars* [Parts II and III]
    * God, the final end of creatures
    * The final end: beatitude (*I-II*, qq. 1–5)
    * The return to God: human action

I-II, qq. 6–114 → General principles
II-II, qq. 1–170 → Particular principles
  * The specific path, salvation:

III, qq. 1–59 → Christ the Redeemer
  * Means of attaining union with Christ:

III, qq. 60–90, and *Suppl.*, qq. 1–68 → The sacraments.
  * The completion of the return, the last things:
      Suppl., qq. 69–99

We can make two observations:

In the first place, among the means for attaining union with Christ, St. Thomas includes the sacraments, of course, but does not devote any question or group of questions to the Church. It is important to emphasize this absence of a treatise on the Church; we will return to it.

In the second place, let us comment briefly on this general outline: the final end, beatitude, is in a certain way unique. It is the only destiny that God has prepared for us: to share forever the intimacy of his Trinitarian life, and everything in us—with grace restoring and elevating nature—leads to this. But this return to God does not depend solely on the requirements and distinctive features of our nature and of the grace that is given to it. This return to God depends also on many other contingent facts that together make up a history wherein God established an *economy* of salvation that could have been quite different, but is exactly what God willed or permitted, and is known to us by his Revelation. In short, Revelation teaches us that man, having destroyed by his sin the economy of grace originally instituted in Adam, henceforth can recover grace and attain his supernatural end only by a *Savior* who is the Son of God made flesh so as to redeem him. So it is that after considering the requirements and modalities of the return to God that are related to the fact that man is a rational creature called to the beatific vision—in our study of anthropology, the natural law, the divine law and grace—we must study the requirements and the modalities that are related to the fact that grace and salvation, because of Adam's sin, exist "concretely" only through Christ the Redeemer and according to a specifically Christian economy that he instituted: the Church.

The *Treatise on God*—in himself and as principle—is studied elsewhere. Our course in ecclesiology aims to study a fundamental point in the Christian economy: the Church. The important thing to grasp here, for the moment, is the subject matter as a whole and how it is divided up.

The admirable and exceptionally balanced plan of St. Thomas's synthesis, however, is not perfect. Nowadays critics point out above all that it lacks a treatise on the Church. It is not a "complete blank," since the major elements of a treatise on ecclesiology are found in the *Summa theologiae;* but they are dispersed throughout the work. With regard to this question, St. Thomas still belongs to the patristic era: the

Church is not nowhere, she is everywhere. What follows will explain further.

7. The place of ecclesiology in dogmatic theology

An adequate answer to this question presupposes the completion of a course on the nature or being [*être*] of the Church. We will be content here to pose the question in precise terms.

The question of a separate treatise "*De Ecclesia*"

Until the fourteenth century we find no dogmatic treatise "*De Ecclesia.*" The example of the synthesis by St. Thomas shows this plainly: God—Christ—the sacraments. This absence is not the sign of an imperfection: the Church is indeed present in medieval theology, as in the Fathers and certainly in Scripture. But she does not constitute the object of a "mystery" clearly distinguished from the others. The ecclesial "mystery" is approached by way of other questions; here are the main ones:

- First of all—and this is fundamental—the Church is part of the mystery of Christ. This is the great theology that is initiated in the letters of St. Paul: the Church is the Body of Christ, of which he is the Head in his humanity that possesses the fullness of grace that he distributes among his members. Many of the Fathers develop a true, rich ecclesiology on this theme.
- Then—and this follows naturally—the Church is intimately bound up with the sacraments, primarily with baptism, which incorporates individuals into the Body, and with the Eucharist, which unites this Body and makes it grow. The sacraments are acts of Christ who, through them, builds up, gives growth, orders and restores his Body. Here too the Fathers elaborate a profound ecclesiology when they speak about the sacraments.
- Furthermore, we must realize that ecclesiology concerns not only dogmatic, but also moral theology. Thus:
- The Church is first of all the community of *faith*. The study of that theological virtue contains precious elements of ecclesiology. Think in the first place about *heresy* (alteration of the faith) and *apostasy* (abandonment of the faith), which in and of themselves

exclude a member from the ecclesial Body. But there is much more. All the teaching activity of pastors is aimed at defending, fostering, and increasing the understanding of the faith and faith itself. This brings us to one of the three great episcopal duties, the *munus docendi,* and therefore prompts us to consider one of the hierarchical aspects of the Church.

- The Church is also and above all the community of *charity.* The study of this theological virtue allows us to address the question of *schism* (breach of charity), but it also serves as a pillar in the study of ecclesial activity (e.g., pastoral and missionary work). Furthermore, charity is the "heart" of the Church, as St. Thérèse of Lisieux so insightfully recognized.[6]
- The treatise on grace is directly concerned with ecclesiology. In particular, the distinction between *sanctifying grace* and *charism* is important for the theology of the ordained ministries that constitute the ecclesial hierarchy and for the theology of the personal ministry of the pope (especially the *charism* of infallibility). But it is of capital importance above all in understanding the doctrine of the Mystical Body of which Christ is the Head: he, full of grace, pours out his grace into our souls.

And the list could go on....

One could say that all parts of dogmatic and moral theology touch directly or indirectly on ecclesiology. This is the reason that before the fourteenth century the subject matter is dispersed, as the *Summa theologiae* testifies. Certainly the Church is more involved in some "mysteries" than in others—for example, Christology is a major area—but one must always keep in mind the need to go to other parts of theology so as to complete, refine, and correct. Hence we can see the very incomplete and imprudent character of a treatise on ecclesiology "*ad mentem Sancti Thomae*" ["according to the teaching of St. Thomas"], of which there were so many before Vatican II, based exclusively on the references to the Church in question 8 of the *Tertia pars* concerning Christ the Head.

---

6. "In the heart of the Church, my Mother, I shall be *Love,*" in *Manuscrits autobiographiques* (Lisieux: Office central, 1957), 229; English edition, *The Story of a Soul,* trans. John Clarke (Washington, D.C.: ICS Publications, 1976), 194.

The appearance of a separate treatise

It is appropriate here to distinguish between the *historical* reasons and the *theological* reasons.

From the historical perspective the great Scholastics of the thirteenth century, as we have said, do not have a separate treatise on the Church. These treatises appear soon afterward in 1301, 1302, 1304 ..., and immediately there are a large number of them. There is a very clear historical fact that is at the origin of this phenomenon: the conflict between Philip IV the Fair and Pope Boniface VIII. This conflict involved all of ecclesiology by way of the particular question about the relation of the temporal and the spiritual orders—more precisely the problem of the pope's authority over the royal power. This problem did not arise in 1300; the papacy in the thirteenth century was acquainted with it, and everyone knows about the very clear-cut differences of opinion between Pope Innocent IV and St. Louis. The pope upheld a very theocratic view resulting from political Augustinianism. With Philip IV the Fair these controversies had more brutal practical consequences. Today we say, to put it concisely:

- there is a *real* distinction between the spiritual and the temporal orders;
- there is a subordination of temporal *ends* to spiritual *ends*;
- the spiritual order has the right to intervene in the temporal order when the latter threatens the spiritual, or so as to enlighten it by the spiritual order.

Above all we must keep the *real* distinction between the two. The Church is not civil society, even in the political age of Christendom. Hence it is necessary to define the boundaries of these two opposing entities, which have different constitutive elements as well as finalities. Yet, it is true, the subjects of a Christian nation—its faithful and its citizens—are the same persons.

This, to put it very schematically, is the reason for the appearance of the first treatises *"De Ecclesia"* in history. Fr. Congar, after giving a long list of these works, says that they deal essentially with the powers in the Church and in civil society and with their relations.[7] We should

7. See Yves Congar, *L'Église de S. Augustin à l'époque moderne* (Paris: Cerf, 1970), 270.

explain however. These are not all legal treatises. *De regimine christiano*, by James of Viterbo, which is probably the oldest (1301), has a long first part that is, properly speaking, theological and of high quality.[8]

From the theological perspective, the appearance of treatises on the Church bears witness to a development in the science of theology. Even when the occasion that gave birth to them receded into the past, authors have continued to compose them down to the present day. If ecclesiology can make a claim to a separate treatise, it is because there is indeed a particular mystery that is the Church. An article of faith has a specific supernatural object, and the Church is one of them: *credo unam, sanctam, catholicam et apostolicam Ecclesiam* [I believe in one, holy, catholic, and apostolic Church]. We will return to this point, because we cannot say that we believe in the Church in the same way that we say we believe *in* God. Still, faith is involved when we profess the Church. Recall that the absolutely first subject of theology and of faith is God himself as he has revealed himself. But in a second, derivative way there are other revealed mysteries connected with him, and among them is the mystery of the Church. Or one can also say that there is a progressive differentiation—at the level of theological understanding—of the various aspects of the mystery of God, starting with the distinction between his being and his action.

At what point in this development do the first treatises on ecclesiology intervene? From the fourteenth century on it was a question of making a clearer distinction between Christ and the Church. These two mysteries are very closely related, so much so that they can be considered as one mystery, but in some important aspects they ought to be distinguished. Thus, from the time of St. Paul, if Christians believe that the Church is indeed the *Body* of which Christ is the Head (1 Cor 12:12ff.), which marks their unity, we also believe that she is his Spouse too (cf. Eph 5:23ff.), which plainly underscores the difference. There is another distinction, too, that views the Church as being simultaneously *the reality of salvation* and *the means of salvation* by which the reality is produced. More penetrating reflection on these two aspects of the one reality called "Church," and on the relations between them, is at the origin of the treatises "*De Ecclesia.*" These studies tend to favor the latter

---

8. Edited by H.-X. Arquillière under the title of *Le plus ancien traité de l'Église: De regimine christiano* (1301–1302) (Paris: Beauchesne, 1926).

aspect, *means of salvation*, but we must never forget to connect this aspect with the first one, *the reality of salvation*, because the Church is inseparably both. This connection is the first object of speculative ecclesiology, as we will see.

The place of the treatise *"De Ecclesia"*

What we have already said on this subject in presenting the Thomistic synthesis will suffice for the moment; a better understanding will develop as we progress. Let us recall briefly:

The treatise on the Church presupposes a complete Christology. It is not just an "outgrowth" of a treatise on capital grace (*ST* III, q. 8). The glorified Christ seated at the right hand of the Father is the one who sends his Spirit that founds the Church. Prior to the treatise on the Church, therefore, we have the treatise on Christ and, of course, even the treatise *"De Deo,"* especially on the Trinity, so that the relation between Christ and the Holy Spirit is situated correctly.

The subject matter subsequent to the Church requires careful explanation.

In the distribution of topics in the *Summa theologiae* we find a very rigorous compartmentalization: Christ—the sacraments—the last things. The treatise on the Church fits neatly between Christ and the sacraments, but there is no watertight division between the Church and the sacraments. The treatise on the Church integrates the study of the sacraments as an essential part, and although the treatise on the sacraments has its own coherence, it is nevertheless constructed in close connection with ecclesiology. All this will become clearer as we proceed, but we should note immediately the very expressive formulation by Fr. de Lubac: "the sacraments make the Church (they build her up), and the Church makes the sacraments (she alone is able to celebrate them)."[9] Furthermore the Church herself, in Christ, is a sacrament (cf. *LG* 1). Hence sacramentality begins before the seven particular sacraments that are an outpouring of the sacrament that is the Church, which likewise takes its sacramental character from Christ, the first and fundamental sacrament.

9. This is a simplified paraphrase of what de Lubac actually wrote, which was as follows: "The Church produces the Eucharist, but the Eucharist also produces the Church"; Henri de Lubac, *The Splendor of the Church*, trans. Michael Mason (New York: Sheed and Ward, 1956; reprinted San Francisco: Ignatius Press, 1986, 1999), 133.

The treatise on the Church therefore is intimately united to the treatise on the sacraments and precedes it. The principles of sacramental theology reside in the treatise on the Church, and they themselves are realized par excellence in Christ.

Furthermore, the treatise on the Church has essential connections with the treatise on the *last things*. The Church present in this world makes her way toward the parousia that will be the final age in the history of salvation. Yet—and this is extremely important—the Church will not be obliterated when Christ returns in glory; she will enter into his glory because she is *already* in this world the Body of Christ. The Church in glory is a fulfillment, not a new reality. This raises the important question of the so-called "*unicity*" or *uniqueness* of the Church. The Church is unique; there are not two or more Churches. The Church on earth and the Church in heaven form only one Church. Similarly, considering the Church on earth, she is unique, and that is the whole question of ecumenism. We will return to it.

Ecclesiology touches also on Mariology. The Virgin Mary is at the heart of the Church, her "prototype," and both the life of Mary and her destiny speak to us about the life and destiny of the Church.

And so speaking about the place of ecclesiology in theology allows us to approach a number of points that will be the object of the whole course. We see also that the subject of ecclesiology, in order to have its own consistency, also makes the connection between many other treatises and, in a sense, with all of them. Ecclesiology is a "crossroads" subject. It is perhaps the treatise that most fully manifests the aspect of synthesis that is necessarily part of theology. The course will have to show what Vatican I calls the *nexus mysteriorum*, the connection among the mysteries. All the mysteries, all the articles of faith, are interconnected and arranged in a certain order of intelligibility. They mutually illuminate and complement and "correct" each other, so that distorting one of them sets off a cascade of deviations in the others.

The Christian mystery as a whole has a profound coherence, a strict unity, and consequently the theology that seeks an understanding of it tends, as we have already said, toward a synthesis. This synthesis is not a summary, as the term is often understood today. A synthesis can be a very long explanation. The essential thing is that it be *organic*—in other words, an explanation of the whole showing the coherence of the constituent elements. It also means that there is a philosophical requirement involved in this work. It is absolutely necessary—at the level of reasoning—to have a philosophy capable of giving an account of this coherent unity, and as we progress in this course we will easily discover that our understanding of the faith cannot be satisfied with a paucity of subject matter without very quickly limiting itself in its investigation and renouncing precisely this task of rendering an account of this coherence of the Christian mystery.

8. The object of ecclesiology

Ecclesiology is the specifically *theological* study of the Church; its object is consequently the *mystery* of the Church. It is neither sociology nor history, nor even philosophy, although these can and must be ancillary disciplines. We should note that it is not apologetics, either. That discipline developed particularly in the nineteenth century in response to a tendency in the liberal current of European thought that refused to acknowledge the Church's place in society. Apologetics is a discipline that does not presuppose faith, but, on the contrary, tries to show, by means of natural reason alone applied to objective facts (for example, the persistence of the Church through the ages), the real existence of the Christian community, its *miraculous* (not mysterious) character. It tries to lead honest minds to the threshold of the mystery, showing that it does not contradict reason even though it surpasses it. Apologetics does not enter into the mystery; for that one must move on to theology, for in order to grasp a mystery faith is necessary. The Church has been one of the preferred fields of apologetics, and in the ongoing dialogue with nonbelievers this discipline remains the only possible line of discussion. Therefore it must not be rejected, but carefully updated, since the old apologetics as such is to a very great extent impracticable nowadays. The difference in perspective with theology can be illustrated as follows: in discussing the one, holy, catholic, and apostolic Church, apologetics will treat these as *notes*—in other words, as *characteristic facts*, whereas theology will regard them as *properties*—that is, as determinations of the intrinsic being of the Church.

This course in ecclesiology is therefore a course in theology. Every science is defined by its object and its method. We have already mentioned the principal points of method; now let us specify the object.

We say: ecclesiology is the part of theology that studies in the light of faith the Church under two aspects, her being and her action.

On the level of being—which comes first—it deals with the Church in the broadest sense—that is, both *the Church in heaven*, also called the Church triumphant or exultant, and *the Church on earth*, also called the Church militant or the pilgrim Church. We have already mentioned the *uniqueness* of the Church. Indeed, we are dealing with one reality. There are not two Churches, one here below and the other in glory, but, once again, *one single Church*. This is to say that the essential element of the Church—what causes the Church to be the Church—is *strictly speaking identical* in the Church in heaven and in the Church on earth. Hence we see plainly that:

- one must *never separate* the Church in heaven from the Church on earth. For example, the communion of saints belongs to both; there is not one heavenly communion and another that is earthly;
- yet one must *distinguish*; the one Church of God is realized differently here below and in glory.

Let us look at this a little more closely, although the point of the whole course is to show this.

No separation into two Churches

At the level of the *reality*, of the very being that we call "Church," at the ontological level, its "heart," its essential element, its "formal constituent," in short, what causes the Church to be the Church, is strictly speaking identical regardless of its earthly or heavenly state. We will see that this "heart" of the Church is made up of two eminently spiritual realities received by human beings, one of them *created*, which is the grace of Christ, and the other *uncreated*, which is the very Person of the Holy Spirit by appropriation.

Now at the level of our *knowledge* of the Church, the question should be addressed here in a precise manner. The two aspects of the Church—celestial and terrestrial—are closely related epistemologically; in other words, one aspect tells us about the other and allows us to know the other, and vice versa.

In the first place, the heavenly Church is the *exemplar* of the earthly Church. The Church in heaven is the model, in some way, after which the Church on earth is fashioned.¹⁰ The "heart" of the Church is, if one can put it like this, in its "pure" state in heaven, not wounded or limited by sin and our present carnal condition. A thorough knowledge of this "heart" of the ecclesial reality, at least as much as is possible here below, is very valuable in coming to know the deepest nature and most intimate workings of the Church on earth. But the Church in heaven is the less well known. We can speak about it thanks to Revelation, but with much humility. That is where the mystery is the most luminous, and we cannot contemplate it in great depth. We must recall the humility necessary for the theologian, which is none other than the humility of faith. Faith is not a kind of knowledge through evidence as the beatific vision will be.

The Church on earth is *the sign* of the Church in heaven. It is appropriate to recall several elements of exegesis concerning the question of the different senses of Scripture.¹¹ We summarize here the teaching of St. Thomas, who offers a good synthesis.¹²

The author of Scripture is God. God speaks to man in human language; otherwise man could not have understood.¹³ In doing so, God uses words to signify something, as we do: this is the *literal sense* of Scripture that expresses first what the inspired author wanted to say. For example, in John 15:5: "Apart from me you can do nothing." "Nothing" must be understood in the order of nature (God the Creator and his Providence), and in the order of grace (God the Savior). The literal sense also concerns the case of metaphors and parables; they must be taken in the proper and figurative literal sense, which explains a reality of grace through an image. For example, Jesus is the door to the sheepfold.

But God also speaks to man through things, institutions, and events,

---

10. This is a very patristic line of theological reasoning that is thoroughly adopted by St. Thomas; see for example *In Ephes*. c. 3, lect. 3 (Marietti 161).

11. The fundamental study of this subject is the one by Henri de Lubac, *Medieval Exegesis: The Four Senses of Scripture*, 3 vol. (Grand Rapids, Mich.: Eerdmans, 1998–2009), which shows that the doctrine of the four senses of Scripture is fundamentally patristic. This is not a question of the *thought* of the Fathers, but of the Fathers as *witnesses to the faith* (the difference between history and theology).

12. See *ST* I, q. 1, art. 10; *Catechism of the Catholic Church* (*CCC*), 2nd ed. (Washington, D.C.: Libreria Editrice Vaticana and United States Catholic Conference, 2000), nos. 115–18.

13. A bit of common sense does not hurt in theology.

and he is the only one able to do so because he directs the course of things and thus gives them a meaning, whether he willed them or simply permitted them.[14] For example, the crossing of the Red Sea signifies and speaks to us:

- about the Passion and Resurrection that it announces by prefiguration;
- about Christian baptism, which it also announces by prefiguration.

Here we are speaking about the *spiritual sense* of Scripture. It is based on the literal sense; it does concern an account of a passage through the sea, but it goes beyond it. This spiritual sense is subdivided into three particular senses that are called the *allegorical sense,* the *moral sense,* and the *anagogical sense.*[15]

The allegorical sense means that things, institutions, and events of the Old Law (OT) signify and announce the things, institutions and events of the New Law (NT). This is true of the example that we took previously of the passage through the Red Sea. The fact—which really happened—refers to another reality that it prefigures or announces allegorically (cf. 1 Cor 10:1ff.; Gal 4:24). We speak too about the *typical* or *typological* sense.

For the moral sense, the things, institutions, and events of the Old Law signify what Christ was later to accomplish (for example, the sacrifice of Isaac), and the things, institutions, and events of the New Law accomplished by Christ manifest what we must do.

The anagogical sense, finally, signifies that the things, institutions, and events that designate the Christ who is to come (OT) or that have been accomplished by Christ (NT) are signs of the realities of eternal glory. This anagogical sense is what we keep in mind here for the Church. The Church on earth, instituted by Christ, is the sign of the Church in heaven. Just as on the ontological level the Church on earth

---

14. In strict theological terms, we say that God *wills* the good and *permits* evil (although liturgical language can make exceptions, and vernacular translations may be inexact).

15. Parenthetically, knowing and being able to read Scripture according to these different senses is the key to Christian preaching. One does not have to limit oneself to the moral sense, which, left to itself, considered alone to the exclusion of the others, causes preaching to degenerate into moralizing and guilt-inflicting sermons.

is the beginning and the Church in heaven is the perfect achievement, there is no break between the two states of the *one* Church; at the epistemological level (level of knowledge) where we are, we say that an understanding of the earthly Church enables us to have a certain understanding of the heavenly Church. And that is very important if we are to avoid presenting as essential to the Church per se realities that are present only in the Church on earth. Thus, for example, the sacraments and the hierarchy were instituted *by Christ,* but they have a reason for being and are present only in the pilgrim Church.[16] This question about the institutions proper to the Church on earth is an important one. Although we must not absolutize these institutions, we must not neglect them, either. To maintain this balance, we will have to study more closely these terrestrial "essentials" that disappear in heaven, while at the same time insisting that the pilgrim Church and the exultant Church make up one Church. And we will see more particularly in what respects these earthly institutions are *signs* of a celestial essential that is *already present* in the Church on earth.

Let us remember for the moment that the two aspects of the one Church must not be confused; still, what we have just noted is enough to make it clear that they must not be separated.

The distinction between the heavenly Church and the earthly Church

On the ontological level we are dealing with a reality that is, strictly speaking, *one.* Yet as long as this world lasts, the Church has two states, two ways of being, two forms of actualization. When we say that the heavenly Church is the exemplar of the Church on earth, we add the converse: that the Church on earth is in the image of the Church in heaven. Expressed in biblical terms, it is a question of an *ontological dependence:* the pilgrim Church receives its "heart" from the Church in glory. But by the simple fact that she is sojourning on earth, she undergoes a certain conditioning that is proper to her. Everyone knows the

16. The *Shepherd of Hermas* presents the Church as a tower being built; once it is completed, the scaffolding—the sacraments and the hierarchy—will be removed; cf. Book I, Vision 3, chapter 2 (PG 1.901–2), and Book III, Similitude 9, chapter 1 (PG 1.981–2).

saying, *Quidquid recipitur, ad modum recipientis recipitur* [Whatever is received is received according to the manner of the recipient]. What is received does not change, but it is received in a certain way by reason of the specific conditions of the one who receives it.

The Church in heaven is a reality of glory. The Church on earth is a reality not *of* but *in* this world, and this insertion into the world gives her particular characteristics. Let us look quickly at the ways in which the world affects the one Church that is found in it.

The earthly Church is a *complex* reality—in other words, is made up of several interconnected elements:

- A purely spiritual element that for the moment we can call in a very general way its "soul";
- A human element that for the moment we can call also in a very general way its "body."

These two elements are very closely connected, like the soul and the body in man; this is the basis of the analogy. Although the spiritual element of the Church on earth is formally identical to that of the Church in heaven, namely the grace of Christ and the Person of the Holy Spirit, the human element, in contrast, is in a form proper to the pilgrim state of the Church on earth. But we should add: the earthly Church is in the image of the heavenly Church, *not* by reason of its spiritual element (for here there is pure and simple identity), but by reason of its human element. To put it briefly, the sacraments and the hierarchy reflect the likewise human, but transfigured elements of the glorious Church. Thus, for example, through the manifold activity of the hierarchy, *vice Christi gerens* [acting in the place of Christ], the Holy Spirit and grace are transmitted to us here below. We are dealing with a form of mediation. This mediation, in its earthly aspect, will indeed cease in glory, but the need for some sort of mediation remains in glory, and the glorious humanity of Christ takes this task upon itself: the mediation of Christ is eternal (Heb 8:6ff. and 9:15ff.). The gifts of God always come to us through the mediation of Christ's humanity, whether on earth through the concurrence of the specifically earthly mediations or in heaven with the sole mediation of the sacred humanity of our Savior.

Thus we see that it is necessary to proceed by making distinctions so as not to confuse everything, but we must not make them so rigid as to end up introducing separations. This is a real danger, for if it happens, it will affect not only the *uniqueness* of the Church, but also her *unity*, the essential bond between her two aspects, between body and soul. It is a question here of avoiding the two capital sins of the mind, which are *monism* and *dualism*. Monism turns a single element into the whole subject. So does traditional Protestant ecclesiology: the real Church is the community of the predestined—in other words, a spiritual, invisible community. Dualism separates elements and consequently makes out of them separated realities instead of a complex reality. Reformed ecclesiology developed in this way by recognizing *two communities* that do not overlap, one called the visible Church and the other the invisible Church.

In order to avoid these two errors, we must be steadfast *in the faith* and try to explain *reasonably* this *uniqueness* and this *unity* in the distinction.

At the level of knowledge

Distinguishing the Church in heaven and the Church on earth without separating them allows us to know one by the other, and here we encounter the two major realist paths of knowledge.

Either we may start from revealed knowledge about the Church in heaven and try to see in what respects the Church on earth is an image of it: the "descending" schema (the key idea here will be the notion of *participation*, so dear to Platonic metaphysics, that initiates the path of *causality*: the heavenly Church engenders the earthly Church [efficient cause] and is its consummation [final cause]); or we may start from revealed knowledge about the Church on earth and try to see in what respects it is the sign of the Church in heaven: the "ascending" schema. The key idea here will be the notion of *analogy* (attribution) so dear to Aristotelian metaphysics; but the Church on earth herself is known only by means of an analogy (of proportionality) to the natural created reality that is human society.

We will have plenty of opportunities to return to all this. Let us say for now that these two major paths of knowledge are mutually dependent; since they do not have the same strengths and weaknesses, they are called to help each other.

9. A brief history of the Church

Here we will review very rapidly, limiting ourselves to a few features, the major historical stages of the pilgrim Church here below, in connection with the major theological questions that are posed in each era. This will allow us to extricate the main question or questions of our time that the course will have to address in particular.

The apostolic age

The Church of the first century is the nascent Church. She experiences a very rapid expansion. The main theological question confronting her, Scripture informs us, is the question of the break with Judaism. How does one understand the fact that Christ came *to fulfill* and not to *abolish*? The question was posed concretely in reference to eating with the Jews (cf. Acts 15:1ff.; Gal 2:11ff.: the "council" of Jerusalem). One must realize that the nascent community did not yet have the New Testament in the form of an established *corpus* of writings.[17] But the ecclesial community lived on the Word of God and the sacraments of Christ through the ministry of its pastors. It was totally Christian, and its first task was to set itself up as such in contrast to the Jews. The Church is Israel according to the Spirit and not according to the flesh; the Church is the new People of God founded on the new and eternal covenant. All these central themes of Christianity were not so much formulated theoretically as lived out by the apostolic Church, which took ownership of them and witnessed to them even to the point of martyrdom. The break with Judaism, and not with the Old Testament, is the great step that it had to take in that age.

The patristic age

Little by little the Church developed an understanding of what she believed so as to conform more fully to it and to respond to serious errors and harmful practices. What appears as the primary thing here is *the faith*, its objective content. The unity of and in the Church was root-

---

17. This Canon will be determined gradually over the course of the second century; the Canon of Muratori dates from around 160, and the complete list of Books recognized as inspired is found in the acts of the provincial councils of Africa in 393 and 397.

ed in the unity of faith. This was the period of the major councils, especially the Christological ones. The faith of the Church is above all the knowledge of a person: Jesus, the Christ.

These "foundational" councils were not meetings of an academy to reflect on this or that question of a particular school of thought. They were convened in response to heresies about the person or the work of Christ or of the Holy Spirit. This is their context, and it is very important if they are to be interpreted correctly. Unlike the medieval councils that were above all councils about moral reform, these first councils took place within the context of a crisis of faith. During this period we encounter those great doctors who are called the Fathers of the Church. They investigated the divine mysteries in a unique way. The authority of their writings is immense, but not absolute. When all (or almost all) of them are in agreement on a point, they constitute a particularly luminous point of Tradition. Today we can see further than they could thanks to the continuous development in our understanding of the faith ("continuous" does not mean peaceful!), and in relation to them we are like "dwarves standing on the shoulders of giants." It is thanks to the Fathers that we have the benefit of a solid doctrine of faith that to a very large extent is shared with the Orthodox East. It is an inestimable treasure.

With respect to ecclesiology, the Fathers are at the beginning of the development of the great theology of the Church as Body of Christ. They made explicit the concepts in the Pauline letters and showed the strict connection between the Eucharist and the Church. After them, with each doctrinal difficulty or in every period of theological renewal, they would always be the ones appealed to in order to discern which formulations truly express the faith. This is why we will cite patristic theology extensively.

The Middle Ages (seventh to fifteenth centuries)

Three major themes, among others, characterize this period:

- At the end of the Western Roman Empire, which was a state of "sacral" Christendom,[18] the Church, overcoming immense diffi-

18. The terms "temporal" or "secular Christendom" and "spiritual" or "consecrational Christendom" are taken from Jacques Maritain, *Humanisme intégral*, in *Oeuvres*

culties, succeeded in integrating the barbarians. The various kingdoms that were born from the collapse of the Roman Empire came to be Christian and, progressively, in communion with Rome. Then there was a slow evolution toward the return of a "sacral" Christendom. A reference point for this development is the reign of Charlemagne. The pope and the emperor were the two great authorities in civil society, and relations between the spiritual and the temporal orders were (relatively) harmonious. Subsequently, because of a decline in faith and therefore in morals, the temporal power would try to assert priority over the spiritual power that was degenerating. This was the famous investiture controversy (1059–1122) that would prompt the Gregorian reform. The major point at stake here is the independence of the Church over against the monarchs. This is first of all a theological question, namely distinguishing the spiritual from the temporal. A whole theology of the Church is involved in it. The question would crop up again at the time of the conflict between Boniface VIII and King Philip IV the Fair.

- From the eleventh century on we see an increase in the power of the papacy. Today this is a very well-known point in Church history, and it allows us to study with very reliable materials the modern genesis of the papal institution. We are talking about a progressive awareness by the papacy of its role in the Church—in modern terms, since it began with St. Clement of Rome. The low Middle Ages were the era that saw the emergence of modern forms of exercising the primacy of the successor of Peter. We are correct in speaking about *forms*, because on the fundamental level of dogmatic content, even though the dogma was not solemnly declared until Vatican I (1870), it was in actual practice from the very beginning. But forms are not just secondary, variable for-

---

complètes, by Jacques Maritain and Raïssa Maritain, edited by Jean-Marie Allion et al. (Fribourg, Switzerland: Éditions Universitaires, 1984), 6:306ff.; English edition, *Integral Humanism: Temporal and Spiritual Problems of a New Christendom*, trans. Joseph W. Evans (New York: Scribner, 1968), 291. For an enlightening theological application, see Charles Journet, *L'Église du Verbe incarné*, 3rd ed. (Bruges: Desclée de Brouwer, 1962), 1:269ff.; English edition, *The Church of the Word Incarnate*, trans. A. H. C. Downes (London: Sheed and Ward, 1955), 214ff.

malities; they are an expression of the fundamental truth. Thus in the medieval period there was an "acceleration" of the unfolding of the dogma, the attainment of a higher consciousness. We should note that the great schism, the separation from the Orthodox Churches, dated 1054 for convenience, did not originate directly in a quarrel over the Roman primacy, but rather in a debate about the *Filioque*, which, it is true, implies a certain exercise of papal primacy.

- The development in the understanding of the Petrine ministry brought with it in the fifteenth century a profound crisis in the West that was to have repercussions down to the present day: the conciliarist crisis. The controversial question was: what is the highest authority in the Church: is it the pope or the general council? "The council," answered the conciliarists, who reached their apogee at the Councils of Constance (1414–1418) and Basel (1431–1445). This was not simply a juridical question, but a profoundly dogmatic one, the settling of which requires that one have a balanced doctrine of the relation between the universal Church and the local churches. We will return to this. For the sake of brevity, we note here that the conciliarist thesis presupposes that one understand the universal Church as a federation of local churches. In that case the universal Church is a *quantitative whole*. There is no more in the whole than in the sum of the parts. This sum, the conciliarists maintained, would be expressed by the general council. Now Catholic doctrine asserts that universality is not primarily a quantitative, but rather a *qualitative* and essential datum, of which the Roman pontiff is the guarantor by virtue of the Petrine succession. *Catholic* is a name denoting quality and not only, or primarily, quantity: a man is Catholic. Therefore the universal Church is the *mother*, in other words, the *principle* of the local churches. Ontologically she precedes the local churches because she transmits to them simultaneously the reality of their being as Church and their unity with one another. This doctrinal point still presents a difficulty in our day for a number of theologians. Once the extremes of the medieval conciliarist current became a thing of the past, this line of thinking was able to persist. The Catholic doctrine was reiterated at Vatican II and even more recently in a document by the Congregation for the Doctrine of the Faith.[19] We will examine this question in detail.

The Reformation and the Counter-Reformation (sixteenth to nineteenth centuries)[20]

The Reformation is the most extensive tragedy that has affected the Church in the West since the Pelagian crisis (a thousand years earlier). In it the "heart" of Catholic ecclesiology was directly challenged.

From a historical point of view, it is necessary to note that the Church saw the danger coming and tried to confront it by holding a general council (Lateran V, 1512–1517). This was a council aimed at reform, especially of clerical morals and the Roman curia. But it was too late, and the will to convert the words of this Council into deeds was indisputably lacking in fervor from "top" to "bottom." Furthermore, the Reformers were much more critical of whole sections of dogma than of ecclesiastical morals.

The Reformation, and chiefly Luther, took as its point of departure a separation in the earthly Church of the human from the "divine." It challenged head-on the *unity* of the ecclesial being. For this entire current of thought, with the nuances proper to each Reformer, the one true Church is only spiritual and "therefore," they add, invisible. The Counter-Reformation (Council of Trent, 1545–1563) subsequently tried to respond to the Protestant theses and tackled in-depth the job of cleaning up ecclesiastical morals, with the important qualification that the erroneous ideas concerning ecclesiology strictly speaking would not be addressed directly by the Council. It taught, for example, that sinners are *in* the Church and not outside, as Calvin claimed, and that the sacraments *contain* the grace that they signify and transmit, and do not merely signify it as Luther said and as Zwingli even more radically maintained. Trent gave no direct teaching on the most important point being debated—namely, the unity of the mystery of the Church. Theologians would later attempt to develop the Catholic

---

19. Cf. *LG* 23; Congregation for the Doctrine of the Faith, *Letter to the Bishops of the Catholic Church on Some Aspects of the Church Understood as Communion*, Rome, May 28, 1992, in *AAS* 85 (1993): 838–50.

20. In some respects the period of the Catholic Counter-Reformation concluded with the Second Vatican Council.

response to this challenge. They tended to say exactly the contrary of the reformers and thus ran the risk of going to the opposite extreme. We will see an example of this in an unfortunate passage by St. Robert Bellarmine, which we will study because it would have repercussions until the eve of Vatican II.

From the ecclesiological perspective, we must also note that in response to the famous Lutheran thesis of the personal interpretation of Scripture, Catholic theology developed a whole dogmatic treatise about the Magisterium that is profoundly rooted in the millennial tradition, but that also became warped toward the opposite extreme.[21] It went so far as to maintain that the Magisterium—especially that of the Roman pontiff—expressed itself with the help of the Spirit of truth, which is correct, but this assistance was sometimes understood to have the same sort of causality as the sacraments, which is plainly and simply inadmissible. Even the exercise of the charism of infallibility by the pope does not bring such causality into play. It is true that the magisterial activity of the Church developed considerably in the nineteenth and twentieth centuries; that the theology of the papal Magisterium is properly Catholic; that some popes like Pius XII taught on this subject very important things that were thoroughly incorporated into Vatican II. But vigilance is always required to ensure a balanced formulation of this doctrine, and from this perspective theology today is just emerging from the Counter-Reformation, with considerable risks of going from one extreme to the other, such as regarding an encyclical as one theological treatise among others.

The contemporary period (twentieth century)

At the purely historical level, we can note during the nineteenth century the rise of nationalism and the development of the separation between Church and State. After the French Revolution the Church had to confront the claims of the new states, especially in Europe, which as a matter of policy deprived her almost completely of her traditional ways of being present and active in society. The suppression of the Papal States, the unilateral abrogation of many concordats, the overt persecution of religious communities and their works,—all this

---

21. We are speaking here about distortions *in theology*, not *of the Magisterium*.

added up to a context of extremely difficult struggles for the Church. Today, in retrospect, we can see that the Christian community did not founder beneath that attack, but on the contrary discovered new ways of approaching the modern world in a manner better adapted to it, and also intensified its internal reform. "Dethroned" and often unjustly despoiled—in a word, persecuted—the Church indisputably gained in spiritual depth. Although she seemed rather tame in the eighteenth century, from the nineteenth century on the Church was very dynamic in its pastoral ministry and missionary work, and a theological renewal got under way.

The outstanding event of the nineteenth century was the holding of the First Vatican Council (1869–1870). Everyone knows that this Council was interrupted when Napoleon III, because of the conflict with Prussia, withdrew his troops that were protecting Rome against the Italian republicans who were trying to seize it. Once the revolutionaries had invaded the City, the Pope deemed that the liberty of the bishops and his own freedom were no longer assured, and consequently suspended the Council. At that moment only part of the Constitution on the Church had been voted on. *Pastor aeternus* was supposed to include teaching about the primacy of the Roman pontiff and on the office of the bishops. Only the first point was voted on and promulgated, however, and consequently an imbalance was created. The Church would have to wait until Vatican II to make up for it.

During this period the major doctrinal questions were related to the nature of the Church, her right to exist.... The pontificate of Leo XIII (1877–1903) witnessed important progress in Catholic theology. From there various renewals went on to develop—in liturgy, exegesis, patristics, Thomistic studies—that would flourish from 1920 until the eve of Vatican II, which in this regard would be their mature fruit, so to speak. It was a period of intense fermentation that would witness returns to Tradition older than the Counter-Reformation as well as significant advances. The wealth that this period (1920–1960) represents for the theology of the Church is immense.

One major fact of contemporary history that can be dated to the time between the two World Wars is the birth and progress of the ecumenical movement. The Protestants were its initiators, and the Catholic and Orthodox Churches followed. Some important advances were made during the 1950s, and the Second Vatican Council—from the Catholic side—benefited from them, making some very clear progress in ecclesiology. The major questions were, What is the *one, unique* Church that we profess in the Creed (*"credo unam Ecclesiam"*)? Where is it? How can we recognize it? In order to answer these queries, it is necessary to have reviewed the essential data of ecclesiology, and we will proceed in carefully gradated stages.

At the present hour we find ourselves under the major influence of Vatican II: the greatest grace given to the Church in the twentieth century, Paul VI used to say. This Council saw the results of the reflections of the hundred years that preceded it, but it is also a fresh point of departure. The Church is the main subject of Vatican II. One could say that Catholic ecclesiology now has a decisive teaching in the last Council. Now it is a question of ensuring that this finding is incorporated into Tradition—in particular that the connection between Vatican I and Vatican II is made—and integrated into the life of the community. We have scarcely begun, and some important problems, not always new ones, remain to be solved. Among the principal questions let us note here the theological understanding of the unity of the ecclesial being, together with the concepts that Vatican II tried to promote—namely, the notion of *sacrament* and the notion of *communion*. There is also the question of the relation between the Roman primacy and the college of bishops, the relations between the universal Church and the local churches, etc. In the speculative part, our course cannot avoid dealing extensively with this.

10. Brief history of ecclesiology

Everything that we said about the appearance of the treatise "*De Ecclesia*" in the fourteenth century showed that ecclesiology, as a distinct part of dogmatic theology, is very recent. This new discipline has gone through four major phases from its birth to our day. We will describe them rapidly.

Nascent ecclesiology

In the fifteenth and sixteenth centuries ecclesiology is a discipline for "combat" against various doctrinal deviations, whether they herald the

Reformation (Huss, Wycliffe) or belong to the Reformation itself. What was at stake in these different movements was the precise understanding of the Church as a *means* of salvation. The theological understanding of the idea of *mediation,* which for centuries had been unproblematic, became one of the most debated points. But this gives nascent ecclesiology a fragmentary aspect; the *whole* ecclesial mystery is not what is being studied, and the works that are published—in ever greater numbers—are not true summas of ecclesiology. One sixteenth-century author would have a considerable following until the eve of Vatican II: St. Robert Bellarmine. His immense work, which is not exclusively ecclesiological, is remarkable in many respects, but it is downright regrettable that it was handed down to posterity primarily through an unfortunate passage of his treatise *"De Ecclesia."* He thereby set the stage for a way of addressing the question of the unity between the "means of salvation" aspect and the "reality of salvation" aspect in the mystery of the Christian community, which culminated in several impasses from which Vatican II would attempt to escape. We will study this much more carefully in the speculative section.[22]

The ecclesiology of the Counter-Reformation

In the seventeenth, eighteenth, and nineteenth centuries, ecclesiology remains piecemeal and not very high-quality. The Dominican Thomists tried to construct a treatise *"De Ecclesia" ad mentem S. Thomae* [according to the teaching of St. Thomas]—for example, Billuart in the eighteenth century—and so did the Jesuit Thomists—for example, Suarez in the seventeenth century and Perrone in the nineteenth century—but these attempts were too much affected by the Protestant innovations to be genuine, calm syntheses. The tone is often polemical, and the work lacks the breadth of vision that an appeal to older Tradition would foster, particularly that of the Church Fathers. During this period the French School of spirituality would rescue the theme of the Church as the Body of Christ. Catholic theologians had tossed it out purely and simply because Protestant theologians made frequent use of it! But in the French School this theme is treated in a manner that is rather individualistic and not sufficiently ecclesial: the assimilation of the believ-

---

22. For a meticulous, well-documented presentation of this founding period of ecclesiology, the reader may refer to Congar, *L'Église de S. Augustin à l'époque moderne.*

ing soul to Christ.²³ Jansenism would have the same tendency. In short, apart from the "spirituality," which is rather individualistic, the theology of that era was mainly concerned with countering the Protestants. We must not exaggerate anything, however. These centuries, as limited as they may have been at the level of ecclesiology, were missionary centuries, and the many martyrs in every corner of the earth testified to a very lively awareness of the mystery that is the Church.

The ecclesiology of the contemporary renewal

The late nineteenth century and the twentieth are an extremely rich period from the perspective of theology, and ecclesiology is one of the topics that benefited the most from it. The Encyclical *Mystici Corporis* (June 29, 1943)—the first magisterial document in history dealing with the Church per se for the purpose of making a synthesis—is a culmination and an attempt at discernment. It gave rise to many studies that also directly prepared the way for Vatican II. The last Council, as we have said, had as its central theme the mystery of the Church. Thus, as Romano Guardini accurately prophesied as early as 1920, the twentieth century was the "century of the Church."

At the outset of this ecclesiological renewal we find the famous School of Tübingen, with its great master Johann-Adam Möhler. In his book *Die Einheit in der Kirche*,²⁴ Möhler reviews the Fathers of the first three centuries and strives to show how the Church appeared to them. Thus he distinguishes the spiritual Church (unity in the Spirit) and the organic Church (unity in the ecclesial institutions). He reintegrates the Holy Spirit into ecclesiology after the omissions and excesses of the Counter-Reformation. Certainly, his thought has its share of defects (he is a Romantic ...), and, although his orthodoxy is sound,

---

23. Even today catechetical and theological publications are perhaps not entirely free of this perspective. Thus, for example, in a recent catechetical commentary on the great mosaic in the Basilica of St. Clement in Rome, in dealing with the theme of Eucharistic communion, the author says, "By receiving the consecrated bread the Christian becomes the Body of Christ"; that is inexact: the Christian becomes a *member* of the Body of Christ that is the Church. St. Paul never speaks about the Christian as the Body of Christ but always as a *member* of the Body of Christ.

24. Johann-Adam Möhler, *Die Einheit in der Kirche* (Tübingen: H. Laupp, 1825); English translation, *Unity in the Church, or The Principle of Catholicism, Presented in the Spirit of the Church Fathers of the First Three Centuries*, ed. and trans. Peter C. Erb (Washington, D.C.: The Catholic University of America Press, 1996).

the value of his theological construct is nonetheless affected by these weaknesses. But we have to give him a lot of credit for getting Catholic ecclesiology out of a rut. By distinguishing somewhat clumsily between the Church of the Spirit and the institutional Church, he was the one who launched the modern debate that revolves to this day around two "poles": charity versus institution, or to put it in other terms, soul versus body. In Möhler's study the body (or the institution) comes after the soul (or the Spirit) that creates the body in which it will express itself. We find here a typically Romantic, vitalist vision. Hence one cannot avoid a certain juxtaposition of institution and love. But Möhler carefully avoids making it an antinomy by correctly emphasizing that the institution is an emanation of the Spirit: the life creates for itself the organs that it needs. This presents the institution as an *effect* of charity, which is true, but it does not take account of the fact that the institution is also the *cause* of charity, which is the main thing. Christ indeed instituted an apostolic hierarchy to preach his word and to celebrate his sacraments, and the Spirit is usually given by means of preaching and sacramental celebration.[25]

Furthermore, during this period, sociology developed—as far as concerns the notion of civil society—the distinction between society and community (or communion), and this distinction, more or less adroitly transposed to ecclesiology to express the classic distinction between the body and the soul of the Church, has made it rather confusing and difficult to explain the unity of the constitutive elements of the Church. We will return to this.

Elsewhere the Jesuits of the Roman College (which in the late nineteenth century would become the Gregorian University), with men such as Passaglia and Schrader, will recover the Pauline theme of the Church as the Body of Christ. The Counter-Reformation had obscured it, as we have said, because people then thought that that theology conveyed the understanding that the Church is a uniquely spiritual reality (*mystical* Body = invisible Body). Now since the Protestants were supporting that view, the Catholics hastily tried to do away with

---

25. In these developments we must not misunderstand the meaning of the word "institution." It does not signify the juridical or political "structure" of a social community, as in modern sociology. The precise ecclesiological (theological) sense is that which has been instituted by Christ. In the Eucharistic Prayer we have the "institution narrative."

the topic. It would have been better to return to a deeper understanding of the Pauline data as the Fathers and the major Scholastic writers had commented on it. To say that *mystical* is the same as *spiritual* and "therefore" purely *invisible* is an odd narrowing of the sense, as we will see. With this ecclesiological renewal, the doctrine of the Church emerged gradually from the legalism with which it sometimes fraternized excessively during the time of the Counter-Reformation.

Later on, after the Second World War, the study of another major ecclesiological theme appeared and developed: the People of God. This was a return to the great Old Testament theology that was very clearly taken up into the New Testament. The Fathers had emphasized it following St. Paul: through Christ there is a passage from the people of the first covenant to the people of the new covenant. This simultaneously implies continuities and discontinuities between Israel and the Church. The People of the new covenant—here we find the novelty—is the Body of Christ. But it remains grafted onto Israel (cf. Rom 11). The ideas of election, vocation, and covenant must be understood initially in the Old Testament, and then it is necessary to see what newness Christ brings along the same lines. There is fulfillment and not abolition. So it is that this theme underscores the history of salvation. The Church has her beginnings in the Old Testament, where she is announced and prepared; this is the patristic theme of *Ecclesia ab Abel* [the Church from the time of Abel].

This whole gigantic effort of renewal restored a great theological depth to ecclesiology: the Church is an integral and integrating part of the Christian mystery. Although today we no longer need to be afraid of falling into a reductive sociological or juridical view of the Church, we will nevertheless still have to be vigilant so as not to lay ourselves open to it. Even in our day too many people understand the word "Church" in a truncated fashion. If a preacher says "Church" in a homily, it is a safe bet that a non-negligible proportion of the listeners will think: the pope and the bishops—in other words, the hierarchy. The secular and sometimes the religious press can fuel this misunderstanding. For example, we frequently read that "the Church says...," meaning that the pope or some conference of bishops has published some document. The word "Church" means *community*, and although it is true that the pastors are part of the community, it does not consist exclusively of them; the Church is made up of the faithful *as a whole,* united among themselves.

Ecclesiology at Vatican II and afterward

Vatican II was an ecclesiological Council: the Church was *the* theme of the Council. We have here an immense theological harvest consisting of judgments that have been discerned, affirmations—whether new or very traditional—and recommendations made for the future.... But a council is not an academic gathering. Its role is to reaffirm the faith in a given context. Its work is a *datum* [*donné*] that must be grasped in *positive* theology. Theologians receive this datum, and their job is to take up the speculative research, to make the connections between one conciliar statement and another, and thus to make progress in theological understanding so as to arrive at a more profound expression of the teaching. This task, as far as Vatican II is concerned, is still a work in progress. Generally it takes two or three generations to reach solid conclusions that the Magisterium will adopt and that will thus become the common property of the faithful as a whole. The 1985 Synod in Rome pointed out a certain number of interpretive errors in this research; it also recalled some important points that unfortunately had been forgotten after the Council—for example, the theme of the Church as the Body of Christ.

This theological project therefore still has a lot on its plate. There are demands that still have not been sufficiently met due to a lack of progress in theological understanding. Let us point out the most important ones:

- We still do not have an ecclesiological synthesis. Nowadays it is rare to find rigorously unified treatises on the Church that clearly distinguish between the study of the sources and the speculative elaboration. This is a clear sign that all the rediscovered elements have not yet been situated in their precise place, and have not been completely decanted either, leaving the dregs behind. The fact that since Vatican II we still do not have an encyclical on the Church plainly shows that the question has not yet sufficiently ripened.
- There are persistent ecclesiological difficulties that—besides the fact that they delay the synthesis—carry over to the pastoral level

and give rise to errors that aggravate difficulties in the life of the Church and in the accomplishment of her mission. The most important of these difficulties, it seems to us, is the separation between the institution and charity that one encounters more often in practice than in theory.[26] At this level, Möhler's insights have had consequences that he certainly did not foresee or intend. This difficulty is one of the primary causes of the current ecclesial malaise that is harmful to the unity of the faithful as well as that of the pastors, and therefore to the Church's pastoral and missionary witness. We will endeavor to examine it as completely as possible.

11. Statement of the general outline of the course

The plan that we will follow is extremely simple. It follows from one distinction at the fundamental level, the distinction between being and action, and from another distinction on the methodological level, the distinction between the theology of sources and speculative theology.

The Church is a specific reality: knowing this reality comes down, in the first place, to studying her *being*. We will first describe this being by taking inventory of her constitutive elements with the help of the data of Revelation: theology of sources. These data can be grasped with the help of biblical images, the expression "Kingdom of God," and especially the revealed themes—namely the Body of Christ, the Temple of the Spirit, and the People of God. All of this information causes one great constant to emerge, which is the sacramentality of the Church. Consequently we will study, for the purpose of making a positive analysis, this "law" of sacramentality that allows us to make the connection among all these data that have been compiled.

After the positive description that reveals to us *how* the Church is,

---

26. See on this point the compilation of the responses from the bishops' conferences to the preparatory questionnaire for the Roman Synod that met in 1985 for the twentieth anniversary of Vatican II, in *Vingt ans après Vatican II: Synode extraordinaire, Rome, 1985*, in the series Documents d'Église 23 (Paris: Le Centurion, 1986), 52: "Understanding the Church as a mystery proves to be difficult for many Christians. Hence a certain inclination to make inappropriate contrasts between the Church as institution and the Church as Mystery; the Church as the People of God versus the hierarchical Church.... The idea of the Church as Communion has not yet imbued the fabric of the Christian people" [translated from French]; see *The Extraordinary Synod, 1985: Message to the People of God* (Boston: St. Paul Editions, 1985).

her constitutive elements and the fundamental relations among them, we will move on to the second phase: according to all that Revelation tells us about the Church, *what* is the Church? On the basis of the points that have been singled out in the first phase, we will inquire into the *definition* of the Church—in other words, one or more concepts capable of expressing the whole set of elements that constitute this *one* reality that is the Church. Once this is done, we will have to investigate (and this is the "fine point") what is the *ontological status* of this being that is the Church, by asking whether it attains the highest perfection of being, which is being a *person*. After that, we will review the *properties* of this ecclesial being—one, holy, catholic, and apostolic—which will provide the opportunity to explain many points only mentioned before. With that our study of the ecclesial being will be completed.

Of course, then comes our study of ecclesial action. This activity is of two sorts. First it is *intra-ecclesial*, dealing with relations among the faithful and more particularly with the relation between the two priesthoods (the priesthood of the faithful and the ministerial priesthood). This is what is most often called *pastoral ministry*. It is necessary to add the study of relations with separated Christians: ecumenism.[27] Secondly this action is also *extra-ecclesial*. We are speaking then about the relations between believers in Christ and non-Christians. This is the place for the study of *missiology*, the *relations between the Church and temporal civil society*, and *relations between the Church and non-Christian religions*. In this course of dogmatic theology we will limit ourselves to the study of the being of the Church. According to the division of the curriculum commonly adopted for Catholic theology, most of the elements concerning ecclesial action are addressed in other courses, in particular the fundamental principles of pastoral ministry in pastoral theology and the course on the sacrament of holy orders, or else can be grasped adequately with the help of appropriate readings.[28] Once we have stud-

---

27. Ecumenism is first studied in the positive part concerning the Church as the Body of Christ. Indeed, we must try to understand how the Church, which is *one* and *unique*—in other words, undivided in herself and singular—exists alongside Christians who themselves are divided. In the part concerning the properties of the Church, specifically the *one* Church, we will look at the ecumenical movement, its institutions, and its particular dynamism.

28. We highly recommend, for pastoral theology, the treatise by Daniel Bourgeois, *La Pastorale de l'Église*, AMATECA 11 (Luxembourg: Saint-Paul, 1999).

ied being and action, we will still have to consider the finality of it all—in other words, the ultimate purpose of the Church, eschatology, the entire Church in glory. But that part is the subject of a separate course (on the Last Things).

This division of the subject matter is simple. It can lead to some repetitions, but we will strive to take advantage of them to deepen and explain further each time. We can summarize the preceding in the following general outline:[29]

The Ecclesial Being

Part One: Theology of sources

Section 1: Description of the Church

> Chapter 1: The biblical images of the Church and the Kingdom of God
>
> Chapter 2: The theme of the Body of Christ
>
> Chapter 3: The theme of the Temple of the Spirit
>
> Chapter 4: The theme of the People of God

Section 2: Summary: The Church is a mystery

> Chapter 1: The first sense of the word mystery: *mystery as truth*
>
> Chapter 2: The second sense of the word mystery: *mystery as reality*

Part Two: Speculative theology

Section 1: The definition of the Church

Subsection 1.1: The nominal definition of the Church

Subsection 1.2: The real definition of the Church

> Chapter 1: The current state of speculative ecclesiology
>
> Chapter 2: The data of Vatican II
>
> Chapter 3: Proposed solution

Section 2: The question of the personality of the Church

---

29. Editor's Note: This version of the outline varies somewhat from the present, revised volume. The current organization of this book is reflected in the table of contents.

Section 3: The properties of the Church
    Chapter 1: The Church is one
    Chapter 2: The Church is holy
    Chapter 3: The Church is catholic
    Chapter 4: The Church is apostolic
    Chapter 5: The question of the Church's indefectibility

Part One

Theology of Sources
Description of the Church

1

Images of the Church and the Kingdom of God

I. Images of the Church

a. Symbolic language

When we use images to speak about the Church, we use so-called symbolic language. A symbol, in the sense in which we understand the term here, is a reality that speaks in a figurative way about another reality. For example, we say about the sacrament of baptism that it is the *door* leading to the other sacraments. The reality named "door" is, in itself, the means of arriving at an enclosed place, and this suggests to us the idea that baptism gives access to all the other sacraments. Symbolic language is not a conceptual, but a metaphorical language. It does not designate the nature of a thing itself, but rather tells something about its action, its effect.

Symbolism is a manner of expressing oneself that has two main qualities. First, it is a simple language that can be understood by everyone. Sacred Scripture, for this reason, is most often composed in symbolic language. The symbols refer to agrarian life or social life, and most people can have access to this language, which gives Sacred Scripture its incomparable flavor. Secondly, this form of expression is an open language—in other words, not locked into a single signification. For example, when we present Christ as a shepherd, this suggests not only that he leads the flock, but also that he feeds, tends and protects it.

This language, however, has two limitations that call for the further work of conceptual language. In the first place, each image is only an introduction to the reality being presented, not a sufficient explanation. For example, to say that the Church is the new Noah's ark suggests that the Church is necessary for salvation. We reason thus: just as entering into Noah's ark was necessary so as not to perish in the flood, so too the Church is the place where God saves us from the evil in this world. But this statement tells us nothing about the necessity itself; it affirms it, but neither explains nor specifies it. In the second place, every image expresses only one aspect of the reality; that is why it must be completed by other images. If one takes an image too far one arrives at absurd conclusions, or at least falls into error, by applying to the Church characteristics that are inappropriate and neglecting or even denying the essential aspects. For example, in discussing the Church as an ark that saves us from spiritual death, we have to explain that we are not in the Church like the passengers in a ship; rather, we make up the Church. The image of the ark must therefore be completed by that of the community: the Church is the People of God, which is to say that she is composed of persons. But here too we run up against a limit, because the meeting of persons is not what forms the Church (as in the case of a people); the Church begets her members, and in virtue of this she is prior to them, since she gave them existence. Therefore we complete the image of the community with that of the mother: the Church is a mother who gives us birth to new life. But here too we encounter a limit: this mother keeps her children in her bosom constantly, and so on.

We must keep in mind the richness and the weakness of figurative language, both so as to benefit fully from the wisdom conveyed by this form of expression, and so as not to fall prey to its limitations.[1] Having recalled this, we shall now present the principal images of the Church as given in the Constitution *Lumen gentium* (no. 6). There are around eighty ecclesial images in Sacred Scripture. The Council mentions about a dozen of them. They fall into two major types, rural images and social images. Those in the first group may no longer speak adequately to modern urban man, which is why the second group should not be neglected.

---

1. For a good presentation of symbolic language in theology, see the book by Fr. Yves de Montcheuil, *Aspects de l'Église*, 19–22, or in the English translation *Aspects of the Church*, 18–21.

b. Biblical images of the Church
1. Rural images
The flock and the shepherd (or pastor)[2]

The focus of the image is not on the flock, which would run the risk of reducing the faithful to the level of dumb sheep, but rather on the shepherd: he leads, guards, tends, feeds.... The image is transcended by the statement that he gives his life for his sheep, and that he is present to his flock not just personally, but also by his vicars, he being the "chief shepherd" (1 Pt 5:4). In these texts the Church appears either as the place where the flock is safe, the sheepfold, or as the flock itself, while taking care to explain that one must not separate the flock from its pastors; the Church gathers in her bosom both the sheep and the shepherds, who are not above but within the flock.

God's field[3]

Here the Church is the place where God's work is carried out. Hence the development or correction of this image by many others: this is the place where the ancient olive tree or the vineyard is planted and grows.... Linked also to this initial image are other images: the sower, the mustard seed, the weeds and the wheat ... that emphasize the time necessary for the Church to grow, and the coexistence within her of the good of holiness with the wounds of the evil that is sin. We should note also that the image of the vine is quite invaluable to help grasp the fundamental idea that is expressed by the theme of the Church as Body of Christ: Jesus is the vine-stock, we are the branches; only if we remain in Christ and share in his sap, his life, can we bear the fruit of eternal life (Jn 15:1–5).

2. Social images
The building[4]

Christians form a spiritual building. This image originates in Matthew 21:42 (and parallel passages), which repeats the Old Testament

---

2. The main scriptural passages: Is 40:11ff.; Ez 34:11ff.; Jn 10:1–18.
3. Cf. 1 Cor 3:9.
4. The most important passages are: 1 Cor 3:9–17; Eph 2:19–22; 1 Tm 3:15; 1 Pt 2:5

theme of the stone rejected which becomes the cornerstone (Ps 118:22–23). St. Paul uses various images, especially that of the rock as foundation, and St. Peter explains the idea of a "living stone" to describe Christ, but also the Christians united to him by baptism. In the teaching of St. Peter, the building thus constructed is the Temple; this underscores the priestly quality of the Christian: the believer, a stone of the holy Temple, is a priest in that Temple (1 Pt 2:4–10). In the pastoral letters, the image is rather that of the Church as God's house to be preserved in order and truth.

Family life

These images are equally numerous and suggestive. Essentially they are about the Church as Bride,[5] or as Mother.[6] The image of the bride is well known in the Old Testament, where it stands for Israel[7] and expresses specifically the theme of the covenant, in particular the violation thereof considered as adultery. In the New Testament the authors emphasize, in contrast with Israel, the fidelity and purity of the new People, either insofar as it has been purified (the OT–NT connection) or else inasmuch as it is immaculate and virgin (Eph 5:26–27 and 2 Cor 11:2).

This brief review of the biblical images shows that they correct and explain one another. Some of them tend to express a very intimate and profound unity of Christ with Christians, while others emphasize more the distinction between them. As such, these images pose the question of the union between Christ and Christians, but do not resolve it; that will require a more speculative effort. But these are the data provided by Sacred Scripture: they affirm a very close union, and at the same time a distinction so that the unity does not go so far as to become confusion. A theological understanding of these data will have to propose models with which to picture this type of unity.

(compare Acts 4:11). A good presentation can be found in Rudolf Schnackenburg, *The Church in the New Testament*, 81–83; 94–102; 167–70.

    5. See especially: Eph 5:22–23; Rv 19:7; 21:2, 21:9; 22:17.

    6. Particularly Rv 12:17; Gal 4:26.

    7. Hos 1:2–3; 2:20; Jer 2:2; 3:2; Is 1:2–3; 49:14ff.; and the Song of Songs in its entirety.

II. The kingdom of God
(*Lumen gentium* 5)

Everyone knows the formula by A. Loisy: "Jesus proclaimed the Kingdom, and what came was the Church."[8] For about a century the question of the relation between the kingdom of God and the Church has become much less clear and certain than it had been before. This situation has resulted from the renewal of biblical studies and the development of interreligious dialogue. The traditional interpretation emphasizes the relation of identity between the kingdom and the Church, adding that the perfection of this kingdom is yet to come;[9] this is expressed in the popular formula, "the already and the not yet."[10] This identification, however, has become problematic for many authors, owing especially to studies on non-Christian religions. Although Vatican II is situated within the classic perspective, we can observe several tentative statements in recent magisterial documents that convey a certain uneasiness. That is why we will first present this teaching in the form of a biblical image with its classic interpretation, and then we will present the more recent data while proposing several reference points.

a. The image of the kingdom of God

The expression "kingdom of God" or "kingdom of Heaven," which appears quite frequently in the synoptic Gospels and is the subject of many parables, is first presented as an image.

1. The basis for the image

It concerns the social community that human beings form by living together. This is divided into two aspects designating, on the one

---

8. Alfred Loisy, *L'Évangile et l'Église*, 153. Insofar as one can claim to understand correctly the thought of this famous modernist—which is rather fluid—the immediate context of this turn of phrase allows it to be understood thus: the Church is on earth the kingdom preached by Christ.

9. This is the classic interpretation of the Fathers in their commentaries on the second petition of the Our Father, "Thy kingdom come"; see, for example, Origen, *De Oratione* 25 (PG 11.495–99); St. Cyprian, *De Oratione Domini* 13–14 (CSEL 3.275–76).

10. In speculative terms this relation has classically been stated as follows: the kingdom on earth is the Church in her state of gradual realization, unfolding her potentialities until attaining her completed act at the Parousia.

hand, the Christ who exercises the kingship,[11] and on the other hand the community itself that is ruled. But often the synoptics concentrate their teaching under the one expression of "kingdom of God" or "of Heaven." For example, the appointment of St. Peter: "I will give you the keys of the kingdom of heaven" (Mt 16:18–20; see also Mt 18:18). Here we have simultaneously a sharing of the apostle in Christ's kingship and a mention of the kingdom itself (the keys). Equally noteworthy, and we will return to this, is the fact that there is also a distinction, well attested in the texts themselves, although there are not many of them, between a kingdom of the Son of Man and a kingdom of God (the Father).[12]

Be that as it may, the image is that of a community of a social type, with its citizens and its governors, the latter being vicars of the one master who is Christ. It is indeed the Church here below that is the kingdom.[13]

2. The content of the image

A political society is formed by the conjunction of several factors, in particular historical and cultural factors, that gather human beings together. The social image has to be transposed in order to understand that the community that is the kingdom is assembled by three essential factors that are clearly listed in *Lumen gentium* 5: the Word of God (cf. the parables of the sower and of the mustard seed), Christ's mighty works which are victories over evil and the Evil One (cf. Lk 11:20 and the parallel passage, Mt 12:28), and the very Person of Christ, source of the Word and his works. Consequently, listening to the Word, these works and professing Christ incorporate the believer into the kingdom.

In this world, this kingdom is at the same time growing and battling against evil, tending toward an accomplishment that will be the end of its history and of world history. It will not be a new kingdom that will follow the one that is already present on earth, but rather the passage from this earthly state to the eternal glory of God. This one kingdom

---

11. A very Pauline theme, cf. Eph 1:22.

12. Cf. Mt 13:41–43: the eschatological judgment will bring the elect from the kingdom of the Son of Man to the kingdom of the Father. But Lk 1:33 says that the kingdom of Christ will have no end.

13. St. Paul clearly states this in Eph 1:13–14: henceforth we are in the kingdom of the Son.

therefore exists already on earth, and the best proof is that it is growing here (Mt 13:31ff. and parallel passages), and its growth means it is not yet set in its perfection. It seems that we must take these statements in the strong sense. The Christian community is not only the sign announcing or prefiguring the kingdom to come; it is this kingdom that is journeying toward its consummation.

3. The data of biblical theology

The two major currents of the Old Testament

In the Old Testament, the kingdom of God is understood in three ways: God is the King of Israel, King of the world, and King of the elect. The concept of Yahweh, King of Israel, is probably the oldest. This dominion pertains to the election of this people by God, to the altogether special covenant that binds the Lord to Abraham and to his descendants (Is 43:15). After the exile, a purer concept of God's transcendence drew attention to the essential attributes of God, notably that he is Creator. That led to the inference of God's universal dominion over all men, which in turn broadened the promise of salvation to mankind. Finally, the kingship of God over the elect appeared later on, owing to the explicit formulation of the reward of the just in the hereafter. Then the supra-terrestrial and more perfect part of the kingdom of God appeared, the realization of which would have to follow the resurrection of the elect. This final stage is attested in few texts, but they are very clear (Ws 3:7–8; 5:15ff.), and it develops in the non-canonical writings, the influence of which was nevertheless very strong in late Judaism (IV Esdras, the Syriac Apocalypse of Baruch).

This kingship of God exists by the very fact that God is God and that he guides the history of salvation. But it is not always recognized by men—far from it. The messianic promise is nothing other than the assurance that God will one day establish his definitive kingdom in justice and peace. This realization of God's plan was the subject of successive and different conceptualizations of the messianic promise. From a purely earthly and collective conceptualization of the kingdom of God, before the exile, the Jews moved on to a more eschatological and spiritual one: the just hope for a better life; they shall rise again (2 Mc 7:9; 11:23). The Book of Wisdom deepens these intuitions (Ws 4:10–14; 6:18–19; 8:13–17).

Thus there are basically two major currents in the Old Testament: one very ancient, Semitic line of thought that ends in a terrestrial and collective eschatological conceptualization of the kingdom of God; and the other more recent one, marked by Greek wisdom, that underscores the spiritual, transcendent character, the "celestial" eschatology of the kingdom to come, but that ignores its social aspect present here below. We have here two concepts that are not unified. So it is that Scripture gives us these different aspects of this mysterious reality that is already present on earth and destined for the future world.

The synoptics

The theme of the kingdom of God is the principal theme in the preaching of Jesus.[14] As it is reported by the evangelists, this preaching is divided into two major groups of *logia*. The first group describes an earthly, temporal phase that is passing, while the second group insists on the transcendent, eternal phase of the kingdom. Some texts explicitly distinguish between these two phases of the same kingdom.[15]

The earthly, historical phase is the time of grace inaugurated by Christ. Signs and wonders manifest it (Jesus driving out demons, cf. Lk 11:20 and parallel passages), and some already strive mightily to enter it (Lk 16:16; Mt 11:12–15). But this inauguration does not have the extraordinary magnificence that was attributed to it in Jewish messianic expectations. The kingdom has humble beginnings; there is no recourse to violence or marvels, one cannot say, "it is here, it is there," and yet it is "in the midst" of the Jews (Lk 17:20–21). This inauguration is unsettling for the whole Jewish current of thought that was fixed on an earthly Messiah: this kingdom preached by Jesus does not have a political dimension. Jesus's response to the Pharisees ("Render to Caesar the things that are Caesar's," Mt 22:21) is clear in this regard: our duties to God and to Caesar are quite distinct, and the kingdom of God does not seek to replace the Empire. The kingdom is not the Jewish nation restored to political independence and power. Although it is spiri-

---

14. The expression "kingdom of God" or "of heaven" occurs 51 times in Matthew, 39 times in Luke, and 14 times in Mark. Luke can therefore write, as Matthew does, that until John there were prophets (the phase of the announcement, of the promise), but since John it has been the kingdom of God (Lk 16:16; Mt 11:12–13).

15. For example, the parable of the weeds and the prayer for the accomplishment of God's will, his kingdom, "on earth as it is in heaven" (in the Our Father), etc.

tual and moral, this kingdom of Jesus is nevertheless visibly organized as a community: Jesus is the shepherd, and he associates his disciples with him in this service of authority. This earthly phase is temporary and transitory. Involved in the vicissitudes of life here below, the kingdom is not fully realized on earth. Besides the inevitable mixture of the good and the wicked, it must face persecutions and false prophets; it encounters the temptation of wealth and the affliction of poverty. This kingdom that has been inaugurated is only a preparation for the second phase, which will be definitive.

This second phase will come about at the close of the age (Mt 13:39–40; 13:49; 24:3 and 28:20), on the "Day of the Lord," the day of general judgment. This is the kingdom "of the world to come," where the blessed will see God (Mt 5:8), where eternal life is presented in terms of joy (banquet) and glory (the just shall shine like the sun), in intimate friendship with the Master.

It is important to note the continuity that, from the Old Testament to the New, maintains this twofold conceptualization of the kingdom, at once earthly and heavenly, inaugurated and yet tending toward a personal and communal fulfillment.

4. The data of Vatican II

The teaching of the Council is situated within the classic perspective that we have just presented. Two citations show this clearly:

> The mystery of the holy Church is already brought to light in the way it was founded. For the Lord Jesus inaugurated his Church by preaching the Good News, that is, the coming of the kingdom of God, promised over the ages in the Scriptures (Mk 1:15; Mt 4:17).... But principally the kingdom is revealed in the person of Christ himself, Son of God and Son of Man, who came "to serve and to give his life as a ransom for many" (Mk 10:45).
>
> ...
>
> The Church, endowed with the gifts of her founder and faithfully observing his precepts of charity, humility and self-denial, receives the mission of proclaiming and establishing the kingdom of Christ and of God, and she is, on earth, the seed and the beginning of that kingdom. While she slowly grows to maturity, the Church longs for the completed kingdom and, with all her strength, hopes and desires to be united in glory with her king (*LG* 5).

This is a clear statement identifying the pilgrim Church on earth with the kingdom that has been inaugurated, is growing, and is journeying toward its eschatological fulfillment.[16] On the other hand, a certain distinction between the kingdom of Christ and the kingdom of God must still be mentioned. This is reinforced by the statement that, in this world, the kingdom is manifested by the very Person of the Incarnate Word and in his work that is recapitulated in the paschal mystery. This distinction, which is initially suggested in Scripture itself, as we have seen, must be examined in greater depth.

b. The current problem resulting from religious pluralism[17]

1. Summary of the moderate position[18]

The main idea is this: although the kingdom of God is indisputably present even here below in the Church, it nevertheless "extends beyond the Church to all humanity.... It is present where Gospel values are at work and where people are open to the action of the Spirit."[19] The commonly held thesis comes down to this: the kingdom of God is "a wider reality than the Church, indeed a universal reality."[20] The argument goes, then, that the ecclesial community resulting from the reception of God's gifts through the institutions of Christ does exist, but non-Christians do not belong to it; they form the *Kingdom of God* that is also a community of salvation, but is not the Church. Here we are dealing with the purely ecclesiological aspect of the question, with an attempt to mitigate or actually eliminate, the adage, "Outside the Church there is no salvation." This would become instead, "Outside the Reign of God there is no salvation." This thesis is based on the real distinction between the Church and the kingdom of God. This way of

---

16. This is also the perspective upheld by the *Catechism of the Catholic Church*, specifically in paragraphs 670–71 and 768–69 (with an explicit reference to *LG* 5).

17. For a good overview of this recent problem, see Jacques Dupuis, *Toward a Christian Theology of Religious Pluralism*, 330ff.

18. We do not discuss here the question of the value and role of non-Christian religions from the perspective of the salvation of all mankind, since that is the subject of a separate course on interreligious dialogue. That is why we limit ourselves here to describing a moderate position and do not take up the extreme theses (salvation solely in an explicit incorporation into the Church—or salvation in all religions that are part of an economy different from the Christian economy).

19. Dupuis, *Toward a Christian Theology of Religious Pluralism*, 340.

20. Ibid., 353.

The Kingdom of God

looking at things is assuredly quite new. It claims authority from several recent magisterial remarks interpreted in this sense.

2. The most recent magisterial formulations

Unquestionably, the papal Magisterium is currently proceeding somewhat tentatively in this matter. One has to admit that a certain number of acts, with varying degrees of authority, have followed one after the other, attempting to clarify the question, but they do not yet present any solid decisions. The *Catechism of the Catholic Church*, as we mentioned, adheres to the formulation of Vatican II. That being so, the *Catechism* does seem to have greater magisterial weight than an encyclical, but the fact that there are several encyclicals and not just one isolated apostolic letter reframes the question. When the ordinary Magisterium repeats the same teaching, such insistence signals the intention to teach authoritatively. Yet, in another sense, these few encyclicals are still very recent, and the teaching contained in them is not very unified. Finally, it must be noted that the Declaration *Dominus Iesus* (*DI*), which is presently the latest magisterial act of any weight in this matter, seems to be backing off somewhat from the position in those encyclicals. The least that one can say is that the time does not seem ripe to make this question the object of a definitive teaching. The main texts are the following:[21]

Pope John Paul II's Encyclical *Redemptoris missio* (*RM*) 18 and 20:

> [O]ne may not separate the kingdom from the Church. It is true that the Church is not an end unto herself, since she is ordered toward the kingdom of God of which she is the seed, sign and instrument. Yet, while remaining distinct from Christ and the kingdom, the Church is indissolubly united to both. Christ endowed the Church, his body, with the fullness of the benefits and means of salvation. The Holy Spirit dwells in her, enlivens her with his gifts and charisms, sanctifies, guides and constantly renews her (*LG* 4). The result is a unique and special relationship that, while not excluding the action of Christ and the Spirit outside the Church's visible boundaries, confers upon her a specific and necessary role (*LG* 18).
>
> It is true that the inchoate reality of the kingdom can also be found beyond the confines of the Church among peoples everywhere, to the extent

---

21. We limit ourselves here to the texts directly related to the problem Church-kingdom.

that they live "gospel values" and are open to the working of the Spirit who breathes when and where he wills (cf. Jn 3:8). But it must immediately be added that this temporal dimension of the kingdom remains incomplete unless it is related to the kingdom of Christ present in the Church and straining towards eschatological fullness (*LG* 20).

Pope John Paul II's Encyclical *Redemptor hominis* 6 speaks about:

the treasures of human spirituality, in which, as we know well, the members of these [non-Christian] religions also are not lacking. Does it not sometimes happen that the firm belief of the followers of the non-Christian religions—a belief that is also an effect of the Spirit of truth operating outside the visible confines of the Mystical Body—can make Christians ashamed at being often themselves so disposed to doubt concerning the truths revealed by God and proclaimed by the Church and so prone to relax moral principles.

Pope John Paul II's Encyclical *Dominum et vivificantem* 53:

The Second Vatican Council, centered primarily on the theme of the Church, reminds us of the Holy Spirit's activity also "outside the visible body of the Church." The council speaks precisely of "all people of good will in whose hearts grace works in an unseen way. For, since Christ died for all, and since the ultimate vocation of man is in fact one, and divine, we ought to believe that the Holy Spirit in a manner known only to God offers to every man the possibility of being associated with this Paschal Mystery" (*GS* 22.5).

The Declaration *Dominus Iesus* 21:

However, from what has been stated above [see no. 20][22] about the mediation of Jesus Christ and the "unique and special relationship" that the Church has with the kingdom of God among men (cf. *RM* 18)—which in substance is the universal kingdom of Christ the Saviour—it is clear that it would be contrary to the faith to consider the Church as *one way* of salva-

---

22. *DI* 20: "The Church is the 'universal sacrament of salvation' (*LG* 48) since, united always in a mysterious way to the Saviour Jesus Christ, her Head, and subordinated to him, she has, in God's plan, an indispensable relationship with the salvation of every human being. For those who are not formally and visibly members of the Church, 'salvation in Christ is accessible by virtue of a grace which, *while having a mysterious relationship to the Church* (*quamquam arcanam habet necessitudinem cum Ecclesia*), does not make them formally part of the Church, but enlightens them in a way which is accommodated to their spiritual and material situation. This grace comes from Christ; it is the result of his sacrifice and is communicated by the Holy Spirit' (*RM* 10); it has a relationship with the Church, which 'according to the plan of the Father, has her origin in the mission of the Son and the Holy Spirit' (Vatican II's document *Ad gentes* [*AG*] 2)."

The Kingdom of God

tion alongside those constituted by the other religions, seen as complementary to the Church or substantially equivalent to her, even if these are said to be converging with the Church toward the eschatological kingdom of God.

Although it is certain that one neither can nor should *separate* the ecclesial mystery from the kingdom of God, a distinction between them is nevertheless being proposed. The result of this approach is that the identification of the Church with the kingdom has become more complex than before, and that it has not yet found a satisfactory formulation.[23] There cannot be a separation between the Church and the kingdom because the Church is "the seed, sign and instrument" of the kingdom (*RM* 18). The term "seed" tells of her existing reality and growth; the terms "sign and instrument" designate the means of this existence and growth. The whole—the means and their end—is the reality, is what fully constitutes the ecclesial mystery. This whole can be found imperfectly established among non-Christians by reason of the action of Christ and the Holy Spirit beyond the visible limits of the Church (*RM* 18), in other words, at the level of the signs that have been instituted as instruments.

These documents include a qualification that too many commentators overlook: it is always a question of *visible* limits, or of the *visible* body, or of the *visible* limits of the Mystical Body.[24] We will study this question at the proper time.[25] When we speak about a situation "beyond the visible limits of the Church," we are not talking about a situation that is purely and simply outside the Church. If the visible signs and instruments (preaching of the Gospel, celebration of the sacraments)

---

23. This theological situation—making the transition from a strict identification to a more complex identification—is encountered in another very closely related ecclesiological question: whereas until the eve of Vatican II the Mystical Body of Christ was narrowly identified with the Catholic Church, since Vatican II the doctrinal formulation of that identity is less exclusive (cf. *LG* 8, §2: the one Church of Christ *subsists* in the Roman Catholic Church, rather than *is*). This question will be discussed during the positive study of the Church as the Body of Christ.

24. With one exception (*Redemptoris missio* 20) that is not really one. The immediate context plainly shows, in fact, that the content of no. 20, as in no. 18, should be taken with the implication "beyond the visible limits of the Church."

25. The controversy with Reformed Christianity began, as far as the mystery of the Church was concerned, with the Lutheran distinction-separation between "visible Church" and "invisible Church"; we will study it in the second part of the course, with the question relative to the speculative definition of the Church.

are really part of the essential "definition" of the Church, since her mystery consists precisely of being simultaneously the sign-instrument and the reality that is signified and obtained, that does not mean that where these are diminished (Christian communities separated from the Catholic Church) or even absent (non-Christian religions) people are purely and simply *extra Ecclesiam* [outside the Church]: one can be in an imperfectly ecclesial situation from either the individual or the communal perspective. Theological research must be conducted in order to understand this imperfectly ecclesial situation.[26]

Finally, we must point out the distinction between the kingdom of Christ and the kingdom of God. For the moment, the classic understanding remains valid: the kingdom of God designates the eschatological accomplishment of the economy of salvation, and the kingdom of Christ is the coming into this world of his signs and instruments in their fullness as well as of the perfection of grace by the work of Christ and in his Person. In other words, the kingdom of Christ is the kingdom of God present in this world through the mediating work of Christ, growing on earth and tending toward its eschatological consummation, which will establish the kingdom of God definitively. In this sense the Church has a "'unique and special relationship' ... with the kingdom of God among men—which in substance is the universal kingdom of Christ the Saviour" (*DI* 21). This "unique and special relationship" is what needs to be explored in greater depth.

Conclusion

The images of the Church, precious though they may be, could not possibly suffice. The modern questions being raised concerning the kingdom of God demonstrate this plainly. The expression "kingdom of God" is not only an image, albeit one with multiple meanings (at the very most the image is that of a kingdom), it is a *theme*. By that we mean to underscore the fact that it is different from simple images. The latter are more or less close comparisons: baptism is *like* a door leading to the other sacraments, the Church is *like* Noah's ark. A theme intends to go further: we do not say that the Church is *like* the kingdom of God, but

---

26. We will present the status of the question at greater length within the framework of our study of the biblical theme of "the People of God."

that she *is* the kingdom of God. The image of a kingdom is surpassed; we are talking about expressing an entity: there is "something" in the human reality called "kingdom" that not only makes us know the mystery of the Church, but also, in a certain way, is really present in that mystery.

Furthermore, a theme gathers together much biblical data that otherwise would remain dispersed and would not converge to form a coherent teaching. Although the theme of the kingdom is the most comprehensive, Tradition has identified three other themes that convey and structure the biblical message. They allow scholars to go further than the theme of the kingdom while illuminating it. These major ecclesiological themes are the Body of Christ, the Temple of the Spirit, and the People of God.[27] With the help of these three themes we will review the sources of the theology of the Church.

Bibliography

Images of the Church

Cerfaux, Lucien. "Les images symboliques de l'Église dans le Nouveau Testament." In *L'Église de Vatican II*, Unam Sanctam 51b, edited by Guilherme Baraúna et al., 243–58. Paris: Cerf, 1966. Good commentary on *LG* 6. The author continues with *LG* 7, on "the Body of Christ," without sufficiently distinguishing between image and theme.

Congar, Yves. *Le mystère du Temple*. Paris: Cerf, 1958. Translated by Reginald F. Trevett as *The Mystery of the Temple*. Westminster, Md.: Newman Press, 1962. A very in-depth study of the image of the building.

de Montcheuil, Yves. *Aspects de l'Église*. Unam Sanctam 18. Paris: Cerf, 1949. Reprinted in the series Cogitatio fidei 255 (Paris: Cerf, 2006). Translated by Albert J. La Mothe, Jr., as *Aspects of the Church*. Chicago: Fides Publishers Association, 1955.

Grelot, Pierre. "Les figures bibliques: Essai de définition et recherche d'un critère." Nouvelle revue théologique 84 (1962): 561–78, 673–98.

Léon-Dufour, Xavier, ed. *Vocabulaire de théologie biblique*. 5th ed. Paris: Cerf, 1981. The 2nd edition was translated under the direction of P. Joseph Cahill and E. M. Stewart as *Dictionary of Biblical Theology*. New York: Seabury Press, 1973. A good basic reference work with a number of entries on the chief biblical images.

Philips, Gérard. *L'Église en son mystère au IIème concile du Vatican*. Paris: Desclée, 1967, 1:98–105. Essentially about *LG* 6.

Schnackenburg, Rudolf. *The Church in the New Testament*. Translated by W. J. O'Hara. New York: Herder and Herder, 1965. Carefully studies most of the major images.

27. Cf. *LG* 17 (*in fine*); *AG* 7, §2.

The Kingdom of God

Congar, Yves. "Royaume, Église et Monde." *Recherches et débats* (July 1951): 2–42.

Deville, Raymond, and Pierre Grelot. "Kingdom." Translated by Eugene C. Ulrich. In *Dictionary of Biblical Theology*, edited by Xavier Léon-Dufour, 292–95. Translated under the direction of P. Joseph Cahill and E. M. Stewart. New York: Seabury Press, 1973. Well done, though a bit hasty; to be supplemented by the entry "King" by Pierre Grelot and translated by Eugene C. Ulrich, *Dictionary*, 288–92.

Hamer, Jérôme. *L'Église est une communion*. Paris: Cerf, 1962, 66–69. Translated by Ronald Matthews as *The Church Is a Communion*. New York: Sheed and Ward, 1964, 64–67.

Loisy, Alfred. *L'Évangile et l'Église*. 4th ed. Ceffonds, near Montier-en-Der, Haute-Marne, France: self-published, 1908. English translation by Christopher Home of an earlier edition first published in 1903 and reprinted as *The Gospel and the Church*. Philadelphia: Fortress Press, 1976.

Philips, Gérard. *L'Église en son mystère au IIème concile du Vatican*. Desclée, 1967, 1:94–98.

Rigaux, Béda. "Le mystère de l'Église à la lumière de la Bible." In *L'Église de Vatican II*, Unam Sanctam 51b, edited by Guilherme Baraúna et al., 228–33. Paris: Cerf, 1966. Gives the essentials.

Schnackenburg, Rudolf. *God's Rule and Kingdom*. Translated by John Murray. New York: Herder and Herder, 1968. A very penetrating study essentially summarized in Schnackenburg, *The Church in the New Testament*, trans. W. J. O'Hara. New York: Herder and Herder, 1965.

The problem resulting from the theology of non-Christian religions

An almost exhaustive bibliography can be found in Jacques Dupuis, *Vers une théologie chrétienne du pluralisme religieux* (Paris: Cerf, 1997), 591–630. Translated as *Toward a Christian Theology of Religious Pluralism* (Maryknoll, N.Y.: Orbis, 1997), 391–424. To our knowledge this is the most complete work on the topic.

2

The Church Is the Body of Christ

The teaching of St. Paul concerning the ecclesial mystery is essentially based on the theme of the Church as the Body of Christ. The Apostle returns many times to this point throughout his ministry so as to complete and develop it. This theme is the main ecclesiological theme of Tradition, which does not mean that it is the only one, nor that it has always been honored in an equally satisfactory way, as we will see particularly in the classical period.[1]

Before starting our presentation of this doctrine, it is advisable to make two important clarifications.

The order in which to study the three themes

We have three major themes, and we propose to begin with the study of the Body of Christ. This is not self-evident, and it is appropriate to justify this decision. Indeed, every time we are faced with several elements in our understanding of a reality, in this case three themes that tell about the one Church, the first thing to ask is the question of how they are related. The order connecting them expresses something extremely important for our comprehension of each element, and their unity provides an understanding of the one ecclesial mystery that they intend to express, each one highlighting those aspects that pertain to it. Now since this order is presented differently depending on the doctri-

---

1. We call "the classical period" the era that other authors call the "Baroque" or "Counter-Reformation."

nal or theological sources, it is advisable to clarify this question at the outset.

We propose to study the three themes in the following order: Body of Christ—Temple of the Spirit—People of God. The two themes of the Body of Christ and the Temple of the Spirit are inseparable, everyone agrees. Each one calls for the other so as to show the close relation that exists between the work of the two Persons of the Trinity who are sent for the salvation of mankind. Normally the theme of the Body of Christ precedes that of the Temple of the Spirit because such expresses the primary role of the Incarnation in the economy of redemption.[2] But the main question is: should the theme of the People of God be placed before or after the Christological and pneumatological themes? Theologians answer this question differently: they either have the People of God precede the Body of Christ and the Temple of the Spirit,[3] or the opposite: they put the People of God third. We have kept the latter order, and we must explain our decision.

The main reason justifying the priority given by some to the theme of the People of God is drawn from the economy of redemption. God, in the expression "People of God," is the Father, to whom is appropriated both the plan of salvation as its source and the sending of the two other Divine Persons to accomplish it.[4] This is quite correct. Nevertheless, this is not the only conceivable order. Indeed, the two first chapters of *Lumen gentium,* which deal with the teaching about the ecclesial mystery as such before beginning a study of each of its elements, are arranged according to another consideration. In the first chapter (*LG* 1–8) we have a presentation of the Church, first in its Trinitarian origin (*LG* 2–4) and then in its constitutive elements, for which purpose the themes of the Body of Christ and the Temple of the Spirit play a role (*LG* 7–8). The second chapter is devoted to the People of God (*LG*

---

2. The Holy Spirit is sent to fructify the Virgin's womb so as to bring about the Incarnation; from then on all the gifts of grace, among them the gift of the Spirit himself, will come to mankind through the mediation of the sacred humanity of the Word.

3. So it is with the two lists of the themes in *LG* 17 and *Ad gentes* 7, §2 and in the *Catechism of the Catholic Church,* 781–801.

4. This order shows that the "economic Trinity" has the same order as the one resulting from the processions in the "immanent Trinity"; in *Lumen gentium* this perspective informs and orders paragraphs 2 (the plan of the Father), 3 (the work of the Son), and 4 (the work of the Holy Spirit).

The Body of Christ 63

9–17). Then it is a question of showing the life of the Church in its principal manifestations, a life that is a journey in this world toward an eschatological fulfillment. In other words, the first chapter of *Lumen gentium* takes an essential perspective; it presents the Church "*in facto esse*" (in her very being), and the second chapter follows an historical, existential perspective; it presents the Church "*in fieri*" (in her becoming).

Obviously it is the same ecclesial entity that is posited in being and that unfolds its potentialities during its life. But it is important to clarify—and this is the deeper reason for the order maintained here among the themes—that what develops in and through history is what was given from the beginning: there is the continuity of one and the same being. This order has priority over the second possible order that puts the People of God first. The order that we will follow is a theological order, from dogmatic theology, according to which we present, first, what constitutes essentially the subject being studied, and second, the acts by which this subject develops its identity through its whole life.[5]

We must add another, more prudential reason for our choice, one that we think is important in our present cultural context in the West. Henri de Lubac expresses this motif as follows: to put preaching about the Church as the Body of Christ before the proclamation of the Church as the People of God "is a decisive reminder of the authentic tradition, barring the way against any attempt at secularization, politicization, and democratization."[6] There is indeed a risk, which is far from being hypothetical, when one begins with the People of God—namely, the risk of understanding this theme reductively (in other words, in a way that is primarily sociological) and of not seeing that it is a question of the form of the historical development of the Body of Christ—a supernatural reality if ever there was one.

---

5. It would be improper to conclude that, since the Body of Christ exists only through the Incarnation, this theme would cause the ecclesial mystery to begin with the coming of Christ, whereas in fact the mystery of salvation—that is, the Church—began as early as the promise of a Savior (Gn 3:15). The Body of Christ exists already under the Old Law; there too it is announced and prepared, already exerting influence in the just. Each one of the three ecclesiological themes concerns Revelation as a whole: both the OT and the NT. We will have the opportunity to demonstrate this in detail during our study.

6. Henri de Lubac, *Entretien autour de Vatican II*, 22.

"Body of Christ," "Mystical Body of Christ"

We find in the writings of St. Paul, throughout the patristic age, and down to the eleventh century that the Church is called "the Body of Christ." Then, rather quickly starting from the twelfth century and then constantly thereafter, it is said that the Church is "the *Mystical* Body of Christ." The reasons for this change are well known since the studies by Fr. de Lubac;[7] we shall summarize them here.

At the start, following the language of St. Paul, the Church is called the Body of Christ, and the expression "Mystical Body" is not found in Scripture. The reader encounters it for the first time at the beginning of the fifth century, and then it designates the Eucharist. The Lord's Supper is a *mystērion* in which we receive Christ himself: in the Eucharist the "mystical" Body of Christ is present (*"en mystērion"*). The expression "Mystical Body" already has a relation with the Church by reason of the profound connection between the two mysteries. In the ninth century in the West, especially in France, there were controversies over the sacrament of the Eucharist that involved in particular the question about the reality of Christ's presence. The terminology would be clarified, making distinctions that resulted in a *triplex Corpus Christi*: the Body born of the Virgin, which was laid in the manger at its birth, led a public life, died, and rose again, and is now seated at the right hand of the Father; the *Corpus mysticum*, the Eucharistic or "sacramental" Body; and the ecclesial Body of Christ, the fruit of the Eucharist, or the *Corpus verum*, where "true" signifies that it is the end to which the first two kinds of presence are ordered. In this context, therefore, the "Mystical Body" is the Eucharist.

In the eleventh century the Eucharistic controversy was revived by the debate that pitted Berengar of Tours against Lanfranc of Caen, again on the subject of the reality of Christ's presence in the sacrament of the altar. This doctrinal difficulty would lead to an interchange of meanings: to affirm the real and not merely symbolic presence—in other words, the identity of the Body born of the Virgin with the Eucharistic Body—theologians would speak about the "true Body" for the consecrated host,[8] and they would speak about the "Mystical

---

7. De Lubac, *Corpus Mysticum: The Eucharist and the Church in the Middle Ages*, 75–122.

8. Cf. the hymn *Ave verum Corpus*, which is sung at Eucharistic adoration.

The Body of Christ

Body" to designate the Church which is the fruit of the Eucharistic mystery. In the West the vocabulary became set in this way down to our time, but one must be attentive to the usage of other Catholic as well as Orthodox Churches, mainly in the East, which did not have the same history. For them the expression "Mystical Body" designates the Eucharistic presence.

In our presentation of this theme and in light of the remarks that we have just made, we will use the expressions "Body of Christ" and "Mystical Body of Christ" interchangeably to designate the Church.

I. The Pauline data

It seems that the whole ecclesiology of St. Paul was defined by the circumstances of his conversion. This grace was, for him personally, a grace pertaining to the mystery of the Church: "I am Jesus, whom you are persecuting" (Acts 9:5). This revelation of the mysterious unity between Christ and Christians that forms the Church was the point of departure for St. Paul's faith. The expression "Body of Christ" to designate the Christian community is the most elaborate expression of St. Paul, yet one must distinguish between the reality being expressed and the terminology being used, because this reality can be found in the Pauline letters without the precise expression. That is why we must recall here the main elements of the Apostle's soteriology.

a. The theology of salvation according to St. Paul

The re-creation, reconciliation, and recapitulation of all creation, above all of man, are the work of Christ in the mystery of the Incarnation and in his Paschal mystery. Salvation is the work of Christ that man appropriates to himself by uniting himself to his Author.

First of all there is the individual perspective: "being in Christ,"[9] along with equivalent expressions such as "being Christ's, belonging to Christ, putting on Christ."[10] Nevertheless the communal perspective is inseparable from this terminology, since to the extent that each one of

---

9. Scholars count 164 occurrences of the expression *"en Christō"* in the Pauline corpus.

10. For example: "If any one is in Christ, he is a new creation" (2 Cor 5:17), or even more forcefully: to become "one in Christ Jesus" (Gal 3:28).

us is "in Christ" we merge into the same reality that is the Savior, and we are thereby united with one another.

Hence the central question: how can one be in Christ? The Spirit of Christ brings about this solidarity among us, and this gift is given by baptism. This new life, which is inseparably individual and communal, is served by various charisms that, in Paul's teaching, are of three sorts: the charisms of ministry, among which that of the apostle comes first because he discerns the other charisms; the charisms of service, in particular that of teaching; and the charisms of manifestation, such as the gifts of healing, miracles, and tongues.

How is this unity with Christ in the Spirit to be understood? Based on our knowledge of creation, we can picture two main types of unity. In the first, so-called "physical" unity starts with various elements and forms one substantial being—for example, the unity that interconnects the members of the human body. This cannot apply to our present subject because this type of unity does not preserve the distinction between persons. To say that the Christian is another Christ in this sense would be an error. In the second place, one can conceive of a "moral" unity that, unlike physical unity, is not a real unity of one being, but only a unity that is brought about intentionally. The same thing is willed by several people, and thereby these persons are united with one another by this purpose that they have in common. So it is, for example, with the social unity that is brought about by the common orientation of citizens toward the common good. For the soteriology of St. Paul, this is insufficient. Our unity with Christ is "real" because we have in common with Christ an essential reality that is his Spirit and his grace. That is why, in order to designate the very specific union that binds Christians to Christ and consequently to one another also, we speak about a "mystical" union, which is a real unity that affects the whole person, body and soul, while preserving the distinction from Christ. This type of unity has no equivalent in creation, and we can picture it to some extent only by situating it "between" real union, pure and simple, and moral union. St. Paul will attempt to explain somewhat this unique type of union by developing the theology of the Body of Christ.

b. The theology of the Church, the Body of Christ

There are two major stages in Pauline teaching that are quite distinct. On the one hand, we have the longer letters, 1 Corinthians and Romans, which are approximately dated between 55 and 60 A.D. and which, for our purposes, have as their central theme the union of all Christians as members of one Body; this is the "horizontal" aspect. Furthermore, we have the so-called captivity letters, Ephesians and Colossians, dated to the time shortly after 60 A.D., in which the central theme is the primacy of Christ and his influence as Head over the entire Body; this is the "vertical" aspect of the teaching.

The expression in St. Paul's writings that we render as "Body of Christ" is "*sōma tou Christou.*" "Body" must not be understood as distinct from the soul. The Greek "*sōma*" is the whole person, whether it be the "body of flesh," Jesus in his earthly condition, similar to ours (Col 1:21–22), or the "glorious body," Jesus in his condition after the Resurrection (Phil 3:21). The Greek word "*sōma*" thereby translates the Hebrew "*bâsar,*" and should also be distinguished from the Greek "*sarx,*" which in St. Paul's writings signifies man in his weak, sinful carnal condition.

1. The major letters

Let us look at the principal texts:

The First Letter to the Corinthians

Do you not know that your bodies are members of Christ? Shall I therefore take the members of Christ and make them members of a prostitute? Never! Do you not know that he who joins himself to a prostitute becomes one body with her? For, as it is written, "The two shall become one" (Gn 2:24). But he who is united with the Lord becomes one spirit with him" (1 Cor 6:15–17).

The Christians of Corinth are known for the anarchy of their charisms, but that was not all! Sexual license reigned rather broadly in Corinth (see the incest in 1 Cor 5:1), and in particular plenty of prostitution. St. Paul intends to oppose it categorically, not in a moralizing way, but by developing an argument that is in the first place dogmatic. This, like the later discussion in Ephesians 5:21–33, is based on the text of Genesis 2:24 affirming that a married man and woman are united in one body. He says in essence to the Corinthians, your bodies, in other words your persons, are members of the Body of Christ; one cannot be one Body with Christ and at the same time with a prostitute; that would be an act of defilement. We know that baptism is what causes a soul to put on Christ (Gal 3:26–28) and establishes the Christian as a member of Christ (as explicitly stated in 1 Cor 6:11). Hence the conclusion of the pericope under consideration may be surprising: "He who is united with the Lord becomes one spirit with him." One would have expected "one body with him." Note "j" at 1 Corinthians 6:15 in *The New Jerusalem Bible* explains it this way: "One would expect 'is one body with him,' but Paul is careful to avoid too materialistic an understanding of the physical realism of union with Christ."

The cup of blessing which we bless, is it not a participation in the blood of Christ? The bread which we break, is it not a participation in the body of Christ? Because there is one bread, we who are many are one body, for we all partake of the one bread." (1 Cor 10:16–17)

We have here the great passage on the connection between the Eucharist and the Church: the Eucharistic Body of Christ engenders his ecclesial Body. It affirms that there is only one Eucharistic bread, and that this bread is the Body of Christ. It is Christ. Every Christian, in receiving this bread, in all truth receives Christ and is transformed into him. All Christians receive the same bread, the same Christ, and thus become one in Christ, forming one Body with him. Whereas the preceding text had baptism as its foundation, this text pertains to the Eucharist. It is one of the rare passages by St. Paul on the Eucharist,[11] but it is of capital importance and is at the origin of the development of the whole Tradition concerning the Church engendered by the Lord's Supper.

For just as the body is one and has many members, and all the members of the body, though many, are one body, so it is with Christ. For by one Spirit we were all baptized into one body—Jews or Greeks, slaves or free—and all were made to drink of one Spirit.

For the body does not consist of one member but of many. If the foot

---

11. Together with 1 Cor 11:23–32, which is the moral extension of it: if the Eucharist makes us one in Christ, it must likewise manifest that unity.

should say, "Because I am not a hand, I do not belong to the body," that would not make it any less a part of the body.... But as it is, God arranged the organs in the body, each one of them, as he chose. If all were a single organ, where would the body be? As it is, there are many parts, yet one body. The eye cannot say to the hand, "I have no need of you," nor again the head to the feet, "I have no need of you."...

Now you are the body of Christ and individually members of it. And God has appointed in the Church first apostles, second prophets, third teachers, then workers of miracles, then healers, helpers, administrators, speakers in various kinds of tongues. Are all apostles? Are all prophets? Are all teachers? Do all work miracles? (1 Cor 12:12–30)

The use of the theme of the body is very broad here: the various charisms have the same origin and the same end. To explain that, St. Paul uses as an example the variety and solidarity of the members of the human body: "we were all baptized into [*eis en* expresses purpose: in order to form] one body" (1 Cor 12:13).

Some have thought that this passage might reveal St. Paul's sources for the ecclesiological theme of the Body. Thus scholars have proposed the hypothesis that St. Paul had received the image of the body from the Hellenistic milieu, which got it specifically from an Aesop's fable wherein the various organs of a human body, out of jealousy, conspired against the stomach and no longer supplied it with food: all of them perished. This fable had been utilized by the senator Menenius Agrippa when the Roman people had revolted against the Senate, which it no longer wanted to obey. The statesman had intended thereby to emphasize the need for all to cooperate for the common good. But these are merely conjectures.[12] It should be noted that the comparison of the political community to a body (the image of many members forming one unity) is well established in Stoic thought.[13] It is therefore possible that St. Paul knew these literary figures of speech, but that is not the decisive factor. Indeed, the image of the human body presents a real, physical union, while the image of the social body presents only a moral union, and both are inadequate for St. Paul's purpose. And so it is

---

12. It seems that the most similar Aesop's fable is "The Stomach and the Feet," but it does not exactly illustrate what St. Paul has in mind.

13. Particularly in Seneca (d. 65 A.D.). On this subject see the comments by Jacques Dupont, *Gnosis: La connaissance religieuse dans les épîtres de S. Paul*, 435ff.

possible to speculate that St. Paul himself originated the image.[14] One could argue that Aesop's fable or the allegory of Menenius Agrippa, if Paul knew of them (which is possible), illustrate the teaching here, but are not the origin of it. The Body of Christ is constituted by and in Christ in a mystical unity, but it also has a human communal aspect. Moreover, this is the immediate context of the pericope: the anarchy of charisms troubling the young church of Corinth.

One can say that the Pauline ecclesiological theme is obtained with the help of a twofold transposition. In the first place, a transposition from the biological (this is clear in the writings of St. Paul) to the social sphere through the idea of the "common good."[15] But if we leave it at that, we still have a union of the moral type. That is why there is a second transposition, from the natural society that is the result of the first transposition to the supernatural ecclesial society that has an incomparably deeper unity than societal groups.

The Letter to the Romans

For by the grace given to me I bid every one among you not to think of himself more highly than he ought to think, but to think with sober judgment, each according to the measure of faith which God has assigned him. For as in one body we have many members, and all the members do not have the same function, so we, though many, are one body in Christ, and individually members one of another. Having gifts that differ according to the grace given to us, let us use them: if prophecy, in proportion to our faith; if service, in our serving; he who teaches, in his teaching. (Rom 12:3–8)

The teaching has become more specific here in one respect: "So we, though many, are one body in Christ" (Rom 12:4). Whereas in 1 Corinthians 12:27 St. Paul said, "you are the body of Christ," here he says, "one body in Christ." St. Paul emphasizes identity with Christ less, because it is necessary to preserve the distinction between Christ and Christians, given that the latter are not purely and simply Christ, but are "in" Christ: Christ has incorporated us into himself; he himself is the unity of the community.

---

14. This is the opinion of Pierre Benoit, "L'Église Corps du Christ," 4:210ff.; see also note "g" in the *Jerusalem Bible* at 1 Cor 12:12.

15. Cf. 1 Cor 12:7: "To each is given the manifestation of the Spirit for the common good" (literally: with a view to being carried together, or gathered together).

The Body of Christ

This first set of texts drawn from the major letters is focused on the "horizontal" aspect of unity: human beings are all united with Christ and among themselves; this forms a whole of which individuals are the parts, each one complementing the others. This unity reflects its principle, Christ, who is this unity in Person and who brings it about in baptism and the Eucharist and the subordinate gifts of the charisms. Paul insists quite forcefully on this "horizontal" solidarity and on the cause of this bond, which is Christ. Christ contributes the decisive, "mystical" element, yet he is still in the whole and insufficiently distinguished from it. That will be the contribution of the second set of texts.

2. The captivity letters

Here Christ is explicitly called Head of the Body. This is how St. Paul shows the supremacy of Christ over the community of his faithful. It must be understood that the word "head" simultaneously connotes the Hebrew idea of the "Lord" who communicates life to all, and the Greco-Latin idea of "Chief" (*"kephalē,"* *"caput"*), which has, first, a moral sense, and emphasizes the function of commanding and teaching.

The Letter to the Colossians

He is before all things, and in him all things hold together. He is the head of the body, the Church; he is the beginning, the firstborn from the dead, that in everything he might be pre-eminent. For in him all the fulness of God was pleased to dwell, and through him to reconcile to himself all things, whether on earth or in heaven, making peace by the blood of his cross. (Col 1:17–20)

This hymn extols the absolute preeminence of Christ in the order of creation (Col 1:12–16), and his unique excellence in the order of redemption (Col 1:17–20). This excellence in the order of grace is expressed by St. Paul in the phrase, "he is the head of the body, the Church" (Col 1:18).[16]

For in him the whole fulness of deity dwells bodily, and you have come to fulness of life in him, who is the head of all rule and authority. (Col 2:9–10)

---

16. A similar teaching is given by St. John in the prologue of his Gospel: "And the Word became flesh and dwelt among us, full of grace and truth; we have beheld his glory, glory as of the only Son from the Father ... from his fulness have we all received, grace upon grace" (Jn 1:14, 1:16).

Christ possesses a fullness of grace that is poured out on human beings, thus associating them with his primacy. Note the clarification: "in him the whole fulness of deity dwells *bodily*," which indicates that this headship belongs to the humanity assumed by the Word. This should be considered in light of the statement in the First Letter to Timothy: "and there is one mediator between God and men, the man Christ Jesus, who gave himself as a ransom for all" (1 Tm 2:5–6). Precisely in his humanity Christ is full of this grace that he instills in us. Paul warns the Colossians about those who are "puffed up without reason ..., not holding fast to the Head, from whom the whole body, nourished and knit together through its joints and ligaments, grows with a growth that is from God" (Col 2:18–19).

This grace that is diffused starting from the Head is the same grace that unites (knits together) men to Christ and men among themselves and that builds up the Mystical Body (growth), for Paul is speaking about a living reality, not a static one. Christ is the "vital principle": just as in a biological body everything necessary for its life comes from the head, so it is in the Body of Christ which receives everything from Christ who is its Head.

The Letter to the Ephesians
In him [Christ] we have redemption through his blood, the forgiveness of our trespasses, according to the riches of his grace which he lavished upon us. For he has made known to us in all wisdom and insight the mystery of his will, according to his purpose which he set forth in Christ as a plan for the fulness of time, to unite [*recapitulare*, Vulgate] all things in him, things in heaven and things on earth. (Eph 1:7–10)

The great hymn with which the letter begins is first of all a profuse thanksgiving for a whole series of blessings that God has showered on us. It is a broad presentation of the Christian mystery: the benevolent divine plan for saving the world. The hymn combines three considerations that are profoundly interconnected: the fact that the world is fallen and needs salvation, the fact that the work of Christ is this salvation, and how we are to be affected by this work of restoration. To save the world is to bring everything back under one Head, Christ (Eph 1:10); the Greek verb *anakephalaioō* can be translated quite precisely as "recapitulate" (to place under a single *kephalē* or *ca-*

put): to make Christ the Head of everything. The whole letter discusses this economy of the mystery while insisting on this manner of being in Christ—in other words, having him as Head by being part of his Body—and emphasizing, as far as man is concerned, the unique role of faith. Thus Ephesians 2:14–16 explains that the reconciliation of the Jews and the Gentiles—that is, all mankind for which redemption is planned—will come about by the gathering of all into "one body." The ecclesial Body is called to gather all of humanity, thereby breaking down all the particular customs that made Israel a people set apart.[17] As the letter continues, the means of incorporating men into this Body are mentioned. St. Paul highlights the primary means, namely faith, and consequently everything related to the preaching of the mystery of Christ. Ephesians 4:11–13 notes that the Body is built up, is edified by apostles, prophets, evangelists, pastors, and teachers. These are the ministries and charisms of teaching. In Ephesians 4:15–16 St. Paul puts it this way:

Rather, speaking the truth in love, we are to grow up in every way into him who is the head, into Christ, from whom the whole body, joined and knit together by every joint with which it is supplied, when each part is working properly, makes bodily growth and upbuilds itself in love.

This passage follows the mention of the ministries (Eph 4:12) and shows the connection between Christ, who builds up his Body, and the ministries that take part in that edification. The unique headship of Christ thus associates ministers to itself, and hence we see that the presentation of the mystery of the Body of Christ includes a consideration of the different ways in which this one headship is exercised. To put it another way, the hierarchical aspect of the Church is included, strictly speaking, in the theme of the Mystical Body.

3. Two complementary clarifications

St. Paul's teaching includes two other important points, the theme of the "*plērōma*" and the theme of the Church as the Bride of Christ.

---

17. This point is repeated in Eph 3:6; in these passages we get a glimpse of the great difficulty that the Church of the apostolic age had in breaking with the synagogue.

The "plērōma"

The Letter to the Ephesians contains a development concerning the *"plērōma."* This idea of fullness is also present in the hymn from the Letter to the Colossians: "He is before all things, and in him all things hold together.... For in him all the fulness of God was pleased to dwell" (Col 1:17, 19), where the notion expresses the primacy of Christ in the work of salvation. In the Letter to the Ephesians this fullness is mentioned once again, but this time along with the Church:

> He [God] has put all things under his [Christ's] feet (cf. Ps 8:6) and has made him the head over all things for the Church, which is his body, the fulness of him who fills all in all. (Eph 1:22–23)

How should this fullness be understood? We can refer the mention of fullness, not to the Church directly, but to Christ.[18] Then it would be appropriate to interpret these verses: Christ is set over all, in the first place over the redeemed, for he is Head of the Church—which is consequently his Body—and he is also the fullness of all creation. St. Paul then would be teaching here the universal presence of Christ throughout the universe that he has redeemed. Another reading refers the mention of fullness more directly to the Church. The proposed interpretation is: Christ is set over all; he is the Head of the Church, which is consequently his Body and is the fullness of all redeemed creation. In the second case the Church is considered in its fullest extent, in other words, "as a cosmic and eschatological reality which in its temporal and earthly existence only unfolds and strives after what in its head, Christ, is already a reality."[19] Indeed, these two interpretations may not be incompatible. The term "body" can only designate human beings redeemed by Christ, whereas the term *"plērōma"* obviously is meant to add the idea that the totality of creation, which certainly was affected by Adam's sin, is likewise the object of Christ's redemptive work. One could then reason that, since redemption in the mode of personal union with Christ concerns only mankind, this redemption also concerns creation as a whole in another mode. What is this other mode?

---

18. See in particular the studies by Pierre Benoit, "L'Église Corps du Christ," 4:232–34.

19. Rudolf Schnackenburg, *The Church in the New Testament*, 175; see general bibliography.

The Body of Christ

It must be admitted that St. Paul does not elaborate on the subject. But one can say (and this is in keeping with the overall Pauline doctrine) that just as all creation had been entrusted to man at the beginning so that he might thus subject it and order it to God,[20] so too creation is entrusted to man after the redemption so that he might place it under the reign of Christ and thus serve the salvation of mankind. In other words, the Church, of which Christ in his humanity is the Head, serves the establishment of the reign of Christ over all creation, thus ordering it to serve its final end, which is the salvation of all mankind.

In summary, we can say that the first *plērōma* is Christ (see Colossians) in the sense that in him is the fullness of the grace of universal salvation. The second, subordinate *plērōma* is the Church (see Ephesians)—that is, the communication-participation by human beings in the fullness of Christ (Head → Body)—and this participated fullness makes it possible to take up again the work of the first six days that had been vitiated by original sin, restoring order and harmony to subhuman creation so that it might once again serve, on its level, the supernatural vocation of man. In this sense the grace possessed in its fullness by Christ touches all that is created: first, in the strong sense, man, and secondarily, through man, creation.

To this it is advisable to add that Christ is likewise Head of "things in heaven" (Eph 1:10), who are the "thrones or dominions or principalities or authorities" (Col 1:16). Christ's headship consequently extends to the angels, as well. This poses a problem, since the angels had no need of salvation. We should note this point made by St. Paul, on which he does not elaborate, and later we will see how Tradition interpreted it.

The Church as Bride of Christ

This Pauline doctrine about the Church is, so to speak, bracketed within a great *inclusio:* the discreet first mention of it is in 1 Corinthians 6:15–17, and the explicit last one is in Ephesians 5:25–27. Let us contrast the two pericopes:

Do you not know that your bodies are members of Christ? Shall I therefore take the members of Christ and make them members of a prostitute? Never!

---

20. See Eucharistic Prayer IV: "so that in serving you alone, the Creator, he might have dominion over all creatures."

Do you not know that he who joins himself to a prostitute becomes one body with her? For, as it is written, "The two shall become one" (Gn 2:24). But he who is united to the Lord becomes one spirit with him." (1 Cor 6:15–17)

Husbands, love your wives, as Christ loved the Church and gave himself up for her, that he might sanctify her, having cleansed her by the washing of water with the word, that he might present the Church to himself in splendor, without spot or wrinkle or any such thing, that she might be holy and without blemish. (Eph 5:25–27)

Some biblical scholars think that the theme of the Church as the Bride of Christ is what led St. Paul to the theme of the Church as the Body of Christ.[21] The account of the creation of woman from the side of sleeping Adam (Gn 2:21) is said to supply the immediate precedent for the theme of the Body of Christ. The bond between husband and wife is indeed a very close tie. Since the woman is derived from the man (which symbolizes their community in the same nature), the argument goes, she forms one body with her husband in marriage, being "flesh of his flesh and bone of his bones." In the theology of the Old Testament, a man who marries incorporates his wife into himself.[22] Moreover, the theme of Christ the Bridegroom is quite evident in the New Testament.[23] Hence there is a certain relation between the quasi-identity of husband and wife and the union between Christ and his Church. St. Paul does not especially develop this point.

This comparison of husband and wife to Christ and the Church is enlightening, but it is to be handled with care. It is enlightening because the Church is the Body of Christ inasmuch as she is Bride. In other words, there is a real distinction between Christ and the Church, between the Head and the Body. To say of Christ and the Church, as St. Joan of Arc did, that "it is all one thing," is not purely and simply correct. Thus, for example, every act performed by the Church is not identically an act of Christ. Moreover, this parallelism allows us to underscore the nature of Christ's dominion over the Church: a domin-

21. For example Henri Cazelles, André-Marie Dubarle, and André Feuillet (see the bibliography at the end of the chapter).

22. Cf. Tb 4:4; the wife must always be buried beside her husband because they are one flesh.

23. Cf. the synoptic Gospels with the preaching of St. John the Baptist, in the wedding feast of Cana in St. John's Gospel, and in St. Paul's writings Rom 7:1–4; Gal 4:24; 1 Cor 11:3.

ion of love. The limitation, however, is that the union between husband and wife is moral; it leaves intact the distinction of persons. But for the union of Christ and the Church this is insufficient. There is a relation in terms of which it is correct to say that Christ and the Church are "all one thing" because one and the same life animates Christ and the Church, and because some of the most decisive acts for salvation (the preaching of the Gospel and the celebration of the sacraments) truly are conjoined acts of Christ and the Church. Here we find again the point that we had emphasized with regard to this more-than-moral and less-than-real/physical union that unites the ecclesial Body to its Head, a union that Tradition would later call *mystical*.

c. Conclusion concerning the Pauline data

The Church is the Body of which Christ is the Head. This implies several important points that are indispensable for the speculative mind, as fundamental elements of the faith, which theology receives as the object of its investigations and the criterion for judging whether or not its propositions are acceptable. Let us recapitulate them:

First, there is an ontological connection (i.e., a special, original tie that is real, on the order of being) that unites Christians with Christ and Christians among themselves. It must go beyond a moral connection, without excluding that, however. In simpler terms, there is "something" essential common to Christ in his humanity and to all Christians. Let us call it, for the moment, "grace." Belonging to Christ is inseparable from belonging to the Church, and vice versa. There is a "quasi-identity" between Christ and *his* Body. This very close relation explains many manners of speaking in Sacred Scripture. It is the source of St. Paul's faith: "I am Jesus, whom you are persecuting" (Acts 9:5), which in turn is an illustration of Matthew 25:40: "As you did it to one of the least of these my brethren, you did it to me." The first Christian community, as shown to us in the Acts of the Apostles, had a strong awareness of this. In Acts 2:41 and 2:47 it says that new believers were "added" or, as the Greek verb implies, "adjoined" to the community, and in Acts 5:14[24] and 11:24 it says that the new believers were "added" to the Lord. The same verb is used (*prostithēmi*): to enter into the com-

---

24. See the note of the *Traduction oecuménique de la Bible* at Acts 5:14: "in joining the community," they were rallying to the Lord.

munity of Christians is to be united to the Lord by reason of this close relationship between the community and Christ.

Second, thanks to this bond, there is an identity of life between Christ and Christians. This life, possessed in its fullness by Christ, is communicated by his humanity to his faithful. This communication comes about through the apostolic preaching that engenders faith, and this leads to baptism, which makes a human being a member of the Body of Christ. The Eucharist nourishes and thus causes the unity of this Body to grow. Hence we see that the theme of the Church as the Body of Christ is not limited to the interior and hence invisible aspect of the unity of grace; it necessarily includes the means of entering into that unity and of making it grow.

Third, this Body has a Head, Christ, from whom everything comes. In the mystery that is the Christian community, in its essential constitutive elements, in its life, everything comes from above: the vertical dimension and the descending motion are altogether primary. The Church continually receives itself from Christ. He is not only its *founder* at the beginning; he is its permanent and perpetual *foundation*. The constant presence of Christ to his Church is a fundamental datum. The last verse of the Gospel according to St. Matthew expresses this in its own way. When Jesus is about to leave this earth to enter into the glory of his Father, he says to his apostles, "I am with you always, to the close of the age" (Mt 28:20). It is advisable to understand this continual presence in the strong sense and not merely in the intentional moral sense.

II. The data of Tradition

a. The Fathers

We remind the reader that we are not presenting a history of doctrines, but rather a study of the *theology* of the sources. The Fathers are considered here as witnesses to the faith. Wherever they are in agreement, the Church has, in effect, recognized the authoritative expression of what she believes.

The study of the Pauline data has shown us two points of capital importance. The scriptural teaching about the Church as the Body of Christ is, in the first place, a doctrine about the union of men with God and among themselves and, second, the revelation of the way in which

The Body of Christ

this union is engendered by a certain connection between the Body born of the Virgin (the mystery of the Incarnation), the Eucharistic Body (the sacramental presence), and the ecclesial Body. The Fathers were intent on making all these data more explicit.

In keeping with their method, the Fathers most often set forth Christian doctrine in its entirety. They are unacquainted with our division into various dogmatic treatises, and many distinctions that are familiar to us today—for example, the distinction between the Church as the reality of salvation and the Church as the means of salvation—are only implicit in their writings. This must be taken into consideration as we read them.

It is well established in patristic writings that the Church as the Body of Christ is understood on the basis of the personal mystery of the Incarnate Word. That means that this unity of men with God and among themselves that is the Church is, like Christ himself, simultaneously a unity of interior, supernatural, and divine life as well as a visible, human unity that can be experienced externally.

In our presentation of these sources, in order to avoid the excess that would be unavoidable if one tried to say everything, we will proceed as follows:

In the first place, we must compile the data of the apostolic Fathers. The first Christian authors (second century) do not furnish well-formulated doctrines, but their insights are often very profound and will be developed subsequently.

The first attempts to express properly Christian Revelation with some degree of comprehensiveness appear in the late second and third centuries.

Finally, the "great patristic age" of the fourth and fifth centuries will bring to light many important connections; it constitutes a peerless treasure.

The Fathers must be situated according to the culture that they actually conveyed and not according to the place of their birth or of their ministry, which may be different. Thus St. Irenaeus of Lyons is a Greek, and St. Hilary of Poitiers, with regard to the question that concerns us, should also be considered part of the Greek tradition. The predominance of Greeks, moreover, is plain. Before the fifth century very few Latins are capable of the same dogmatic influence.

1. The apostolic Fathers

The principal writers classified as apostolic Fathers are St. Clement of Rome, St. Polycarp, St. Ignatius of Antioch, the author of the *Didache* (also called *The Teaching of the Twelve Apostles*), and the Pastor of Hermas.

The *Didache* offers a symbolic image that will be repeated by all the Fathers and even in our day because of the important point that it makes:

As this broken bread was scattered over the hills [i.e., the stalks of wheat in the fields] and then, when gathered, became one mass [i.e., one bread], so may Thy Church be gathered from the ends of the earth into Thy Kingdom.[25]

The same symbolism is applied to the many grapes that make up one wine. This is the first reception of the teaching of 1 Corinthians 10:16–17, and it is quite clear: the Eucharist unites all who participate in it, for in receiving Christ they receive union with God and among themselves.

St. Clement of Rome is a Latin. The moral aspect is more familiar to him, and since he has to intervene in the Church of Corinth because of disturbances that were dividing it, he prefers to accentuate the unity of concord, but not by linking it solely to a common discipline: Christ is the one who, by his Spirit, unifies the whole Church.[26]

St. Ignatius of Antioch wrote letters to several churches that he encountered during his journey to Rome where he was to die as a martyr. All these letters are dominated by his concern for keeping the Church, which is first of all local, in unity.[27] Christ is the principle of unity; he is the "invisible bishop"[28] who acts through the ministry of the bishop:

---

25. *Didache* 9.4, in ACW 6:20; see also 10:2 and 10:5–6.
26. See in particular St. Clement, the (first) *Epistle to the Corinthians* 46.5–6: "Why are quarrels and outbursts of passion and divisions and schisms and wars in your midst? Or do we not have one God and one Christ and one Spirit of grace, a Spirit that was poured out upon us?" in *The Epistles of St. Clement of Rome and St. Ignatius of Antioch*, trans. James A. Kleist, ACW 1:37–38.
27. See the fine introduction by Pierre-Thomas Camelot to *Lettres de S. Ignace*, SC 10:20–55.
28. See *To the Magnesians* 3.2, in ACW 1:70; see also *To the Romans* 9.1, in ACW 1:84.

The Body of Christ

"It is needful then ... that you do nothing without your bishop,"[29] who is above all the liturgical minister of the Eucharist.[30] The Eucharist, presided over by the bishop, surrounded by the presbyterate and assisted by the deacons, is what brings about and manifests the Church. The moral aspects of this same unity (peace, concord) are connected with the charity that is the very life of God.

In summary, these very first testimonies already offer an overall vision that is rather clear and easy to bring to light: the Word of God, who has become incarnate, then makes himself present in the Eucharist celebrated by the ministers, thereby uniting in himself all the faithful as the Church.

2. The Alexandrians

The School of Alexandria gathered, above all, masters of the spiritual life. Their perspective is therefore primarily moral; it presupposes the dogmatic basis present in St. Paul, but does little to explicate it. On the moral level where they situate themselves, to be in Christ is principally to imitate the model that is Christ so as to live as he lived. The Mystical Body here consists of the group of those who lead an upright life in conformity to the Savior's teaching. The perspective is both individual and communal: the believer, like the entire Church, reproduces in his life the life of Christ:

> We say that according to the teaching of the divine scriptures the body of Christ, the soul of which is the Son of God, is the whole Church of God, and that the limbs of this body, which is to be regarded as a whole, are those who believe, whoever they may be.[31]

This line of theological thought is invaluable: from the moment when a person or a community imitates Christ's way of life, one can speak about Christians and Church. The accent is placed on apostolic preaching and on the Word as "interior Master." These are Christian gnostics. The certification of moral rectitude is what allows one to as-

---

29. *To the Tralliens* 2.1–3, citation at 2, in ACW 1:75–76.
30. *To the Philadelphians* 4.1, in ACW 1:86; see also the *To the Ephesians* 5.1–2, in ACW 1:62.
31. Origen, *Contra Celsum* VI.48 (PG 13.1374); trans. Henry Chadwick (Cambridge: Cambridge University Press, 1965), 365.

cend to its cause. Thus those who have never heard apostolic preaching, but who live an upright life, have been able to receive the preaching of the Word that enlightens every man in this world (Jn 1:9).[32] St. Clement does not hesitate to acknowledge that the just Greek philosophers can express the truth about God, but he does not distinguish clearly between the insights of reason and the illumination of faith.[33]

The limitation of this School is that Christ is presented only as an interior Master, leaving in obscurity the role of Christ's humanity, which is the foundation of pastoral ministry and the sacraments.

3. The beginnings of Greek patristic literature

St. Irenaeus

The doctrine of recapitulation is at the heart of the teaching of St. Irenaeus. It originates in the Pauline teaching about the two Adams: just as the first Adam, who was made head of the human race, failed, so too Christ has been made the second Adam, the perfect Head of the restored human race. Salvation therefore means that all mankind is recapitulated in Christ:

There is therefore, as I have pointed out, one God the Father, and one Christ Jesus, who came by means of the whole dispensational arrangements [i.e., the Old Testament], and gathered together all things in Himself. But in every respect, too, He is man, the formation of God; and thus He took up ["recapitulated"] man into Himself, the invisible becoming visible, the incomprehensible being made comprehensible, the impassible becoming capable of suffering, and the Word being made man, thus summing up all things in Himself: so that as in super-celestial, spiritual, and invisible things, the Word of God is supreme, so also in things visible and corporeal He might possess the supremacy, and, taking to Himself the pre-eminence, as well as constituting Himself Head of the Church (Col 1:18), He might draw all things to Himself at the proper time.[34]

---

32. See, for example, St. Justin, *First Apology* 46: "Those who lived by reason [according to the *Logos*, the Word] are Christians, even though they have been considered atheists; such as, among the Greeks, Socrates, Heraclitus, and others like them"; in *Saint Justin Martyr*, trans. Thomas B. Falls, FOC 6:83.

33. St. Clement of Alexandria, *Protrepticus* IV; *Exhortation to the Greeks*, trans. G. W. Butterworth, Loeb Classical Library 92 (Cambridge, Mass.: Harvard University Press, 1960), 101–43, esp. 129ff. and 143.

34. *Adversus Haereses* III.16.6, in ANF 1:442–43.

The Body of Christ

St. Irenaeus clearly shows the two aspects of Christ's work: solidarity with fallen man—that is, the Incarnation—and reuniting fallen man with God in the work of redemption. We see here the grand movement of Greek soteriology: God became man so that man might become God. While combating the Christological heresies that deny either the true humanity or the true divinity of the Savior, St. Irenaeus bases his arguments on the preaching of the apostles, which is guaranteed by the Holy Spirit. Although the theme of the Body of Christ is not explicitly developed, one can nevertheless see the extremely close tie that connects Christ and the Church:

The Church, indeed, though disseminated throughout the world, even to the ends of the earth, received from the apostles and their disciples the faith in the one God the Father Almighty, ... and in the one Jesus Christ, the Son of God, who was enfleshed for our salvation; and in the Holy Spirit.... She likewise believes these things just as if she had but one soul and one and the same heart; she preaches, teaches and hands them down harmoniously, as if she possessed but one mouth.[35]

If the Church here on earth is the community of faith, she owes this to the apostolic preaching that continues visibly within her. Hence the importance of the lists of bishops, which allows us to trace their lines of succession back to the apostles.[36] Yet this ministry is only the manifestation of a deeper, defining cause.

But [unlike that of the heretics], the preaching of the Church is everywhere consistent, and continues in an even course.... [This] well-grounded system ... [is] our faith; which, having been received from the Church, we do preserve, and which always, by the Spirit of God, renewing its youth, as if it were some precious deposit in an excellent vessel, causes the vessel itself containing it to renew its youth also.

For this gift of God has been entrusted to the Church, ... for this purpose, that all the members receiving it may be vivified; and the [means of] communion with Christ has been distributed throughout it, that is, the Holy Spirit, the earnest [i.e., down payment] of incorruption, the means of confirming our faith, and the ladder of ascent to God. "For in the Church," it is said, "God hath set apostles, prophets, teachers," (1 Cor 12:28) and all the other means through which the Spirit works; of which all those are not partakers who do not join themselves to the Church, but defraud themselves of

---

35. *Adversus Haereses* I.10.1–2, in ACW 55:48–49.
36. *Adversus Haereses* III.3.3, in ANF 1:416a.

life through their perverse opinions and infamous behaviour. For where the Church is, there is the Spirit of God; and where the Spirit of God is, there is the Church, and every kind of grace.[37]

The Holy Spirit is the Master of this work of apostolic preaching, through which faith is engendered, preserved, and increased in each person and in the whole community. The mystery of the Church is formed by this alliance. Hence it can only be in the Church that the divinization of man is wrought by Christ and his Spirit, and this Church reproduces in some way the mystery of the Savior: true ecclesiastical organism (the apostles) and true organism of grace (communion in divine life):

[The schismatics] cut in pieces and divide the great and glorious body of Christ, and so far as in them lies, destroy it.... True knowledge is the doctrine of the apostles, and the ancient constitution ["organism"] of the Church throughout all the world, and the distinctive manifestation of the Body of Christ according to the successions of the bishops, by which they [i.e., the apostles] have handed down that Church which exists in every place.[38]

Note the very strong expression that St. Irenaeus uses to speak about the Body of Christ (the Church)—namely, "organism of the Church"; there is no distinction, much less separation, between what is human and the divine gift in this mystery: if anyone breaks away from the apostolic preaching, by that very fact he departs from the Body of Christ.

St. Athanasius

St. Athanasius is not, strictly speaking, a theologian of the Mystical Body. In opposing Arius he is the champion of Christ's divinity, of the reality of the Incarnation of the Word, in a long, drawn-out battle that would culminate in the Council of Nicaea (325 A.D.). His writings testify to the typical schema of Greek theology, which originates in the Most High, in the Trinitarian mystery itself: life is communicated from the Father to his eternal Son, the Word, and then from the Son to the humanity that he assumed by the Spirit and, through that assumed humanity, to all men who, finding themselves thus incorporated into

37. *Adversus Haereses* III.24.1, in ANF 1:458.
38. *Adversus Haereses* IV.33.7–8, in ANF 1:508.

Christ, thereafter have access to the divine life. Elaborating on Christ's prayer, "That they may be one even as we are one," (Jn 17:22), Athanasius writes:

"[Father,] I am Thy Word, and since Thou art in Me, because I am Thy Word, and I in them because of the body, and because of Thee the salvation of men is perfected in Me, therefore I ask that they also may become one, according to the body that is in Me and according to its perfection; that they too may become perfect, having oneness with It, and having become one in It; that, as if all were carried by Me, all may be one body and one spirit, and may grow up unto a perfect man." For we all, partaking of the Same [Christ], become one body, having the one Lord in ourselves.[39]

If we look at things starting from man and retrace the chain of salvation, then man once again becomes a son of God by being united to the humanity of Christ, which is one with his divinity, consubstantial with the Father and the Spirit; this is the ascending schema:

For as we are all [made] from earth and die in Adam, so being regenerated from above of water and Spirit [in baptism], in the Christ we are all quickened; the flesh being no longer earthly, but being henceforth made Word, by reason of God's Word who for our sake became flesh.[40]

But this movement of man's salvation remains entirely dependent upon the first movement of the Incarnation, which is the descending schema:

For as the Lord, putting on the body, became man, so we men are deified by the Word as being taken to Him through His flesh, and henceforward inherit life everlasting.[41]

It would take many more investigations to discern what this "life" communicated by the Incarnation of the Word is and to understand better how this communication of divine life to the humanity assumed by the Word and to the human beings touched by this humanity of Christ comes about, but with St. Athanasius we are at the decisive Christological source of the doctrine of the Mystical Body. Indeed, if Jesus, this man, is not God, then no Mystical Body is possible, for only the divine life can save us. St. Athanasius does not explain in detail the

---

39. *Contra Arianos* III.22 (PG 26.367–70), in NPNF, 2nd series, 4:405–6.
40. *Contra Arianos* III.33 (PG 26.395), in NPNF, 2nd series, 4:412.
41. *Contra Arianos* III.34 (PG 26.398), in NPNF, 2nd series, 4:413.

ecclesiological part of the mystery (How does this incorporation into Christ come about?), but he does set up the general schema that later patristic literature will strive to elaborate.

4. The beginnings of Latin patristic literature

St. Cyprian

We possess a short treatise on the unity of the Church composed by the bishop of Carthage on account of heresies. His insistence on the need for unity is clear:

> God is one, and Christ is one, and His Church is one; one is the faith, and one the [Christian] people cemented together by harmony into the strong unity of a body.[42]

The word "harmony" is rather tame as a description in this fine teaching on unity because it suggests a merely moral requirement (and we know that the Latin Fathers were particularly attentive to this aspect). But other writings allow us to see that St. Cyprian is acquainted with other foundations for this bond of unity:

> [The Church is] a people united in the unity of the Father and of the Son and of the Holy Spirit.[43]

In other words, what unites the three Persons of the Trinity is, in a way, the same thing that unites human beings in the Christian people. Missing, however, is any mention of Christ's own mystery through which this communication of the Trinity to men comes about. Other remarks by St. Cyprian show that he is not unaware of this economy. Thus, with regard to the Eucharist, he writes:

> And what is more, the very sacrifices offered by our Lord demonstrate how in Christianity men are of one mind, linked together by the bonds of a powerful and unbreakable charity. For when the Lord calls bread His own body—and bread is a conglomerate of many individual grains, made into one—He signifies that we, the people whom He bore, are united into one. Similarly, when He calls wine His own blood—and wine is pressed from a great many clusters of individual grapes, squeezed into one juice—He again

---

42. *On the Unity of the Catholic Church* 23 (PL 4.517), in ACW 25:65.
43. *On the Lord's Prayer* 23 (PL 4.553), in St. Cyprian, *Treatises*, FOC 36:125–62, at 148.

The Body of Christ

indicates that we, His flock, being a multitude gathered together, are mingled and joined into one.[44]

For just as numerous grains are gathered, ground, and mixed all together to make into one loaf of bread, so in Christ, who is the bread of heaven, we know there is but one body and that every one of us has been fused together and made one with it.[45]

Similarly, in discussing the bishop, on whom St. Cyprian insists just as much as St. Ignatius:

Even when a whole host of proud and presumptuous people may refuse to listen and go away, the Church herself does not go away from Christ.... The Church consists of the people who remain united with their bishop, it is the flock that stays by its shepherd. By that you ought to realize that the bishop is in the Church and the Church in the bishop, and whoever is not with the bishop is not in the Church.[46]

The Latin teaching appears to be less elaborate than that of the Greeks, but it does articulate the same points.

5. The beginnings of Greek High Patristic literature

This was the age of the first fundamental definitions.

St. Hilary[47]

St. Hilary is very attentive to the role of the Savior's humanity in the divinization of men and in the formation of the ecclesial Body. The general idea is that the humanity of the Savior is the servant of his divinity:

The body that Jesus assumed as a servant accomplished in itself the whole mystery (*sacramentum*) of our redemption.[48]

Starting from this axiom, his statements are particularly powerful:

If the Word has indeed become flesh [Jn 1:14], and we indeed receive the Word as flesh in the Lord's food, how are we not to believe that He dwells

---

44. *Epistle* 69.5.2, in ACW 47:36.   45. *Epistle* 63.13.4, in ACW 46:105.
46. *Epistle* 66.8.3, in ACW 46:121.
47. St. Hilary of Poitiers is a Latin Father, but his teaching here is influenced by the Greeks.
48. *Commentary on the Gospel of Matthew* II.5 (PL 9.927) [translated from French].

in us by His nature, He who, when He was born as a man, has assumed the nature of our flesh, bound inseparably with Himself, and has mingled [i.e., conjoined] the nature of His flesh to His eternal nature in the mystery [sacrament] of the flesh that was to be communicated to us? All of us are one in this manner because the Father is in Christ and Christ is in us.... If, therefore, Christ has truly taken the flesh of our body, and that man who was born from Mary is truly Christ, and we truly receive the flesh of His body in the mystery [sacrament] (and we are one, therefore, because the Father is in Him and He in us), how can you assert that there is a unity of will [alone], since the attribute of the nature in the sacrament is the mystery of a perfect unity?[49]

He Himself thus testifies how natural is this unity in us: "He who eats my flesh, and drinks my blood, abides in me and I in him" [John 6:56]. No one will be in Him unless He Himself has been in him, while He has assumed and taken upon Himself the flesh of [that person] only who has received His own. Previously, He had already given an explanation of the perfect unity when He declared: "As the living Father has sent me and as I live through the Father, so he who shall eat my flesh shall live through me" [John 6:57].[50]

Note that St. Hilary interprets the Pauline data concerning the ecclesial Body in the most realistic sense, thanks to his reference to St. John (discourse on the bread of life in Jn 6 and Jn 17). This relation between the teaching of St. Paul and that of St. John is a classic feature of Tradition. On the other hand, St. Hilary's vocabulary should not be surprising. He speaks of a "natural" unity (based on the Greek notion of "*physis*"), which here means substantial or real. St. Hilary thus opposes those who acknowledge only a moral union of wills.[51] However, and this is his limitation, St. Hilary does not specify the mode of this divine "consubstantiality" of the Father and the Son, nor does he explain how the human "consubstantiality" between Christ and men comes about; of course, they should not be understood in the same sense.

Following St. Hilary, Tradition definitively acknowledges that the unity of the Mystical Body is real and not merely moral.

---

49. *The Trinity* VIII.13 (PL 10.246), trans. Stephen McKenna, C.Ss.R., FOC 25:285.
50. *The Trinity* VIII.16 (PL 10.248), in FOC 25:287.
51. He does so explicitly in *The Trinity* VIII.17 (PL 10.249), in FOC 25:287–88.

St. John Chrysostom

An enthusiastic admirer of St. Paul, the preacher of Constantinople upholds the realism of the Eucharistic union with the Savior that makes the Church. With reference to the discourse on the bread of life (Jn 6), he comments:

We must learn the wondrousness of the [Eucharistic] Mystery, what it is, why it was given, and what is the benefit to be derived from it. "We are one body," Scripture says, "and members made from his flesh and from his bones" (Eph 5:30). Let the initiated attend studiously to these words.

Therefore in order that we may become of His Body, not in desire only, but also in very fact, let us become commingled with that Body. This, in truth, takes place by means of the food which He has given us as a gift, because He desired to prove the love which He has for us. It is for this reason that He has shared Himself with us and has brought His Body down to our level, namely, that we might be one with Him as the body is joined with the head.[52]

With reference to 1 Corinthians 10:16–17 ("The bread which we break, is it not a participation in the body of Christ?") he comments:

"For why speak I of communion?" saith he, "we are that self-same body." For what is the bread? The Body of Christ. And what do they become who partake of it? The Body of Christ: not many bodies, but one body. For as the bread consisting of many grains is made one, so that the grains nowhere appear; they exist indeed, but their difference is not seen by reason of their conjunction; so are we conjoined both with each other and with Christ.[53]

Here one can make the same remarks as in the case of St. Hilary. The Word comes into us in Eucharistic communion in somewhat the same way as he came into a single human being at the Incarnation. Note also the absence of individualism: each of the communicants does not become a Body of Christ, but all of them together form one ecclesial Body.

---

52. *Homilies on the Gospel of St. John* 46.3 (PG 59.260), trans. Sr. Thomas Aquinas Goggin, S.C.H., FOC 33:468.
53. *Homilies on 1st Corinthians* 24.4 (PG 61.200), in NPNF, 1st series, 12:140a.

6. The Greek Nicene and post-Nicene period
This was the era of doctrinal synthesis.

St. Cyril of Alexandria

St. Cyril centers his discussion on the mystery of the Incarnate Word. Although the arguments of St. Athanasius and St. Hilary were rooted in the mystery of the Trinity, from now on everything is concentrated on the Incarnation. In this context theologians attain greater precision in their formulas.

In the first place, the realism of the Incarnation upholds the realism of the Mystical Body. Christ's own mystery is the mystery of the real union between the Word and man in a single hypostasis. With this as the starting point, attention is concentrated on the assumed humanity: if the assumed humanity is one with the Word, then from that Word it receives life itself, incorruptible, enlivening, eternal, subsistent. From then on the body and blood of Christ (his humanity) are therefore the body and blood of the Word, of life, and hence are life-giving. The humanity of Christ "contains" supernatural life, and we see in the Gospels the works that Christ performed while he was among us: through his humanity, filled with the life-giving power of God, Christ cured the sick and raised the dead. This is the very mystery of the Savior:

> Although the natures [divine and human] are different which were brought together to a true unity, there is one Christ and Son from both. The differences of the natures are not destroyed through the union, but rather the divinity and humanity formed for us one Lord Jesus Christ and one Son through the incomprehensible and ineffable combination to a unity.[54]

This union, which constitutes Christ's identity, is in a certain way communicated to human beings for their salvation:

> In order, then, that we ourselves also may join together, and be blended into unity with God and with each other, although, through the actual difference which exists in each one of us, we have a distinct individuality of soul and body, the Only-begotten has contrived a means which His own due Wisdom and the Counsel of the Father have sought out. For by one Body, that is, His own, blessing [literally: "eulogizing," which is Eucharistic vocabulary]

---

54. *Epistola* IV (PG 77.46), Cyril's Second Letter to Nestorius, FOC 76:39.

through the mystery of the Eucharist those who believe on Him, He makes us of the same Body with Himself and with each other. For who could sunder or divide from their natural union with one another those who are knit together through His holy Body, Which is one in union with Christ? For if *we all partake of the one Bread,* we are all made one Body (1 Cor 10:17); for Christ cannot suffer severance. Therefore also the Church is become Christ's Body, and we are also individually His members, according to the wisdom of Paul (Eph 5:23ff.). For we, being all of us united to Christ through His holy Body, inasmuch as we have received Him Who is one and indivisible in our own bodies, owe the service of our members to Him rather than to ourselves.[55]

The Eucharist makes us "of the same body" [*concorporels*] with the sacred humanity of Christ, which, because it is the most intimately united with the Word, unites us to God. St. Cyril emphasizes the fact that our union with God depends on the constitutive union of the mystery of Christ more than he does the difference between the hypostatic union on the one hand and the mystical union on the other. Both unions are real, and this is what they have in common; the reality of the hypostatic union guarantees the reality of the mystical union that brings about the mystery of the Church. To put it yet another way, although the union brought about by the Incarnation of the Word is unique and incommunicable, the consequence thereof is that the humanity assumed by the Word is filled with divine life. Since this humanity is connatural with us, it can be received into us and hence can enliven us, making us participants by grace in what the Son is by nature. Thus the union of God with human beings depends essentially on the union of God with one man, Christ.

Consequently in his humanity Christ is the life of all human beings, mediator and Head of his ecclesial Body. This humanity, because it subsists in the Person of the Word, is "mystical": its union with the Word is the reason for its union with us; Christ's title of Head is not something superadded, but is an intrinsic part of his mystery; he is the one "full of grace and truth" (Jn 1:14) so as to communicate to us what he has and is in fullness.

---

55. *Commentary on the Gospel of John* XI.11 (PG 74.559), trans. Thomas Randell as *Commentary on the Gospel according to S. John,* vol. 2, *A Library of Fathers of the Holy Catholic Church* (London: Walter Smith, 1885), 549–50.

7. The Latin post-Nicene period

St. Augustine is the only Latin author who can rival the Greeks in speculative power. That is why we will confine ourselves to the Doctor of Hippo here.

St. Augustine

St. Augustine developed the doctrine of the Mystical Body, not for its own sake, but in the course of his battles on two fronts: against the Donatists, who had caused a schism, and against the Pelagians, who were heretics. Against the former he developed above all the criteria for recognizing the true Church; against the latter he pursued a more in-depth understanding of what the ecclesial Body is. We will also mention some homilies that the bishop of Hippo preached to his people.

Regarding his controversy with the Donatists, it is a question of knowing who acts in the celebration of a sacrament. The schism had taken place in Carthage around eighty years before St. Augustine. It had started with an episcopal ordination celebrated by a bishop suspected of unworthy conduct, and Donatus had maintained that consequently the rite had been invalid. St. Augustine tirelessly responded that the true minister of a sacrament is Christ himself. Everyone knows the formula, "Let Peter baptize, ... let Judas baptize; Christ it is who baptizes."[56] Christ is the one Head of the Mystical Body, the unique source of all grace; the minister does not produce, but rather transmits. The unworthiness of a minister therefore does not affect the truth of the sacrament. In his anti-Donatist writings, St. Augustine does not strictly speaking develop the doctrine of the Mystical Body; he argues starting on the grounds on which his adversaries have positioned themselves. He understands the question posed by the Donatists as follows:

1. Where is the Body of Christ that is the Church?

> This, certainly, is the question that we are discussing: Where is the Church? Is it with us [Catholics] or with them [the Donatists]? In any case there is only one; our ancestors called it Catholic so as to show by its very name that it extends everywhere.... Now this Church is the Body of Christ, as the Apostle says: "for his Body, which is the Church,"

---

56. See *In Johannem* VI.7, in FOC 78:135.

The Body of Christ

(Eph 5:23). Hence it is quite plain that someone who is not among the members of Christ cannot possess salvation in Christ. Now the members of Christ are joined with one another by the unity of charity, and this is what attaches them to their Head, who is Christ Jesus.... Now the question in the debate between us and the Donatists is this: Where is this Body, in other words, where is the Church?[57]

2. The unity of the Head and the Body: to be outside the Body is to be outside the influence of the Head.

> The whole Christ is Head and Body. The Head is the only-begotten Son of God, and his Body is the Church; they are the Bridegroom and the Bride, two in one flesh (Eph 5:23). Anyone who dissents from the Sacred Scriptures concerning the Head ... is not in the Church [theme of unity in faith about Christ] Again, anyone who ... does not share in the unity of the Church [theme of the universal episcopal communion] is not in the Church, because he dissents from the testimony of Christ himself concerning the Body of Christ that is the Church.[58]

3. The unity of the Head and the Body: To be outside the influence of the Head is to be outside the Church.

> [The Donatist bishops] anoint their heads with the oil of flattery (Ps 140 [141]:5). They themselves wish to be their own heads, because they do not want to be under the one Head who is in heaven, in the unity of the Body that is throughout the earth.[59]

Plainly his employment of the doctrine of the Mystical Body is still embryonic and does not reach the level of sophistication already attained by the Greek Fathers.

Against the Pelagians, St. Augustine went on to elaborate a doctrine about original sin and grace. Pelagius greatly diminished the gravity of the first sin and diminished just as much the value and necessity of grace. For him, man can lead an upright, moral life alone and unaided. This point of view destroys two essential forms of solidarity: the mystery of the solidarity between sin and death and the mystery of the solidarity between good and life. The Pauline doctrine of the two Ad-

---

57. *Epist. ad Catholicos* II.2, in CSEL 52:232 [translated from Latin with reference to the French].

58. *Epist. ad Catholicos* IV.7, in CSEL 52:238 [translated from Latin with reference to the French].

59. *Contra Epist. Parmeniani* III.5.26 (PL 43.103) [translated from Latin with reference to the French].

ams is thus emptied of meaning. For Pelagius original sin is only a bad example (moral causality), and the grace of Christ (the good example of his life and teaching) can be useful, but is not necessary. St. Augustine responds by basing his argument on St. Paul: in Adam, all have sinned and are deprived of divine life; in Christ, all those who make up his Body are saved. Everything depends here on the grace of Christ:

> Therefore, in him who is our head (*caput*) let there appear for us the very fountain of grace, whence he pours himself out through all his members, according to the measure of each one. For the grace that makes any man a Christian from the time he begins to believe is the same grace by which one man [Jesus] from his beginning became Christ. That Spirit by which the Christian is reborn is the same Spirit by which Christ is born. It is the same Spirit that brings about in us the remission of sins as brought about in Christ that he had no sin.[60]

The Mystical Body is presented clearly here as the great organism of grace, both in its source in Christ and communicated to men by the door of faith.

Outside his polemical works, St. Augustine preached to the people of Hippo. These sermons show us that the bishop of Hippo had a broad, Pauline view of ecclesiology. To complete this presentation we shall cite several texts, in a style that is more homiletic than academic, in which the union of men in Christ is the subject of very strong formulas. Yet they testify to the realism with which the preacher conceives of our union in Christ that makes the Church.

> If you want to understand the Body of Christ, listen to what the Apostle says to the faithful: "Now you are the Body of Christ and members of it" (1 Cor 12:27). Therefore if you are the Body of Christ and its members, then your mystery is placed on the altar of the Lord; you receive your mystery....
>
> Why then is this mystery received in [the form of] bread? Let us make no statement of our own; let us listen to the Apostle himself who says, when he speaks of this Sacrament, "We, being many, are one bread, one body" (1 Cor 10:17). Understand and rejoice. Unity, truth, piety, charity. "One bread"; what is this one bread? One Body made from many. Consider that bread is not made of one grain, but of many. When you were being exorcised [during the baptismal ceremony], you were, so to speak, being ground up [like grains of wheat]. When you were baptized you were, so to speak,

---

60. *De praedestinatione sanctorum* XV.31 (PL 44.982), in *On the Predestination of the Saints*, FOC 86:254.

The Body of Christ

moistened [like flour made into dough]. When you received the fire of the Holy Spirit, it was as though you were baked....

My brethren, recall how wine is made. On the cluster there are many grapes, but the liquid that flows from the grapes mingles in unity. Thus Christ the Lord ... consecrated on his altar the mystery of our peace and our unity.[61]

The grace, or the Spirit, possessed in fullness by the humanity of Christ, pours out from the Head to all the members of the Body through baptism and the Eucharist, joining them together in the most profound unity. The result is that Head and members form as it were one being, which St. Augustine calls, with an expression that is peculiar to him, the "whole Christ":

If we consider ourselves, if we reflect on [Christ's] Body, we will see that we too are he. For if we were not he himself, it would not be true that "As you did it to one of the least of these my brethren, you did it to me" (Mt 25:40). If we were not he himself, it would not be true: "Saul, Saul, why do you persecute me?" (Acts 9:4). Therefore we too are he, because we are his members, because we are his Body, because he is our Head, because the whole Christ is the Head and the Body.[62]

"No one has ascended into heaven but he who descended from heaven, the Son of man, who is in heaven" (Jn 3:13). Christ said this because of the unity whereby he is our Head and we are his Body.[63]

The art of the sacred orator goes as far as possible to show the unity of Christ the Head and Christians, the members of the Body. The expression, taken literally, could cause concern that St. Augustine is confusing the Head and the Body in an indistinct whole (cf. "we are he"), but there is always a continuation of the sentence that rectifies and balances the force of the expression by recognizing the unique excellence of Christ, who personally possesses what he communicates to us, to each his share.

8. Summary of the patristic data

The survey of the Fathers that we have just made could have been much longer and more complete. We limited ourselves to the main

---

61. *Sermon* 272 (PL 38.1247–48) [translated from Latin].
62. *Sermon* 133 (PL 38.742) [translated from Latin].
63. *Sermo* 263 "*De Ascensionis Domini*" III (PL 38.1210) [translated from Latin].

clarifications for which the Fathers are irreplaceable witnesses. The initial teaching, the very first reception of Scripture, was as follows: Christ saves us by uniting us to himself by the faith that leads to baptism and the Eucharist, all of which is the object of the apostolic service that the bishops continue. To be saved is thus to be "in Christ," with each one doing his part to build up his Body. Patristic literature as a whole deepens this fundamental basis along three closely interrelated lines:

1. At the Trinitarian level, it was necessary to establish that Christ is God, consubstantial with the Father (cf. the effort of St. Athanasius and St. Hilary);

2. At the Christological level, it was necessary to establish the reality of the Incarnation and the mode of union between the Word and the humanity that he assumed (cf. the battles of St. Cyril of Alexandria).

3. Finally, on the ecclesiological level, what was at stake was the communication of the fullness present in the humanity of Christ (the Head) to all human beings (his Body), which required a precise teaching about the preaching of the faith, about baptism and the Eucharist, and also about the ministry charged with serving these means of unity in Christ.

The patristic doctrine about the Church as the Body of Christ is all this. It is a considerable accomplishment and has enormous ecumenical value because it is radically shared by our Orthodox brethren and by us.

b. The medieval data: St. Thomas Aquinas

The medieval period was an extraordinarily prolific age. With respect to the Masters of the Augustinian tradition, St. Thomas Aquinas is original on many points. We limit our presentation to him because his doctrine was adopted to a great extent by the subsequent Magisterium. At first we will present his teaching in a synthetic form, then we will single out three important points, and we will conclude with three more precise and "technical" observations. However, before entering upon this subject, it is advisable to introduce briefly the originality of the medieval theological endeavor.

With Scholastic theology we enter—and this is the novelty—the era of speculative syntheses. Until then the theological research of the

Fathers chiefly followed the movement of Revelation itself. Let us explain what we mean.

The last word of scriptural Revelation on the mystery of Christ, the most explicit formulation thereof that St. John and St. Paul give to us, is that Jesus of Nazareth, the son of Mary, the village carpenter, *is* the Son of God by nature, begotten of the Father before all ages and, like him, God by his unity with the Divine Word: "My Lord and my God!" said St. Thomas the apostle in the presence of the man whose wounds he touched (Jn 20:28). The progressive discovery of the mystery of the Incarnation was made by the disciples through the preaching of Jesus and through the interior teaching of the Holy Spirit after Easter. This followed an *ascending* line, moving from what was externally explicit—the reality of his humanity—to what was more interior and secret, his divine personhood. This is an order of *knowledge* or also of *discovery*.

Nevertheless, considered in itself, the mystery of the Incarnation is not the mystery of the exaltation of a creature to the level of God (adoptionism); it is the mystery of the coming of God to us in a particular human nature that he assumed. Although the man Jesus was proclaimed Christ and Lord on Easter morning, "designated Son of God in power" (Rom 1:4) and exalted at God's right hand, this was not the apotheosis ("*apotheōsis*" in Greek = deification) of a mere creature, it is the return to God of the one who had come from God to us; it is the glorification in his humanity of him who possesses that glory from all eternity. Here we are following the *real* order.

It is necessary therefore to distinguish carefully between the order of knowledge and the order of the reality itself: the mystery of Christ is the mystery of the eternal Son who is God and who was sent to us, was born of a woman (Gal 4:5) a man like us: the *descending* real order.

Thus—and this is a general rule of knowledge—we proceed, in our investigation of reality, "against the grain," as it were, ascending from effects to their cause, from accidents to the substance, from properties to the essence. But once we have arrived at a certain stage of knowledge, we can from then on manage to make the real order and the order of knowledge coincide, and this is the stage where *science* occurs. Its discourse is *descending*, like the real order; it goes from the cause toward the effects. This order of science is what began in the theology of the Church in the thirteenth century, and it is important to grasp this: the

Thomistic treatment in the *Summa theologiae* that we will present follows an order of scientific synthesis. So it is that the patristic heritage of the theology of the Body of Christ is taken up by St. Thomas. Let us look at the principal passage: *Summa theologiae* III, q. 8.

1. Overall explanation

The mystery of the Savior: The hypostatic union

St. Thomas takes as his point of departure the mystery of the Incarnate Word in its source, which is the divine action itself that brings about the Incarnation (*ST* III, qq. 1–6). This is the hypostatic union in the sense of the unitive action by which the two natures are conjoined: the grace of union represented by *the fact* that these two natures are so intimately united that they form one single *being*.

The first consequence for the assumed humanity

Then St. Thomas considers the effect that such a union caused in the individual humanity thus assumed (*ST* III, q. 7): the personal grace of Christ. By the fact of the union, this individual humanity that has been assumed is supremely filled with grace, perfectly holy.

The second consequence for the assumed humanity

Finally St. Thomas considers the purpose of this union and of its individual consequence in the humanity of Christ—namely, *our salvation:* Christ possesses grace in its fullness *so as to transmit it to us;* this is the grace of the Head or capital grace (*ST* III, q. 8).

These passages [from the *Tertia pars* of the *Summa theologiae*] are the principal texts in St. Thomas that we must investigate in terms of their theological methodology and of their context. For convenience' sake, we speak about the three graces of Christ, but theologians speak more precisely about the *triplex gratia Christi*—that is, about one grace in its three distinct aspects.

To say that Christ is "full of grace and truth" (Jn 1:14), and that "from his fullness have we all received, grace upon grace" (Jn 1:16) is to emphasize correctly that Christ gives us *his* grace. The grace that he possesses in fullness is the same grace that is poured out on us, without ceasing, of course, to be fully present in him. Consequently Christ

The Body of Christ 99

is sanctifying because he is holy (Heb 2:11). We will see, in the speculative [part of this course], the importance of this assertion.

Let us look now at several particular points in this doctrinal synthesis (the complete study of question 8 depends on Christology).

2. Particular points

The metaphor of the Head (*ST* III, q. 8, art. 1)

St. Thomas utilizes here, as the basis of the comparison, some physical findings from the natural history of Aristotle,[64] but it is very discreet; the only explicit citations in the article are biblical.

On the natural level, the head of a man, while having the same nature as the rest of his body, is superior to it in two ways: it alone possesses all the senses, while the other members have only the sense of touch; from it comes all that is necessary for the life of the whole organism (air, food, direction). This can be applied to Christ. He is consubstantial with us according to his humanity, yet he is superior to us in this order because he possesses the spiritual life in its fullness and it is through him that we receive it. This image, however, has its limits: the head of the body cannot live without the other members that help and complete it. Now Christ is in no way helped nor completed by the members of his Mystical Body. We find again here the two paths already attested in the writings of St. Paul: Christ as the supereminent member of this Body of which he is the Head; and Christ who is in no way completed by his Body, because he is above the Church. In other words, there is an aspect of unity (Head-Body): Christ as man is in the Church as its Head; and an aspect of distinction: Christ is indissociably God and, as such, above the Church.

The efficiency of grace (*ST* III, q. 8, art. 5)

St. Thomas recalls that the grace of the Head (capital grace) is formally the same as the personal grace. Christ transmits to us something *of himself.* The influx of grace, from the Head to the members, is not *only* on the moral order, but also "physical" in some way; there is a communication of something real.[65] We speak here about physical ef-

64. *Historia animalium* I.7 and *De partibus animalium* II.10 and IV.10.
65. See other passages in St. Thomas: *ST* III, q. 13, art. 2; *Quodlibet* II, in the Leonine edition *Opera omnia* 25 (Rome: 1996), art. 6, q. 4, ad 3.

ficient causality, and this is important in the debate with Protestants: Catholics insist that we are justified *intrinsically*. In order to grasp this point better, it is good to recall several points from the doctrine of redemption. We cite here *ST* III, q. 48 and q. 49.[66] How was redemption won for us? St. Thomas shows that all causalities (both moral and physical) are at work in Christ, and we will find them again in the Church in a certain way.

To put it succinctly, redemption is understood according to two distinct and complementary lines that are well attested in the Fathers of the Church: there is the "real" (or better: "physical") theory of redemption and the moral theory of redemption. According to the physical theory, Christ, assuming human nature totally, thus created a solidarity, a mystical union with all human beings; he is one of us and not "only" One of the Trinity. We are one with Christ in the same human nature and in the same grace bestowed on that nature.

According to the moral theory of redemption—a prolongation of the first—it is said that our deliverance comes from God who, out of mercy, applied to us the superabundant merits of Christ. God found in his creation a perfect man who returned love for his love, and because of him pardoned all the others. In this sense Christ expiated in our place (St. John Chrysostom), paid our debt for us (St. Anselm). This interpretation has strong scriptural support.[67] Let us not forget that the very word "redemption" means buying back, and that this notion has its origin in the Old Testament notion of the "*gō'ēl*," the one who ransomed.

It must be understood that the moral theory has to be linked to and dependent on the physical theory. If Christ can make satisfaction in our place (moral theory), it is because he is one of us and really united to us. In the absence of that real unity (our grace is the grace of Christ that is poured out on us), the moral theory, left to itself, becomes untenable. It becomes the expression of an arbitrary decree by God who agrees to appease his wrath—that of an outraged king or an unpaid

---

66. On this point see the book by Bernard Catão, *Salut et rédemption chez S. Thomas d'Aquin*.

67. See especially the parable of the debtor who could not repay in Lk 7:42ff. and the remark that Christ gave his life as a ransom for many in Mt 20:28 and parallel passages.

The Body of Christ

creditor—by making an innocent man (Christ) pay for the sins of others (we ourselves). This offends one's innate sense of justice. We have to go further. God found in his creation a man who loves him perfectly, who responds fully to his love, *and* this man really unites all men and women to himself, thus making them capable of such a love, the most consummate example being the Blessed Virgin. The "channel" of perfect love has been reopened by Christ, and we are not saved without our participation.[68]

This explains the fact that a redemption that is totally accomplished in the Head is really communicated to the Body, which is thus capable of participating in its redemption or, as St. Paul puts it, of "complet[ing] what is lacking in Christ's afflictions for the sake of his body, that is, the Church" (Col 1:24). Christ the Redeemer does not act in place of man; he gives him the ability to act perfectly himself by means of this real "physical" communication of the principle of supernatural life, which is grace.[69] All this depends on the very important statement that the personal grace and the capital grace of Christ are the same grace considered under two different aspects. Protestants accept only the moral theory of redemption and accordingly believe in *extrinsic* and merely moral justification, which devaluates man's participation in salvation.

To summarize, we can say: the Incarnation, inasmuch as it causes the Savior's humanity to be one, in the strong sense, with the Word, is for that assumed humanity the grace of union. This union gives to this humanity an intrinsic sanctity that is personal grace. This sanctity is so great and perfect that it is made to "overflow" and pour out upon us, which is capital grace. We have the following schema:

---

68. Cf. St. Augustine: "God created thee without thee, but will not justify thee without thee"; *Sermon* 159.XI.13 (PL 38.923).

69. This is not some impotence in the Savior that would require us to complete something that was lacking in him in order to assure the salvation of humanity. But it is the perfection of the divine love that is expressed thereby: indeed, it is more respectful of the dignity of the human being who is to be saved to restore within him the capacity to collaborate in his salvation and in that of his brethren than it is to save him "passively." We are not only saved individuals, but our assimilation to Christ also configures us to him to the point where we become "saviors"—in other words, participants, in our position and according to our capacity, in the salvation of the world.

Word > assumed humanity: *the grace that is their union*

Consequences of this union:

1. a peerless sanctity: *personal grace*

↓

2. the capacity to diffuse *his* sanctity: *grace of the Head* (*capital grace*)

↓

Human beings: *ecclesial body*

We are at the heart of Christology that is also the heart of ecclesiology: the Church is the community of Christian grace, *Christic* grace; it comes from Christ and *conforms souls to Christ*. We will add what comes second (which is by no means secondary): the means by which Christ diffuses his grace to men—in other words, the preaching of the Gospel and the celebration of the sacraments. In doing so we follow this order of understanding: 1. The purpose; 2. The means of attaining it (efficient causes).

The question of the members of the Church (*ST* III, q. 8, art. 3)

This question can be treated in two ways. Either we consider as members those who are *capable* of being the receptacles of grace—in this case we understand the Mystical Body to consist exclusively of men (minus the damned) and angels. This is the position of St. Thomas, who distinguishes between actual members (the blessed, those in a state of grace here below, the angels) and potential members (sinners, unbelievers). Or we consider only those who receive grace *effectively*—in other words, the predestined: this is the area of difficulty pondered by Calvin in particular.

We will return to this question "*De membris,*" because this was historically the point of departure for modern speculative reflection on the Church.

3. Particular observations
The instrumental causality of Christ's humanity

A fundamental affirmation of Greek patristic literature is that, in Christ, his humanity is the instrument of his divinity.[70] Among the Fathers of the Church, the common, general notion of instrument is the one that is still used most often as an image. But in the writings of St. Thomas, with the help of Aristotelian metaphysics, this affirmation acquires a very functional and "technical" value; here it is a question not just of a simple *image*, but of instrumental *causality* (see *ST* III, q. 19, art. 1).

The instrumental cause is situated in the order of efficient causality: it is a question of producing an effect. It is the kind of cause that *produces its effect only when moved by a principal agent*. Thus far the pattern applies neatly to Christ: his humanity is indeed in this sense the instrument of his divinity. As God, Christ, by his own authority, can give grace; as man, it pertains to him to do so instrumentally. To put it differently—in a manner of speaking that is close to that of Scripture—his *human* acts, by virtue of his divinity, caused grace in his contemporaries by instrumental efficiency.[71]

Pursuing this application of instrumental causality to the case of Christ, however, poses major problems. Indeed, an instrument *is moved* by the principal cause and *moves* toward the ultimate effect. We say that the instrument is *movens motum*, "the moved mover": this is the notion of *intermediary*. In doing this, joining the principal cause to the effect, the instrument makes the influence of the principal cause pass *through itself* so as to attain its effect. In other words, the characteristic of an instrument is that it operates not according to its own power, but according to the power of the principal agent. For example a saw, according to its own power, cuts; but as an instrument, operating by the power of the artisan (principal cause), it makes a piece of furniture. Hence this important consequence: it is not part of the definition of an instru-

---

70. For the patristic history of this notion, see Theophil Tschipke, *L'humanité du Christ comme instrument de salut de la divinité*.
71. In the case of human beings who were born after the Ascension, Christ touches them through his glorified humanity, which acts through ministers celebrating the sacraments: two subordinate causalities that are instrumental.

ment to have some *habitus*, but rather to be capable of being moved by the principal agent. And although Christ, in his humanity, is Head inasmuch as he pours out grace upon mankind, that does not require that he possess grace in its fullness. He could transmit grace as do the ministers of the Church who do not give a grace that is their own, but are true instruments: grace passes through them like the power of the principal agent passes through the saw so as to be completed in the piece of furniture, thus the "transitive" power of the instrument. This is the objection noted in *De Veritate* q. 29, art. 5, arg. 2.

Yet the scriptural data oblige us to hold that Christ sanctifies because he is personally holy: of *his* fullness we have all received, grace upon grace (Jn 1:16). In Scholastic terms we say—and this amounts to the same thing—that Christ possesses perfectly *ut res* [as a thing per se] what he must transmit *ut instrumentum* [as an instrument]. We find here a unique sort of instrumental causality that is not based on any metaphysical necessity, but is obligatory by reason of the data of Revelation. The question has the utmost importance for speculative ecclesiology. Indeed, if that is the case in the Head, then how is it with the Body?

We have two extremes of instrumental causality:

- Christ: his humanity possesses fully what it must transmit as an instrument.
- The ministers and the sacraments: instruments in the strict sense, which is to say that grace passes through them, but does not stay in them.

What about the Church? Should we take her sanctity in the strong sense? Is she holy and does she consequently sanctify in a certain way like Christ? Or is she holy because she sanctifies by a transitive power, like the ministers and the sacraments? We note here the beginning of a solution that we will develop in the speculative part: one must start from the Eucharist, the fruit of which is the unity of all the baptized in one Body, the Body of Christ that is the Church. The Eucharist is *the only one* of the seven sacraments in which God's action is not transitive, but assumes a certain permanence: the consecrated bread *is* the sacramental Body of Christ and remains such as long as the species continue to exist. The Eucharist *sanctifies because it is holy*, unlike the water of baptism, for example, which sanctifies only transitively. The Church,

The Body of Christ

the Mystical Body of Christ, should be understood in terms of the Eucharist that engenders her.

The complexity of the Mystical Body

We know that in the teachings of St. Paul and in all patristic literature, the Church, the Mystical Body, is a complex being that is at the same time spiritual (the fellowship of grace) and quite incarnate (the sacraments, the ministries). And so there is on the one hand the *reality* of supernatural communion in the grace of Christ and, on the other hand, *the order of the means* for entering, remaining, and growing in this communion, and also for returning to it if one has cut oneself off from it. Now at the end of the Second World War, some authors objected that St. Thomas had elucidated the vital influx of Christ on the Church without allowing sufficient room for the incarnate aspect of this mystery, without including the whole order of the means of grace. Indeed, they said, St. Thomas includes in the Mystical Body all the just of the Old Testament and even the angels; where then is the outward aspect of the Mystical Body?[72]

This objection to St. Thomas appears to be unfounded for many reasons:

The place of ministers is explicitly considered (*ST* III, q. 8, art. 6); we will get to that. The place of the sacraments—in keeping with the plan of the synthesis—is underscored in the treatment of each one in turn, and it is clear that the central role of the Eucharist has not been omitted.[73] St. Thomas even says crudely, "*Ecclesia fabricatur* [*sacramentis*]."[74] We will see in the speculative part the profound reasons for these objections to St. Thomas. But let us remember that, like Scripture (St. Paul) and the Fathers, St. Thomas includes under the name "Mystical Body" *the entire ecclesial mystery* and not only its interior aspect of grace. Consequently we will have to see how it is with the just of the Old Testament and the angels.

---

72. See the summary of this debate by Jérôme Hamer in *The Church Is a Communion*, 71–82.

73. See in particular *ST* III, q. 60, art. 3, *sed contra;* q. 73, art. 6; and especially q. 80, art. 4; also *Super Ephesios* c. 4, lect. 4 (Marietti 214–16).

74. "The Church is *made* (by the sacraments)"; 4 *Sent*. D. 18, q. 1, art. 1; see also *Super 1 Cor*. c. 11, lect. 2 (Marietti 348).

The twofold influence of the Head (*ST* III, q. 8, art. 6)

If Christ is the Head of the Mystical Body, it is, we repeat, because he pours out his own life into the whole organism. This is the most profound reason for his headship. Since the Middle Ages the word *influx* has become the "technical" term designating this physical efficient causality. In other words, Christ causes his vital force to pass into the whole Body; he infuses into it his own life and all its riches: his light (Jn 8:12, for example) according to the biblical symbolism in which light is faith under the aspect of knowledge, his holiness (Jn 17:19), or even his grace (Jn 1:16). And he does this by the most immanent, most intimate action that there is: it touches the soul of the recipient and his body. This influence of the Head is twofold:

- an *internal* influx. Christ communicates grace by his power alone, independently of any external act—for example, the miracles that he worked at a distance such as the healing of the centurion's servant (Lk 7:1–10).
- an *external* influx. Christ communicates grace by his external-corporeal actions; he pronounces an efficacious word of pardon, he puts mud on the blind man's eyes, he raises the dead son of the widow of Naim.

Since the Ascension, the internal influx is still possible for Christ; it is no more restricted to external acts than it was before. But the external influx is no longer possible for Christ now that he has withdrawn his bodily presence from the world. This is why, in order to continue this activity, he instituted ministers who would dispense the sacraments to the faithful.[75] For this reason these ministers are called "Heads" of the Church in a *secondary, derivative* way (*vice Christi gerentes;* literally, vicars "replacing" Christ).

There are many differences between these ministers who are "vicarious Heads" and Christ the Head:

- They do not transmit a grace of their own; unlike Christ, they illustrate totally the concept of instrument, as we saw earlier. St. Thom-

---

75. See *SCG* IV, c. 74.

as says it clearly: "The definitions of a minister and of an instrument are the same" (*ST* III, q. 64, art. 1).⁷⁶
- They are "Head" for only a specific time and/or place, whereas Christ is Head of all and everywhere.
- They are "Head" only in and for the Church on earth, whereas Christ is Head of the Church in her various states.

From this it follows that the ministerial hierarchy is formally distinct from the hierarchy of holiness, the latter being the only one that is eternal.

Conclusion on St. Thomas

The position of St. Thomas, we believe, does assume the data of Revelation. It makes possible a profound understanding of them, especially concerning one point that has yet to be mentioned: the distinction between the universe of creation and the universe of redemption.

If Christ essentially came to save mankind, the Church that is his Body and was therefore founded by him attains its definitive status only through the Incarnation (which establishes the Head) and through Pentecost (which establishes the Body). Yet at the same time it began to exist—not in the first days of creation, nor even by the gift of the first grace bestowed on the angels and on humankind in the age of innocence—but rather *on the day after the Fall*, when the graces given to mankind (sinful and repentant humanity) were given in view of the future merits of Christ, the case of Mary Immaculate being the summit thereof.

From the "protoevangelium" on (Gn 3:15), God orients the hope of fallen humanity toward the future Savior. This Savior is what mankind then awaits. The Church begins to be gathered in this expectation; it journeys toward the Messiah, preparing his ways under the influence of a grace that *already* is Christic and conforms souls to Christ. In its definitive, perfected status, the Church is born on the cross from the open side of Christ as Eve was born from the side of slumbering Adam, and she manifests herself at Pentecost. But in her previous phases of formation, somewhat like the fetus in the mother's womb, she is *already* the work of Christian grace, the grace of Christ, and she remains

---

76. This is the answer elaborated by Augustine in confronting the difficulty of the Donatists (see the discussion on Augustine and Donatism earlier in this chapter).

the same, substantially identical, throughout all time and through the profound transformations that she experiences in the various ages of her formation.

In a word, the Church is the universe of redemption.[77]

Consequently, whatever is earlier than the regime of Christian grace—creation, the order of supernatural values as such, the elevation of the angels to supernatural life, their trial and the determination of their eternal destiny (glory for the good angels and disgrace for the wicked), the institution of humanity in a state of supernatural life (original justice)—all that makes up the universe of creation and is *anterior* to the Church.

It follows that two orders, two universes, coexist: that of creation and that of redemption. The Church—the order/universe of redemption—is really distinct (by her "nature") from what survives here below of the universe of creation: the order of temporal things (nature and culture). But this is not a duality that separates. The two orders are meant to agree with one another according to the principle of the subordination of the temporal to the spiritual.

This duality exists, however, only on earth. The order of creation present here below will pass away with this world. Only the universe of redemption has eternal life as its purpose; only the Church is *eschatological*. She is therefore, here below, the *first fruits* of the reconciled universe; she is called to be in eternity the *fullness* of the reconciled universe.

But the universe of creation that continues to exist includes also the angelic world. What will be its relation with the universe of re-

---

77. Our discussion, which reserves the mystery of the Church for the time of the redemption, does not completely adopt the thesis maintained by François Daguet, *Théologie du dessein divin chez Thomas d'Aquin: Finis omnium Ecclesia*. According to that author, for St. Thomas the Church would be that creation destined to beatitude, whether before or after Adam's sin. It is true, and Daguet has shown it clearly, that the remaking of the work that fell by sin presupposes major continuities with the order of creation, for the latter was not fundamentally destroyed by Adam. And so the two must never be set in opposition. It seems possible to us to maintain—and it is certainly the thought of St. Thomas—that if man had lived in familial and social community before the Fall, he would have received grace with respect to his nature as an embodied, social spirit—in other words, in an economy that would have been comparable in many aspects to that of the redemption. It seems perfectly tenable to us to give the name "Church" to the community of believers in that era. But we know nothing from Revelation about man's life before the Fall, which is why we limit ourselves to the Church of the redemption.

demption, with the Church? Christ came to save human beings, not angels (Heb 2:16).

The position of Duns Scotus and his School on this subject is quite consistent. Affirming that the Word became incarnate in order to perfect creation, so that the Incarnation would have taken place even if man had not sinned, he concludes that every grace bestowed on every creature was given in view of the merits of Christ, whether of his passion (for *in fact* the Incarnation led to that), or else of any meritorious activity whatsoever (if man had not sinned). Hence the grace given to the angels is, from the outset, a Christic grace. The weakness of this thesis is that it lacks any positive basis: nothing in Scripture or Tradition supports it; it is a good example of speculative theology that is not based on an adequate theology of the sources.[78] But this thesis concerning the grace of the angels is the obligatory consequence of the Scotist position on the motive for the Incarnation: if the Incarnation was willed unconditionally, then it is certain that every grace, of whatever order, in every historical age and to every creature endowed with personhood, could be given only through Christ and dependent on his merits: there is no grace but Christian grace.

In the perspective of St. Thomas, it seems to us that matters are different: the first grace of the angels is not a Christian grace. However, having come to save mankind, the Incarnate Word comes as head of the angels, and he is this so truly and profoundly (Heb 1:4) that he will introduce them into his Body. Christ is, according to St. Paul, the one who recapitulates all things in the heavens and on earth (cf. Eph 1:10 and Col 1:19). Out of angels and men he makes one Body, of which he is the Head. The grace of the angels then becomes, over the course of time, a Christian grace, and the angels thus pass from the universe of creation to the universe of redemption. In thus drawing the angels closer to himself, Christ draws them at the same time closer to mankind, gathering both groups into the one Church that is the fullness of his Body.

This rapprochement that "adds" to the initial grace of the angels is explained by St. Thomas as follows (*ST* III, q. 8, art. 4): citing Colossians 2:10 ("[he] is the head of all rule and authority"), we have the schema:

78. The patristic Tradition does not envisage the possibility, considered abstractly, of an Incarnation intended to complete and perfect creation, but stays with the perspective enunciated in the Creed: "For us men and for our salvation, he came down from heaven."

	→ angels	
One Head	and	→ one Body.
	→ men	

The notion of "Body" that is at work here is clarified by St. Thomas: a multitude of members ordered in the unity of one and the same purpose according to their various activities and functions. Since angels and men are ordered to the same end (the glory of divine beatitude) and attain it by different activities and functions, one can say that, together with blessed human beings, the angels form the Church in heaven.

But what does that add to the angels? They did not need to be saved; their beatitude had been acquired well before the Fall and redemption from it. Although Christ is the Head, thus pouring out Christian grace upon the angels, that does not enter into the *end* at which the Incarnation aims, but is only a *consequence* thereof.[79] The Christian grace of the angels is not the grace of beatitude *"simpliciter"* as it is for men, but rather an increase in beatitude.[80] To put it another way, Christ does not merit for them the grace of a blessed life, but through fittingness augments it for them. Indeed, we must recall that the beatitude of created beings (angels and men) is not an absolute (i.e., being God, possessing without limitation the life of God), but rather a *participation* in divine beatitude, a share that is greater or smaller, not only according to one's degree of holiness, but also—for the angels—according to the history of salvation.

Christ's headship over the angels therefore is not identical to his headship over men, but analogous, because:

- Christ is not of the same nature as the angels; he is man.
- The angels do not depend absolutely on the Head for grace; they were already blessed before the Incarnation.

As with the notion of instrumental cause, it was the particularly clear data of Revelation (St. Paul) that obliged St. Thomas to renounce a pure and simple application of the comparison of the body (whether on the biological level or on the social level) in a univocal figurative sense.

---

79. St. Thomas Aquinas, *De Veritate* q. 29, art. 4, ad 5.
80. St. Thomas Aquinas, *De Veritate* q. 29, art. 4, ad 4.

St. Thomas does take into account the fact that the Mystical Body is the communion in the theological virtues (which is primary) *and also* the order of means for bringing souls into it (word, sacraments, ministries, which are secondary); we are dealing here with *one complex being*. The Mystical Body is an utterly spiritual (*théologale*) *and* incarnate reality. This complexity recalls the complexity of Christ's being (true God *and* true man: one being).

The developments elaborated by St. Thomas are dominated by final and efficient causality. But we must not forget what St. Thomas says elsewhere (in particular in *ST* III, qq. 48–49), that Christ also is an *exemplary* cause. This is another aspect that must not be omitted, although it depends more on the moral dimension. To say that the Church is the Body of which Christ is the Head underscores that grace is *Christic* in the manner in which it is given (by Christ: efficient cause) and in its finality (to become one with Christ: final cause). It is also to say, in a secondary and subordinate way, that grace *conforms one to Christ*—in other words, that the life of the members, both individually and communally, reproduces somehow the life of Christ (cf. moral theology as the study of Christ's morals in us). This is part of the moral elaboration of the doctrine of the Mystical Body.

c. The modern rediscovery of the Mystical Body

As profound, important, and constant as it was in Tradition, the doctrine of the Church as the Body of Christ nevertheless underwent a harmful eclipse following the crisis in the sixteenth century marked by the Reformation. Protestants had an understanding of the Pauline doctrine that made the Mystical Body into an invisible, entirely inward community quite distinct from, if not even sometimes separate from, the outward community that is visible in ecclesiastical institutions. Failing to ground their arguments deeply in Scripture as the Church Fathers and the medieval writers in their turn had understood it, Catholics preferred to distance themselves from this now controversial theme so as not to appear to grant Protestants their dualist vision of the Church, which moreover they vigorously disputed.[81] So it happened that this ecclesiology was shrouded, so to speak, from the

---

81. We will examine these controversies and related issues at length at the beginning of the speculative part of this book.

sixteenth to the nineteenth centuries. The Pauline doctrine persisted, however, notably in the French School,[82] but as a theme in "spirituality"—in other words, in moral theology, from a perspective that was primarily individual: the baptized person "becomes part" of Christ intimately because he is a member of his Body; consequently he must "reproduce" throughout his life the mystery of Christ, the mystery of obedience to the Father for love of God and for the salvation of mankind.[83] This line of thinking is not incorrect, and it enjoys a long Tradition among moralists, but although it is based on Pauline doctrine, it is presented here as though separate from that foundation.

At the beginning of the nineteenth century, particularly thanks to the School of Tübingen and the Roman College, the ecclesiological theme resurfaced. It had been sufficiently rehabilitated [*réapproprié*] at the time of the First Vatican Council to be chosen as the principal ecclesiological theme of the teaching that the Council intended to give concerning the Church.

In this part we will give longer citations so as to demonstrate in this review of the sources the growing role played by speculative reflection in magisterial teaching.

1. The schema *De Ecclesia* of Vatican I

Everyone knows that the schema on the mystery of the Church was closely studied and debated several times by the Council Fathers, but that there was not enough time to revise it definitively so as to put it to a vote before the Council was suspended. Decreed by the pope because of the political troubles that were agitating nascent Italy and Rome in particular, this suspension was in fact a closure, since it was never possible to resume the work of the Council. As a result, there was no conciliar document, but the schema was nevertheless the source from which Leo XIII would draw in his numerous encyclicals with ecclesiological overtones. He testifies to the return of the theme in Catholic doctrine and to the way in which it was understood, in particular with regard to its use by Protestants. That is why it is useful to present this document in its major subdivisions.

---

82. Raymond Deville, *L'École française de spiritualité*.
83. For an example, see St. John Eudes, *Treatise on the Admirable Heart of Jesus* I.5, in the *Oeuvres complètes* 6:107–15.

The Body of Christ

The overall structure of the document[84]

The schema consists of five carefully ordered chapters. Chapter 1, entitled "The Church is the Mystical Body of Christ," begins by situating the mystery of the Church within the divine plan of salvation:

> The only-begotten Son of God who enlightens every man coming into this world, and whose help for the miserable children of Adam has never been lacking in any era, when the time had arrived at that fullness appointed in advance by the eternal counsel, having become like men (Phil 2:7), appeared in the visible form of our body that he had assumed, so that earthly, carnal men, by putting on the new man that had been created after the likeness of God in the true righteousness and holiness (Eph 4:24), form a Mystical Body of which he himself is the Head.

The point of departure is therefore the mystery of the Incarnation, and from the outset Christ is situated as Head of the Body. The document continues:

> In order to bring about the union of this Mystical Body, Christ our Lord instituted the sacred bath of regeneration and of baptismal renewal, through which the children of men, divided amongst themselves by so many different names, and above all cast into disgrace by sin, now washed of all the stains of their faults may become members of one another (Eph 4:4–25) and united to their divine Head by faith, hope and charity, may all be enlivened by his one Spirit, and may receive abundantly the gifts of heavenly graces and charisms. Such is the sublime appearance (*species*) of the Church which must be proposed to the minds of the faithful so as to be deeply impressed on them and which cannot be emphasized enough; the Head of the Church is Christ (Col 1:18); from him the whole Body, firmly joined and united by the bonds of mutual assistance, with each member working in its proper way, receives its growth so as to be built up in charity (Eph 4:16).

This preliminary development therefore presents the Church as the great organism whose interior life is the grace of Christ, whose unity is received from above and whose growth has an eschatological terminus. Here we are in the order of the Church as a reality of grace, with a very quick reference to the means of being born to that life (baptism).

---

84. The entire Latin text is in Giovanni Domenico Mansi, J. B. Martin, and L. Petit, eds., *Sacrorum Conciliorum nova et amplissima collectio* (Paris: H. Welter, 1901–27), 51:539–53. The French translation used by the author is by Humbert Clérissac in *Le Mystère de l'Église*, 245ff. (with several minor corrections). [Citations from the schema are translated from French.]

Chapter 2, entitled "The religion of Christ can be practiced only in the Church and through the Church founded by Christ," is rather brief and intends to present the order of the mediations in the reality of grace:

> Jesus, the author and perfecter of the faith, himself founded and established this Church which he won at the price of his Blood and loved from all eternity as a uniquely chosen spouse; and he commanded that she should be gathered continually by his apostles and their successors, until the end of the world, throughout the earth and from every creature, and that she should be taught and governed by them so that she might be one holy nation [*gens*], a people of his own zealous for good deeds (Ti 2:14). For what defines the evangelical Law is not that every social tie should be rejected and that true worshippers should worship the Father in spirit and in truth individually, each in his own way; but rather our Redeemer willed that his religion should be joined by such intrinsic ties to the society that he founded, that it might remain entirely united to it and, so to speak, become one body with that society, and that outside of it there would be no true Christian religion.

Immediately after the general presentation of the community of which Christ is the Head, the schema mentions hierarchical mediation, according to the idea that Christ the founder is "continued" by the apostles and their successors. One drawback is that this mediation specializes, as it were, in the tasks of teaching and governing; the office of sanctifying through the celebration of the sacraments is not mentioned, perhaps because baptism had already been mentioned (and the Eucharist, too, though not explicitly) in the first chapter. What is at stake in this emphasis on the mediation of the ministers is the visibility of this gathering of human beings into one people. Obviously this is an anti-Protestant remark. In other passages this view of the "one true religion" is again emphasized, and one would search in vain here for any ecumenical overture. However, the insistence on these features serves a truth that we must not lose sight of: the visible, communal character of the mystery of salvation in this world. The following chapter will insist on this point.

Chapter 3, entitled "The Church is a true, perfect, spiritual and supernatural society," begins in a particularly solemn way:

> We teach and declare that the Church possesses all the qualities of a true society. This society was not left incomplete or formless by Christ; rather, just as it has its existence from him, so too by his will and from his Law it

received its form and constitution. Nor is it a member or part of any other society, nor can it be confused or enter into composition with another. Instead it is so perfect in itself that, while being distinct from all human societies, it nevertheless surpasses them absolutely. Indeed, sprung from the inexhaustible source of the mercy of God the Father, founded by the ministry and work of his Incarnate Word, it was established in the Holy Spirit who, after first having been poured out on the apostles with the utmost generosity, continues ceaselessly to be poured out abundantly on the children of adoption, so that they, illumined by his light, might cleave to God and be united among themselves by one and the same faith; so that, carrying in their hearts the pledge of their inheritance, they might renounce the desires of the flesh and the corruption of concupiscence which is in the world; and, strengthened by the same blessed and common hope, they might desire the eternal glory of God that is promised to them, and might confirm, by their good works, their call and election (2 Pt 1:10). Since men increase in the Church by the Holy Spirit from the wealth of all these benefits, and since they are joined in unity by the ties of that same Holy Spirit, the Church is indeed a spiritual society of an order that is supernatural to the highest degree.

In order to grasp thoroughly the meaning of this mention of the "perfect society," one would have to recall some points from social philosophy. This will be done within the context of our study of the theme of the People of God. For the moment note that the communal aspect of salvation takes the form of a human society with all its visibility and its institutions. However, the human sociability that is assumed here is brought to a very high degree that is unique among human communities, since it is elevated by grace and the Holy Spirit in Person. That in no way diminishes the visibility of this society; the following chapter recalls this.

Chapter 4, entitled "The Church is a visible society," essentially considers itself to be within the framework of the controversy with Protestant Christians:

Let no one think, however, that the members of the Church are joined only by interior, hidden ties, and that she is consequently an invisible society. The mighty, eternal wisdom of God willed that, corresponding to the spiritual, invisible ties by which the faithful adhere through the power of the Holy Spirit to the supreme and visible Head of the Church, there should also be external, visible ties, so that this spiritual, supernatural society might appear outwardly and show itself in broad daylight. Hence the visible Magisterium, by which is proposed publicly the faith that must be believed inwardly and confessed outwardly (Rom 10:10). Hence also the ministry by which a public office regulates and carries out the visible mysteries of God whereby internal sanctification is given to men, and to God—the worship that is his due; hence the visible government that orders the communion of the members among themselves and disposes and directs the whole external and public life of the faithful in the Church; and finally the whole visible body of the Church, to which not only the just or the predestinate belong, but also sinners, provided that they are joined to her by their profession of faith and by their communion. It follows from this that the Church of Christ is neither invisible nor hidden on earth; rather she is made conspicuous (St. Augustine, *In Ps.* 18.2.6), like a shining city high upon a mountain (St. Cyril of Alexandria, *Comm. in Isa.* 1.3.c.25.4), which cannot be hidden and like a lamp on a lampstand which, illumined by the sun of justice, enlightens the whole world with the light of its truth.

This chapter insists on the visibility of the causes of grace. The Lord himself, during his service on earth, visibly communicated his grace to men by his ministry, and the apostolic mission continues this deliberate mode of giving salvation to mankind. Notice that here the three major mediations—sanctification, teaching, and governing—are reunited. Incorporation into the ecclesial Body therefore has a note of visibility that is essential to it. The schema expounds this still within the context of the Protestant denials and with the teaching of St. Robert Bellarmine as its more immediate source. We will encounter it again in the speculative part of this course.

Chapter 5, finally, is the result of all the preceding. Entitled "On the visible unity of the Church," it shows where this Church can be discerned:

Since the true Church of Christ is such, We declare that this visible and prominent society is that same Church of the promises and divine mercies that Christ willed to distinguish and adorn with so many prerogatives and privileges. We declare also that it is so perfectly defined in its constitution that any societies whatsoever separated either from the unity of the faith or from the communion of this body cannot in any way be considered as a part or member of it; nor is it dispersed and diffused throughout the various groups that go by the name of Christian, but completely united in itself, and absolutely consistent, it presents in its manifest unity an undivided and indivisible body, which is the very Mystical Body of Christ. This is what the Apostle says: "There is one body and one Spirit, just as you were called to the one hope that belongs to your call, one Lord, one faith, one baptism, one God and Father of us all, who is above all and through all and in all." (Eph 4:4–6)

Although it is not named explicitly, it is clear that the Roman Catholic Church is the one that is declared here to be, on earth, the one Mystical Body of Christ. No overture is made to the other Christian communities, just as in the preceding chapter separated Christians were not considered at all to have the qualifications to be members.

Some observations

In the first place—and this is the exemplary feature that we must retain above all—the schema proceeds from the more spiritual, the reality of grace, to the more "incarnate," so to speak, the order of the means of grace, which is dependent on grace. This is the same path that St. Paul followed in his letters, and it remains the standard. There is no disputing that the text is old-fashioned, not only in its style, but also in what it says about the means of grace—notably, it recognizes no place for the common priesthood—but its overall approach remains correct: the reality of grace which is the heart of the ecclesial mystery is inseparable from the means by which this reality comes to us. In the second place, we must emphasize its univocal concept of the Church—it is the Roman Catholic Church, and outside of her there is no Christian communal reality—which prevents any positive consideration of the separated brethren. That is a serious limitation. Third, the consequence of this is a very rigid, all-or-nothing perception of belonging to the Church, with a major difficulty: the statement, which is difficult to prove and yet true,[85] that sinners can remain members of the ecclesial Body.

The Magisterium after Vatican I would have to consider these questions, which were not satisfactorily explained by this schema, and it would do so while remaining within the doctrinal framework set forth here, which indicates that one must not separate grace and the mediations of grace. This would be a difficult task that the whole ecclesiological renewal of the twentieth century would tackle and that we will explain as fully as we can in the speculative part.

---

85. This is the teaching with which the Council of Trent countered the Protestants; see Session 6, Decree on Justification, chap. 13.

2. The Encyclical *Mystici Corporis Christi*[86]

This magisterial document was published right in the middle of the contemporary theological renewal. It benefits from much of the progress that had been made in the research, and it intends to make a number of judgments so as to avoid errors. We emphasize here two major points.[87]

The elaboration of the notion of Mystical Body

The Encyclical situates the ecclesial Body in relation to the two other meanings that the expression "Body of Christ" has in Scripture:

> There are several reasons why [the expression "Mystical Body"] should be used; for by it we may distinguish the Body of the Church, which is a Society whose Head and Ruler is Christ, from His physical Body, which, born of the Virgin Mother of God, now sits at the right hand of the Father and is hidden under the Eucharistic veils; and, that which is of greater importance in view of modern errors,[88] this name enables us to distinguish it from any other body, whether in the physical or the moral order. (no. 58 [60])

Here we find again the *triplex Corpus* in a precise order of presentation: he who is born of the Virgin—Christ in his humanity—is the one who makes himself present in the Eucharistic mystery in order to engender the new humanity as his Body, which will be called mystical so as to distinguish it from the first two meanings. Next Pius XII strives to capture, with the help of two erroneous extremes (physical body and moral body), the type of unity that brings about the Mystical Body:

> In a natural body the principle of unity unites the parts in such a manner that each lacks in its own individual subsistence; on the contrary, in the Mystical Body the mutual union, though intrinsic, links the members by a bond which leaves to each the complete enjoyment of his own personality. More-

---

86. The author cites a French edition with paragraphs numbered according to the Latin edition edited by Sebastian Tromp, *Litterae encyclicae de mystico Iesu Christi corpore deque nostra in eo cum Christo coniunctione: Mystici Corporis Christi*. [Those paragraph numbers are given with the citations, followed in brackets by the numbering from the English translation at the Vatican website that is used here.]

87. We will address the question of the identity between the Mystical Body on earth and the Roman Catholic Church during our study of Vatican II on that point.

88. The errors targeted here tended toward a "fused" understanding of Christ and Christians.

over, if we examine the relations existing between the several members and the whole body, in every physical, living body, all the different members are ultimately destined to the good of the whole alone; while if we look to its ultimate usefulness, every moral association of men is in the end directed to the advancement of all in general and of each single member in particular, for they are persons. And thus—to return to Our theme—as the Son of the Eternal Father came down from heaven for the salvation of us all, He likewise established the Body of the Church and enriched it with the divine Spirit to ensure that immortal souls should attain eternal happiness according to the words of the Apostle: "All things are yours; and you are Christ's; and Christ is God's." For the Church exists both for the good of the faithful and for the glory of God and of Jesus Christ whom He sent. (no. 59 [61])

Unlike the physical body, the Mystical Body does not fuse the mass of its members into a single whole. Physical unity is too deep, in the sense that it makes only the whole exist, each member having its existence only as a part. The personal dignity of each of the members of the Church is contrary to that type of unity. This leads us to conceive of the Mystical Body as resembling human social communities, which are groups of persons. But here too there is a limit to the comparison:

But if we compare [the Mystical Body] with a moral body, it is to be noted that the difference between them is not slight; rather it is very considerable and very important. In the moral body the principle of union is nothing else than the common end, and the common cooperation of all under the authority of society for the attainment of that end; whereas in the Mystical Body of which We are speaking, this collaboration is supplemented by another internal principle, which exists effectively in the whole [organism] and in each of its parts, and whose excellence is such that of itself it is vastly superior to whatever bonds of union may be found in a physical or moral body. As We said above, this is something not of the natural but of the supernatural order; rather it is something in itself infinite, uncreated: the Spirit of God, who, as the Angelic Doctor says, "numerically one and the same, fills and unifies the whole Church." (*De Veritate* q. 29, art. 4) (no. 60 [62])

The transition from the physical to the social is followed by a transition from what is natural and social to what is supernatural and communal. The mention of the Holy Spirit, traditionally called "the soul of the Church,"[89] recalls the altogether peculiar nature of this ecclesial

---

89. This point will be studied along with the theme that follows: the Church as the Temple of the Spirit.

whole, which is as interconnected as a physical body, while allowing its members to continue their existence as distinct persons.

We have here the best classical expression of the doctrine of the Mystical Body as the unity of everyone in God, through Christ and in the Spirit.

The complexity of the ecclesial being

The second important point of the Encyclical, for our purposes, is in its affirmation of the complexity of the ecclesial being. The Church is formed of diverse elements, and the principal distinction in this regard is the one that distinguishes the reality of salvation and the means of salvation. Since the Church is inseparably both, it is appropriate to demonstrate it, because the contemporary ecclesiological renewal had difficulty perceiving it. *Mystici Corporis* is in basic continuity with a teaching of Leo XIII that is readily connected with the deliberations of Vatican I that resulted in the schema *De Ecclesia*. Moreover, as we will see, Vatican II intended to pursue that Tradition, and it is good to bring this magisterial consistency to light. The teaching of Leo XIII is as follows:

The connection and union of both elements [i.e., the body and soul of the Church] is as absolutely necessary to the true Church as the intimate union of the soul and body is to human nature. The Church is not something dead: it is the body of Christ endowed with supernatural life. As Christ, the Head and Exemplar, is not wholly in His visible human nature, which Photinians and Nestorians assert, nor wholly in the invisible divine nature, as the Monophysites hold, but is one, from and in both natures, visible and invisible; so the mystical Body of Christ is the true Church, only because its visible parts draw life and power from the supernatural gifts and other things whence spring their very nature and essence.[90]

Here we must pay attention to two points. In the first place, the complexity of the Church, which is at the same time outward (visible) and inward (invisible), had been compared ever since the controversy with Protestants to the complexity of man, who is at the same time corporeal (visible) and spiritual (invisible). Leo XIII recalls that theological line. But most importantly he develops a theological comparison with the mystery of Christ, who is at the same time man (visible)

---

90. Encyclical *Satis cognitum*, June 29, 1896, paragraph 3, in *Acta Sanctae Sedis* 28 (1895–1986): 710; English translation from Vatican website.

and God (invisible). The parallel is delicate, because although the mystery of the Savior is indeed a mystery of one Person in two natures, the mystery of the Church is a mystery of one nature—graced human nature. This idea, which during the theological renewal would be called ecclesiological "theandrism," is not unproblematic. Although Monophysitism is a Christological heresy, it is not an ecclesiological heresy; quite the contrary. Yet, it is true, we still have to understand correctly the manner in which the Holy Spirit, the soul of the Mystical Body, accomplishes this mystical union. We will make several clarifications during our study of the theme of the Church as the Temple of the Spirit, but we will have to wait for the speculative question about the personality of the Church in order to take this inquiry further.

Pius XII also addresses the Church's complexity in the Encyclical *Mystici Corporis*:

From what We have thus far written, and explained, Venerable Brethren, it is clear, We think, how grievously they err who arbitrarily claim that the Church is something hidden and invisible, as they also do who look upon her as a mere human institution possessing a certain disciplinary code and external ritual, but lacking power to communicate supernatural life. On the contrary, as Christ, Head and Exemplar of the Church "is not complete, if only His visible human nature is considered ..., or if only His divine, invisible nature ..., but He is one through the union of both and one in both ... so is it with His Mystical Body"[91] since the Word of God took unto Himself a human nature liable to sufferings, so that He might consecrate in His blood the visible Society founded by Him and "lead man back to things invisible under a visible rule." (no. 62 [64])

The comparison of the mystery of the Church with the mystery of the Incarnate Word is more nuanced than in the presentation by Leo XIII, which, however, is cited. Here it does not concern the ontology of the human community or suggest that it is at the same time human and "divine," which is strictly speaking the unique prerogative of the Savior; instead it indicates the active, pedagogical aspect whereby what is human in the Church (the visible society), because it has been consecrated, has a certain role in pointing out and supplying the invisible realities of grace. Furthermore, the comparison with the human soul and body is purely and simply omitted.

---

91. Citations from *Satis cognitum*; see previous note.

As we see, the modern Magisterium has noticed two principal difficulties in the contemporary understanding of the doctrine of the Mystical Body. The first concerns the nature of this union of men in Christ and among themselves. It is clear that one must insist on a union that is real, rather than moral, but without going so far as to posit a physical union, much less a union of the hypostatic type, which is proper to Christ and incommunicable. The second is the union of the "means of grace" aspect and the "reality of grace" aspect. This unity, of a kind that is quite unique to the Church, indicates that the distinction of the aspects must remain a distinction and never lead to a separation, however small. Hence we see that the development of Tradition involves it in questions that require for their resolution a speculative approach.

d. The outcome at Vatican II

The theme of the Church as the Body of Christ is considered in paragraphs 7 and 8 of the Constitution *Lumen gentium*.

1. *Lumen gentium* 7: Biblical theology

In paragraph 7 we have an extensive presentation of the biblical theology that follows closely the two stages that can be observed in the writings of St. Paul (his major letters and the captivity letters). It is a model of biblical synthesis that does not enter into questions disputed among exegetes, but sticks to what is most certain. It adds nothing to what we have already seen.

2. *Lumen gentium* 8: Speculative precisions

Paragraph 8 considers the theology of the Mystical Body principally in its speculative consequences. These precise details are extremely important.

LG 8, §1: The unity of the ecclesial being

The first paragraph takes up the distinctions proposed during the contemporary ecclesiological renewal (hierarchical society/Mystical Body, or else inward element/outward element) so as to make clear that we can speak only about *distinctions* and not about separations:

The Body of Christ

Christ, the one Mediator, established and continually sustains here on earth His holy Church, the community of faith, hope and charity, as an entity with visible delineation through which He communicated truth and grace to all. But the society structured with hierarchical organs and the Mystical Body of Christ are not to be considered as two realities, nor are the visible assembly and the spiritual community, nor the earthly Church and the Church enriched with heavenly things; rather they form *one complex reality* which coalesces from a divine and a human element. For this reason, by no weak analogy, it is compared to the mystery of the incarnate Word. As the assumed nature serves the divine Word as a living organ of salvation inseparably united to Him, so, in a similar way, does the visible social structure of the Church serve the Spirit of Christ, who vivifies it, in the building up of the body. (cf. Eph 4:16)

In short, the reality of the Church is *a complex reality* made up of a "divine" element (namely, God himself, by appropriation the Holy Spirit, and the grace of Christ which is of divine origin) and a human element (the entire order of the means of grace). It is extremely important to recall that the order of grace and the order of the means of grace are not two realities, but only one, a *complex* reality, to be sure, but *one* that is really *undivided*, even though our mind can apprehend it only through distinctions. Hence it cannot be said that the Church is the hierarchical society *plus* the Mystical Body: the reality called "Mystical Body" is *simultaneously* an inward *and* an outward reality. We will see this again in the speculative part, but here at the level of positive theology it is important to determine exactly what we will have to try to explain.

On the other hand, the comparison with the mystery of the Incarnate Word is placed clearly on the level of action: all that is human in the Church is raised to be a sign and instrument of the divine gift of grace, just as the humanity assumed by the Word was the sign and instrument through which salvation was accomplished.

LG 8, §2: The unicity of the ecclesial being

The Council continues: this one reality is also *unique:*

This is the *one* Church of Christ which in the Creed is professed as one, holy, catholic and apostolic, which our Savior, after His Resurrection, commissioned Peter to shepherd.... This Church constituted and organized in the world as a society, *subsists in* the Catholic Church, which is governed by the successor of Peter and by the Bishops in communion with him, although many elements of sanctification and of truth are found outside of its visible structure. These elements, as gifts belonging to the Church of Christ, are forces impelling toward catholic unity.[92]

Here we are at the level of the very first principles of Catholic ecumenism. The "classic" Catholic perspective was to affirm that the one, unique Church of Christ, the Mystical Body, was the Roman Catholic Church.[93] This identification was thought to be exclusive: the Mystical Body—in this world—is the Roman Catholic Church and it *alone*. Consequently the other separated Christian communities are not the Church of Christ. We pointed out in this regard, especially in the schema from Vatican I, a univocal approach to the Church.

Vatican II opted—without major debates—for another perspective: the Church of Christ, in this world, *subsists in* the Roman Catholic Church, and no longer *is* the Roman Catholic Church. What does this mean? To clarify the matter somewhat we must consider this section 2 in its entirety. Note that there are two elements in the conciliar statement:

- The Church of Christ in this world subsists in the Roman Catholic Church.
- At the same time many elements of sanctification (sacraments) and truth (preaching) can be found outside this community, such elements being *identical* to those of this community. This positive way of looking at the separated communities is one of the great novelties of Vatican II. The Decree on Ecumenism will develop this point.[94]

Unity and unicity should be kept together, but in a way that does not exclude the ecclesial character of other separated communities.

92. For the presentation of the text at the Council, see *AS* III/I:176–80. The identical text is found in the Decree on Ecumenism, *UR* 4 (cited later).

93. See the Schema from Vatican I, chap. 5; Pius XII's Encyclical *Mystici Corporis* [no. 13 in the English translation]: "If we would define and describe this true Church of Jesus Christ—which is the One, Holy, Catholic, Apostolic and Roman Church—we shall find nothing more noble ... than the expression 'the Mystical Body of Christ'"; see also the reminder about this teaching in the Encyclical *Humani generis*, in *AAS* 42 (1950): 571.

94. We will encounter it again when we study the Catholic principles of ecumenism in the third part of the course, "The Properties of the Church: The Church is *One*."

The Body of Christ

The Roman Catholic Church is still the Mystical Body as it is present in this world, but that does not mean that the other Christian communities are deprived of all ecclesial character. To demonstrate this, Vatican II reasons as follows:

- *All* the means of grace instituted by Christ, together with the reality of grace thus obtained, produce the Church that is *fully one*—namely, the Roman Catholic Church *alone.*
- *Some* true means of grace and also the reality of grace result in something that is still *one,* and also ecclesial, but diminished: separated communities.

Furthermore, what is present in the separated communities, LG 8, §2 finally adds, impels them toward Catholic unity; for there are not in fact more means of grace in the Christian communities taken together than in the Roman Catholic Church alone. To define even more precisely the significance of the doctrinal progress that this teaching represents, we must strive to understand what this verb "*subsistit in*" means.

The ordinary meaning of *subsistit in*

In the ordinary dictionary definition, the verb *subsistere in* means either *adesse in* (to be present in) at the level of reality or *invenire in* (to be found in) on the level of knowledge. This reality is present in that subject; the former can be perceived in the latter. Then one can say, with reference to the question that we are discussing, the one, unique Church, as God gives it to us in Christ, is found in the Roman Catholic Church; in her one can see the institution of Christ as he willed it.[95] This is what the Decree on Ecumenism (*Unitatis redintegratio* [UR]) declared in paragraph 4:

We believe that this unity [with which Christ endowed his Church] subsists in the Catholic Church as something she can never lose, and we hope that it will continue to increase until the end of time.

This common meaning of *subsistere in* allows for the remark that follows immediately in *Lumen gentium* 8, §2 concerning the ecclesial elements preserved by the separated communities. To say that the

---

95. The common connotation *subsistere in* = *adesse in* was clearly affirmed in the *relatio* by the Doctrinal Commission of the Council in reference to LG 8 (see AS III/I:176).

Church of Christ is surely and fully present in the Roman Catholic Church does not exclude—at the level of that statement alone—the possibility of other communities retaining some realities in common. To illustrate this point, we can make the following comparison, which is only a comparison and should not be forced: French culture is fully realized in France. But that does not rule out the possibility that some cultural elements originally belonging to French culture (language, customs, artistic expressions, judicial rules) might be present and alive in Quebec. Some realities on the spiritual order—here the natural spiritual phenomenon that is culture—are not necessarily tied to specific places. A more theological example is the one sacrament of holy orders, which is possessed in its fullness by the bishop alone and in a diminished, yet real way by the priest and the deacon.

The elements preserved by the separated communities come from the one, unique Catholic Church, it is something that the separated brethren took with them when they left and that has been kept up after they broke away. To say that these elements within the separated communities impel them from within toward reunion is to affirm that these elements have preserved their salvific value (cf. *UR* 3). No Catholic ever doubted that the baptism administered by Protestants is true baptism.

We see that a relation of identity (Mystical Body—Roman Catholic Church) can be thought of in two ways: in an exclusive way (see *Mystici Corporis* and *Humani generis*) or in a nonexclusive way, and that is the whole significance of the progress made by Vatican II. The identity Mystical Body—Catholic Church remains, and this underscores a *fullness* present in her alone, but the other communities are also *ecclesial* communities. The unicity of the Church is thus indeed affirmed: the one, unique Church of Christ is fully formed in the Roman Catholic Church; she and she alone possesses the *complete set* of the means of salvation instituted by Christ and, of course, the reality of grace, *and this same Church is the one that is more or less formed in the other communities.*

Two interpretations that should consequently be rejected:

- The one, unique Church is formed by the combination (the quantitative sum) of all the communities; thus it does not yet exist, it is a goal to be reached.

- The one, unique Church once existed, but no longer exists since the separations, and must be reconstituted (the object of ecumenism).[96]

This common connotation of *"subsistere in"* indisputably has a positive significance with regard to the separated communities, and that is certainly the intention of the Fathers at Vatican II.

The *technical* sense of *"subsistere in"*

In philosophy we say that a reality *subsists;* we speak about its *subsistence* to underline the fact that this reality exists by itself in its perfection and not in something else. This is the dignity proper to a substance as opposed to an accident; *"subsistentia"* is the most perfect mode of existing.

If we apply this sense to *LG* 8, §2 we will say, The Roman Catholic Church represents integral fidelity to the original institution of Christ and is in no way completed by the separated communities; she and she alone has full subsistence. Vatican II did not mean to express this idea in paragraph 8, §2 of *Lumen gentium,* which is intended to have a positive meaning with respect to the separated communities. But the Council expressed it in another way in the Decree on Ecumenism in paragraphs 3 and 4: Catholic *fullness.* It seems to us that the notification to Leonardo Boff that mentions this interpretation,[97] although it basically recalls a common doctrine, is wrong in stating that the Council intended to give this technical, philosophical sense to the verb "subsist." Nothing in the *Acta Synodalia,* to our knowledge, allows this statement. But that in no way diminishes the fact that this meaning is acceptable and quite expressive of the Catholic Church's self-awareness.

In our opinion, the two meanings of the verb *subsistere in* should be kept together. At the present time we are dealing with the concept that is called the *gradation of ecclesiality* due to a fullness that is shared to a greater or lesser extent. This leads to an analogous approach to the ecclesial reality, starting with a first and even chief (*princeps*) type—the Roman Catholic Church—and other secondary and later types, which are the separated communities. They are arranged along this spectrum

---

96. On this subject see the Declaration *Mysterium Ecclesiae* (see bibliography at the end of the chapter).

97. See the documents in the bibliography at the end of the chapter.

according to the number and the quality of the means of salvation that they have preserved: the correctness of their faith and the number of their sacraments. It is clear that between the Orthodox Churches that have preserved all the sacraments along with their apostolic succession and the Protestant communities that have only baptism there is a gradation in their ecclesial situation.

We can say then that the Roman Catholic Church *actually* is the one, unique Church of Christ; the separated communities *potentially* are the one, unique Church, not by a pure potentiality, but by a potentiality that is actualized progressively if they follow the dynamism of the ecclesial elements preserved within them. Charles Journet, for example, says that the Orthodox Churches appertain *initially and tendentially* to the Roman Catholic Church.[98]

The Council applied this concept of gradualism to a similar, related question: that of individual incorporation into the Church. Vatican II says that those persons are *fully incorporated* into the Church of Christ who fulfill "in heart" and "in body" the conditions that are mentioned in LG 14, §2, these conditions being Catholic conditions. Those persons are *imperfectly incorporated,* yet joined to the one, unique Church, who fail to satisfy some of these conditions: these persons are the separated brethren (LG 15). Considering these persons—not individually but as a community—we can say that the community within which all the prerequisites for incorporation are offered is *fully* the Church of Christ, and the community that does not offer its members the entire set of these prerequisites is *imperfectly* the Church of Christ.

This dogmatic perception could have a particular application in the field of ecumenism. There is, we think, a specifically ecumenical meaning of the expression *subsistit in* that could complement the dogmatic meaning by imparting to it a certain dynamism that was not expressed by the earlier *est.*[99] In short, the Catholic Church's awareness of being the Church born on Pentecost is a reality of her faith that cannot be called into question. Nevertheless, it is advisable to situate this identity in time. With regard to the past and the present, the one Church

---

98. Charles Journet, *L'Église du Verbe incarné,* 2:688 and 730 (1067 and 1222 from the individual perspective of the members); see general bibliography.

99. I am summarizing here one of my earlier essays, "Vocabulaire et notions à Vatican II et dans le magistère postérieur," 245–73 (esp. 264–68).

The Body of Christ

of Christ in this world has always been and still is today the Church led by the bishop of Rome and the bishops in communion with him. So be it. But what about the future delineated by the grace of ecumenism? We suggest saying that the future, under the action of the Spirit of Christ, will move all the Christian communities so that they will become capable of converging in order to bring about the perfect unity of Christians. This convergence will have to result from progress made by all the Churches and ecclesial communities in grasping the mysteries more profoundly and in living the Christian life more fully. Although the progress to be made is not the same for all, there is nevertheless a need for all to make progress.[100]

Thus the meaning of *subsistit in* emerges. It is an ecumenical meaning that tries to express with a single verb two things that are to be distinguished clearly. In the first place, a past and ever-present ecclesiological reality, namely the indefectibility of the Church that is fully assured—by the mercy of God—in the Catholic Church. In the second place, with regard to the future, the necessary moral and dogmatic progress that *all the Churches and ecclesial communities* must make, through dialogue, in order to converge, each one by its own path of progress, into the full unity that, once attained, will enrich them all.

If one agrees to these clarifications, one then sees that Vatican II—*Lumen gentium* 8 read together with *Unitatis redintegratio* 4—gives us three juxtaposed propositions: 1) the indefectibility of the Church, of which the Catholic Church is the witness; 2) the genuine elements of truth and sanctification preserved by the separated brethren; 3) the progress to be made by all toward a more perfect unity that will be not only moral but also dogmatic.[101]

To conclude this discussion of the unity and unicity of the Church, and especially of Catholic fullness, we remind the reader that we have treated the question *dogmatically*, dealing with the *ecclesial being* as such, in its ontology. We have not treated the question from the perspective of *moral* theology. Let us say a word about this final point, to which we will return in the third part of the course in the chapter concerning the holiness of the Church.

---

100. For example, John Paul II clearly indicated that the Catholic Church had to progress in her understanding of the exercise of the Roman primacy and that this progress demands the collaboration of all the Churches and ecclesial communities; see his Encyclical *Ut unum sint* 95.

101. De La Soujeole, "Vocabulaire et notions," 267.

3. *Lumen gentium* 8, §3: The moral aspect

To affirm, on the dogmatic level, that the Catholic fullness cannot be lost does not necessarily mean that the members of that community have an unchangeable moral fidelity to the deposit of faith that they have received. That the community as such cannot err in the faith is certain, and even an article of faith, but it cannot be taken for granted that all the members within it, clerics as well as laymen, actually do live in keeping with that fullness, as history demonstrates. The insistence of Pope John Paul II within the context of the Jubilee Year 2000 on asking forgiveness for the moral faults of Catholics is part of the ecumenical attitude, the frank and honest *moral* (not dogmatic) ecumenism that is required of us. *Lumen gentium* declares:

> While Christ, holy, innocent and undefiled (Heb 7:26) knew nothing of sin (2 Cor 5:21), but came to expiate only the sins of the people (Heb 2:17), the Church, embracing in its bosom sinners, at the same time holy and always in need of being purified, always follows the way of penance and renewal.... By the power of the risen Lord [the Church has] strength that it might, in patience and in love, overcome its sorrows and its challenges, both within itself and from without, and that it might reveal to the world, faithfully though darkly, the mystery of its Lord. (*LG* 8, §3)

Here we run into another speculative difficulty that we will have to address: the Church is holy and composed of sinners. The statement appears contradictory: How can a community that subsists in its members be holy if its members are sinners? How can the Church be holy and sanctifying in the image of Christ who is holy and sanctifying, when her members here below are all wounded by their own sins? For now we note this finding to which the sources attest.

Catholic fullness by no means rules out the possibility that, morally speaking, Catholics may be less holy than their separated brethren, or even that genuine saints may exist in the separated communities. Indeed, on the one hand, the members of the separated communities are not personally guilty of the sin of schism or heresy that is at the historical origin of their community, a sin to which many Catholic members at the time might well have contributed.[102] But on the other hand, if a

---

102. There is no doubt that, if the Reformation started at the beginning of the sixteenth century, it was particularly due to the moral frailties of the Catholics of that era, both clerics and laity.

Protestant brother, for example, is holy, it is not because of what makes him Protestant, which separates him from the Catholic fullness and is itself the dogmatic principle of that separation, but because of what we have in common.[103]

Finally—and this is something that one must always remember—the Catholic fullness is to be understood among Catholics according to the teaching of the parable of the talents (Mt 25:14ff.): those to whom much has been given will have to "render" more. We Catholics will be more severely judged. This fullness is not a cause for boasting or pride, but a particularly demanding call to practice the humility of a servant.

Conclusion

This doctrine of the Church as Mystical Body of Christ has great breadth. Its fundamental richness is that it benefits from a very firm basis in Scripture and has been handed down to us by an extremely profound Tradition that is largely shared with our Orthodox brethren. It is the heart of the Christian community that is expressed here: it is the community of Christian grace. This justifies all the rest (the whole order of the means of grace) and is the basis for the correct understanding of it.

We have emphasized repeatedly the speculative questions that spring from this theology of sources; the two most important concern the nature of this mystical unity and the complexity of the ecclesial being. Consequently we will meet with them again in the second part of the course.

As it emerges from the sources, the theme of the Mystical Body expresses the Church along a line that relates to her essence above all else, *in facto esse:* what the Church actually has been from the first day and what she will never cease to be. This does not exclude, however, a perspective that is also more historical (salvation history). Indeed, the Body of Christ includes the just of the Old Testament, all those who faithfully awaited Christ. For the Body of Christ was formed progressively: the Church is young under the Patriarchs and attains adulthood with Christ.[104]

103. Journet, *L'Église du Verbe incarné*, 2:921.
104. An Augustinian theme taken up by St. Thomas, *In Psalmos Davidis expositio* 36:18 (Parma edition, 286).

The question about the members of the Church is also included in the study of the Mystical Body theme, even though Vatican II preferred to consider it instead in the theme of the People of God, which is perfectly justifiable. But we must pay attention to one important point: when situated within the framework of the doctrine of the Mystical Body, the question *"De membris"* is discussed in terms of incorporation—in other words, chiefly in view of the life of grace and, secondarily, in relation to the means of grace. If we are not careful, the study of this question in the context of the People of God theme can lead us to consider first its relation with the means of grace, with the unfortunate consequence of excluding from the life of grace those who do not benefit from those means.

Finally (and this is not the least important aspect), the doctrine of the Mystical Body presents the Church as the whole community of grace. That is to say that the pastors are part of the Church; they are not above her at all, but are members of her. The point may appear obvious today, but that was not always the case. The darkest day at Vatican II was the one on which the Council Fathers had to vote on the question of whether the Marian teaching of the Council should be in the Constitution *Lumen gentium* or should be the topic of a separate document. That came down to asking the question of whether or not Mary was part of the Church. The assembly divided into two almost equal parts over this issue, since the majority that favored introducing Mariology into the ecclesiology was very weak.[105] There can be a similar difficulty with the hierarchy: certainly it is the vicarious Head of Christ, but it is made up in the first place of baptized men. A correct insight into the Mystical Body theme allows one to dispatch these questions easily.

The illustration of this theme in the liturgy is an important point with which to complete this presentation. The doctrine of the Mystical Body was much neglected after Vatican II in the life of the community, whereas the liturgical reform fully retained its place. A few citations from the Eucharistic Prayers will suffice to show the connection between the Eucharistic Body and the Church, the Mystical Body.

Humbly we pray that, partaking of the Body and Blood of Christ, we may be gathered into one [Body] by the Holy Spirit. (Eucharistic Prayer II)

---

105. A change of around twenty votes (out of 2,200 voting members) would have been enough to reverse the result.

The Body of Christ

Look, we pray, upon the oblation of your Church and, recognizing the sacrificial Victim by whose death you willed to reconcile us to yourself, grant that we, who are nourished by the Body and Blood of your Son and filled with his Holy Spirit, may become one body, one spirit in Christ. (Eucharistic Prayer III)

Look, O Lord, upon the Sacrifice which you yourself have provided for your Church, and grant in your loving kindness to all who partake of this one Bread and one Chalice that, gathered into one body by the Holy Spirit, they may truly become a living sacrifice in Christ to the praise of your glory. (Eucharistic Prayer IV)

BIBLIOGRAPHY
The Church, the Body of Christ, in biblical theology

Benoit, Pierre. "Corps, Tête et Plérôme dans les épîtres de la captivité." In *Exégèse et théologie*, 2:107–53. Paris: Cerf, 1961–82.

———. "L'Église Corps du Christ." In *Exégèse et théologie*, 4:205–62. Paris: Cerf, 1961–82.

———. "L'unité de l'Église selon l'épître aux Éphésiens." In *Exégèse et théologie*, 3:335–57. Paris: Cerf, 1961–82.

Cambier, Jules. "Le grand mystère concernant le Christ et son Église: Éphésiens 5:22–33." *Biblica* 47 (1966): 43–90 and 223–42.

Cerfaux, Lucien. *La Théologie de l'Église suivant saint Paul*. 2nd ed. Paris: Cerf, 1965. The first edition was translated by Geoffrey Webb and Adrian Walker as *The Church in the Theology of Saint Paul*. New York: Herder, 1959.

d'Aragon, Jean-Louis. "Le caractère distinctif de l'Église johannique." In *L'Église dans la Bible*, 53–66. Paris: Desclée de Brouwer, 1962. On the corresponding theology of St. John (allegory of the vine).

de La Potterie, Ignace. "Le Christ, Plérôme de l'Église, Ep 1:22–23." *Biblica* 58 (1977): 500–24. Nicely complements Feuillet's article.

Dubarle, André-Marie. "L'origine dans l'Ancien Testament de la notion paulinienne de l'Église 'Corps du Christ.'" In *Studiorum Paulinorum Congressus Internationalis Catholicus 1961*. Analecta biblica 17. Rome: Pontifical Biblical Institute Press, 1963. Pages 231–40. On the realism of the OT that is the basis of St. Paul's doctrine.

Dupont, Jacques. *Gnosis: La connaissance religieuse dans les épîtres de S. Paul*. Louvain: E. Nauwelaerts; Paris: J. Gabalda, 1949.

Feuillet, André. "L'Église, Plérôme du Christ d'après Éphés., 1:23." *Nouvelle revue théologique* 78 (1956): 449–72 and 593–610.

Léon-Dufour, Xavier. *Le Corps et le Corps du Christ dans la première épître aux Corinthiens*. Lectio divina 114. Paris: Cerf, 1983. Particularly "Corps du Christ et Eucharistie selon saint Paul," 225–55.

Remy, Pierre. "Le mariage, signe de l'union du Christ et de l'Église: Les ambiguïtés d'une référence symbolique." *Revue des sciences philosophiques et théologiques* 66 (1982): 397–415.

Robinson, John A. T. *The Body: A Study in Pauline Theology.* London: SCM Press, 1957. A fundamental study of the realist meaning to be given to the Body of Christ.

Traduction oecuménique de la Bible (TOB). Paris: Cerf, 1977.

The Church, the Body of Christ, in patristic writings

Dictionary articles provide valuable elements either on the general theme (art. "Mystical Body," "Church"), or for an individual Church Father, or even in discussions of the sacraments (in particular the articles on "baptism" and "Eucharist"). Old articles can be valuable in identifying important passages in a particular Father; the recent articles (particularly in the *Dictionnaire de Spiritualité*, edited by Marcel Viller et al. [Paris: Beauchesne, 1932–95]) provide noteworthy bibliographies.

- The works of the Church Fathers can be found in the *Patrologia* by Migne (Greek or Latin); more recent editions of the texts (particularly in the *Corpus christianorum* and in the collection *Sources Chrétiennes*) are *always* preferable.
- English translations are listed in the English edition of Johannes Quasten, *Patrology* (see later); those in the series *Ancient Christian Writers* and *The Fathers of the Church: A New Translation* are generally the most reliable. The series *The Ante-Nicene Fathers* and *The Nicene and Post-Nicene Fathers* (1st and 2nd series) were prepared by Protestant scholars and may be tendentious at crucial places. English translations of the complete works of many Fathers of the Church can be useful (especially the index), but always check the exact meaning of the original text and the accuracy of the translation for every important passage.
- The historical, philological, and doctrinal introductions to the volumes in the *Sources Chrétiennes* series are often high-quality, detailed studies.
- To begin studying a Church Father, the periodical *Connaissance des Pères de l'Église* provides a good historical and literary basis as well as an initial bibliography that is usually quite recent. Some issues have a theme and study several Fathers on the subject. (To our knowledge there is no issue on the Body of Christ.) Recommended.

Bardy, Gustave. *La Théologie de l'Église de saint Clément à saint Irénée.* Paris: Cerf, 1945.

———. *La Théologie de l'Église de saint Irénée au concile de Nicée.* Paris: Cerf, 1947. Both works by Bardy are serious studies, always worthwhile.

Camelot, Pierre-Thomas. "Le sens de l'Église chez les Pères latins." In *Sentire Ecclesiam: Das Bewusstsein von der Kirche als gestaltende Kraft der Frömmigkeit*, edited by Jean Daniélou and Herbert Vorgrimler. Freiburg im Breisgau: Herder, 1961. Part 1 of this essay, on the Latin Fathers except St. Augustine, was reprinted in *Nouvelle revue théologique* 83 (1961): 367–81 (part 2 on St. Augustine is missing). An overall study of the Latin patristic typology for the Church, including the Body of Christ.

Delahaye, Karl. *"Ecclesia Mater" chez les Pères des trois premiers siècles.* Unam Sanctam 46. Paris: Cerf, 1964. Holy Mother Church is an image connected with that of the Church as Bride, and thus to the theme of the Church as the Body of Christ.

Jaki, Stanley. "Recherches récentes sur l'ecclésiologie des Pères." In *Les tendances nouvelles de l'ecclésiologie,* 170–87. Rome: Herder, 1957. Useful for an appreciation of the findings of the contemporary patristic renewal, especially the question of the "theandric" character of the Church.

Kelly, J. N. D. *Early Christian Doctrines.* San Francisco: Harper, 1978. See particularly chap. 15, "Christ's Mystical Body," 401–21. Studies the period from Nicaea to Chalcedon, which nicely complements Gustave Bardy.

Mersch, Émile. *Le Corps mystique du Christ.* 2nd ed. 2 vols. Paris: Desclée de Brouwer, 1936. A reference work for the source theology. A posthumous work by the same author was translated by Cyril Vollert as *The Theology of the Mystical Body.* St. Louis: Herder, 1951.

Pagé, Jean-Guy. *Qui est l'Église?* Montreal: Les Éds. Bellarmin, 1979, 2:39–52. A quick summary of the patristic data that is very dependent on Émile Mersch.

Quasten, Johannes. *Patrology.* 4 vols. Westminster, Md.: Newman Press, 1950–1960. A veritable summa of patristic theology with important bibliographical notes.

Ratzinger, Joseph. "L'idée de l'Église dans la pensée patristique." In *Pour une nouvelle image de l'Église,* 31–48. Gembloux, Belgium: Duculot, 1970.

Tromp, Sebastian. *Corpus Christi, quod est ecclesia.* 2nd ed. Rome: Pontificia Universitas Gregoriana, 1946. Translated by Ann Condit as *The Body of Christ, Which Is the Church.* New York: Vantage Press, 1960. An extensive collection of patristic texts by one of the principal authors of the Encyclical *Mystici Corporis* (June 29, 1943).

The Church, the Body of Christ, after the patristic period

The High Middle Ages

Congar, Yves. *L'Ecclésiologie du haut Moyen Âge.* Paris: Cerf, 1968.

———. *L'Église: De saint Augustin à l'époque moderne.* Paris: Cerf, 1970. Provides a considerable amount of additional bibliography.

de Lubac, Henri. *Corpus mysticum: l'Eucharistie et l'Église au Moyen Âge.* 2nd ed. Paris: Aubier, 1949. Translated by Gemma Simmonds et al. as *Corpus Mysticum: The Eucharist and the Church in the Middle Ages.* Notre Dame, Ind.: University of Notre Dame Press, 2007.

Mersch, Émile. *Le Corps mystique du Christ.* 2nd ed. Paris: Desclée de Brouwer, 1936, 2:139–57. A rapid, but suggestive overview with an initial bibliography.

Scholasticism

Mersch, Émile. *Le Corps mystique du Christ*. 2nd ed. Paris: Desclée de Brouwer, 1936, 2:158–70. An interesting overall presentation.

St. Thomas Aquinas

The main passages:

- *Summa theologiae* III, q. 8: capital grace. This treatment is valuable as a recapitulation; clarifications should be sought, however, in the following passages:
- III *Sent.* dist. 13, q. 2, art. 1.
- *De Veritate* q. 29, art. 4 and 5 (particularly important for instrumental causality). For the Latin original, see the Leonine edition, *Opera omnia* 22, 3 vols. (Rome: 1970–76). Translated by Robert W. Mulligan, James V. McGlynn, and Robert W. Schmidt as *Truth* (Chicago: H. Regnery, 1952–54; repr., Indianapolis: Hackett, 1994).
- *Compendium theologiae*, chap. 213–17 (esp. chap. 214). For the Latin original, see the Leonine edition, *Opera omnia* 42 (Rome: 1979). Translated by Richard J. Regan as *Compendium of Theology* (Oxford: Oxford University Press, 2009).
- The following Scripture commentaries can be found in the volumes *Super Epistolas S. Pauli* and should not be neglected:

    I ad Cor. c. 11, lect. 1;
    Ad Rom. c. 12, lect. 2;
    Ad Ephes. c. 1, lect. 8;
    Ad Colos. c. 1, lect. 5.

Studies on the ecclesiology of St. Thomas

N.B. These studies are all interesting because of the great variety of texts by St. Thomas that are cited, but they are based on a philosophical preconception that we will have to bring to light in the speculative part of the course so as to evaluate it. They should therefore not be read uncritically.

Bainvel, J. Vincent. "L'idée de l'Église au Moyen Âge: S. Thomas." *La Science catholique* (1899): 975–88. Old, but well-documented for that time; a study that is always cited.

Catão, Bernard. *Salut et rédemption chez S. Thomas d'Aquin*. Paris: Aubier, 1965.

Congar, Yves. "The Idea of the Church in St. Thomas Aquinas." In *The Mystery of the Church*, 53–74. Rev. translation. Baltimore and Dublin: Helicon Press, 1965. The original French edition may be found in *Esquisses du mystère de l'Église* (Paris: Cerf, 1940), 59–91. Fr. Congar has nicely elucidated the key texts needed to understand the ecclesiological approach of St. Thomas. Fr. Congar's personal elaboration of the subject, however, is more debatable.

———. "Vision de l'Église chez Thomas d'Aquin." In *Thomas d'Aquin, sa vision de la théologie et de l'Église*. London: Variorum, 1984. This is an edition of an article that appeared in the *Revue des sciences philosophiques et théologiques* 62

The Body of Christ

(1978): 523–41. A well-documented study to which we will return in the speculative part of our course. For a critical presentation of the views of Fr. Congar concerning the ecclesiology of St. Thomas, see Jean-Pierre Torrell, "Yves Congar et l'ecclésiologie de S. Thomas," *Revue des sciences philosophiques et théologiques* 82 (1998): 201–42.

Daguet, François. *Théologie du dessein divin chez Thomas d'Aquin: Finis omnium Ecclesia.* Bibliothèque thomiste 54. Paris: Cerf, 2003.

Darquennes, Achille. "La définition de l'Église d'après S. Thomas." In *L'organisation corporative du Moyen Âge à la fin de l'Ancien Régime,* 1–53. Louvain: Bureaux du Recueil, 1943. A much-noted study in its time and often cited since. It takes the notion of "Body" or "Corporation" in such a way that it means only the idea of a *multitude ordered by a common finality;* this is insufficient to understand the use of the idea of body in the ecclesiology of St. Thomas.

Hamer, Jérôme. *The Church Is a Communion.* Translated by Ronald Matthews. New York: Sheed and Ward, 1964. For a good clarification concerning the critiques formulated against St. Thomas after the Encyclical *Mystici Corporis,* see 71–82.

Mersch, Émile. *Le Corps mystique du Christ.* 2nd ed. Paris: Desclée de Brouwer, 1936, 2:172ff.

Sabra, George. *Thomas Aquinas' Vision of the Church: Fundamentals of an Ecumenical Ecclesiology.* Mainz: Matthias-Grünewald-Verlag, 1987. The author's idea is that the basic ecclesiological insights of St. Thomas—particularly his doctrine of the Mystical Body—could be of great help in the current ecumenical debate.

Travers, Jean C. M. *Valeur sociale de la liturgie d'après Saint Thomas d'Aquin.* Paris: Cerf, 1946. See in particular Part II, "Valeur sociale des signes chrétiens," 139ff.

Tschipke, Theophil. *L'humanité du Christ comme instrument de salut de la divinité.* Translated from German by Philibert Secrétan. Studia Friburgensia 94. Fribourg, Switzerland: Academic Press Fribourg, 2003.

From the end of the Middle Ages to the modern era

Clérissac, Humbert. *Le Mystère de l'Église.* Paris: Téqui, 1921.

Congar, Yves. *L'Église: De saint Augustin à l'époque moderne.* Paris: Cerf, 1970.

———. "*Lumen gentium* no. 7: L'Église 'Corps mystique du Christ' vue au terme de huit siècles d'histoire de la théologie du Corps mystique." In *Le Concile de Vatican II: Son Église, peuple de Dieu et corps du Christ,* 137–61. Paris: Beauchesne, 1984.

Deville, Raymond. *L'École française de spiritualité.* Bibliothèque d'histoire du christianisme 11. Paris: Desclée, 1987.

Eudes, Jean. *Le Coeur admirable de Jésus.* Vol. 6 in *Oeuvres completes.* Paris: Beauchesne, 1905–09.

Kerkvoorde, Augustin. "La théologie du 'Corps mystique' au dix-neuvième siècle." In *Nouvelle revue théologique* 67 (1945): 415–30, 1025–38. A valuable study on the progressive "exhumation" of this theme in Catholic theology.

The theology of the Mystical Body was studied widely between 1920 and 1940; during that period many treatises "*De Ecclesia*" appeared that more or less incorporate the renewal of this theme. Some of these works will be cited in the speculative part of the course.

Concerning the Encyclical *Mystici Corporis*, there is a very extensive literature that varies in quality. Note particularly the following titles:

Bouyer, Louis. "Où en est la théologie du Corps mystique?" *Revue des sciences religieuses* 22 (1948): 313–33. Makes useful judgments about the vast scholarship previously mentioned.
Hamer, Jérôme. *The Church Is a Communion*. Translated by Ronald Matthews. New York: Sheed and Ward, 1964. See especially the section "Meaning and Implications of the Encyclical *Mystici Corporis*," 13–34.
Jaki, Stanley. "Recherches récentes sur l'ecclésiologie des Pères." In *Les tendances nouvelles de l'ecclésiologie*, 170–87. Rome: Herder, 1957. A relatively complete review and critique of the theological renewal surrounding the theme of the Mystical Body.
Malevez, L. "Quelques enseignements de l'encyclique *Mystici Corporis Christi*." In *Nouvelle revue théologique* 67 (1945): 994–1015.
Nothomb, D. M. "L'Église et le Corps mystique du Christ." *Irénikon* 25 (1952): 226–48.
Pagé, Jean-Guy. *Qui est l'Église?* 3 vols. Montreal: Les Éds. Bellarmin, 1977–79. Brief remarks on the nineteenth and twentieth centuries (on 2:63–72) that allow the reader to situate matters correctly.
Pius XII. *Litterae encyclicae de mystico Iesu Christi corpore deque nostra in eo cum Christo coniunctione: Mystici Corporis Christi*. Edited by Sebastian Tromp. 3rd ed. Textus et Documenta, Series theologica 26. Roma: Pontificia Universitas Gregoriana, 1958.

Concerning the teaching of Vatican II there are very few studies, since the theme of the Mystical Body was neglected after the Council. See, however:

Congar, Yves. "*Lumen gentium* no. 7: L'Église 'Corps mystique du Christ' vue au terme de huit siècles d'histoire de la théologie du Corps mystique." In *Le Concile de Vatican II: son Église, peuple de Dieu et corps du Christ*, 137–61. Paris: Beauchesne, 1984.
de Lubac, Henri. *Entretien autour de Vatican II*. Paris: Cerf, 1985.
Philips, Gérard. *L'Église en son mystère au IIe concile du Vatican*. Paris: Desclée, 1967–68, 1:105–26. A good commentary by the principal author of *Lumen gentium*.

Paragraphs 1 and 2 of *LG* 8, however, have been the subject of numerous studies. These particular points will be studied in the speculative part of the course.

The question of the *subsistit in* (*LG* 8, §2)

There is abundant literature after Vatican II. The main studies are the following:

Baum, Gregory. "The Ecclesial Reality of the Other Churches." In *Concilium*, English edition, 4 (1965): 34–46.

The Body of Christ 139

Congar, Yves. "Le développement de l'évaluation ecclésiologique des Églises non catholiques." *Revue de droit canonique* 25 (1975): 215ff.
de Halleux, André. "Les principes catholiques de l'oecuménisme." *Revue théologique de Louvain* 16 (1985): 318–26.
Dejaifve, Georges. "Un tournant décisif de l'ecclésiologie à Vatican II." *Le Point théologique* 31 (1978): 97–106.
de La Soujeole, Benoît-Dominique. "Et pourtant ... elle subsiste!" *Revue thomiste* 100 (2000): 531–49. Review of magisterial teaching from Vatican II to the Declaration *Dominus Iesus* and a comparison with Orthodox thought and the various Protestant interpretations.
———. "Vocabulaire et notions à Vatican II et dans le magistère postérieur." *Revue thomiste* 110 (2010): 245–73.
Pagé, Jean-Guy. *Qui est l'Église?* 3 vols. Montreal: Les Éds. Bellarmin, 1977–79. See especially the section "Le Corps mystique et la communion," 2:162–75.
Philips, Gérard. *L'Église en son mystère au IIe concile du Vatican*. Paris: Desclée, 1967–68, 1:119ff.
Sullivan, Francis. "The Significance of the Vatican II Declaration That the Church of Christ 'Subsists in' the Roman Catholic Church." In *Vatican II, Assessment and Perspectives: Twenty-five Years After (1962–1987)*, 2:272–87. New York: Paulist Press, 1988. With recent bibliographical references.

The aforementioned question about *subsistit in* has been mentioned repeatedly by the Magisterium since the Council; the main documents are [all available in English at the Vatican website]:

Catechism of the Catholic Church. 2nd ed. Washington, D.C.: Libreria Editrice Vaticana and United States Catholic Conference, 2000. Number 816.
Congregation for the Doctrine of the Faith. Declaration *Dominus Iesus*. August 6, 2000. Number 16, §3.
———. Declaration *Mysterium Ecclesiae*. June 24, 1973. *Acta Apostolicae Sedis* 65 (1973): 396–408. The document is followed by a supplementary note.
———. Notification on the Book *Church: Charism and Power*, by Fr. Leonardo Boff, OFM. February 12, 1982. *Acta Apostolicae Sedis*, 77 (1985): 758–59.
———. Responses to Questions concerning Certain Opinions Pertaining to the Doctrine of the Church. June 29, 2007. *Acta Apostolicae Sedis* 94 (2007): 604–8.
Council for Promoting Christian Unity. *Directory for the Application of Principles and Norms on Ecumenism* (1993). Number 17.
John Paul II. Encyclical *Ut unum sint*. 1995. Numbers 10–11. Should be read in the official Latin text published in the *Acta Apostolicae Sedis* 87 (1995): 926–27.
Kasper, Walter. *Intervention at the Conference on the Fortieth Anniversary of the Promulgation of the Conciliar Decree "Unitatis redintegratio."* November 11, 2004. See the analysis by Emmanuel Lanne in *Irénikon* (2004): 548ff.
Paul VI. *Credo of the People of God*. June 30, 1968.

3

The Church Is the Temple of the Spirit

We are entering here on what is usually called *ecclesiological pneumatology*—in other words, the doctrine about the place and role of the Holy Spirit in the Church.

The theme of the *Temple of the Spirit* is not as clear-cut in Scripture, and consequently in Tradition, as that of the *Body of Christ*. The subject matter emerges less readily. In the New Testament there are no comparably clear expressions of it. Formally speaking, it is advisable to trace the precise outlines of it by showing the specific contribution that it makes. Now Scripture clearly connects the Christological and pneumatological aspects. For example, in John 2:21, "he [Jesus] spoke of the temple of his body." Our investigation in positive theology will therefore be less strictly connected with the expression "Temple of the Spirit." Before coming to the heart of the matter, let us make three general observations about pneumatology.

Holy Spirit or Spirit of Christ?

Christ and the Spirit are inseparable. On the one hand, the Divine Persons constitute only one God; on the other hand, the humanity of Christ is the work of the Holy Spirit who made the Virgin's womb fruitful. Consequently, what is so intimately united in being is so also in acting. The work of building up the Church is that of Christ and of the

Spirit jointly. What is *appropriated* to the Holy Spirit, as we will see, is the spread of Christ's work in time and space. Let us recall (very) briefly what in Trinitarian theology is called *appropriation*.[1]

Theologians attribute to the Spirit, for example, the unity of the Church and of Christians, the inspiration of the Scriptures, assistance to pastors, the sanctification of the faithful. Does this mean that the two other Persons have nothing to do with these things? Certainly not. Every work *ad extra* of one Divine Person is in reality a joint operation of the three Persons. What is at stake is the unity of the Trinity, which remains such in salvation history (connection between the immanent Trinity and the economic Trinity). Would this prohibit our manner of speaking that attributes certain particular works to one Person in particular? Note that these *appropriations* are initially expressions from Scripture itself that liturgical language follows faithfully. In the creeds, for example, creation is referred to the Father, the work of salvation to the Son (this causes less difficulty because he is the only Person of the Trinity to have become incarnate, but it also says that he upholds the universe by his word; cf. Heb 1:3), and sanctification to the Holy Spirit. Obviously one cannot suppose that only the Spirit is the sanctifier because he alone is holy!

How then are we to understand, first, the *fact* of these appropriations?

The first answer is to point out, on the linguistic level, that we are dealing with a figure of speech called *antonomasia*. Antonomasia is a rhetorical device whereby, in place of a common noun, for example, "miser," one uses a proper name, for example, "Harpagon" [from the comedy on that subject by Molière] that illustrates the essential quality designated by the common noun. The point of this figure of speech—besides the rhetorical effect—is to express what one means to say more vividly, more suggestively, and thereby to emphasize more clearly an essential aspect of the reality. Thus the appropriation used for the *ad extra* workings of the Trinity is initially a manner of speaking—of biblical origin—for the sake of greater clarity.

But the question is to determine what basis it has. Why, when we want to speak about the sanctification of men, do we refer this work

---

1. For an elaboration of this point of Trinitarian theology, see Jean-Hervé Nicolas, *Synthèse dogmatique*, 218ff; see general bibliography.

to the Holy Spirit and not to the Father? Certainly, again, there is no question of denying that the Father is holy and therefore a sanctifier too, but why say this more particularly about the Spirit? If the Father and the Spirit are equally holy and sanctifying—which is true—would not attributing sanctification to the Spirit be, ultimately, a purely verbal convention without any real significance? No. There is a deeper reason.

We are acquainted with the essential divine attributes (power, wisdom, holiness, etc.), which as such are attributes of the One God. But since the One God is also triune, there are also personal properties that as such are proper to each Person (the fact that the Father is unbegotten, for example). Appropriation is situated between these two poles. On the one hand it does not designate a strictly personal aspect of one of the Persons of the Trinity, but on the other hand it does reveal an affinity between an essential attribute and one particular Divine Person. If creation is appropriated to the Father it is because he alone is unbegotten—in other words, without principle—just as creation is *ex nihilo*. Another example: Scripture says, "It is the spirit that gives life" (Jn 6:63), or again, "The Spirit of truth ... will guide you into all the truth" (Jn 16:13). In doing this, Scripture helps us to track down the mysterious personal property of the Third Person of the Trinity. A property of the latter is that he proceeds from the two other Persons by love. Consequently we appropriate to him the attributes of goodness, love, and holiness—attributes that per se are common to the three Persons.

Appropriation is a manner of speaking that reveals a manner of knowing, that leads us into the reality. By Revelation we know the attributes of the One God and we know that there are three Persons who are one God. When Scripture tells us that the attribute "holy" serves to designate the third Person (the Holy Spirit), it helps us to track down what is proper to this Person in the Trinity: the fact that he proceeds by love from the two other Persons. As such, appropriation is a noetic, pedagogical procedure, the legitimacy of which is based on the authority of Scripture. We have recalled this point from Trinitarian theology in order to draw attention to a potential difficulty: everything that we will say about ecclesiological pneumatology will be attributed to the Holy Spirit by appropriation and will make us understand better what each *divine mission* (mission of the Son or mission of the Spirit) accomplishes jointly with the other. Ecclesiological pneumatology is inseparable from ecclesiological Christology. We have an indication of this in the Constitution *Lumen gentium:* the two themes of the Body of Christ and the Temple of the Spirit are intermingled in paragraphs 7 and 8. The simultaneous need to appropriate and not to separate what is always joined will become clearer with regard to the second point, which we will now take up.

The doctrine of the different ages of salvation

A serious difficulty in Trinitarian theology was at the origin of a heresy that troubled the life of the Church in the twelfth and thirteenth centuries and still remains as a temptation in Christian life. The heresy in question is that of Joachim of Fiore (1130–1202).[2] Its point of departure is the common patristic teaching about the different ages of the world (see table 3-1). This sequence of ages is divided into three fundamental stages. The first is the so-called age "of the Father," the second "of the Son," and the third "of the Spirit." But whereas this sequence involves successive *manifestations* of the three Divine Persons (the cognitive aspect), Joachim of Fiore makes of it a succession of *actions*. By way of Pentecost (the one in Acts or else another yet to come: millenarianism), the age of the Son is followed by the age of the Spirit, characterized by a different economy, the specific feature of which is not to be incarnate, but rather very "spiritual." It is easy to see the ecclesiological applications of this: the whole system of mediations instituted by Christ (preaching of his Word, celebration of his sacraments, service of the ministers) disappears or is minimized in favor of relations with God and among men that are much more informal, spontaneous, or rather freely "inspired" by the Spirit. This sequence of actions presupposes a non-substantial unity in the Trinity: what one Person (the Son or the Spirit) accomplishes is not necessarily a *joint* action with what the other does, because the Persons are not united to the point of making one God.

2. For a discussion of this error, which has persisted under many forms down to the present day (cf. the so-called "spirituals" of the fourteenth century and in our days those who set a Church "of the Spirit" in opposition to an "institutional Church"), see Henri de Lubac, *La Postérité spirituelle de Joachim de Flore*; see also Charles Journet, *L'Église du Verbe incarné*, 3:617ff. ("the 'dreams' of Joachim de Fiore"); see general bibliography. The common basis for this error is apparent from the beginnings of Christianity, particularly with the second-century Montanist heresy.

TABLE 3-1
History of Salvation according to the Church Fathers*

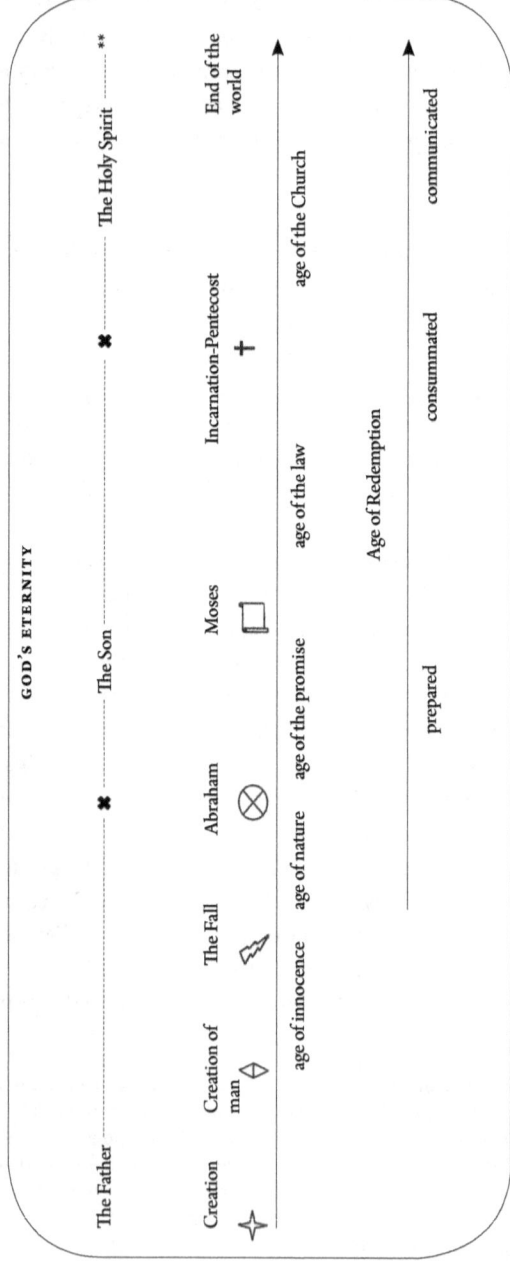

*Cf. A. Luneau, *L'histoire du salut chez les Pères de l'Église: la doctrine des âges du monde* (Paris, 1964).
** This line indicates a series of *manifestations* or *revelations* of the Divine Persons, not a sequence of actions (heresy of Joachim of Fiore).

This patristic teaching about the different ages of the world is valuable also for the rest of our ecclesiological study, particularly in the speculative part of it. Let us note for the moment that this sequence of ages is first of all a *chronological* sequence (an age replaces the previous one) that represents the history of salvation. It is the slow ascent of history toward the Christ who is to come, then its "passing away" ["*écoulement*"] starting with Christ until his return. But it is also a *theological* sequence in the sense that these ages coexist in our days. Depending on the knowledge of the divine mediations that they have and receive in faith, men belong to one or another age of salvation. Whether in the heart of the tropical rainforest or in the middle of our modern cities, there are men who, by no fault of their own, have never heard the Word of God directly or indirectly. These men belong to the age of nature, in which the divine mediation is taken up by creation (the works of God speak about their Author: cf. Psalm 19:1, "The heavens are telling the glory of God") and the individual conscience.[3] The Muslims in some respects can be considered to be in the age of the promise, since they have an Abrahamic kind of monotheism.[4] And so on.

The explicit proclamation of the divinity of the Holy Spirit

The divinity of the third Person of the Trinity was not proclaimed solemnly until the Council of Constantinople (381). This does not mean that the Church did not profess this faith before then; the liturgy, especially in its Trinitarian formulas of baptism and doxologies, sufficiently attests to that. This point of doctrine therefore was lived and professed from the very beginning. But on the level of theological understanding things went more slowly.

The nascent Church had a multiform experience of the Spirit. There was an experience of a power (Lk 24:49; Acts 1:8) that was ascribed at first to the power that inspired the prophets: the breath coming from God. This gift, which in the Old Covenant was intermittent and most often could not be handed on, was bestowed on "all flesh" and became transmissible in the New Testament. But there is still some indeterminacy concerning the Holy Spirit as a divine Person in theology. In the

---

3. The main NT passage: Rom 1:18–32.
4. This is the viewpoint of *LG* 16.

first centuries the Father and the Son were firmly grasped, but the Holy Spirit—who is more difficult to conceptualize—was the subject of few developments. Some formulations and even confusions reflect that tentative search. For Hermas, Christ is the Holy Spirit incarnate (*Similitudes* V.6.5). The first successful theological attempt to expound a trinity of Persons in God is, to our knowledge, that of St. Irenaeus.[5] The solemn formulations of faith occur very early, at Nicaea (325) and Constantinople (381). They would never be called into question.

It should not be surprising, therefore, if our patristic research, in the first three centuries, does not allow us to elucidate satisfactorily the most important declarations relative to the Holy Spirit and his role in the Church.

I. The Church, Temple of the Holy Spirit, in Scripture

The history of salvation is the history of the Father's plan accomplished by the Son in the Holy Spirit. The liturgy has an unchanging formula: salvation is the work of the Father, *through* the Son, *in* the Spirit. Salvation is, at the level of its purpose, the gathering of all men into one People of God that is the Body of Christ, built into one Temple of the Holy Spirit (*Ad gentes* 7). What does the mention of the Holy Spirit add to what we already know from our study of the Body of Christ?

a. The image of the Temple in Scripture

The Temple is, in its most material sense, a building, common to most religions, where God makes himself present to men, where he dwells among them so as to bestow his favors and receive their worship in return. The Temple is therefore the place of God-to-man and man-to-God communication; it is a symbol in the strong sense, in other words, simultaneously a sign of the presence of God and a means of establishing a religious relationship with the divinity.

In the Old Testament this symbolism is clearly found in the Temple of Jerusalem: God is present there, he manifests himself in the midst of the cloud and declares that he lives there because it is his dwelling

---

5. See in particular *Demonstration* 3 and 6; *Adv. Haereses* IV.33.15.

The Temple of the Spirit

place.⁶ But God, whom the heavens cannot contain, is not bound by this sign.... Starting with the reign of Solomon, the Temple quickly becomes the center of the worship rendered to the Lord, a center to which everything converges: pilgrimages, daily liturgies ...; that is where the holy assembly of the People (the *Qᵉhal YHWH*, translated into Greek as *Ekklēsia*) gathers to celebrate the covenant. This sign given by the Lord himself is not completely free of ambiguity, however. The prophets respect it; there God reveals himself to Isaiah in the great inaugural vision of his ministry (Is 6), and the pious Jew is known by the zeal that he has for the House of the Lord (Ps 69:9 → Jn 2:17). But the same Isaiah, as well as Ezekiel and Jeremiah (two priests of the Temple), also denounce the superficial character of the worship that is celebrated and even the idolatry that the Temple can harbor. Instead of being the place where the profane is consecrated, the Temple can become the place where the sacred is profaned. The trial of the exile to Babylon thus begins with the departure of the glory of God from the Temple (Ez 10:18ff.).

Two major periods can be distinguished in the history of Israel: they are referred to as "the period of the first Temple" (from Solomon to the exile) and "the period of the second Temple" (from the return from exile to 70 A.D.). The period of the second Temple is characterized by a religious reform effort marked by a very clear concern about promoting a more spiritual form of worship. There is no lack of prophetic warnings against overly sense-oriented veneration of the Temple (for example Is 66:1ff.); God dwells primarily in the heavens, where he receives prayers of his faithful wherever they are (Tb 3:16). Shortly before the coming of Christ, a group called the Essenes broke with the Temple, which they viewed as defiled by an unfaithful priesthood.⁷ This dissident community considered itself to be a spiritual Temple in which God received praise that was worthy of him. Here, with the idea of the community as a Temple and not just the material sign, we are at the cutting edge of the Old Testament that awaits the Messiah.

The New Testament has a profound theology of the Temple. Christ is first of all a pious Jew. He has the greatest respect for the Temple in Jerusalem. He observes the practices of the Law, in particular by mak-

---

6. An important passage for a theology of the Temple: 1 Kgs 8. Good discussion by Yves Congar, *Le Mystère du Temple*, part I.

7. There is a possible allusion in Jn 2:13–17.

ing the pilgrimage to Jerusalem and paying the Temple tax. And yet, from the beginning of his ministry in the Gospel of St. John, Jesus announces the destruction of the Temple. During his trial, the accusation on which they try to base his condemnation would be blasphemy against the House of God, since he had declared that he could destroy it and rebuild it in three days.[8] But this was a prophecy that subsequent events would explain.[9] Hence it should be understood that the new and definitive Temple is Christ himself, a Temple that is no longer bound to a particular place, but will be present everywhere, in any place where he is celebrated, particularly in the Eucharist.[10]

The initial apostolic preaching would also understand the profound unity between Christ and Christians with the help of the theology of the Temple as adopted by Jesus. This is the theme of Christ as the cornerstone of the Temple, of which the baptized are the living stones (1 Pt 2:4–10). The early Church, after maintaining some relations with the Temple (the apostles went there to pray; cf. Acts 3:1), understood very early on that it had to separate. The speech of St. Stephen before the Sanhedrin marks the Christian break with the Temple. St. Stephen exhorts his listeners to spiritual worship and does not hesitate to suggest that from now on the Temple is an idol.[11] Christians quickly became aware that they themselves constituted the new and definitive Temple. St. Paul would express this in very strong terms, as Rudolf Schnackenburg remarks:

> This is the explicit teaching of Paul: the Church is the Temple of God built on Christ (1 Cor 6:15 and 12:27), and His body is the Temple of the Holy Spirit (1 Cor 6:19; Rom 8:11). The two statements are connected: since the risen body of Jesus, in which deity dwells bodily (Col 2:9), is the Temple of God par excellence, Christians, who are members of that body, are the spiritual Temple with Him.... This is the definitive Temple that was not made by human hands: this is the Church, the Body of Christ, the meeting place between God and men, the sign of the divine presence here below. The ancient sanctuary was only a suggestive but imperfect figure of this Temple.[12]

---

8. See Mk 14:58ff. and parallel passages; the accusation is not correct, because Jesus had said, "Destroy this temple, and in three days I will raise it up" (Jn 2:19).

9. Jn 2:21: "But he spoke of the temple of his body."

10. See in particular the discourse to the Samaritan woman, Jn 4:20–24.

11. This is the meaning of the expression used by St. Stephen: "yet the Most High does not dwell in houses made with hands" (Acts 7:48); see Ps 114:2.

12. *Vocabulaire de théologie biblique*, col. 1271–72.

The Temple of the Spirit 149

b. The Church, Temple of the Holy Spirit

We should first examine the two "Pentecosts" that are reported in the New Testament, one in the Gospel of St. John and the other in the Acts of the Apostles. Then we will present the teaching of St. Paul.

The Johannine Pentecost occurs in two phases, since St. John mentions twice that Jesus gives the Spirit within the context of the Paschal mystery. The first time, Jesus is on the cross: The Church is born from the pierced side of the Crucified and is first realized in the Virgin Mary and St. John at the foot of the cross. The symbolism (the water and the blood in Jn 19:34 → baptism and Eucharist), together with the words ("I thirst," Jn 19:28; "he ... gave up his spirit," Jn 19:30 → "to expire" here means to give the Spirit), and the remark, "the disciple took [Mary] to his own home" (Jn 19:27): all these things indicate that the Church is born in the Virgin Mary and St. John from his pierced side through the gift of the Spirit that enables the two privileged witnesses to see the event on Calvary through the eyes of faith. The second time, Jesus appears on the evening of the Resurrection and gives the Spirit to the disciples who were absent during the Crucifixion (Jn 20:19–23). Here too the symbolism reported by the evangelist is very expressive: the event takes place on the first day of the week, referring back to creation, which began on a first day when the breath of God moved over the waters, and by the action of that breath Adam was brought to life. On this second "first day of the week," Jesus breathes on his disciples; the gesture is creative: the Church is born in the Spirit of the risen Jesus.

St. John therefore reports the birth of the Church twice, but it is one teaching: the gift of the Spirit is the fruit of Christ's death and Resurrection; it is given in the mystery of his death (Virgin Mary and St. John) and in the mystery of his Resurrection (the disciples). These are two sides of a single mystery. Through this gift, faith is born in the heart of man. There is a very close connection between the gift of the Spirit and the paschal faith: the Spirit is given so as to make the disciples into men of faith in Christ who has died and is risen. This is a key theme of the Gospel of St. John: it is not so important to have seen Jesus; the important thing is to believe in him (Jn 20:29, the episode of doubting Thomas).

The Pentecost in Acts (Acts 2) is well known. In the theology of

St. Luke, the Church is born on the day of Pentecost when the Holy Spirit promised by Christ at his Ascension (Lk 24:49 → Acts 1:4–5) is actually sent to the disciples. Here too, the biblical symbolism of the account is very rich. Pentecost is the realization of the event predicted by the prophets (Is 2:2–4 and 43:5–6; Jer 16:19–21): the eschatological gathering on Mount Zion of those who were dispersed. This is the meaning of the list of nations assembled in Jerusalem (Acts 2:5–11). Similarly, the eschatological outpouring of the Spirit announced in the Old Testament (Jl 2:28–32, cited in Acts 2:17–21) is the moment when the new People of God is established. St. Luke reinforces this symbolism: the twelve (Judas was replaced earlier by Matthias; see Acts 1:15ff.) represent the new Israel. Moreover, in Judaism Pentecost (the fiftieth day after Passover) had become the feast of the covenant and of the giving of the Law. St. Luke consequently indicates that the outpouring of the Spirit causes us to arrive at the fullness of time: the Spirit is simultaneously the new and eternal covenant and also its Law.

The two theologies harmonize well. St. Luke, in a more narrative style, describes the mission of the Spirit as the gathering of men: Pentecost is above all the reunion of those who had been scattered. The crowd in which everyone hears the preaching in his own language manifests the reversal of Babel. St. John, for his part, insists on the condition for such a gathering: faith in Christ. Finally, St. Luke adds that this gathering is missionary. It is quite evident from reading these passages that the Spirit is the principle of the unity of Christians, thanks to the gift of faith: the Spirit is the one who causes Christ and his work to be accepted.

After these notes concerning the gift of the Spirit and the birth of the Church, we should look at the presence of the Spirit in the life of the Church that has been constituted in this way. The Acts were traditionally called *The Gospel of the Holy Spirit*. Indeed, on almost every page St. Luke shows us the Spirit at work in the life of the community. The Spirit is not only the *founder*, but also the *"dynamic principle"* of the apostolic witness that ensures the expansion of the community. The Church in Acts goes from [the first two] Pentecosts to [further] Pentecosts that manifest the accomplishment of the missionary plan announced by Christ.[13] Thus we can count four Pentecosts:

13. See in particular Lk 24:47–49, Mk 16:15, and Mt 28:19.

The Temple of the Spirit

- The one in Jerusalem (Acts 2): salvation had been promised first to the Jews.[14]
- The one in Samaria (Acts 8:15): salvation offered to the lost sheep of the House of Israel.
- The one in Caesarea (Acts 10:44): salvation offered to the pagans.
- The one in Ephesus (Acts 19:1): salvation extends beyond the promised land.[15]

Each time (except in Acts 10:44) the imposition of hands by the apostles is a unique ritual connected with the planting of the nascent Church and signifying the gift of the Spirit. One can say that in Acts the Church goes from birth to birth under the impulse of the Holy Spirit who sweeps aside many misgivings (evident in Acts 10:44). Although the work of salvation is always attributed to Christ in the major discourses in Acts, the Spirit is the one who communicates this same salvation in time and space and who for this purpose leads the apostles and missionaries in general (cf. the deacon Philip in Acts 8:28). Scholars have noted that St. Luke had an exclusively ecclesiological pneumatology. Indeed, for the composer of Acts, the action of the Spirit is a building-up and an expression of the Church. Here there is no theology of the individual spiritual life as in St. Paul (especially Rom 8). For St. Luke, the life of the Christian is an ecclesial life (see in particular Acts 2:42, the first summary).

The teaching of St. John is extremely rich, too. For the sake of brevity we can note just two aspects that the evangelist intended to emphasize: the Spirit of truth and communion and the Spirit of mission. For the first aspect, truth and communion, St. John insists on the fact that the revelation of the Father, source of all faith and all charity, must be experienced by the faithful in the midst of a hostile world (one of the aspects of the Johannine "world"; see Jn 15:18ff.). The role of the Spirit Paraclete is to help the faithful, to defend them in their need (Jn 16:7). He is the Spirit of truth who neither declares innovations nor invents anything new, but causes Christ's teaching to be put into practice

---

14. This fundamental Pentecost has a sort of doublet in Acts 4:31 (the same basic structure: the group was praying, the place shook, they were all filled with the Spirit, they proclaim Christ boldly) that introduces the second summary (Acts 4:32) describing the unity of the faithful ("they were of one heart").

15. See the synoptic table, table 3-2.

TABLE 3-2

The Four Pentecosts in the Acts of the Apostles

	Jerusalem Acts 2:1–4	Samaria Acts 8:14–18	Caesarea Acts 10:44–48	Ephesus Acts 19:1–6
The group is gathered before the outpouring	v. 1 When the day of Pentecost had come, they [the apostles] were all together in one place.	vv. 15–16 [Peter and John] came down and prayed for [the Samaritans] that they might receive the Holy Spirit; for the Spirit had not yet fallen on any of them.	v. 24 Cornelius… had called together his kinsmen and close friends. v. 34 And Peter opened his mouth and said.…	v. 1 Paul… found some disciples [v. 7 There were about twelve of them in all.] v. 5 On hearing this, they were baptized in the name of the Lord Jesus.
The visible and audible sign of the outpouring	vv. 2–3 And suddenly a sound came from heaven like the rush of a mighty wind, and it filled all the house where they were sitting. And there appeared to them tongues as of fire, distributed and resting on each one of them.	v. 17 Then [Peter and John] laid their hands on them		v. 6 And when Paul had laid his hands upon them,
The outpouring of the Spirit	v. 4 And they were all filled with the Holy Spirit	v. 17b and they received the Holy Spirit.	v. 44 While Peter was still saying this, the Holy Spirit fell on all who heard the word.	v. 6b the Holy Spirit came on them;
Charisms	v. 4b and began to speak in other tongues, as the Spirit gave them utterance.		v. 46 They heard them speaking in tongues and extolling God.	v. 6c and they spoke with tongues and prophesied.
The reaction of the witnesses	v. 6 At this sound the multitude came together, and they were bewildered.	v. 18 Simon saw that the Spirit was given through the laying on of the apostles' hands.	v. 45 And the believers from among the circumcised who came with Peter were amazed, because the gift of the Holy Spirit had been poured out even on the Gentiles.	

1. Table compiled by Fr. David Macaire, OP.

among the disciples, preserving them in the communion of the same faith and the same love. The second aspect, mission, is clearly emphasized. The gift of Jesus is directly connected with the communication of the mystery (Jn 17:18; 20:21–23). More precisely, the mission proceeds from a twofold witness: that of the Spirit and that of the apostles (Jn 15:26–27). Those who hear the apostolic preaching come to believe through the Spirit, and thus the mystery of Christ is preached. In believing, the new Christian enters into the communion of the children of God.

The teaching of St. Paul, according to his genius and his special graces, agrees with many of the themes present in the writings of St. Luke and St. John, but has its own personal character. We present it in two points that are fundamental for our ecclesiological purpose: the relation between Christ and the Spirit and the presence of the Spirit in the life of the Church.

The Spirit is completely relative to Christ. Fr. Congar, in table 3-3,[16] shows that St. Paul does not hesitate to use almost identical formulas for Christ and the Spirit. Indeed, whereas the center of the faith is the declaration that Jesus is Lord, this is precisely what the Spirit leads the believer to profess: "No one speaking by the Spirit of God ever says 'Jesus be cursed!' and no one can say 'Jesus is Lord' except by the Holy Spirit" (1 Cor 12:3). The Spirit reveals Christ and makes the believer adhere to him. St. Paul does distinguish the action of the Spirit: he "searches everything, even the depths of God" (1 Cor 2:10ff.); he is "sent … into our hearts" (Gal 4:6); he "apportions to each one individually as he wills" (1 Cor 12:11); but he is "the Spirit of Christ" (Rom 8:9) or "the Spirit of [the] Son" (Gal 4:6), or else "the Spirit of the Lord" (2 Cor 3:17), or finally "the Spirit of Jesus" (Acts 16:7 and Phil 1:19). The unity of the two Persons and their unity of action are notably underscored, and therefore it is not surprising that some effects of that action are attributed indifferently to one or the other, and that the formulas "in Christ" and "in the Spirit" are often used interchangeably. This will leave its imprint on the identity of Christians: configured to Christ, they are filled with the Holy Spirit and thereby reproduce in some way in their lives the life of Christ.

---

16. Yves Congar, *I Believe in the Holy Spirit*, 1:37–38. Part of this table is reprinted as table 3-3.

TABLE 3-3

The Holy Spirit and Christ in the Writings of St. Paul[1]

Christ	The Holy Spirit
So that in him [Christ] we might become the righteousness of God (2 Cor 5:21)	Righteousness and peace and joy in the Holy Spirit (Rom 14:17)
Justified in Christ (Gal 2:17) Those who are in Christ Jesus... (Rom 8:1)	Justified in the name of the Lord Jesus Christ and in the Spirit of our God (1 Cor 6:11)
If Christ is in you... (Rom 8:10)	But you are not in the flesh, you are in the Spirit, if the Spirit of God really dwells in you (Rom 8:9)
Rejoice in the Lord (Phil 3:1)	Joy in the Holy Spirit (Rom 14:17)
The love of God in Christ Jesus (Rom 8:39)	Your love in the Spirit (Col 1:8)
The peace of God ... will keep your hearts and your minds in Christ Jesus (Phil 4:7)	Righteousness and peace and joy in the Holy Spirit (Rom 14:17)
Sanctified in Christ Jesus (1 Cor 1:2, 1:30)	The offering ... sanctified by the Holy Spirit (Rom 15:16; parallel in 2 Thess 2:13)
Speak in Christ (2 Cor 2:17)	Speaking by the Spirit (1 Cor 12:3)
Filled with Christ (see Col 2:10)	Filled with the Spirit (Eph 5:18)
One body in Christ (Rom 12:5) Baptized into Christ (Gal 3:27)	By one Spirit we were all baptized into one body (1 Cor 12:13)
In whom [Christ] the whole structure ... grows into a holy temple in the Lord (Eph 2:21)	for a dwelling place of God in the Spirit (Eph 2:22)

1. According to Y. Congar, *Je crois en l'Esprit Saint* (Paris: 1979), 1:64; English edition *I Believe in the Holy Spirit* (New York: Seabury, 1983), 1:37–38.

This joining of Christ and the Spirit will be quite characteristic of St. Paul's ecclesiology. Two verses mentioning it, among others, can be mentioned: "For by one Spirit we were all baptized into one Body (of Christ)" (1 Cor 12:13). And also: "There is one Body (of Christ) and one Spirit" (Eph 4:4). Although, as we have seen in the preceding chapter, the doctrine of the Church as Body of Christ is a doctrine about the unity of all Christians in Christ, Pauline pneumatology shows us that the Spirit is the principle of this unity: "the unity of the Spirit in the bond of peace" (Eph 4:3).

For St. Paul, in perfect harmony with St. John, the gift of the Spirit fulfills the promise made to Abraham: "I will make of you a great nation" (Gn 12:2). This is accomplished in the economy of faith and not of the Law (Gal 3:14). As in the writings of St. John, the transmission of the Spirit depends on Christian preaching (1 Cor 2:4–5, 13; Gal 3:2). St. Paul notes at great length that the Christian life is a life in the Spirit (Rom 7 and 8), a holy life, the principle of which is charity (Rom 5:5, 13:8). God himself communicates himself to the Christian, making of him his adopted son, in order to elicit acts of this filial life, acts "of Christ in us" (Gal 2:20; see also Phil 2:5). Dynamism, power, a principle of action, the Spirit is in Person the Law of the New Covenant. As we have already noted, this life of the Christian is not solitary, but profoundly ecclesial: "By one Spirit we were all baptized into one Body" (1 Cor 12:13).

One comment about vocabulary should be made here: never in St. Paul's writings is the Church called "the Church of the Holy Spirit." St. Paul speaks about "the Church of God" (1 Cor 1:2 and 2 Cor 1:1), or about "the Church of Christ" as the Body of the Head (Col 1:18, 24); the Church is also set in relation with the Father and the Son (1 Thes 1:1; 2 Thes 1:1), but never so directly with the Spirit. This indicates that the relation of the Holy Spirit with the Church is not a simple relation of dependence; it is more difficult to grasp. The Spirit leads persons to Christ so as to form his Body. To a great extent the crisis in Corinth was related to this point. That young Church was "charismatic," and it made a wrong turn because it did not allow itself to be led to Christ by the Spirit. The Corinthians wanted to penetrate the depths of God that the Spirit fathoms (1 Cor 2:10); they were seeking a quasi-Gnostic wisdom in an all-too-human way. Now the wisdom that the Spirit of God reveals, St. Paul repeated forcefully, is the wisdom of the cross (1 Cor 1:23ff.). The truly "pneumatic" soul is not one who claims to know what God thinks, but the one who has the mind of Christ (1 Cor 2:16). The Spirit builds up the Church by ceaselessly gathering believers and building up their communion (2 Cor 13:11–13), and in the writings of St. Paul this is done in three principal ways:

The Holy Spirit raises up ministers

The ecclesial hierarchy is a gift of the Spirit; it is charismatic. Several times St. Paul lists charisms (1 Cor 12:4ff. and 14:1ff.), and the grace of being an apostle is always mentioned first because it is the first "dispensation" or ministry (*diakonia*) of the Spirit (2 Cor 3:8).

The Holy Spirit pours out his gifts

The gifts of the Spirit are *always* ecclesial—in other words, given in view of the common good (1 Cor 12:7). This explains why the gift of apostleship is the first: the apostle must discern the other gifts and make them work for the good of the unity of the whole Body.

The Holy Spirit, baptism, and Eucharist

We are indebted to St. Paul for some essential remarks concerning baptism. This rite of new birth introduces the recipient to life in the Spirit (Rom 6 and 8). Although St. Paul did not develop his teaching on the Eucharist to the same extent—even though his references to it in the First Letter to the Corinthians are the earliest ones that we have—his vocabulary leaves no room for doubt: the Eucharist is the work of the Spirit. A parallel should be drawn between the major reference in 1 Cor 10:16–17 ("The cup of blessing which we bless") and 1 Cor 10:3–4 (the "spiritual" food and drink of Israel in the desert), which does deal with "pneumatic" realities. This is reinforced in 1 Cor 10:18 by the contrast with Israel "according to the flesh" [*kata sarka*]. The Eucharist is a pneumatic (spiritual) food. However in 1 Cor 11:23, which deals with the correct celebration of the Lord's Supper, to eat and drink worthily is to discern what these realities are: the Body and Blood of the Lord; there is no mention here of the Holy Spirit.

c. Conclusion of this scriptural section

The metaphor of the Temple chiefly expresses the idea of the indwelling of the Spirit in the Church. St. Paul acknowledges the communitarian aspect ("Do you not know that you are God's Temple and that God's Spirit dwells in you?" 1 Cor 3:16) and the individual aspect ("Do you not know that your body is a temple of the Holy Spirit within you ...?"

The Temple of the Spirit

1 Cor 6:19). The Spirit does not only act in or on the Church; he *is* there, and this indwelling is first of all ecclesial.

We should note the very close connection between the Body and the Temple (cf. Jn 2:21): the Body of Christ is the place where the Spirit is present, and this is altogether in keeping with the close relations between Christ and the Spirit.

As for the action of the Spirit, it is expressed fundamentally by the idea of *life:* the Spirit gives birth to the Church; out of nothing the Spirit makes a community of believers. This work of creation is accomplished through the outpouring of the Spirit that is brought about in a certain way by the institutions of Christ (apostles, preachers and ministers of the sacraments). From there we arrive at the idea of the principle of unity. This is mentioned frequently by St. Paul (one Spirit in them all). We find in the writings of St. Paul an expression that was to become a very technical term in Tradition. After considering the diversity of charisms, the Apostle of the Gentiles says repeatedly that this diversity comes from the same Spirit, from the one Spirit (1 Cor 12:4ff.), and he continues: "All these are inspired by one and the same Spirit" (Cor 12:11). He concludes: "by one Spirit we were all baptized into one body" (Cor 12:13). The expression "one and the same" will recur later to describe the type of unity that the Spirit brings about. We will see this again. For the moment we should note that the frequent use of the words "one, same, only" highlights the central theme: the Spirit of *unity.*

II. The Church, Temple of the Spirit, in Tradition

a. The patristic data

We will organize the vast amount of material by taking note of the main emphases in successive historical periods.[17] The events of the fourth century, especially the Arian crisis and the discussions on the subject of the Spirit (heresy of the Pneumatomachi or Macedonians), resulted in important modifications in the way Christians thought about the

---

17. We borrow this subdivision of the topic from the rich study by André Benoit, "Le Saint-Esprit et l'Église dans la théologie patristique grecque des quatre premiers siècles," 138–39.

relation between the Holy Spirit and the Church. After the question of the Son, true God and true man, which was settled as a matter of principle at Nicaea, people wondered about the "nature" of the Spirit in the same terms as for the Son: is he God? Is he consubstantial with the Father? The answer of Constantinople I (381) is affirmative. Before that decision the Spirit was viewed most often as the power of God at work in the Church. Consequently, during this period we find patristic writings that develop a theology of the Holy Spirit in the Church, with the question, what is his action in and through the Church? They stuck to the level of *action*. After the Council of Constantinople, the Holy Spirit is clearly considered as a personal subject, and the question that arises then is deeper: what is the relation between the Spirit and the Church? At that moment a theology of the Holy Spirit and the Church was born, concerning the relation between two distinct *beings*.

1. Before the fourth century: The Holy Spirit *in and through* the Church

What is accomplished by the Spirit in the Church? Everyone knows that Scripture is already quite clear on this subject; that the fundamental role of the Spirit is to spread, to communicate the saving action of Christ in time and space: to bring about in a "sacramental" way [*de façon "mystérique"*] what Christ accomplished to some extent in a "physical" way. How, specifically?

The first Fathers of the Church, the Apostolic Fathers, are still rather succinct, but they give us the irreplaceable point of departure, which further reflections would unceasingly develop. The Spirit of truth guarantees in the Church true speech by the ministers:

If any prophet speaks in ecstasy [literally: in the Spirit], do not test him.[18]

You have looked deep into the sacred writings, which tell the truth and proceed from the Holy Spirit.[19]

Consequently, the Church is first of all one in the truth of the faith and in charity:

You consider yourselves stones of the Father's temple, prepared for the edifice of God the Father, to be taken aloft by the hoisting engine of Jesus

---

18. *Didache* 11.7–8, in ACW 6: 22.
19. St. Clement of Rome, *Epistle to the Corinthians* 45:2, in ACW 1:36–37.

The Temple of the Spirit

Christ, that is, the Cross, while the Holy Spirit serves you as a rope; your faith is your spiritual windlass and your love road which leads up to God.[20]

Why are quarrels ... in your midst? Or, do we not have one God and one Christ and one Spirit of grace, a Spirit that was poured out upon us? And is there not one calling in Christ?[21]

These two elements, truth and unity, are the basis for an incipient theology of ecclesial ministry:

Assured through the resurrection of our Lord Jesus Christ, as well as confirmed in faith by the word of God, [the apostles] went forth, equipped with the fullness of the Holy Spirit, to preach the Good News.... From land to land, accordingly, and from city to city they preached, and from among their earliest converts appointed men whom they had tested by the Spirit to act as bishops and deacons for the future believers.[22]

You will certainly give us the keenest pleasure if you prove obedient to what we have written through the Holy Spirit.[23]

It was the Spirit who kept preaching [despite the troubles in the community of Philadelphia] in these words: "Apart from the bishop do nothing; preserve your persons as shrines of God; cherish unity, shun divisions."[24]

The transmissibility of the Spirit is one of the great innovations brought about by Christ. This Spirit, transmitted by the apostles to their successors, makes possible an initial, still somewhat sketchy theology of the help given by the Spirit to pastors.

There we have the main contribution of the early Fathers of the Church. Note the very strong emphasis on ecclesial unity (cf. the theme of the Body of Christ), which is above all a unity in the faith and charity maintained by the legitimate pastors. The power of the Spirit is what accomplishes this.

The Greek Fathers are important here for more than one reason. St. Clement of Alexandria is a Christian Gnostic. The primary thing for him is the knowledge of the truth; that is what liberates and makes a soul live a truly spiritual life. The Church is compared to a mother who feeds her children with the milk of holiness, this latter being in the first

---

20. St. Ignatius of Antioch, *Epistle to the Ephesians* 9:1, in ACW 1:63–64.
21. St. Clement of Rome, *Epistle to the Corinthians* 46:5–6, in ACW 1:37–38.
22. St. Clement of Rome, *Epistle to the Corinthians* 42.3–4, in ACW 1:35.
23. St. Clement of Rome, *Epistle to the Corinthians* 63.2, in ACW 1:48.
24. St. Ignatius of Antioch, *Epistle to the Philadelphians* 7.2, in ACW 1:88.

place the possession of right doctrine in a pure, unchangeable faith.[25] The Spirit sanctifies: he is consequently the Author of true knowledge (the true "gnosis"). In this sense he is the principle of life[26] and of intelligence,[27] he who inspired the Scriptures;[28] moreover he is the one who explains them.[29] The true Church is the one made up of true Gnostics; it is a spiritual Church. The limitations of St. Clement are of two sorts. In the first place, a strong insistence on the spiritual Church causes him to neglect the Incarnation of this reality and hence, in particular, the place of the ministers; he really knows only "the invisible bishop," Christ. Then he has a rather defensive attitude—in keeping with the context of the persecutions—that is focused primarily on the need to be saved by faith, thus neglecting the missionary aspect of the community in which the Spirit plays a strong role.

Origen, another Alexandrian, also insists a lot on the aspect of revelation. The Spirit is the one who reveals God;[30] in this capacity he inspires the Scriptures. He is the guarantor both of the truth of Scripture and also of its effectiveness: through Scripture the Spirit is poured out; he not only inspired it, but dwells within it.[31]

Because of this, Scripture possesses a spiritual sense beside the literal sense.[32] This spiritual sense is not known by all, but by those who have received a special grace from the Spirit.[33] This grace is given to the baptized and chiefly to the apostles:

He is high priest ... who knew the Law both according to the spirit and according to the letter.[34]

---

25. *Paedagogus* I.6.42, in *Christ the Educator*, trans. Simon P. Wood, in FOC 23:40.
26. *Stromata* V.98.4, in ANF 2:467b.
27. *Stromata* V.25.5 and V.88.4, in ANF 2:450a and 2:465a–b.
28. *Protrepticus* I.5.3 and VIII.68.1, in *Exhortation to the Greeks*, Loeb Classical Library 92 (Cambridge, Mass.: Harvard University Press, 1919), 11–12 and 181.
29. *Protrepticus* VIII.68.4, in *Exhortation to the Greeks*, 181.
30. *De Principiis* I.3.4; English trans. G. W. Butterworth, *On First Principles* (Gloucester, Mass.: Peter Smith, 1973), 31–33.
31. One of the main themes of the *Homilies on Leviticus*.
32. *De Principiis* IV.1.1 and IV.1.7, in *On First Principles*, 256–57 and 265–68; see also note 3 in the edition of the *Homilies on Leviticus*, SC 286, 357.
33. *De Principiis*, Preface no. 8, in *On First Principles*, 5.
34. *Homilies on Leviticus 1–16*, Hom. VI.3; trans. Gary Wayne Barkley, FOC 83:121; see also V.5, in FOC 83:99–100.

The Temple of the Spirit

More novel are his remarks about the Holy Spirit in relation to the unity of the community:

From the fullness of the Spirit, the fullness of love is infused into the hearts of the saints ... so that ... the word which the Lord said might be fulfilled: "As you, Father, are in me and I am in you, may they also be one in us." This is, of course, to be sharers of the divine nature by the fullness of love furnished through the Holy Spirit.[35]

The unity of Christians is related here to the Spirit who gives the theological virtue of charity. This is a further step: if faith is the radical principle, charity is the perfection of Christian unity, and together faith and charity constitute Christian holiness. Origen does not forget to mention that baptism and the imposition of hands empower the new man who thus receives the Spirit. Furthermore, the great Alexandrian teacher is invaluable because he initiates a theology of Tradition. The Holy Spirit assures the permanence of the deposit of faith in and through its transmission. The preaching of the Gospel and the teaching of the Church are one and the same thing because apostolic teaching, also called Church teaching,[36] is animated by the Holy Spirit:

The teaching of the church, handed down in unbroken succession from the apostles, is still preserved and continues to exist in the churches up to the present day, [and] we maintain that that only is to be believed as the truth which in no way conflicts with the tradition of the church and the apostles.[37]

But these themes will take on much broader dimensions in the writings of St. Irenaeus. He assumes what we have just seen in the Alexandrian Fathers, but he is the theologian of Tradition. For St. Irenaeus, who is fighting against the Gnostic heretics, the Church is in the first place a community of faith, a faith given and taught by the Holy Spirit. The Spirit is primarily the Spirit of truth. And in the Church the apostolic college continued by the bishops is what guarantees, thanks to the Spirit, a message that is neither changed nor corrupted. This is the idea of the charismatic hierarchy:

---

35. *Commentary on the Epistle to the Romans* IV.9 (PG 14.997c); trans. Thomas P. Scheck, FOC 103:292–93.
36. *De Principiis*, Preface, 4.1, 4.8, in *On First Principles*, 2.3.
37. *De Principiis*, Preface, 2, in *On First Principles*, 2.

The preaching of the Church is everywhere consistent, and continues in an even course, and receives testimony from the prophets, the apostles, and all the disciples.... Our faith, which, having been received from the Church, we do preserve, and which always, by the Spirit of God, renewing its youth, as if it were some precious deposit in an excellent vessel, causes the vessel itself containing it to renew its youth also. For this gift of God [the Spirit] has been entrusted to the Church, as breath was to the first created man (Gn 2:7), for this purpose, that all the members receiving it may be vivified; and the communion with Christ has been distributed throughout it, that is, the Holy Spirit.... "For in the Church," it is said, "God hath set apostles, prophets, teachers" (1 Cor 12:28), and all the other means through which the Spirit works; of which all those are not partakers who do not join themselves to the Church, but defraud themselves of life through their perverse opinions and infamous behaviour. For where the Church is, there is the Spirit of God; and where the Spirit of God is, there is the Church, and every kind of grace; but the Spirit is truth (1 Jn 5:6).[38]

Wherefore it is incumbent to obey the presbyters who are in the Church—those who, as I have shown, possess the succession from the apostles; those who, together with the succession of the episcopate, have received the certain gift [charism] of truth, according to the good pleasure of the Father. But [it is also incumbent] to hold in suspicion others who depart from the primitive succession, and assemble themselves together in any place whatsoever.[39]

Because of their historical context (heresies), the Greek Fathers accentuated the Spirit of truth, the source of right faith, and the foundation of the unity of Christians. An ancillary development was a theology of apostolic preaching, of Tradition, and of the episcopal ministry. For St. Hippolytus of Rome, who was culturally a Greek, there is a perfect correspondence between the Spirit and the Church in the sense that the Spirit is found only in the Church:

The believer who does not keep the commandments is deprived of the Holy Spirit, because he is expelled from the Church.[40]

---

38. *Adversus haereses* III.24.1, in ANF 1:458.
39. *Adversus haereses* IV.26.2, in ANF 1:497a.
40. *Commentary on Daniel* I.17, in SC no. 14, 107 [translated from French]. This formulation is similar to that of St. Cyprian ("You cannot have God for your Father if you have not the Church for your mother" [*De unitate Ecclesiae* VI (PL 4.503), in *Treatises*, FOC 36:48–49]), and refers back to the adage, "There is no salvation outside the Church" (Letter 73, XXI.2, in ACW 47:66). For the moment this is aimed only at those

The Temple of the Spirit

If anyone thinks that he is a citizen the Church, without having the fear of God, his companionship with the saints will avail him nothing, since he does not possess the power of the Holy Spirit.[41]

The liturgy is the major place where the Spirit manifests himself to sanctify the baptized. For example, the Eucharistic Prayer, right after the Institution narrative, says:

And we ask that you should send your Holy Spirit to the offering of the holy church: gathering it into one, may you grant to all the saints [the baptized] who receive [of your holy mysteries] for the fullness of the Holy Spirit, for the confirmation of their faith in truth, that we may praise and glorify you.[42]

The Spirit guards the Church, especially by giving himself in a particular way to the ministers, by communicating to them the different charisms necessary for their duties. Again in a liturgical context we can quote the prayer for consecrating a bishop:

Even now pour out from yourself the power of the Spirit of governance, which you gave to your beloved child Jesus Christ, which he gave to the holy apostles, who set up the church in every place as your sanctuary, for the unceasing glory and praise of your name.... Grant that your servant, whom you have chosen for oversight [= the episcopate], should shepherd your flock and should serve before you as high priest without blame.[43]

Note in this last passage the subtle statement that the Church is the Temple of the Spirit ("in place of the sanctuary" = the Temple of Jerusalem).

Tertullian, also, emphasizes the Spirit of truth, who gives to the Church the "orthodoxy," the doctrinal correctness necessary for the faith. We limit ourselves here to studying the rich passages from *De praescriptione* on this theme. This work is one of Tertullian's masterpieces. He is a lawyer and uses here a well-known argument from Ro-

---

who, having once been members of the Church, separate themselves from it (heresy, schism), and not at those who have never been in a position to enter the Church. We will see this question at the conclusion of our study of the theme of the People of God.

41. *Commentary on Daniel* IV.38, in SC 14:341 [translated from French].

42. *Traditio apostolica* 4.12–13, in *On the Apostolic Tradition*, trans. Alistair Stewart-Sykes (Crestwood, N.Y.: St. Vladimir's Seminary Press, 2001), 190n47.

43. *Traditio apostolica* 3.3–4, in *On the Apostolic Tradition*, 61; see also *Traditio apostolica* 2, 8, & 9.

man trial law. This argument, called the "argument of prescription," as its name indicates, is placed at the beginning of the memorandum that the litigant submits to the judge. It is a matter of invoking an exception—in other words, a legal maneuver—that, if it is accepted, concludes the litigation in the litigant's favor without the judge having to address the facts of the matter. For example, a creditor, despairing of ever being paid amicably by his debtor, summons him before a judge so as to obtain a court order (in particular to seize property). Now the debtor counters this legal action by asserting that the creditor did not choose the right judge:[44] a plea that the judge has no competency in the case. If the judge accepts this argument, the matters will stop there, and the evidence for the creditor's claim will not even be examined.

Tertullian uses this form of argumentation against the heretics: he does not intend to discuss the basis for their teachings but, from the start, he means to show that they cannot be true—whatever they may say—for reasons logically prior to the content of their statements. For example, because they are not in the apostolic succession, the heretics cannot speak the truth:

[The Lord] instructs [his disciples] to "go and teach all nations, and baptize them," when they were so soon to receive "the Holy Ghost, the Comforter, who should guide them into all the truth."... If the apostles, who were ordained to be teachers to the Gentiles, were themselves to have the Comforter for their teacher, far more needless was it to say to us, "Seek, and ye shall find," to whom was to come, without research, our instruction by the apostles, and to the apostles themselves by the Holy Ghost.[45]

Or again, because they do not accept the Acts of the Apostles as a canonical book, the heretics cannot be enlightened by the Holy Spirit; their teachings are merely human:

No doubt He had once said, "I have yet many things to say unto you, but ye cannot hear them now"; but even then He added, "When He, the Spirit of truth, shall come, He will lead you into all truth." He [thus] shows that there was nothing of which they were ignorant, to whom He had promised the future attainment of all truth by help of the Spirit of truth. And assuredly He fulfilled His promise, since it is proved in the Acts of the Apostles that

---

44. The common rule of law most often requires that in this sort of legal action the proper venue for the creditor is the court that has jurisdiction over the debtor's domicile.
45. *De Praescriptione* [*On Prescription against Heretics*], VIII.14, in ANF 3:247b.

The Temple of the Spirit

the Holy Ghost did come down. Now they who reject that Scripture [cannot] belong to the Holy Spirit, seeing that they cannot acknowledge that the Holy Ghost has been sent as yet to the disciples.[46]

Many other important statements by Tertullian could be noted, but for that the reader can refer to specialized studies.[47] In short, the essential data of the Church Fathers in this period is unanimous: the Spirit communicates divine life through the institutions of Christ that he animates (apostolic preaching, sanctification, ecclesial ministry).

2. After the fourth century: The Holy Spirit *and* the Church

We are now entering the golden age of patristics. Gradually the reflection ascends from the action of the Holy Spirit in and through the Church[48] to the very fact that this relation exists: how can we picture the union of the Spirit and the Bride?

Among the Greek Fathers, we must first mention St. Basil of Caesarea. He quotes one of the major passages from St. Paul (1 Cor 12), while insisting on the unity of the community thanks to the Holy Spirit:

Again, when we consider the distribution of gifts, we perceive that the Spirit is a whole divided *into* parts, since we are all members one of another, having gifts that differ according to the grace given to us ... so that the members may have the same care for one another, since from the beginning they are spiritually united in sympathy. "If one member suffers, all suffer together; if one member is honored, all rejoice together" (1 Cor 12:26). We live in the Spirit as individual members of a body, because we were all baptized into one Spirit, in one body (cf. 1 Cor 12:13).[49]

---

46. *De Praescriptione* XXII.8, in ANF 3:253b.

47. Concerning, in particular, Tertullian's interesting formulation, "The Church, the 'body' of the Trinity" (in the context of an anthropology in which the body is the instrument of the soul), see the remarks by Fr. Refoulé in his edition of *De Baptismo*, SC 35:75 and note 3.

48. We will not repeat here what the Fathers keep saying and what is now quite certain about this action; except for one special case we will concentrate on new observations.

49. *De Spiritu Sancto* XXVI.181b, in *On the Holy Spirit*, trans. David Anderson (Crestwood, N.Y.: St. Vladimir's Seminary Press, 1980), 94.

Note in the texts above that sanctification is expressed in terms of unity. This does not cause St. Basil to forget the institutional system, which is also related to the Spirit:

> Is it not indisputably clear that the Church is set in order by the Holy Spirit? [For St. Paul says,] "God has appointed in the Church first apostles, second prophets, third teachers, then workers of miracles, then healers, helpers, administrators, speakers in various kinds of tongues."[50]
>
> So ambitious, self-elected men [i.e., the Arian bishops] divide the government of the Churches among themselves, and reject the authority of the Holy Spirit.[51]

St. John Chrysostom is very valuable for a more in-depth understanding of ecclesial unity in connection with the Spirit. The first idea in the oeuvre of the preacher from Constantinople is that the Spirit plays *ad extra* (in creation) the role that he fulfills within the Trinity.[52] Just as, in the Trinity, the Holy Spirit shows that the Father and the Son are distinct, yet one in essence and united by love, so too the Spirit consecrates us as distinct persons while building us up into the Church by uniting us in communion. St. John Chrysostom is not a speculative theologian, but rather an orator. He makes statements that lead the understanding toward the heart of the question, but he does not explain. Starting from the Pauline data (1 Cor 12), he applies to the Spirit and the Church the comparison of the human body, a unity of body and soul:

> In the human body there is a spirit (*pneuma*) which holds all together, though in different members. So is it also here [with the Church]; for to this end was the Spirit given, that He might unite those who are separated by race and by different manners; for old and young, rich and poor, child and youth, woman and man, and every soul become in a manner one, and more entirely so than if there were one body. For this spiritual relation is far higher than the other natural one, and the perfectness of the union more entire.[53]

There is a very strict view of the body-soul unity:

50. *De Spiritu Sancto* XVI.141a, in *On the Holy Spirit*, 65–66.
51. *De Spiritu Sancto* XXX.216a, in *On the Holy Spirit*, 116.
52. Trinitarian theology studies precisely this connection between *theology* and *economy*: the missions *ad extra* of the Persons who are sent (Son and Spirit) are a prolongation of the divine processions.
53. *Homilies on the Epistle to the Ephesians*, Hom. IX.3 (PG 62.72), in NPNF, 1st series, 13:97a.

The Temple of the Spirit

"There is one body, and one Spirit, even as ye are called in one hope of your calling: One Lord, one faith, one baptism" (Eph 4:4–5). Now what is this one body? The faithful throughout the whole world, both which are, and which have been, and which shall be.... The body is not disjoined from the spirit (*pneuma*), for then would it not be a body.[54]

As then ... our body is one thing though it be composed of many: so also in the Church we all are one thing....

... That which established us to become one body and regenerated us, is one Spirit.... Not only is that which hath baptized us one, but also that unto which He baptized us.[55]

This view of the unity between the Spirit and the Church as resembling the body-soul unity in a living human being leads St. John Chrysostom to the following conclusion:

If the Spirit were not present in the midst of her, the Church would not perdure; if she perdures, it is a clear sign of the presence of the Spirit.[56]

This comparison with the body and the soul will become common property in Tradition, and through more in-depth speculation on this datum theologians will arrive at the clearer teachings, as we will see.

For St. Cyril of Alexandria, as for all the Greek Fathers, pneumatological reflection is situated at the heart of the doctrine of the Mystical Body, but for the famous Alexandrian it is based more on the Gospel of St. John than on Pauline teaching. The theme of the unifying Spirit is now classic:

For that which knits us together, and, as it were, unites us with God, is the Holy Spirit.[57]

The "process" of unification is studied by carefully connecting the work of the Spirit to Christ's work:

We all, receiving one and the same Spirit, I mean the Holy Spirit, are in some sort blended together with one another and with God. For if, we be-

---

54. *Homilies on the Epistle to the Ephesians*, Hom. X.1 (PG 62.75), in NPNF, 1st series, 13:99a.

55. *Homilies on the First Epistle to the Corinthians*, Hom. XXX.1–2 (PG 61.250), in NPNF, 1st series, 12:176a.

56. *Homily 1 on Pentecost* 4 (PG 50.459) [translated from French].

57. *Commentarius in Iohannem* XI.10 (PG 74.543c), in *Commentary on the Gospel according to S. John*, trans. Thomas Randell, vol. 2, *A Library of Fathers of the Holy Catholic Church* (London: Walter Smith, 1885), 537.

ing many, Christ, Who is the Spirit of the Father and His own Spirit, dwells in each one of us severally, still is the Spirit one and indivisible, binding together the dissevered spirits of the individualities of one and all of us, [insofar] as we have a separate being, in His own natural singleness into unity, causing us all to be shown forth in Him, through Himself, and as one. For as the power of His holy Flesh [the humanity of Christ] maketh those in whom It exists to be of the same Body, so likewise also the indivisible Spirit of God That abideth in all, being one, bindeth all together into spiritual unity.... For while the Spirit, Which is One, abideth in us, the One God and Father of all will be in us, binding together into unity with each other and with Himself whatsoever partaketh of the Spirit.[58]

This unity in Christ (being "of the same body") and this "spiritual" unity in the Spirit are accomplished in the Eucharist:

For the Son dwells in us in a corporeal sense as Man, commingled and united with us by the mystery of the Eucharist; and also in a spiritual sense as God, by the effectual working and grace of His own Spirit, building up our spirit into newness of life, and making us partakers of His Divine Nature.[59]

This passage is very dense and intends to give due regard also to the humanity of Christ in the process of unification. The purpose of all this is, as the liturgy unceasingly proclaims:

Thus all thoughts are uplifted through the Son to the Father, from Whom He proceeds by the Spirit.[60]

As for the Latin Fathers, we will limit ourselves to St. Augustine.[61] The Doctor of Hippo did not develop an ecclesiological pneumatology, but his statements are of capital importance and became the basis of all Latin theology on the subject.[62] In his writings the relation between

---

58. *Commentarius in Iohannem* XI.11 (PG 74.559d–62a), in *Commentary on the Gospel according to S. John*, 551. Other passages in St. Cyril: *Dial. De S. Trinit.* I; *De adoratione in spiritu et veritate* XV and XVII.

59. *Commentarius in Iohannem* XI.12 (PG 74.653c), in *Commentary on the Gospel according to S. John*, 554.

60. *Commentarius in Iohannem* XI.10 (PG 74.542c), in *Commentary on the Gospel according to S. John*, 536.

61. For other authors, see the references in the bibliography, especially Stanislas Isnard Dockx, "L'Esprit Saint, âme de l'Église," 67ff.; see also Sermon 77 on Pentecost by St. Leo the Great, III.1 (PL 54.412a).

62. We have noted in the bibliography a debate in the theological discussion that is rather petty and nicely illustrates certain dangers in reading texts from Tradition.

The Temple of the Spirit

the Spirit and the Church is clearly stated by way of the comparison with the relation between the soul and the body in man. St. Augustine starts from the following anthropological observation:

If a member is cut off from the body, ... the soul doesn't follow, does it? ... When it was in the body, it was alive; once it is cut off it loses its life.[63]

Yet the member can be recognized for what it is; it is a finger, a hand, an arm, an ear. Apart from the body it still has its form, but it has no life.[64]

When it is merely sick or wounded, the member remains capable of reviving, but only if it is not cut off from the body.[65]

This anthropological basis gives priority to the idea of efficient cause: the soul is the principle of the body's life and movement. The ecclesial application is then:

If you wish to have the Holy Spirit, listen, my brothers: our spirit by which every human being lives is called a soul, and you see what the soul does in the body. It quickens all the members. It sees by the eyes, hears by the ears, smells by the nose, speaks by the tongue, works by the hands, walks by the feet. It is present to all the members at once, so that they might live. It gives life to them all, and to each one its function. The eye does not hear, nor does the ear see. The tongue does not see, nor do the ear and the eye speak. But nevertheless the eye lives, the ear lives, the tongue lives. Their functions are different; their life is shared. So it is with the Church of God. In some saints this life produces miracles, in other saints it preaches the truth, in other saints it preserves virginity, in other saints it preserves conjugal modesty. In some this and in others that. Each one has its own work but all are equally alive. *Now what the soul is to the body of man, the Holy Spirit is to the Body of Christ, which is the Church. The Holy Spirit does throughout the Church, what the soul does in all the members of one body.*[66]

To him [the Holy Spirit] belongs this fellowship (*societas*) by which we are made into the one Body of the only-begotten Son of God.[67]

On account of this fellowship those [disciples] on whom the Spirit descended for the first time spoke the languages of all nations. For association within the human race exists through languages. And so it was fitting that this society of the children of God and of the members of Jesus Christ, which

---

63. *Serm.* 267.4 (PL 38.1231) [translated from Latin].
64. *Serm.* 268.2 (PL 38.1232) [translated from Latin].
65. *Serm. Denys* 19.7 [? sic] [translated from French].
66. *Serm.* 267.4 (PL 38.1231) [translated from Latin].
67. *Serm.* 71.28 (PL 38.461) [translated from Latin].

was to be among all peoples, was symbolized by the languages of all nations; and just as at that time someone who spoke with the languages of all nations had evidently received the Holy Spirit, so today someone recognizes that he has received the Holy Spirit by the fact that he is held fast by the bond of peace in the Church that is spread through all the nations. Hence the Apostle says: "Be eager to maintain the unity of the Spirit in the bond of peace" (Eph 4:3).[68]

Finally, we can note the individual application of this teaching:

A Christian ought to dread nothing so much as to be separated from the body of Christ. For, if he is separated from the body of Christ, he is not a member of him; if he is not a member of him, he is not enlivened by his Spirit.[69]

The heretic has become cut off [from the church], and the life does not follow the amputated member.[70]

Everyone, therefore, who is guilty of impenitence against the Holy Spirit, in whom is gathered the Church's unity and fellowship of communion, will never obtain forgiveness, because he has shut himself off from the source of forgiveness.[71]

He who abandons unity violates [the law of] charity, and whoever violates charity, whatever greatness he may have, he himself is nothing. Even though he may speak with the tongues of men and Angels, and know all mysteries ... he is nothing, and it does him no good. All the things that he has are useless, because he does not have the one thing by which he might put them all to good use.[72]

They cannot attain to life eternal save through the charity of unity.[73]

We see that Latin patristic writings are quite consistent with the teaching of the Greek Fathers, even though there is a different emphasis: the Greeks are more speculative and like to go to the Trinitarian roots of the doctrine; the Latins are more accustomed to the anthropological basis. This difference should not be overemphasized,[74] but it expresses well the distinctive genius of each of these two cultural periods.

68. *Serm.* 71.28 (PL 38.461) [translated from Latin].
69. *In Joh.* 27.6 (PL 35.1618), in FOC 79:281.
70. *Serm.* 267.4 (PL 38.1231) [translated from Latin].
71. *Serm.* 71.34 (PL 38.463) [translated from Latin].
72. *Serm.* 88.21 (PL 38.550) [translated from Latin].
73. *De Baptismo* VI.34.66 (PL 43.219), in NPNF, 1st series, 4:495a.
74. For St. Augustine, in particular, the Trinitarian foundation of his ecclesiological

3. Note concerning the anthropological basis

The doctrine of the Holy Spirit as the "soul of the Church" is based on the comparison with the soul and body in a human being.

First of all, we must note the fact that such talk about soul and body—which was still relatively clear for most people fifty years ago—has quickly become obscure or even incomprehensible for our contemporaries. People do not speak much about the soul today, except as a simple metaphor with a rather vague meaning that is merely a figure of speech: for example, "This house has no soul," or "Switzerland is losing its soul." Neurologists now talk about "consciousness," psychologists about "psychic apparatus," biologists about genes and even about a "germinal line," while philosophers insist more on "the person." Does this mean that the doctrine of the Holy Spirit as the soul of the Church no longer has any meaning today? That would be to deprive ourselves of a long and profound Tradition. But in order to preserve it and to preach it, one must be conscious of the present difficulties. We intend here to provide some notes on how to understand correctly the Fathers and their irreplaceable contribution.

Let us put the matter as simply as possible: fundamental anthropology recognizes that man, this particular human being, has two closely united dimensions: his "corporeality" or exteriority and his "animality" (the fact that he is animated) or interiority. We find a very general statement of this initial observation—quite independent of this or that philosophy or theology—in *Gaudium et spes* 14, §§1 and 2.

> Man, though made of body and soul, is a unity. Through his very bodily condition he sums up in himself the elements of the material world. Through him they are thus brought to their highest perfection and can raise their voice in praise freely given to the Creator....
>
> For by his power to know himself in the depths of his being he rises above the whole universe of mere objects.... So when he recognizes in himself a spiritual and immortal soul, he is not being led astray by false imaginings that are due to merely physical or social causes. On the contrary, he grasps what is profoundly true in this matter.

---

pneumatology is assuredly in evidence; in the chapter bibliography see especially the studies by Bertrand de Margerie, "La doctrine de S. Augustin sur l'Esprit Saint comme communion et source de communion," and François Bourassa, "Le Saint-Esprit unité d'amour du Père et du Fils."

This initial finding means that man is an animated corporeal whole—that these two dimensions are equally essential, since the combination of the two is what makes up a human being. This broad, general view takes a very clear stance against any "materialism" that retains in a human being only what is derived from his corporeality, against any "spiritualism" that, on the contrary, devalues the corporeal dimension by recognizing only the interior dimension, and against any dualism (of the Manichean type) that would make man the battlefield between these two dimensions, a battle that could end only by the disappearance of one of the two terms (generally corporeality). On the contrary, the notion of "person" appears as a result of reflection on this complex whole, the human being.

This commonplace view is already an affirmation of the utmost importance, and on the basis of it, theological anthropology develops its subject matter as follows:

The human person, created in the image of God, is a being at once corporeal and spiritual. The biblical account expresses this reality in symbolic language when it affirms that "then the LORD God formed man of dust from the ground, and breathed into his nostrils the breath of life; and man became a living being" (Gn 2:7). Man, whole and entire, is therefore *willed* by God.

In Sacred Scripture the term "soul" often refers to human *life* or the entire human *person*. But "soul" also refers to the innermost aspect of man, that which is of greatest value in him, that by which he is most especially in God's image: "soul" signifies the *spiritual principle* in man.

The human body shares in the dignity of "the image of God": it is a human body precisely because it is animated by a spiritual soul, and it is the whole human person that is intended to become, in the body of Christ, a temple of the Spirit (Cf. 1 Cor 6:19–20).

The unity of soul and body is so profound that one has to consider the soul to be the "form" of the body: i.e., it is because of its spiritual soul that the body made of matter becomes a living, human body; spirit and matter, in man, are not two natures united, but rather their union forms a single nature.[75]

The question is of particular importance for morality. Since corporeality is an essential dimension of the human being, consideration of it is *intrinsic* to the morality of human acts. To consider the human body as a datum deprived of significance or moral value is seriously contrary to Revelation:

---

75. *Catechism of the Catholic Church*, 362–65.

The Temple of the Spirit 173

This moral theory ... contradicts the Church's teachings on the unity of the human person, whose rational soul is *per se et essentialiter* the form of his body. The spiritual and immortal soul is the principle of unity of the human being, whereby it exists as a whole—*corpore et anima unus* (GS 14)—as a person.... It is in the unity of body and soul that the person is the subject of his own moral acts.... A doctrine which dissociates the moral act from the bodily dimensions of its exercise is contrary to the teaching of Scripture and Tradition.... In fact, body and soul are inseparable: in the person, in the willing agent and in the deliberate act they stand or fall together.[76]

Once the distinction between body and soul and their substantial unity have been affirmed, we must now consider the question of the relation between these two truths.[77]

Briefly, the dominant current in patristic thought is dependent especially on the Platonic concept of the soul as a complete substance that makes use of a body as an instrument. To borrow a classic image from antiquity, the soul is to the body what the pilot is to the ship that he steers. The relation is that of the mover to the thing moved.

This is the notion behind the theology of the Holy Spirit as the soul of the Church in the Fathers. Indeed, the Holy Spirit is not the Church, and vice versa. They are, however, very closely related—namely, in a relation of instrument and thing moved to the principal author and mover. The medieval project would add to this the typically Aristotelian perspective of the soul as the principle of unity of the body, because it is the *form* of the body. In this regard the principle of distinction between the Holy Spirit and the Church yields to the principle of their unity.

These two paths illustrate what we have already encountered with respect to the relation between Christ and the Church. The mystery obliges us to maintain *at the same time* the distinction and the closest possible unity (not just a moral unity, but somehow a unity of being). We will see this from St. Thomas on, for he is the source of the later magisterial references to this theme.

To conclude this section on the contribution of the Fathers, let us summarize our findings in a short outline:

76. Encyclical *Veritatis splendor* 48–49.
77. Bibliography: Gilles Emery, "L'unité de l'homme, âme et corps, chez saint Thomas d'Aquin" (nicely situates the Platonic and Aristotelian views along with their influence on the Church Fathers); Norbert A. Luyten, "L'homme dans la conception de S. Thomas."

- Everything is rooted in the Trinitarian doctrine.

    Within the Trinity, the Spirit is the communion of love between the Father and the Son, and by being communicated himself, he communicates this gift of the unity of men with God and with one another.

- It is the Spirit of Christ.

    The humanity of Jesus, consecrated from the beginning by the Spirit (cf. Lk 4:18 → Lk 1:35), is the humanity of the Word. This consecration effects the hypostatic union whereby Christ's sacred humanity is the sign and instrument through which the Word communicates God to men. First aspect: The Spirit presides in some way over the economy of the Incarnate Word. Throughout his ministry Jesus acts in and through the Holy Spirit, promising to give him to his disciples (Mt 4:1; Lk 4:14; Jn 3:34). In Christ's resurrection this role and this gift of the Spirit are fully manifested; it is the Spirit who raises Jesus, thus establishing him as the principle and source of glorification for every human being. Since the Passover of the Head has been accomplished, that of the Body can begin, and here too we will find again the place and the role of the Spirit.

    Therefore no separation or opposition is possible between the action of the Son and that of the Spirit.

- The Spirit in the ecclesial economy of salvation.

    The Spirit is the one who makes God communicable; he is at the source of our deification by which we are "sons in the Son." For this reason he is said to be the "soul" because he is the one through whom and in whom Christ gives us his life, conforming us to his image. The Spirit enlivens by giving us faith, charity, the forgiveness of sins.... He is also "soul" because he is the one through whom and in whom we are all united to Christ; he is the seal of the unity between man and God in the mystery of Christ, and he it is who brings about the unity of men in the Body of Christ that is the Church.

    In keeping with the Pauline data, the Fathers do not speak about a "Church, Body of the Spirit"; this is because the action of the Spirit is to configure us to Christ, to join us increasingly to his Body so that we may realize our vocation as children of God. In this sense, if the Spirit is at the source of our salvation, Christ is the end thereof: through and in the Spirit we become sons and daughters of God by being members of the Body of Christ that is the Church. To this work of unity in Christ—forming his ecclesial Body—we must add a work of diversification: the Spirit distributes his gifts and watches

The Temple of the Spirit

over their interdependence; the Spirit here is at the source of a theology of charisms, especially the hierarchical charisms.

All this is expressed by the doctrine of the Spirit as soul of the Church. The very clear consequence in the writings of the Fathers is that there is complete and utter unity between the Church of Christ and "the Church of the Spirit."

b. Tradition after the patristic era

We will limit our presentation for the medieval period to St. Thomas Aquinas, because he is the one who adds something new, thanks to the Aristotelian contribution. For the modern period we will discuss the Counter-Reformation rather quickly because of its limitations, and we will present the essentials of the modern magisterial proclamation that culminates in Vatican II.

1. St. Thomas Aquinas

Saint Thomas compiles the patristic heritage—in particular that of St. Augustine—which can be summarized by the following idea: the Spirit *enlivens* the Church, as the soul enlivens the body. One citation from among many others illustrates this point:

Just as man has only one soul and one body composed of various members, so too the Catholic Church forms only one body composed of various members; the soul that enlivens this body is the Holy Spirit. (*In Symb.*, art. 9).

Along these very patristic lines the soul is understood, consonant with Platonic philosophy, as the principle of the body's life and movement; this is the perspective of *efficient* causality: the soul gives the body certain powers of being and action, and in this sense the soul enlivens and moves it.

But the Aristotelian contribution adds the concept of the soul as the principle *of unity* among the members of the body.[78] This is along the complementary line of *formal* causality. And surprisingly, this is consistent with St. Paul (in particular 1 Cor 12:11).[79] St. Thomas goes

---

78. See the *Commentary* on De anima, Book II, lecture 7.
79. There is even a striking similarity of expression. In 1 Cor 12:11 we read, "All these are inspired by one and the same Spirit"; the expression "one and the same" translates the Greek *to hen kai to auto* and the Latin *unus atque idem*. "*Unus et idem (numero)*"

on to develop the theme along this line of the quasi-formal causality of the Spirit acting upon the Church, and his teaching later became part of Tradition through magisterial teaching, as we will see.

The Holy Spirit, principle of life and movement

St. Thomas prefers to resort here to the image of the heart according to the findings of Aristotelian physics. The heart is the central, hidden organ, the starting point from which the vital force spreads throughout the body. St. Thomas thus assigns the respective places of Christ and the Spirit in the Church. In the *Summa theologiae*, one objection to the expression "Head of the Church" to designate Christ reads:

> The head of a man is a particular member, receiving an influx from the heart. But Christ is the universal principle of the whole Church. Therefore He is not the Head of the Church. (*ST* III, q. 8, art. 1, obj. 3)

We saw during our study of the theme of the Body of Christ that calling Christ the Head means that he is the "source of everything"; if it is true that in the biological comparison the head is not the source of everything because the head itself receives an influx from the heart, then the expression cannot be correctly applied to Christ. That is the whole meaning of the objection. St. Thomas replies:

> The head has a manifest pre-eminence over the other exterior members; but the heart has a certain hidden influence. And hence the Holy Ghost is likened to the heart, since He invisibly quickens and unifies the Church; but Christ is likened to the Head in His visible nature in which man is set over man. (*ST* III, q. 8, art. 1, ad 3)

The metaphors of the head and the heart do not have the same extension. The head designates Christ *in his humanity*; the heart designates the *Divine Person* of the Holy Spirit who exerts an influence as God (by appropriation) on the humanity of Christ and, through it, on all mankind. In other words, the image of the head befits Christ as man, and in this regard he prevails over all mankind. As for the Spirit, his role refers to the "whole Christ," the Church (Head *and* Body).

["(Numerically) one and the same"] is the favorite expression of St. Thomas and occurs frequently in magisterial documents.

The Temple of the Spirit

At the level of the image, the heart has a hidden influence, which is to "quicken" or *enliven* first the head, because it is the noblest member and has a vital influence on the other members. In the Church, the transposition is as follows: the Spirit first enlivens Christ in his humanity and then, in a derivative way, all those who are united to his humanity. Christ therefore, in his humanity, exercises his influence as Head only in dependence on the Spirit. From this we see that the Spirit accomplishes in the Church what he realizes *first* in the humanity of Christ. To put it differently: the Spirit gives life *directly* (immediately) to the humanity of Christ, and *indirectly* (by mediation), through the humanity of Christ, to all mankind.

This should not pose any particular problem; it is a somewhat technical way of presenting the subject, but it is the common property of the patristic Tradition.

The Holy Spirit, principle of unity

This doctrine, which is the most original of St. Thomas's teachings, will enable us to make real progress with respect to previous findings. It appeals to refinements that belong to other areas in theology; we will recall these points so as to get an overall view of this theological perspective.

The doctrine of the Mystical Body *united* under one Head poses a rather complex problem: the derivation of Christ's grace in us (the influx) must not be understood in the manner of the transfusion of a bodily/physical reality. "Something" corporeal does not go from Christ into us, as though it were no longer in Christ so as to come to pass in us. What we call "grace," in the sense of gifts given by God to men in Christ, is what is born in man by the fact that he is loved by God. Grace, in this sense, is a personal perfection, a strictly personal perfection; it is this personal relation between this human being and God resulting from an infused *habitus*, by a process of drawing out and raising up (in Latin *eductio*) [something latent] within the person. God raises our soul to a dignity that allows it from then on to place acts that are above its natural capacities: to know God as he knows himself (by faith here below, in the beatific vision in heaven); to love him as he loves himself and us. Sanctifying grace is the gift of a *habitus* or quality that is entitative (on the order of being) and subsequently operative (on the order of action). This *habitus* does not pass from Christ to us; it is created by eduction in the person and from the person as a quality of his or her soul, for this soul has an obediential potency for such elevation, which God actualizes.

To say that grace is a *created gift* means then that there is no transfer of something from Christ to the human being: God creates this disposition in the human being. Hence we see that grace is multiplied as many times as there are subjects in whom it is educed. The implication is clear: on the level of created grace, there is no single reality common to Christ and men; there are only *similar* realities. Through Christ each human being is endowed with a *strictly personal* sanctification, such that the grace given to Peter is not identical to the grace given to Paul, but is only similar. From this strictly personal aspect we conclude likewise that grace cannot be transmitted from one human being to another: I cannot have faith for my brother. The unity brought about in the Church by the theological virtues (unity of faith, hope, and charity) is consequently first a *moral* unity, owing to the fact that each of the members of the Church believes, hopes in, and loves the same object (God himself); it is a unity brought about by the same end pursued by all. It is also a *real* unity in the sense that it resides in the possession of an infused *habitus* that is similar in all [the members of the Church].

These refinements concerning the nature of created grace allow us to understand the following passage:

In the natural body there are four types of unity among the members:
- The first results from their natural conformity ... ; we say then that the members are one by genus or species.
- The second is brought about by the sinews and joints that connect the members with one another; we say then that the members are one by continuity.
- The third results from the diffusion of the vital spirit and the powers of the soul throughout the body.
- The fourth results from the fact that all the members are perfected by the soul, which is numerically one in all the members.

These four types of unity are found also in the Mystical Body:
- The first, inasmuch as all its members are of the same nature by genus or species.
- The second results from the fact that all the members are bound to one

The Temple of the Spirit

another by faith, because they are connected in this way in the one object that is believed.
- The third results from the fact that all the members are enlivened by grace and charity.
- The fourth results from the fact that all the members have in them the Holy Spirit, who is the final and principal perfection of the whole Mystical Body, somewhat as the soul is in the natural body.

The first of the aforementioned unities is not unity simply speaking, because the thing that brings about this unity [human nature] is not unique,[80] as is the case for the three other types of unity. For by faith and charity all the members are united in the numerically one object that is believed and loved. Similarly the Holy Spirit, who is one numerically, fills them all....

Believers in a state of grace are united according to the third unity, which is a formal unity [i.e., a unity that forms or perfects] with respect to the second, and again according to the fourth unity that completes it all." (III *Sent.* dist. xiii, q. 2, art. 2, qla. 2, corpus)

The unity brought about by the Holy Spirit is the strongest numerical unity: the same reality (the same being) is present in all in the manner of a formal cause—in other words, so as to bring about the most complete unity: a being that is *one* and not just *united* (while preserving the distinction of persons: and here we find again the *unum mysticum*).[81]

On the basis of this teaching, we find frequent statements such as these:

The Holy Spirit is the *first, radical* principle of unity of the Mystical Body, because he is equally and simultaneously present in the Head and in the members. (III *Sent.* dist. xiii, q. 2, art. 1, sol. 1)

In the Mystical Body there is a certain continuity because of the Holy Spirit who, being numerically one and the same (*unus et idem numero*), fills and unites the whole Church. (*De Veritate* q. 29, art. 4, corpus)

Hence we can note the two major principles of unity of the Mystical Body. The first and radical one is the *uncreated gift* of the Holy Spirit who is really (*in re*) transmitted from the Head to the members and

---

80. "*Non est unum numero*," literally, "is not one numerically"; this means, "is brought about as many times as there are individuals." The passage is translated from Latin with reference to the French.

81. In the Latin prose of St. Thomas, not always but frequently, a distinction is made thereby between what is *unum* or "one" (intrinsic cause) and what is only *unitum* or "united" (extrinsic cause).

dwells in each one; the second is the *created gift* of the grace of the virtues that is given by the eduction (quasi-creation) of the obediential potency of the soul of each human being. This second principle is indeed a *real* principle (a spiritual reality), but it is numerically plural because it is realized as many times as there are subjects; it is not one, but rather *similar* in each human being, and produces its effect of unifying persons only by reason of the tendency toward the same end that it imprints and maintains in each one, namely, the same God who is believed and loved.

Note in conclusion several scriptural commentaries by St. Thomas in which this doctrine is indeed assumed:

(On 1 Cor 12:12–13) "For just as the body is one and has many members, and all the members of the body, though many, are one body, so it is with Christ. For by one Spirit we were all baptized into one Body ... and all were made to drink of one Spirit."

Commentary: [The] one ground of unity is the Holy Spirit, as it says in Eph 4:4: "There is one Body and one Spirit." But we receive a double benefit by the power of the Holy Spirit [namely baptism and the Eucharist]. (*Super 1 Cor.*, c. 12, lect. 3 [Marietti 734], translated by Fabian Larcher, OP)

(On Col 1:18) "[Christ] is the head of the body, the Church; he is the beginning, the first-born from the dead, that in everything he might be pre-eminent."

Commentary: The Church is called a "Body" because of its likeness to a single human being. This likeness is twofold: first, in that it has distinct members (Eph 4:11); secondly, because the members of the Church serve each other in ways that are different: "[So that] the members may have the same care for one another" (1 Cor 12:25; Gal 6:2). Again, just as a body is one because its soul is one, so the Church is one because the Spirit is one (Eph 4:4; 1 Cor 10:17). (*Super Col.*, c. 1, lect. 5 [Marietti 46], translated by Fabian Larcher, OP)

(On Rom 8:9) "Any one who does not have the Spirit of Christ does not belong to him."

Commentary: Just as what is not enlivened by the spirit of the body (the soul) is not a member of the body, so too someone who does not have the Spirit of Christ is not a member of Christ. (*Super Rom.* c. 8, lect. 2 [Marietti 627]; translated from French)

Conclusion concerning St. Thomas

The distinction between unity through the created gifts and unity through the uncreated gift will become a commonplace in Tradition; we will see it again in the teaching of the popes. This doctrine has a very solid scriptural basis. The distinction between the Spirit in Person who is God and sanctifying grace (faith, hope, charity) that is *created* is in Scripture. It is not the conclusion of our reasoning, but rather a given that we have to understand.

The resulting distinction between the uncreated unity and the created unity of the Church allows us to situate better [in the overall context] the following points:

The Church is a *created* being. She does possess within her "something" divine (a supernatural reality created by God), but she is not God! Since she is a created being, her formal principle, that by which the Church is the Church, must be of a like nature [*homogène*]—in other words, must be *created* also. God, by reason of his absolute transcendence, does not enter into composition with any created being, except in the unique case of the hypostatic union that brings about the mystery of the Word Incarnate. In this sense God is extrinsic to the Church. This formal principle for the Church is the created gift, the grace of the theological virtues, in particular charity. This grace has a twofold relation with the Holy Spirit:

- It is a gift of the Holy Spirit; it comes from him; he it is who, through the humanity of Christ, educes or elicits it from our soul.
- Grace disposes the believer, by renewing and elevating his nature, to receive the Holy Spirit in Person so as to be united with him and to act at his prompting.

If the Holy Spirit is called "soul of the Church" along the line of formal causality, this is because he constitutes the highest unity of the Church (a reality that is one and the same in all her members), but he does not enter into composition with the Church so as to bring about a being. In this sense he is not immanent in the Church; he ensures a participation in the communion of the Divine Persons. The Church is not the Trinitarian communion as though it included human beings *simpliciter* [simply speaking]; she is only a participation therein.

It must be carefully noted:

The grace of the theological virtues is immanent to the Church; for this reason it deserves the name of "created soul," with this qualification: while this grace is one in its species, it is numerically plural. As for the Holy Spirit, he is not immanent to the Church (he surpasses the Church on all sides and does not enter into composition with her to form a being), but he deserves the name "uncreated soul" because he is numerically one and the same in all the members. The two causes of the unity of the Church call for one another; moreover these causes cannot exist separately.

The terms "created soul" and "uncreated soul" were introduced by Charles Journet. They are not found in magisterial writings. They are a theological manner of speaking that remains on the level of theologians. Everyone remains free to adopt this terminology or not. But what they intend to express, the revealed reality that we seek to understand, is part of ordinary magisterial teaching, as we will see.

Let us note for the moment, as a positive datum, the fact that there are several principles that concurrently contribute to the unity of the Church. In other words, these principles bring about the unity of persons who make up the community that bears within it the means of grace and is in fact the reality of grace.

A passage by Cajetan nicely sums up this finding.[82] We summarize it here. In the church there are three causes of unity that are ordered among themselves:

The unity of *order*

This unity consists essentially of the fact that all believers have the same head, Christ and—because of the pilgrim status of the Church in this world—his vicar, the pope. This is the simplest form of unity, which consists above all in the obedience of *subordinates*. It is a simply moral unity. It does not bring about the Church as one (*una*), but through it the Church is said to be *sub uno* (under one). For example, Spain and Austria had the same king in the sixteenth century, but they

---

82. Thomas de Vio Cajetan, *In Summa theologiae*, at ST II-II, q. 39, art. 1, no. II.

were two distinct countries. The unity of the Church is much deeper, but it requires this first form.

The unity of *similarity*

Here we mean the unity that is engendered by the theological virtues. All the faithful believe in (faith), hope in (hope), and love (charity) *the same object* (God himself), thanks to this infused *habitus* educed from the soul of each one. In this unity there is at the same time a moral aspect and a real aspect. The moral aspect comes from the tendency of all to converge on the same object; the real aspect comes from the similar *habitus* educed in each one. Thus the faithful are *brought together* because they gather in acts of the theological virtues that are formally *similar*. However, these acts of faith, hope, and charity remain strictly personal acts (one cannot believe, hope or love in place of someone else). This cause of unity does not make the faithful *one*, but they are *similar* and thus *brought together*.

Simply *numerical* unity

The faithful belong to the same whole (the Body of Christ), of which each one is a member; in other words, he exists and actualizes his own identity only *as part of a whole*. The Holy Spirit in Person, who is "one and the same" (*unus et idem numero*)—in other words, totally present at the same time in the whole and in each part (like the soul in the human body)—is the one who brings about this unity. Each of the faithful believes, hopes, and loves—not just personally—but together with the others. One believes, hopes, and loves *as a member of the Church*. The baptized person receives spiritual goods and lives them out as someone who is taken up into a whole [*un ensemble*] that surpasses him and causes him to participate in the whole.

These three forms of unity are inseparable. To break with one of them is to break with the whole. This connectedness is easy to grasp insofar as the unity of similarity and numerical unity are concerned. The unity of order may seem less important. Certainly, it is subordinate to the other two in the sense that the pope's authority is exercised as a service to the two other kinds of unity. But to refuse this service is to neglect a dimension of the Church that is part of her mystery—in other words, that affects the rightness of the faith and therefore injures the unity of similarity. This will be clarified in the speculative part.

2. The Counter-Reformation

We will pass rather rapidly over this era of Tradition for two main reasons. In the first place, as we already noted with reference to the Body of Christ theme, we find in this period a strong tendency to consider the Christian life to be more individual than communitarian. Furthermore the Holy Spirit is presented more as the "guest of the pious soul" than as the soul of the Church. The spiritual theology of the seventeenth century gives priority to this perspective. In the second place (and this is more decisive), Catholic theologians, within the context of their controversies with Protestant Christians, would follow St. Robert Bellarmine in imagining a distinction between "the body of the Church" and "the soul of the Church" that is by no means equivalent to the traditional distinction between the Mystical Body and its soul. Even though the new distinction can be rendered acceptable by means of important clarifications and corrections—we will return to this in our discussion of speculative theology—this is an important change of perspective: the soul of the Church is no longer the Holy Spirit in Person, or even the grace of the theological virtues, but rather the persons who are actually under the dominion of the Spirit and of grace, whether or not these individuals are visibly in the Church, whether or not they have received the supernatural gifts through the institutions of Christ. Here is the passage:

> The Church is a living body in which there is a soul and a body. The internal gifts of the Holy Spirit (faith, hope, charity, etc.) are the soul. The external profession of faith and participation in the sacraments are the body. Hence we see that some men belong to the soul and the body of the Church and accordingly are united internally and externally to Christ the Head. They are perfectly and completely in the Church.... [O]thers are part of the soul and not of the body, such as catechumens.... Finally others are part of the body and not of the soul [e.g., serious sinners].[83]

---

83. St. Robert Bellarmine, *De controversiis,* chap. I, in Naples edition, 2:74.

The Temple of the Spirit

Tradition (the Church Fathers, St. Thomas, etc.) has shown us that the soul of the Church is the Spirit in Person as the principle of the created gifts. The ecclesial Body is made up by men in whom the Spirit and his gifts are received. With St. Robert Bellarmine, there is a considerable change of perspective: the soul of the Church is made up of persons who have the Spirit and his gifts; the body of the Church is made up of the persons who are externally members of the Church. The consequence is clear: the soul and the body of the Church are separable; they form two distinct communities that are normally united, but can be separated.[84] Hence we cannot avoid the following conclusion: the Holy Spirit—more by his gifts than by himself—is strictly speaking the soul of "the invisible Church" but not of "the visible Church." That is where the break appears, and it is fearsome.

3. The contemporary ecclesiological renewal

As with the doctrine of the Mystical Body, the way was prepared by two theological Masters, Möhler and Scheeben. By way of example we can quote the former:

Christ [is] the center of our faith.... But I did not wish to discuss what might reasonably be assumed as already known; rather, I wished to begin with the topic that belonged fully to the matter at hand. The Father sent the Son, and the Son sent the Spirit: in this way God came to us. We come to him in the reverse way: the Holy Spirit guides us to the Son, and the Son to the Father. Therefore I began with what is temporally first in our becoming Christians."[85]

The concept of the church is defined in a one-sided manner if she is designated as a construction or an association, founded for the preservation and perpetuation of the Christian faith. Rather, she is much more an offspring of this faith, an action of love living in believers through the Holy Spirit.[86]

Little by little magisterial documents will bring this Tradition back to the surface. For example:

---

84. This is the case of the catechumen who, in this perspective, is already a member of the "invisible Church" without yet being a member of the "invisible Church"; on the other hand, we find the Christian in a state of mortal sin who is a member of the "visible Church" while he is not a member of the "invisible Church."
85. Johann Adam Möhler, *Unity in the Church*, 77.
86. Möhler, *Unity in the Church*, 209.

We have resolved to address you ... concerning the indwelling and miraculous power of the Holy Ghost; and the extent and efficiency of His action, both in the whole body of the Church and in the individual souls of its members.[87]

As Christ is the Head of the Church, so is the Holy Ghost her soul.[88]

The references by Leo XIII are not very elaborate, and there is still a strong insistence on the individual aspect of sanctification by the Spirit, but at least the patristic and medieval Tradition is cited and is thus put back into circulation, so to speak. But the decisive references are found in the teaching of Pius XII:

To this Spirit of Christ, also, as to an invisible principle is to be ascribed the fact that all the parts of the Body are joined one with the other and with their exalted Head; for He is entire in the Head, entire in the Body, and entire in each of the members. To the members He is present and assists them in proportion to their various duties and offices, and the greater or less degree of spiritual health which they enjoy. It is He who, through His heavenly grace, is the principle of every supernatural act in all parts of the Body.... This presence and activity of the Spirit of Jesus Christ are tersely and vigorously described by Our predecessor of immortal memory Leo XIII in his Encyclical Letter *Divinum Illud* in these words: "Let it suffice to say that, as Christ is the Head of the Church, so is the Holy Spirit her soul."[89]

The Spirit is present here in his work of quickening; as we have seen, this conveys the first stage of the patristic period. To this Pius XII adds:

In the moral body the principle of union is nothing else than the common end, and the common cooperation of all under the authority of society for the attainment of that end; whereas in the Mystical Body of which We are speaking, this collaboration is supplemented by another internal principle, which exists effectively in the whole and in each of its parts, and whose excellence is such that of itself it is vastly superior to whatever bonds of union may be found in a physical or moral body. As We said above, this is something not of the natural but of the supernatural order; rather it is something in itself infinite, uncreated: the Spirit of God, who, as the Angelic Doctor

    87. Leo XII, Encyclical *Divinum illud munus*, 1897, par. 2 (prologue) [EWTN archives].
    88. Leo XII, Encyclical *Divinum illud munus*, 1897, no. 6.
    89. Pius XII, Encyclical *Mystici Corporis* (1943), no. 57 [English translation at Vatican website].

The Temple of the Spirit

says, "numerically one and the same, fills and unifies the whole Church." (*De Veritate* q. 29, art. 4, corpus)[90]

Here we have the formal aspect, the Spirit as the unity of the Mystical Body.

Taking this modern reception of the Tradition as our point of departure, we can state the two principal characteristics of pneumatological ecclesiology. On the one hand, the Spirit constitutes the Church as *one* because he is in Person her principle of unity; this is the "static" aspect. On the other hand, the Spirit constitutes the Church as something alive, in other words active, for he is her principle of life; this is the "dynamic" aspect. The Spirit unites and enlivens the Church: these are the two pillars of pneumatology pertaining to our subject: the original gift and the continual gift, the permanence of Christ's work (*his* Gospel, *his* sacraments, *his* ministers) and their fruitfulness in every age that must meet ever-new challenges.[91]

This is the stage of Tradition in which the Second Vatican Council assembled.

4. The teaching of Vatican II (*Lumen gentium*)

The Trinitarian presentation of the Church

The Constitution *Lumen gentium*, after an introductory paragraph, immediately presents the Church as having come forth from the Trinity, the product of the ordered work of the three Divine Persons. Paragraph 2 sets forth the Father's plan to bring all things back to himself; paragraph 3 is devoted to the mission of the Son accomplishing the Father's plan by his Incarnation, and paragraph 4 teaches about the mission of the Holy Spirit who has come to communicate the work of the Son.[92] Concerning the Spirit, Vatican II declares:

---

90. Pius XII, Encyclical *Mystici Corporis*, no. 62.

91. By way of illustration we can mention consecrated life: founded on the life and example of Christ, its qualitative and quantitative developments over history are attributed to the work of the Holy Spirit (*LG* 43; *Perfectae caritatis* 1).

92. This Trinitarian presentation of the *being* of the Church is followed, in the Decree on the Missionary Activity of the Church, by a Trinitarian presentation of the ecclesial action: "The Church on earth is by its very nature missionary since, according to the plan of the Father, it has its origin in the mission of the Son and the Holy Spirit" (*Ad gentes* 2).

When the work which the Father gave the Son to do on earth (cf. Jn 17:4) was accomplished, the Holy Spirit was sent on the day of Pentecost in order that He might continually *sanctify* the Church, and that, consequently, those who believe might have access through Christ in *one* Spirit to the Father (cf. Eph 2:18). (*LG* 4, emphasis added)

This first mention sets forth in general terms the works of sanctification and unity that are appropriated to the Spirit. The passage continues:

Guiding the Church in the way of all truth (cf. Jn 16:13) and unifying her in communion and in the works of ministry, he bestows upon her varied hierarchic and charismatic gifts, and in this way directs her; and he adorns her with his fruits (cf. Eph 4:11–12; 1 Cor 12:4; Gal 5:22). By the power of the Gospel he permits the Church to keep the freshness of youth. Constantly he renews her and leads her to perfect union with her Spouse....

Hence the universal Church is seen to be "a people brought into unity from the unity of the Father, the Son and the Holy Spirit" (St. Cyprian, *De Orat. Dom.* 23). (*LG* 4)

Here the ecclesial work of the Spirit is presented more explicitly. This paragraph 4 is descriptive in the manner of patristic teaching before the fourth century, as we have seen. The Council, further on, integrates the later, more speculative contributions:

Giving the body unity through himself, both by his own power and by the interior union of the members, this same Spirit produces and stimulates love among the faithful. From this it follows that if one member suffers anything, all the members suffer with him, and if one member is honored, all the members together rejoice (cf. 1 Cor 12:26). (*LG* 7, §3)

Much biblical theology is interwoven into this paragraph 7, which marks a development concerning the Body of Christ that is the Church. The theology of the Mystical Body thus integrates ecclesiological pneumatology with its principal theme of unity. Several lines further on, *Lumen gentium* completes this presentation with the following statement:

In order that we might be unceasingly renewed in him (cf. Eph 4:23), [Christ] has shared with us his Spirit who, *being one and the same* ("*unus et idem*") in head and members, gives life to, unifies and moves the whole body. Consequently, his work could be compared by the Fathers to the function that the principle of life, the soul, fulfills in the human body.[93] (*LG* 7, §7)

---

93. Another related passage: "As the assumed nature, inseparably united to him, serves the divine Word as a living organ of salvation, so, in a somewhat similar way ('*non*

The Temple of the Spirit

The three points attributed to the Spirit are the enlivening, the unification, and the movement. The enlivening, as we saw, is the Platonic perspective (efficient causality): the Holy Spirit gives us grace and the various gifts, and gives himself. The gift par excellence is love, since the Spirit is the conjoined love of the Father and the Son, and since charity is created participation therein. That is the distinctive life of the Church. In saying this we are not dealing with "spirituality," but with dogmatic theology. Any definition of the Church that does not necessarily and primarily include uncreated and created love can only be seriously deficient. Ecclesiological pneumatology is the surest way of avoiding the ecclesiological exaggerations that tend toward legalism. We have here the most profound structure of the theology of the Church, a structure that affects all the rest of the subject matter, not only in terms of our theological comprehension of the mystery, but also in terms of discernment for an ecclesial life correctly understood.[94] Let us review briefly these notes attributed to the Spirit:

The Spirit of unity

Unity among Christians is received from the Holy Spirit in Person; it is not "produced" by human initiative. This allows us to appreciate correctly the secondary means of unity and in particular the place of the apostolic hierarchy. The pastors do not bring about the deepest unity of the Church as a colonel brings about the unity of a regiment—in other words, principally by commanding and by being obeyed. The primary and decisive thing—without which there will be no secondary means at all—is that the hierarchy receives unity from the Spirit so as to transmit it to all the faithful. The hierarchy is not "productive" of the fundamental unity (as in a socio-juridical scheme), but rather the servant of the gift of unity. This service (the first charism given by the Spirit) is a preferred means of the Spirit for receiving, increasing, defending—in short for serving—a unity that comes from God. The apostle does this by preaching the Gospel, by celebrating the sacra-

---

dissimili modo'), does the social structure of the Church serve the Spirit of Christ who vivifies it, in the building up of the body" (*LG* 8.1).

94. Thus all "malfunctioning" in ecclesial life (dissensions, lack of docility, disobedience) cannot be reduced to acts of insubordination alone, but are more deeply signs of a charity that is growing cold.

ments, and by leading the community thus gathered toward its eschatological goal.

But the Spirit also makes other gifts without going through the pastors.[95] The Spirit thus edifies in many ways a community of which he is personally the unity, and he is the great conductor of this symphony that ecclesial life should be.

The life-giving Spirit[96]

Life is the fundamental movement by which a living being actualizes its potentialities. It is the process by which a living being attains its perfection by its acts. From the embryo to the mature human being we find this passage, this trajectory toward the perfection of the subject. This is the fundamental movement that constitutes life. To say that the Spirit enlivens and moves the Church is to say that he leads her toward her perfection, which is entrance into the heavenly Jerusalem. Her perfection as a holy, immaculate assembly is realized little by little in this world. It comes about by way of the healing of her wounds (ecumenism) and by her extension to all mankind (the missions).

The Holy Spirit is the one who stirs up the desire and the initiatives that tend toward the visible unity of all baptized persons in the one Church (*LG* 15; *UR* 3). This entails the search for unity of the faith professed in a diversity of legitimate expressions (*UR* 4), and unity of charity in action. By pouring out faith and charity on all, the Holy Spirit moves toward unity. Consequently, in the ecumenical movement it will always be necessary to give priority to the practice of the theological virtues over theology, since spiritual ecumenism is the root of doctrinal ecumenism.[97]

The mission to the non-Christians is an important field. We know from Scripture that the apostles received the commission to bring the Good News to the ends of the earth. That is why Christ announces to them that he will send "power from on high" (Lk 24:46–49; Acts 1:8).

---

95. Particularly charisms in the service of the faith and charity of the whole community, such as the charism of consecrated life.

96. We classify under this heading also the aspect of movement, since "life" is a movement.

97. In this regard the reader can refer to the Encyclical *Ut unum sint* (1995), which sets this forth quite clearly in its first chapter.

The Temple of the Spirit

This power, the Spirit, is the real motor driving the missionary expansion of the Church that the world has witnessed starting with the book of Acts. We have noted the Trinitarian structure of this sending on mission (*Ad gentes* 2); a little further on the same Decree mentions the role of the Spirit:

This [missionary] task ... is one and the same (*"unum idemque"*) everywhere and in all situations, although, because of circumstances, it may not always be exercised in the same way. (*AG* 6)

The expression *unum idemque* refers back to the Holy Spirit who is one and the same throughout the Church, her most radical principle of movement, especially of missionary activity. This states the place of pneumatology in missiology, not only so as to reconcile unity and the diversity of situations, but first and foremost so as to grasp the intrinsic unity of the missionary movement, whatever the differences in times and places: always and everywhere to extend the one, unique Church.

Conclusion

In conclusion, we wish to give several liturgical illustrations of the doctrine that we have just set forth. We take them from the Eucharistic liturgy, which is par excellence the place where the Incarnate Word and the Spirit manifest their joint action:

Preface of the Mass of Pentecost:
> It is truly right and just, our duty and our salvation,
> always and everywhere to give you thanks,
> Lord, holy Father, almighty and eternal God.
> For, bringing your Paschal Mystery to completion,
> you bestowed the Holy Spirit today
> on those you made your adopted children [→ the Holy Spirit
>   in Person]
> by uniting them to your Only Begotten Son.
> This same Spirit, as the Church came to birth,
> opened to all peoples the knowledge of God [→ the gifts of the
>   Spirit, e.g., faith]

and brought together the many languages of the earth
in profession of the one faith.

Preface of the Mass for Christian Unity

It is truly right and just, our duty and our salvation,
always and everywhere to give you thanks,
Lord, holy Father, almighty and eternal God,
through Christ our Lord.

For through him you brought us
to the knowledge of your truth,
so that by the bond of one faith and one Baptism
we might become his Body.
Through him you poured out
your Holy Spirit among all the nations, [→ the Holy Spirit in Person]
so that in a wondrous manner
he might prompt and engender unity
in the diversity of your gifts, [→ the gifts of the Spirit, efficient causality: life]
dwelling within your adopted children [→ the gifts of the Spirit, formal causality: unity]
and filling and ruling the whole Church.... [→ the gifts of the Spirit, efficient causality: movement]

Sanctifying Epiclesis of Eucharistic Prayer II:[98]

Humbly we pray
that, partaking of the Body and Blood of Christ,
we may be gathered into one [Mystical Body] by the Holy Spirit.

Sanctifying Epiclesis of Eucharistic Prayer III:

Look, we pray, upon the oblation of your Church
and, recognizing the sacrificial Victim by whose death

---

98. The sanctifying epiclesis, generally *after* the consecration, which invokes the Spirit to gather the Church, is distinguished from the consecratory epiclesis, generally *before* the consecration, which invokes the Spirit for the consecration of the gifts that are offered.

you willed to reconcile us to yourself,
grant that we, who are nourished
by the Body and Blood of your Son
and filled with his Holy Spirit,
may become one body, one spirit in Christ.

In their sobriety, the epicleses, as we can see, express only the aspect of unity and imply the aspect of sanctification, since the latter is conditional on unity: only if one is in the unity of the Mystical Body of Christ, thanks to the Spirit, can one receive the sanctifying gifts of the same Spirit.

Pneumatological ecclesiology, of which we have just presented the essential elements, is therefore of considerable importance. The principal difficulty with it resides in the fact that it is based on an appropriation to the Spirit of what is common to the three Divine Persons, but this does not mean that it is merely a manner of speaking without any real import. Indeed, it is quite clear that the work of the Incarnate Word possesses an "incarnate" note that is evident and relatively easy to grasp (Christ's institutions). But the mention of the Spirit of Christ adds two refinements: on the one hand, these institutions of Christ can be devoid of all salvific value if they are not understood, served, and lived out in the Spirit; on the other hand, the Church also lives out other gifts that are not made through the intermediary of Christ's institutions (consecrated life is the best, but not the only illustration); therefore these gifts are attributed to the Holy Spirit. These gifts do not constitute another way of salvation, but their purpose is to serve the one salvific economy that is the one Church.

This allows a reading of history that is perhaps more precise than the one that is usually made. For example, it is customary to present the time of the Catholic Counter-Reformation as a period when the hierarchical aspect of the Church and a certain religious formalism became increasingly influential. It is said that the Christological path tended to monopolize attention at the expense of the pneumatological consideration. This observation tells only part of the truth. Indeed, at the same moment the Church experienced an extraordinary flowering of consecrated life and a considerable missionary movement. This shows that this period is also in many aspects the time of a Catholic Reform that bore fruit on a very large scale. It is possible that theology has not always followed the same line, but the reality of ecclesial life must not be neglected, since it is constantly teaching lessons.

BIBLIOGRAPHY

The Church, Temple of the Spirit, in Scripture

Amiot, François. "Temple." Translated by John P. Langan. In *Dictionary of Biblical Theology*, edited by Xavier-Léon Dufour, 594–97. New York: Seabury Press, 1973.

Borremans, John. "L'Esprit Saint dans la catéchèse évangélique de Luc." In *Lumen vitae* 25 (1970): 103–22.

Cerfaux, Lucien. *La Théologie de l'Église suivant saint Paul*. 2nd ed. Paris: Cerf, 1965. Good classic study. The first edition was translated by Geoffrey Webb and Adrian Walker as *The Church in the Theology of Saint Paul* (New York: Herder, 1959).

Congar, Yves. *Je crois en l'Esprit Saint*. 3 vols. Paris: Cerf, 1979–80. Translated by David Smith as *I Believe in the Holy Spirit*. 3 vols. New York: Seabury, 1983. The first part of volume 1, "The Canonical Scriptures," is a careful presentation in about a hundred pages. The author remarks, however, that ecclesiological pneumatology is on the whole not studied much for its own sake by biblical scholars. Extensive bibliography.

———. *Le mystère du Temple*. Lectio divina 22. Paris: Cerf, 1958. Translated by Reginald F. Trevett as *The Mystery of the Temple*. Westminster, Md.: Newman Press, 1962.

Credo in Spiritum Sanctum: Atti del Congresso internazionale di Pneumatologia. 2 vols. Vatican City: Libreria editrice vaticana, 1983. Many valuable essays; see in particular Ignace de La Potterie, "L'Esprit Saint et l'Église," 791–808.

Durrwell, François-Xavier. *L'Esprit Saint de Dieu*. Paris: Cerf, 1985. Translated by Benedict Davies as *Holy Spirit of God: An Essay in Biblical Theology*. London: G. Chapman, 1986. See especially chap. 5, "The Spirit of Christ in the Church."

Feuillet, André. "Le temps de l'Église d'après le IVe évangile et l'Apocalypse." *La Maison-Dieu* 65 (1961): 60–79. With bibliography.

Guillet, Jacques. "Spirit." Translated by Arthur F. McGovern. In *Dictionary of Biblical Theology*, edited by Xavier-Léon Dufour, 569–71. New York: Seabury Press, 1973.

———. "Spirit of God." Translated by Arthur F. McGovern. In *Dictionary of Biblical Theology*, edited by Xavier-Léon Dufour, 571–76. New York: Seabury Press, 1973.

Harlé, Paul-André. "Le Saint-Esprit et l'Église chez saint Paul." *Verbum caro* 76 (1965): 13–29. Rather dependent on Lucien Cerfaux and Pierre Benoit.

Haya-Prats, Gonzalo. *L'Esprit, force de l'Église: Sa nature et son activité d'après les Actes des Apôtres*. Lectio divina 81. Paris: Cerf, 1975. Extensive bibliography.

Lémonon, Jean-Pierre. "L'Esprit Saint dans le corpus paulinien." In *Dictionnaire*

de la Bible: Supplement, edited by Louis Pirot, André Robert et al., 11:192–326. Paris: Letouzey and Ané, 1987. See especially "Esprit et communauté," 11:216–40.
Schnackenburg, Rudolf. *The Church in the New Testament*. Translated by W. J. O'Hara. New York: Herder and Herder, 1965.

The Church, Temple of the Spirit, in the Church Fathers

Because of the connection between this theme and that of the Body of Christ, useful references can be found among the titles cited in the bibliography of the preceding chapter (especially Émile Mersch, Johannes Quasten, and J. N. D. Kelly).

Congar, Yves. "The Holy Spirit and the Apostolic College, Promoters of the Work of Christ." In *The Mystery of the Church*, translated by A. V. Littledale, 105–45. Rev. ed. Baltimore and Dublin: Helicon Press, 1965.
———. *Je crois en l'Esprit Saint*. 3 vols. Paris: Cerf, 1979–80. Translated by David Smith as *I Believe in the Holy Spirit*. 3 vols. New York: Seabury, 1983. In particular see vol. 1, part 2 for the patristic era.
Credo in Spiritum Sanctum: Atti del Congresso internazionale di Pneumatologia. 2 vols. Vatican City: Libreria editrice vaticana, 1983. Note in particular Georges Khodr, "L'Esprit Saint dans la tradition orientale," 1:377–408.
de Durand, Georges-Matthieu. "Pentecôte johannique et Pentecôte lucanienne chez certains Pères." *Bulletin de littérature ecclésiastique* 79 (1978): 57–126.
Dockx, Stanislas Isnard. "L'Esprit Saint, âme de l'Église." In *Ecclesia a Spiritu Sancto edocta. Lumen gentium 53: Mélanges théologiques offers à Mgr Gérard Philips*, 65–80. Gembloux, Belgium: Duculot, 1970.
L'Esprit Saint et l'Église: L'avenir de l'Église et de l'oecuménisme; Actes du Symposium de l'Académie internationale des Sciences Religieuses. Paris: Fayard, 1969. Good essays, in particular André Benoit, "Le Saint-Esprit et l'Église dans la théologie patristique grecque des quatre premiers siècles," 125–52.
Galtier, Paul. *Le Saint-Esprit en nous d'après les Pères Grecs*. Rome: Pontificia Universitas Gregoriana, 1946.
Tromp, Sebastian. *De Spiritu Sancto anima Corporis mystici*. 2 vols. 2nd ed. Rome: Pontificia Universitas Gregoriana, 1948 and 1952. Volume 1 treats the Greek Fathers; volume 2 treats the Latin Fathers. A good, wide-ranging review of some of the most important patristic passages; supplements Émile Mersch.

On the Holy Spirit, soul of the Church

Gribomont, Jean. "Esprit Saint chez les pères grecs." In *Dictionnaire de Spiritualité*, edited by Marcel Viller et al., 4:1266–68. Paris: Beauchesne, 1961.
Le Guillou, Marie-Joseph. "Esprit Saint." In *Catholicisme: Hier, aujourd'hui, demain: Encyclopédie*, edited by G. Jacquemet, G. Mathon et al., 4:492–94. Paris: Letouzey et Ané, 1956.
Liégé, Pierre-André. "Ame de l'Église." In *Catholicisme: Hier, aujourd'hui, demain: Encyclopédie*, edited by G. Jacquemet, G. Mathon et al., 1:434–36. Paris: Letouzey et Ané, 1948.

Tromp, Sebastian. "Esprit Saint, âme de l'Église." In *Dictionnaire de Spiritualité*, edited by Marcel Viller et al., 4:1296–1302. Paris: Beauchesne, 1961.

On St. Augustine

Batiffol, Pierre. *Le Catholicisme de S. Augustin*. 2 vols. Paris: Gabalda, 1920. A rather outdated work that we cite because of the "quarrel" mentioned in the following section.

Bourassa, François. "Le Saint-Esprit unité d'amour du Père et du Fils." *Sciences ecclésiastiques* 14 (1962): 375–415.

Cavallera, Ferdinand. "La doctrine de Saint Augustin sur l'Esprit Saint à propos du *De Trinitate*." *Recherches de théologie ancienne et médiévale* 2 (1930): 365–87; 3 (1931): 5–19. Despite its title, this study does not limit its investigation to the *De Trinitate*.

de Margerie, Bertrand. "La doctrine de S. Augustin sur l'Esprit Saint comme communion et source de communion." *Augustinianum* 1 (1972): 107–19.

Lamirande, Émilien. *Études sur l'ecclésiologie de Saint Augustin*. Ottawa: Éd. de l'Université Saint-Paul, 1969. A precise, invaluable study.

Rondet, Henri. "L'Esprit Saint et l'Église dans saint Augustin et dans l'augustinisme." In *L'Esprit Saint et l'Église: L'avenir de l'Église et de l'oecuménisme; Actes du Symposium de l'Académie internationale des Sciences Religieuses*, 178ff. Paris: Fayard, 1969.

Note concerning a "quarrel"

At the time of the renewal of patristic studies, scholars were led to observe that the way in which the soul of the Church had been spoken of since the Counter-Reformation was new in relation to Tradition (see the section on speculative theology). Some authors, taking the Counter-Reformation sense as the only accepted meaning, consequently declared that St. Augustine had never spoken about the Holy Spirit as the soul of the Church; see, for example, Pierre Batiffol, *Le Catholicisme de S. Augustin*, 1:250; the argument is repeated by Henri Rondet, "L'Esprit Saint et l'Église," 180. Now in the anthology by Sebastian Tromp, *De Spiritu Sancto anima Corporis mystici*, we find no fewer than 73 citations from St. Augustine (chiefly excerpts from the *Enarrationes in Psalmos* and the *Homilies*) that contain either the expression or the idea. Émilien Lamirande, *Études sur l'ecclésiologie de Saint Augustin*, cleared up these mistakes. Based on the current state of the scholarship, we can say that St. Augustine uses the expression "soul of the Body of Christ" frequently and the phrase "soul of the Church" at least twice (see his *Enarrationes in Psalmos* 9.6 and 66.4).

The Church, Temple of the Spirit, after the patristic era

de Lubac, Henri. *La Postérité spirituelle de Joachim de Flore*. 2 vols. Paris: Lethielleux, 1979–81.

St. Thomas Aquinas

See also in the bibliography of the preceding chapter many studies on the theology of the Mystical Body in St. Thomas's writings, which include some elements of pneumatology, in particular Yves Congar, *The Mystery of the Church*, 66–67. Dictionary and encyclopedia articles are generally rather misleading as far as St. Thomas is concerned (except the one by Marie-Joseph Le Guillou in his entry "Esprit Saint" in *Catholicisme*).

Cajetan, Thomas de Vio. *In Summa theologiae*. In Thomas Aquinas, *Opera omnia iussu impensaque Leonis XIII P. M.* Vols. 4–11. Rome: Propaganda Fide, 1888–1906.
Emery, Gilles. "L'unité de l'homme, âme et corps, chez saint Thomas d'Aquin." *Nova et Vetera* (French edition) 75 (2000): 53–76.
Journet, Charles. *L'Église du Verbe incarné*. Vol. 2. Paris: Desclée de Brouwer, 1951, 454–705. The author does distinguish the Spirit as efficient cause and as formal cause. A high-quality study (see particularly the alphabetical table on pages 1323–24 for the different passages). The distinction between "created soul" and "uncreated soul" that Journet always defended (see 565–79) has been much debated, notably by Ernest Mura, "L'âme du Corps mystique, est-ce le Saint-Esprit ou la grâce sanctifiante?" *RT* 41 (1936): 233–52; and Journet's response in the same volume, 651ff. For the general debate, see Stanley Jaki, *Les tendances nouvelles de l'ecclésiologie*, 217–18.
Luyten, Norbert A. "L'homme dans la conception de S. Thomas." In *L'Anthropologie de Saint Thomas*, 35–53. Fribourg, Switzerland: Éditions Universitaires, 1974.
Vauthier, Émile. "Le Saint-Esprit principe d'unité de l'Église d'après S. Thomas d'Aquin." *Mélanges de sciences religieuses* 5 (1948): 175–96; 6 (1949): 57–80. The first part of the essay offers a review of the principal passages in St. Thomas's writings; the second part attempts a synthesis of this teaching. See the critical assessment by Fr. Yves Congar in *Sainte Église* (Paris: Cerf, 1963), 647–49.

The period of classical theology

Bellarmine, Robert. *De controversiis*. Naples: Giuliano, 1857.
Congar, Yves. *I Believe in the Holy Spirit*. 3 vols. Translated by David Smith. New York: Seabury, 1983, 1:151ff.
Liégé, Pierre-André. "Ame de l'Église." In *Catholicisme: Hier, aujourd'hui, demain: Encyclopédie*, edited by G. Jacquemet, G. Mathon et al, 1:434–36. Paris: Letouzey et Ané, 1948. A quick demonstration of the gradual shift caused by classical theology.
Möhler, Johann Adam. *Unity in the Church, or The Principle of Catholicism, Presented in the Spirit of the Church Fathers of the First Three Centuries*. Edited and translated by Peter C. Erb. Washington, D.C.: The Catholic University of America Press, 1996.

The contemporary period

The articles "Esprit Saint" in the encyclopedia *Catholicisme,* vol. 4(1956), and in the *Dictionnaire de Spiritualité,* vol. 4, edited by Marcel Viller et al. (Paris: Beauchesne, 1961), mention the findings of the contemporary renewal.

Charue, André-Marie. "Le Saint-Esprit dans *Lumen gentium.*" *Ephemerides theologicae lovanienses* 45 (1969): 358–79.

Congar, Yves. *I Believe in the Holy Spirit.* Translated by David Smith. New York: Seabury, 1983, 2:5–66. The entire first part of volume 2 is a good overall synthesis of the subject.

———. "La pneumatologie dans la théologie catholique." *RSPT* 51 (1967): 255ff.

———. "Pneumatologie ou 'christomonisme' dans la tradition latine?" *Ephemerides theologicae lovanienses* 45 (1969): 394–416. Allows the reader to perceive the gradual shifts in Latin theology, but without making the serious charge of "Christo-monism"; rather, it is "Christo-centric," which is not the same and is a fairer assessment.

Credo in Spiritum Sanctum: Atti del Congresso internazionale di Pneumatologia. 2 vols. Vatican City: Libreria editrice vaticana, 1983. Note in particular: Yves Congar, "Actualité de la pneumatologie," 1:15–28; Jean-Marie Roger Tillard, "L'Esprit Saint dans la réflexion théologique contemporaine," 2:905–19; with bibliography; Georges Chantraine, "L'enseignement de Vatican II concernant l'Esprit Saint," 2:993–1010; and Jean-Hervé Nicolas, "Le Saint-Esprit, principe d'unité de l'Église," 2:1370ff.

Dewailly, Louis-Marie. "L'Esprit et les Chrétiens dans l'Église du Christ." In *Le Saint-Esprit: Auteur de la vie spirituelle,* Cahiers de la vie spirituelle, 67–83. Paris: Cerf, 1944.

Mühlen, Heribert. *L'Esprit dans l'Église.* Translated by A. Liefooghe, M. Massart, and R. Virrion. 2 vols. Paris: Cerf, 1969. Attempts to strike some new balances in favor of pneumatology in modern ecclesiology, starting from a renewed vision of the relation between Christ and the Spirit. Rather attractive. See the critical review by Yves Congar in *RSPT* 55 (1971): 334–39; see also Marie-Vincent Leroy, *RT* 72 (1972): 288–91.

Vonier, Anscar. *The Spirit and the Bride.* London: Burns, Oates, and Washbourne, 1935. Good popularization.

4

The Church Is the People of God

Our elaboration of this third ecclesiological theme may seem unusually long in comparison with the two preceding chapters. We do not intend to suggest thereby that this is the main theme. These three approaches to the mystery of the Church are interdependent and form a whole that is very rich, to which each one contributes something irreplaceable. However, in our day the theology of the People of God in particular has been distorted and misunderstood in ways that are fraught with consequences. It is important therefore to present this aspect of Revelation anew in all its breadth. That is why we are proposing here an overall view, especially insofar as the modern Tradition is concerned.

We have already seen that the Church began from the moment following Adam's fall, from the beginning of the age of redemption.[1] The theme of the Church as Body of Christ does not mean that the Church of Christ was born purely and simply from the Cross of Christ and was not manifested until Pentecost. Tradition speaks extensively about the

1. To be more thorough, one would have to emphasize the fact that the mystery of the Church can be considered as the mystery of the return of rational creatures to God. This includes the angels and the time before original sin. The Church of the redemption is the recovery, in the precise perspective of salvation, of the original economy that one can term "Church of the creation." There are, indeed, some basic continuities between the two economies that elucidate them reciprocally. We limit ourselves here to the study of the Church of the redemption. The main book that shows the continuity between the two economies is that of François Daguet, *Théologie du dessein divin chez Thomas d'Aquin: Finis omnium Ecclesia* (Paris: 2003).

Ecclesia ab Abel to emphasize that the just men and women of the Old Testament are members of the Body of Christ.[2]

The theme of the People of God, which is also quite pervasive in Scripture and Tradition, was rediscovered at the time of the twentieth-century theological renewal after the theme of the Body of Christ.[3] It was taken up by Vatican II, which devoted to it a whole chapter of the Constitution *Lumen gentium*. In order to present this theme to the Council Fathers, the spokesman for the drafting commission spelled out two major reasons.[4] In the first place, the theme of the People of God allows one to underscore properly the progressive character of the manifestation of the ecclesial mystery in time as the Church marches toward her eschatological end; the Church here below has a historical status. In the second place, the Church must be seen first in what is fundamentally common to all the faithful, so that what is most important is more evident—namely, the community of charity making its way toward its fulfillment. The hierarchy, under the aspect in which it engenders the faithful, precedes them; this is the perspective of efficient causality that is often favored in Latin theology. But there is another aspect that is just as important for our understanding of the mystery and of this ministerial efficacy itself. According to this aspect, the Church is willed for her own sake in the divine plan. This is the perspective of final causality, eternal beatitude, which the People of God theme expresses well. In other words, the consideration of the end, even if it is attained only gradually, does shed light on the whole order of means that are arrayed with the view to that end—means that are not limited to the apostolic hierarchy. Catholic unity can thus be better manifested in the variety of duties, offices, and vocations, a variety that does not destroy unity, but rather enriches it.[5]

We can see better, then, what this theme contributes in relation to the two preceding themes. The more specifically New Testament themes (Body of Christ and Temple of the Spirit) present the Church

---

2. See in particular *LG* 2. This commonplace of Tradition is assumed by St. Thomas when, within the context of the question in the *Summa theologiae* related to the headship of Christ, he mentions the just who lived before Christ (see *ST* III, q. 8, a. 3).

3. The most productive moment was during the 1950s; see the bibliography at the end of the chapter.

4. See *AS* III/1, 500–1.

5. *Lumen gentium* therefore put the People of God (chap. 2) before the consideration of the hierarchy (chap. 3); we will examine again this decision and its implications at the conclusion of this chapter.

along a more "essential" line (*in facto esse*): what the Church is and does not cease to be in her perfection, which is brought about by the accomplishment of the mission of the Son and the Spirit. The theme of the People of God, because it directly takes up the historical dimension, presents the same Church along a more "existential" line (*in fieri*): what the Church becomes during the time of her earthly pilgrimage. Hence the sequence in which the Constitution *Lumen gentium* presents things is explained. The first thing to be taught is what the Church is, her "fundamental ontology," with the accent on her note or mark of unity; this is the subject of the first chapter (mainly paragraphs 7 and 8), with the help of typically New Testament themes, since Christ is the one who gave the community of salvation its essential perfection. In the second place the document presents the life of this being that in time develops its potentials and its diversity, with an emphasis on its universal vocation. This development is the subject of the whole second chapter (paragraphs 9–17), which deals with the People of God theme, for the Church was prepared and announced, she began to exist from the moment following the sin of our first parents.[6]

A note on biblical vocabulary

In the Hebrew Old Testament, the word *am* (singular) designates Israel as the People of God, and word *goyim* (plural) generally designates foreigners who are not part of the divine election and make up the pagan nations. The Septuagint did justice to this difference in terminology because the Greek language lent itself to this distinction. Indeed, conscious of the excellence of their culture, the Greeks saw themselves as forming a civilized political society, the *laos*, that was superior to foreign communities, which were considered to be barbarian, the *ethnē*. Thus the Septuagint translated *am* as *laos*, resulting in the expression "*laos tou Theou*" (People of God), and *goyim* as *ethnē*. Latin was less well-suited to translating this distinction from Hebrew and Greek. Certainly the Romans too considered themselves to be a civilized people,

---

6. It must be understood that we are dealing here with theological emphases and not with features [*notes*] that exclude each other. In other words, the People of God that tends toward the reception of Christ (OT) is already the Body of Christ and Temple of the Spirit, but this subject lacks some essential elements that will be given only by the Savior. These elements are announced and prepared under the regimen of the first covenant, which looks forward to and prepares the way for the new covenant.

beyond which there were only barbarians, but the vocabulary was not strictly established to express this. Often the (Roman) *populus* was distinguished from the (foreign) *gentes,* but the word *gens* could also signify race and especially family (lineage), and in this case it applied to the Romans, as well. Moreover, within the *populus* they sometimes distinguished between the *plebs* (those who were governed) and the political elite, but not always.[7] Generally the Vulgate rendered the distinction *am* = *laos* and *goyim* = *ethnē* by the words *populus* and *gentes,* but this is not always the case. There is a loss of nuance here.

Since Hebrew and Greek are the two cultures present in the New Testament, the use made therein of the terminological distinction (in Greek) is very significant theologically. One of the best examples is the prophecy of Caiphas (Jn 11:49ff.): "It is expedient for you that one man should die for the people (*laos*), and that the whole nation (*ethnos*) should not perish." Dying for the *laos* is the prophecy, for Jesus does die to save the People of God. The perishing of the *ethnos* is the secular political unit threatened by the Romans. And since Caiphas is a politician, we must understand his concern to preserve the *ethnos* so as to save the *laos.* And this recalls all the prophetic denunciations in the Old Testament against the kings of Israel who made alliances with the pagans, who put their trust in chariots and horsemen in order to save the *laos,* whereas it is in the hands of God alone by virtue of the covenant.

St. John the Evangelist was not mistaken when he commented on this prophecy: "He prophesied that Jesus should die for the nation (*ethnos*), and not for the nation (*ethnos*) only, but to gather into one the children of God who are scattered abroad" (Jn 11:51f.). The use of the one word *ethnos* to designate Israel is clear: in rejecting Christ, Israel becomes an *ethnos* like the others. The only word that St. John places on the lips of Pilate to designate Israel (Jn 18:35) is *ethnos,* because the perspective was exclusively political for the Roman administrator (who was to remain unaffected by this theology).

Ethnos also designates the Church two times in the New Testament, and this is very instructive. In Mt 21:33–46, the parable of the murderous vineyard tenants concludes with a major teaching of Jesus: "The kingdom of God will be taken away from you and given to a na-

---

7. Thus the well-known expression *"Senatus Populusque Romani"* (SPQR).

The People of God

tion (*ethnos*) producing the fruits of it" (Mt 21:43). The sentence has an unprecedented severity, because it clearly indicates that Israel ceases to be the *laos*; the Church will be born of the pagans; the *goyim* will become the *laos!* In 1 Pt 2:9, "you are ... a holy nation (*ethnos hagion*), God's own people (*laos*)," the point is less explicit than in Mt 21, but in light of Matthew's theology we can read this verse from the First Letter of St. Peter in this sense: out of the sanctified pagans, God makes his People.

To summarize, we can present the New Testament data as being articulated along two major lines:

On the one hand, the new People (*laos*) is born from the old: the Jews are the first ones called to enter into the new People of God. In this sense we can read the clear references at the beginning of the Gospel of St. Luke (Lk 1:17; 2:32: Jesus, the glory of Israel). On the other hand, the new People has sprung from the pagans. This is a theme in the initial Christian preaching.[8]

In both cases the Jewish people is no longer the Chosen People. St. Paul even goes so far as to say that the first election of Israel was not so glorious: Israel is [likened to] the son of Hagar, the slave woman, whereas the Church is a People born of the promise, and the slave woman is rejected (Gal 4:21ff.). The new People therefore comes from two sources: the Jews, and this is in continuity, but no longer as Jews per se: the covenant is new, and the pagans are invited to share in it—that is the novelty.[9]

The New Testament is sometimes very harsh toward the Jews who refuse to enter into the new People (See Mt 21:33ff.): although they are greatly exalted when one considers the Old Testament, they are just as greatly condemned if they remain Jews when the New Covenant is promulgated before their eyes. The discourse of St. Stephen (Acts 7) underscores both the greatness of their past sacred history and the present misery of the Jews who reject Christ.

---

8. For example, Acts 15:14—the discourse of St. James that becomes the baseline of St. Paul's ministry.

9. It is not completely new, however, inasmuch as the preaching of the prophets had announced that Israel's election is open to the pagans. The Book of Isaiah (esp. Is 56–66) contains a real and profoundly universal design, the work of the Messiah who is to come. Therefore, once Jesus is recognized as Savior by a Jew, the extension of the covenant to the pagans does not appear to be contrary to the doctrine of Israel's election.

Having made these clarifications, our study of the sources follows the well-known plan that goes from Scripture to Vatican II.

I. The People of God in Scripture

Our study of the Bible first shows in the Old Testament the similarities between Israel and other peoples, but also the fact that these similarities do not constitute identity: there are original and radically specific features in Israel. These specific features very strikingly announce the New Testament, the Church, in a way that is easier to see than the Old Testament announcements of the Body of Christ theme. Then, in the second prong of our biblical survey of the Old Testament data, we will see how the Church was grafted onto Israel (Rom 11:17).

a. The People of Israel
1. Similarities and specific features of Israel

The first element of Israelite society is its territory. Like any people, Israel has a territory that it must organize, make fruitful, and defend as needed. For Israel the land has the importance that it has for all its neighbors: it is a pledge of political independence and an economic element. But there is much more: it is the land that is promised and then given as an inheritance. It is a *gift* and not a conquest, the fulfillment of the promise made to Abraham (Gn 12:7). This gift can be lost, not by some military mishap, but by infidelity. This is the tragic experience of the exile in Babylon. But the People is always preserved; it is reformed starting with a remnant that comes to Jerusalem after the exile. At that moment, meditation on the major prophecies (Ez 11:14–21; 36:24ff.; Jer 31:31ff.) leads to an understanding that God will renew the covenant, while enlarging it to include all humanity. Consequently this land is holy because it is God's gift, the place of his presence, and it is destined to receive all nations (Is 65:17), which indicates a transcendence of the idea of an enclosed geographical territory.

Israel forms a political community. It exploded onto the scene as a federation of diverse tribes founded by the great statesman David, and Solomon maintained it with difficulty, but it was subsequently divided into two unequal communities that had to face the dangers of neigh-

The People of God 205

boring kings. In Israel there is a true political history. But there is much more. This People has its origins in one man, Abraham, of whom it is the posterity. Through fleshly descent is transmitted a spiritual heritage that consists of knowledge of the one true God and a unique covenant with him. Thus the "race" of Abraham is more sublime than a merely biological reality; it is indeed founded on descent according to the flesh, but the flesh is the sign and the means of a spiritual descent. This knowledge of the one true God and Israel's unique relation with him can be read in the life of this people (deliverance from Egypt, exile, restoration), which thereby becomes an instrument of Revelation.[10]

At the cultural level, Israel's culture is chiefly religious, like that of all its neighbors. It can be seen in its architecture, customs, sacred books; it is not without foreign contributions. But this culture is essentially rather than chiefly religious. It is expressed above all in a type of worship, whether public or private, that has the specific feature of recalling events from the past, the central fact being the Passover from Egypt. Moreover, it intends to actualize these events and to that end ceaselessly stirs up faith in a personal God who is always present and active (see esp. Jo 24). This cult also stimulates the People's hope and their expectation of the day when God will inaugurate his kingdom among his own. This eschatology would be developed especially after the experience of the exile (Ez and Jer). This religious culture is thus very specific. Besides, if we remain exclusively at the cultural level, it is less brilliant than the cultures of its large neighbors (Babylon and Egypt), but it contains and expresses a faith that demands fidelity, for which a son of Israel must be ready to endure the cruelest persecutions (2 Mc).

Like any nation, in order to become established and to last over time, Israel little by little built up political, judicial, economic, social, and military institutions; they are the product of its specific genius, but foreign influence also had its part in it. Here too we can observe that these institutions cannot be reduced to their sociological aspect alone.

10. Revelation consists not solely of words, but also of historical deeds, the meaning of which is given by the prophets. This is the most profound and original historical aspect of the Revelation made to the Jews, an aspect that is accomplished in the acts of the man Jesus. The life of the Church, which is also made up of events, is likewise a path by which to penetrate more deeply into the meaning of the fulfillment brought by Christ (cf. GS 4.1: the theology of the *signs of the times*).

Take, for example, the monarchy. This is the most widespread system of government in the regions surrounding the Jews. In the ancient East, the institution of royalty is always closely connected to the mythical concept of divine royalty: either the king is the embodiment of a higher god (Egypt), or else he is the one chosen by the tutelary god to be his steward on earth (Babylon). We find nothing of the sort in Israel. Monarchy is not one of the fundamental institutions of the chosen people: the only true king is God. He alone has sovereignty over the People;[11] the institution of monarchy involved the risk of obscuring this, and that is why it was granted only with misgivings (Jgs 9:8ff.). The king of Israel is therefore a servant, a man like all the rest, liable to sin. Besides, although the King has the particular duty of preserving the religion, he is neither priest nor prophet. With the disappearance of the royal house during the exile to Babylon, Israel's hopes were fixed on the kingship of God that must be recognized by all nations. The expectation of the Messiah, who is often depicted as king (Zec 9:9), eliminates the need for this ambiguous political authority in the life of Israel.

We could elaborate much more on this discussion of Israel, but we prefer to turn now to the reasons that explain both these similarities and these differences.

2. Basis for the similarities and the specific characteristics

Israel is a People in many ways similar to all its neighbors. In a word, Israel is a rather common reality of the social type. It is not a religious sect; it is not an army. But this social nature, banal in itself, manifests some very strongly original features with respect to its neighbors because it has its origin, its ongoing life, and its hope in God's redemptive action. The existence of Israel, even at the basic level of a particular nation, ultimately can be explained only by a faith that takes account of all that this nation possesses that irreducibly sets it apart from the others. This faith can be summed up in three main points, the themes that structure the entire Old Testament, which are important keys for the interpretation of the New Testament also. We mean the themes of election, vocation, and covenant.

---

11. See 1 Sm 8:7; Ex 19:6; this is the basis for the prohibition against taking a census of the people (2 Sm 24).

The People of God

Election

The experience of election, of being chosen, is the experience of a singular condition due not to a blind concurrence of circumstances or to a series of human accomplishments, but rather to a deliberate, sovereign initiative by God: the gratuitous initiative of a love that remains faithful, despite everything, to all that was promised to Abraham. This choice by God situates Israel among the nations as a People set apart. This awareness is quite vivid and very ancient in Israel, and the prophets constantly recall it.

Vocation

For what purpose did God choose Israel? Israel is established and set apart to accomplish a mission: to bear witness, to make known in truth to the whole world the one true God and to love him with all its heart. This is the *Shema Yisrael* (Dt 6:4–8), which is like the charter for the Chosen People, the clearest statement of its vocation. The founding of Israel in Abraham is a decisive stage in salvation history: starting with one man who will be like a new rootstock of humanity, God begins to unite all men with himself and with one another. The first step—in this world that is under the curse of Babel—is to establish a people that is small at first, but will grow until it encompasses all nations (Gn 12:3: "By you all the families [nations] of the earth shall bless themselves," according to the Septuagint and the New Testament; see parallel verse Jer 4:2). This is the universalism of Israel's vocation, which is developed especially after the return from exile (Is 45:14ff.). In other words, all the privileges of Israel, and they are considerable, exist only to make of this People a faithful witness at the service of all humanity. The vocation of all nations is the same: to join Israel one day in the common adoration of the one true God and mutual love.

Covenant

This vocation utterly surpasses the strength of the Chosen People; that is why God makes a covenant with them. God binds himself to his People so that, despite its radical powerlessness, it can carry out the vocation for which it was chosen. Men bind themselves to one another by pacts, contracts, and treaties to bring their enterprises to a successful conclusion. This reality of juridical, economic, and political life enabled the sacred authors to picture the manner in which God assures Israel of his cooperation. This covenant has its terms: the Law (Ex 34). It concerns in the first place the worship to be rendered to God, and therefore the proscription of idolatry: the absolute rejection of any other god; strict monotheism. Furthermore, there is a categorical prohibition of any compromise or pact with pagan nations: salvation comes from God alone. Finally, we recognize in this Law a whole set of observances whose object is both to promote religious fidelity and to express it and witness to it. Over the course of history a closely woven fabric of ordinances (613 commandments at the time of Jesus), encompassing all aspects of life, would develop. The pious Jew can be recognized by his zeal in observing them. The sealing of the covenant is the subject of a ceremony reported by two different traditions. On the one hand there is the tradition of the sacred meal that Moses, Aaron, and the elders had in the presence of the Lord (Ex 24:1–2; 9–11), and on the other hand the sacrifice of an animal with the sprinkling of its blood (Ex 24:3–8 and the expression "blood of the covenant"). In the Temple, which houses the Ark of the covenant, the people gather to celebrate the major feasts (each one being a memorial of the covenant); these great cultic assemblies, which perpetuate those in the desert, are known under the title "*Qᵉhal YHWH*," what the Septuagint would later translate with the word *Ekklēsia*.

3. Three fundamental titles

We find here the triad *priest, prophet, and king*.

The individual as priest, prophet, and king

Within the chosen people, in order to ensure its fidelity to the covenant and thus to its vocation, which justifies its election, there are three titles given to particular persons. Priest, prophet, and king are special inasmuch as they are the three types of persons who, under the first covenant, received an anointing as a sign of their personal consecration; they were "*christs*" in the sense of the Greek word. The consecratory anointing was an outward sign manifesting that the one who received it was chosen by God to become his servant for a precise purpose. For this reason God communicated a share of his Spirit to the

The People of God

one whom he had chosen. The king was anointed to govern the people, to defend it, and to secure justice. The priest was anointed to offer sacrifices. The prophet was anointed (most often by a metaphorical anointing) to speak in God's Name.

The community as priest, prophet, and king

The three individual titles recalled above are telling; they reveal something essential about the People as a whole, because it is the People as such that is consecrated (Ex 19:6). Later, when the Davidic monarchy was suppressed during the exile, royalty became a more spiritual and mystical theme. The Jew is king because he participates in God's sovereignty, ruling as God rules—in other words, by wisdom and love he leads men to God. In doing so the holy People participates in the kingdom of God for the benefit of the nations. Gradually this kingdom is thought of as a kingdom entrusted to the People (Ex 19:6): "The righteous ... will govern nations and rule over peoples" (Ws 3:8). Israel is likewise a People of priests. Israel must ensure the worship of God, which is centered on the Passover. The central text is in Exodus 19:6: "I shall make you (*or* you shall be to me) a kingdom of priests." The Book of Leviticus not only gives rules for worship that every Jew must observe, but also makes provisions for the sacrifices offered by the whole people (Lv 4:13ff.; Lv 16 and 23). Finally, Israel is a People of prophets. Personal prophetic activity is knowledge by an individual divine revelation that is destined to become public. In this sense, a few are prophets, and the rest are not. But prophetic activity also includes the understanding of written Revelation, the holy books that everyone can read or hear as they are read aloud. This understanding is granted by the same Spirit by whom the Book originated through a personally inspired author. "Would that all the Lord's people were prophets," said Moses (Nm 11:29); he is not talking here about the prophetic activity of the inspired author; rather, since the Word of God is addressed to all the People, they can and must have a right knowledge of God and of his plans so as to witness to them. The prophetic activity of the People as such is fundamentally the mission to witness (Is 43:10ff.; 44:8ff.).

The findings from our survey of Old Testament biblical theology can be summarized in three points:

A plan of communal salvation

Nothing is more foreign to the Old Testament than individualism. Receiving a true knowledge of the One God and in return loving God faithfully and witnessing to him is inconceivable outside of a community. This is what we can call the "social structure": God brings men together with himself and, as a necessary corollary, with one another. Salvation is the recovered unity of the human race, and being established as a People is a very expressive sign of this. The major acts in the life of a pious Jew are communal acts, whether it is a question of cultic acts or of the mission of witnessing in the sight of the nations.

Equality and inequality in the People of God

As we see it in the Old Testament, the People of God is made up of men who are radically equal in their dignity and vocation. If the People as such is priest, prophet, and king, it is because, in a certain way, each of its members is. Election by God is not measured by personal criteria. But to this we must add that there is necessarily an organic, functional inequality among the persons. In Israel the royal, priestly and prophetic nature of the People does not rule out, but on the contrary calls for, the existence of an institutional royalty, an ordained priesthood at the service of public worship, and prophetic activity by some individuals with reference to that of the People.

The universality of the promised salvation

At the moment of his election, Abraham receives the promise of a universal salvation, and this is recalled several times (Gn 17:5; 22:18). This universalism is quite clear at the very beginning of the establishment of the People. At the end of the Old Testament this universalism reappears. This is the appearance of the theme of the eschatological covenant expressed in terms of the marriage of Yahweh with the New Jerusalem (Is 54). It is concluded by the Servant whom God establishes as "a covenant to the People, a light to the nations" (Is 42:6 and 49:6). The apocalypse of Daniel takes up this theme (Dn 2). Israel has been set apart, but this appears then as a provisional stage in the divine plan, since all nations are invited to travel to Jerusalem so as to

The People of God

know and love the One God there.[12] We know that in Jesus's time Israel did not yet fully comprehend this original universalism; it was still more vividly aware of its separation from other peoples. Yet this universalism is the true divine election (the salvation of the human race), the true vocation of the People of God (to witness to this divine intention), the very reason for the covenant that announces and prepares for the *new* covenant to come (Jer 31:31).

Although the annunciations to Zechariah and to Mary, the *Benedictus* and the *Magnificat* that begin the Gospel according to St. Luke, remain within the framework of the election of Israel and its salvation, the canticle of Simeon, the *Nunc dimittis*, gives the interpretation thereof: the salvation prepared by Israel for all peoples, a light to illumine the nations and the glory of Israel. Thus the consummation of the first covenant must be its disappearance so as to allow all peoples to enter.

b. The Church, the new People of God

To designate the community of salvation of the new covenant, the New Testament most often uses the word "*ekklēsia*," which the Septuagint had chosen to name the cultic assembly of Israel. But the word "*laos*" is often used as well, and the expression "*laos tou Theou*" ["People of God"] is found very clearly about ten times. It is plainly evident that the community of Christians understands itself as a people and not just any group, and on the other hand it is perfectly aware that it is the successor of Israel in its election, vocation, and covenant. This is quite clear in Rom 9:25–26, 2 Cor 6:16, and 1 Pt 2:9–10, pericopes that cite Old Testament verses and apply them to the Church.[13]

Even more than a successor, the Church is conscious of being the eschatological People foretold and prepared by the first covenant, of which Israel was consequently only the symbol. Israel had only the promise; it is fulfilled in Christ and gives birth to the Church.

---

12. This theme recurs frequently in the Book of Isaiah: Is 2:2ff.; Is 45 and 60; Is 66:18–21 clearly shows that this is a matter of reversing the situation that started in Babel; see also Zec 14:16.

13. See especially the study by Rudolf Schnackenburg, *The Church in the New Testament*, 149ff.

1. The continuities and discontinuities with Israel

The trilogy election—vocation—covenant is essential to the structure of the New Testament, as well.[14] If election, as the choice of Israel already testifies, is an absolutely gratuitous initiative of God that endows his elect with a status and a destiny different from that of other peoples, then it is clear that the Church is founded on an election. But this election no longer concerns a particular people; rather, humanity as a whole has been chosen. Moreover, it is no longer a question of preparing the world to receive salvation, but rather of effectively receiving it through salvific acts: from now on this is the sole path of salvation for the human race.

Vocation (as a call from God to accomplish a specific task within the framework of man's cooperation in salvation) was another constitutive element of Israel. It is likewise manifest in the Church. Israel and the Church are both signs and means forged by God to work with him in his plan of salvation. From this perspective, Israel and the Church are not different: both are supposed to witness to the one true God. Nevertheless, there is a difference of scale: Israel was to witness to the expectation of the Savior-Messiah, while the Church testifies that the Messiah has come and that from now on all nations are to enter into this salvation that has been accomplished once and for all.

Covenant means the same thing for Israel as for the Church: God binds himself to his partner. But there is a profound difference. The Old Testament covenant is a conditional covenant (Jo 24:1–28): God binds himself to his People, and his commitment is valid only if the People remains faithful to the Law. Now Israel's history is the history of its infidelities, or, if one prefers, the history of an impossible fidelity. It is an entirely different matter with the new (not "renewed") covenant concluded by Christ in his Blood. This is an eternal (Heb 13:20), unfailing (Mt 16:18 and 28:20) covenant with "the many" or the multitude (Mk 14:24; Mt 26:28), that renders the first one void.

All these elements allow us to say that the Church does not simply succeed Israel; there is not simply the replacement of a failing partner with another that is thought to be better suited to continue the same

---

14. See, for example, Col 3:12, "[You,] God's chosen ones, holy [vocation] and beloved [covenant]."

The People of God

"economy" or plan. There is continuity inasmuch as it is still a question of the one, fundamental plan of God that is continued through history, but the discontinuity is profound: the salvation that had been prepared is now effectively given. The universalism that had been announced is now offered, and all the things that militated against it before (race, language, territory) no longer define the new People.

2. The radical novelty of the Church

The Church appears from the start as the eschatological People. This People is the new humanity.[15] It is God's last word (literally, *eschatos logos*), the final stage of his plan of salvation that has been gradually brought to perfection since the fall of Adam. In Christ everything has been given. This eschatology contains an aspect of becoming, because the passage of unified humanity into the eternal kingdom that is not of this world is something still awaited, not in the manner of a new event that has yet to occur, but rather in the manner of a crop that must grow until the fruit matures. Eschatology has therefore been inaugurated, and everything in this New People, the Church, is turned toward this consummation that will be the final coming of Christ. Thus what the Church lives on and hopes for is not of this world.

Furthermore, the Church understands herself as a People that is not only on earth, but partly in heaven already. This is in keeping with the eschatology that has been inaugurated. The People of the new and eternal covenant does not belong to this world (Jn 18:36); its homeland is in the heavens (Heb 11:16), where its members have their citizenship (Phil 3:20), for they are the children of the Jerusalem on high (Gal 4:26). Nevertheless this People dwells here below. The Church is on pilgrimage on earth, marching toward heaven where she will be perfected, but since the eschatology has been inaugurated, it is one People, the unique Church of Christ, in two distinct states.

This eschatological character and the consequences thereof will allow us to understand how the Church is the priestly, prophetic, and royal people in each of her members and as a whole.

---

15. Cf. Eph 2:15; see also the themes of the New Adam (1 Cor 15:45), the new stock or root (Rom 5:12).

3. Priest, prophet, and king in the New Testament

The trilogy priest-prophet-king is present in the New Testament, but one has to be able to recognize it without those precise words. It is manifested most often and most clearly by Christ, the Anointed One par excellence. His priesthood is the main theme of the Letter to the Hebrews. His prophetic character is expressed from the beginning of his public life when Jesus applies Isaiah 61:1 to himself ("The Spirit of the Lord is upon me; because he has anointed me to preach good news to the poor" Lk 4:18–21). His royal status is manifested in his glorious entrance into Jerusalem (Mt 21:5 refers to Is 62:11 and Zec 9:9); during his sorrowful passion he also lays claim to it before Pilate (Jn 18:36ff.). These references are scattered, but two passages from the Gospels gather them in a way and allow us to rediscover this trilogy as a summary expression of Christ's character. In John 14:6, Jesus declares that he is "the way, and the truth, and the life." Although classical exegesis since patristic times sees here an affirmation of the Savior's humanity (the way) and divinity (truth and life), we can also understand this to refer to the three messianic qualities: "the way" expresses the fact that Jesus guides the faithful toward the Father's house; he is the one who walks ahead of his followers in his capacity as leader or king. "The truth" signifies that Jesus preaches in all truth because he himself is the Word of God, the Logos, the perfection of prophecy. Finally "the life" refers to the Paschal mystery through and in which Jesus gives his life in a sacrificial act of which he is simultaneously priest and victim. Another passage can be cited. In Matthew 23:8–10 Jesus relates himself to various sorts of authorities among the Jewish people (rabbi = teacher; Father = author of life; master = king).[16]

In the final verses of the Gospel of St. Matthew (Mt 28:19–20), the trilogy is found again in terms of the mystery of Christ. All *"exousia"* (authority) has been given to Christ, and he communicates a share in it to his apostles so that they may make disciples of all nations (of-

---

16. One could also cite other passages, particularly in John 6: Jesus leads the multitude (Jn 6:2), who upon seeing the miracle of the multiplication of the loaves try to make him king (Jn 6:15); Jesus works signs (Jn 6:2), and the people say, "This is indeed the prophet who is to come into the world" (Jn 6:14); Jesus presides at the cultic meal (Jn 6:11) provided for the people by the multiplication of the loaves, which are the sign of his flesh offered for the salvation of the world (Jn 6:51) as part of his priestly office.

The People of God

fice of preaching—prophecy), baptize those who believe (baptism as the gateway to all the sacraments—priesthood), and make them observe all the commandments of Christ (conduct—kingship). The disciples are not successors to Christ; they are his vicars, representing him thanks to a specific participation in the anointing that he has received.[17] The threefold character is consequently found in the ministers of the new People.

Finally—and the New Testament is extremely clear about this—the triad designates the Christian status received at baptism and expresses the common Christian identity in the Church. The believer is often considered as a priest inasmuch as his interior acts and dispositions are concerned: Christian life is a liturgy, a sharing in the priesthood of Christ. This teaching is Pauline above all: life as sacrifice, as spiritual worship (esp. Rom 12:1–2). The People in its entirety is priestly based on the common title of its members, the subject of true worship (1 Pt 2:9–10; Rv 1:6; 5:10; 20:6). On the day of Pentecost, Peter declares that the wish of Moses (Nm 11:29) and the prophecy of Joel (Jl 2:28–29) have been fulfilled, that the Spirit would be poured out on all flesh and the sons and daughters of the chosen People would prophesy.[18] St. Paul holds in very high esteem the charism of prophecy in the young Church; it builds up, encourages and consoles (1 Cor 14:3) because it is a proclamation of Christ. The expression "a People of prophets" is not found in Scripture, but the idea is present (cf. Acts 4:31), and even affirmed quite clearly in 1 Jn 2:20 and especially in 1 Jn 2:27 ("but the anointing which you received from him abides in you, and you have no need that any one should teach you"). The kingly title likewise designates a spiritual sovereignty of the Christian and of the communi-

---

17. Note that the conclusion to the Gospel of St. Matthew is ecclesiological (it depicts the privileged position of the apostles as the hierarchy of the new People), whereas that of the Gospel according to St. Luke (Lk 24:36–48) is broader, because Christ appears to all those who were present (the apostles "and those who were with them"; cf. Lk 24:33), making them all his witnesses and promising the Spirit to them all. There is no contradiction between these two evangelists, but rather a clear indication that Christ's anointing has a twofold configuration, one ministerial, the other general or common to all members of the new People. The beginning of the Book of Acts (Acts 1:2–8) emphasizes the apostles alone, but without overlooking other persons (Acts 1:14).

18. Here too we should note the twofold manner of participation: Acts 2:4 = Pentecost of the apostles; Acts 4:31 = Pentecost of the faithful (on this point see the preceding chapter).

ty as well, which is expressed by combining the two terms of priest and king (1 Pt 2:9, "royal priesthood"; Rv 5:10, "a kingdom and priests").

In conclusion, the theme of the People of God allows us to express a certain number of very valuable elements.

The meaning of the OT and its fulfillment by the NT

The Old Testament reality designated by the expression "People of God" has a very rich theological basis, but it is still limited by the ethnic aspect of the Chosen People. The messianic People, tied in the old covenant to a land and a race, becomes in the mystery of Christ a universal People, without any secular defining characteristic, detached from any political or temporal formation. This point is of capital importance in making sure that in Christian theology this theme does not regress to its Old Testament status.

Similarities and dissimilarities between Israel and the Church

Israel is the first-fruits, the olive stock on which the Church is grafted (Rom 11:16–19); in this respect there is a necessary continuity that we must keep in mind along with the elements of discontinuity. For since the coming of Christ, the Church is now the only true Israel, the People of the true covenant of which the old covenant was only a shadow (Col 2:17). Although, in the history of Christian reflection, the specificity of the Church—the element of discontinuity—has been emphasized, in our days we must take care to note also the element of continuity. We will return to this point.

The social structure of salvation

This aspect is extremely important. "People of God" indicates that the messianic community is a reality of the social order—in other words, not just any, but a certain type of human community. We will have to examine this point in greater depth in our study of Tradition, since Scripture limits itself to noting this aspect without elaborating further. Indeed, the Church, unlike Israel, does not assume a sociotemporal dimension in the manner of a political society, but this dimension is not totally foreign to her.

The title "citizen" of this People

The Christian status expressed by the triad priest-prophet-king cannot be reduced to a sociological interpretation: it is fundamentally theological. It can be understood only with reference to the mystery of the humanity assumed by the Word. "People of God" is a reality in the order of grace.

These two last points, social structure and reality of grace, should be kept together. Any distortion that would emphasize one at the expense of the other would falsify our understanding of this theme, thus opening the way for considerable ecclesiological errors.

II. The data of Tradition

The theme of the People of God is omnipresent in Scripture and remains so in Tradition. Tradition goes on to develop in two distinct directions that call for one another to complement and correct each other. There is the development along the lines of the biblical theology based on election, vocation, the covenant, and the three titles (priest, prophet, and king), and the more dogmatic development that emphasizes an interpretation of the People of God starting from the common concept of people.

These two directions are found in the writings of the Fathers. Later on the biblical line of thought is less developed starting with Scholasticism, which becomes more involved in the dogmatic line. With Protestantism the biblical theme returns with considerable force, and this frightens the Catholics who underestimate it.[19] The contemporary theological renewal at first promoted the Body of Christ theme, and only later was the biblical theology of the People of God revisited.

a. Tradition in biblical theology
1. The Church Fathers

So as not to go to excessive lengths in examining these developments, we will be content with short citations illustrating one or another point of the scriptural data; in this way we will show how the Church Fathers appropriate Scripture.

19. We have seen the same thing happen with the Body of Christ theme.

In patristic writings the expression "People of God" is first and foremost the expression of a biblical theme. This theme can be found also in related expressions such as "Zion, Jerusalem, holy city." The Fathers very frequently underscore election, vocation, and covenant. It is difficult to find in their writings a synthetic presentation.

The letter attributed to Barnabas has two parts, one dogmatic, the other moral. The most significant references are found in the dogmatic part:

> Their covenant [at Sinai] was shattered, that the covenant of the beloved Jesus might be sealed in our heart through the hope which the faith in Him holds out.[20]

> If the Lord submitted to suffering for our souls ... [it was] to redeem the promise made to the fathers, and—while preparing for Himself the new people—to give proof while still on earth that He would raise Himself from the dead and then judge.[21]

> I am going to offer my body for the sins of the new people.[22]

> But let us inquire whether our people [the Christians] or the former [the Jews] is the heir, and whether the covenant is intended for us or for them.[23]

The connection between the person of Christ, his sacrifice by which he establishes the new covenant, and the birth of the new People is very neatly made at the very beginning of Tradition. It is true that the teaching of St. Paul is already quite clear. The line of thought here emphasizes the discontinuity between Israel and the Church.

St. Irenaeus, with greater balance, underscores the fulfillment (element of continuity) of Israel in the Church just as much as the entry of the pagans into the new People (element of discontinuity). Commenting on Rom 9:25 ("those who were not my people I will call 'my people'"):

> [Preaching to the pagans, the apostles proclaimed] Christ, who redeemed us from apostasy with His own blood, so that we [the pagans] should also be a sanctified people.[24]

---

20. *Epistle of Barnabas* 4:8 (ACW 6:41).
21. *Epistle of Barnabas* 5:5 and 7 (ACW 6:43).
22. *Epistle of Barnabas* 7:5 (ACW 6:47).
23. *Epistle of Barnabas* 13:1 (ACW 6:56).
24. *Adversus Haereses* III.5.3 (ANF 1:418b); see also I.10.3 and IV.20.12. On the theme of the Church as the true posterity of Abraham, cf. *Adv. Haer.* V.32.2 and V.34.1.

The People of God

The expression "redeemed ... with His own blood" refers to the covenant.

Tertullian, who was more willing to engage in polemics, harped on the theme of the Jews being succeeded by the Church:

And accordingly we, who "were not the people of God" in days bygone, have been made His people, by accepting the new law ... and the new circumcision before foretold.[25]

As for St. Augustine, he underscores the continuity between Israel and the Church:

[God] indeed blessed a certain [family] tree and made it the olive tree, as the Apostle said, the holy Patriarchs themselves, from which blossomed the People of God.[26]

St. Leo the Great speaks about an adopted People:

Among the People of God's adoption, which is priestly and kingly when taken as a whole ..., it is the approval of heavenly grace that engenders the prelate.[27]

St. Basil of Caesarea speaks about election in a passage that we mention because it seems to show that the distinction between *laos* and *ethnos* is becoming blurred:

"Blessed the nation (*ethnos*) whose God is the LORD, the People (*laos*) whom he has chosen as his heritage" (Ps 33[32]:12). No one calls blessed the People (*laos*) of the Jews, but rather this People (*laos*) that has been chosen from among all peoples (*laos*). We are that nation (*ethnos*) whose God is the LORD: we are the People (*laos*) whom he has chosen as his heritage.[28]

To sum up, the Fathers clearly testify to this fundamental conviction about the unity of Revelation and of faith since Abraham. Now this is what constitutes the People of God in the first place in both Testaments: Abraham, Isaac, Jacob are our Fathers, the two covenants form a whole.[29]

---

25. *Adv. Iudaeos* 3 (ANF 3:155a).

26. *Enarrationes in Psalmos* 134.7 (CCSL 40:1943). [Translated from Latin.]

27. *Sermon* III, in PL 54.145b; FOC 93:21–22. The same idea can be found in St. Ambrose, *Apologia of the prophet David* IV.18 (PL 14.859).

28. *Homily on Ps.* 32:7 (PG 29.342b–c). [Translated from French.]

29. St. Irenaeus has some very strong formulas to express this. See *Adv. Haer.* V.32.2 ("For his seed [i.e., the posterity of Abraham] is the Church") (ANF 1:561b).

As for the trilogy priest-prophet-king, the Fathers of the Church do not have synthetic presentations, but they do repeat the scriptural affirmation that only one is truly, totally priest, prophet, and king, namely Christ, and that the faithful are such also by their baptismal configuration to Christ, and for certain ones also by their consecration as ordained ministers.

St. Eusebius of Caesarea is often presented as an initiator of this trilogy, based on the meaning of the word "christ" (anointed one) in the OT:

> Now, the name of Christ adorned not only those among the Hebrews who were honored with the prepared oil as a symbol, but also the kings whom the Prophets at the bidding of God anointed and, as it were, constituted typical Christs [i.e., prefigurations of Christ].... We have also learned through tradition that some of the Prophets themselves had already through anointing become Christs in type, so that all these [the priests, kings, and prophets of the old covenant] have reference to the true Christ, the divine and heavenly Word, who really is the only High Priest of all, the only King of all creation, and the Father's only Archprophet of the Prophets.[30]

This connection between the Old Testament and Christ allows us then to make the connection between Christ and Christians. Thus St. John Chrysostom preaches:

> And what is "anointed" and "sealed" [i.e., what do these words mean in 2 Cor 1:21–22, "Now he ... that hath anointed us is God, who also hath sealed us"]? [Jesus] gave the Spirit by Whom He did both these things, making at once prophets and priests and kings, for in old times these three sorts were anointed. But we have now not one of these dignities, but all three preeminently. For we are both to enjoy a kingdom and are made priests by offering our bodies for a sacrifice (cf. Rom 12:1) and withal we are constituted prophets too: for what things "eye hath not seen, nor ear heard" (1 Cor. 2:9), these have been revealed unto us.[31]

Among the Latin Fathers, St. Augustine says nothing different:

> The name Christ means "the anointed one." ... God anointed [our Lord Jesus Christ] with the oil of gladness, that is, with the Holy Spirit, before

---

30. *Hist. eccl.* I.3.7–8 (PG 20.71a–b); FOC 19:47–48. The whole following passage and chapter 4 show how Christians are configured to Christ according to these three titles. For St. Eusebius, see also *Comm. on Psalm* 2 (PG 29.82).

31. *Homilies on 2 Cor*, Hom. 3.4 (PG 61.411); NPNF 1.12:290a.

The People of God

all His fellows. From that time, those who believed in Him and who were cleansed by the sanctifying power of His baptism have been anointed, not in a limited number as formerly under the old Law, but all, in addition to prophets, priests, and kings.[32]

Concerning the ministers, we can limit ourselves to this very explicit statement concerning the blessing of the oil used during the consecration of a bishop:

If anyone offers oil he [the bishop] shall render thanks in the same manner as for the offering of bread and wine, not saying it word for word, but to the same effect, saying: "O God, sanctify this oil; grant holiness to all who use it and who receive it, and as you anointed kings, priests and prophets, so may it give strength to all who consume it and health to all who use it."[33]

Just as in Scripture these titles are combined in different ways (for example, "royal priesthood"), so too in the patristic Tradition.[34] The kingship, however, tends to be concentrated on the domination of one's passions. Thus St. Hilary of Poitiers:

Those in whom sin does not reign are kings.[35]

The same observation can be made for the Greek Fathers. For example, St. John Chrysostom:

And in another way too we become kings: if we have the mind to get dominion over our unruly thoughts.[36]

---

32. *De vita christiana* I.1, (PL 40.1033); translation in *Treatises on Various Subjects* (New York: Fathers of the Church, 1952), 10–11.
33. *On the Apostolic Tradition* 5, an English version with introduction and commentary by Alistair Stewart-Sykes (Crestwood, N.Y.: St. Vladimir's Seminary Press, 2001), 76.
34. Christ received a unique anointing that constitutes him priest and king at the same time: St. Hippolytus of Rome, *Comm. on Daniel* IV.30 (SC 14:325). See also St. Clement of Alexandria, II *Stromata* V.21–22 (ANF 2:449b) (prophet and king). The titles of prophet and priest call for each other, as St. Paul teaches: to win souls by teaching the doctrine of the Gospel is to prepare for God a true priestly oblation (cf. Rom 15:15–16, "the grace given me by God to be a minister of Christ Jesus to the Gentiles in the priestly service of the gospel of God, so that the offering of the Gentiles may be acceptable, sanctified by the Holy Spirit"). Similarly, for the titles of prophet and king, St. Ambrose declares, "Those are kings who have received the grace to speak..., those who have been appointed by Christ as ministers of the New Testament"; *In Ps 118* 6.34 (PL 15.1279c) [translated from French].
35. *In Ps 135* 6 (CSEL 22:717) [translated from French].
36. *Homilies on 2 Cor 1:21*, Hom. III.5 (PG 61.411); NPNF 1.12:290a.

From these examples, selected from among many others, we should take away the testimony of the lively awareness among the Fathers of the Church that they have received the novelty of Christ along with all the announcements and preparations of the Old Testament. This attitude is exemplary.

2. Tradition after the patristic era

The themes of election, vocation, and covenant are omnipresent. The traditional patristic schema, according to which the Church succeeds Israel, which has lost all its privileges, also persists. The Church is the people that has received the fulfillment of the Promise. In other words, the dissimilarity between Israel and the Church prevails over the element of continuity. Above all we wish to elaborate on the triad priest-prophet-king because some have maintained that the Latin Catholic tradition had forgotten it during the Middle Ages, and that it was retrieved only by the work of the Reformers.[37] A much more nuanced account is necessary.

St. Thomas Aquinas

St. Thomas is not unaware of the triad, which he mentions several times. In his works it gains a clarity that is due to the development of the doctrine of the grace of Christ. Christ, as Head of redeemed humanity, has the fullness of grace. This fullness is manifested at first in the fact that he personally holds all three titles, whereas in Israel they were assigned to distinct persons:

> Christ, as being the Head of all, has the perfection of all graces. Wherefore, as to others, one is a lawgiver [similar to a prophet], another is a priest, another is a king; but all these concur in Christ, as the fount of all grace. (ST III, q. 22, art. 1, ad 3)

There were three anointings under the Old Law: Aaron was anointed for the priesthood (Lv 8:12); Saul was anointed by Samuel for the kingship (1 Sam 10:1), and so was David (1 Sm 16:13); and Elisha was anointed to become a prophet (1 Kgs 19:16). That is why Jesus is rightly called "christ" because he was a true priest ..., king, and prophet.[38]

---

37. This is the thesis of M. Fuchs, presented by Yves Congar, "Une trilogie ecclésiologique," *RSPT* (1969): 185–211.

38. *Super Mt.*, c. 1, lect. 1, Marietti no. 19 [translated from French]; cf. also no. 20 and

The People of God

The trilogy is applied also to the apostles:

A threefold office has been conferred by Christ. First to teach ["go and make disciples"]; second, to baptize ["baptizing them"]; third, to regulate everything concerned with behavior ["teaching them to observe all that I have commanded you"].[39]

[The apostles are God's ministers in three matters]: first inasmuch as they dispense the sacraments.... Secondly inasmuch as they govern the People of God.... Thirdly inasmuch as many are converted by their ministry and preaching.[40]

Finally, it is applied to the baptized:

This anointing [of Christ] also befits Christians, for they are kings and priests (1 Pt 2:9).... Furthermore, He has the Holy Spirit, Who is the spirit of prophecy.... Therefore, all are anointed with an invisible anointing.[41]

This demonstrates that the Latin medieval period had indeed received this patristic doctrine. But we must explain why references to this trilogy at the time of the Reformation were less clear-cut in Latin Catholic writers. Indeed, after the thirteenth century a certain concentration on the idea of priesthood occurred. The precise notion of priesthood (offering sacrifice) came to coexist with a broader notion, for which indications can be found as early as the thirteenth century in St. Thomas. The broad notion includes the two other titles, because it expresses the idea of *mediator*. In the *Summa theologiae*, in the treatise on the Incarnate Word, we find only one question about the offices of Christ, which are classified under the broad term of priesthood (III, q. 22). This priesthood-mediation brings about the descending relation from God to men (he transmits divine things to men) and the ascending relation from men to God (he presents to God what comes from men). In the descending direction, the priest-mediator, in the first place Christ, transmits truth (prophet), divine life (priest), and guidance (king). This question 22 (a. 1, corpus and ad 3) is where St. Thomas spells out the trilogy. In the Middle Ages both the broad and the

---

c. 16, lect. 2, 1374. See also *ST* III, q. 31, art. 2, corpus, which says that Christ is the son of Abraham and of David because Christ is king, prophet, and priest; cf. also *In Ps. 44*, no. 5.

39. *Super Mt.* c. 28, lect. 1, Marietti no. 2462.
40. *Super 2 Cor.*, Prologue, no. 2; translation by Fabian Larcher, OP.
41. *Super Heb.* c. 1, lect. 4, no. 64; translation by Fabian Larcher, OP.

strict notions of priesthood were still kept together, but later the tendency was increasingly to retain only the broad notion.[42] From the nineteenth century on the precise notion would be used again, bringing with it the complementary features of the two other offices.

b. Tradition in dogmatic theology

Parallel to the biblical tradition, the People of God theme lent itself to the development of a concept of the Church starting from the common experience of human social life. Here, too, as in biblical theology, we must not follow particular words slavishly; although the word "people" is often used, its content can be expressed by other terms also, such as "civil society," "kingdom," and "Sion."

1. The Fathers of the Church

Several testimonies by church Fathers from different cultures neatly illustrate this Tradition. Thus St. John Chrysostom writes:

> The other cities can be called cities of God only by the sole title of creation, whereas Zion is such also by virtue of the intimate ties that unite it to God, and because that is where God worked all his miracles. That city (Jerusalem) was called the City of God, but now we all belong to God.[43]

Here we have two levels that are carefully distinguished: on the one hand the general plan that is valid for all mankind, which regards any people as already being the People of God because it is a work of God, the Creator of all that exists. Every people, consequently, bears a certain stamp of divine creation. Israel was People of God at that level already, but above and beyond that by a more particular title: in the midst of this People, God performed his marvelous works, which implies election, vocation, and the covenant. The Church is called People of God because now these "intimate ties" belong to those who profess Christ.

---

42. For the tradition after St. Thomas until the twentieth century, see in the bibliography the study by R. Vaillancourt.

43. *Super Ps. 47*, no. 1 (PG 55.217) [translated from French]. Cited in a more literary French translation (Bareille, *Oeuvres* [Paris: 1868], 9:243) by Yves Congar, "Peuple de Dieu dans l'Église ancienne," in *Rencontre: Actes du colloque judéo-chrétien sur le Peuple de Dieu* (Strasbourg: 1970), 36.

The People of God

Among the Latin Fathers, St. Augustine seems to treat the subject most extensively:

when God is in you, you will be of Zion, a member of Zion, a citizen of Zion, belonging to the society of the People of God.[44]

The word *societas* in the expression "society of the People of God" does not have the restricted sense that it has acquired in French and other modern languages (the juridical structure of the State). In Latin it has the sense of "community," expressing the fact of coexistence in general.

Of course, *The City of God* is the work in which the Bishop of Hippo gives his definition of "people" at the natural level:

[A people is] a multitude bound together by a mutual recognition of rights and a mutual cooperation for the common good.[45]

However, this definition, it seems, is not applied by St. Augustine to the People of God, either of the Old Testament or of the New.[46] Cicero's definition, however, through St. Augustine, would dominate all of Latin theology, not only for political theology, but also, later on, for ecclesiology. Indeed, we find in it the initial elements: a consensus about the law (which presupposes the law that expresses it and is the work of a legislator: the perspective of authority); a community of interests, in other words, mutual service for the common good governed by political friendship (the perspective of the flourishing of the subjects). These elements can easily be transposed to the People of God. St. Augustine did not elaborate on it; medieval theology would do so.

2. St. Thomas Aquinas

St. Thomas often uses the Ciceronian definition of people that St. Augustine had adopted. For example:

---

44. *Enarr. in Ps.* 98 (CCSL 39:1381) [translated from Latin].
45. Augustine, *City of God* II.21.2; FOC 8.1:108. This definition is taken from Cicero, *De Republica* I.25.42. It is mentioned also in *City of God* XIX.21.1; FOC 8.3:232.
46. See the references in the previous note and also *City of God* XIX.23.5; FOC 8/3:242–43, which clearly deals with the Roman people. On this point see Yves Congar, "People de Dieu dans l'Église ancienne," 38. Probably St. Augustine's Platonism was what prevented him from seeing in natural social reality an analogy for the social aspect of grace that constitutes the Church.

When [men] consent to the rights of the divine law in order to be useful to each other and tend toward God, then they are God's People.[47]

Unanimity in the divine Law reflects unity of faith, and serving the common good and tending toward God reflects charity.

It is interesting to cite another passage in this regard. Commenting on Eph 4:5–6, "One Lord, one faith, one baptism, one God and Father of us all, who is above all and through all and in all," St. Thomas writes:

> Since the Church is likened to civil society [*civitas*], it is one and distinct, although this unity is not uncomposed but composed of different parts. Thus the Apostle does two things: First, he shows what is common in the Church. Secondly, he shows what is distinctive [to each member] in her (Eph 4:7).
>
> The solidarity of any civil society demands the presence of four common elements: one governor, one law, the same symbols, and a common goal. The Apostle affirms that these are present in the Church also.
>
> Hence, he says: You ought to have one body and one spirit since you belong to the one unified Church.
>
> First, she has one leader, Christ. Obeying "one Lord," not many, conflicts do not arise from trying to comply with divergent commands....
>
> Secondly, her law is one. For the law of the Church is the law of faith.... "One faith" [as the Apostle says] designates the unity of the habit of faith by which all believe....
>
> Thirdly, the Church shares the same symbols. They are Christ's sacraments, of which baptism is the first and the entrance to the rest. Hence [the Apostle] says "one baptism...."
>
> Fourthly, the Church has the same goal, God. The Son leads us to the Father.... In reference to this the Apostle adds "one God."[48]

This Tradition, however, would undergo in the modern era, from the nineteenth century on, an important modification that is the cause of its relative disappearance.

---

47. *Super Heb.* 8:10, 406; translation by Fabian Larcher, OP. In the passage commented on, the Letter to the Hebrews cites Jer 31:31–34: "I will put my law within them, I will write it upon their hearts; and I will be their God, and they shall be my people."

48. *Super Eph.* 4:5–6, Marietti 198–201; English translation by Matthew L. Lamb, OCSO, *Commentary on Saint Paul's Epistle to the Ephesians* (Albany, N.Y.: Magi Books, 1966), 154–57.

3. Modern developments[49]

The dogmatic tradition of the People of God theme is based on an analogy with social reality (or civil society). The concept was provided either by Stoic philosophy or else by Aristotelian philosophy. The latter was increasingly preferred after the time of St. Thomas. Now in the modern age a new philosophical approach has gradually replaced the old one. Hence there is a serious risk of misunderstanding. Since Vatican II gave a highly developed teaching about what a civil society is, it is appropriate to make the distinctions necessary for the ecclesiological analogy. We will present briefly these three main points.

The classical analysis of society and ecclesiology

Ancient philosophy was unanimous in recognizing that man is a *social* animal (Stoics) or a *political* being (Aristotelians). We will show how St. Thomas Aquinas repeats, explains, and completes the Aristotelian view.

St. Thomas faithfully cites Aristotle to give the fundamental data of the social reality—namely, its natural character, its end (which is the common good), and the means for its unity.

Man is a political animal. This is a statement made very frequently in various forms (for example *ST* I-II, q. 95, art. 4), so often that St. Thomas usually does not bother to justify it; it goes without saying, given the previous demonstrations. The proof in *De Regno* (I.1) shows that Aquinas adopts as his own the statements of Aristotle, which he paraphrases at length. Man cannot live alone and lives in society. This necessity *of nature* can be observed in the *fact* that human beings—unlike animals—are not naturally endowed with food, clothing, and means of self-defense. In short, they are not equipped to live alone. A human being does, however, possess the distinctive gift of reason, which is expressed in language, thus making him capable of communicating with others of his species. Through this association of several

49. I summarize here two of my articles published in the *Revue Thomiste:* "'Société' et 'communion'" chez Saint Thomas d'Aquin: Étude d'ecclésiologie," *RT* 90 (1990): 587–98 (for the notion of society in St. Thomas); "L'Église comme société et l'Église comme communion au deuxième concile du Vatican," *RT* 91 (1991): 219–26, 236–43 (for the notion of society in modern philosophy and at Vatican II).

individuals (society), man can live. This strict dependence on Aristotle shows us that St. Thomas adopts as his own the Philosopher's method, which, as we know, is based on observation of the social *fact*.

The purpose of society is the *common good*. Its aim is to assure that its members *live well*: "The aim for which civil society was originally established is to provide a living—in other words, to prepare the conditions allowing men to have a sufficiency of what they need to live."[50] This statement is about the *natural and temporal* common good. This common good is primarily of a spiritual nature. It aims at the *moral* formation and development of man: "Man is aided by the multitude of which he is a part to ensure a perfect life, i.e., not only to live but to live well, having at his disposal all that he requires to live ..., not only with regard to bodily goods ..., but also with regard to spiritual goods."[51] This *moral* end is essential in order for a group of human beings to be a society. The other ends (economic, self-defense) are secondary. Civil society thus appears as a framework for life that, by reason of its end, has the role of an instrument of perfection so that men might progress in virtue, the only means of living *well*.

This social end is already a principle of unity. The *common* pursuit of the *common* good of all brings about an initial form of unity. Subordinate to this service are other causes of unity that must assure, in turn, the continuation of the tendency toward the end. Here too St. Thomas faithfully follows Aristotle in noting the predominant role of government and law.

The common good unites the whole [of society] with regard to the particular interest, which, in and of itself, does not unite, but distinguishes or even sets up an opposition; the government of the multitude is what ensures that the tendency toward the common good prevails. The government is what moves the multitude toward the good that is *common* to the whole, as an application of the principle that we can call "hierarchy": "In all things that are ordained towards one end,

---

50. Thomas Aquinas, *Sententia libri Politicorum*, in *Opera omnia*, Leonine ed. 48 (Rome: 1972), Book I, lectio 1b, A77, 19ff. [translated from French, which interprets the Latin]; see also Aquinas's commentary, book 3, lectio 5.

51. Thomas Aquinas, *Sententia libri Ethicorum*, in *Opera omnia*, Leonine edition, vol. 47/1 (Rome: 1969), Book 1, lectio 1, page 4, lines 68–75. Note that "spiritual" does not necessarily mean "supernatural" but rather "incorporeal."

The People of God

one thing is found to rule the rest."⁵² This principle guiding the parts so that they constitute a *social* whole takes the form of a government (a person or a group of persons who are members of that society), which is responsible for making sure that the tendency toward the common good prevails and, in case of conflict, for giving priority to the common good over a particular interest.

The government acts in the first place by enacting laws: "A law, properly speaking, regards first and foremost the order to the common good."⁵³ The law regulates, stimulates, and orders the life of the people with a view to the common good; this is affirmed everywhere in the treatise devoted to law in the *Summa theologiae*.

These explanations already indicate to us the nature of the unity that makes society. We are not talking here about a substantial unity like the one that holds together the members of a biological body, but about a particular *moral* unity that aims at a precise *order* among the parts for a common end: to establish the common good. For this reason it is called the *unity of order*.

This is the Aristotelian foundation for the subsequent Thomistic developments.

To declare that man, by virtue of a natural requirement, is *political* amounts to saying that society is fundamentally good, like the human nature that requires it; it is, in a certain way, like the prolongation thereof. This gives a very positive content to social reality. St. Thomas thereby sidesteps the whole Augustinian line of thinking, which regards society instead as an inevitable affliction resulting from original sin, or at least as a remedy to its effects. Aquinas clearly states, "man is naturally a social being, and so in the state of innocence he would have led a social life."⁵⁴ It follows that the means necessary to social life that are connected with this requirement of nature (government and law) are not founded on a deliberate agreement of the subjects, nor is their existence subject to man's consent. Nature demands them and is the basis for their legitimacy in principle. Society and its main institutions are founded in nature; they are not solely or even primarily the work of culture. In this respect the Thomistic view of society diverges radically

---

52. *De Regno* I.1.9; trans. Gerald B. Phelan, rev. I. Th. Eschmann, OP.
53. *Summa theologiae* I-II, q. 90, art. 3.
54. *ST* I, q. 96, art. 4.

from modern theories resulting from the thesis of the social contract.

The second specifically Thomistic development is what we can call the "law of solidarity." When one accentuates the intellectual dimension of man, one sees that the human intellect is essentially *reason*. Man does not grasp truth immediately as an angel does, but rather arrives at it gradually starting from sensory experience, and by way of instruction, since no one by himself can make all the necessary observations. Thus man only attains his full, typically human development little by little with the help of others. He is teachable and trainable. Here again we are talking about something given by nature and not about any consequence of original sin.[55]

Consequently it is part of the nature of a rational being—a nature as God created it and before the wound of original sin (which only reinforces this need for solidarity, but does not create it)—to need others in order to be truly oneself. This is the natural foundation of society, which is obviously more profound than the mere requirements of economic life or of the biological reproduction of the species. This "law of solidarity," decreed by the Creator at the very beginning of our world, is what leads man to the necessity of living with others like him.

However, this natural solidarity does not produce a community that is fully realized by nature, as is the case for animals that live together (bees, ants). The human community demanded by nature is brought about by reason (culture), which achieves the goal of nature. For example, the precise constitutional form of the government (monarchy, aristocracy, democracy) will be determined by the culture of the place and of the moment.

This obligatory solidarity is manifested also by the fact that the gifts generously distributed by the Creator to his creatures are not identical in everyone, but rather are different, varied, and *complementary*. One person will have intellectual qualities, another manual dexterity, another an accurate memory. Only in the aggregate do human beings combine all the qualities necessary for the life *of each one*. St. Thomas thus affirms without hesitation that in the age of innocence—if there had been social life—the men better endowed with knowledge and justice would have had to watch over the others, particularly in governing civil

55. *ST* I, q. 101, art. 1 and 2.

society.[56] We have here, as it were, the root of man's natural sociability: because the Creator has deposited with one individual what his neighbor lacks in order to be truly himself, he is naturally drawn to will what is good for his neighbor and vice versa. That is why this bond of social exchanges is called *political friendship*. This friendship is in the first place *useful*. We are still in the order of nature here.

This aspect of the law of solidarity is called political friendship. Friendship is not only an act or a series of acts; it is a *state*, a certain stable affective situation (which is therefore voluntary) between two or more persons or within a group.[57] It is expressed in acts, but does not cease with them. The virtuous progress of this *useful* friendship makes it tend to become a form of benevolence (willing another's good for his own sake), which, when it is reciprocal, is fulfilled in a perfect friendship. The friendship becomes disinterested so that imperfections in reciprocity do not cause it to disappear. This reciprocity indicates that a certain good is willed by all—the good of the whole—and this is why it is called the *common good*.

When the group in question is civil society, this friendship will be called *political* friendship. This friendship brings about at its level the unity of the group by providing its truly formal principle: through it, everyone knows that he is and wills to be part of a whole that surpasses him and, in due order, has a prior claim to his service. Through this virtuous disposition each one pursues the flourishing of all, and it is in pursuing this flourishing of the group as such that the particular subject benefits from the conditions necessary for bringing about his own good. In other words, it is a question first of everyone building the common good together and then proceeding to the distribution of this common good to each one; this is a major sphere of the virtue of justice: *distributive* justice.

Thus political friendship, *convivium*, is like the "soul" of society. Where it is absent (discord or, worse, sedition), society disappears. For St. Thomas and his School, one cannot speak about civil society without necessarily including its formal element, which is, so to speak, its principle of life, unity, and dynamism. This "soul" of civil society announces its presence in the acts by which men exchange among them-

---

56. *ST* I, q. 96, art. 4.
57. *ST* II-II, q. 23, art. 1.

selves, by benevolence and friendship, what is necessary for the good of the whole and, consequently, of each one.

Solidarity, therefore, is something given that presides over the foundation and the life of civil society. It shows that, of all the forms of human sociability (the family, the clan), only civil society has in and of itself the wherewithal to meet all the indispensable conditions for the full flourishing of its members. Civil society and it alone can respond to all the needs of each member. The family is too restricted a context, one that "specializes," so to speak, in the generation and initial education of the child. Its development into the village and then into a federation of villages[58] results not only from biological constraints (population growth) and their economic corollaries, but in the first place from the need to be able to educate the human being suitably—in other words, to make him grow up *morally*. This complete character of civil society is expressed in the classical remark that civil society alone is the perfect society. "Perfect" is understood here in its *ontological* sense (a "complete" being) and not in the moral sense (a sinless being).

Finally, there is a third point where the adoption of Aristotle's thought by St. Thomas is clearly marked by Christianity. We mean the relations of the individual with the group. It is important to avoid two excesses: individualism that gives the individual priority over the group and totalitarianism that gives the group priority over the individual. In short, the common good is logically prior to the particular good, since the latter depends on the former; hence from the perspective of the common good that is to be attained, the part exists for the whole. Society therefore has a claim on the whole man, body and soul, in all his faculties, for its end, which is the common good. But the common good is called to guarantee the conditions for the particular good. Thus there will be a distribution that terminates in the particular. This shows that the social end is not man's ultimate end; his end is his own good. This proper end requires solidarity, not only as a means, but also as an end: it is in developing his altruism that man perfects himself morally. These refinements are not typically Christian per se. What is specifically Christian is the intervention of an end that is not temporal: the supernatural end. Man has a transcendent end (beatitude) that

---

58. This is the process that, according to Aristotle, gives rise to civil society; St. Thomas adopts it: see *De Regno* I.2.

is not of the same order as the social end and is neither detrimental to nor in competition with it. Yet these ends are interrelated, because the same persons have these two ends. The final and ultimate (supernatural) end must be served—in due order—by all the other ends that are only intermediary. This is the basis for the distinction and the relation between the temporal and the spiritual.

Therefore, it will be up to the social authority to make sure that the social end remains *subordinate* to the supernatural end, which does not necessarily mean that civil society must be confessional when some Christians are members of it. There must be at least *respect* for this order, and therefore civil society cannot *require* anything in the social order that would be contrary to the supernatural order. (One can and one must often tolerate something contrary, however.) The effective principle of order in society (the government) has here something like a criterion for moral goodness in its actions.

We should emphasize, finally, that St. Thomas found in Scripture the justification of the natural need for every social group to have a government: "Where there is no governor, the people shall fall" (Prv 11:14, according to the Douay-Rheims translation). This need for a principle of order is formulated as follows: "In every multitude there must be some governing power."[59] In a Christian and more immediately theological context, this clarification is important. The governmental institution in a society is necessary for its life. The distinction frequently made nowadays between "structure" and "life" proves to be very ticklish to apply, because the structure transmits, educates, guides, and regulates life, which could not grow normally and endure without it.

Summary definition of society

In order to formulate a definition of society we can make use of the four causes of natural philosophy. This demonstrates nicely that the various elements form a *single* reality called "political society."

- At the level of the material cause, it is about man as a political animal. We can add, secondarily, the place where the group is established (the territory), which is more or less extensive depending on the intensity of the formal cause.

59. *De Regno* I.1.9.

- At the level of the formal cause, *convivium*, political friendship, will be what causes each member always to live and act in social life as part of a whole.
- At the level of efficient cause we should mention nature that is supported and fulfilled through reason by means of a government, the first competence of which is to enact laws (secondary competence: seeing to it that they are carried out—*executive*—and imposing sanctions when they are disregarded—*judiciary*).
- At the level of the final cause, it is a question of "living well," the pursuit of the common good of the whole as the prerequisite for the particular good.

Hence the following definition: society is the group that men form by political friendship, assisted by authority, with a view to living well.

Based on this reality—society in its proper and not metaphorical sense—St. Thomas proposes an analogy to define the Church. We looked earlier at the commentary on Eph 4:5–6 by St. Thomas. We find in it the analogy of civil society. It can be summarized as follows:

- The head: just as every civil society must have a governor, so too the Church must have a head, who is Christ.
- The law: just as civil society is ruled by one and the same law, so too for the Church there is the law of faith, an object to be believed (God) that is identical for all.
- The *insignia* (distinctive marks): just as all the members of the same civil society have a common mark (citizenship), so too in the Church all the faithful have this common distinctive sign—namely, the sacraments, in particular baptism, the gateway to all the others.
- The end: just as civil society is established with a view to the common good, so too for the Church this common good is a share in the beatitude of God the Father, through the Son, in the Spirit.

In his close reading of the passage from the Letter to the Ephesians, St. Thomas does not explicitly mention political friendship, which corresponds by way of analogy to charity. Nevertheless, it is implied, if only in the *insignia:* the citizens in the Church are those who are united by the political friendship that is the charity communicated by the sacraments. We could summarize this definition as follows: The Church is

The People of God 235

the City of God—in other words, the totality of human beings governed by Christ, united in faith and charity, for the sake of eternal glory.

The analogy with political society, on this philosophical basis, produced in the nineteenth century the ecclesiology called *Ecclesia, societas perfecta inaequalis*.[60] This is clearly attested to, for example, in the writings of Leo XIII.[61] But since the end of the nineteenth century this line of ecclesiological thought has been disturbed by important developments in social philosophy, so that many ecclesiological accounts have assumed the form of a "hierarchology," as Fr. Congar put it.[62] In order to understand this, we must now present the major trends in modern social philosophy. We will look then at the refinements brought about by Vatican II (*Gaudium et spes*). It is necessary to be aware of this: to speak today about the Church as a "perfect society" can lead to the most serious misunderstandings. Let us see why.

Trends in modern social thought

The nineteenth century was a time of great social upheavals. The characteristic approach of those who reflected on human reality, i.e., *social reality*, was to consider predominantly the *will* in their analysis of human acts and to limit their reflection to *phenomena* (lack of metaphysics). The prevailing tendency was to consider political society as a reality that is above all juridical and utilitarian: it was a question of expressing with this old word *society* the political power necessary for the development and protection of economic structures. Thus people would talk, for example, about democratic society (power structure) and liberal society (economic system). But authors noted also that the true human good of all the citizens could not be reduced to these technical considerations: it is of a spiritual nature. As before, philosophers persisted in thinking that man, by living with others like himself, pursued his own *moral* fulfillment. Hence, if the objective of the so-called social group is not to respond to this demand, it will be up to another sort of group to do so: the *communion* or the *community*.

60. The "inequality" signifies that in this community there is a distinction—not moral, but official—between the governors and the governed.
61. Analysis by Charles Journet, *L'Église du Verbe incarné*, 2:1186ff.
62. The expression means that the Church is understood above all in terms of her hierarchical part (which accounts for efficient causality alone), and not as a total community of pastors and faithful (the perspective of final causality above all).

These preliminaries seem to set the tone for all modern social philosophy. Human life in common depends on *two* formally distinct groups. Communion expresses the predominant attention to the person and to "life"; society represents the necessary, but subordinate technical structure.

Historical events (phenomena) at the time of the birth of this new worldview allow us to explain the appearance of this distinction within social reality. The nineteenth century in Europe was the age of the birth of the great modern nations, a birth that did not take place without difficulties. The question at stake in all the political battles was to determine the meaning of a constitutional government. Many revolutions were attempted or succeeded. As a result of this instability, the economy was unstable. In short, the immediate institutional and economic future was never certain. In that context it was indeed necessary to be able to give an account of some kind of permanence in social reality, and this permanence could be observed only at the level of more restricted groups that were neither institutional nor directly economic; these were the ones that were called communions or communities. However, once those political and economic circumstances were gone, the distinction between society and communion would persist and would even become surprisingly widespread.

The closeness of union in communion is noted in contrast to the external unity in society. Many philosophers, especially those whose approach is personalist (one of the first was Max Scheler), would develop this simple idea, which maintains that the "material" demands of men are satisfied by society, and that his spiritual and moral requirements, his private and emotional life, are the province of more informal groups that would most often be called communions. For example, for Emmanuel Mounier society is the legal, juridical, social, and economic system of the common life, and the community is formed by the love that one "I" bears for a "thou," from which results a "we."[63]

Right away we see that this broad current of modern social philosophy has broken up the unity of the social *reality* with its notion of two *formally* different kinds of human groups. Society is a group with a unifying principle of a juridical sort (the submission of the will to the au-

---

63. *RT* (1991): 221–23 (in particular note 5).

thority and its laws), which imposes constraints with a view to *utilitarian* and especially economic ends. The social bond is purely external; it in no way implies the equality of the members, but rather their classification into those who command and those who obey. Moreover, this group assumes various forms in different times and places. This contrasts, point by point, with a communion: its principle of unity is love, which implies stability, intimacy, and equality, and its end is strictly moral (the flourishing of its members). The conclusion that can be drawn from this approach is the following: in man's life it is not society, but communion that allows him to respond to his deepest demands. Therefore it will be necessary to make sure that society remains within its subordinate parameters, that it does not succumb to the totalitarian temptation by suppressing the communion or communions that coexist, not within it, but "alongside" of it.

It is easy to gauge the profound change of perspective in comparison to the classic concept inherited from Aristotle and St. Thomas. The point of departure seems to be the abandonment by modern thinkers of the affirmation that man is *naturally* inclined to social life, an inclination that is perfected by reason, which achieves nature's purpose. Once it is affirmed that social life originates in the *will* (the idea of the social contract as an agreement of wills is the implicit or explicit presupposition of contemporary reflection), society can only appear as a construct of the mind (a cultural datum) in order to respond to *utilitarian* needs. It is a question of a (more or less empirical) technical framework that can vary according to the culture. On the contrary, the flourishing of the individual, which is a demand that everyone bears within himself, requires a freedom that is understood as the absence or maximum limitation of constraint. What makes this freedom possible is not the social framework, but rather a communitarian life that is as informal as possible. Consequently the notion of the common good has changed. It is no longer made up of the *totality* of the conditions necessary for the flourishing of man in *all* his aspects, and thus a reality that is *prior* to the particular good, but rather is merely an economic datum of a technical sort; this is called *the general interest*.

These philosophical perceptions directly influenced sociology, unless the converse is true. Sociology analyzes the *external* manifestations of the social *phenomenon*. It does so in freedom from any philosophy (at least of any explicit philosophy), and the notions that it employs can vary greatly from one author to the next. This science appears like a dense forest in which it is not easy to clear a path. One trail can be discerned, however, and it is precisely the distinction or separation between society and communion (or community). Generally accepted nowadays, it is used extensively, so that one can detect real affinities between sociology and modern social philosophy.

This distinction in sociology seems to have late-nineteenth-century German beginnings.[64] For brevity's sake, we can say that these thinkers conceptualize two forms of human groups, one modeled on the living organism (the community), the other analogous to a machine produced by human industry (society). The community is a natural datum (the typical community is the family), and society is a cultural datum that comes into existence through human reason in the following circumstances: close solidarity, caused by the unity of sentiments that forms the community, ceaselessly runs the risk of breaking up as a result of personal rivalries, economic difficulties, and demographic growth. Therefore a supplementary, constraining framework of a juridical sort is necessary in order to fight constantly against this tendency toward the fragmentation of the community: this is society. The latter is therefore a sort of structure, a solution of practical reason to mitigate the disorderly swarming of "life." But the richness, depth, and reality of human life are found in the community.

This fundamental perception is adopted by twentieth-century sociology and elaborated with the help of scientific psychology. From this distinction between community and society (thus understood) it follows that "the communitarian hold on men is always deeper than the societal hold. The awareness of the 'we' is more intimate and radical than pressure and constraint. The community therefore surpasses society."[65] The authors take care to explain that no community exists in a pure state, separate from any sort of society whatsoever, because no community can do without the stability provided by juridical society.

By society sociologists mean the product of the will that constrains for economic reasons: this is the juridical framework necessary for

---

64. *RT* (1991): 223–26.
65. F. Perroux and R. Prieur, *Communauté et société*, 2nd ed. (Paris: 1942), 15. These authors belong to the personalist school (E. Mounier).

material subsistence. In return, the community or the communion is the work of the will of its members that thus constructs the immediate framework for life and flourishing. This emphasis on the will is the main thing that sociology borrows from modern social philosophy. In both cases, thinkers refrain from inquiring into the determining causes: the will to live together in communion and the consent to social constraint are observed absolutes, and there is no attempt to bring to light the basis for them: It is a fact to be taken for granted.

In a word, in sociology as in social philosophy, it is postulated that man in this world will have *two* ways, neither reducible to the other, of being with others like himself: On the one hand the personal, intimate, egalitarian, and voluntary relation, and on the other hand the purely utilitarian, hierarchical association to which one must necessarily consent. This thesis of the voluntary origin of common life is an unproven postulate. The point of departure of Aristotle and St. Thomas seems more reliable: we observe that man never lives alone because *in all aspects of his life* he needs others like himself. Thus we posit an empirical basis for the fact of human life in common, whereas modern thought is wrong, in our opinion, to consider in the abstract fully formed subjects who supposedly decide to join in communion and to consent to society. In the one view, one recognizes a prior cause for common life that reason receives and harnesses (the nature-nurture relation), while in the other view only a voluntary cause is postulated (culture). Whether we like it or not, this modern concept is not based on observation of the (universal and constant) social reality, but on what must be called a myth (such as the one about the noble savage by Jean-Jacques Rousseau).

The concept of social authority is also quite different. What modern thinkers picture as a juridical, constraining structure limited to material life was perceived in a broader, all-encompassing way by ancient philosophers. For them government is responsible for right dispositions concerning the common good (the broad, all-encompassing concept of the common good) and of leading the citizens to it and of distributing its fruits. Finally, political friendship as the social bond in civil society seems to us richer and deeper than the mere notion of interest that supposedly justifies social life (love being found only in communion).

There has been no lack of theologians who have constructed an analogy to define the Church upon such foundations from social philosophy (if not simple sociology). They say then that the Church is at the same time a society because of all its hierarchical, external, and constraining features and a communion because of all that is egalitarian, intimate, and free within it. We will run across this notion again in the speculative part, because what is at stake here is the *unity* of the ecclesial being. Indeed, society and communion are formally distinct groups: what makes up society *is not* what makes up communion, and vice versa. Consequently, to say that in the Church everything involved with its aspect as the means of salvation is accomplished in ecclesiastical society, and everything involved with its aspect as the reality of salvation is accomplished in ecclesial communion, *necessarily* leads to recognizing that *two realities* make up the Church, and not one reality—which is complex, to be sure, yet *one*—as we saw noted in *Lumen gentium* 8, §1. That is the very substantial defect of this theology. Vatican II carefully avoided talking about the Church in these terms, and it is not by accident.

The principal social data of Vatican II

After the elements of social philosophy that we have reviewed in the preceding discussions, it is good to know how Vatican II spoke about the social reality. The council did so extensively in the Constitution *Gaudium et spes* (Part I, chap. 2). The Council refers explicitly to the Encyclicals *Mater et magistra, Pacem in terris,* and *Ecclesiam suam.* We limit ourselves here to the main references. The details would be a matter for an academic course or treatise on justice (the social teaching of the Church).

Man is *naturally* sociable (*GS* 25).

Life in society is necessary for the full development of man. This is a necessity of nature that gives rise to two fundamental communities, the family and civil society. The others kinds of groups are only useful. Note in this regard that the Fathers of Vatican II did not adopt the distinction between society and communion. The terms "society," "community," and "communion" are interchangeable in *Gaudium et spes*.

The purpose of social life (GS 26).

The Council elaborates here the traditional notion of the common good, understood as the sum total of conditions necessary for the flourishing of both the group and the individual. The perfection of the group is to serve the perfection of the individual. Thus every society as such must tend toward a good that is proper to it but ordered to the good of each member.

Government and laws (GS 74).

The necessity of civil government has its basis in nature since it is indispensable to society, which is itself required by nature. Its role is to unify the group by orienting all toward the common good; it acts in the first place by establishing just laws.

The social bond that unites the citizens (GS 24–25).

This bond is fundamentally love of neighbor (political friendship), which is manifested in just relations with others, mutual service, and peaceful dialogue. Pride and selfishness are the two vices that undermine the *convivium* necessary for all social life.

This rapid survey of what is implied by the notion of society demonstrates that the Council essentially adopted the findings of classical social philosophy. Although the expression *societas perfecta* is not mentioned—in our opinion due to the risk of it being understood in a moral and not ontological sense—the substance of it is presupposed: man naturally is part of a group, society, that ought to assure him of the *sum total* of social conditions necessary to attain his personal and social fulfillment (GS 26). This is a natural given; only its cultural form for our time is not defined precisely, because the Council notes that we have gradually moved toward a process of globalization. It is possible that tomorrow international society, instead of national society, will deserve the title of perfect society.

Conclusion concerning these modern developments

The dogmatic tradition of the People of God theme has been affected by the vicissitudes of the developments of social philosophy in the modern era. This explains the malaise that came to light after the Council. The ambiguity of the word "society" was and may still be such that very often it was difficult to understand correctly the thought of one author or the other, not to mention the excesses resulting from an inept use of sociological schemes. Perhaps this was why Paul VI was rather hesitant to preach about the Church as the People of God.[66] Furthermore, and also because of these dogmatic difficulties, the biblical Tradition of the People of God theme was what theologians developed above all after the Council. Presently it seems that it is necessary to preserve these two Traditions that easily complement each other, the first being biblical Tradition, while keeping careful watch so as to cure dogmatic Tradition of its wavering. This does not mean that we must purely and simply repeat the old findings in identical terms, which would be contrary to the very idea of Tradition; rather, on the basis of a refined and enriched philosophy (think, for example, of the principle of subsidiarity), we should rework the social analogy so as to arrive at a richer understanding of the theological data.

c. The teaching of Vatican II

This is the subject of the whole second chapter of *Lumen gentium*, which we will review.

1. General presentation of the Tradition

Lumen gentium 9 introduces the chapter; it is divided into three carefully organized paragraphs. The first is a good summary of biblical theology with the three themes of election, vocation, and covenant. This presents no particular difficulties; the reader can consult the passage. The second paragraph is a summary of dogmatic theology that is very close to the medieval line of thought.[67] Because of our earlier presentation, we consider it unnecessary to give any additional explanations. In contrast, the tone of the third paragraph is quite novel and deserves a leisurely examination.

66. See the well-documented study by J.-P. Torrell, "Paul VI et l'écclésiologie de Lumen gentium," in *Paolo VI e i problemi ecclesiologici al concilo*, Colloquio internazionale di studio (Brescia: 1989), 155–60.

67. This is no accident. Fr. Congar, one of the chief draftsmen of this passage, commented, "In composing this text, I recalled ... the commentary of St. Thomas on Eph 4:5–6"; see Yves Congar, *Un peuple messianique*, 77–78 and note 5.

2. A new question: Israel, a present sign

The conciliar text reads as follows:

Israel according to the flesh, which wandered as an exile in the desert, was already called the Church of God (2 Esd. 13:1; cf. Nm 20:4; Dt 23:1ff.). So likewise the new Israel which while living in this present age goes in search of a future and abiding city (cf. Heb 13:14) is called the Church of Christ (cf. Mt 16:18). For He has bought it for Himself with His blood (cf. Acts 20:28), has filled it with His Spirit and provided it with those means which befit it as a visible and social union. God gathered together as one all those who in faith look upon Jesus as the author of salvation and the source of unity and peace, and established them as the Church that for each and all it may be the visible sacrament of this saving unity. While it transcends all limits of time and confines of race, the Church is destined to extend to all regions of the earth and so enters into the history of mankind. Moving forward through trial and tribulation, the Church is strengthened by the power of God's grace, which was promised to her by the Lord, so that in the weakness of the flesh she may not waver from perfect fidelity, but remain a bride worthy of her Lord, and moved by the Holy Spirit may never cease to renew herself, until through the Cross she arrives at the light which knows no setting. (*LG* 9, §3)

The classic perspective gave priority to the view of the Church as the fulfillment of Israel, which prefigured it and prepared the way for it. This remains true, of course, but it should be added—and this is the new idea—that Israel exists also in the present.[68] By this we mean to emphasize that as a result of the mysterious persistence of the Jewish people, despite their dispersion and persecutions, there is a theology of present-day Israel.[69] The point of comparison that allows us to liken Israel today and the Church is the fact that these two coexisting Peoples of God are both Peoples that were brought into existence by God in order to tend toward a fulfillment that is to transform them profoundly. They are Peoples in which and through which a slow and profound

---

68. Considering Israel solely as something in the past leads to the disparagement of the first Chosen People (which still says no to the fulfillment accomplished by Christ). This line of argument is indisputably the basic current of thought among the Church Fathers. On this point the reader may consult issue 28 of the review *Connaissance des Pères de l'Église*.

69. When we say "present-day Israel" we do not mean the country that is a member of the international community, but rather the theological reality of the Jewish community; on this problem, see J. Stern, "Marcionisme, néo-marcionisme et tradition de l'Église," *RT* 105 (2005): 473–506 (esp. 486ff.).

process of giving birth is accomplished. Hence we see how this consideration supplements the simple pattern of the fulfillment of Israel by the Church, in which Israel only prefigures and prepares the way for a future event—and it is true that this event, the Christ, has come in salvation history—but Israel also lives by a hope, an eschatological promise, and its *present* life should enable Christians to revive unceasingly their sense of the fulfillment of the promise. This is because, for Christians also, the final fulfillment is yet to come.[70] This is an initial point: the present-day pedagogical value of Israel for the Church. The sins committed by Israel during the time when this People carried the hope of the world can reoccur today within the Christian People.[71] The same goes for the glories of Israel, which still teach us about the true criteria for fidelity.[72]

Can we go further and speak about two Peoples that are *presently* messianic? Although the covenants by which God bound himself to men in history have a successive aspect, in the sense that the previous covenant was to announce and prepare the following one that replaces it—and in this case the covenant sealed by Christ is the new, definitive, perfect, and eternal covenant—it is commonly admitted today that the earlier covenants were not revoked.[73] They coexist today for the benefit of those who, by no fault of their own, do not have access

---

70. In other words, the Church does not just "manage" an acquisition (the fulfillment of Christ under Pontius Pilate); she tends toward a fullness of which she possesses presently only the pledge and down payment. The fidelity and infidelity of Israel should serve as an example to Christians, for although the basic fidelity of the Church is promised by Christ (Mt 16:18), the persons who make up the community can individually lose it. This is the speculative question about the indefectibly holy Church, whereas in this world she is made up of sinners. We will address this question within the context of our study of the Church's holiness.

71. It is not difficult to draw parallels between the Old Testament and the Church of Christ: temptations to secularization (when Israel made alliances with neighboring kings), the temptation of power (cf. the prohibition of the census), the temptation of wealth, etc.

72. Think in particular about the religious reforms in Israel (the reform of Josiah, the return from exile) that express an important teaching concerning the "return to the sources" that is not something archaic or mere romanticism.

73. *Lumen gentium* 16; address by John Paul II in Mainz, November 17, 1980 ("the Old Covenant, never revoked by God"); documented at the website of the Institute for Jewish-Catholic Relations at Saint Joseph's University (Philadelphia), www.sju.edu/academics/centers/ijcr.

The People of God

to the fullness of Christianity. This survival is a divine mercy. In dealing quite specifically with the covenant made with Israel, we can explore more deeply the substance of this mercy. We should recognize that certain prophetic passages (notably in Is 60–66, particularly Is 66:15) announce to the Jews the *parousia* (the end of history), and not just the coming of the Savior. Might there not be here an element that could shed light on the curious statement in Rom 11:26, which is also about the consummation of history: "And so all Israel will be saved"? In other words, present-day Israel, a witness to the future fulfillment of the promises, remains a messianic People in the plan of divine wisdom, "for the gifts and the call of God are irrevocable." Israel, presently, would then be a People tending toward the same parousia as the one awaited by Christians. Certainly, this duality of messianic Peoples is not the perfect fulfillment of the divine will manifested in Christ, but this mercy on behalf of Israel is also a gift for the Church, which thus possesses a living testimony of its origins and of its future, its "root" on which it is "grafted" (Rom 11:16ff.). Might not the obstinate and miraculous survival of Israel be justified by this divine mercy, which thus allows Jews and Christians to support each other mutually in the hope for the Day of the Lord's coming?

One might think that we are deriving a lot of things from this third paragraph of section 9 of *Lumen gentium*, which at first glance seems quite "classical," but it would not be the first time that Council Fathers had composed a text, the richness of which was partially unknown to them and was to be revealed later on.[74] However that may be in the case of this particular question, we are only suggesting certain developments.[75] We are dealing here with *theology*, not with a presentation of received *doctrine*. We think that there is no contradiction between the two.

---

74. One would also have to consider writing a commentary on the teaching of the Declaration *Nostra aetate* 4, in which the Fathers discussed in very plain terms the "graft" of the Church onto Israel.

75. About this additional consideration of Israel, see the suggestive study by M.-D. Chenu, "Un peuple messianique," *NRT* 99 (1967): 164–82. Another approach to the same idea: M. Sales, *Le Corps de l'Église* (Paris: 1986) (a collection of articles; we recommend for our subject "La constitution israélite de l'Église," 13–103). One could also read the stimulating reflections by D. Cerbelaud, *Ecouter Israël* (Paris: 2002), 81ff.

3. Developments of the theme

Citizenship in this People (*LG* 10–12)

After having considered the People in its entirety, the Council considers the individual members who make up that community. Following the medieval Tradition that we have seen, Vatican II employs the broad notion of priesthood (expressing the three offices of priest, prophet, and king) in order to describe the common fundamental quality that results from baptism. Special mention is given to the offering of spiritual sacrifices (priesthood in the strict sense) in paragraphs 10–11 and the witness of the Gospel (Christian prophecy) in paragraph 12.[76] These developments constantly accentuate the common basic identity (principle of unity) and the variety of charisms (principle of diversity), all this in the broadest possible interdependence for the benefit of all. The question is particularly important insofar as it concerns the distinction and the relation between these two priesthoods that share in the priesthood of Christ, the baptismal priesthood and the ministerial priesthood. In teaching that the two priesthoods "differ essentially and not only in degree" (*LG* 10), Vatican II made a statement that is extremely important if we are to grasp the very nature of the ministerial priesthood and its relation with the baptismal priesthood. We will encounter this question again at the conclusion of this chapter.[77] Another important note: the *sensus fidei* (*LG* 12). Succinctly recalling this common doctrine—the fundamental ecclesial reality is the faith of the believing People, that faith being served by its ministers—Vatican II manifests the unity of the Christian community by situating the hierarchy not above, but within the People of God.

---

76. As for the kingly office of the faithful, the Council sets this forth in the Decree for the Lay Apostolate, while not always distinguishing as rigorously as one might have wished between the prophetic mission and the kingly mission. See, for example, *Apostolicam actuositatem* 2, "to establish the right relationship of the entire world to Christ."

77. The developments of this teaching would be a matter for an academic course or treatise on the sacrament of holy orders. We mention here only what concerns the hierarchical nature of the Church. For what pertains to ecclesial action (pastoral theology), we refer the reader to the excellent work by D. Bourgeois, *Traité de théologie pastorale* (Paris: 2002).

The extent of the People of God (*LG* 13–17)

Vatican II accommodates here the teaching that since the sixteenth century has been called "*De membris Ecclesiae*," but with a rather large difference in perspective. Classical theology, following the Middle Ages and relying somewhat on the Church Fathers, treated this question within the framework of the doctrine of the Church as the Body of Christ. The Council resolutely decided to approach the question differently. Rather than consider membership in the Church in an exclusively "essential" way, at the level of the conditions for receiving the grace of Christ and of its effects in the believer, the Council Fathers opted for a dynamic presentation that was made possible by the historical aspect conveyed by the People of God theme: all human beings are situated positively in relation to the Church, although to various degrees. The question thus undergoes a rather profound renewal, and this teaching still keeps shedding light on many contemporary questions, as we will show further on. It is fair, however, to note that these developments sometimes repeat what has already been said by way of the Body of Christ theme.

Section 13 is a pivotal development, as the *relator* [drafting committee spokesman] points out to the Council Fathers:

The purpose [of this paragraph] was to set forth the principles of the unity and universality of the People of God, before going on to describe the various ways in which human beings are connected to the People of God (nos. 14–16). Consequently this paragraph is like a hinge or a link between two parts: the first indicates the general necessary conditions of the People of God, and the second deals with the members, whether actual or potential.[78]

The outline of this second part of Chapter 2 is consequently as follows: I. The situation of all human beings in relation to the mystery of the Church (no. 13); II. The principal distinctions among human beings (nos. 14–16); III. The justification for missionary activity (no. 17). Let us examine this text, step by step.

Section 13 is very well constructed in three paragraphs.

The first paragraph situates God's plan with respect to the reunion of the human race under one Head, Christ, through his Spirit, in other words, the Church; here we find the intentional perspective.

78. *Relatio* on the new no. 13, *AS* III/I:200.

All men are called to belong to the new People of God. This People therefore, whilst remaining one and only one, is to be spread throughout the whole world and to all ages in order that the design of God's will may be fulfilled: he made human nature one in the beginning and has decreed that all his children who were scattered should be finally gathered together as one (cf. Jn 11:52). It was for this purpose that God sent his Son, whom he appointed heir of all things (cf. Heb 1:2), that he might be teacher, king and priest of all, the head of the new and universal People of God's sons. This, too, is why God sent the Spirit of his Son, the Lord and Giver of Life. The Spirit is, for the Church and for each and every believer, the principle of their union and unity in the teaching of the apostles and fellowship, in the breaking of bread and prayer (cf. Acts 2:42).

The second paragraph considers the progressive realization of this call by the development of this People of God, which is simultaneously highly unified and quite diverse:

The one People of God is accordingly present in all the nations of the earth, since its citizens, who are taken from all nations, are of a kingdom whose nature is not earthly but heavenly. All the faithful scattered throughout the world are in communion with each other in the Holy Spirit so that "he who dwells in Rome knows those in most distant parts to be his members."[79]

The third paragraph concerns the relation of every human being with this People, whether he is actually a member of it or is ordered to it.

All men are called to this catholic unity.... And in different ways to it belong, or are related (*variis modis pertinent vel ordinantur*): the Catholic faithful, others who believe in Christ, and finally all mankind, called by God's grace to salvation.

Note the vocabulary for which we have provided the original Latin in parentheses. This is very technical language that must be understood correctly.[80] After this important paragraph 13, nos. 14–16 will describe in somewhat greater detail the various degrees of relationship between human beings and the People of God.[81]

---

79. Here follows a rather long development concerning the Catholic Church, her means of unity, and the diversity within her. We will return to it.

80. For a more in-depth discussion we refer the reader to my essay "Être ordonné à l'unique Église du Christ," *RT* (2002): 5–41.

81. *Lumen Gentium* describes the situation starting with *individuals* in light of God's

The People of God 249

Section 14 is devoted to the Catholic faithful. Its first paragraph recalls the doctrine resulting from the saying, "No salvation outside the Church." This must be understood to mean that no salvation is possible for someone who, knowing that the Church established by God in Christ is the path of salvation, would refuse to enter it or to persevere it.[82] We will return to this point in the conclusion of this chapter. The second paragraph considers incorporation into the Church. The manner of addressing this question is very different from the approach taken by theologians since the sixteenth century. Briefly, it is not a matter of distinguishing between "the visible Church" and "the invisible Church"; instead the passage situates within individual persons the conditions for their ecclesiality [ecclesial membership]: being in the one and only Church *in heart and in body*.[83] This is the patristic (in particular the Augustinian) and medieval line of thought. The incorporation is said to be *full* when the person adheres thoroughly to the two aspects, Christological and pneumatological, of the ecclesial mystery. This means persons who "possessing the Spirit of Christ, accept all the means of salvation given to the church"; consequently, they are in the visible assembly of the Church. This change of perspective in relation to classical theology is important; we will return to it in the speculative part. The third paragraph recalls what one could term "the ecclesiality of desire" of the catechumen, based on his explicit desire for baptism; there is no particular problem here.

Section 15 concerns non-Catholic Christians. Sacramental baptism

---

universal salvific will and then goes on to speak about the quality (ecclesial or not) of the *communities* to which these individuals belong. This communitarian perspective is also the object, for separated Christians, of the Decree on Ecumenism (*UR*), and for non-Christians the object of the Declaration on Non-Christian Religions (*Nostra aetate* [*NA*]).

82. The saying, which is not repeated verbatim, is found in two other contexts (*LG* 26 and *AG* 7) with different emphases.

83. As we emphasized, the approach here is individual; it should be interpreted with reference to the presentation of the Church in *LG* 8, where the perspective is communitarian. In other words, Vatican II first presented the one and only Church in the fullness of Christ's gifts (the Catholic Church) and mentioned that this fullness has not been preserved in the other Christian communities (*LG* 8, §§1 and 2). Then, in *LG* 14–15, the Council addresses the same question from the perspective of the individuals who are or are not fully members of the one and only Church. Finally, the communitarian perspective, the principles of which are stated in *LG* 8, will be developed in the Decree on Ecumenism.

is what makes the Christian. Among the separated brethren there are those who do not profess the faith integrally (their community originated in a heresy), and there are those who, professing the same faith, are not united in communion with the successor of Peter (their community originated in a schism). Vatican II opted for a positive presentation, in other words, by highlighting what unites more than what separates. But it was also advisable not to minimize the fact and the causes of this situation of division. The Fathers swung back and forth during the conciliar discussions. Indeed, if these separated brethren have the Holy Spirit, the soul of the Church, they share with us the very foundation of the ecclesial mystery. But on the other hand, the objective lack that they suffer from, the Christological "deficit," is no mere detail. The conciliar decision was to underscore at the same time the union and its imperfection by composing in this way the key phrase: "*vera quaedam in Spiritu Sancto coniunctio*," that is, underscoring that the unity is *true*, and yet that it is a *kind of* unity and not purely and simply unity.[84] This conciliar teaching repeats and develops the teaching in *LG* 8, §2 that we have already presented. These two passages should be read together.

Section 16 is devoted to non-Christians—in other words, to persons who are not sacramentally baptized. To say that these persons are outside the Church would be very hazardous. We already know that they are *called* to belong to the People of God (*LG* 13), and, intentionally, the first phrase of section 16 repeats this: "Those who have not yet received the Gospel are related to the People of God in various ways." It seems quite clear that Vatican II, as it did for the separated Christians, was unwilling to use all-or-nothing reasoning here (a person is either in or outside the Church), but rather framed the question in terms of a fullness that is shared in different ways.[85] Adopting here terminology suggested by Jacques Maritain, we propose making distinctions between the *potential* (pure existing possibility), the *virtual* (possibility that is incompletely actualized) and the *actual* (what has attained the fullness).[86] Non-Christians can be not only potential but also virtual members.

The Jewish people are mentioned before all the others:

84. For the explanation of this formulation see *AS* III/I:205.
85. As the *relator* says in note 78, there are actual members and potential members.
86. Journet and Maritain, *Correspondance*, vol. 2 (1930–1939) (Fribourg: Éditions

The People of God

There is, first, that people to which the covenants and promises were made, and from which Christ was born according to the flesh (Rom 9:4–5): in view of the divine choice, they are a people most dear for the sake of the fathers, for the gifts of God are without repentance (cf. Rom 11:28–29).

This reference is brief, but not unimportant.[87] This People is great not only because of its past—for this is the people from which the Church came—but also at present, because the gifts of God are without repentance. Note the extreme sobriety of this reference, which does seem to show that the Council wishes to leave the door open to a consideration of the present positive value of Judaism.

The Muslims are considered next. Note here that there is no question of "Islam"[88]—in other words, the religious community as such—but rather of the persons that are part of it: the Muslims. Indeed, Islam poses a formidable and unique problem in the interreligious debate because it is a religion founded after Christianity and in part against it. The reference by Vatican II is therefore extremely cautious. Then follows the consideration of persons of other religions "who in shadows and images seek the unknown God." The perspective is likewise individual, without any particular consideration of the religions of these persons.[89]

The document continues—and this is new—with a consideration of two types of persons who do not belong to any religious community. Indeed, one should not confuse those who have only the testimony of God in their conscience and strive to live according to that absolute, whatever the expression thereof may be—something transcendent is

---

universitaires Fribourg (Suisse); Paris: Éditions Saint Paul, 1997), 318–19. This distinction is proposed to the question of membership in the Church. The *virtual* degree intends to take into account the ecclesiality of Christians belonging to a community that is separated from the Catholic Church; it is extended here to those who may possess, within a non-Christian religion or without having any religion, the baptism of desire.

87. It is advisable to refer also to the longer discussion by Vatican II of the Jewish People in *Nostra aetate* 4. The Church is mentioned seventeen times in that Declaration. Out of these seventeen occurrences, we can count eleven concerning the *mystery* of the Church, the Church *of Christ*, the new *People of God*, that are concentrated in section 4 dedicated to the Jews. The Council recognizes that the Church is already present in her mystery, *mystically prefigured*, the document says (*NA* 4, §2), in the first chosen People.

88. Nor, incidentally, in the Declaration *Nostra aetate*.

89. One should consult the Declaration *Nostra aetate* for a consideration of non-Christian religions.

recognized here—and those who have not yet arrived at an express knowledge of God (their speech may even be atheistic or agnostic to outward appearances), but who strive to lead an upright life. In both cases, if the situation of these persons is *by no fault of their own*, the grace of God is not refused, and the baptism of desire can even come about.[90]

Bearing in mind this resolutely positive perspective, the Council wished to conclude these discussions with paragraph 17, which is abundantly clear in recalling the traditional teaching about the mission of the Church.[91] In short, the teaching of Vatican II decisively follows the so-called "fulfillment" line of thinking. According to this perspective, the entire past and present work of God has its finality in the Mystical Body of Christ, the Temple of the Spirit, and the People of God. Anything positive outside of the perfectly formed ecclesial mystery is ordered to that mystery and already tends to be part of it and finds its accomplishment therein. We know that the research currently being done in interreligious dialogue tends, in many cases, to try to open up other perspectives. Some in particular try to conceive of the possible salvation of non-Christians in a way that is not ecclesial. The least that one can say is that such research cannot find support in the teaching of Vatican II. If we remain within the perspective of ecclesial salvation for all human beings, two possibilities are presently being investigated. The first highlights the potential or virtual ecclesiality of the non-Christian considered individually. In this case the person can be saved in his religion, but not by his religion.[92] The second goes one step further and tries to picture the non-Christian religion as sharing in the mystery of the Church, thus being able to offer, through everything true and good that it possesses, a disposition to the grace of salvation. In the latter case, the person can be saved in and *in a certain manner* through his religion.[93]

---

90. The reference in *Gaudium et spes* 22, §5 complements *LG* 16 in this sense: "For since Christ died for all, and since all men are in fact called to one and the same destiny, which is divine, we must hold that the Holy Spirit offers to all the possibility (*possibilitatem offerre*) of being made partners, in a way known to God, in the paschal mystery."

91. The missionary doctrine is recalled and developed in the Decree *Ad gentes*.

92. The most recent study from this perspective is the one by Fr. Daguet, "L'unique Église du Christ en acte et en puissance," *Nova et Vetera* 2 (2004): 45–70.

93. This is the proposal that we make, in particular in the article "Être ordonné à

Conclusion
Two questions by way of recapitulation

The People of God theme is a key theme in *explaining* many aspects of the Body of Christ theme. For example, whereas we say, together with the whole theology of the Mystical Body, that the Christian *is* a member of this Body, we specify with the People of God theology the *activity* to which these members are called (priest, prophet, king). Moreover, the Church as Body of Christ appears to us initially in its fundamental *being* (the great organism of grace), and the Church as People of God appears to us initially in its fundamental *activity* (the acts proper to this organism by which it grows). These are valid observations about the respective emphases of these two themes, but we must not overstate matters; Body of Christ and People of God both speak to us about the being and the activity of the Church. As we stressed in the introduction, the People of God theme situates the Church in a more *historical* perspective, while the Body of Christ theme situates the Church in a more *essential* perspective. It is the same being in either case, but the historical aspect shows how this being develops its potentialities over time. For grace that has been received, inasmuch as it qualifies a *being*, is also and inseparably a *principle of action* in the person, and thereby of the community, and this action is the way by which the subject attains his perfection. This set of themes (the Temple of the Spirit theme is more directly connected to the Body of Christ theme), studied in the order followed by *Lumen gentium*, forms a whole that is incomparably rich in meaning.

Until now we have presented things mainly from the perspective of the ecclesial community. We should now say a word about the individual perspective, about personal membership in the Church. This is the aspect that we will discuss in studying the saying, "No salvation outside the Church." Finally, just as we showed within the Church the inequality of the members (in the sense that we specified), we will now note the principles for distinguishing within the People of God three major categories of "citizens": clerics, laity, and consecrated persons.

---

l'unique Église du Christ: L'ecclésialité des communautés non chrétiennes à partir des données oecuméniques," *RT* 102 (2002): 5–41.

a. The saying "No salvation outside the Church"

This is a very ancient saying that nowadays is so poorly understood that one cannot repeat it, in a homily, for example, without running the risk of seriously shocking people and of being judged intolerant (or fanatical) and reactionary. Now this saying, correctly understood, of course, expresses a *doctrine* that is indispensable. What it expresses is extremely profound. And it is extremely important to understand it correctly so as to be able to express the substance thereof without the classic formula, which is a booby trap for the modern mindset. Moreover, this study constitutes a particularly enlightening example of dogmatic development. The way in which this truth has been understood has progressed continually in history, and the Second Vatican Council incorporates a recent acquisition that has a wealth of applications in our de-Christianized world.[94]

1. The scriptural foundation

There is no doubt about the scriptural basis for this doctrine. Scripture, indeed, tells us in a thousand ways that salvation is obtained by faith, which is born of preaching (Rom 10:17), which leads to baptism, the gateway to all the other sacraments. To be saved is to be graced, to be a member of the Body that has Christ as its Head,[95] in other words, a member of the Church. All this is well established, particularly in the writings of St. Paul, but also in the Synoptic Gospels (cf. Mk 16:15–16: "Go into all the world.... He who believes and is baptized will be saved; but he who does not believe will be condemned"). It is necessary, however, to explain the revealed truth correctly.

God wants all men to be saved (1 Tm 2:4). Hence the ones exclud-

---

94. From the perspective of positive theology, we have a very complete study of the patristic, medieval, and modern tradition in the two volumes by L. Caperan, *Le Problème du salut des infidels:* vol. 1, *Essai historique*, and vol. 2, *Essai théologique*, 2nd ed. (Paris: 1934). It does not include recent contemporary developments, but is still an excellent foundation. The most recent essay of value on this subject is the one by B. Sesboüé, *Hors de l'Église pas de salut: Histoire d'une formule et problèmes d'interprétation* (Paris: 2004). It is indicative, however, of the minimizing approach that is currently very widespread (see my review in *RT* (2004): 667–74).

95. Acts 4:12. There is salvation in no one else [than Jesus], for there is no other name under heaven given among men by which we must be saved.

The People of God

ed from salvation are those who reject it—in other words, those who are enlightened by grace, yet close themselves off from Christ (cf. the parable of the sower in Mt 13:1–23 and parallel passages). This grace can reach them in different ways:

Either *by means of* the mediations instituted by Christ, and in this case:

- they reject the preaching of the Gospel (Lk 2:34);
- they accept the Gospel, but then abandon it by leaving the community (1 Jn 2:18–19), or remain in the community "in body" only, but no longer "in heart" as well (Mt 13:41–42).

Or else *without* the mediations instituted by Christ, and in that case:

- they reject the interior prompting [*motion*] of the Spirit that occurs in every human being and makes up for the absence of any preaching, sacraments, and ministry. This is the case for all men before or after Christ who were unable, by no fault of their own, to encounter the mediations instituted by Christ. This direct prompting is an "abnormal" system of salvation, a substitute system, but the Word enlightens every man that comes into this world (Jn 1:9).

This is the scriptural testimony of which Tradition would develop an understanding.

2. Development by Tradition

The patristic contribution

The easiest point to grasp is the following: someone who benefits from the mediations instituted by Christ, but rejects them by leaving the community, cannot be saved. For St. Ignatius of Antioch, "If a man runs after a schismatic, he will not inherit the Kingdom of God."[96] For St. Irenaeus, those who reject the apostles, prophets, and doctors—that is, the ministers through whom the Spirit offers the faith by preaching—"defraud themselves of life." This is the context in which the famous formula occurs: "For where the Church is, there is the Spirit of God; and where the Spirit of God is, there is the Church, and ev-

---

96. *To the Philadelphians* 3.3 (ACW 1:86).

ery kind of grace."[97] St. Cyprian is the author of the formula "*Extra Ecclesiam non salus est.*"[98] He is aiming this passage at heretics. There is a related formula by the same author: "You cannot have God for your Father if you have not the Church for your mother."[99] At that time there was no formal distinction between heresy (an attack on the faith) and schism (breach of charity), and the various citations apply to both cases. Origen's teaching is identical: "*Extra Ecclesiam nemo salvatur.*"[100] St. Jerome takes the same perspective: "Whoever is not in Noah ark will perish when the flood prevails."[101] Lactantius also says that since the Church is God's Temple, "if one does not enter this and goes out from it, he is cut away from the hope of life and salvation."[102] St. Augustine is the one who gives the most complete teaching. He distinguishes those who are in the Church "in heart and in body" and are saved, from those who are in the Church "in body" only and not "in heart" and are not saved, and also from those who are in the Church "in heart" but not "in body" and are saved by an invisible substitute for sacramental baptism.[103]

Not all membership in the Church is salvific after all, and a lack of the means of salvation instituted by Christ can be "supplied" or made up for. This supplementation will be the object of dogmatic development.

The supplementary system of salvation

This is a matter of understanding how faith and baptism, both of which are absolutely necessary for salvation (cf. the conclusion of Mk) can be "supplied" or substituted for.

---

97. *Adv. Haer.* III.24.1 (ANF 1:458b).

98. "There is no salvation outside the Church"; Letter 73, xxi, 2, in ACW 47:66.

99. *De Ecclesiae unitate*, chap. VI (PL 4.503); *Treatises* (New York: Fathers of the Church, 1958), 48–49, but the whole treatise should be cited here.

100. "Outside the Church, no one is saved"; *Homilies on Joshua*, Hom. III.5 (PG 12.841–42); FOC 105:50 (a related formula can be found in *Homilies of Jeremiah*, Hom. V.16).

101. *Letter* 15.1 (ACW 33:71) (in this context, the ark is the *communio Petri*, i.e., union with the bishop of Rome).

102. *Inst. Div.* (PL 6.543); FOC 49:325.

103. *De Bapt.* V.xxviii.39 (PL 43.197); NPNF 1.4:477–78; V.xviii.24 (PL 43.189); III.xix.26 (PL 43.152). One could also cite VI.xiv.23 and IV.xxii.29.

Faith

All human beings are enlightened by the Word (Jn 1:9). The School of Alexandria that develops this point does not yet distinguish between the illumination of reason and the illumination of faith. But the theological conclusions are solid. For St. Justin, those who lived before the Incarnation of the Word were ignorant of him by no fault of their own, but they were able to "live by reason [the Logos]"; they are Christians. If they "did not live by the Logos," they are already enemies of Christ.[104] The same teaching is found in the writings of St. Clement of Alexandria: the Word is hidden from no one; he shines for all human beings.[105] Thus in Alexandria there was no hesitation to canonize Socrates or Plato.

Baptism

Here the doctrine of baptism by desire appears. We must distinguish between the desire for baptism (in catechumens, for example) from the baptism of desire. Someone who desired sacramental baptism but died before its celebration received the grace that he was asking for. This is the argument developed by St. Ambrose of Milan, who was catechizing Emperor Valentinian when the latter was assassinated: "Has he not, then, the grace which he desired? ... And because he asked, he received."[106] So-called baptism of desire (non-sacramental baptism) is a different case. This is an *unformulated* desire for the grace of salvation as a result of ignorance that is not culpable. On the basis of Scripture (especially Rom 2) and the findings of the School of Alexandria, rich developments are possible. They will occur in the medieval period.

The medieval period

The Middle Ages, like the patristic period, was convinced that the preaching of the Gospel had reached all the nations on the earth. It was assumed, therefore, that explicit faith in the principal revealed truths was possible for every human being and therefore required for salva-

---

104. *Apol.* I.46 (PG 6.398); *First Apology*, trans. Thomas B. Falls (New York: Fathers of the Church, 1948), 83; *Apol.* II.10 (PG 6.459–60); FOC (1948), 129–30.
105. *Protrepticus* XI.88.2; *Exhortation to the Greeks*, Loeb Classical Library 92:241, 243.
106. *De obitu Valent. consol.* 51 (FOC 22:288).

tion. In that case non-culpable ignorance was not an issue. This minimum of explicit faith concerns the first two *credibilia* [objects of belief] according to Hebrews 11:6: God exists and he rewards good and evil. This conviction about the total expansion of evangelical preaching was based on a remark in Psalm 19:4, "Their voice has gone out to all the earth, and their words to the ends of the world," as it is cited in the context of the Letter to the Romans (Rom 10:18). St. John Chrysostom interprets it literally: the Gospel has been spread by the apostles throughout the world.[107] St. Augustine is more nuanced: this apostolic preaching is certain, but it has not completely built up the Church everywhere.[108]

St. Thomas attempts to reconcile the two statements:

For in the days of the apostles some report about their preaching had reached all nations, even to the ends of the world, at least through their disciples and even through the apostles themselves. For Matthew preached in Ethiopia, Thomas in India, Peter and Paul in the West. And this is what Chrysostom means. However, during the times of the apostles it had not been fulfilled in such a way that the Church had been built up in all nations, but it would be fulfilled before the end of the world, as Augustine says.[109]

St. Thomas explains the consequences of this view: every human being can know and adhere to the Gospel, either by encountering a preacher, or else by an interior inspiration that will guide him to the Church. Every human being therefore belongs to the Church or is led toward her, so that in the case of rejection there can only be a culpable refusal. Consequently the medieval Magisterium developed the conditions for belonging to the Church, which is conceived of only as full incorporation.[110]

This teaching can be understood only within the context of the pa-

107. *Sup. Mt.* 24:14; *Hom.* 75–76 (PG 58.689).
108. *Letter* 199.12 (CSEL 57:284–85).
109. *Sup. Rom.* c. 10, lect. 3, 848; trans. Fabian Larcher, OP.
110. One can cite, among others: Innocent III, "Profession of faith imposed on the Vaudois" (see FC 422); Boniface VIII, in his famous Bull *Unam sanctam* (FC 422): "We declare, say, define, and proclaim to every human creature that they by necessity for salvation are entirely subject to the Roman Pontiff"; the Ecumenical Councils, in particular the Council of Florence: "[The Church] firmly believes, professes, and proclaims that those not living within the Catholic Church, not only pagans, but also Jews and heretics and schismatics cannot become participants in eternal life"; *A Decree in Behalf of the Jacobites* (FC 433).

The People of God

tristic tradition relative to the extent of the apostolic preaching. If the Gospel has been preached to all, or at least if the interior prompting of the Spirit leads to the Church that is already established, the only rejection or ignorance possible is *culpable*. The subsequent developments would have bearing on the extent of the apostolic preaching and on the nature of the *culpable* ignorance or rejection.

The modern period

The discovery of the New World would bring about an awareness that the apostolic preaching never reached immense regions where millions of persons had been living. The interior prompting of the Spirit could not lead to the already established Church because the Church was not present in the place where the person lived. Furthermore, some peoples that were discovered showed no evidence of an explicit faith, not even one limited to the first two *credibilia*. These questions would be debated extensively in the universities and would give rise to profound investigations that little by little would allow a doctrinal refinement by the Magisterium.

Pius IX

This nineteenth-century pontiff stated:

It must be held by faith that outside the Apostolic Roman Church, no one can be saved; that this is the only ark of salvation; that he who shall not have entered therein will perish in the flood; but, on the other hand, it is necessary to hold for *certain* that they who labor in ignorance of the true religion, if this ignorance is invincible, are not stained by any guilt in this matter in the eyes of God.... "For the hand of the Lord is not shortened" (Is 50:2), and the gifts of heavenly grace will not be wanting to those who sincerely [i.e., with an upright heart] wish and ask to be refreshed by this light.[111]

This is the first development: non-culpable ignorance of the "true religion" (the public Revelation preached by the Church) does not impede salvation. This statement has not been reconciled with the necessity of belonging to the Church for salvation. In the present state of the question, therefore, the two propositions should be kept together, although it is not possible to give an account of the connection between

---

111. Allocution *"Singulari quadam,"* December 9, 1854 (FC 440).

them. Pius IX returned to this question in a second, more solemn document:

They who labor in invincible ignorance of our most holy religion and who, zealously keeping the natural law and its precepts engraved in the hearts of all by God, and being ready to obey God, live an honest and upright life, can, by the operating power of divine light and grace, attain eternal life, since God who clearly beholds, searches, and knows the minds, souls, thoughts, and habits of all men, because of His great goodness and mercy, will by no means suffer anyone to be punished with eternal torment who has not the guilt of deliberate sin. But, the Catholic dogma that no one can be saved outside the Catholic Church is well-known; and also that those who are obstinate toward the authority and definitions of the same Church, and who persistently separate themselves from the unity of the Church, and from the Roman Pontiff, the successor of Peter, to whom "the guardianship of the vine has been entrusted by the Savior," cannot obtain eternal salvation.[112]

The clarification here bears on what "upright heart" means in the previous teaching from *Singulari quadam*. It has to do with an upright moral life, in keeping with the demands of conscience, which apprehends the precepts of the natural law. Very little explanation of this faith is given (cf. "to obey God"); above all it is "existential." Note that Pius IX keeps two ideas together: the necessity of the Church for the salvation of those who are in a position to encounter the preaching of the Gospel, and possibility of salvation for those who are non-culpably ignorant of this preaching. The connection between these two statements is not always made. This is due, we think, to a concept of the Church, and thus of membership in the Church, that is still too juridical. The distinction is not yet made between full membership and belonging "*voto*" [by desire]. On this point Pius XII would make a little progress.

Pius XII

According to the Encyclical *Mystici Corporis*, persons who do not belong to the visible organism of the Church—in other words, the non-evangelized and those who belong to separated Christian commu-

---

112. Encyclical *Quanto conficiamur*, August 10, 1863; trans. Roy J. Deferrari from the 30th edition of Denzinger's *Enchiridion Symbolorum*, in *The Sources of Catholic Dogma* (St. Louis: Herder, 1957), 425.

The People of God

nities—"by an unconscious (*inscio*) desire and longing ... have a certain relationship with the Mystical Body of the Redeemer."[113] "Having a certain relationship to," or "being ordered to (*ordinentur*)," as we read in the Latin original, is already realizing a bit of potential, being somewhat in act.[114] The Encyclical goes no further, but it opens the way to the recognition of an ecclesial character in non-evangelized persons of upright heart and in our separated brethren.

Vocabulary notes

During this time of intense doctrinal ferment, the vocabulary of the theologians has not yet been well established, and some expressions used here and there need to be understood correctly. Non-evangelized persons of upright heart are called "positive unbelievers," and their interior dispositions are designated by the expressions "implicit faith" or else "natural faith." The expression "positive unbeliever" should be avoided: an unbeliever is someone who has no faith; objectively there could be no question of his salvation since without faith "it is impossible to please God" (Heb 11:6). The expressions "implicit faith" and "natural faith" are more subtly nuanced.

It is often said that the person who has the baptism of desire—an unformulated, preconceptual desire for grace—has an "implicit" faith; what does that mean? The implicit and explicit aspects of faith are characteristics of the *interior* act of faith (adherence of the mind to God who reveals himself as truth). Moreover, there is no such thing as a "totally implicit" faith, because the notion of implicit is a correlative notion. In order for there to be something implicit there must be something explicit. "Implicit" means that a truth is grasped, not directly in itself, but *in another truth that is explicit*. The implicit aspect is *in* the explicit aspect; there must necessarily be something explicit for there to be something implicit. For example, when someone believes that he should do good for its own sake and not just to be rewarded or to avoid

---

113. Encyclical *Summi pontificatus*, October 20, 1939, *AAS* (1939): 418–19; Encyclical *Mystici Corporis*, June 29, 1943, no. 101 in the Latin edition numbered by Sebastian Tromp [no. 103 at Vatican website].

114. A clear distinction should be made between "being ordered to," which signifies a potential already being actualized (which, following Jacques Maritain, we propose calling it something "virtual"), and "being oriented toward," which only signifies a simple potential that is not yet actualized (something "simply potential").

punishment, this proposition is held *explicitly in mind,* and at the same time the person affirms *implicitly* a transcendence of the good toward which he is tending. Therefore, in order to use the expression "implicit faith" correctly, we must specify what the explicit element is in which the implicit faith is contained. If we use the expression "implicit faith" without any reference to the explicit aspect, then we are expressing the common notion of "good faith." In other words, the well-disposed ignorance (a mere potentiality) of someone who will believe if the truth is presented to him but who, in his present state, does not yet believe, does not yet adhere to the truth. That person does not yet have supernatural faith. He is perhaps *oriented toward ...,* but not *ordered to.*

What then is this explicit thing that is always necessary in order for "implicit faith" to exist? This is the point on which the most recent developments have bearing, as we will see a little further on.

As for the expression "natural faith," the question is simpler. The word "faith" designates, in a general way, firm adherence of the mind to some certain knowledge without having evidence for it, on the basis of testimony: I have "faith" in my physician who prescribes such and such a remedy for me. Faith, per se and always, excludes doubt. If this certitude is acquired through revelation by God—who can neither deceive nor be deceived—its total certitude comes from the excellence of the one who reveals (God as the motive of faith). This faith is *supernatural.* Strictly speaking, we use the term *natural* faith to designate the same fundamental psychological reality (firm adherence to a truth that is not evident because of testimony), but with a different motive and a different object. The thing believed, but not evident—if not per se, then at least for the subject—is not a transcendent truth, but a created one. For example, we believe Einstein in things concerned with the theory of relativity, which for us is not evident. It is quite certain that only *supernatural* faith saves. Consequently, it is formally incorrect to use the expression "natural faith" for the faith of someone who is in invincible ignorance about the true religion.

The state of the question before Vatican II

Theologians were investigating the explicit component necessary in order for there to be "implicit faith." Normally faith is fully explicit, so that what is believed is conceptually present in the mind.

The People of God

As for partially explicit faith, until the modern era it consisted of the presence in the mind of two first *credibilia* [things that can be believed]: namely that God exists and that he rewards human acts; thus two explicit things implicitly "contain" the two others (the Trinity and God as Redeemer in Christ). This may be the situation, for example, of a Muslim of upright heart. But the modern difficulty, encountered by missionaries and now present in Europe also with atheism, comes from the fact that there are human beings who do not even seem to have the first two *credibilia* in mind, or who even deny them externally (in particular Buddhism or, for different reasons, modern atheism). In this case, what will be the explicit component in the mind in which the implicit component of the faith can be discerned? Would a person who does not seem to hold any of the *credibilia*, or even rejects the conceptual statement of them, be without any faith whatsoever? This is the point on which the whole contemporary effort is centered.

The scriptural basis that would be cited for these modern developments is essentially Rom 2:10–15:

> Glory and honor and peace for every one who *does good,* the Jew first and also the Greek. For God shows no partiality.... When Gentiles who have not the Law do by nature what the Law requires, they are a law to themselves [i.e., they act according to their conscience, cf. the note "c" in the *Jerusalem Bible* (1966) at Rom 2:14b], even though they do not have the Law. They show that what the Law requires is written on their hearts, while their conscience also bears witness and their conflicting thoughts accuse or perhaps excuse them.

We can also add other Scripture verses that are more concise, but are explained by Romans 2. Thus, "Every one who does right is born of [God]" (1 Jn 2:29), and "He who loves is born of God" (1 Jn 4:7).

Scripture refers to a morally right *way of acting* that testifies to a previous, but not necessarily conceptual adherence to God and to his will through the mediation of moral conscience.

The affair of the Jesuit Leonard Feeney caused the Holy Office to take a position that clarified the debate. We know that, according to the Encyclical *Mystici Corporis,* those who are not fully in the Church by a faith that is quite explicit can nevertheless be "ordered" to the Mystical Body. L. Feeney interpreted this *ordinantur ad Ecclesiam* purely and simply as a non-membership in the Church, and thus as a mark of reprobation (damnation). The Holy Office responded clearly:

The same in its own degree must be asserted of the Church, in as far as she is the general help to salvation. Therefore, that one may obtain eternal salvation, it is not always required that he be incorporated into the Church actually as a member, but it is necessary that at least he be united to her by desire and longing. However, this desire need not always be explicit, as it is in catechumens; but when a person is involved in invincible ignorance, God accepts also an implicit desire, so called because it is included in that good disposition of soul whereby a person wishes his will to be conformed to the will of God.[115]

This explicit component may be present in an experienced, preconceptual, nonreflexive way; it will have to do in particular with the person's morals. By living an upright life and striving to accomplish what is truly good because of its intrinsic value, and not so as to be rewarded or to avoid punishment, the person existentially professes a certain transcendence of that good. This practical knowledge of God can even coexist with a theoretical ignorance of God, or even with an external negation: such a man declares himself an atheist, but he follows his conscience, which reveals to him the true good to be done for its own sake. The God that he rejects conceptually is perhaps a God "distorted" by a false philosophy, bad preaching, or deviant spirituality..., but the God that he accepts experientially by following his right conscience is the true God. In doing this, he adheres to and tends toward the Lord. That person then belongs to the Church in a way that is *real* and salutary, albeit still imperfect and precarious. Imperfect, because he does not share the means of salvation instituted by Christ; precarious likewise because these means of salvation are not ornamental "details," but purposeful gifts that help a person remain and grow in friendship with God, in this world where evil and error are present and active. Communicating these gifts and helps is the very foundation of the Church's mission.

How does this baptism of desire come about? What is the *single act* that inaugurates this life of grace in the individual person? The magisterial documents say nothing about it. For the moment this remains a matter for discussion by theologians. In our opinion the most fruitful proposal is that of Jacques Maritain.[116] We will only summarize it here

---

115. Letter of the Holy Office to the Archbishop of Boston, August 8, 1949, FC 505.
116. The reader can find it expressed in "La dialectique immanente du premier acte de liberté," in *Nova et Vetera*, 1945; reprinted in *Raison et raisons* (Paris: 1947), 131–65.

because it is a point that properly would be a matter for an academic course or treatise on faith.

Maritain's point of departure is St. Thomas's teaching about mortal and venial sin in a child (*ST* I-II, q. 89, art. 6, corpus). The context is as follows: The question under discussion is, at what moment does a child baptized at birth become capable of sinning (cf. "the age of reason")? St. Thomas considers the first act by which a child who has attained the age of reason deliberates about himself and by himself. If this act is performed for the good, for the sole reason that it is good, it is his first act of freedom, and from that moment on the child orients himself toward his final end and becomes capable of sinning personally. That act constitutes the beginning of his personal moral life. Maritain transposes this teaching to the case of the non-baptized child. This person, who has arrived at a certain stage in the development of his conscience, will place a first act of freedom by choosing, with regard to some matter or other, to do good because it is good and not so as to be rewarded or to avoid punishment. This act that he places is his baptism "*voto*" (of desire). This transposition has the merit of being very close to the scriptural data (Rom 2). And obviously this situation does not concern only a child at a tender age. Since it is a question of *moral* maturity, it may not occur until later, at the age when the person is physically an adolescent or even an adult. This delay—for the so-called "age of reason" is reached on average between the ages of five and seven—can be caused by psychological defects, a bad education, a morally very primitive or very aberrant culture. This so-called "baptism of desire" is based on this conceptually unformulated, but "existential" or "experienced" desire, and the precise moment of it is not always known. This does not keep it from occurring in a precise act, the act by which the choice of the good for its own sake was made with regard to such and such a concrete choice: put in a position to be able to steal with impunity, the individual did not; being able to lie profitably and without risk, the individual did not. What we call "desire" in this way is a purely interior deliberation that the individual who has attained the age of reason makes concerning his life, about what will orient him fundamentally and the "values" that he accepts as "principles" of moral life. The faith obtained is the true supernatural faith that alone justifies. It is made explicit in the mind in a subconceptual way, whereby the first two *credibilia* are grasped. The intellectual "support" may be very poor, limited for example to the sole notions of good and evil, but it is open to all further progress.

Baptized *"voto,"* by desire, having thus received supernatural faith that lives by charity, this person is a member of the Church, the reality of salvation, and thereby can be saved. The person is an imperfect and precarious member, but a real one. This membership is already salutary.

Doctrinal recapitulation of Vatican II

This question, which closely concerns the very notion of Church inasmuch as it considers membership in the Church, was addressed by Vatican II in the conclusion of chapter 2 on the People of God, which deals with ecclesial incorporation.

The maxim "No salvation outside the Church" is clearly adopted in *LG* 14, §1 as it was understood in the patristic writings:

> The one Christ is mediator and the way of salvation; he is present to us in his body which is the Church. He himself explicitly asserted the necessity of faith and baptism (cf. Mk 16:16; Jn 3:5), and thereby affirmed at the same time the necessity of the Church which men enter through baptism as through a door. Hence they could not be saved who, *knowing that the Catholic Church was founded as necessary by God through Christ*, would refuse either to enter it, or to remain in it.

The maxim "No salvation outside the Church" applies quite clearly to someone who would refuse to enter the Church, the means of salvation, by a *culpable* refusal or ignorance. He is then excluded from the Church, the reality of salvation, precisely because of his lack of supernatural faith, which makes a person adhere to the Church in all her aspects. It goes without saying that such a judgment can be passed on such and such an individual concretely only by God alone.

An application of this is made, in no. 15, to non-Catholic Christians. Their refusal or ignorance of the Catholic fullness of the Church is presumed to be *non-culpable,* because they are presumed innocent of the sin of heresy or schism that is at the historical origin of their communities. They have received *sacramental* baptism, and not only the baptism of desire. As a result, *a true union in the Holy Spirit is added to all the means of salvation that we may have in common with them.* Hence it is

The People of God

clear that these non-Catholic believers belong to the Church and consequently can be saved.

On the subject of the situation of non-Christians (*LG* 16), the Council proceeds in two very distinct stages. The first concerns those who explicitly profess the first two *credibilia*. Mentioned first are the Jews, who are ordered to the People of God. This ordering, as we said, is already the actualization of a potential, and not a pure potentiality. Here, too, incorporation into the Church will take place depending on whether or not the refusal to enter it fully is culpable. The second stage concerns the other belief systems that profess monotheism, first of all the Muslims, but also those who seek "in shadows and images" a God whom they do not know. In this case the first two *credibilia* are always present explicitly in a more or less elaborate form. The Council repeats here the teaching that has become traditional since Pius IX:

> Those who, through no fault of their own, do not know the Gospel of Christ or his Church, but who nevertheless seek God with a sincere heart, and, moved by grace, try in their actions to do his will as they know it through the dictates of their conscience—those too may achieve eternal salvation.

Finally, the Council—still in no. 16—considers expressly those who do not even have an explicit knowledge of God, or even those who reject it (practical or theoretical atheism).

> Nor shall Divine Providence deny the assistance necessary for salvation to [such persons] ... who, not without grace, strive to lead a good life.[117]

We have therefore in this doctrinal summary a wide-ranging teaching that, for every conceivable spiritual situation, takes care to show how the maxim "No salvation outside the Church" applies. From the full, total acceptance of the idea of Church (Catholic fullness) to its imperfect realizations that are still founded on sacramental baptism (separated communities) and then to its imperfect realizations that do not include the means instituted by Christ (the Jewish religion, monotheistic faiths, extra-biblical religions, a-religious situations), it is always through some kind of more or less perfect belonging to the Church that one is saved. For the faith received through sacramental baptism or baptism of desire always makes the subject a member of the Body of Christ.

---

117. This "necessary assistance" is, in other words, the means that make possible a baptism of desire and a largely implicit supernatural faith.

Inevitably, some concluded from this that belonging to the Catholic Church had now become useless for salvation; in order to avoid such reasoning, the Council recalled the "abnormal" and precarious situation of those who do not benefit from the fullness of Catholic life and consequently the responsibility of Catholics in God's sight. In the final lines of chapter 2, the Council reiterates the necessity of the missions, which strive "to procure the glory of God and the salvation of all these [men]" (no. 16 and 17 at the end).

In conclusion, once the main clarifications have been made, it is evident that the maxim "No salvation outside the Church" does not smack of imperialism or intolerance. It expresses in its own way the heart of ecclesiology by showing how the analogy of ecclesial membership can be applied in different situations. We will return to this in the speculative part. This is a particularly noteworthy example of dogmatic development. Now we see better why and how the Spirit of truth assures a *homogeneous* development. The ancient doctrine does not need to be attenuated, much less suppressed, but rather *deepened*. The point is not that belonging to the Church needs to be relativized; rather, the *mode* of this incorporation needs to be refined.

b. The order and the distinction between clergy, laity, and consecrated religious

1. The classification "clergy vs. laity"

In deliberately placing its treatment of the People of God (chap. 2) before the discussion of the hierarchy (chap. 3), the Council meant to speak first about all of Christ's faithful before making any distinction. The expression *Christi fideles* is the most universal; this is the common status of all the children of God: to be baptized is the real treasure.[118] And so it is important to recall—and the Council did so in this way—that before studying the distinctions between members of the Body of Christ, the first thing is to be a member!

It has also been said and repeated almost *ad nauseam* that this presentation meant to break with the practice of manuals on ecclesiology before the Council, which always presented the clergy before the laity,

---

118. See the remark attributed to Pius XI: "The most beautiful day in the life of a pope is the day of his baptism."

The People of God

thus reducing ecclesiology to a sort of "hierarchology." In short, Vatican II is said to have brought about a "Copernican revolution" in this regard. This has to be understood correctly. It is quite accurate to say that the prevailing ecclesiological teaching followed the classification "clergy vs. laity" and ran the risk of reducing the vision of the Church to a hierarchical vision. There were historical reasons for that presentation, which, properly situated within a much larger context, is still correct. Indeed, according to one important perspective, the hierarchy should be placed before the laity. The Church is the work of God, and this work is accomplished in Christ and through the Holy Spirit, who act through "intermediaries" or *mediators* (the hierarchy). These mediators, at their own level, are true causes of grace.[119] Now a cause always has priority in relation to its effect. This is the sense in which the hierarchy precedes the laity. If the primacy of the assembly of the baptized over its ministers is absolutized, we run the risk of thinking about the hierarchy as the product, the effect of the charity of the faithful: the constituted community internally "secretes" the pastoral service that is entrusted to some of its members. But then the question arises of *how* that grace of charity made its way into this community. If we answer "directly from Christ," we are not considering the ministers as *mediators* in the line of efficient causality instituted by Christ, but rather as a merely human disposition that proceeds from the community and can vary according to its needs. That would be to acknowledge the typically Protestant view, which rejects any mediation between Christ and the faithful. This explains why during the era of the classical theology of the Counter-Reformation there was an insistence on the efficient causality exercised by ordained ministers. This answer is correct, but, if only this aspect is honored, there is a risk of concentrating all of ecclesiology in a "hierarchology"; this was the case in many manuals from the late nineteenth and early twentieth centuries. The reaction against the Reformation must not lead to the opposite extreme. Therefore the line of reasoning about efficient causality must be supplemented by other considerations. Two principal ideas should be emphasized.

The first boils down to noting that charity, once it has been received among the faithful, "circulates" throughout the organism of

---

119. According to the expression of Charles Journet, the causality of ordained ministers is a "ministerial efficient causality."

grace that is the Church. It comes from Christ through his ministers; it is the first thing in the order of efficient causality. Once received in the ecclesial Body, however, it acts in turn upon the ministers, so that all the acts for which the ministers are secondary causes (preaching and governance) will be more or less "successful" depending on the specific state of the charity in the whole organism. Charles Journet expresses the matter thus:

> The hierarchy ... is the cause of the Church before it is her effect.... But there is an influence flowing the other way, too, inasmuch as the quality and functioning of the hierarchy in a given period—the precise state of its historical development, the choice perhaps of its declarative pronouncements, the nature above all and the quality of its canonical decisions—may be explained in a large measure by the state of the inner charity of the Church at the time.[120]

The fact that *Lumen gentium* 2 gives priority to a consideration of all the faithful, before any distinction, is therefore not a denial of the causal role of ordained ministers. Besides, the discussion of the Body of Christ theme (chap. 1, nos. 7–8) already mentions it clearly.

The second consideration will give us the profound reason for the order followed by *Lumen gentium*. The notion of *service* (*"diakonia,"* "ministry") makes it comprehensible. All of Christian life is service. All baptized persons are charged with a *diakonia* for the whole world in the image of Christ, the first Servant. It is a question of transforming the world by causing it to live better and better, more and more by grace and in grace. For this purpose all Christians are priests, prophets, and kings, so that the Reign of God might extend to the whole world in all aspects of its life. This is Christian service *par excellence;* here is the fundamental Christian vocation. The hierarchy exists so that this service might be rendered by all. This is the sense in which every cleric is a *servant of the servants.* We must therefore add to the line of reasoning about efficient causality a complementary perspective, that of *finality:* in order that the whole community might fulfill properly its vocation to service, there is within it a particular ministry given and instituted by Christ, which derives its purpose from that general vocation: this is the hierarchy. For this purpose it exercises its authority over a given group (the community) that must be true to its vocation. Here the

---

120. In *L'Église du Verbe incarné,* 1:670–71; cited from *The Church of the Word Incarnate,* 519–20.

The People of God

consideration of the hierarchy is second (but by no means secondary): an understanding of the end precedes an understanding of the means, because it makes them intelligible.[121]

In summary, the classification "clergy vs. laity" differs according to the vantage point in which one is situated. As for efficient causality, the cleric engenders the layman personally and communally. As for final causality, the laity are served personally and communally by the clergy. This second point of view—finality—was the decisive thing in determining the order of the first two chapters of *Lumen gentium.*

These clarifications are important to understand what an *order* between various realities is. Contrary to what our present-day culture thinks, the notion of order does not express a "rigid" or "authoritarian" concept of things (as in the expression "moral order"). On the contrary, this notion, if it is considered correctly, tries to express the relations between certain realities—in other words, the dynamism that results from their interdependence. To show this better, it is interesting to note how Vatican II presented simultaneously the distinction and the relations between the two types of priesthood shared with Christ: "Though they differ essentially and not only in degree, the common priesthood of the faithful and the ministerial or hierarchical priesthood are none the less ordered one to another; each in its proper way shares in the one priesthood of Christ."[122]

The difference between these two priesthoods (the baptismal priesthood that makes a person a lay Christian and the ministerial priesthood that makes a man a priest) is both an essential difference and a difference of degree. This twofold difference is what manifests their relation.[123] We can summarize this in terms of the major liturgical expression of these two priesthoods. In the celebration of the Eucharist, the baptismal priesthood appears first as something essentially different from the ministerial priesthood, because these two priesthoods

---

121. On this point, cf. the intervention of the drafting committee spokesman on chap. 2 of *Lumen gentium*, AS III/I:205ff. See also G. Philips, *L'Église en son mystère au deuxième concile du Vatican*, 1:129–30.

122. "Sacerdotium autem commune fidelium et sacerdotium ministeriale seu hierarchicum, licet essentia et non gradu tantum differunt, ad invicem tamen ordinantur; unum enim et alterum suo peculiari modo de uno Christi sacerdotio participant"; LG 10.

123. See Benoît-Dominique de La Soujeole, "Différence d'essence et différence de degré dans le sacerdoce," *RT* 109 (2009): 621–38.

do not perform the same act: the baptized person offers the spiritual sacrifice of himself, while the minister offers the sacrifice of Christ. Each priesthood is the ultimate purpose of the other: the reason the priest carries out Christ's sacrifice is so that the baptized person might join his own to it, and the reason the baptized person carries out the sacrifice of himself is so that it might be taken up into the sacrifice of Christ. In this way the Eucharist achieves its perfection of being the sacrifice of the whole Christ, Head and members. But there is, furthermore, a difference of degree. In effect, during the Eucharist, when Christ's sacrifice is made present by the act of the priest (consecration), the faithful cooperate in offering this sacrifice to the Father.[124]

This twofold difference is structural. It is found again analogically in the other two qualities (prophetic and royal). The faithful simultaneously witness personally to their faith and to the faith of the Church, in cooperation with the ministers; the faithful simultaneously govern the world themselves according to the Gospel and cooperate with the clergy in governing the Church. Consequently, as a general rule, the order clericvs. layman is a complex order that orders these two qualities to each other so that the life of the Church is fostered and grows and is fully manifested. For this reason we must beware of oversimplification and, above all, of reducing the relations between clergy and laity to the purely sociological level (governors vs. governed).

2. The distinction between cleric and layman

This distinction per se is simple: the cleric is the baptized man who has received the sacrament of holy orders (active definition) in order to beget human beings to supernatural life, in the ecclesial community, for the service of that community's mission. The layman is the baptized person who is not a cleric—in other words, who *is begotten,* and who *is served.* As one can see, the definition of the layman is thus "negative": a so-called definition "by privation." This type of definition is not well received in our days because it is thought to be demeaning. Therefore people tried to give a positive definition of the layperson. To do that, many authors took as their basis the reference in *Lumen gentium* 31,

---

124. See the prayer following the consecration in Eucharistic Prayer I: "Therefore, O Lord, ... we [priests], your servants and [= together with] your holy people [the baptized], offer to your glorious majesty ... this pure victim, this holy victim."

which says that "Their secular character is proper and peculiar to the laity." What does that mean? On this subject there is plenty of literature that should be read with a critical eye; it tries to exalt this secular character, arguing that the laity has been treated for too long in the Church as "inferior." It must be admitted that a narrow, dangerous clericalism developed in the Church, especially during the nineteenth century,[125] but trying to react against that state of affairs can lead to the opposite extreme, which is no better. The evolution of some Catholic Action groups since 1950 has not avoided that pitfall.

What, then, is this *secular character*? In order to circumscribe a reality, one must first look at its *being*. Thus, on the ontological level, we will say that the secular character—as its name indicates—is the fact of belonging to the *saeculum*—in other words, the world that has been created and redeemed by God. This is—obviously—common to the cleric (who is not a superman), the layman, and the consecrated religious (who is not an angel). The secular character is not an *ontological* mark proper to the layman. Moreover, it is clear that before being a cleric or a consecrated religious (as an adult), one is a layman; upon ordination or profession of the evangelical counsels nothing ontological is removed. What distinguishes the cleric (and the consecrated religious) from the layman under the heading "secular character" should be sought, not along ontological, but along *operative* lines. Consequently we will call *the secular character* the vocation of having to deal with temporal (secular) affairs, according to their own logic (cf. the autonomy of the temporal order in GS 36) and to order them to God. This is *Lumen gentium* 31 verbatim.

The term "laity" is here understood to mean all the faithful except those in holy orders and those who belong to a religious state approved by the Church. That is, the faithful who by Baptism are incorporated into Christ, are placed in the People of God, and in their own way share the priestly, prophetic and kingly office of Christ, and to the best of their ability carry on the mission of the whole Christian people in the Church and in the world.

---

125. People used to say in those days that the layman had two basic postures: kneeling before the altar and seated before the pulpit. Some added maliciously: reaching for their wallets at the collection! [See "Pray, Pay, and Obey."] If those are the three chief acts of the *tria munera Christi* of the layman, one cannot say that the baptismal vocation is exalted! See Yves Congar, *Jalons pour une théologie du laïcat*, 7.

Their secular character is proper and peculiar to the laity. Although those in Holy Orders may sometimes be engaged in secular activities, or even practice a secular profession, yet by reason of their particular vocation, they are principally and expressly ordained to the sacred ministry. At the same time, religious give outstanding and striking testimony that the world cannot be transfigured and offered to God without the spirit of the beatitudes. But by reason of their special vocation it belongs to the laity to seek the kingdom of God by engaging in temporal affairs and directing them according to God's will. They live in the world, that is, they are engaged in each and every work and business of the earth and in the ordinary circumstances of social and family life which, as it were, constitute their very existence.

This activity belongs specifically to the laity. The cleric and the consecrated religious are not *ontologically* incapable of it, but they are—with some exceptions—excluded from it, since their vocation places them in another type of relation to the world, a relation complementary to that of the layman.[126] The cleric serves grace with a view to this work, while the consecrated religious witness to the fundamental orientation of this world toward another world.[127]

Finally let us note one clarification with regard to the layman that should be understood.

Fr. Congar maintained that the term *laïkos*, which is derived philologically from *laos*, expressed the whole theological substance of the People of God theme.[128] In short, the *laïkos* is said to be a member of the *laos* [the people] and thus is a "believer"; in the People of God all would then be primarily and fundamentally *laymen*. This point was critiqued by Fr. de La Potterie in an article that appeared in 1958.[129] Fr. Congar acknowledged that the critique was well-founded ("a study as decisive as it is learned")[130] and consequently modified his position.[131] Here, in summary, are their findings:

---

126. The appendix of D. Bourgeois, *L'Un et l'autre sacerdoce* (Paris: 1991), makes for interesting reading on this subject.

127. This is the eschatological character of consecrated life (*LG* 44, §3).

128. See *Jalons pour une théologie du laïcat*, 2nd ed. (Paris: 1954).

129. *NRTh* 80 (1958): 840–53. A revised version of the article was published in *La vie selon l'Esprit: condition du Chrétien*, US 55 (Paris: 1965).

130. In the preface to *La vie selon l'Esprit*.

131. In *Jalons*, 3rd ed., in US 23 (Paris: 1964), 647–48.

The People of God

In profane Greek, *laïkos* does designate a member of the *laos*, but always as distinguished from those who govern, the *archontes*. Biblical Greek (LXX and NT) knows nothing of the word *laïkos*. The Church Fathers use it very little, and always in keeping with the profane usage. The conclusion is certain: a *laïkos* is a Christian who is neither bishop nor priest nor deacon—in short, who does not belong to the clergy. The word cannot be made to signify more than that, except that it designates someone whom the ordained ministers serve.[132]

3. The situation of the consecrated religious

We understand this expression to mean a person who belongs to the consecrated life, whatever the particular type may be (monk, religious, hermit, consecrated virgin). With the help of the preceding discussion, we can declare that the consecrated religious, whether or not he is a priest (if a man), is "ontologically" secular: he belongs to the *saeculum*. But at the level of activity, he does not have the "secular character." In other words, he does not have to engage in temporal affairs according to their rules (cf. *LG* 31). Although he belongs to this world with all his being, he does not act in the secular manner upon the realities of the world. On the other hand, the consecrated religious is defined positively: he is a baptized person who is oriented toward the common perfection of all the baptized, the fullness of charity, by the particular path of the evangelical counsels.

What about the consecrated religious cleric, however?

The state of the consecrated religious is a *state of life*. The clerical state, though, does not imply a particular state of life. Per se, the priesthood can be lived in the diocesan clergy as well as in the consecrated life. It is an office, exercising ministerial efficient causality—in other words, preaching, sanctifying, and governing: these are actions. They do require a preliminary ontological quality, the priestly character, in order to be placed, but this is not *per se* connected with a particular state of life.[133]

---

132. On the theology of the laity, see the recent study by G. Magnani, "Does the So-Called Theology of the Laity Possess a Theological Status?" in *Vatican II: Assessment and Perspectives* (New York: Paulist Press, 1988), 1:586–633.

133. We might have cited, as an example of the variety possible in the form of priestly life, the existence of both a celibate and a married priesthood. However, the question of priestly celibacy is particularly complex, and that is why we do not take that example.

276   Theology of Sources

The consecrated religious who has received the sacrament of holy orders is first—at the level of state of life—a consecrated religious, and then at the level of office, a cleric. The specificity of his vocation to consecrated life sets conditions to some extent on his way of acting as a cleric. What is this relation? The purpose of the religious state is to promote the acquisition of the perfection of charity, and thereby the religious cleric benefits from a special, very precious aid in carrying out his clerical duties better and better.[134] Furthermore, not infrequently the consecrated religious, according to his specific vocation, actualizes this or that aspect of the clerical office in a more particular way and another aspect not as much, without however being radically incapable of those other aspects. Thus a Dominican friar performs above all the duties of teaching and sanctifying, but he performs only slightly, or not at all, the duty of governing a specific part of the People of God.[135] The monk who is a priest performs above all the duty of sanctifying and normally does not carry out the duty of teaching and governing. The Carthusian Order is an order of priests sustained by a very exalted spirituality of the Eucharist; it is practically the only priestly act that a Carthusians carries out. But there are also institutes of consecrated life in which the vocation of the members allows them to put into action all the aspects of the priestly office—for example, the canons regular who, by their vocation, are in charge of parishes.[136]

To sum up, how are we to understand the ecclesiological situation of clerics, laymen, and consecrated religious? Keeping in mind the preceding discussion, we see clearly that the criteria for distinguishing among these three categories of persons are of two sorts:

From the perspective of *efficient causality*, we distinguish within the Church:

- those who administer grace: the clerics;
- those *to whom* grace is administered: the faithful (both lay and consecrated persons).

---

134. This, of course, is true *objectively* and not at the personal, interior level: a faithful parish priest is worth more than a religious priest who has gone astray.

135. A Dominican can be a parish priest; he is made capable of it by the sacrament of holy orders, but normally he is not a parish priest.

136. Cf. the tradition of Augustinian Canons and the Premonstratensian Order.

From this perspective, the consecrated religious per se is not distinguished from the layman if he is not a cleric. The criterion is functional. This is the criterion that determines the sequence of chapters 3 (on ministers) and 4 (on the laity) of *Lumen gentium*. What distinguishes these persons is their place, their rank in the community (*ordo*).

From the perspective of *final causality*, we distinguish within the Church:

- those who tend toward Christian perfection by the common path: clerics and laypeople;
- those who tend toward Christian perfection by the particular path of the evangelical counsels: consecrated religious.

From this perspective, the cleric does not have a *state of life* that is per se distinct from that of the lay faithful. He is not bound to practice poverty; he owes obedience to his bishop just as a layman does: the bishop is his *father*, as he is for the layman, not his "superior." His Christian perfection is attained *first and foremost* by the exercise of his ministry (the *tria munera Christi*), and this ministry *per se* does not require a particular state of life. The criterion here is state of life (*status*), and this is the criterion that determines the sequence of chapters 5 (the universal call to holiness) and 6 (the consecrated life) in *Lumen gentium*.

We must be careful, however, about texts that adopt limited definitions suited to the context. Thus, for example, the passage from *Lumen gentium* 31 that was already cited: "The term 'laity' is *here* understood to mean all the faithful except those in Holy Orders and those who belong to a religious state approved by the Church." Here the document focuses on the layman *simultaneously* by the criteria of efficient causality and final causality. The layman *here* is someone who is not a priest (criterion of office, *ordo*) and who is not a consecrated religious (criterion of state of life, *status*). This distinction is not tripartite, but still bipartite, based on involvement in temporal affairs. This is clear in the next lines of the document: the layman *here* is someone who acts in the world, on the world, and according to the laws of the world. The document recalls that engaging in temporal matters is the business of those who are neither priests nor consecrated religious;[137] it does not pres-

---

137. The same point is made in *LG* 40, §2.

ent the ecclesiological situation of these three categories of persons in terms of a proper ontological character. Moreover, in conclusion, we can point out that those who maintain that there is only one division into three states of life are thwarted by the existence of consecrated religious who are priests: could it be that those persons have two states of life? We prefer to say that in this case we have a state of life properly speaking (consecrated), which is understood in terms of the finality of the Christian life, and a precise place in the Church, which is understood in terms of the ministerial efficient causality of grace.

BIBLIOGRAPHY
The Church, the People of God, in Scripture

The ecclesiological theme of the People of God was promoted in the 1950s, particularly by Lucien Cerfaux, *La Théologie de l'Église suivant saint Paul*. See also Rudolf Schnackenburg, *The Church in the New Testament*. See both in the general bibliography.

Carrez, Maurice. "Le Nouvel Israël: Réflexions sur l'absence de cette désignation de l'Église dans le Nouveau Testament." *Foi et Vie* 58 (1959): 30–34. Although brief, this study helps to show why the expression "New Israel" would become an important patristic commonplace. Should be read with Marcel Simon's *Verus Israël*.

Concilium 1 (1965). The whole issue is devoted to the theme of the People of God. See in particular the reports by Rudolf Schnackenburg and Jacques Dupont on the recent biblical studies at that time.

Congar, Yves. "L'Église comme Peuple de Dieu." *Concilium* 1 (1965): 11–34. The article is not exclusively a biblical study, but starts out from a solid scriptural basis.

———. *Un Peuple messianique: L'Église, sacrament du salut, salut et libération*. Paris: Cerf, 1975. Offers a good understanding of the People of God theme after the extremes of the postconciliar period.

Coppens, Joseph. "L'Église, nouvelle alliance de Dieu avec son peuple." In *Aux origines de l'Église*, edited by Jean Giblet, 13–21. Recherches bibliques 7. Paris: Desclée de Brouwer, 1965.

de Vaux, Roland. *Les Institutions de l'Ancien Testament*. 2 vols. Paris: Cerf, 1958–60. Translated by John McHugh as *Ancient Israel*. New York: McGraw-Hill, 1961. A valuable study of the similarities and differences between Israel and other peoples.

Giblet, Jean, and Pierre Grelot. "Covenant." Translated by John J. Kilgallen. In *Dictionary of Biblical Theology*, edited by Xavier-Léon Dufour, 93–98. New York: Seabury Press, 1973. A good general presentation.

Grelot, Pierre. "People." Translated by John J. Kilgallen. In *Dictionary of Biblical*

The People of God

Theology, edited by Xavier-Léon Dufour, 416–22. A good general presentation.

Guillet, Jacques. "Calling." Translated by Donald F. Brezine. In *Dictionary of Biblical Theology*, edited by Xavier-Léon Dufour, 65–67. A good general presentation.

———. "Election." Translated by Glicerio S. Abad. In *Dictionary of Biblical Theology*, edited by Xavier-Léon Dufour, 137–41. A good general presentation.

Le Peuple de Dieu, a special issue of the journal *Foi et Vie* 6 (1964). Good studies; most importantly it includes a summary of the article *laos* from Kittel's *Theological Dictionary of the New Testament*.

Schnackenburg, Rudolf, and Karl Thieme. *La Bible et le mystère de l'Église*. Tournai: Desclée, 1964. See in particular Thieme's essay on "Le mystère de l'Église et la vision chrétienne du Peuple de l'ancienne alliance," 139–202.

Simon, Marcel. *Verus Israël*. Paris: Boccard, 1964. Jewish-Christian relations in the second and third centuries, mainly from a literary and historical perspective. Important for an understanding of the climate in which the transition from the old to the new People was experienced.

Spicq, Ceslaus. *Vie chrétienne et pérégrination selon le Nouveau Testament*. Lectio divina 71. Paris: Cerf, 1972.

Vonier, Anscar. *The People of God*. London: Burns, Oates, and Washbourne, 1937. A groundbreaking book in a rather outmoded style, yet it nicely shows the historical and communal dimensions of salvation. The biblical basis is not very substantial, but it is a good example of quality "popular" preaching.

The Three Titles of Priest, Prophet, and King

Studies have proliferated with the rediscovery of the People of God theme. They have dealt above all with Tradition because scholars thought, at first, that this theological line of thought was unknown between Eusebius of Caesarea and Calvin. From the biblical perspective, we might note (beside the preceding titles, which may address the subject):

Amsler, Samuel. "Les ministères de l'ancienne alliance: rois, prêtres et prophètes." In *Ministères et laïcat*, 29–41. Taizé: Presses de Taizé, 1964.

Cazelles, Henri. "Royaume de prêtres et nation consacrée (Ex. 19:6)." In *Humanisme et foi chrétienne*, edited by Charles Kannengiesser and Yves Marchasson, 540–45. Paris: Beauchesne, 1976.

Cerfaux, Lucien. "Regale sacerdotium." In *Recueil Lucien Cerfaux*, 2:283–315. Gembloux, Belgium: J. Duculot, 1954. Reprinting of an article that appeared in *Revue des sciences philosophiques et théologiques* 28 (1939): 5–39.

Colson, Jean. *Prêtres et peuple sacerdotal*. Paris: Beauchesne, 1969.

Congar, Yves. *Le Sacerdoce chrétien des laïcs et des prêtres*. Brussels: La Pensée catholique, 1967.

Coppens, Joseph. "Le messianisme sacerdotal dans les écrits du Nouveau Testament." In *La Venue du Messie: Messianisme et eschatologie*, 101–12. Recherches bibliques 6. Paris: Desclée de Brouwer, 1962.

———. "Le sacerdoce royal des fidèles." In *Au service de la parole de Dieu*, 65–75. Gembloux, Belgium: Duculot, 1969. Very good bibliography up to 1969.

———. "Le sacerdoce vétérotestamentaire." In *Sacerdoce et célibat*, 3–21. Gembloux, Belgium: Duculot, 1971.
Cothenet, Édouard. "Le sacerdoce des fidèles d'après la Prima Petri." *Esprit et Vie* 79, no. 11 (March 13, 1969): 169–73.
Feuillet, André. "Les chrétiens prêtres et rois d'après l'Apocalypse." *Revue thomiste* 75 (1975): 40–66.
Hanson, Paul D. *The People Called: The Growth of Community in the Bible*. San Francisco: Harper and Row, 1986.
Vanhoye, Albert. "Sacerdoce commun et sacerdoce ministériel." In *Nouvelle revue théologique* 97 (1975): 193–207.

The Church, the People of God, in Tradition
Patristic Literature
The theme of the People of God in general

The reader may consult the general works of patrology already cited and particular authors (especially Ratzinger and Camelot; cf. chapter 3).

Dictionary and encyclopedia articles are rather poor because they are dated. See however the article "Peuple de Dieu" by Jan Grootaers in the encyclopedia *Catholicisme*, 11:98–121. A rather quick summary of the patristic literature; completely ignores the dogmatic tradition of the theme.

Bardy, Gustave. *La Théologie de l'Église de S. Clément de Rome à S. Irénée*. Paris: 1945. Also by Bardy: *La Théologie de l'Église de S. Irénée au concile de Nicée*. Paris: 1947. By the same author, a series of articles on the priesthood of Christians in patristic writings, in *La Vie spirituelle*, suppl. 1937 and 1939, as well as "Le sacerdoce chrétien du Ier au Ve s." In *Prêtres d'hier à aujourd'hui*. US 28. Paris: 1954, 23–61.
Congar, Yves. "L'Église comme Peuple de Dieu." *Concilium* 1 (1965): 15–31.
———. "Peuple de Dieu dans l'Église ancienne." In *Rencontre*, Actes du colloque judéo-chrétien sur le Peuple de Dieu. Strasbourg: 1970, 35–53. This very well-documented essay aims in particular to emphasize the Fathers' understanding of the persistence of Israel. A copious survey of the Fathers.
Simon, Marcel. *Verus Israël*. Paris: 1948.

St. Augustine in particular

Jourjon, M. "L'évêque et le peuple de Dieu selon S. Augustin." In *S. Augustin parmi nous*. Lyons: 1954, 151–78.
"Peuple de Dieu," special issue of the journal *Les Quatre Fleuves* 5 (1975); note particularly the essay by A. Jaubert, "D'Israël à l'Église," and the one by Charles Pietri, "Des ministères pour le nouveau Peuple de Dieu?" Not very patristic as a whole.
Ratzinger, Joseph. *Volk und Haus Gottes in Augustins Lehre von der Kirche*. Munich: 1954. This was the author's doctoral thesis, which was highly influential. The study is not limited to St. Augustine, but considers all of African theology. A

great classic and, before the Council, a powerful help in rediscovering the patristic tradition on the People of God theme. Italian translation: *Popolo e casa di Dio in sant'Agostino.* Milan: 1971.

The trilogy priest-prophet-king

Congar, Yves. *Jalons pour une théologie du laïcat.* Paris: 1953. English translation by Donald Attwater: *Lay People in the Church: A Study for the Theology of the Laity.* Westminster, Md.: Newman Press, 1957. A great classic. The author arranges the material according to the *tria munera* applied to the lay faithful. In each instance the author cites fundamental patristic testimonies.

———. "Sur la trilogie: prophète-roi-prêtre." *RSPT* 67 (1983): 97–115. This is a long review of the thesis by L. Schick, *Das Dreifache Amt Christi und der Kirche* (Frankfurt and Bern: 1982). Congar adds many erudite or fundamental remarks that make this review the equivalent of a scholarly article.

Dabin, P. *Le Sacerdoce royal des fidèles dans la tradition ancienne et moderne.* Brussels and Paris: 1950. A reference work.

Fuchs, J. *Magisterium, Ministerium, Regimen.* Bonn: 1941. Translated into French in *RSPT* 53 (1969) under the title "Origines d'une trilogie ecclésiologique à l'époque rationaliste de la théologie," 185–211. The author's thesis is that the trilogy priest-prophet-king was of Protestant origin; that nothing was written between several isolated Fathers and Calvin that could serve as a basis for the modern use of those terms. The author's mistake is to limit himself to excessively literal observations (the words priest-prophet-king used together). Since then learned studies (cf. Dabin and Congar) have corrected these overly hasty remarks. The article is still instructive in showing how Catholics, particularly canonists, "re-tamed" the trilogy starting in the nineteenth century so as to overcome the impasses caused by the distinction *ordo-iurisdictio.*

Vaillancourt, R. "Le sacerdoce et les trois pouvoirs messianiques." *Laval théol. et Phil.* 22 (1966): 248–303. Limited to the consideration of the ministerial priesthood, this article is devoted mainly to a presentation of the tripartite tradition as compared with the bipartite tradition (*ordo-iurisdictio*). Contains a valuable review of the Magisterium and authors from the Renaissance to the eve of Vatican II.

St. Thomas Aquinas

de La Soujeole, Benoît-Dominique. "Les *tria munera Christi;* contribution de saint Thomas à la recherche contemporaine." In Actes du colloque Saint Thomas d'Aquin et le sacerdoce, *RT* 99 (1999): 59–74.

Journet, Charles. *L'Église du Verbe incarné.* Paris: 1951: "Les trois privilèges de la grâce capitale," 2:607ff. A rather close reading of passages cited from St. Thomas, which opts for a different tripartite division (priesthood, sanctity, kingship, the last-mentioned including prophecy).

Torrell, Jean-Pierre. *Saint Thomas d'Aquin, maître spirituel.* Paris and Fribourg: 1996, 198–200. Major passages from St. Thomas.

Vaillancourt, R. "Le sacerdoce et les trois pouvoirs messianiques." A review of several passages, but the commentary is limited.

The Church, the People of God, in the contemporary period

For an introduction to the history of the modern rediscovery of the People of God theme, see the articles "Peuple de Dieu" in the *Dictionnaire de Spiritualité* and the encyclopedia *Catholicisme*. Note also:

Napiwodzki, Piotr. *Eine Ekklesiologie im Werden: Mannes Dominikus Koster und sein Beitrag zum theologischen Verständnis der Kirche.* Freiburg [CH]: 2005. See particularly pages 46–71 for the modern reintroduction of the People of God theme in dogmatic theology and the difficulty of articulating it in terms of the Body of Christ theme.

The following titles are essentially commentaries on chapter 2 of *Lumen gentium*.

Bouyer, Louis. *L'Église de Dieu.* Paris: 1975, 213–84. English translation by Charles Underhill Quinn: *The Church of God.* Reprinted San Francisco: Ignatius Press, 2011, 181–248.

Concilium 1 (1965). See the reports by Rudolf Schnackenburg and Jacques Dupont on the recent theological literature at that time, 91–100.

Congar, Yves. "L'Église comme Peuple de Dieu." *Concilium* 1 (1965): 15–31. Provides a precise theological analysis of the theme, showing in what ways it needs to be supplemented by the Body of Christ theme.

———. "Richesse et vérité d'une vision de l'Église comme Peuple de Dieu." *Les Quatre Fleuves* 5 (1975): 46–54. The article was reprinted in *Le Concile Vatican II: Son Église, Peuple de Dieu et Corps du Christ.* Théologie historique 71. Paris: 1984.

Dupuy, B.-D. "Le 'Peuple de Dieu' dans la théologie et l'exégèse chrétienne contemporaine." In *Rencontre 1972.* Actes du colloque judéo-chrétien sur le Peuple de Dieu. Strasbourg: 7–9 Feb. 1970, 54–67.

Fransen, F. "L'Église comme Peuple de Dieu." In *La nouvelle image de l'Église.* Paris: 1967, 102ff. More detailed than Semmelroth.

Holstein, H. *Hiérarchie et Peuple de Dieu d'après Lumen gentium.* Théologie historique 12. Paris: 1970. Nicely situates the new perspective, which is to consider *all* members of the Church in one community.

Nicolas, Jean-Hervé. *Synthèse dogmatique.* Paris and Fribourg: 1985, 646ff. Clearly shows the limits of this theme.

Pagé, Jean-Guy. *Qui est l'Église?* Vol. 3, *Le Peuple de Dieu.* 2nd ed. Montreal: 1985. See particularly 24–36 for a balanced presentation of Vatican II (with bibliography).

Philips, Gérard. *L'Église en son mystère au deuxième concile du Vatican.* Paris: 1967, 1:131ff. The best general presentation of the conciliar teaching by one of the principal authors of *Lumen gentium*.

The People of God

Semmelroth, O. "L'Église, nouveau Peuple de Dieu." In *L'Église de Vatican II*. US 51b. Paris: 1966, 395ff. A somewhat rapid presentation.

The rediscovery of the People of God theme has promoted a renewal of relations between the Church and Judaism. The question has had bearing especially on the idea of Messianism. Among the chief contributions are:

Chenu, M.-D. "Un peuple messianique." *NRTh* 99 (1967): 164–82. An important essay that had been drafted in *Peuple de Dieu dans le monde* (Paris: 1963), particularly 123ff., where the author studied the various secular messianic movements of the modern world.
Congar, Yves. *Un Peuple messianique*. Paris: 1975. With an extensive bibliography.
Dupuy, B.-D. "Le 'Peuple de Dieu' dans la théologie et l'exégèse chrétienne contemporaine."
Gonzalez-Ruiz, J.-M. "L'Église, Peuple de Dieu dans le monde." *Lumière et Vie* 72: 69–86. On the basis of *LG* 9 it proposes a new meaning for the expression "New Israel."
Rijk, C. A. "La recherche de l'unité primitive du Peuple de Dieu; juifs et gentils." In *La nouvelle image de l'Église*. Paris: 1967, 269ff.

On the trilogy: priest, prophet, and king

Alafaro, J. "Les fonctions salvifiques du Christ comme prophète, roi et prêtre." In *Mysterium Salutis*. Dogmatique de l'histoire du salut 11. Paris: 1975, 241ff. Not directly concerned with ecclesiology, it nevertheless gives the fundamental Christological basis.
de Smedt, E.-J. "Le sacerdoce des fidèles." In *Le Concile Vatican II*. US 51b. Paris: 1966, 411ff.
Hamer, J. *L'Église est une communion*. Paris: 1962. English translation by Ronald Matthews: *The Church Is a Communion*. New York: Sheed and Ward, 1965. See particularly chap. 5, "The Royal Priesthood of the People of God," 97ff. The author presents the state of the question (the three messianic offices of Christ, of the faithful, and of ordained ministers) on the eve of Vatican II. The theological presentation is very precise. Concerning ministers, he critiques the classic *ordo-iurisdictio* division and notes the status of the debate (especially with Charles Journet). This study is the first one to be consulted on the question.
Pagé, J.-G. *Qui est l'Église?* Vol. 3, *Le Peuple de Dieu*. 2nd ed. Montreal: 1985, 91ff.
van Leeuwen, B. "La participation universelle à la fonction prophétique du Christ." In *Le Concile Vatican II*. US 51b, Paris: 1966, 425ff.

See also the articles cited in the review of L. Schick by Yves Congar (*RSPT* 1983).

The distinction between cleric and layman

de La Soujeole, Benoît-Dominique. "Différence d'essence et différence de degré dans le sacerdoce," *RT* 109 (2009): 621–38.

The question of the relation of non-Christians to the Church

The Church Fathers and non-Christian religions

Daniélou, Jean. *Message évangélique et culture hellénistique aux IIe et IIIe s.* Tournai: 1961, especially on St. Justin.

de Lubac, Henri. *Paradoxe et mystère de l'Église.* Paris: 1967, chap. IV: "Les religions humaines d'après les Pères."

Fedou, M. "Les Pères de l'Église face aux religions de leur temps." *Pontificium Consilium pro dialogo,* Bulletin 80, no. 2 (1992): 173–85.

Luneau, A. "Pour aider au dialogue: Les Pères et les religions non chrétiennes." *NRTh* 89 (1967): 820–41; 914–39.

The classic problem of the salvation of nonbelievers

Caperan, L. *Le Problème du salut des infidels.* Vol. 1, *Essai historique (théologie positive).* Vol. 2, *Essai théologique (théologie speculative).* 2nd ed. Toulouse: 1934.

———. *L'Appel des non chrétiens au salut.* Paris: 1961.

Contemporary research
Before Vatican II

In the context of the so-called fulfillment theory:

Daniélou, Jean. *Le Mystère du salut des nations.* Paris: 1946. English translation by Angeline Bouchard: *The Salvation of the Nations.* New York: Sheed and Ward, 1950.

———. *Le Mystère de l'avent.* Paris: 1948. English translation by Rosemary Sheed: *Advent.* New York: Sheed and Ward, 1951.

———. *Essai sur le mystère de l'histoire.* Paris: 1953. English translation by Nigel Abercrombie: *The Lord of History: Reflections on the Inner Meaning of History.* Chicago: Regnery, 1958.

———. *Les Saints "paiens" de l'Ancien Testament.* Paris: 1956. English translation by Felix Faber: *Holy Pagans of the Old Testament.* London and New York: Helicon Press, 1957.

de Lubac, Henri. *Le Fondement théologique des missions.* Paris: 1946.

———. *Catholicisme: Les aspects sociaux du dogme.* 2nd ed. Paris: 1952. English translation by Lancelot C. Sheppard: *Catholicism: A Study of Dogma in Relation to the Corporate Destiny of Mankind.* New York: Longmans, Green, 1950; especially chapter V: "Christianity and history," 67–82.

Maurier, H. *Essai d'une théologie du paganisme.* Paris: 1965.

von Balthasar, Hans Urs. *The Moment of Christian Witness.* Translated by Richard Beckley. Glen Rock, N.J.: Newman Press, 1969. Moreover, see the general presentation in Jacques Dupuis, *Toward a Christian Theology of Religious Pluralism* (Maryknoll, N.Y.: Orbis, 1997), 140–43.

In the context of the theory of Christ in pagan religious traditions:

Fedou, M. *Les Religions selon la foi chrétienne.* Paris: 1996. A small but well-done book that presents the question nicely. Good supplemental bibliography.

Panikkar, R. *The Unknown Christ of Hinduism.* London: Darton, Longman, and Todd, 1964. The author developed his insights considerably after Vatican II. For one approach to his theology, see J. Dupuis, *Toward a Christian Theology of Religious Pluralism* (Maryknoll, N.Y.: Orbis, 1997), 149–53.

Rahner, Karl. "Theos in the New Testament." In *Theological Investigations.* Baltimore: Helicon Press, 1961, 1:79–148.

———. "Membership in the Church according to the Teaching of Pius XII's Encyclical '*Mystici Corporis Christi.*'" In *Theological Investigations.* Baltimore. Helicon Press, 1963, 2:1–88.

Rahner, Karl, and J.-B. Metz. *L'Homme à l'écoute du Verbe: fondements d'une théologie de la religion.* Tours: 1968.

Thils, G. *Propos et problèmes de la théologie des religions non chrétiennes.* Tournai: 1966.

Karl Rahner's widely popularized theory of the "anonymous Christian" was first formulated in his essay "Die anonymen Christen," in *Schriften zur Theologie* (Einsiedeln: 1965), 6:545–54; English translation "Anonymous Christians," in *Theological Investigations* (Baltimore, Helicon Press, 1969), 6:390–98. This intuition was taken up in *Foundations of Christian Faith: An Introduction to the Idea of Christianity,* trans. William V. Dych (New York: Crossroad, 1982). An enlightening study on the subject was written by Bernard Sesboüé: "Karl Rahner et les 'chrétiens anonymes,'" in *Études* 361 (Nov. 1984): 521–35. A friendly critique by Yves Congar can be found in "Les religions non bibliques sont-elles des médiations de salut?" In *Essais oecuméniques* (Paris: 1984), 271–96. See also H. van Sraelen, *Ouverture à l'autre: Laquelle?* (Paris: 1982); van Straelen, *L'Église et les religions non chrétiennes au seuil du XXIe s.* (Paris: 1994).

In the Thomistic school, note in particular:

Journet, Charles. *L'Église du Verbe incarné.* Paris: 1969, 3:354–412.

Lacombe, O. "Incidence de la rencontre des religions sur la théologie." *RT* 71 (1971): 589–98.

General studies surveying this literature

Labourdette, Marie-Michel. Chronicles in *La Revue Thomiste,* "Foi chrétienne et religions," *RT* 69 (1969): 93–126; *RT* 70 (1970): 96–116; *RT* 74 (1974): 643–55. Note also the essay by the same author, in collaboration with M.-J. Nicolas, "Théologie de l'apostolat missionnaire," *RT* 46 (1946): 575–602.

Willems, B. "La nécessité de l'Église pour le salut; aperçu bibliographique." *Concilium* I (1965): 101–14, with an extensive bibliography on the period leading up to Vatican II.

Vatican II

The Declaration *Nostra aetate*

A collection of essays can be found in *Les relations de l'Église avec les religions non chrétiennes.* US 61, Paris: 1966.

The Decree *Ad gentes*

A collection of essays can be found in *L'activité missionnaire de l'Église*, US 67 (Paris: 1967); in particular: Joseph Ratzinger, "La mission d'après les autres textes conciliares," 121–47; Yves Congar, "Principes doctrinaux," 185–217; H. Maurier, "Lecture de la Déclaration par un missionnaire d'Afrique," 119–60 (particularly 133ff., the presence of values outside the Church that the Church may not possess); A.-M. Henry, "Missions d'hier, mission de demain," 411–40.

Scholarship after Vatican II

An almost exhaustive bibliography can be found in Jacques Dupuis, *Toward a Christian Theology of Religious Pluralism* (Maryknoll, N.Y.: Orbis, 1997), 391–424. To our knowledge this is the most complete study. See the critical reviews: C. Geffré, "Le pluralisme religieux comme question théologique," *La Vie spirituelle* (1998): 580–86 (esp. 583–84). Editorial committee of *La Revue Thomiste*: "'Tout récapituler dans le Christ': À propos de l'ouvrage de Jacques Dupuis, *Vers une théologie chrétienne du pluralisme religieux*," *RT* 98 (1998): 591–630. Dupuis responded to the critiques of his arguments in a long article, "The Truth Will Make You Free," *Louvain Studies* 24 (1999): 211–63.

Académie internationale des Sciences religieuses. *Le Christianisme vis-à-vis des religions*. Chief editor J. Doré. Namur: 1997. Proceedings of the 1995 Athens colloquium. Conferences given by Catholics, Orthodox, and Protestants. Interesting illustration of the approaches of the different Christian confessions.

Aebischer-Crettol, M. *Vers un Oecuménisme interreligieux: Jalons pour une théologie chrétienne du pluralisme religieux*. Paris: 2001. Wide-ranging review of authors and trends with a good bibliography. The thesis attempts a middle path between religious "absolutism and relativism" that in our opinion is not conclusive.

"Le dialogue interreligieux," a dossier in the series *Questions actuelles: Le point de vue de l'Église*, published in September–October 1999 by DC. Interesting especially as an introduction to the nature and activities of the Pontifical Council for Interreligious Dialogue.

Generally speaking, the research can be divided into three currents or "paradigms" according to the predominant note: ecclesiocentrism, Christocentrism, theocentrism. Concerning this presentation, see Jacques Dupuis, *Toward a Christian Theology of Religious Pluralism* (Maryknoll, N.Y.: Orbis, 1997), 185–201.

The contribution of Thomists

In the wake of the publication of the above-cited book by J. Dupuis, we can cite the following studies:

Cagin, M. "Tout récapituler dans le Christ." *Nova et Vetera* (1999/2): 87–90. Favorable review of the *RT* article.

Cottier, G. "Sur la mystique naturelle." *RT* 101 (2001): 287–311 (esp. 288–97). Discussion with J. Dupuis on non-Christian mysticism; one must not be too quick to declare it supernatural.

Dupuis, Jacques. "The Truth Will Make You Free: The Theology of Religious Pluralism Revisited." *Louvain Studies* 24 (1999): 211–63. General response by Dupuis to the critiques of his book.

Editorial Committee of *La Revue Thomiste*. "'Tout récapituler dans le Christ': À propos de l'ouvrage de Jacques Dupuis, *Vers une théologie chrétienne du pluralisme religieux*." *RT* 98 (1998): 591–630.

Elders, L. "Les théories nouvelles de la signification des religions non-chrétiennes." *Nova et Vetera* (1998/3): 97–117. A very critical review of Dupuis's book, yet it remains within the perspective on non-Christian religions as being merely "natural."

Vallin, P. "Sur une suggestion thomasienne à l'adresse du dialogue interreligieux." *Nova et Vetera* (2002/3): 19–45. More critical with regard to the position of the *RT*.

Further developments concerning the Christology of Jacques Dupuis:

Donneaud, H. "Chalcédoine contre l'unicité absolue du médiateur Jésus-Christ?" *RT* 102 (2002): 43–62. Very closely argued critique of the following article by Jacques Dupuis, especially at the level of fundamental theology.

Dupuis, Jacques. "Le Verbe de Dieu, Jésus-Christ et les religions du monde." *NRTh* 123 (2001): 529–46. The author proposes a reading of Chalcedon and Constantinople III that could make room for the activity of the Word both before and after the Incarnation.

———. "Le Verbe de Dieu comme tel et comme incarné." *Was den Glauben in Bewegung bringt: Fundamentaltheologie in der Spur Jesu Christi*, Mélanges offerts à Karl H. Neufeld, SJ, sous la direction de A. R. Batloog, M. Delgado, et R. A. Siebenrock. Freiburg, Basel, and Vienna: Herder, 2004, 500–16. Dupuis's response to Donneaud. Beyond the Christological debate, it does seem that their clash is in the first place over theological method (Thomism not being a "hermeneutical theology").

Emery, Gilles. "Le Christ et la mission de l'Esprit selon S. Thomas." In Actes du colloque *Saint Thomas d'Aquin et la théologie des religions*.

Pottier, B. "Note sur la mission invisible du Verbe chez saint Thomas d'Aquin." *NRTh* 123 (2001): 547–57. The author consults St. Thomas and thinks that he allows for the possibility of a twofold action of the Word in the world, that of the Word as such and that of the Incarnate Word. In response, see the preceding study of Gilles Emery.

Later, more specialized studies on the ecclesiological question:

Daguet, François. "L'unique Église du Christ en acte et en puissance." *Nova et Vetera* (2004/2): 45–70. An ecclesiological approach that disputes the following study on certain points.

de La Soujeole, Benoît-Dominique. "Être ordonné à l'unique Église du Christ: L'ecclésialité des communautés non chrétiennes à partir des données oecuméniques." *RT* 102 (2002): 5–41. Develops the ecclesiological aspect of the question by proposing to manifest the analogical realization of the one and only Church.

Proceedings from the colloquium *Saint Thomas d'Aquin et la théologie des religions*, Institut Saint Thomas d'Aquin, *Revue Thomiste*. Toulouse: May 13–14, 2005; in particular the essays by Gilles Emery, "Le Christ et la mission de l'Esprit selon S. Thomas"; Gilbert Narcisse, "L'universalité de la médiation du Christ: Médiation du Verbe ou médiation du Christ?"; and Benoît-Dominique de La Soujeole, "La foi implicite" (reprinted in 2006 in *Revue Thomiste*).

Various authors. *Thomistes: ou de l'actualité de Saint Thomas d'Aquin*. Paris and Les Plans: Parole et Silence, 2003. Note in particular the essays by Gilles Emery, "Question d'aujourd'hui sur Dieu," 87–98 (esp. 96ff.); Gilbert Narcisse, "Le Christ selon S. Thomas," 115–29 (esp. 121–23); Benoît-Dominique de La Soujeole, "Enjeux actuels du dialogue interreligieux," 155–62; and T.-D. Humbrecht, "S. Thomas et la Providence," 227–37. Overall presentation of Thomistic thought indicating its current interest for interreligious dialogue.

The post-conciliar Magisterium

The reader may consult *Le Dialogue interreligieux dans l'enseignement officiel de l'Église catholique (1963–1997)*, documents compiled by F. Gioia, Edition de Solesmes, 1998. An almost exhaustive collection of pontifical documents that mixes, however, very diverse sources of widely varying degrees of authority. Note in particular the following documents:

John Paul II. Encyclical *Redemptor hominis* (March 4, 1979), esp. nos. 6 and 11.

———. Encyclical *Dominum et vivificantem* (May 18, 1986), esp. no. 53.

———. Apostolic Exhortation *Redemptionis missio* (December 7, 1990), esp. nos. 9, 18, 20, 28–29, 55–56.

———. *Catechism of the Catholic Church* (May 1994), esp. nos. 839, 841–45, 846, 847, 856, 2104.

———. Apostolic Letter *Tertio millennio adveniente* (November 10, 1994), esp. nos. 6, 19, 38, 46, 52–53.

Paul VI. Encyclical *Ecclesiam Suam* (August 6, 1964), esp. no. 60.

———. Apostolic Exhortation *Evangelii nuntiandi* (December 8, 1975), esp. no. 53.

Dicasteries and commissions

Congregation for the Doctrine of the Faith. Declaration *Dominus Iesus* (August 6, 2000). English edition: *On the Unicity and Salvific Universality of Jesus Christ and the Church*. Boston: Pauline Books and Media, 2000.

———. "Notification Relative to the Book of Jacques Dupuis, *Toward a Christian Theology of Religious Pluralism*" (January 24, 2001). English translation at Vatican website.

International Theological Commission. "The Single Church of Christ." Part IX of "Select Themes of Ecclesiology on the Occasion of the Twentieth Anniversary of the Closing of the Second Vatican Council" (1984). In *International Theolog-*

ical Commission: Texts and Documents. 2nd ed. San Francisco: Ignatius Press, 2009, 1:302–5.

———. "Christianity and the World Religions" (1997). In *International Theological Commission: Texts and Documents.* San Francisco: Ignatius Press, 2009, 2:145–86.

Pontifical Biblical Commission. *Foi et culture à la lumière de la Bible.* Turin: 1981.

Pontifical Commission for Justice and Peace. *Assisi: World Day of Prayer for Peace* (October 27, 1986). The Vatican: 1987.

Secretariat for Non-Christians. "The Attitude of the Church toward Followers of Other Religions: Reflections and Orientations on Dialogue and Mission" (May 10, 1984). http://www.cimer.org.au/documents/DialogueandMission1984.pdf.

5

Recapitulation

The Church Is a Mystery

All the features of the Church that we have just described through biblical themes lead us to grasp an important idea that can broadly be called *Christian realism*. What does this mean?

Christian Revelation is not only the communication of a set of truths preached by the prophets and Christ. More fundamentally, it is a *Mystērion:* in other words, a Revelation-reality, a salvation history in which the divine reality, insofar as it directly concerns humanity, manifests itself in a visible, earthly reality. Revelation, as Saint Augustine says, is *"historia ... dispensationis temporalis divinae Providentiae"* ["the history of the temporal dispensation of Divine Providence"].[1] The *kerygma* or Revelation-word expresses and analyzes the contents of this Revelation-reality. The latter consists in the temporal economy of salvation, and behind it appears the hidden Trinitarian life of the saving God.[2]

This distinction between Revelation-truth and Revelation-reality is terminology that has already been elaborated, but it has its basis in Scripture. For example, when St. Paul says to the Colossians concerning question about food and drink, "These are only a shadow of what was coming: the reality is the body of Christ" [Col 2:17, *Jerusalem Bible*,

---

1. *De vera religione* VII.13 (CCSL 32:196).
2. Edward Schillebeeckx, from the French-language Introduction to his thesis *De sakramentele Heilseconomie* (Antwerp: 1951); published in French as *L'Économie sacramentelle du salut* (Fribourg: 2004), 537.

1985], he distinguishes between the Jewish observances (announcements of things to come: *truths*) and their fulfillment in the New Testament (the gift that was announced is given: *reality*).³ This is very deeply rooted in Sacred Scripture. The Hebrew *dābār* can be translated, depending on the context, as "word" or "reality," "event," "fact," "action." The Word, when it is God's, says what will be accomplished and accomplishes what it says. From the beginning of the Book of Genesis it is noted that every time "God said ...," it comes to pass (Gn 1:3ff.). The Christian era begins in a similar way when the angel Gabriel announces to Mary that the words of the Lord to her will be fulfilled, for "with God nothing will be impossible" (Lk 1:37). This refers back to the annunciation of Isaac's birth, which says that Sarah will have a child despite her old age: "Is anything too hard for the Lord?" (Gn 18:14). Literally, Genesis 18:14 should be translated, "Is there anything [any "*dābār*"] too wonderful for the Lord?" Finally, as far as Greek and Latin are concerned, the *Logos-Verbum* is the Word of God who is a Person, the Christ who expresses himself and acts.

And so therefore this economy of salvation, which is prepared in the Old Testament, reaches its summit in the appearance of God in the world through the Incarnation of the Word: the human, earthly *reality* of Christ is the Revelation-presence of the divine realities, for "in him [Christ] the whole fulness of deity dwells bodily" (Col 2:9). The human community born from Christ's work of salvation, his Body, understands itself according to this pattern because of its connection with its Head: it is not only the sign of salvation, but the *reality* thereof.

In Christ Revelation-truth and Revelation-reality are joined, just as they are, in a certain way, in the Church. There is a word in Scripture that expresses this very precisely: the word "mystery." This idea of mystery will serve as a recapitulation of the positive data that we have compiled thus far. Here we are at the fine point of source theology where it touches on speculative theology. The latter will receive from this last definition something like the specifications for the explanatory effort that it will have to make.

The word "mystery" can be understood in two correlative senses that will be the object of the two parts of this chapter:

---

3. The same distinction is found in Heb 8:5 and 10:1.

- As for the Revelation-truth, the "mystery" is a truth inaccessible to unaided reason, which can be grasped only by accepting Revelation through supernatural faith.
- As for the Revelation-reality, the "mystery" signifies that the reality of God's gift is present in this world, where it is communicated and received in ways adapted to the human beings for whom it is destined.

I. The mystery-truth

This is about a supernatural revealed truth that exceeds the capacities of unaided reason. This truth requires faith in order to be received by the human mind, and thus it is situated at the beginning of every theological effort as its source, and likewise at the end as the criterion for verifying it.

a. The biblical data

In the Septuagint the word "mystery" has the initial sense of "secret, hidden thing." It appears only in the late books (Tobit, Judith, Wisdom, Sirach, 2 Maccabees), and it does not occur frequently. It is derived from the Aramaic *rāz*, which signifies something secret, which corresponds to the classical Hebrew *sôd*. The first Hebrew meaning applies first of all to God himself: he is unfathomable, incomprehensible, unknowable, hidden, veiled. All of God's transcendence is expressed initially by man's unknowing. But this meaning is very soon refined by the nuance of the word "secret." A secret thing is not unknowable per se, but it is known in fact only to some. With reference to God and his designs, the biblical man combines transcendence and knowledge as follows: this knowledge is not given to everyone, but to some in order to be communicated: "Surely the Lord God does nothing, without revealing his secret (*sôd*) to his servants the prophets" (Am 3:7). Thus God speaks by his envoys, to whom the Hebrews must listen. The theme of *hearing* (cf. the "*Shema Yisrael,*" Dt 6:4ff.) the Word of God announced by those whom he has sent is a central theme throughout Scripture.

These secrets that God communicates give to those who receive them *wisdom* (a major theme in the books of Daniel and Wisdom). This wisdom—and this is a Jewish characteristic—does not concern myths about the origins of the world or the conduct of the gods, but

The Church Is a Mystery

rather an understanding of the history of this particular People, a history oriented toward an end that is salvation. The culmination of the Old Testament can be seen in the testimony of the writings at Qumran: the "mystery to come" will arrive on the "day of the visitation" and will decide the fate of the just and the sinful.

The New Testament, by reason of Christ's coming, brings about a very clear, but progressive deepening of the idea of mystery. In the first place, scholars note that the word is found only once in the Gospels (Mk 4:11): "To you has been given the secret (*mystērion*) of the kingdom of God, but for those outside everything is in parables." In the parallel passages (Mt 13:11 and Lk 8:10) the expression is spelled out: "to know the secrets." "Those outside," according to the context, are those whose "hardness of heart" prevents them from understanding (Mk 4:12 refers to Is 6:9ff.). The mystery here is the coming of the Kingdom announced by the prophets: the Kingdom is now here.[4] This synoptic context shows that the word "mystery" refers here to the fundamental disposition that allows man to grasp this Revelation: faith. God reveals his plans (God speaks), and grants understanding with which to grasp the truth of his statements (God gives).

In the theology of St. Paul the specifically Christian "mystery" is more fully present. In the writings of the Apostle to the Gentiles, the term "mystery" always implies a relation with Christ. Thus in 1 Corinthians 1:23 to "preach Christ crucified" means to "proclaim the mystery of God" (1 Cor 2:1 in some ancient versions).[5] Similarly, in 1 Corinthians 2:7, where the folly of the cross is contrasted to the wisdom of the world, "we impart a secret (*en mystēriōi*) and hidden wisdom of God, which God decreed before the ages for our glorification.... God has revealed [this] to us through the Spirit." Also in 1 Corinthians 13:2, "And

---

4. Christ's preaching on this subject developed. The Kingdom is presented at first as being very near (Mt 4:17 and parallels), then as present (Lk 17:21 and parallels). At the end of his ministry, when he instituted the Eucharist, Jesus said, "From now on I shall not drink of the fruit of the vine until the kingdom of God comes" (Lk 22:18). This refers not only to the eschatological feast in heaven, but also to the Eucharist in which Christ in person presides over our meal (see also Lk 22:30). The Kingdom is an eschatological reality, but this eschatology has already started, still existing in a mixed state in its historical condition (Mt 13:24ff.; 22:2; 22:11, for example).

5. Another reading is "the testimony of God"; in the manuscript tradition, the Greek words *martyrion* and *mystērion* have sometimes been interchanged. The reading with *mystērion* is well attested in the East.

if I ... understand all mysteries ... but have not love," and in Ephesians 3:3, "the mystery was made known to me by revelation."

We must note the well-known passage in Ephesians 5:31–32: "For this reason a man shall leave his father and mother and be joined to his wife, and the two shall become one. This is a great mystery, and I mean in reference to Christ and the Church." St. Paul emphasizes here the allegorical sense of Genesis 2:24, which he cites. This Old Testament quotation alludes to the relations of unity between Christ and the Church; to put it more accurately, there is in Genesis 2:24 a veiled, mysterious announcement of what will be accomplished by Christ when he unites the Church to himself—in other words, when mankind accepts his wisdom.

The word "mystery" is also used by St. Paul and the Book of Revelation to designate the eschatology to come (the parousia). This is a great mystery that the Father has reserved for himself, yet it will be announced by remarkable events (cf. 2 Thes 2:3ff., for example).

In all these passages the "mystery" designates in the first place the revealed truth to which faith adheres in its cognitive aspect.[6]

b. The data of Tradition
1. The Fathers of the Church

In the Apostolic Fathers the word "mystery" is rather rare.[7] It is not surprising that in the writings of the Alexandrine Fathers the mystery is the object of true *gnōsis*, of a profound, decisive understanding of Scripture: access to its allegorical sense. This idea is found again in St. Augustine, who shows that Noah's ark is an allegory for the Church, the figure of such a great "mystery."[8] To avoid losing this richness in meaning, the Greek *mystērion* was not translated, but transliterated, producing the Latin word *mysterium*.

Since this fact is well known, we will not dwell on it.[9]

---

6. Cf. 1 Tm 3:9, "the mystery of faith": the mystery (of Christ) to which faith gives access.

7. It occurs three times in St. Ignatius of Antioch (for example *To the Ephesians* 19:1: Mary's virginity, the birth of Jesus, and his death are "three mysteries ... proclaimed to the world, though accomplished in the stillness of God" [ACW 1:67]). It is used once in the *Didache*.

8. See *De Civit. Dei* XV.26 (FOC 7:478); *De catechizandis rudibus* 19.32 (PL 40.334).

9. An excellent patristic survey on this subject is given by E. Schillebeeckx, *L'Économie sacramentelle du salut*, 36ff.

2. Subsequent Tradition

The Latin tradition would preserve the word "mystery" in order to designate this aspect of knowledge. This is well attested in St. Thomas—thus, for example, "The mysteries, in other words, the secret things, since the word comes from the Greek and denotes that which is secret."[10] This was to become the common property of Latin theology and led to the well-established usage of the Magisterium, as attested in the Constitution *Dei Filius* of Vatican I: a "mystery" is an order of knowledge concerning things "which, had they not been divinely revealed, could not become known."[11] This meaning is still present in the documents of Vatican II. For example, we can cite, "sometimes one tradition has come nearer to a full appreciation of some aspects of a mystery of revelation than the other."[12] Or "The words [of Revelation] proclaim the works [of God], and bring to light the mystery they contain" (Dei verbum [DV] 2). This poses no problem.

The title of chapter 1 of the Constitution *Lumen gentium*, "*De mysterio Ecclesiae*," must be understood in the first place at the level of this first Tradition of the word "mystery."[13]

c. The Church is a mystery
1. The Church as a whole is mysterious, an object of faith

To say that the Church is a mystery means, in this first sense of the word "mystery," that knowledge of it is *supernatural* and depends on the super-

---

10. *In Isaiam*, Prologue. See also I *Contra Gentiles* VI: "The mysteries surpass all human understanding," and *S.Th.* I, q. 1, a. 9, ad 2, which shows that scriptural Revelation uses figures that are sometimes obscure in order to "protect the mysteries from the mockeries of unbelievers."

11. Vatican I, *Dei Filius*, chap. 4. See also in the same chapter: "Reason when it is illumined by faith ... attains with the help of God some understanding of the mysteries, and that a most profitable one, not only from the analogy of those things that it knows naturally, but also from the connection of the mysteries among themselves.... Nevertheless, it is never capable of perceiving those mysteries in the way it does the (natural) truths that constitute its own proper object. For, divine mysteries by their nature exceed the created intellect so much that, even when handed down by revelation and accepted by faith, they nevertheless remain covered by the veil of faith itself."

12. *UR* 17. In this Decree, the expression from Vatican I, "*nexus mysteriorum*" (the connection of the mysteries), is rendered by the phrase "hierarchy of truths"; cf. *UR* 11.

13. Along these lines see Pius XII, *Mystici Corporis* 11: the union of believers with the Redeemer that is the *mystery* of the Church.

natural virtue of *faith;* the exposition of the Church's self-understanding is *doctrinal,* and the quest for an ever deeper understanding of it, as much as this is possible, is the object of *theology.*

The Church *as a whole* is mysterious. What is human and visible in the Church, as well as what is "divine" and invisible in her, constitutes *one whole* that *is* the Church and that consequently is a *mystery.* For example, knowledge and understanding of what the ecclesial hierarchy is and accomplishes is possible only by faith, and in this respect is above all a matter of doctrine. *Mystery* must not be equated with the *invisible;* what is visible is as mysterious as what is invisible. It is like a miracle: it has its visible component—for example, an eye without a retina that sees normally—but accepting it as a *sign* and understanding it as a sign of something specific is a matter of faith.

Faith is therefore necessary in order to know and confess the mystery of the Church. We *believe* that this being, the Church, is *one, holy, catholic and apostolic;* that is why we *profess* this in the Creed. There is, however, a difference between *believing in God* and the belief that has the Church as its object. The virtue of faith is not involved in the same way in these two cases. The present English and French translations of the Creed, as far as this article of faith related to the Church is concerned, do not express this difference, whereas it is in the Latin text. There is a difficulty here that we must acknowledge and that may help us to appreciate a criticism that Protestants level at Catholic and Orthodox Christians: that we make out of the Church an article of faith identical to those that have God as their object. Recall: although it is true that the Holy Spirit (by appropriation) is the soul of the Church, more particularly in the manner of a formal cause, he nevertheless does not enter into composition with a "body of the Church" in such a way that the result would be an individual being that subsists independently (as is the case with the body-soul union in a human being). In short, the Church is not God, but that does not make her merely human; she is the great organism of grace. We will encounter this question again in the speculative theology with regard to the personality of the Church. Here, let us just emphasize (succinctly, since this would be a matter for an academic course or treatise on faith) what pertains to the faith by which we know the ecclesial mystery and adhere to it.

The current standard text (the liturgical Latin text) reads:

The Church Is a Mystery

> *Credo in unum Deum, Patrem omnipotentem ...*
> *Credo in unum Dominum Iesum Christum ...*
> *Credo in Spiritum Sanctum, Dominum ...*
> ...
> *Et unam, sanctam, catholicam et apostolicam Ecclesiam.*

- Therefore, we have the expression *Credo Ecclesiam* (without the preposition *in*).

With the promulgation of the revised *Roman Missal* in 2011, the liturgical English translation (like the French and the Spanish, but not the Italian and German) reads:

> I believe *in* one God, the Father Almighty ...
> I believe *in* one Lord, Jesus Christ ...
> I believe *in* the Holy Spirit, the Lord ...
> I believe *in* one, holy, catholic and apostolic Church.

- Therefore, it is as if the original Latin reading were "*Credo in Ecclesiam.*"

This translation considers two formulas, *credere* + *in* + accusative (*credere in Deum*) and *credere* + accusative (*credere Ecclesiam*) as equivalents; now the presence or absence of the preposition *in* has an important theological significance.

At the linguistic level in Latin, *credere* + accusative indicates the object of knowledge: *credere Deum* (with the infinitive *esse* implied) = I believe God (to be) = "I believe that God exists." The construction "*credere* + *in* + accusative" has a richer meaning that is based on the preceding one, but surpasses it. The preposition "*in* + accusative" expresses the idea of movement: *credere in Deum* = "I believe into or towards God, I adhere to God, I unite myself to God." To put it another way, thanks to the revealed knowledge that I have of God and receive in faith (*credere Deum*), I can tend toward the final purpose of that knowledge, which is to unite myself to God (*credere in Deum*). Note for the sake of completeness that we have also the expression *credere Deo* (dative) = "I believe God," in the sense that "I take what he tells me to be true." Note a fourth possible formula: *credere in Deo* (*in* + ablative) = "I believe in God," but without the idea of movement implied by "*in* + accusative." The ablative case has a static meaning: the fact of being permanently in something (*in domo*) or, figuratively speaking, in someone (*in Christo*). In this sense, *credo in Deo* means, "I am established, I abide in God because I know him in truth." Evidently Latin (like Greek on this point) has a wealth of nuances. They will be used in theology as the doctrine of the supernatural virtue of faith develops—a virtue of which *credere* is the proper interior act.

At the theological level, at the beginning of Christianity in the first creeds, which were often baptismal examinations, the candidates professed that they believed "into/toward the Holy Spirit ('*eis* + accusative' in Greek; '*in* + acc.' in Latin) who works in ('*en* + ablative' in Greek; '*in* + abl.' in Latin) the holy Church."[14] This is a very precise usage that is able to distinguish faith in the Holy Spirit (*in* + acc.) from the permanent presence of the Spirit in the Church (*in* + abl.). The other creeds or "symbols of faith"—notably the Creed of Nicaea-Constantinople as formulated in 381—do not make a distinction between belief *in* the Holy Spirit and belief *in* the Church.[15] This is because they do not distinguish the different aspects within the act of faith. St. Ambrose illustrates this: "He who believes in God the Creator (*in* + acc.), believes also in the work of the creator (*in* + acc.)."[16] St. Augustine is the one who later makes the fundamental analysis. The doctor of Hippo distinguishes the three aspects of the act of faith:

- *Credere Deo*: "I believe God, I acknowledge God as the source of truth." This is about believing *the One* (God) who reveals. When I say in English, "I believe Edward," this means that I have confidence in what he tells me. Here the faith pertains to *the one* who speaks. This is the motive for the faith.
- *Credere Deum* (*esse*): "I believe (that) God (exists), I acknowledge the fact that God exists." This is about believing *what* is revealed. In English we might say, "Believing the treatment, the patient slept peacefully." Expanding the sentences illustrates this construction of "believe + accusative": "Believing the treatment described to him by the trustworthy doctor to exist and to be effec-

---

14. See, for example, St. Hippolytus of Rome, *Apostolic Tradition* 21, Stewart-Sykes edition, 113.

15. Most often we find in Greek "*eis* + acc." and in Latin "*in* + acc."

16. *Explanatio symboli* 6 (CSEL 73:9); in this regard St. Ambrose cites Jn 10:38, "Even though you do not believe me, believe the works [that I do]."

The Church Is a Mystery

tive, the patient slept peacefully." Here the faith pertains to *what* is said. This is the object of the faith.
- *Credere in Deum:* "I believe into or toward God, I tend toward God as my unique destiny." Here there is movement (*in* + acc.) that brings the person to adhere to God, to unite himself to him by knowledge and love.[17]

The classic doctrine on this subject was elaborated by the medieval Masters, in particular St. Albert the Great and St. Thomas Aquinas.[18] We present it briefly here.

There is one and the same act of faith, but this one act has various relations with its object, which is God *and God alone*. Thus we must distinguish between (1) God who reveals himself, who makes himself known, who is the Author of the light that manifests him; (2) the God who is known in this way, for what God reveals and illuminates is himself; and (3) God as man's final end.

- *Credo Deo:* "I believe God"—in other words, I agree to receive this supernatural light that elevates my faculty of knowing (intellect) beyond its natural capacities. Here, the act of faith pertains to the testimony given by God.
- *Credo Deum:* "I believe unto or for God," or "My belief is leading toward God"—in other words, I believe what the light given by God manifests to me. Thus I believe that God exists, that he is one in three Persons, and so on. This is the substance of the testimony that God gives: what God reveals is himself.
- *Credo in Deum:* "I believe in God"—in other words, I tend toward God by knowledge and love so as to be with him and to live eternally in his presence. Faith here is a movement that will terminate

---

17. It must be emphasized that in St. Augustine's writing it is most often a question of Christ (*credere Christo, Christum, in Christum*) and not of God, but it amounts to the same thing, since he is discussing the Word. The main passages in Augustine: *Tract. In Ioan.* XXIX.6 and 8 (FOC 88:17–21); and LIII.10 (FOC 88:297); *Enarr. In Ps.* LXXVII.8 and CXXX.1. These distinctions are not pointlessly subtle. Certainly, if faith, in order to be supernatural, must be integral and keep these three aspects together, then it can happen that they occur separately (sins against faith); besides, these explanations allow us to understand certain statements in Scripture that would otherwise be very obscure, such as this one about the faith of demons: "You believe that God is one; you do well. Even the demons believe—and shudder" (Jas 2:19).

18. Main passages: St. Albert, *III Sent.* d. 23, a. 7; St. Thomas, *ST* II-II, q. 2, art. 2.

in the beatific vision. This faith, entirely informed by charity, is living faith, the only sort that saves. A human being in a state of mortal sin might very well preserve the first two aspects of the faith, but he does not have this third one.

These clarifications suffice to explain the theological difficulty with the English translation, "I believe in one God, the Father almighty, ... in Jesus Christ, ... in the Holy Spirit," and the theological importance of the translation, "I believe *in* the Church."[19] The Church is not God, and the virtue of faith informed by charity does not lead us toward her as our final, beatifying end. We are right in saying "*Credo in unum Deum ..., in unum Dominum ..., in Spiritum Sanctum*," because these are the Divine Persons toward whom a living faith leads us so as to unite us with them. [This aspect of supernatural faith is not expressed in the current English liturgical translation. If we look again at the Latin,] the formula "*et (credo) unam, sanctam, catholicam et apostolicam Ecclesiam*" is quite correct, because it signifies, "I believe that the Church exists, that she is one, holy, catholic and apostolic." It is about a *belief* because God has revealed to us—and therefore it is *de fide*—that the community of his sons and daughters in the Son is one, holy, catholic and apostolic. This is an instance of *credere Deum* [believing *what* God says], more precisely, an instance of *credere* that pertains to the revelation of a work of God (*Ecclesiam*), a *credere* that follows from the *credere Deo* and shows us the path of *credere in Deum*.[20]

To summarize: the act of faith (*credere*) is directed toward God. Faith carries us in him, to him, and toward him. However, in adhering thus to the mystery of God, faith causes us to enter into the saving work of God that can be expressed by the one word "Church." Hence

---

19. Translator's note: Due to the differences between the French verb *croire* and the English "to believe," this paragraph had to be altered insofar as it specifically discusses the current liturgical translations of the Latin Creed. This was done in order to respect the author's theological goal—namely, to establish that there is a difference between God and the Church insofar as the theological virtue of faith is concerned.

20. Some bibliographic references on this subject: T. Camelot, "*Credere Deo, credere Deum, credere in Deum:* pour l'histoire d'une formule traditionnelle," *RSPT* (1941–1942): 149–55; Charles Mohrmann, "*Credere in Deum:* sur l'interprétation théologique d'un fait de langue," in *Études sur le latin des chrétiens*, 2nd ed. (Rome: 1961), 1:195–203; Charles Journet, *L'Église du Verbe incarné* (Paris: 1951), 2:595, note 2 (a rapid but rigorous overview dealing with the subject in its traditional context: the relations of the Church with the Holy Spirit).

The Church Is a Mystery

St. Thomas does not hesitate to write, "If we say: 'I believe *in* the holy Catholic Church (*in sanctam Ecclesiam catholicam*),' this must be taken as verified in so far as our faith is directed to the Holy Ghost, Who sanctifies the Church; so that the sense is: 'I believe in [i.e., tend toward] the Holy Ghost sanctifying the Church (*Credo in Spiritum Sanctum sanctificantem Ecclesiam*).'"[21] Gilles Emery subtly adds:

> This perspective, which starts from God [the Holy Spirit] in considering the Church, is objectively first.... [There is a] second perspective [that] takes things according to the inverse movement. It considers the Church herself, in which the Trinity is present, as an object of properly theologal faith: I believe in the Church, which is a mystery. By reason of the indwelling of the Trinity in the Church (the indwelling of the Holy Spirit), this second perspective emphasizes that, when faith living through charity embraces the mystery of the Church, it attains to God himself. One can say that this second perspective is subjectively primary.[22]

2. The three levels of intelligibility of the Church

Since we are dealing with a mystery, its intelligibility is a matter of faith in its connection with reason—in other words, the domain of doctrine and of theology. However, since we are dealing with an incarnate mystery like that of the Savior, we must allow room for a purely rational grasp of the subject that, even though it does not have access to the mystery as such, does grasp one aspect thereof, the aspect under which it appears at first to man by taking on a human dimension. In order to grasp this it is particularly helpful to start from the mystery of Christ and from the Gospel testimonies concerning the ways in which he was perceived by his contemporaries.[23] Those who encountered Christ walking on the roads of Galilee and Judea saw, heard, and touched his humanity. In relation to that humanity, three reactions are reported in the Gospel.

There were those for whom Jesus was only the son of the carpen-

---

21. *ST* II-II, q. 1, art. 9, ad 5; English translation modified for this linguistic argument.

22. Gilles Emery, *The Trinity: An Introduction to Catholic Doctrine on the Triune God*, trans. Matthew Levering (Washington, D.C.: The Catholic University of America Press, 2011), 79.

23. We summarize here a very suggestive teaching by Charles Journet, *Théologie de l'Église* (Paris: 1962), 10ff.; English edition: *Theology of the Church* (San Francisco: Ignatius Press, 2004), 1ff.

ter from Nazareth and nothing more. They considered him an insignificant man and, if they encountered him at all, they neither listened to him nor, *a fortiori,* followed him. So it is with the Church yesterday, today, and tomorrow. It is possible to see in her only a religious organization like so many others, with its rules, rituals, and prayer formulas. This is the view of a certain sort of journalism, and of statisticians, sociologists, and political society in the Western world. This first view encompasses only the mere phenomenon. To be sure, this consideration is not necessarily false, just as saying that Jesus weighed seventy kilos [154 pounds] is not necessarily false (assuming that it could be verified!), but it is still ignorance of the mystery, properly speaking.

Crossing paths with Christ, there were those—often the lowly—who on seeing him were struck by the dignity of his life and the authority of his words (Lk 4:22). They were also intrigued by the miraculous signs that he performed. All this was not insignificant. They then thought that this Jesus of Nazareth was inhabited by a force that could not be merely human. Therefore they thought he might be a prophet (Mk 8:27–28 and Lk 9:18–19). These people arrived at the threshold of the mystery. They still had not entered in, but they were very close. So it is with the Church. Someone may observe without too much difficulty that this community carries within it and transmits a particularly sublime wisdom. In every age, in all places, men and women within this fellowship have shined with an extraordinary quality: the saints, whether or not canonized. For two thousand years this community has existed and expanded, despite many persecutions, while keeping its living identity intact despite the passage of generations and the variety of cultures. Within this community there are indeed miracles, not only those certified at Lourdes, but also the infinitely more numerous miracles of heroic charity. Does this community then not appear to be "something" that surpasses mere human capabilities? There is a limit, however, to this parallel with Christ. Jesus was completely without sin (Jn 8:46), but the Church here below is made up of sinners. And it is true that in every age and in all places, besides the grandeur of Christian culture, we can also observe serious faults in Christians. We must admit this honestly, but also reflect: precisely, how can this community continue to exist in this way, to preserve its sublime message, and always to have such influence, despite the serious contrary wit-

The Church Is a Mystery 303

nesses that affect it? From the human perspective, it ought to have disappeared long ago, like any kingdom divided against itself. And yet it continues to exist and even expands. This makes the inquiry even more complex. It leads the honest mind to take a look at this phenomenon that goes further, a look that we can metaphorically call metaphysical: there is in this particular entity, the Christian community, "something" unique and not directly perceptible that raises a question. Not everything in the Church is explained at first glance, and even the second look does not produce a definitive answer; it sets one on the path to seeking something more. Here we have reached the level of apologetics, a discipline that ought to be renewed in-depth today. The second look remains exclusively rational—it does not presuppose faith at all—but it consists of that docility of reason that allows itself to question and to be oriented toward more than it can find by itself; thus reason itself—if the apologetic is proposed correctly—asks for help to surpass its own limits.

Among these people who take a second look, there will be a certain number, sometimes more, sometimes less, who will cross the decisive threshold. "Who do you say that I am?" (Mt 16:15), Jesus asked the Twelve. And this is Peter's profession of faith, on which the Church is founded: "You are the Christ, the Son of the living God!" (Mt 16:16). This is the decisive response, the whole truth that comes from God and is professed by a human heart (Mt 16:17). So it is with the Church. The threshold is crossed when someone confesses, "Truly, this community, the very one that I have before my eyes, is the Body of Christ, the Temple of the Spirit, the People of God!" This is the profession of faith concerning the mystery of the Church: this visible, human, quite observable community *is* the community of human beings with God, of which Christ is the Head and the Holy Spirit—the soul.

Every Christian, as his conscious faith has awakened, has traveled this path slowly or rapidly—no matter! The important thing is not to lose any of the truth of the three looks; they must be kept together, and what makes this possible is the last look, the look of faith, which recapitulates and elevates the two preceding ones.

The existence of the ecclesial community is therefore a question asked of every human being who encounters it, and the only answer to it is either yes or no. Not to respond, to withhold one's answer, saying "We will hear you again about this" (Acts 17:32), is already to answer "no" to the mystery that presents itself. One cannot be a member of this community unless one embraces its mystery. To be sure, it will always be possible to be a member externally without being a member in one's heart, but this membership is only an appearance. In fact, one has not entered into its mystery. Even those who had acclaimed Jesus as a prophet (the second look) ended up leaving him. At the time of Christ's Passion, where were they? Similarly, those who salute the Church for her originality, her historical greatness (it is no mean feat to have produced European civilization), her remarkable quality among the religious movements of humanity, are not yet fully members of her, living her life entirely, because they do not profess her to be what she is in the fullness of her truth.[24]

Since this is a question of the faith that is involved in professing the ecclesial mystery, it would be futile to try to convince anyone of it, but we are asked to preach it, which is something else altogether.[25] The preacher will encounter much opposition, surely, but it is not right to diminish the mystery so as to make it more acceptable. The Christian mystery, starting with the mystery of Christ, will always be a folly or a scandal for men left to their own intellectual and moral capabilities. But present-day difficulties seem to us to require a particular effort in order to foster the passage from the first to the second look, and to nourish the second look by a truly modern apologetic, for here it is a matter of preparations for the faith that ought not to be neglected.

II. The mystery-reality

The aspect of truth, important as it is, is not the highest aspect. There is also an aspect of *knowledge*—in other words, of the presence of the reality in our mind. Now the reality is vaster than anything we can grasp;

---

24. This is, and rightly so, the most decisive reproach leveled against Charles Maurras [an early-twentieth-century French author, nationalist, and theorist of Catholic Action]: that he considered and admired "Christendom" (the second look), but knew nothing about "Christianity" (the third look), if he didn't reject it outright (cf. his remark about the "venom of the Magnificat").

25. Preaching to non-Christians consists in the first place of a living witness ("By this all men will know that you are my disciples, if you have love for one another," Jn 13:35), whereas preaching with words deciphers, so to speak, the preaching by example.

The Church Is a Mystery

furthermore, we live by the full, entire reality, and not only by what little we can perceive of it, even by faith. The perfection of charity is what completes the perfection of faith. What, then, does our use of the word "mystery" add to our understanding of the reality?

a. The origins of this term

In secular Greek, although a "mystery" is in the first place something secret, another sense of the word is also well attested. It is a religious ceremony reserved to those who are initiated—and therefore a secret for the common man—by which a certain "contact" with the deity or deities is brought about. Thus texts from antiquity speak about the "mysteries of Eleusis." More generally, we refer to these cults as "mystery religions." The ritual aims to assure some participation in what is manifested. Thus, for example, the cult of Zeus is celebrated so that the participants can appropriate somehow the power of this god, with a view to some project or other (long voyage, war). In this context a "mystery" is the cultic celebration during which and through which the god invoked bestows his gifts on those who beg for them.[26]

In the writings of St. Paul the word "mystery," as we have seen, most often signifies the hidden and revealed secrets of God, his plan of salvation, of which Christ is the centerpiece. There are some instances of the word, however, as used by the Apostle to the Gentiles, in which a richer connotation can be discerned, one that is related to the meaning in secular Greek. Thus when St. Paul proclaims "the mystery of faith" (1 Tm 3:9), this is not just about the truth to which faith adheres; it is, as he says a little further on (1 Tm 3:16), "the mystery of our religion: He was manifested in the flesh [Incarnation], vindicated in the Spirit [Resurrection]..., taken up in glory [Ascension]." In other words, the "mystery" is Christ himself, as opposed to the "mystery of lawlessness/iniquity" (2 Thes 2:7); it is the way in which God not only reveals to us his plan of salvation, but actually saves us.

Christ himself is mystery—in other words, he is the reality of salvation by God, and this is the sense in which the apostle who is charged with communicating this salvation is said to be a "servant of Christ and

---

26. For a minutely detailed presentation of this substructure in Greek culture, with testimonies in its philosophy also, see the study by Edward Schillebeeckx, *L'Économie sacramentelle*, 25ff.

steward of the mysteries of God" (cf. 1 Cor 4:1). In the Letters to the Colossians and the Ephesians the explanations are the most thorough. To the Colossians, St. Paul says that he is a minister of the Church with the responsibility "to make the word of God fully known, the mystery hidden for ages ... but now made manifest to his saints.... This mystery ... is Christ in [*or* among] you" (Col 1:25–27). The aspect of knowledge is clear (and is repeated in Col 2:2–3), but the real aspect is added: that which is revealed is a presence; the presence of Christ now at work that engenders the Body of which he is the Head (Col 1:18).

This teaching is repeated in the Letter to the Ephesians, and it concerns the Church. In Ephesians 3 St. Paul describes in detail his ministry of the mystery of Christ, and he plainly declares: he must announce the unfathomable riches of Christ, bring fully to light "the plan of the mystery" (Eph 3:9).[27] This communication of salvation is the building up of the Body of Christ that is the Church (Eph 2:16 and 3:10). The word "mystery" here is not limited to the aspect of knowledge—which it does express, of course, in its initial sense—but also designates the thing to which this knowledge brings us: the real reception of the very thing that is revealed.

At the level of the translation from Greek into Latin, there is an interesting point worth noting. Although most often the Greek word for *mystērion*-knowledge is rendered in Latin by its transliteration *mysterium*, the *mystērion*-participation is quite frequently rendered in Latin by *sacramentum*. For example, the Vulgate translates "the mystery of our religion" in 1 Tim 3:16 as *pietatis sacramentum*, or again the "communication of the mystery" in Ephesians 3:9 is translated as *dispensatio sacramenti*.[28] We have here a beginning of what Tradition would later develop considerably, but relying also on non-biblical sources.[29]

---

27. Literally the *oikonomia tou mystēriou*, which can be translated "the placing at our disposition" or "the communication of the work of God in Christ."

28. One must be cautious here about any attempt to systematize, for this is only a tendency, and not a rule that is always followed. For example, in 1 Cor 4:1, St. Paul presents himself as the "steward of the mysteries," and one might expect the Latin translation *dispensatio sacramentorum*, yet the Vulgate here has *mysteriorum*.

29. We remain here within the perspective of a general presentation. A more advanced study of this vocabulary question would be a matter for our course on the sacraments in general. On this point Edward Schillebeeckx, *L'Économie sacramentelle*, 5–92, is quite thorough and very enlightening.

b. The patristic tradition

In the Greek world that received the Gospel, the mysteries (most often the word is in the plural) designate Christian belief (the initial sense: knowledge), but also the symbolic practices representing the holy realities. From the third century on, among the Alexandrians, the rites of Christian initiation are called the "little mysteries," and gradually the Eucharist—the source, center, and summit of the whole Christian economy—is called everywhere, even in the Latin world, "the holy mysteries." This expression designates the entire celebration—rituals, prayers, and postures. In the fourth century, the *"mystery"* is the divine operation that touches us by means of the symbolic rites.[30] It is remarkable that this liturgical sense of the word *mystery* is not explicit in Scripture—nowhere does St. Paul speak about baptism as a mystery—but we have seen that the New Testament is open to that interpretation. In fact it is likely that the Greek Fathers adopted here the terminology of the mystery religions, which thus acquired its full significance in and through Christianity.[31]

The Latin Fathers, as we said, adopted the word *"sacramentum"* to mean that. Etymologists, without being certain of it, propose the following origin: *sacrare* from *sanctio*: "to sanction, to establish"; and the suffix *–mentum* expressing the instrumental aspect. The *sacramentum* then would be the way of obtaining or realizing something sacred. In one of the principal pagan uses, the word designates the oath of allegiance that new soldiers had to make to the emperor. By reason of the divinization of the emperor, we have here a good example of a pagan sacred thing.[32] We will skip over the history (St. Cyprian, St. Hilary, St. Ambrose are pertinent to this topic) to get to St. Augustine, who was to settle things for Latin theology. In the abundant writings of the Doctor of Hippo we note the following uses of the term *sacramentum:*

The first and decisive use is *sacramentum Christi*.[33] This is quite close

---

30. The terminology is clearly fixed in the writings of St. John Chrysostom, particularly in his treatise on baptism.

31. For very interesting remarks by Schillebeeckx on this subject, see *L'Économie sacramentelle*, 47–57.

32. This civil usage is the reason Tertullian would call baptism a *sacramentum*, for it is the oath par excellence. Hence the faith professed and the ritual initiation would be called *sacramenta*.

33. See the references to the studies by Pierre-Thomas Camelot, C. Couturier, and M.-F. Feret in the bibliography.

to St. Paul (cf. "*Mystēriou tou Theou, Christou*" in Col 2:2 and "*Mystērion tou Christou*" in Eph 3:4; Col 1:26–29 and 4:3). Christ is *the* mystery par excellence because God's plan of salvation is revealed and accomplished in him. St. Augustine adopts the sense of knowledge that is frequently found in St. Paul, but also develops the active sense whereby what is revealed is the very thing that is communicated. For example, in reference to the two names of the Savior, *Jesus Christ*, St. Augustine notes that *Jesus* is the proper name of a person, like Abraham, Elijah, Moses ..., and *Christ* is the name of a *sacrament*[34]—in other words, the name not only of his priestly, prophetic, and royal office, which he received by the anointing of the Spirit, but also of his "ontology": the union of the Divine Person of the Word with a particular human nature. The divinity of Christ is of course hidden to us, but it is revealed and truly communicated to us by his humanity. Hence we see why the heralding figures of the Old Testament deserve the name of sacrament: because they announce the Christ, and we clearly see how the *realities* of the New Testament fully accomplish the notion of mystery-sacrament.

It must be noted carefully that when speaking about the *sacramentum* that is Christ, the entire reality of the Savior—true God and true man—is what is called "sacrament." From this it follows that in the writings of St. Augustine the term "sacrament" would be applied to the Church also by the Doctor of Hippo.[35] If Christ is the sacrament par excellence, his Body and his Bride are, too, by reason of the strict unity between the Head and the community of the members. The mystery of the Church thus resides in the fact that she is a human community through which and in which the divine reality of salvation intervenes.

We owe to the Fathers, both Greek and Latin, the clarification of what could be called the "fundamental structure of salvation." By this we mean that the distinguishing feature of the Christian faith is the economy of the Incarnation: the divine reality touches and saves us in and through the mediation of human realities, the first of which and the source of all the others is the humanity assumed by the Word.

34. Cf. *Tract.* 3 on the Epistle of St. John (PL 35.2000; FOC 92:164). See also *Serm.* 91, no. 3: "it is a great thing to know the mystery of how Christ is both David's Lord and the son of David," (PL 38.568); and no. 5: "to understand the mystery [*sacramentum*] of God, how Christ is both man and God," 568–69 [translated from Latin].

35. "This testimony professes ... the whole mystery of all the Scriptures, that is, Christ and the Church"; *Enarr. in Ps.* 79.1 (PL 36.1021) [translated from Latin].

Christ *is* God in the flesh; he touches us in a human way so as to save us in a divine way. His Body, filled with his Spirit, is a human community in which and through which the community of grace comes about. Scripture is sacred because the Word of God is given by it, in and through the human words of the inspired author. The rites are sanctifying because the grace of salvation is in them and comes to us through them. This economy of salvation is what forms the Christian *"mystery,"* or typically Christian sacramentality.

c. The medieval period: St. Thomas Aquinas[36]

The Middle Ages are a key moment in the elaboration of the notion of sacrament that would fix the Latin Tradition down to our times.

Before the thirteenth century, the word *"sacramentum"* had a rather broad sense designating a very large part of sacred symbolism. Although the Eucharist and baptism are the principal sacraments, various blessings and minor rites are also called sacraments. Little by little a distinction would be made between the *sacramenta maiora* and the *sacramenta minora*, depending on whether the symbolism signifies a reality that is effectively communicated through and in them or the significance is limited to the aspect of knowledge. Although one still encounters the expressions *sacramentum Christi* and *sacramentum Ecclesiae*, this usage is in decline, but the expression *"mysterium Christi"* understood in the sense of *"sacramentum Christi"* remains current.[37]

Although St. Thomas is acquainted with the patristic tradition and continues to speak about Christ as the sacrament of salvation,[38] or equivalently as the mystery of salvation,[39] his particular contribution was to elaborate speculatively the notion of *sacramentum* based on the patristic data. He finds himself initially confronting these multiple uses of the word and, in keeping with his method, he attempts to single out a first sense that can serve as a basis for the secondary and derived

---

36. Cf. E. Schillebeeckx, *L'Économie sacramentelle*, 131–53.
37. Schillebeeckx, *L'Économie sacramentelle*, 131–33.
38. Cf. *Compendium*, chap. 227, no. 3: "Christ also willed to die, not only so that His death might be a satisfactory remedy, but also that it might be the sacrament of our salvation."
39. Cf. *Compendium*, chap. 201: "The divine wisdom that had made man assumed a bodily nature and visited man who was lying prostrate among corporeal things so as to lead him back to spiritual things by the mystery of His body."

senses. This is the whole point of *ST* III, q. 62, art. 1. In the three objections of this article St. Thomas mentions the main senses of the word *sacramentum* known to Tradition: "sacrament" derived from *sacrare–mentum* (to make sacred), "sacrament" as a simple translation of *mystērium* in the sense of secret, and "sacrament" in the sense of oath (cf. Tertullian). The body of the article affirms that all these senses have a common tie: in different respects, the realities thus expressed are ordered among themselves and to one reality from which they take their name. What is this first reality that provides the formal notion of sacrament, while the others are an analogical application of it? St. Thomas determines the first sense: a sacrament is *something that has within it a certain hidden sanctity*. This sense is the principle and center of the analogy by virtue of which everything that has any relation whatsoever to this first reality can be called sacrament, too, but in a derivative sense.

Thus baptism, the Eucharist, confirmation, and the four others will be called sacraments only analogically and in a derivative way, because they are in a relation of sign with the holy and salvific reality that is divine life. St. Thomas says explicitly at the beginning of his treatise on the sacraments, "But now we are speaking of sacraments in a special sense, as implying the habitude of sign" (q. 60, art. 1), and he goes on to add in article 2, "the sign of a holy thing so far as it makes men holy" (insofar as it is communicated). We must therefore situate the *mystērion-sacramentum* precisely in its first and fundamental sense: a sacred reality that comes to us in a reality that per se is profane. The profane reality (washing with water made specific by the words in the case of baptism, for example) directs us to the sacred reality in two ways: it makes it known (sign-symbolic content), which is always the first way; then it communicates it in different ways, either really (efficient causality—real content: the seven sacraments), or to make an oath solemn (God taken as witness—moral content), or else to dispose the heart to receive the sacred reality (sacramentals—moral content). In this effort by St. Thomas there is a structuring and a clarification of data that is fundamentally that of the Fathers. When they call Christ the sacrament par excellence, thus expressing his fundamental ontology, they correctly say that the humanity that he assumed—in itself a profane thing—has within it a hidden sanctity (the fullness of grace dependent on union with the Divine Person), and they develop this along two ma-

The Church Is a Mystery

jor, inseparable lines: the humanity of Christ is the *sign* of his divinity—and the humanity of Christ is the means, the Greeks say the *organon* (instrument), of his divinity. This is the common patristic exegesis of John 14:6, "I am the way, and the truth, and the life": Christ is the way according to his humanity, which leads to the truth and the life that he is in his divinity.[40]

The Thomistic clarification is important. It is situated, however, within a historical context that increasingly reserves the word *sacrament* to the seven acts of divine worship, so that the analogy derived from Christ and the Church is not elaborated. It is ceaselessly implied, in the sense that the whole Christian economy is indeed sacramental, but the precise application to the *mystery-sacrament* that is the Church is not made.

d. Between the end of the Middle Ages and the modern renewal

Two principal features mark this period. On the one hand, the term *"sacrament"* becomes specialized so as to denote only the seven acts of Christian worship, and, on the other hand, a certain anthropological impoverishment affects the general understanding of the Christian economy.

Very quickly after St. Thomas—this is the down side of the success of his speculative definition of sacrament—the word came to denote only the seven particular acts by which Christ effectively gives his grace.[41] This is, in fact, a specialization of the word, which is legitimate per se, but causes theologians to lose sight of the fact that this was an analogical sense; it becomes instead the first if not the only sense of the term. What was still very clearly recognized in the writings of St. Thomas was no longer so later on. Thus theologians would tend to forget the great "law" of the sacramentality of salvation.

Then the notion of sacramentality underwent some contortions that were fraught with consequences. Considering the sacraments formally as signs (that was the contribution of St. Thomas), theologians

---

40. See St. Augustine, *In Joan.* XXXIV.9 (FOC 88:68); and LXIX.3 (FOC 90:70).
41. See for example the bulls of union of the Council of Florence that define the set of seven and the teaching of Trent.

went on to discuss[42] and then to deny[43] the necessarily sensible character of the sign, which nonetheless had been emphasized so much by St. Augustine[44] and by St. Thomas after him: a sign is something that is addressed to the senses.[45] This negation of the sensible nature of the sign would have an immediate effect on the understanding of the sacramentality of the seven cultic acts. "Sign" would no longer designate a present *reality*, but purely and simply a *knowledge* of the gift of grace.

These shifts in meaning are fraught with consequences. The seven sacraments become the focus of all sacramentality, which no longer holds together, as closely connected, signification (the order of knowledge) and causality (the real order): what is signified—not necessarily in a way perceptible to the senses, since what is known can be just a divine decree—is no longer *ipso facto* what is realized. It is possible to signify something that has already happened or is yet to come, not through and in the sacrament, but parallel with the sacrament. The concepts of Luther and Calvin are nothing but a consequence of these premises. We will see in the section on speculative theology that the Catholic understanding of the Church suffered during the classic period of this development.

e. The modern rediscovery of sacramentality

From the end of the Middle Ages to the modern era, Latin Catholics understood the word *"sacrament"* to mean only the seven acts of divine worship. But increasingly, from the nineteenth century on, stimulated initially by German theology, there was a rediscovery of the full breadth of the sacramental perspective.[46] This is an interesting histori-

---

42. Cf. W. of Occam, *IV Sent.* q. 1: God could have signified the sacramental gift of grace without *external* signs, for example in a pious meditation, but he did not do so.

43. Cf. R. Bacon (a contemporary of St. Thomas), *Opus maius, De signis* 2: not every sign is necessarily presented to the senses as the colloquial connotation of the word sign implies, but certain signs are given to the intellect alone without the mediation of the senses.

44. A sign is necessarily presented to the senses; cf. *De Doctrina christiana* L.2.I.1 (CCSL 32:32); see also L.2.III.4 (CCSL 32:33–34).

45. Intelligible effects (for example, the concept formed by abstraction) cannot be called signs except in a secondary fashion and in a certain way, inasmuch as they themselves are manifested by signs; thus the sacramental character of baptism (see *ST* III, q. 60, art. 4, ad 1).

46. John Henry Newman also had remarkable insights on this subject. For him, all

The Church Is a Mystery

cal development, about which there are few general studies.[47] Here we give a general overview of this movement so as to have a better perspective on the choices made by Vatican II. This rediscover can be presented in two major phases, before and after the Second World War.

1. The return to the sacramental idea starting in the nineteenth century

M. J. Scheeben had a very broad perspective, thanks to his assiduous reading of the Church Fathers. He develops what he calls the "sacramental mystery" so as to go beyond the limitations on the aspect of truth that are entailed in "mystery." The mystery hidden in the sacrament is the grace hidden in the sign. There is a *real* union of mystery and sacrament, first of all in Christ:

> Since ... the mystery is actually present in the visible object, it is also actually present to him who sees the visible object, not indeed in the sense that he thereby perceives the mystery as it is in itself, but in the sense that when *by faith* he is apprised of the union of the two elements, he knows upon seeing the visible object that he actually has the mystery before him.[48]

The first application is made to Christ: his visible humanity (sacrament) in which his divinity is present (mystery). The second application concerns the Eucharist, which is the life-giving flesh of the Word. Finally, the third application is made to the Church that is born of the Eucharist. He is talking about the Church in her very being:

> The Church, by virtue of its connection with Incarnation and the Eucharist, becomes a great sacrament, a sacramental mystery. Although the Church

---

Christianity is sacramental; this is what he calls "the sacramental principle," according to which "All that is seen,—the world, the Bible, the Church, the civil polity, and man himself,—are types, and, in their degree and place, representatives and organs of an unseen world, truer and higher than themselves"; Newman, *Essays*, 194n11.

47. M. Deneken, "Les romantiques allemands, promoteurs de la notion d'Église sacrement du salut? Contribution à l'étude de la genèse de l'expression 'Église sacrement du salut,'" *Rev. Sc. Rel.* 67, no. 2 (1993): 55–74; Deneken, "Sacramentalité de l'Église et théologie," *Rev. Sc. Rel.* 67, no. 3 (1993): 41–58. More particularly concerning the twentieth century, see M. Bernards, "Zur lehre von der Kirche als Sakrament: Beobachtungen aus der Theologie des 19 und 20 Jhds.," in *Münchener theologische Zeitschrift* 20 (1969): 29–54 ; see also, in the bibliography, the thesis by Jean-Marie Pasquier.

48. Matthias Joseph Scheeben, *The Mysteries of Christianity* (New York: Herder, 1951), 560; original German edition, 1868.

is outwardly visible and according to its visible side appears to be no more than a society of mere men, it harbors in its interior the mystery of an extraordinary union with Christ made man and dwelling within it, and with the Holy Spirit who fructifies and guides it.[49]

It must be added that the ecclesial action conforms to its being:

As the mystical body of Christ, the Church is His true Bride who, made fruitful by His divine power, has the destiny of bearing heavenly children to Him and His heavenly Father, of nourishing these children with the substance and the light of her bridegroom, and of conducting them beyond the whole range of created nature up to the bosom of His heavenly Father.[50]

This line of thought can be found in France somewhat later:

It is Christ, the person of Christ, that is the sacrament *par excellence,* the first sacrament, the sole sacrament, since whatever we call a sacrament is only a continuation of His symbolic and real action; symbolic, since He is a manifestation of God; real, because He is God given to us.[51]

With this application to the Church:

The Church is a sacrament so far as she is a symbol and means of unity between God and man, just as Christ—her Chief, the Head of the organised Mystical Body—is a sacrament, because He is the expression of God as given to man, and of man as given to God.[52]

After that the author naturally moves on to discuss all the significant activity of the Church in which the sacramentality of her being is put into action, not only in the seven sacraments, but also in all the sacramentals.[53]

Thus scholars rediscovered the patristic breadth of sacramentality: it is first and foremost in Christ, and it is communicated in a certain way to the Church that is thus actualized.

Another movement during that same period reconstitutes the sac-

---

49. Scheeben, *Mysteries of Christianity,* 561.
50. Scheeben, *Mysteries of Christianity,* 541–42 (the reader will have noted that Scheeben reasons in his account from action to being).
51. A. G. Sertillanges, *The Church,* trans. A. G. McDougall (New York: Benziger Brothers, 1922), 139.
52. Sertillanges, *The Church,* 187. The English translator cautiously writes "sacramental" twice instead of "sacrament."
53. Sertillanges, *The Church,* 2:40–41 in the French edition.

ramental schema by starting from the other end—namely, the seven acts of divine worship. The idea here is that the seven particular sacraments presuppose a fundamental type that is expressed through them, of which they are the manifestation, so to speak. This particular action allows us to infer the being that places it: the Church. The sacramental activity of the Church—in the strict sense of the performance of the seven precise acts of divine worship—is the continuation of the priestly office of Christ in these specific acts placed by the Church, which accomplishes for the time of this generation what Christ himself accomplished when he lived on earth. Thus, early on in the theological renewal, it was noted:

> The Church, as a general means of sanctification, as an institution of sanctification, and therefore the Church in the visible form in which she appears—supported by the Holy Spirit—must be called not a kind of sacrament but rather *the* Christian sacrament. The Church herself is the sacrament, being the means of salvation, in the broadest sense of the word.[54]

The reader will note that the word *sacrament* here designates the visible aspect of the sanctification and not the sanctification itself; this was inevitable because of the development of sacramental theology from the thirteenth century on. Thus sacramentality designates only the "means of salvation" aspect of the ecclesial mystery, not the "reality of salvation" aspect. This "functional" sacramentality does not have its origin in the "essential" sacramentality that Scheeben had demonstrated so well. Generally speaking, the later theology of ecclesial sacramentality narrows the notion somewhat: theologians speak about sacrament only to designate the visible aspect of the ecclesial mystery and, since they do not go back to the mystery of Christ himself, the Church tends to become the fundamental sacrament. For example:

> Generally speaking, we can call the Church the unique sacrament inasmuch as participation in her outward, visible community communicates to us in general the grace and truth of Christ, just as participation in one of the particular outward signs of the Church (the seven sacraments) produces special sacramental graces in us.[55]

---

54. J. H. Oswald, *Die dogmatische Lehre von den heiligen Sakramenten der Katholischen Kirche* (Münster: 1856), 10 [English citation translated from French].

55. J. Schwam, *Dogmengeschichte der vornicänischen Zeit* (Münster: 1862), 553 [English citation translated from French].

The first attempts at speculative elaboration came to light above all through the influence of the liturgical movement inaugurated by Dom Odo Casel after World War I. It was a question then of restoring unity between the inward reality of grace and the outward reality that signifies and procures the inward reality. A sacrament is not initially an action (the aspect of efficient causality), but first of all an ontology (the aspect of formal causality), a particular being that is profoundly one, although composite. Thus we rediscover the initial (abstract) sense that St. Thomas had derived. For example:

> According to this nomenclature (Church-sacrament), we designate first an inward reality, namely our union with God (and with one another), in other words, the very state of our sanctification.[56]

Speculatively, it is important to describe, first, the being that is called sacrament, in terms of which one can then arrive at the sacramental action placed by that being. Although, in the order of empirical observation [*invention positive*], we ascend from action to being, in the order of speculative exposition the reverse is true: we go from being to action, from cause to effect. But this speculative path was not yet highly developed before World War II; that would occur especially afterward and in various ways that are not all equally valuable.

2. Recent development of the sacramental idea

An initial effort was made to try to understand the sacramental idea with the help of the speculative findings of the Thomistic theology of the sacraments: *sacramentum tantum—res et sacramentum—res tantum*. Fr. Congar was a precursor in this approach. From his very first published work he presented the general schema of ecclesial sacramentality as follows:

> *Sacramentum tantum:* the ecclesiastical institution.
> *Sacramentum et res:* the value of this institution to procure:
> → the *res tantum:* the purely inward reality of the Church.[57]

He returned to this subject some years later:

---

56. A. Stolz, *De Ecclesia* (Freiburg im Breisgau: 1939), 16 [English citation translated from French].
57. Yves Congar, *Divided Christendom* (London: Centenary Press, 1939), 83ff.

The Church Is a Mystery

The whole Church is a great sacrament, whose soul is the Eucharist, whence flow and whither tend all the other sacraments and sacramentals, powers and ministries. This sacrament considered outwardly is, as it were, a *sacramentum tantum*: the institution with its rites, organization, hierarchy, law. But the sacrament also includes a *res et sacramentum*, calculated to produce, in varying degrees, a spiritual effect.... This *res et sacramentum* in turn is the sign and source of a pure, inward reality of grace, the *res tantum*. After the pattern of the Eucharist, and thanks to it, the Church-as-institution, considered as a great sacrament, produces this *unitas corporis mystici*. This last [as St. Thomas says] consists of faith and supernatural love in the life of living faith.[58]

We have here one of the first applications of the technical sacramental schema to the ecclesial mystery. It does not seem to be entirely satisfactory; in particular the dissociation of institution from reality of grace endangers the unity of the ecclesial being, and the true nature of the *res et sacramentum* remains rather obscure. But the idea was launched, and it was to run its course. K. Rahner adopted and developed this intuition within the framework of the difficult question of membership in the Church according to the determinations made in the Encyclical *Mystici Corporis*.[59] Rahner summarizes in a way the Scholastic view of the sacraments by pointing out that the word *sacramentum* designates directly (*in recto*) the sacramental sign and indirectly (*in obliquo*) the sacramental grace.[60] For the sacrament Church this means:

The same is true of the ecclesiastical usage regarding the term "Church."... Like the notion of "sacrament," the word "Church" refers in ecclesiastical usage directly [*in recto*] to the external, visible and legally structured community of believers. It refers only indirectly [*in obliquo*] to men's inner faith and union with Christ by grace.[61]

General sacramental theology teaches that in the celebration of a sacrament, the sacramental sign (the *sacramentum tantum*) can be placed

---

58. Congar, *Esquisses du mystère de l'Église*, 2nd ed. (Paris: 1953), 87; English edition: *The Mystery of the Church*, trans. A. V. Littledale, rev. ed. (Baltimore: Helicon Press, 1965), 72.
59. Karl Rahner, "Membership in the Church According to the Doctrine of the Encyclical *Mystici Corporis Christi*," in *Theological Writings* (Baltimore: Helicon Press, 1961–1979), 2:1–88.
60. Rahner, "Membership in the Church," 2:16.
61. Rahner, "Membership in the Church," 2:16.

without the occurrence of the reality of grace (the *res sacramenti*) that it signifies (because of an *obex* or obstacle in the recipient, for example). The conclusion is as follows: someone who belongs only to the outward society is already a member of the Church. A certain dissociation is possible between the outward appearance and the inward membership. We will encounter again in the section of speculative theology this particular question about incorporation into the Mystical Body. For the moment we note that one tends to dissociate the *sacramentum* ("the Church") from the *res sacramenti* ("the Mystical Body"),[62] which seems to be a risk inherent to the sacramental approach to the Church starting with the seven sacraments.

On the eve of Vatican II, the author who had the best view of ecclesial sacramentality, in our opinion, was Edward Schillebeeckx.[63] He returned to the profoundly patristic insight that bases our understanding of all sacramentality on the mystery of Christ:

Christ himself *is* the Church, an invisible community of grace with the living God (the Son made man with the Father), manifested in visible human form.[64]

The ecclesiological thesis is therefore:

[The Church is the] earthly "Body of the Lord"..., [the] earthly sacrament of Christ in heaven.... The earthly Church is the visible realization of this saving reality in history. The Church is a visible communion in grace.... The Church ... is Christ's salvation itself, this salvation as visibly realized in this world.[65]

No dissociation between the visible and the invisible is posited here, even though the distinction between these two aspects is legitimate. But the "homogeneity" of Christ the Head and the Church the Body/Spouse does not allow us to separate that which is constitutive of the being of both of them.

---

62. See, for example, O. Semmelroth, *L'Église, sacrement de la rédemption* (Paris: 1962), 35.
63. In Edward Schillebeeckx, *Christ, the Sacrament of the Encounter with God*, trans. Paul Barrett, rev. ed. (New York: Sheed and Ward, 1963); first Dutch edition published in 1957.
64. Schillebeeckx, *Christ, the Sacrament of the Encounter with God*, 13.
65. Schillebeeckx, *Christ, the Sacrament of the Encounter with God*, 47–48.

The Church Is a Mystery

f. The teaching of Vatican II

The reader will have noted that the teaching about the sacramentality of the Church was not explicitly adopted by the Magisterium during the whole intense ecclesiological ferment that characterized the contemporary renewal. That was a sign that the time was not yet ripe. Now Vatican II very clearly adopts the sacramental perspective for the Church, although it is not entirely developed. It is above all the sign of a discernment: this theological path is worthwhile, but it still requires some clarifications. We present here this conciliar discernment.[66] Our study will concentrate on the two principal references that are at the very beginning of *Lumen gentium*.

The first important reference is the title itself of the first chapter of *Lumen gentium*, which opens the whole Dogmatic Constitution as follows: *De Ecclesiae mysterio* [On the mystery of the Church]. As we pointed out before, this is in the first place about recalling that the conciliar perspective is doctrinal and that consequently this teaching addresses the faith. This is the classic sense of the word "mystery." But given what is about to follow (*LG* 1), the Theological Commission of the Council explained to the Fathers that it is necessary also to understand this in the second sense, the one equivalent to "sacrament."

The word *mystery* does not just indicate something unknowable or hidden but, as is recognized by many, it designates a divine, transcendent and salvific *reality* that is *revealed* (= known) and *manifested* (= in the strong sense: really present) by some visible means. This nomenclature, which is above all biblical, appeared particularly apt to designate the Church.[67]

The word "mystery" is found several times in the first chapter of *Lumen gentium*, both in the first sense (truth) and in the second (sacrament); the reader must pay attention to this. For example, in no. 3 it says that Christ inaugurated the Kingdom of God on earth "and re-

---

66. A list of the references: "Since the Church, in Christ, is in the nature of sacrament—a sign and instrument, that is, of communion with God and of unity among all men" (*LG* 1); the passage is repeated twice in *Gaudium et spes* (nos. 42 and 45); "All those, who in faith look towards Jesus, the author of salvation and the principle of unity and peace, God has gathered together and established as the Church, that it may be for each and everyone the visible sacrament of this saving unity" (*LG* 9); "The Lord founded his Church as the sacrament of salvation" (*AG* 5; see also *SC* 26 and *LG* 48).

67. *Acta Synodalia*, III/I, 170. [Translated from French.]

vealed to us his mystery" ("mystery" here means "truth") and that the Church is this Kingdom already present "*in mysterio.*" In rendering this second meaning of the word, the translations are sometimes too pale in that they seem to stay with the meaning of "truth" by rendering "*in mysterio*" by the adverb "mysteriously," whereas it must be translated with a noun, in keeping with the significance of this expression in the Church Fathers: the Church is the Kingdom already present here on earth "in mystery"—in other words, she is the sacrament of the Kingdom; she points to it and "contains" it in some way so as to give it.

The statement in no. 1 of *Lumen gentium* is obviously of great importance:

Christ is the light of humanity; and it is, accordingly, the heart-felt desire of this sacred Council, being gathered together in the Holy Spirit, that, by proclaiming his Gospel to every creature (cf. Mk 16:15), it may bring to all men that light of Christ which shines out visibly from the Church. Since the Church, in Christ, is in the nature of sacrament—a sign and an instrument, that is, of communion with God and of unity among all men—she here purposes, for the benefit of the faithful and of the whole world, to set forth, as clearly as possible, and in the tradition laid down by earlier Councils, her own nature and universal mission.

These two sentences are extremely "well-wrought," ordered to each other, each one made up of two clauses, a main clause and a subordinate clause. This construction invites us to read them carefully. The first sentence situates the entire paragraph in a Christological context that is made clear by two references, the one that begins and the other that completes the exposition: Christ is the light of the nations, and this is the light, resplendent on the face of the Church, that the Council wants to spread over all mankind. How are we to understand that the light that is Christ shines upon the Church? This is the purpose of the second sentence:

Cum Ecclesia sit ...

The sentence consists of a main clause (the Church intends to clarify her nature and mission) and a subordinate clause introduced by "*cum sit*" (in the sense of "because she is ..."). The intention is to teach the nature of the Church and then her mission by noting at the outset the sacramentality of the Church as that which best presents her in

The Church Is a Mystery

her being as well as in her action. This is how the sequence of chapters 1 and 2 of *Lumen gentium* is presented, the first insisting on the origin and the unity of the Church, the second setting forth her journey in time, a journey entirely dedicated to the spread of salvation.

in Christo veluti sacramentum ...

Immediately afterward comes the reference "in Christ" that echoes in a way the beginning of the paragraph: "*Lumen gentium cum sit Christus.*" This is the hallmark of the "Christocentrism" of the conciliar ecclesiology that we have already noted.[68] To put it another way, the context of the mystery of the Church is the mystery of Christ, and the sacramentality of the Church must be grasped in relation to the sacramentality of Christ; the latter is the fundamental thing. The Church participates in the sacramentality of Christ.[69] Understanding the sacramentality of the Church in terms of the sacramentality of the seven sacraments was therefore not the path taken; one must start with Christ. But what is this "fundamental sacramentality" of Christ? It cannot be his theandric character (the union of the two natures in the Divine Person), since the Church does not participate in that, but rather it is his humanity inasmuch as it is overflowing with grace (Christ's personal grace) and, for that reason, communicates grace to mankind (Christ's capital grace).

In other words, for Christ in the strong sense and in a certain way for the Church, we must consider, first of all the reality of grace and second, this same reality inasmuch as it is communicated—being be-

---

68. This Christological context for the sacramentality of the Church is underscored also in *LG* 9, which concerns activity: the People of God *established by Christ* is *in his hands* the instrument of redemption. This indicates that one must not separate the Church from Christ, either in being or in action, and that there is no basis to the charge that applying sacramentality to the Church makes the latter independent of Christ; on this point, see Yves Congar, *Un Peuple messianique*, 43.

69. Gérard Philips, *L'Église en son mystère*, 73. That point was to finish the debate on the Church-as-primordial-sacrament that was conducted before the council, and that the German draft revision of the initial conciliar schema upheld; cf. *AS* I/IV, 601–9. This draft was quite cogent; it started with the words "*Lumen gentium cum sit Ecclesia,*" and several lines later, speaking about sacramentality, it declared, "[The Church] recognizes that she is the sacrament of the close unity of the whole human race in itself and in its union with God" (610); clearly, the Christological context of sacramentality was one of the main things added by the debates to produce the final text that we have now; on this textual development, cf. Jean-Marie Pasquier, *L'Idée sacramentelle*, 189–201.

fore operation, for that which is given is that which is possessed. The humanity of Christ is not an instrument through which the grace coming from God passes. It is holy, full of grace, and that which it signifies and gives instrumentally is what it possesses in fullness. This shows once again that ecclesial sacramentality cannot be apprehended in terms of the seven sacraments (making the necessary qualification for the Eucharist), because they are instruments communicating a grace that is not their own, if one may put it that way, but that "passes through" them. Christ, in contrast, sanctifies us because he is holy; the Church, in Christ, sanctifies us because she is holy.[70] This reference to Christ, the principle of all sacramentality, shows us that one must take things "from above" according to the following schema: the grace possessed in fullness makes itself visibly present and communicates itself visibly. The order is, therefore, first, the *reality* of salvation, and second, the *manner* of its communication—in other words, first Christ who *is* salvation, because of which he *communicates* to us what he *is*. If one were to take matters "from below," according to a classical schema resulting from the seven sacraments—symbolic cultic activity laden with a saving power—the accent would be placed on the means of salvation, and there would be a risk of overlooking the fact that they are the expression of a fullness that is "poured out" through them. At the very least this fullness would be situated in Christ, which is correct, but not in the Church; this explanation would not notice that she is the reality of salvation, that she receives from her union with Christ—she is the Body of which he is the Head, the Bride with whom he has united himself in one flesh—this fullness that she communicates.[71]

---

70. Once again we must note that this passage from sanctity (being) to sanctification (action) is well marked by the sequence of chapters 1 and 2 of *Lumen gentium*. As for the sanctity of the Church in particular, her "description," the reader can refer to chapter 5, "The universal vocation to holiness in the Church," which begins with these words: "The Church, whose mystery is set forth by this sacred Council, is held, as a matter of faith (*creditur*), to be unfailingly holy" (*LG* 39). Next come the themes of Church as Bride united to Christ as his Body, filled with the gifts of the Spirit. On this point see in particular Y. Congar, *Un Peuple messianique*, 38: "[The Church] lives already the realities of which she is the sign and of which she exercises the ministry"; see also P. Smulders, "L'Église, sacrement du salut," in *L'Église de Vatican II*, US no. 51b, 332ff.

71. Hence we see that the sacramentality of the Church appeals more directly to the theme of the Mystical Body (being) than to the theme of the People of God (action). Fr. de Lubac remarked, "The Church is the sacrament of Jesus Christ. This means also, in other words, that she is in a mystical relation of identity with him"; de Lubac, *Médita-*

The Church Is a Mystery

seu signum et instrumentum intimae unionis cum Deo ...

This reference is closely connected with the preceding expression (*"seu"* = "or," "in other words"). It explains what is meant by "sacrament," but always with reference first to Christ and only then secondarily to the Church. The notions of sign and instrument must first be distinguished. The fully graced humanity of Christ is visible, thanks to its corporeal nature. His life, as it is manifested, signals a peerless sanctity by reason of its unfailing righteousness, and the eyes of faith make it possible to profess this (Mt 16:16–18). The human activity of Christ, on the other hand, communicates grace visibly through words and deeds, through all his "*acta et passa in carne*" ["deeds and sufferings in the flesh"], which are also received in faith.

In and of itself the sign produces only the signification; in other words, it causes us to know.[72] As such it does not have a real efficacy; it communicates intellectually that which it causes us to know, but not really. Its efficacy, however, is of the nature of an instrument. The nature of an instrument does not require that it possess in itself that which it confers; it accomplishes its effect as it is moved by the principal agent. In the case of Christ, however, the instrument (which is his humanity) possesses the fullness of the grace that it transmits. It is somewhat the same for the Church: she is sanctifying because she is holy in Christ.

There are two levels of visibility: the visibility of the subject and that of the instrument through which the subject acts. In Christ, at the highest point, we can say that the sacrament of his humanity contains the grace that it transmits, since the humanity of Christ is at the same time the reality of grace and the instrument for communicating that reality. What extrapolation can we make from this point concerning the Church? One the one hand we can say that the Church is the Mystical Body of Christ, and by virtue of this she visibly manifests the fullness of grace in the form of a social sign. As Fr. Edward Schillebeeckx puts it:

> The Church ... is Christ's salvation itself, this salvation as visibly realized in this world. Thus it is, by a kind of identity, the body of the Lord.[73]

---

tions sur l'Église, 161; see also Fr. Congar: "It is indeed because she is the Body of Christ that the Church can be *in Christ* the sacrament (cf. *LG* 1)," in *Un Peuple messianique*, 83.

72. Cf. *ST* IIIa, q. 62, art. 3, corpus: grace is in the sacraments as in a sign.

73. Edward Schillebeeckx, *Christ, the Sacrament of the Encounter with God*, 48 (rather than "by a kind of identity" we would say "mystically").

This visible manifestation of a fullness of grace is confirmed at the level of its properties: one, holy, catholic, and apostolic. This visible sign is made up of the life of the community as a whole, clergy and laity:

> The whole Church, the people of God led by the priestly hierarchy, is "the sign raised up among the nations." The activity, as much of the faithful as of their leaders, is thus an ecclesial activity. This means that not only the hierarchy but also the believing people belong essentially to the primordial sacrament which is the earthly expression of this reality [since the Ascension of Christ].[74]

This fullness exists, after the pattern of the fullness residing in the humanity of our Savior, in order to communicate itself. The Church is, inseparably, the means of salvation, the instrument through which God saves.[75] The topic here, at this stage of our consideration, will be the particular acts of Christ that the Church places significantly and instrumentally, the seven sacraments in the precise sense of the term (always with a reservation concerning the Eucharist, which we will discuss in detail in the speculative part). The gift of grace is given in a visible form proper to it. Unity, holiness, catholicity, and apostolicity will be reduced to act in a sign that will be a specific activity—namely, the sacramental liturgical action.

With reference to Christ, thanks to him and in constant dependence upon him, the Church that is his Body and his Bride really contains the grace that she signifies and communicates. She is, in this order, at the same time the reality of salvation and the means of salvation. This presentation of the general economy of the sacramentality of Christ, which is the basis for that of the Church, shows that there is a profound affinity between the two. All that we have said about the Church is completely dependent on her configuration to Christ: if the Church is not the Body and the Bride of Christ, all her sacramentality vanishes.

But at this point in our study, a difficulty specific to the Church arises. Although one can and must say that the communion of life resulting from the theological virtues is *in* the ecclesial society, and thereby

---

74. Schillebeeckx, *Christ, the Sacrament of the Encounter with God*, 48–49.

75. Charles Gouyau, *L'Église instrument du salut* (Paris: 2005), particularly pages 219ff., although it reduces the instrumental ecclesial activity to the action of the ministers. In this perspective, the whole ecclesial community would not be the sign-instrument.

the unity of the subject is posited, one must recognize that the ecclesial society is composed of sinners. What is inconceivable in Christ—this man *is* certainly, constantly, and perfectly the Son of God because sin has no control over him, he is perfectly deserving of this title—will pose a formidable question for the Church: how can we be sure that the reality of salvation is unfailingly present *in* this earthly community when there is no discernible guarantee of the sanctity of its members, and when such sanctity is doubtful because every human being is capable of sin? We must examine therefore in greater depth the configuration of the Church to Christ and the question of sin in the Church. These are questions that we will address in the speculative part. For the moment, let us recall the data that the sources give us, which is precisely what we will have to try to explain. The parallelism between Christ and the Church that is the basis for sacramentality can be set forth as follows:

TABLE 5-1

Christ, full of grace and truth (Jn 1:14)	The Church is the fullness of Christ (Eph 1:23)
Christ is holy	*The Church is holy in Christ*
From his fullness we have all received (Jn 1:16)	This fullness is communicated to mankind (Eph 3:10)
Christ sanctifies	*The Church sanctifies "in Christo"*
The humanity of Christ is sign and instrument; it is united to the Word in his Person.	The Church is the sign and instrument; united to Christ, forming with him as it were a single mystical Person (his Body and his Bride).

We see the clarification that this teaching about ecclesial sacramentality provides. Many times, as we were studying the themes of the Body of Christ, the Temple of the Spirit, and the People of God, we remarked that Revelation used the name "Church" to refer to two distinct things: the community of knowledge and love with God and among men, in which is found salvation, and the whole order of means to signify and obtain it. Sacramentality tells us that the relation between these two aspects is twofold: a relation of *sign* to notify and a relation of *instrument* to communicate really what is known. This twofold relation is so close and solid that the mystery of the Church consists fundamentally in the inseparable unity between the reality procured and the signs-instruments that procure it. We hold this by faith, and this will be one of the very first speculative questions to resolve: to give an account of this unity between such dissimilar elements.

Let us say a word about the aftermath of Vatican II on this subject. After the Council theology concentrated, so to speak, on the biblical theme of the People of God and neglected to continue the effort concerning sacramentality. A good observer remarks on this subject:

> After the Council, however, this important statement [about the sacramentality of the Church] came to be forgotten for the most part, and indeed discredited. Some people see it as theological window-dressing, if not actually an ideological self-enhancement of the church as it really and specifically is.[76]

Vatican II had intended to show the unity of the different aspects of the ecclesial being through sacramentality. The fact that this theological path was neglected explains why post-conciliar ecclesiology has still not resolved this question. It is plain that today the Church is still presented as a "composite" of a human reality (all that is sign and instrument) and a "divine" reality (all that falls under the heading of grace itself). The reality of grace and the means of grace are still not unified conceptually. This will be our primary speculative effort in the future. The International Theological Commission drew up a report for the Extraordinary Roman Synod in 1985, which was convoked for the twentieth anniversary of the close of the Council. This question about the unity of the ecclesial being is *the* great contemporary ecclesiological question, and the fact that it has been inadequately explained is the source of many difficulties of a pastoral sort. If one *separates* the ecclesial means from the ecclesial reality—for example, by speaking about the Church-the-visible-institution as really distinct from the Church-the-invisible-communion (and this separation is lived rather than thought by a great number of people)—then one mutilates the ecclesial being, somewhat as if one were to separate the body from the soul of a human being. The accounts of the bishops with a view to the Synod have often pointed out this difficulty, which is at the origin of many anti-ecclesial sorts of behavior (relativization of the profession of faith, of the reception of the sacraments, of ecclesial discipline).

---

76. Walter Kasper, *Theology and Church* (New York: Crossroad, 1989), 112.

The Church Is a Mystery

This is why the International Theological Commission recalled in its report the importance of the sacramentality of the Church.[77] But this document is not magisterial. That is why it is important to see how the final Synod report voted on by the Fathers keeps the Commission's suggestions in mind. This final report insists on the mystery of the Church, her sacramentality.[78] One can also read the final Message of the Synod to the People of God, which likewise insists on this in its first paragraph. All of this shows us the importance of a correct understanding of ecclesial sacramentality. We will examine this in greater depth in the speculative part.

To finish this section we propose placing more clearly in context the reasons for the contemporary difficulty in grasping the fundamental unity that makes the mystery-sacrament.

g. The unity of the mystery-sacrament: modern difficulties

What is unique about the Christian faith is the precise manner of the alliance between the divine and the human, the transcendent and the immanent, the mysterious and the knowable, the temporal and the eternal. This is not only about the relation whereby creation proclaims the glory of God—in other words, about a symbolism that can be called "natural" and does not belong solely to the Christian religion (which nevertheless adopts it), but rather about a relation that is deeper in another way, founded on the very mystery of the Savior, the object of all Judeo-Christian Revelation: it is the most profound and decisive mode of the relation of God to man and of man to God that is addressed here and that is specifically Christian. The theological significance of the world is part of this perspective: secular realities, which as such are human, immanent, temporal, receive this ability to speak of divine, transcendent, eternal realities, and for some of them—the ones that have been chosen by Christ—this leads them to be in some way the mode in which divine, transcendent, and eternal realities are present in this world. We have on the one hand the world as such, which is the great book through which God speaks about himself and on the other hand certain worldly reali-

---

77. Report of the ITC, chap. 8.
78. Final Report of the Synod Fathers, II. Particular subjects; A. The mystery of the Church; 2. The mystery of God through Jesus Christ in the Holy Spirit.

ties that have a more precise expressive power and a capacity to engender that which they express. For example, the washing of water accompanied by a word signifies and brings about the purification that is the new birth to divine life.

The *age* in the Christian perspective is fraught with meaning and sometimes even with the active presence of realities that go beyond it, but are somehow contained in it: transcendence and immanence have to be held together. This way of thinking has been accused, in the twentieth century, of harking back to a mythical, magical stage of human awareness that saw the world as a sort of "great visible God."[79] This awareness has been outmoded by the development of knowledge, especially scientific knowledge. Modern, functional society regards things only as useful things, since the world is thought of as a set of material realities and human actions on those things. A thing remains a thing; by itself it is mute, and if a higher meaning is given to it, that meaning is given and added by man as something apart from the thing. This is a kind of secularization that leads to the loss of transcendence and universality.

In fact, transcendence and immanence can be kept together—in a Christian context—only with the help of a third term that can be called *transparency*.[80] The divine reality is not only *above* the world, transcending it, and is not just immanent *in* it, but is also transparent *to* the world and *through* it. We mean that the behavior of God toward the world cannot be understood fully if one keeps only the "above" and the "in." There is a third specific dimension that we can find in St. Paul: "There is ... one God and Father of us all, who is above all [transcendence] and through all [transparency] and in all [immanence]" (Eph 4:6). Transparency is the golden mean between transcendence and immanence, and it is what explains the things of the world as symbols. The symbol, from its etymology that is religious, is the meeting of the transcendent and the immanent. The symbol is neither immanent nor transcendent; it is the encounter of the two, one in the other and vice versa.

Transparency is therefore a quality of a thing that is worldly per

---

79. See Aristotle, *Peri philosophias*, frag. 18; Plato, *Timaeus* 92b. This is the typical problematic in the writings of R. Bultmann.

80. This does not mean a kind of transparency like that of a clear window, but rather that of a stained-glass window that adds its colors and projects its image on the space that is illumined. This idea could be expressed by other words, such as *transfiguration, manifestation, epiphany*.

The Church Is a Mystery 329

se, which allows transcendence to occur "through it." It is very precisely the sacramental thought of the Fathers who set Christianity on a path toward self-understanding that we think is basically definitive: worldly transparency is what ties together the divine and the human, the transcendent and the immanent, the historical and the eternal; it is the place where transcendence becomes visible in and through immanence; the absolute is not grasped "with" the symbol, but rather "in" the symbol, which by its transparency opens up a view of the infinite.

Because it is situated midway, transparency possesses a sort of ambivalence, depending on the direction from which one looks at it. On the one hand, the simpler aspect starting from the "natural" symbolism—the world, immanence—is the *sign* of a higher reality: washing in water accompanied by a word *signifies* new birth; this function results in knowledge. On the other hand, the transcendent reality speaks itself and gives itself in and through the worldly reality: the symbol has an additional function of *accomplishing* what it signifies; it is the visibility and the actuality of the transcendent reality itself in and for the world.

The Christian community adopts this "symbolism" in its very identity. According to its faith, the Church is immanent—fully human—and transparent to the transcendence that dwells somehow within it. The simplest approach begins by recognizing its sociological aspect: being a reality of this world, it consequently assumes the human sociability from which it cannot free itself without disappearing. Secularization does not deny this sociological dimension, but makes it the whole of the reality: immanence alone, without any sign-relation to transcendence given from above.[81] Secular or "laicist" legislation of the French sort considers only that. A community of the religious type is thus a bit of the social civil totality, most often considered in terms of its ethical and social utility. Another approach—in reaction to this secularization—places the emphasis on the transcendent aspect, the communion of saints, but with the risk of not situating this transcendence *in* the sociological reality, depriving the latter of all transparency.

The absence of symbolic thinking—the absence of *transparency*—leads to keeping the two aspects separate, in a dualistic way, instead of one through and in the other. This view is one of the foundations of

---

81. This is what we noted, in the discussions concerning the mystery-truth, as being the first glance at the Church.

Protestantism (the duality: visible Church—invisible Church), which rests largely on the abandonment of the properly Christian symbolic dimension of the world. This dualist mindset seems to us to be at the origin of modernity and the secularist movement that proceeds from it.[82] Today it has reached a crisis and is about to explode. It is urgent to return to this sacramental view of the world.

Bibliography

General studies of vocabulary

The noun "mystery" has a great breadth of meaning (mystery-truth, with its adjective *mysterious,* and mystery-reality, with its adjective *mystic*). The rediscovery of this breadth is rather recent in Latin theology. Among the main studies we can mention:

Bouyer, Louis. "'Mystique': Essai sur l'histoire d'un mot." *La Vie Spirituelle,* Supplément (1949): 3–23.

———. "Mysterion." *La Vie Spirituelle,* Supplément (1952): 397–412.

Mystery-Truth

Please refer to the course on fundamental theology (particularly concerning the Constitution *Dei Verbum,* nos. 2–6) and to the course on morality concerning faith. Furthermore, many of the titles cited within the context of the mystery-reality (see later) also address this aspect. Generally speaking, one can also profitably read the following titles, which have inspired us more particularly:

Journet, Charles. *L'Église du Verbe incarné.* Vol. 2. Paris: 1951. Especially 1193ff. on the distinction between mystery and miracle that serves as the basis for the distinction between theology and apologetics; very enlightening.

———. *Théologie de l'Église.* Paris: 1960. English edition: *The Theology of the Church.* Translated by Victor Szczurek, O. Praem. San Francisco: Ignatius Press, 2004. Particularly the parallel between the three ways of looking at Christ and the three ways of looking at the Church; see. chap. 1.

Schillebeeckx, Edward. *L'Économie sacramentelle du salut.* Fribourg: 2004, 129–32.

The Mystery-Reality (sacrament)

Biblical Studies

Bornkamm, G. "Mystērion." In *Theological Dictionary of the New Testament* ("Kittel").

Coppens, Joseph. "Le mystère dans la théologie paulinienne et ses parallèles qumraniens." In *Recherches bibliques.* Paris: 1960, 5:142–65.

---

82. For lack of transparency, the symbolic function retains, at best, only the aspect of *sign,* but not that of *accomplishment;* as things develop, this "pure sign" tends to disappear.

Deeden, D. "Le mystère paulinien." *Eph. Th. Lov.* 13 (1936): 405–42.
Follet, R., and K. Prumm. "Mystères." In *Supplément au Dictionnaire de la Bible,* vol. 6, col. 1–225.
Richter, G. "Mystère: I—Étude biblique." In *Encyclopédie de la foi.* Paris: 1966, 3:155–61.
Rigaux, B. "Le mystère de l'Église à la lumière de la Bible." In *L'Église de Vatican II.* US no. 51b. Paris: 1965, esp. 223–28.
Rigaux, B., and Pierre Grelot. "Mystère." In *Vocabulaire de théologie biblique.* Paris: 1981.
Schlier, H. *Le Temps de l'Église.* Paris: 1961. Collection of articles; see particularly "L'Église d'après l'Épître aux Éphésiens," 169ff.; "L'Église, mystère du Christ, d'après l'Épître aux Éphésiens," 302ff.; and "L'unité de l'Église dans la pensée de saint Paul," 291ff.
Schnackenburg, Rudolf. *The Church in the New Testament.* Translated by W. J. O'Hara. New York: Herder and Herder, 1965.
Schnackenburg, Rudolf, and Karl Thieme. *La Bible et le mystère de l'Église.* Paris: 1964. Essentially repeats the findings of the preceding title; see esp. 88ff. Clear, descriptive presentation of the complexity of the ecclesial being; the speculative assumptions are much more liable to criticism.

Patristic Theology

Ruffini, E., and E. Lodi. *"Mysterion" e "Sacramentum": La sacramentalità negli scritti dei Padri e nei testi liturgici primitivi.* Bologna: 1987. An extensive collection of patristic texts that shows the consistency of patristic theology, with differences in emphasis between the Greek and the Latin Fathers.

Greek world

Chenevert, J. *L'Église dans le commentaire d'Origène sur le Cantique des cantiques.* Studia 24. Bruxelles, Paris, and Montréal: 1969. See particularly chap. 5, "L'Église et le Verbe incarné," 159ff., and the conclusion, 276ff.
Daniélou, Jean. *Sacramentum futuri.* Paris: 1950.
Marsh, H. G. "The Use of 'Mystērion' in the Writings of Clement of Alexandria." *Journal of Theological Studies* (Oxford) 37 (1936): 64–80. Good review of the texts.
Mondesert, C. "Le symbolisme chez Clément d'Alexandrie." *Rech. de Sc. Rel.* 26 (1936): 158–80.
Verriele, A. "Le plan du salut d'après S. Irénée." *Rech. de Sc. Rel.* 14 (1934): 493–524. Important for understanding the union of the human and the divine in the way in which God chose to save the world.
Visentin, P. *"Mysterion—Sacramentum* dai Padri alla scolastica." *Studia Patavina* 4 (1957). See especially 399–402 on the Greek Fathers.
von Balthasar, Hans Urs. "Le mysterion d'Origène." *Recherches de Science Religieuse* 26 (1936): 513–62; *Recherches de Science Religieuse* 27 (1937): 34–64.

The Latin world

de Ghellinck, J. *Pour l'histoire du mot "sacramentum."* Vol. 1, *Les Pères anténicéens.* Louvain: 1924. Vol. 2, *Patristique et Moyen Âge.* Louvain: 1947. An extremely valuable set of essays. The reader should be familiar with these works.

Mohrmann, Charles. "'Sacramentum' dans les plus anciens textes chrétiens." *Harvard Theological Review* 47 (1954): 141–52. Reprinted in *Études sur le latin des chrétiens.* Rome: 1961, 1:233–44. Discusses the hasty comparisons made by many authors (in particular Odo Casel) between the pagan "mysteries" and the Christian "mysteries."

Particular church fathers

Duval, Y. M. *"Sacramentum" et "mysterium" chez s. Léon le Grand.* Lille: 1958.

Camelot, Pierre-Thomas. "'Sacramentum,' notes de théologie augustinienne." *RT* 57 (1957): 429–49.

———. "Le Christ, sacrement de Dieu." In *L'homme devant Dieu,* mélanges H. de Lubac. Paris: 1964, 355–63.

Couturier, C. "*Sacramentum* et *mysterium* dans l'oeuvre de S. Augustin." In *Études augustiniennes.* Paris: 1953, 163–332. The most complete positive investigation, listing the 2,279 occurrences and attempting to classify them.

Feret, M.-F. "*Sacramentum res* dans la langue théologique de S. Augustin." *RSPT* 29 (1940): 218–43.

Hocedez, P. H. "La conception augustinienne du sacrement dans le *Tractatus 80 in Johannem.*" *Rev. de Sc. Rel.* 9 (1919): 1–29.

Mandouze, A. "À propos de '*sacramentum*' chez S. Augustin: Polyvalence lexicologique et foisonnement théologique." In *Mélanges offerts à Chr. Mohrmann.* Utrecht and Anvers: 1963, 222–32. A clarification by a man of letters concerning the sometimes too hasty conclusions of the theologians.

Testard, M. *Le mot "sacramentum" dans les sermons de s. Léon le Grand.* Paris: 1950.

Van der Meer, F. "*Sacramentum* chez S. Augustin." *La Maison Dieu* 13 (1948): 50–64.

Medieval Theology

Chenu, M. D. "Théologie symbolique et exégèse scolastique aux XII-XIIIe s." In *Mélanges offerts à J. de Ghellinck,* Museum Lessianum "section historique" 2, no. 14 (1951): 509–26. Concerns the two major ways possible of understanding the symbol.

de Ghellinck, J. "L'histoire de la définition des sacrements au XIIe s." In *Mélanges Mandonnet.* Vol. 2. Paris: 1930.

———. *Pour l'histoire du mot sacramentum.* Vol. 2. 1947 (already cited).

de Lubac, H. *Corpus mysticum.* Paris: 1949. Important survey of the use of the word "*sacramentum*" before the Thomistic definition.

The Church Is a Mystery

Saint Thomas Aquinas

Roguet, A.-M. Treatise "Des sacrements en général" in the edition of the *Summa theologiae* of the *Revue des Jeunes*. Paris: 1951. Excellent notes, in part, see 255–62, for the data prior to the Thomistic reflection.

Schillebeeckx, Edward. *L'Économie sacramentelle du salut*. Fribourg: 2004, 122–34.

Schoot, H. J. M. *Christ the "Name" of God: Thomas Aquinas on Naming Christ*. Louvain: 1993. The first chapter, entitled "Christ, the Mystery of God," studies St. Thomas's usage of the word "*mysterium.*" The author discovers four fundamental meanings that emphasize above all the aspect of knowledge (mystery-truth). He emphasizes very little the possible connection between mystery and sacrament. It is true, though, that St. Thomas uses the word "sacrament" only in the restricted sense.

We refer the reader to the course on the sacraments for the sacramental theology of St. Thomas.

After St. Thomas: varying connotations of sacramentality

English, E. D. *Reading and Wisdom: The "Doctrina christiana" of Augustine in the Middle Ages*. Medieval Studies 6. Notre Dame, Ind.: University of Notre Dame Press, 1995. Collaborative work. See in particular the essay by T. S. Maloney, "Is the *De doctrina christiana* the Source for Bacon's Semiotics?" 126–42. The author points out that, unlike St. Augustine, R. Bacon insists that a sign is not necessarily presented to the senses; see in particular 131ff.

Gy, P.-M. "Sur la théologie sacramentaire du Bienheureux Jean Duns Scot." *Rev. de l'Inst. Cath. de Paris* 49 (1994): 19–25. Concerns the beginnings of the relativization of the necessarily sensible character of a sign and thus of the sacraments.

The Modern Rediscovery of Sacramentality in the Wider Sense

Before Vatican II

Congar, Yves. *Chrétiens désunis: principes d'un oecuménisme catholique*. US 1. Paris: 1936, esp. 106–8. English translation by M. A. Bousfield, OP: *Divided Christendom: A Catholic Study of the Problem of Reunion*. London: Centenary Press, 1939, esp. 83ff.

———. *Mystery of the Church*. Baltimore and Dublin: Helicon Press, 1965. Note in particular the essay "The Idea of the Church in St. Thomas Aquinas," 53ff.

Gribomont, Jean. "Du sacrement de l'Église et de ses réalisations imparfaites." *Irénikon* 22 (1949): 345–67. One of the first attempts to apply ecclesial sacramentality to ecumenism by the analogy of the Church that follows the various degrees of realization possible of her sacramentality.

Hamer, Jérôme. *The Church Is a Communion*. New York: Sheed and Ward, 1964. Severe, but justified critique of Rahner and Semmelroth (particularly 87–90, which states the essentials well).

Oswald, J.-H. *Die dogmatische Lehre von den heiligen Sakramenten der Katholischen Kirche*. Münster: 1856.

Pasquier, Jean-Marie. *L'Église comme sacrement: Le développement de l'idée sacramentelle de l'Église, de Moehler à Vatican II*. Studia Friburgensia 105. Fribourg: Academic Press Fribourg, 2008. Thorough review of nineteenth- and twentieth-century authors. Very analytical.

Rahner, Karl. "Membership in the Church according to the Teaching of Pius XII's Encyclical *Mystici Corporis Christi*." In *Theological Investigations*. Baltimore: Helicon Press, 1963, 2:1–88.

Scheeben, Matthias Joseph. *Le Mystère de l'Église et de ses sacrements*. Paris: 1946. Original German edition, 1869. This remains the most profound study of the period; it was to have a great influence on the contemporary renewal. Worth reading.

———. *The Mysteries of Christianity*. New York: Herder, 1951. Original German edition, 1868.

Schillebeeckx, Edward. *Christ, the Sacrament of the Encounter with God*. New York: Sheed and Ward, 1963. This is the most decisive study for a correct understanding of sacramentality, starting from Christ. A major, must-read work.

Schwane, J. *Dogmengeschichte*. Münster: 1872.

Semmelroth, O. *L'Église, sacrement de la rédemption*. Paris: 1962.

Sertillanges, A. G. *The Church*. Translated by A. G. McDougall. New York: Benziger Brothers, 1922.

Stolz, A. *De Ecclesia*. Freiburg im Breisgau: 1939.

Vatican II and the aftermath

Congar, Yves. "L'Église, sacrement universel du salut." In *L'Église aujourd'hui*. Paris: 1967, 5–30. Reprinted in *Cette Église que j'aime*. Paris: 1968, 41–63.

———. *Un peuple messianique: Salut et libération*. Paris: 1975. All of chapter 1 is devoted to the sacramentality of the Church.

International Theological Commission. *The One Church of Christ*. Report written for the Extraordinary Synod of 1985. See chap. 8, "The Church as sacrament of Christ"; nicely recalls the essentials of sacramentality. Useful in discerning the deficiencies and weaknesses of the post-conciliar theology on this topic.

Journet, Charles. "Le mystère de la sacramentalité." *Nova et Vetera* (1974): 161–214. Essay that develops sacramentality in terms of Christ so as to discover the sacramentality of the Church. This study is the speculative continuation of a retreat preached in Geneva in 1973 and likewise published under the title *Le Mystère de la sacramentalité*. A very dense, Scripture-based meditation; worth reading.

Kasper, Walter. "The Church as a Universal Sacrament of Salvation." In *Theology and Church*. New York: Crossroad, 1989, 111–28. Deceptive study that separates the "*sacramentum*" from the "*res*" (along the lines of Rahner and Semmelroth).

Le Guillou, Marie-Joseph. "La sacramentalité de l'Église." *La Maison Dieu* 93 (1968): 9–38. One of the best authors on this subject. Concerning the author, see M. Cagin, "L'Église sacrement, ou l'Église dans sa transparence au mystère." In *Quand un homme témoigne de Dieu: Le Père Marie-Joseph Le Guillou*. Saint Maur: 1998, 113–33.

Martelet, G. "De la sacramentalité propre à l'Église, ou du sens de l'Église inséparable du sens du Christ." *NRTh*. 95 (1973): 25–42. A study focusing more immediately on the post-conciliar difficulties; shows the usefulness of the concept of sacramentality to avoid separating "the human from the divine" in the Church.

Nicolas, Jean-Hervé. *Synthèse dogmatique*. Paris and Fribourg: 1985, 630ff. States the essentials well and shows the relevance of sacramentality to the unity of the ecclesial being.

Pagé, Jean-Guy. *Qui est l'Église?* Vol. I, "Le mystère et le sacrement du salut." Montreal: 1977, esp. 240–75. Well-balanced, overall presentation. Good bibliography.

Philips, Gérard. *L'Église en son mystère au IIe concile du Vatican*. Paris: 1967, 1:71–76. Rapid overview.

Smulders, P. "L'Église, sacrement du salut." In *L'Église de Vatican II*. US 51b. Paris: 1966, 313–38.

Tillard, Jean-Marie Roger. "Église et salut: Sur la sacramentalité de l'Église." *NRTh*. 106 (1984): 658–85. Interesting for the ecumenical aspect of sacramentality.

Warnach, V. "L'Église comme mystère." In *La nouvelle image de l'Église: Bilan du concile Vatican II*. Paris: 1967, 39–47; see also Warnach, "L'Église comme sacrement," in *La nouvelle image de l'Église*, 47–55. Good overall presentation of the concepts in a perspective that is at the same time historical and theological; mostly German bibliography.

Part Two

Speculative Theology
Definition of the Church

Introduction

I. Speculative theology: Necessity and possibility

As we already explained in the general introduction to the course, theology—as the rational understanding of what one believes—begins by apprehending its *sources*, the data of faith (Revelation: Scripture and Tradition). This is positive theology or source theology. The result is a certain "mass" of information that *describes* the reality that one is trying to understand. This was the object of Part One. Having arrived at this point, we need to take another step that is decisive for our understanding. On the basis of the elements collected from the sources, we pose the following question: what is the Church? Although positive theology strives to answer the question "*quomodo sit?*" ["How is it?"], speculative theology follows up the effort with the question "*quid sit?*" ["What is it?"]. This is the final phase of the quest for knowledge. Speculative theology therefore has the higher aim, but also the humbler one: the divine *realities* cannot be strictly circumscribed by *truths*, even if they are truths of faith or speculatively certain. Despite this, the speculative effort is necessary, and because it is necessary one hopes that it is possible.

- The speculative effort is indispensable.

This final stage of the quest for knowledge is indispensable. It corresponds to the deepest and most spontaneous question of our mind when it considers a reality: *What is it?* Faith, in enabling us to grasp a *Revelation*, is at the beginning of this effort that aims to understand that which is revealed. This theological knowledge holds the middle position between two errors: fideism and rationalism. We will not dwell on this because it is part of the course on faith.[1] But in a course on ecclesiology it is necessary to note the ecclesial pertinence of the preceding material. An understanding of the faith, insofar as it progresses, promotes the Christian life in its communitarian, ecclesial aspect, and that is essential. The higher we advance, each one personally, in knowledge of reality, the more we all converge toward that reality, the more we are united by our knowledge of that reality. What we may call "subjectivism" in the broad sense (the attitude, "as for me personally, I ...") runs the risk of reducing the faith to a strictly personal dimension that thus can vary from one person to the next and is, strictly speaking, incommunicable. On the contrary, our faith is the faith of the community, and this faith is at the basis of our unity.[2] These reminders are important in our age, when speculative efforts are rarely in agreement.

It should be recalled, however, that the faith is not the work of the intellect; it is a grace, a gift from God. We do not seek to understand in order to believe, but rather we believe in order to understand. The assent of the theological virtue of faith comes first in relation to theological study, whether positive or speculative. Furthermore, a theological understanding of the content of our faith is important to show that faith is not contrary to reason (the reproach of "obscurantism"). It is very important these days not only to "give a reason (Greek: *logos*; Latin: *ratio*) for the hope that is in you" (cf. 1 Pt 3:15), but also to show that the faith does not mutilate the human being, but elevates him to one of the truest and highest orders of knowledge.[3]

Having noted this necessity of understanding what we believe, we must show the possibility thereof.

- Speculative theology is possible.

God and his works that Revelation has made known to us are neither absurd, nor random, nor arbitrary. God speaks and acts in such a

---

1. See in particular the Constitution *Dei Filius* of Vatican I, chap. 4.
2. See, for example: "Consensus in the unity of the faith is the principle of communion in charity; this is why dissent in faith excludes friendship," in *IV Sent*. D. 13, q. 2, art. 3, sol. 1, ad 1.
3. See our discussion of the *mystery-truth*: the *super*intelligibility and not the *un*intelligibility of revealed truth.

way that man may understand who he is and what he does. In doing so, God respects the faculty of reason that he gave us, which is called to make us not only receive impressions of God passively [*pâtir Dieu*], but also participate in him and in his works. As we have already seen, this is the most decisive reason of fittingness in grasping the reason for the "law of sacramentality" that God has chosen to save the world: the divine reality comes to dwell in a human reality so as to make itself known through it and to communicate itself through it.

Furthermore, there is an overall coherence in God's action, whatever the highs and lows there may have been in the history of salvation because of the malice of mankind. God acts by beginning in this way and continuing in another ... there is a "logic" to it. This is what Vatican I calls the *nexus mysteriorum*,[4] the connection between the mysteries. We saw some examples of it in Part One on positive theology. Thus Christological errors bring about ecclesiological errors. By ceaselessly investigating these connections, by examining them in depth, one progresses in an understanding of the faith and eventually comes to propose what is the terminus of the theological effort: a synthesis capable of showing the architecture of the whole. Even though these syntheses are always precarious (for that which our intellect penetrates slightly is infinite), the acquisition thereof is irreplaceable. Thanks to them we can make still further progress.

Everything that we have just recalled implies a certain concept of God that is not always well understood, or may even be denied. Indeed, anything closely or remotely connected to fideism (which denies the capacity of human reason to have a certain understanding of the mysteries) originates in a view of God that is not always quite explicit, but can be lived. God is thought to be a "king-dictator" who gives orders and consequently requires blind obedience. Someone states that such and such is "the will of God," and faced with that, the religious person has no alternative but to humble himself. Now all of Revelation presents God to us in a different light. He is not a master the way men are, nor is he simply a friend; he is Father. Paternal love for sons and daughters is the "driving force" of divine action. This love never ceases to speak in order to make itself understood; it acts in such a way that

---

4. Constitution *Dei Filius*, chap. 4.

we can participate in what it brings about. When he is received in faith, we go to meet him in an intelligent, voluntary way. We are not in competition with God, either, and we do not think it necessary to annihilate man in order to exalt God. On the contrary, he draws us to himself by grace so as to be, through participation, that which he is by nature. The theological effort on its level, which is the level of the intellect, is at the service of this profound spiritual progression.

II. Presuppositions of Speculative Theology

Speculative theology does not describe reality as positive theology does; instead it aims to express its being by definition. To the question, "what is it?" it answers, "It is this." To aim at the being of a thing is to try to give an account of its essence. What represents (i.e., makes present) in our mind the essence of a thing is the *concept*, which is expressed by the *name*. The following diagram recalls several important ideas:

TABLE 6-1

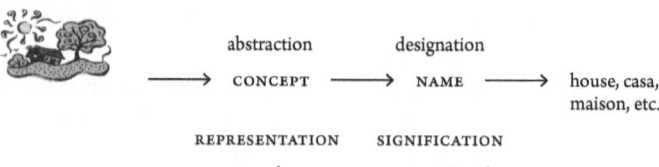

	abstraction	designation	
⟶	CONCEPT ⟶	NAME ⟶	house, casa, maison, etc.
	REPRESENTATION	SIGNIFICATION	
	real	conventional	

- The *concept* in the mind represents the *real* thing.
- The *conventional name* signifies the concept.

All knowledge comes from the senses. Now the senses apprehend *singulars* (*this* house). The mind abstracts (etymologically: "draws out") from the singular object under consideration its *form:* that by which it is what it is. Based on this the mind expresses the *formal aspect*, or the concept, which is always universal (we speak about the concept of "house" and not the concept of "this house"). The concept is the same everywhere because it is *real*. Hence, since the concept is universal, it can be applied to every reality possessing the same formal aspect (middle-class house, castle, villa, hut). Since these realities are formally the same, they are said to be *univocal;* the same concept is abstracted from each one of them.

For realities that do not exhibit the same formal aspect, yet have a similarity, we will say that they are *analogous,* and, to begin with, we will make an analogous application of the concept.[5] For example, the staff of officials in the service of a sovereign or his progeny are called his "house" (e.g., the "house of Savoy").

Everything on the order of the concept is *real* and by no means *conventional.* If two realities are really in an analogous relation, the concept will be analogical. On the contrary, when one and the same *name* designates concepts that represent formally different realities, we say that the name is *equivocal.* For example, the word "table" designates a piece of furniture, an array of integers (multiplication table), a list (table of contents). The equivocal character of a name is a phenomenon peculiar to each language or culture, because the name is by nature conventional.

We can summarize this with the following diagram:

TABLE 6-2

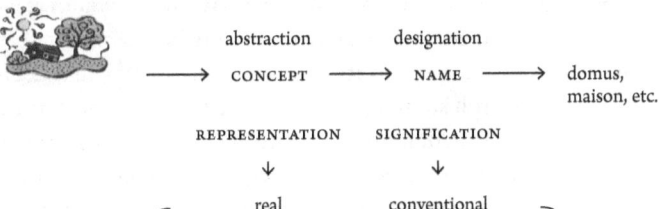

- *Real* application → univocal (same form → same concept)
  →Analogical (analogous form → analogous concept)
- *Conventional* application of the *word* → equivocation.

---

5. Recall: the analogy *of the reality* is what implies the analogy of the concept. This ensures that we avoid what we might call a certain "conceptualism" that has disastrous consequences that we will see later on.

The concept is therefore the representation in the intellect of the reality from which it is abstracted—more precisely the representation of the *form* of that reality. When the reality is *simple*, in other words, not composed of matter and form (God, angels), the concept is the faithful representation of the reality. For all the realities of this world that are *complex*—in other words, composed of matter and form—it must be noted that the abstraction causes the mind to pass from the singular to the universal. Now what *exists* is the singular. The universal, as such, is a *being of reason* that does not exist, because the form does not exist without the matter that it informs and by which it is individualized. Thus, for example, we have a concept of "man," but what really exists is Peter, or Paul, or John.... These reminders are of capital importance for speculative theology. To abstract from the concrete ecclesial reality—the only one truly existing—one aspect, "the reality of salvation," or another aspect, "means of salvation," is legitimate so as not to mix everything together, just as abstracting from Paul what constitutes his bodily nature and his spiritual nature is right and necessary, *provided that* one does not lose sight of the fact that what truly exists is the Church as the one whole made up of these aspects, just as Paul is the one whole made up of body and soul.

- The notion of speculative truth

This is generally expressed in the following way: "*adequatio rei et intellectus.*" A concept is true if it faithfully represents in the intellect the form of the object understood, in its relation to the matter that is informed. This type of truth should not be confused with *practical* truth, which is found in the suitability of means to the end that is pursued. Such suitability fluctuates greatly because achieving a precise end depends on many elements, some of which are contingent. Practical truth therefore is never definitively established; it is a matter for the virtue of prudence. On the contrary, *speculative* truth is stable. This does not mean that it is without progress. The relation of correspondence between the thing and the intellect can and must always progress. The intellect comes closer and closer to the thing; it is always in truth, but ever more deeply. This is how dogma progresses, without contradiction, but in continuity; it is *the same relation* that intensifies and is enriched.

The first and decisive effort of speculative theology in ecclesiology is this: to provide a concept of the Church. All of ecclesiological research aims to answer the question, "What is the Church?" Theologians therefore seek a *definition* of it. For that it is fitting to proceed in two stages.

- The two stages in defining the Church

When a child has reached the age of asking "why?" and "what is that?" he spontaneously shows us the two stages of speculative research. The child sees a pen and asks, "What is that?" We answer, "It is a pen." And the child continues. "What is a pen?" We have two sorts of definition: the *nominal* definition by which we attribute a conventional *name* to something, and the *real* or *conceptual* definition by which we designate the *essence* of that reality.

- The *nominal* definition

The nominal definition is—roughly speaking—what everyone understands, more or less confusedly, to be the meaning of the word being used: the French word *stylo* comes from *stylographe* and designates a writing implement. Since words are not natural signs, but rather conventional signs (otherwise there would not be several languages), their meaning is made more precise by etymology. This is an indication of their real signification. The name can be more than an indication; its etymology can indicate the overall genus in which the designated reality is classified. As we will see, this is precisely the case with the word *Ekklēsia*, which is the nominal definition of the reality that we are studying.

- The real definition

This definition aims at expressing the essence signified by the name. It is found at the conclusion of the speculative effort, and it depends entirely on the demonstration of the unity of the being that one intends to define. This definition is not contained in a descriptive phrase, but rather in a concept, or else in two interrelated concepts, one expressing the genus and the other the specific difference (for example, man: rational animal). This definition, unlike the preceding sort that is given at first by Scripture, is obtained by the inductive method that, starting with the data from the sources, brings to light the concept or concepts that express abstractly the positive data that have been acquired. Here we have the subject of Section I: The definition of the Church.

Having made this effort, we will have to pose the question: what is the degree of perfection of this ecclesial being? In other words, we will have to determine whether it possesses the highest quality, which is being a *person*. This will be the subject of Section II: The question of the personality of the Church.

Finally, once the ecclesial being has been identified in this way, we will have to take into consideration its *essential properties*—in other words, the differentia that necessarily follow from its essence. In fact we have already mentioned them, but we will take them up again for their own sake so as to consider several specific problems. This will be the subject of Section III: The properties of the Church.

SECTION I
The Definition of the Church

SUBSECTION 1
The Nominal Definition

Out of a multitude of names used to designate the kingdom inaugurated on earth "*in mysterio*," the Christian community reserved the name *Church*. The study of the meaning of this word and of its use in Scripture already teaches an important lesson.

6

Ekklēsia in Scripture

I. The meaning of the word *Ekklēsia*

a. The secular meaning

In the Romance languages, the word for "church"—*chiesa, église, iglesia*—comes from the Latin *ecclesia*, which is the transliteration of the Greek *ekklēsia*. The Latin term does not translate the Greek, because the authors of the *Vetus latina*, as well as St. Jerome (*Vulgate*) and all the writers of the Western Tradition, were conscious of a particular meaning of the term that a translation would have impoverished or distorted.[1] *Ekklēsia* comes from the verb *ek kaleō:* to call to convoke. The *ekklēsia* is an assembly, but not just any gathering: it results from a call, a convocation; it is not a spontaneous phenomenon like a crowd. In Greece, the *ekklēsia* is the assembly of citizens convoked by the public herald. It is the *Agora*, which functioned in different ways in Sparta and in Athens. But it is still the plenary assembly of the *dēmos* officially gathered by the magistrates to deliberate on the most important business of civil society. The conditions for participating in it were strict: only those who had the status of citizen (men only, no slaves or foreigners) and who had not been convicted of a crime or misdemeanor were allowed and obliged to respond to the convocation. In its internal functioning, the assembly observed an order among the citizens, be-

---

1. Note incidentally that the names "church" and *"Kirche"* come from the adjective *kyriakon*, derived from the Greek noun *Kyrios* (Lord), meaning "which belongs to the Lord."

cause there were various ranks and particular offices to ensure that it ran properly. Here we find the fundamental distinction between the *laïkoi* (from *laos*, the people, from which we get "laity") and the *archontes* (those who governed).

In [ancient] Greek the word *ekklēsia* therefore had no religious meaning at all; it did not even allow for one, as the word *mystērion* did. It was a term from political vocabulary. We have a clear use of it in Acts 19:32, where it designates the assembly of the citizens of Ephesus.

b. The religious meaning

The LXX [Septuagint] uses the word *ekklēsia* ninety-six times to translate the Hebrew *qāhāl* or its derivatives. *Qāhāl* belongs to the vocabulary of the Deuteronomic school; one of the major emphases thereof is the call to the fidelity owed to God. In 2 Kings 22 and 23 we find the account of the discovery of the book of the Law (or of the covenant) by the High Priest, a discovery that would be the start of the abortive reform of Josiah in 622 B.C. Among the major themes of the Deuteronomic preaching we have the key ideas of any religious reform: The Lord is the One God; he has chosen for himself a People (election) that must love him and bear witness to him (vocation); he has bound himself to that people (covenant). This fidelity to God is expressed first in the liturgy in which the People, an assembly convoked (*Qāhāl*) by God, remembers (memory) and hears the Word of God that is ever-present (memorial) in the solemn reading of the Law.

The term *Qāhāl* is above all liturgical. It designates the Chosen People when it is assembled to worship God. Originally the *Qāhāl* is seen during the march toward the promised land; this is the Horeb-type *Qāhāl* in Deut 4:10; 4:23; and 31:30. We find the word again used for the assemblies that were held once they had arrived at their destination, particularly during the dedication of the Temple by Solomon (1 Kgs 8) and at the time of the restoration of the Temple after the exile (Neh 8; Ezr 3).

The *Qāhāl* has four fundamental components:

- The convocation *by God* and the actual gathering of the People who have been convoked.

- The presence of God among his People.
- The announcement or proclamation of the Word of God to the People.
- The sacrifice, during which the covenant is concluded or renewed.²

For the sake of completeness it must be noted that the LXX has another term alongside *ekklēsia*, which is *synagōgē* (etymology: *syn*, together—and *agōgē*, action of leading, bringing). The synagogue is a place where certain business matters are conducted together, where certain actions are performed together. The meaning is first of all material, and the word could be translated "meeting place." A related word is *synaxe* (*synaxis*), the gathering, and by extension the assembly that has gathered.³

The New Testament uses the word *Ekklēsia* 114 times, especially in the writings of St. Paul. This is the term that caught on. Why? One can argue that the term is broader than *synagogue*, which has a more directly material connotation. Two historical reasons can be added. The first was the very real concern of the first Christians to distinguish themselves as much as possible from the Jews after the break with the Temple. The second is recorded for us by St. Epiphanius:[4] it is no longer about the Jews, but about Christians setting themselves apart from heretics. The Ebionites, true sectarians, had their own places of worship that they called *synagogue*, and they categorically refused to use the word *ekklēsia*. Here the word "choice" revealed a doctrinal choice.

Ultimately the adoption of the word *ekklēsia* was the result of a profound doctrinal step. *Ekklēsia* is the term that adopted the entire sense of *Qāhāl*, and the *Qāhāl* of Israel is an exact prefiguration [French: *annonce*] of the sacred assembly of the New Testament. The new People that Christ brought into existence, starting from the old one, becomes the true Israel assembled by the divine initiative. *Ekklēsia* designates this continuity in novelty.

2. Note parenthetically, since the subject would be discussed during the course on the Eucharist, that these characteristic elements are found again to a unique degree in the Christian Eucharistic celebration. This is why the Eucharistic assembly is the Christian *Qāhāl* par excellence, the principal manifestation of the Church (see *SC* n. 41).

3. This term will acquire a Christian meaning that is still used in the Eastern Churches to designate liturgical actions, particularly the chief one that is the Eucharist.

4. St. Epiphanius of Salamis, *Panarion* XX, Discourse against the Ebionistes (PG 41.435a).

The word *Ekklēsia*, however, was not automatically extended to all Christians. Originally the Christians of Jerusalem saw in the expression *Ekklēsia tou Theou* a title that ought to be their monopoly. They rejected the use of it for the pagan-Christians (baptized Gentiles). But very soon the Christian assembly in Antioch called itself *an Ekklēsia;* that meant that there were several *Ekklēsiai*. It seems that the attitude of Antioch was not a deeply theological choice at first. Secular Greek usage was enough to justify the use of the term for the Christian assembly. Indeed, although *ekklēsia* still designated the political assembly of Athens, abroad, in the sphere of influence of Greek culture, this word was used to designate local political assemblies and sometimes even domestic groups.

II. The theological development of the Pauline *corpus*

a. The data in the letters

St. Paul clearly claims the word *ekklēsia* for the Gentile Christian assemblies. In his letters we encounter two sorts of usage. In the salutations that begin several letters (1 and 2 Thes in particular), the word *ekklēsia* directly designates the local assembly. But in the course of the letters St. Paul shows that, given the multiplicity of particular communities, he knows that he is confronted with one *Ekklēsia* that is the community formed by all baptized persons, wherever they may be: the *Ekklēsia tou Theou*. This is especially clear in the captivity epistles: there is one calling and therefore one *Ekklēsia* (e.g., Col 1:18, 1:24; Eph 1:22; 3:10, 3:21; 5:23, 5:32). Here it is a question of accentuating the unity of all Christians in Christ. Christ destroyed the law that separated the two peoples (the *laos* from the *ethnē*); he united the things of heaven with those of earth, and the Gentiles are *fellow citizens* (a strong expression that should be correlated with *ekklēsia-agora*), as we read in Eph 2:19 and 3:6. This *Ekklēsia* is at the same time the heavenly Jerusalem, the Bride of Christ who is his Body, the edifice of God built on the apostles of his Son.

The Pauline data therefore includes two very clear uses of the word *ekklēsia:* one that designates the local community of the baptized, and another that designates the universal community of Christ's disciples. This gives rise to an important question: which is the primary sense?

b. The primary sense of *Ekklēsia*

The question was posed in the twentieth century: what is the decisive sense of the word *ekklēsia*? Three main theses confronted each other.[5]

Pierre Batiffol thinks that, starting from the secular Greek usage, the word *ekklēsia* then came to designate first the various local communities and then, finally, the universal Church. In this account there was first an "empirical" meaning and then a theological meaning. Adolf von Harnack, a Protestant and an historian of dogma, taking a stance against nineteenth-century liberal Protestantism, which maintained that the universal Church was born in the second and third centuries out of a progressive federation of local churches, tried to show that in the New Testament the word *ekklēsia* always has the sense of universal Church, the mysterious Church that God is building in heaven. According to him the notion of local church comes later: what comes first is the heavenly Church. He adds (and this is a typically Protestant view) that this heavenly Church is partially, defectively incarnated here below in the local communities. Finally, Karl Ludwig Schmidt, author of the article "*Ekklēsia*" in Kittel's lexicon, the *Theological Dictionary of the New Testament*, remarks that the meaning of *Ekklēsia* is not secular, but biblical: *Ekklēsia tou Theou*. This is the equivalent of "People of God." Hence when St. Paul says, "the Church of God which is at Corinth" (1 Cor 1:2), he is not speaking about the local community in Corinth as such, but about the assembly of God that is the one Church present in every place where God assembles his People.

We think that the solution to this interesting debate in biblical theology has been proposed by Lucien Cerfaux. This author proposes that three stages should be distinguished in the semantic development of the term *ekklēsia* in the New Testament:

- The point of departure: Together with Harnack and Schmidt, one must recognize that the first thing was the notion and the expression *Ekklēsia tou Theou*. The first community of Jerusalem is conscious of being the "remnant," the People of the last days, the true Israel of God. It takes from the Hebrew Bible and the LXX the terms *qāhāl* and *ekklēsia* and applies them to itself. This is attest-

---

5. The documents of the debate, with bibliographical references, are listed at the end of the chapter.

ed in St. Paul's writings. The name *Ekklēsia tou Theou* belonged first and exclusively to the Jerusalem community (Gal 1:13); this is "the Church of God" that St. Paul began by persecuting (Acts 8:1, 8:3).
- Second stage: Christianity spreads beyond the Jewish world. Starting first in Antioch, which is a mixed community (Jews and Greeks, cf. Acts 11:20–21), it then takes root in communities entirely made up of former pagans. We observe here a break in the semantic unity. The term *ekklēsia* did not immediately extend to the whole community. The Christians of Jerusalem first believed that they were privileged, being descendants of Abraham: the biblical sense of *Ecclesia*. Under Greek influence, the community of Antioch designated itself as an *Ecclesia* (Acts 11:26), in the everyday sense of a local assembly. But St. Paul adopts this nomenclature and gives it a religious sense. In this period, therefore, Christians had the word in the singular, which designated the local assembly, and the word in the plural, which designated the whole set of local assemblies.
- The conclusion of the development: The word *ekklēsia* returns to the singular and designates the whole People of God. St. Paul, who founded multiple Christian communities, knew very well that in each one of the he was confronting the one *Ekklēsia tou Theou*. The Church is therefore realized in each of the Churches through one convocation that gathers one assembly. This final stage can be observed in the captivity epistles.

This data leads us to pose the speculative question concerning the distinction and the relations between the universal Church and the particular churches.

III. THE MAJOR TEACHINGS ABOUT THE NAME *EKKLĒSIA*

a. Local assemblies and universal assembly

The speculative question just mentioned, which will be reserved for our discussions on the catholicity of the Church, is formulated by the findings of biblical theology: there is a relation, in the mystery of the Church as this mystery makes its pilgrimage here below, between the group of

Christians who form one community and the multiplicity of local communities in which Christians are distributed. This relation is not simply quantitative, the relation of a whole made up of parts, but more profoundly qualitative. In a certain way the whole ecclesial mystery is present in the local community, but from another perspective, the local community is in a relation of strict dependency on the universal community, which precedes it somehow.

b. The Church and her communal nature

The name *ekklēsia* signifies initially "community"—that is, in the most common connotation, "set of individuals who make up a unity." This reminds us in the first place that salvation is of a communal nature. We meet again here a finding that was brought to light by the People of God theme, which we called "the social structure of salvation." This leads us therefore to two questions. The first, of a moral nature, is the question as to the relation between the individual and the community. These two aspects go together. Absolutizing either of the two—absolute primacy of the individual (individualism) or absolute primacy of the community (totalitarianism)—leads to complete ruin. This question is connected with the problem of the relation between communal unity and the diversity of the members. The second question, concerning the communal aspect, deals with the permanence of the community. The Church does not die with the deaths of the individuals who make up the Church. Unceasingly there are new members within her. The permanence of this ecclesial community poses the question as to her identity: does she remain herself through the succession of generations? This is the question about the indefectibility of the Church. These questions will be addressed later on, after we have proposed a speculative definition of the Church.

Bibliography

The nominal definition of *Ekklēsia*

Biblical studies

The preliminary data are supplied by dictionaries and encyclopedias; see in particular *Catholicisme*, vol. III, article "Église," cols. 1408–1409; *Dictionnaire de Spiritualité*, vol. IV (Paris: 1960), cols. 370–83 (the most complete discussion).

The debate over universal Church vs. local church

Is the primary meaning of the word *ekklēsia* in the NT the local church or the universal Church? The main contributions to the debate are:

Batiffol, Pierre. *L'Église naissante et le catholicisme*. Paris: 1909, 88ff. English edition: *Primitive Catholicism*. New York: Longmans, Green, 1911, 138ff. The author maintains that the name church came from secular Greek usage and initially designated the local church then, ultimately, the universal Church. The same thesis is found in H. Leclercq's article "Église," in *Dictionnaire d'archéologie chrétienne*, vol. IV (1921), cols. 2200ff.

Braun, F.-M. *Aspects nouveaux du problème de l'Église*. Fribourg: 1942, 32ff. Good summary of the question to date.

Cerfaux, Lucien. *La théologie de l'Église suivant S. Paul*. US 54. 2nd ed. Paris: 1965 (particularly chap. V, "Les Églises"). This thesis seems to us to be the most probable one.

Schmidt, Karl Ludwig. Article "*Ekklēsia*" in the *Theological Dictionary of the New Testament* ("Kittel"), 3:501–536 (see the general bibliography). The author remarks that the meaning of *ekklēsia* has a biblical origin (the LXX translation of *Qāhāl*)—hence the connotation of universal Church is the first meaning. The same thesis is found in A. Fridrichsen, "Église et sacrement dans le N.T.," *Rev. Hist. Phil. Rel.* 17 (1937): 345.

von Harnack, A. See the references mentioned in Schmidt. At a time when liberal Protestantism maintained that the unified Church as seen in the second and third centuries was the result of the combination of autonomous communities that were governed by laymen, Harnack was the first to show his coreligionists that the word *ekklēsia* in the New Testament always has the sense of *universal* Church, the Church that God is building in heaven. The notion of local church would therefore come later.

The Fathers of the Church

Bardy, Gustave. *La Théologie de l'Église*. US 13–14 (see the references in the general bibliography at the end of the volume). States the essential points in the patristic understanding.

Journet, Charles. *L'Église du Verbe incarné*. 2:50–52.

By way of example, the reader may consult Cyril of Jerusalem, *Pre-baptismal Catechesis on the Symbol of Faith*, no. 18, 23–25 (PG 33.1043–47).

Overall presentations

Hamer, Jérôme. *The Church Is a Communion*. New York: Sheed and Ward, 1964, 35–67.

Pagé, Jean-Guy. *Qui est l'Église?* Vol. I, "Le mystère et le sacrement du salut." Montreal: 1982, 136–48. Good summary of the biblical and patristic data; includes a helpful bibliography.

SUBSECTION 2

The Real Definition of the Church

The search for a real or conceptual definition of the Church has its point of departure in the immediate data provided by the nominal definition: the Church is a community. In order to advance in our understanding of this particular community, we must try to bring to light the various elements that contribute to the unity, both of the members who make up the community and of the community itself that is thus constituted. Source theology enabled us to list a certain number of important elements pertaining to this subject. We consider decisive the requirement for the unity of all the elements that contribute to the formation of this particular subject that we call "Church." Briefly, we can say along with *Lumen gentium* 8, §1 that the means of salvation aspect and the reality of salvation aspect "are not to be thought of as two realities [but] form one complex reality." Although distinctions among the various aspects are legitimate and necessary so as not to confuse everything, they nevertheless must not become separations that would break the unity of the subject and consequently the subject itself.

The question of the constitutive unity of the ecclesial mystery, understood in this way, is one of the greatest challenges in contemporary ecclesiology. This question, which arose in the sixteenth century during the Reformation crisis, has still not found a theological answer sufficiently clear and solid to be adopted by the Magisterium. Although we hold by faith that the various aspects of the mystery of the Church constitute a unity, we have not yet arrived at a theologically satisfactory explanation of this unity. In other words, we are still at the stage of research, and the following discussions are non-binding.

We plan to proceed in four chapters: the first is a *status quaestionis* that investigates the research that has gone before and accompanying magisterial documents; the second will give a general critique of this data; the third will explain the important points of a philosophical nature that are preliminary to the theological work; and the fourth will propose our definition.

7

History of the Question

The question concerning the definition of the Church was formulated during the early sixteenth-century crisis with the Reformation. Of course, it had been latent in the preceding century, but it did not crystallize until the polemic between the Catholics and the Protestants. The Reformed Christians owed their major insights to Luther and Calvin.

I. The terms of the debate

a. The statements of the Reformers

Because of his presuppositions pertaining to the doctrine of justification and its consequences for his understanding of the mediating humanity of Christ, Martin Luther opted very early for a "split" view of reality:

[Two realities are meant by the word "Church."] The first, which is natural, basic, essential, and true, we shall call "spiritual, internal Christendom." The second, which is man-made and external, we shall call "physical, external Christendom." Not that we want to separate them from each other; rather it is just as if I were talking about a man and called him "spiritual" according to his soul, and "physical" according to his body, or as the Apostle is accustomed to speak of an "internal" and "external" man [Rom. 7:22–23]. So, too, the Christian assembly is a community united in one faith according to the soul, although, according to the body, it cannot be assembled in one place.... But those who are in the second [external] community without faith and outside the first [internal] community are dead before God.[1]

1. Martin Luther, "On the Papacy" (1520), in *Luther's Works*, ed. Jaroslav Pelikan, 39:70.

Within Lutheranism there are many discussions over whether Luther thought of the Church as made up of two separate communities or as a complex community.[2] Without attempting to enter into this discussion, it seems undeniable that, in Luther's writings, belonging to the "internal community" can be separated from belonging to the "external community." Note also the terminology: the binomial spiritual-internal (invisible) and the binomial physical-external (visible).

Calvin's writings contain the more precise terminology of "visible" and "invisible":

> I have observed that the Scriptures speak of the Church in two ways. Sometimes when they speak of the Church they mean the Church as it really is before God [the community of those who are in the state of grace].... Often, too, by the name of Church is designated the whole body of mankind scattered throughout the world, who profess to worship one God and Christ.... In this Church there is a very large mixture of hypocrites....
>
> Hence, as it is necessary to believe the invisible Church, which is manifest to the eye of God only, so we are also enjoined to regard this (visible) Church which is so called with reference to man, and to cultivate its communion.[3]

Essentially this position is the same as Luther's. Calvin verbally maintains that there is a unity between the invisible Church and the visible Church, but in fact one is obliged to consider these two communities as separable, since within the visible Church the good coexist with the wicked. In the writings of Luther and Calvin, apart from their respective originality, there are significant points of convergence due to a common orientation:

1. The question "What is the Church?" originates in the question as to the members of the Church: who belongs to it? Are sinners included? The Reformers absolutely refuse saving membership in the Church for sinners: only the just really belong to the community of salvation.

2. The terminology is quite fixed: the contrasting terms "visible-external Church" and "invisible-internal Church" are born.

3. The relation between the visible Church and the invisible Church

---

2. See H. Strohl, *La Pensée de la Réforme*, 178; A. Birmelé, "Église," in *Encyclopédie du Protestantisme*, 488.

3. John Calvin, *The Institutes of the Christian Religion*, book four, chap. 1, 7, trans. Henry Beveridge (Grand Rapids, Mich.: Christian Classics Ethereal Library, 2002), 628.

is the great ecclesiological question. Some texts tend to imply a strict duality, while others tend toward a stronger connection that nevertheless remains extrinsic: The visible Church is a purely human reality; the invisible Church is a reality of "pure" grace.

b. The response of Catholic theology

We have no direct magisterial response to the statements of the Reformers. The Council of Trent did not address the ecclesiological question explicitly, but many of its statements (intrinsic justification, the sacraments as containing grace, sinners are members of the Church) have obvious ecclesiological implications. The Catholic response to the ecclesiological question of the Reformers came from the theologians. Among them we can distinguish three major categories:

- The controversialists (St. Francis de Sales and Bossuet).
- The Scholastics who attempt to include in the synthesis of St. Thomas (commentaries on the *Summa theologiae*) a unified presentation of ecclesiology, often starting from the treatise on faith.
- The authors of manuals, the famous treatises *De Ecclesia*, starting in the nineteenth century, which are mainly designed for the formation of the clergy.

We should note the particular place of St. Robert Bellarmine in this major current. His chief ecclesiological contribution is part of his controversial work, but his influence goes far beyond that genre because his major insight was repeated by all theologians until the twentieth century.[4] That is why we must present this writer separately and first.

1. The contribution of St. Robert Bellarmine[5]

The point is to respond to the Reformation theologians with regard to the question of membership in the Church, as we have seen. St. Robert begins with the nominal definition of the Church: *Ecclesia id est coetus fidelium* [The Church is the assembly of the faithful] (chap. I). The

---

4. To be fair to St. Robert Bellarmine, we must explain that he himself did not intend his polemical work to be distributed widely, aware that it was by nature limited. Posterity unfortunately did not realize that.

5. *De controversiis*, chaps. I and II, Naples ed., vol. 2, 73–74.

Church is therefore a community of human beings. But which ones? In order to establish the real definition, it will therefore be necessary to specify which human beings we are talking about. The question of defining the Church is therefore the question of belonging to the Church (chap. II).

In order to formulate a response, St. Robert proceeds in two phases. In the first place he proposes a purely external definition of the Church:

> To our way of thinking, the Church is only one, not two, and this one true Church is the community of men gathered by their profession of the same Christian faith, and their communion in the same sacraments, under the government of legitimate pastors, especially of the one Vicar of Christ on earth, the Roman pontiff. By this definition it is easy to tell which men belong to the Church and which ones do not belong to her. For there are three parts to this definition: the profession of the true faith, the communion of the sacraments, and subjection to the legitimate pastor, the Roman pontiff. The first part excludes all infidels ..., heretics, and apostates. The second element excludes the catechumens and the excommunicated.... The third excludes the schismatics.... All the other persons are included, even if they are reprobates, wicked, and impious.
>
> The difference between our definition and all the others is that all the other definitions require internal virtues in order to determine that someone is in the Church, and they thereby make the true Church invisible; we, on the other hand, also believe that all the virtues are found in the Church (faith, hope, charity, and the rest), nevertheless, in order that someone may be said, in a certain way, to be a member of the true Church about which the Scriptures speak, we do not think that any interior virtue is required, but only the external profession of faith and the communion of the sacraments—things that the senses can perceive. The Church is, indeed, a group of men as visible and palpable as is the group of the Roman people, or the Kingdom of France, or of the Republic of Venice.

As the last sentence indicates, this first definition is of a purely sociological nature. It is manifestly inadequate, and that is why St. Robert continues with a second, more theological definition:

> It should be noted, based on what Augustine says in the *Breviculus collationis*, chap. 3, that the Church is a living body in which there is a soul and a body. The internal gifts of the Holy Spirit (faith, hope, charity, etc.) are the soul. The external profession of faith and participation in the sacraments are the body. Hence we see that some men belong to the soul and the body of

the Church and accordingly are united internally and externally to Christ the Head. They are perfectly and completely in the Church; for they are like living members in the body, although among them there are some who share more or less in this life, and some who have only the beginning of this life—the faculties of sense but not of motion, so to speak—such as those who have faith alone without charity. Still others are part of the soul and not of the body, such as catechumens and the excommunicated, if they have faith and charity, which can happen. Finally others are part of the body and not of the soul, like those who have no interior virtue and nevertheless, through some worldly hope or fear, profess the faith and receive the sacraments under the government of the pastors; they are like the hairs, the nails or the bad humors in the human body.

The comparison with the soul and the body provides a basis that is interesting in itself, but St. Robert jeopardizes it by depriving it of its main feature—namely, the inseparability of soul and body that makes a substantially unified subject. It must be realized that St. Robert first presents the three external elements that the senses can perceive (profession of faith, participation in the sacraments, obedience to the pastors); then he adds the three internal elements, which are faith, hope, and charity.[6] But it is clear that the external elements can exist independently without the internal elements, and vice versa. There is indeed a duality.

2. Comparison with Reformation theology

For the Reformers as for St. Robert, the question "*Quid sit Ecclesia?*" relates to the members of the Church: The Church is what it is depending on what one learns about those who make up that society. But whereas the Reformers consider the conditions for full ecclesial membership—the just are the only true members of the Church—St. Robert declares himself content with the minimum required. This option is diametrically opposed, but still within the same conceptual framework:

Our definition therefore includes only this last way of being in the Church, [in other words, those who are only part of the body,] because only the minimum is required in order for someone to be included in the visible Church.[7]

---

6. Note that the Holy Spirit is absent, whereas he, in Person, is the one called "soul of the Church" in Tradition.

7. *De controversiis*, chap. II, Naples edition, 75.

In other words, sinners are still truly members of the Church.[8] It is appropriate therefore to include them in her essential unity. Hence Bellarmine looks for the elements that are found in sinners so as to justify their membership. To enumerate them, consequently, will be to define what is essential to the Church because it is common to all her members, both the just and the sinners. These elements come down to external social behavior.

The expression "visible Church" is understood by the Reformers as well as by Bellarmine to mean men whose external behavior is in conformity with the established discipline. The community thus formed is a reality visible to the eye, of a natural order, that the senses perceive. The two sides seem to agree in considering the "invisible Church" as a purely spiritual and supernatural reality. This agreement is based on a concept of "internal virtues" (e.g., faith, hope, charity, gifts of the Holy Spirit) as purely and simply spiritual, immaterial and hence invisible. Thus the internal act is disconnected from the external act of the virtues, and the two no longer form a whole.

The relation between "visible Church" and "invisible Church" involves the same characteristic on both sides of the polemic: they are separable and have different natures. The visible-sensible is of the natural order, and the invisible-internal is supernatural. What is visible is connected to what is sensible and only to that. In other words, the spiritual-supernatural *is not visible*. This contradicts all Catholic theology of grace, which maintains that grace [once granted] inheres in nature so as to heal and elevate it. To put it another way, the unity of nature and grace is at stake here, and the idea that they are separable is connected in fact with the concept of extrinsic justification so dear to the Reformers. Bellarmine subscribes to the Catholic affirmation of the unity of the interior and the exterior, but his treatment does not make this evident; quite the contrary.

c. The patristic and Thomistic antecedents

The question of membership in the Church, which is the point of departure for the ecclesiological question that we are studying, was posed

---

8. This is what the Council of Trent teaches (session VI, chap. XIII) and what Bellarmine intends to uphold vis-à-vis the Protestants.

in a very different way in the history preceding the Reformation. We should note first that when St. Thomas Aquinas asks the question about the members of the Church (*ST* III, q. 8, art. 5), he does not try, as Luther or Calvin do, to determine who is *effectively* a member, but rather who is *capable* of being a member of the Church; and to answer that question, St. Thomas develops an analogous concept that distinguishes between potential members and "members in act" according to various degrees. This is a whole different perspective.

But in an even more decisive way we see clearly in the writings of St. Augustine, as in St. Thomas, that the conditions for ecclesial membership are situated *within* persons. In St. Augustine we find the passage:

> I do not hesitate for a moment to place the Catholic catechumen, who is burning with love for God, before the baptized heretic; ... [and] we acknowledge that some catechumens are better and more faithful than some baptized persons. For the centurion Cornelius, before baptism, was better than Simon [the magician], who had been baptized. For Cornelius, even before his baptism, was filled with the Holy Spirit; Simon, even after baptism, was puffed up with an unclean spirit. Cornelius, however, would have been convicted of contempt for so holy a sacrament, if, even after he had received the Holy Ghost, he had refused to be baptized.[9]

This passage nicely shows that the principle of ecclesiality is *within* persons. Consequently we will distinguish very clearly between the two expressions: being in the Church *in a bodily way* and being *in the Body of the Church*. The Augustinian perspective talks about the body of the person and not about the Body of the Church. This is all the more remarkable, since St. Augustine, if he had wanted, could very well have spoken about the Body of the Church, given that he speaks in many other passages about the soul of the Church.[10] There are, we believe, precise reasons for this, which we will spell out later on. The same goes for St. Thomas Aquinas:

> *ST* II-II, q. 1, art. 9, obj. 3: The confession of faith, which is contained in the symbol [i.e., creed], concerns all the faithful. Now the faithful are not all competent to believe in God, but only those who have living faith. Therefore it is unfitting for the symbol of faith to be expressed in the words: "I believe in one God."

---

9. *De baptismo contra donatistas* IV.xxi.28.
10. See our remarks on the Church as Temple of the Spirit.

The response is:

ST II-II, q. 1, art. 9, ad 3: The confession of faith is drawn up in a symbol in the person, as it were, of the whole Church, which is united together by faith. Now the faith of the Church is living faith; since such is the faith to be found in all those who are of the Church not only outwardly but also by merit (*numero et merito de Ecclesia*). Hence the confession of faith is expressed in a symbol, in a manner that is in keeping with living faith, so that even if some of the faithful lack living faith, they should endeavor to acquire it.

It is easy to see that St. Thomas aligns himself with the Augustinian tradition that locates *in persons* the criteria for church membership. We can give a second example of this:

ST III, q. 69, art. 5, obj. 1: It seems that certain acts of the virtues are unfittingly set down as effects of Baptism, to wit: "incorporation in Christ, enlightenment, and fruitfulness." For Baptism is not given to an adult, except he believe; according to Mark 16:16: "He that believeth and is baptized, shall be saved." But it is by faith that man is incorporated in Christ, according to Ephesians 3:17.... Therefore no one is baptized except he be already incorporated in Christ. Therefore incorporation with Christ is not the effect of Baptism.

The response is:

ST III, q. 69, art. 5, ad 1: Adults who already believe in Christ are incorporated in Him mentally [or interiorly, *mentaliter*]. But afterward, when they are baptized, they are incorporated in Him, corporally (*corporaliter*), as it were, i.e. by the visible sacrament; without the desire of which they could not have been incorporated in Him even mentally.

Here too incorporation into the Church must be evaluated *in persons*, and one apprehends the Church in herself by proceeding from the individual members to the community that they form.

What we have just seen of the Protestant position and of the response by St. Robert Bellarmine can be described as the framework of the modern ecclesiological question that will shape theology until the twentieth century. We should make two general observations about this subject:

First observation: a community subsists in its members.

A community is a whole made up of parts that are its members. The community "in itself" does not exist; its members are the things that exist. We must recall here several major elements of social metaphysics. A human community is a social whole made up of *persons*—in other words, a group of beings subsisting on their own who are not "depersonalized" by the fact that they live together. The social whole does not subsist by itself, but in its members. Take away the parts and the whole disappears. To put it another way, the parts as parts—in other words, in their mutual relations—are what make up the whole. The holistic principle is the same one that governs the relations of the parts among themselves. In order to grasp this principle, one must start from *the persons themselves,* since they are the subjects of these relations. Furthermore, we must consider simultaneously from this perspective the relations that *engender* the whole—that is, the community—and the relations that *express* the life of the communitarian whole that is thus constituted. For the specific community that is the Church, it is a matter of taking into account the different ways in which the members *receive grace* and the various ways in which they *manifest the fruitfulness of that grace in them.* The life of the ecclesial community does not exist "in itself"; it is rather the life of each member—beginning with Christ—and of all the members in their mutual relations.

This fact explains why the question *"De Ecclesia"* necessarily includes a question *"De membris."* In this the ecclesiological basis of St. Robert Bellarmine is reliable. But he makes inept use of it. Like the Reformers whom he opposes, he considers only the relations among the members that engender the community (justification by faith alone on the one hand, mediations on the other), but not the relations that manifest the life of that community (the "works"). St. Robert Bellarmine did not go beyond this framework, and that is why his definition is based only on the profession of faith, participation in the sacraments, and obedience to the pastors, inasmuch as these acts engender the community and express the necessary mediations. He added no considerations relative to the active charity that expresses the life that is received through the mediations. That is a serious limitation.

Second observation: the notion of ecclesial visibility.

For St. Robert Bellarmine, the Church is visible to the *eye*—in other words, in her physical qualities and not as a mystery.[11] This visibility

---

11. The clearest critique, to our knowledge, was made by Charles Journet, *L'Église du Verbe incarné,* 2:1181ff.

is focused, so to speak, on the means of grace considered in their purely external aspect. For example, it is a question of the *profession* of faith (external act) and not about the *confession* of faith (an act that is both internal and external).

It is necessary to distinguish between material visibility and formal visibility. The visibility to the eye of physical qualities (in the case of the Church: the sociological qualities)[12] has no direct relation with the soul: a reality with a beautiful external (physical) appearance may very well be a ruin internally (morally). And so ecclesial visibility is addressed not so much to the eye as to faith. The various ecclesial acts, in other words, the various relations among the members—whether these relations cause grace or are the effect of graces received—are indeed manifestations visible to the eye (*material* visibility), but they refer to their invisible principle as *signs* of the latter: this is their *formal* visibility. One must say, therefore, to adopt the terminology of St. Robert Bellarmine, that the body of the Church allows the eye to see the manifestations of her soul, which faith alone can recognize. The thing that one sees is one thing, and the thing that one believes is another.[13] This is the *epiphanic* status of visible Christian reality: just as Christ's humanity by its actions manifests to faith the divinity that dwells within it, so too the community of human beings manifests to faith by its actions the community of grace that it is.

This relation of signification can be called a relation of *real* signification in the sense that the Church-body signifies not another reality, but what she is in her inmost being, her soul. When we talk about the communitarian relations by which grace is transmitted or in which grace acts, we must say that the ecclesial Body "contains" what it signifies, not only so as to live by it, but also so as to give and transmit it, so that through its activity all men may unceasingly flock to it to be

---

12. This is the first glance that we mentioned in discussing the *mystery-truth*.

13. With respect to the apparitions of the risen Christ, St. Ambrose notes: "*Species ... uidetur; uirtus uero narratur; illa oculis, haec mente conprehenditur.*" ["The appearance is seen, but the power is told. The former is grasped by the eyes, the latter by the mind."] *Commentary on the Gospel of St. Luke*, I.25 (SC 45:59–60). What the witness sees with his eyes is not what he believes by his faith, but rather the sign of what he is called to believe. St. Thomas put his hand into the side of Christ the man; he confessed his divinity ("*Tetigit hominem, confessus est Deum*"); St. Augustine, *Commentary on the First Letter of John* I.3 (SC 75:119).

saved. The reduction of ecclesial visibility to a material visibility on the sociological order, however, was inevitable for St. Robert Bellarmine precisely because of his point of departure. St. Robert Bellarmine and his successors in the approach that he started do not present ecclesiology for its own sake, for the purposes of a synthesis, but solely from the perspective of refuting Reformation thought. Now the latter on this subject is based on two main theses: the underestimation or even the denial of the mediations of grace and the rejection of works. In his ecclesiology St. Robert Bellarmine argues only about the first point. The question of ecclesial visibility is focused on the means of grace and works insofar as they are ecclesial are purely and simply omitted. The controversialist cardinal says, as if in passing, the thing that appears to go without saying:

> The difference between our definition and all the others is that all the other definitions require internal virtues in order to determine that someone is in the Church, and *they thereby make the true Church invisible;* we, on the other hand....[14]

In other words, faith, hope, and charity are considered only as entirely internal and spiritual qualifications, and not also and inseparably principles of action, a source of acts that are external as well: works. This aspect of works is so closely connected with the internal aspect that if the works are rejected, the grace dies. This concept of ecclesial visibility reduces it to the means of grace. This leads to considering the Church only under its aspect of mediation of grace to the detriment of the other aspect, which is reality of grace. Although visibility is essential to the Church—which Bellarmine correctly maintains—in his thought it nonetheless affects only one aspect of the mystery, and not both aspects. Because of the context of anti-Protestant polemics this choice was made. It is clear that we are not looking at a comprehensive theology.

Every polemical theology has its limits. The chief limit of Bellarmine was that he let himself be drawn onto his adversaries' terrain and thus incautiously accepted their major premise: the separation within the ecclesial mystery of the means of grace aspect from the reality of grace aspect.

---

14. *De controversiis,* chap. II.

II. The Consequences in Catholic Theology

The insights of St. Robert Bellarmine and particularly his distinction-separation between the soul and the body of the Church, were subsequently repeated widely. We cite here several authors by way of illustration:

Charles-René Billuart (1685–1757):

We can distinguish two parts in the Church. One is internal, which many call the *soul* of the Church; this is the faith by which the members of the Church are united with one another and with their head. The other is external, which is called the *body* of the Church, to wit the external society of those who are one through their public profession of the same faith, and by their communion in the same sacraments and with the same pastors. And although the internal part is invisible per se, the Church is nevertheless said to be visible by reason of its external part: thus man is visible by his exterior, although his soul per se is invisible.[15]

Giovanni Perrone (1794–1876):

(By the name *soul of the Church*) we designate first of all the internal justice or the sanctifying grace by which the just are closely united to God.... Moreover we designate faith, hope, and charity, without which no one would be able to live.... All these gifts, which make up the soul of the Church, come from God and are poured out by Christ, who is the Head, into the Church, which is the body, so as to give her life. Consequently some have given to the soul of the Church the name "divine element" and to the body that it pervades the name "human element."[16]

Jan Vincent de Groot (1859–1929):

The Church consists of an internal part and an external part, which are like her soul and her body. Just as the soul and the body make one being, so too one Militant Church results from the internal part and the external part of the Church. Her *body* is made up of the external profession of the faith, the administration of the sacraments, the visible government, while her *soul* consists of faith, hope, charity, the internal gifts of the Holy Spirit, in short, all supernatural virtue and every grace that enables the Church to have life and to have in that grace the principle of her movement.[17]

---

15. *Summa Sancti Thomae*, Tractatus "De regulis fidei," D. 3, a. 3 [translated from French].
16. *Praelectiones theologicae*, Pars I, "De locis," chap. 2.
17. Tractatus, *De Ecclesia* 64.

The Bellarminian lineage is clearly evident: body and soul of the Church express the exterior and the interior aspects of the mystery. Thus Catholic writers intend to keep the body and the soul properly united. We have a good speculative testimony in the following author:

Louis Billot (1846–1931):

According to the analogy of the human composite, we distinguish in the Church founded by Christ a body and a soul. The *body* is the social organism or aggregate of the members resembling an organic physical body. The *soul* consists in the interior gifts of habitual grace and supernatural life. And just as the body and the soul do not constitute two human beings in the human composite, they do not constitute two Churches here but only one.[18]

The unity of the external and internal aspects is always clearly affirmed. This is the center of the Catholic opposition to the Protestant ecclesiological vision. Nevertheless, the question recurs and takes a surprising turn with regard to the membership of persons in the Church. In response to the question about the Church's members, the same Billot does not hesitate to declare:

The *form* of the body of the Church insofar as she is specifically a social body is one thing, and the *form* insofar as she is living the life of grace is another.[19]

Hence, as a *necessary* consequence, it follows that being incorporated into the body of the Church (visible membership) is not per se incorporation into Christ (invisible membership).[20] Although the two communities, the social body and the life of grace, are "normally" united as a substantial form and an accidental form can be, they can nevertheless be separated in extreme (which is not to say rare) cases: the case of the upright pagan (invisible membership only) or of the baptized person in a state of mortal sin (visible membership only). It must be noted that all this remains within the same limits as St. Robert Bellarmine's.

In the early twentieth century we find in this regard the following summary of a very common teaching shared by most theological schools:

---

18. Tractatus, *De Ecclesia Christi* 1:100.
19. Tractatus, *De Ecclesia Christi* 1:272.
20. Tractatus, *De Ecclesia Christi* 1:320–21.

The body [of the Church] includes the visible element or the visible society to which one belongs by an external profession of the Catholic faith, by participation in the sacraments, and by submission to the legitimate pastors, and the soul includes the invisible element or the invisible society, to which one belongs by the fact that one possesses the interior gifts of grace.[21]

Therefore we have a Church made up of two formally distinct communities, in such a way that a person can be part of one without being a member of the other. The inevitable consequence of this is that *in reality* a distinction is made between two communities whose union "normally" makes up the Church, but that are separable. These two communities can indeed be united, but their unity is not substantial. This is tantamount to saying that this theology does recognize two Churches, the visible Church and the invisible Church. This position, in effect, joins the Protestants in their major ecclesiological premise.

III. The contemporary ecclesiological renewal

This renewal began by criticizing the Bellarminian line of argument. Given the difficulties posed by this mindset, theologians came to propose new ideas.

a. The critique of the Bellarminian tradition

We are talking about the distinction between the body and the soul of the Church as it was made and developed by St. Robert Bellarmine. It should not be confused with other ecclesiological proposals that utilize in an entirely different way a body-soul distinction with reference to the Church.[22]

One of the first things discovered was that Bellarmine's citation of St. Augustine is faulty. Materially, nothing in the *Breviculus* indicates the distinction that St. Robert Bellarmine seems to see in it. Admittedly, the controversialist does not say *"sicut dixit Augustinus"* ["as Augustine said"], but rather *"notandum ex Augustino"* ["it should be noted,

---

21. E. Dublanchy, "Église," in *Dictionnaire de Théologie Catholique*, 4:2154 (essay dated 1911).

22. This is the case particularly with Charles Journet, in his ecclesiological synthesis, *L'Église du Verbe incarné*, vol. 2.

based on Augustine"]; this is therefore a freer use of the Augustinian source, *ad mentem Sancti Augustini* ["to St. Augustine's way of thinking"].

Next the authors note the following points:

Recourse to the Bellarminian distinction was generally abandoned over the course of the 1920s:

The expression itself, "the soul of the Church," after being very popular for a certain time, is generally criticized at the present day.[23]

We observe progressively a reversal of perspectives brought about by the Bellarminian tradition in relation to the Church Fathers and medieval writers:

Theological tradition ..., instead of drawing the distinction in the *actuality* of the Church and dissociating body and soul ..., places it in the *manner of belonging* to that actuality.[24]

Finally, theologians addressed the core of the problem: if the body and the soul are separable, the very basis of the analogy is ruined. Charles Journet is one of the principal authors at this juncture. He recalls that soul and body are coextensive by citing Hugh of St. Victor, for example:

In body is one spirit [= soul]. Nothing dead in the body, nothing alive outside the body.[25]

Journet develops three consequences of this substantial unity of body and soul for ecclesiology:[26]

- Where the soul of the Church is, her body is there, and vice versa: where the body of the Church is, her soul is there. This recalls St. Irenaeus: "Where the Spirit is, there is the Church."
- Where the soul is perfect, the body is fully manifested, and where the soul is imperfect, the body is imperfectly manifested. This

---

23. H. de Lubac, *Catholicism: Christ and the Common Destiny of Man*, 235n50.
24. Yves Congar, *Divided Christendom*, 225 and n2.
25. Hugh of St. Victor, *De sacramentis christianae fidei* II.2, chap. 1 (PL 176.415–16); *On the Sacraments of the Christian faith*, trans. Roy J. Deferrari (Cambridge, Mass.: The Medieval Academy of America, 1951), 254.
26. Charles Journet, *L'Église du Verbe incarné*, 2:281–82; see also Yves Congar, *Divided Christendom*, 80–82 and 225ff.

must be understood first of all at the communal level. At the individual level this means that the one charity is shared in differently by the members of one and the same community, and those in whom charity is most perfect will best manifest the visible aspect of the Church by their works (this is the example of the saints). From this we must conclude that the more spiritual the Church is, the more visible she is, just as in the comparison with the living thing, the more life-giving the soul is, the healthier the body.
- Where something of the soul of the Church appears, something of her body necessarily appears, since the latter is the sign and instrument of the soul.

In other words, the Church is inseparably visible and invisible, bodily and spiritual. She gathers in her bosom some who are just and others who are sinners, each one being to a varying degree members both of her body and of her soul. The sheer hypocrite does not belong to the body of the Church—*contra* Bellarmine—but to her corpse, if one may say so. The just "outside" manifest somehow their incorporation, if only by their upright lives and their tendency toward full integration [in the Church].

The main advantage of this critique is that it absolutely rules out the concept of the Church composed of *two* communities, one being the means of salvation (the body) and the other the reality of salvation (the soul), which of course are "normally" connected, but in fact are separable, each having its own principle of being and of unity.

It must be admitted that the critique of the Bellarminian line of argument is incontestable. But even if one agrees in recognizing *the unity* of this complex being, it still must be demonstrated theologically. This is the contemporary challenge for theological research.

b. The theology of the Mystical Body

We know that, after it was obscured somewhat from the sixteenth century to the beginning of the nineteenth century, this major ecclesiological theme of St. Paul came back strongly in Catholic theology (e.g., in Vatican I). It even became the theme of the contemporary renewal in the years 1920 to 1940. The chief author who worked on this theme in source theology was Fr. Émile Mersch.[27] At the level of positive theology, this

---

27. Émile Mersch, *Le Corps mystique du Christ*, vols. 1 and 2.

work is quite remarkable and of lasting value. However, when the author proposes a more speculative sort of reflection on the data that he has accumulated, he expresses himself in a surprising way:

> The notion of the Mystical Body and the idea of the Church are very closely related. No decision, no recent usage of the terms allows us to establish a clear-cut division between the meaning of one and that of the other. To help classify the ideas, it seems to us, here is the most acceptable thing that can be said. These two notions both express the work of Christ in this world, but the first, the notion of the Mystical Body, designates first of all the invisible element of this work (interior life, Christ continued, etc.) and the second, the notion of Church, designates primarily the visible element of this same work (society, authority, etc.).[28]

According to this way of thinking, the catechumen is a member of the Mystical Body, but not of the Church.[29] Indeed:

> It is *certain* ... that the notion of Mystical Body is not absolutely identical to that of the Church. One may ask, for example, whether sinners are members of the Mystical Body, and whether fervent catechumens are outside of that Body, whereas it is *certain* that the former are members of the Church and that the latter are not.[30]

It is easy to see that the theology of the Mystical Body espouses the Bellarminian line of argument. The word "Church" then designates the Body, and the expression "Mystical Body" designates the soul. As a result, the critiques that can be leveled at this part of the contemporary renewal are fundamentally the same the ones that can be made of Bellarmine and his followers.

---

28. *Le Corps mystique du Christ*, 2:218, note 3.
29. *Le Corps mystique du Christ*, 2:219.
30. *Le Corps mystique du Christ*, 2:335. In the posthumous work *La Théologie du Corps mystique*, vol. 2 (Paris: 1946), translated by Cyril Vollert as *The Theology of the Mystical Body* (St. Louis: Herder, 1951), we can read also: "A person can be a member of the visible society of the Church without actually living the life of Christ as a perfect member of the mystical body.... Likewise one can truly live the life of Christ without being actually attached to the visible society that is His Church.... Accordingly, the great number of souls effectively living the life of Christ is one thing, and the visible Church is another; in a matter so delicate dealing with such important subjects, we shall find it useful to have two different words to designate *two realities* that differ *de facto*, however closely they may be related *de jure*" (196; English. ed. 480). This binomial Church/Mystical Body is present also in the writings of Yves Congar, particularly in *Divided Christendom*, 90.

c. Other distinctions in the renewal

Other distinctions have been proposed, such as *society-community* (or *communion*),[31] or else on the basis of the general theory of the sacraments, the *sacramentum tantum* and the *res sacramenti*.[32] Actually, this is still a matter of the influence of the Bellarminian current. It is easy to tell when the authors address of the question of membership in the Church. Thus, for example, Karl Rahner:

> For this reason therefore, all those and only those points which affect the Church as a visible, public and juridical society are significant and decisive for the question of membership of the Church understood in this precise manner. Since the visibleness and visible unity of the Church are constituted by the sacramental and juridical authority of the Church, ... *all and only those belong to the Church as members who are visibly, i.e., in the external forum, subject to these two powers of the Church.*[33]

We can say, therefore, that the contemporary ecclesiological renewal has indisputably discovered a great wealth of positive theology, but when it is a question of elaborating on these data in a more speculative way, the "habits" of the Bellarminian tradition persist.

IV. THE SITUATION OF ECCLESIOLOGY AFTER VATICAN II

a. General situation

The references to this topic in *Lumen gentium* 8, §1 are too clear to be debated: the Church is a *complex reality made up of a twofold element*. The Council meant to respond to the whole current of thought that we presented earlier. The Council Fathers pronounced no condemnation

---

31. This distinction originates in German sociology, which conceptualizes the common life of men according to two well-defined categories: *Gemeinschaft* (community) and *Gesellschaft* (society). The first expresses the internal life and the second the purely external life. On this point, see our presentation of the People of God theme.

32. Thus, for example, Yves Congar: "After the pattern of the Eucharist, and thanks to it, the Church-as-Institution, considered as a great sacrament, produces this *unitas Corporis mystici* [unity of the Mystical Body]"; *The Mystery of the Church*, 72. See also Karl Rahner, "Membership in the Church according to the Teaching of Pius XII's Encyclical 'Mystici Corporis Christi,'" in *Theological Investigations*, 2:16.

33. Karl Rahner, "Membership in the Church," 2:17 [emphasis added].

of any author, but their response is clear. The theological question after the Council, therefore, has become this: How to give an account of this unity? By far the prevalent theological path is the one that expresses the *tension* between two *poles*. Let us look at a few texts on this subject. We chose them deliberately from very different disciplines so as to show that this is indeed a broad current in post-conciliar theology.

- Biblical theology:

The Church may be regarded as a unity in tension combining what is human and divine, earthly and heavenly, temporal and eternal; all these categories unite in the Church and link the various contrasted elements in its life to produce its characteristic appearance and efficacy.[34]

- History of the Church:

Along with a great deal else in modern culture, polarity of the argument [in French: "dialectical polarity"] offers genuine and fruitful criteria in the field of knowledge, and guarantees close consideration of whatever is under review. When a subject is isolated from its context one runs the risk of not understanding it fully, because every matter is only real in so far as one can see where it comes from and where it is going to: its growth, associations and anticipated polarities. It is clear from a study of the past that there have always been tensions in the Church: and also that it has been customary to make reference to a system of theoretical justifications which supports now this side and now that of the argument.[35]

- Speculative theology:

All life moves in tension, as J. A. Möhler showed; where tension ends, there is death.... But a distinction must be made between genuine tensions, where the poles are related to one another in a complementary way, and unconnected, indeed irreconcilable differences, which shut themselves off mutually and exclude one another, both in logic and in attitude.[36]

No seemingly definitive institutional solution has been found for any [conflict] and ... I do not think that one can be found if a definitive solution is the aim. Indeed, the *tensions* that have repercussions in the law are a reflection of the sacramental character of the Church. In her, unlike in Christ, the

---

34. Rudolf Schnackenburg, *The Church in the New Testament*, 142.
35. L. Sartori, "The Structure of Juridical and Charismatic Power in the Christian Community," in *Concilium*, English ed., 109 (1977): 56–66; reprinted in *Charisms in the Church*, edited by Christian Duquoc and Casiano Floristan, 56–66, citation at 56 (New York: Seabury, 1978).
36. Walter Kasper, *Theology and Church*, 163.

tension between the constitutive elements is a state that is part of her constitution.[37]

These examples—and we could provide many others—allow us to point out something that is characteristic of the predominant current in speculative theology since Vatican II, for which we propose the name "binomial thinking." Let us present this sort of thought briefly.

b. The general structure of "binomial thinking"

The idea undergirding this sort of thinking is as follows: one grasps a being (in this case the Church, but we are dealing here with a veritable substitute "metaphysics" that is supposed to be applied to all of reality) not in its *unity*, but rather in its *composition*, with the proviso that the unity is not the "sum" of the two poles or elements that one could call a third term, as the substantial "sum" of the body and soul is called "human being"; instead, the unity is situated "between" the two poles. The notion of unity is replaced here by the notion of *equilibrium*, and this equilibrium is, somewhat as in physics, brought about by the equal play of contrary forces. For, it should be noted, the two fundamental poles are for the most part understood as *antinomies*, seemingly irreconcilable antitheses (for example living organism/juridical organization, or else life-freedom-flourishing/structure-constraint-limitation), and they are harmonized insofar as they tend to correct one another. Thus it is said that life is by nature growth, development, and progress, whereas a juridical structure is in itself static and conservative. This is the sort of equilibrium that is called *tension*, and that is always precarious. The process that juxtaposes the two *poles* is most often called a *dialectical process*. The following chart attempts to regroup the different terms used by this mode of thinking:

- All of this makes up an *equilibrium:*
  - an ideal to pursue,
  - that is experienced as unstable.

---

37. A. Acerbi, "L'ecclésiologie à la base des institutions ecclésiales post-conciliaires," in *Les Églises après Vatican II: dynamisme et prospective*, 257.

History

TABLE 7-1

Divine	Tension	Human
Reality of salvation		Means of salvation
Heavenly		Earthly
Eternal		Temporal
	Complexio oppositorum	
Life		Institution
Eschatology		History
"not yet"		"already"
	Incarnation	
Agent of change		Element of continuity
	Mutual inclusion	
Realism of God		Formalism of human conditions.
Affective knowledge		Intellectual knowledge (concepts…)
Spiritual	*Bipolarity, antithesis, etc.*	Rational
Fraternal communion	*Complementarity or else*	Hierarchical society
Internal	*incompatibility*	External

There we have a veritable Vulgate of contemporary ecclesiology, especially in the use of the binomial *institution—communion*, in which the term *institution* is taken in its sociological connotation, and not in its theological sense.[38]

Having recalled this, it is necessary now to include in our investigation the data consisting of magisterial judgments.

V. MAGISTERIAL JUDGMENTS

Before Vatican II, the Magisterium did not venture into the ecclesiological arena to resolve ongoing debates and investigations. So it is always when a question is not yet ripe. But if a deviation of some importance occurs (especially one that is widespread), the Magisterium does not do theology, but rather recalls what must be held in faith—namely, the requirements of the deposit of faith [*du donné positif*]. Here, for our

---

38. The word *institution* in sociology means the juridical structure of the authority, whereas in theology, particularly in ecclesiology and sacramental theology, it means, "what Christ has instituted," has brought into being in some way.

specific question, the Magisterium recalls in many ways that the various aspects that can be distinguished within the Church *should always be considered within the unity of the ecclesial being, in other words, in their inseparability*. This is what we are going to look into now.

a. On the distinction between body and soul in the Church

It is important to note that this distinction has *never* been adopted in magisterial teaching. Although the following document is not strictly speaking magisterial, we have here a clear indication that this absence is not fortuitous but quite deliberate:

"This distinction must not be repeated *because it is scholastic and above all novel in the way in which the councils express themselves.*"³⁹

We have here a typical attitude of the Magisterium, because the Council would follow the Preparatory Dogmatic Commission on this point. This was a matter of *prudentially* rejecting the Bellarminian distinction in what concerns the question about the constitution of the Church. And in fact, in chapters 1 through 5 of the draft Constitution *De Ecclesia* devoted to the being of the Church, this distinction is not found. It is found, however, in another context, that of ecclesial membership, but only in a note. We already said that this draft Constitution had not been voted on by the Council because the latter was interrupted. Many remarks in this document provided the basis for the later teaching of Leo XIII, but—and it is important to note this—the distinction was never adopted by Leo XIII, neither with regard to the being of the Church nor with regard to membership in the Church. On the contrary, the inseparability of the different constitutive elements of the Church is what was continually recalled by the Magisterium:

It is assuredly as impossible that the Church of Jesus Christ can be the one or the other, as that man should be a body alone or a soul alone. The connection and union of both elements is as absolutely necessary to the true Church as the intimate union of the soul and body is to human nature.⁴⁰

---

39. Preparatory Dogmatic Commission, Vatican I, Mansi, *Sacrorum conciliorum*, vol. 49, col. 624d–25a [translated from French].

40. Leo XIII, Encyclical *Satis cognitum*, June 29, 1896. According to Fr. Congar, this is the only magisterial use of this comparison before Pius XII.

There can, then, be no real opposition or conflict between the invisible mission of the Holy Spirit and the juridical commission of Ruler and Teacher received from Christ [by the pastors and doctors], since they mutually complement and perfect each other—as do the body and soul in man—and proceed from our one Redeemer.[41]

These magisterial documents are extremely cautious. Without making a declaration about the ground(s) for the pertinence of the distinction, they recall the essential thing that must be held: the inseparability of the different elements that make up the Church in order for the ecclesial being to be *one*.

b. On the theology of the Mystical Body

The Magisterium has *never* articulated either the distinction between Mystical Body and Church or the distinction between Mystical Body and society. It has always considered that the expression *Mystical Body* designated the whole ecclesial mystery in all its internal and external aspects. We can cite, for example:

Since the true Church of Christ is such, we declare that the visible and evident society that we just spoke of is the Church of the promises and of the divine mercies that Christ willed to distinguish and adorn with so many prerogatives and privileges.... [This society] is entirely self-contained and fully forms a whole, and its splendid unity reveals within it the undivided and indivisible body that is the Mystical Body of Christ himself.[42]

But He, indeed, Who made this one Church, also gave it *unity*, that is, He made it such that all who are to belong to it must be united by the closest bonds, so as to form one society, one kingdom, *one body*.[43]

As Savior of the human family, he had a spiritual and mystical body, the society, namely, of those who believe in Christ.[44]

The mystical body of Christ [i.e., the Church], in the same manner as His physical body, is one, compacted and fitly joined together....[45]

---

41. Pius XII, Encyclical *Mystici Corporis*, June 29, 1943, Vatican website translation, par. 65.
42. Vatican I, schema *De Ecclesia* (not voted on), chap. 5, "De visibili Ecclesiae unitate," Mansi, vol. 51, col. 541 a–b [translated from French].
43. Leo XIII, Encyclical *Satis cognitum*.
44. Pius X, Encyclical *Ad diem illum* (1904).
45. Pius XI, Encyclical *Mortalium animos* (1928).

If we would define and describe this true Church of Jesus Christ—which is the One, Holy, Catholic, Apostolic and Roman Church—we shall find nothing more noble, more sublime, or more divine than the expression "the Mystical Body of Christ."[46]

But, the society structured with hierarchical organs and the mystical body of Christ ... are not to be thought of as two realities. On the contrary, they form *one complex reality* which comes together from a human and a divine element.[47]

This last citation might seem to distinguish between hierarchical society and Mystical Body, but in fact that is by no means the case. Basically this is the passage that asserts most clearly the constitutive unity of the ecclesial mystery. Moreover we should recall that here the conciliar Magisterium is responding explicitly to the works of theologians; therefore it adopts their vocabulary while showing them what must absolutely be held as a matter of faith: the unity of the ecclesial entity. The Magisterium makes no direct pronouncement on the different distinctions then current in the theological renewal, but since it aligns itself in continuity with the magisterial tradition that we cited in the preceding passages, it would be a distortion to cite this paragraph to "canonize" this distinction; everything proves the contrary. One need only reread the explanation of *Lumen gentium* 7 about the theology of the Mystical Body to be readily convinced of it: the expression *Mystical Body* expresses the ecclesial mystery *as a whole*.

c. On the distinction between society and community

The distinction basically has a sociological and philosophical origin, and it has been applied to the Church by way of analogy. Therefore the magisterial point of departure on this subject is to be found in the social teaching of the Church. Now it is striking to note that the social teaching does not adopt this distinction:

One of the most striking features of today's world is the intense development of interpersonal relationships due in no small measure to modern technical advances. Nevertheless genuine fraternal dialogue is advanced not so much on this level as at the deeper level of personal fellowship (*personarum communitate*), and this calls for mutual respect for the full spiritual dig-

---

46. Pius XII, Encyclical *Mystici Corporis* (1943), 13.
47. Vatican II, Constitution *Lumen gentium* 8, §1.

nity of men as persons. Christian revelation greatly fosters the establishment of such fellowship (*communionem inter personas*) and at the same time promotes deeper understanding of the laws of social living (*vitae socialis*) with which the Creator has endowed man's spiritual and moral nature.

Some recent pronouncements of the Church's teaching authority have dealt at length with Christian teaching on human society (*de societate humana*). The Council, therefore, proposes to repeat only a few of the more important truths.[48]

In this passage—and likewise throughout the Constitution—the words "fellowship" (community), "communion," and "society" are used as equivalents. It should be noted, however, that sometimes Vatican II uses the distinction between *structure* and *life* that is equivalent to the distinction between *society* and *community* (or *communion*), but this never has any bearing on the question of the Church's constitution or on the question of membership in the Church. This distinction, insofar as it can clarify, is applied, for example, to situate within the ecclesial mystery certain realities such as consecrated life: the latter does not belong to the *structure* of the Church, but falls under the heading of her *life* (cf. *LG* 44). This means, to put it plainly, that Christ's gift of consecrated life does not fall under the category of hierarchical mediations of grace (the sacrament of holy orders), but under the reality of grace. Therefore, this language does not adopt the distinction that originated in sociology.

d. On sacramentality

Paragraph 1 of *Lumen gentium* clearly enunciates the sacramental relation, as we saw before:

Since the Church, in Christ, is in the nature of sacrament—a sign and instrument, that is, of communion with God and of unity among all men....

One might think that this sacramentality applies only to the humanity of the ecclesial mystery, because *sign and instrument* were understood by many theologians as being separable from the *"res,"* namely "communion with God and unity among all men." That is why, in other passages, the Council is careful to specify that the entire mystery constitutes the sacramentality of the Church:

---

48. Constitution *Gaudium et spes* 23, §§1 and 2.

Christ lifted up from the earth, has drawn all men to himself. Rising from the dead he sent his life-giving Spirit upon his disciples and through him set up his Body which is the Church *as the universal sacrament of salvation.*[49]

In other words, although it is legitimate to distinguish the *sign-instrument* from the *reality* that it brings about, one must never separate them: one cannot be without the other, for this sacramentality defines first the ontology of Christ and [then] that of the Church. In the preceding citation (*LG* 48) the equivalence between Mystical Body and sacrament says this clearly.

e. The question of membership in the Church

We have already showed how the Bellarminian paradigm was different from the patristic and medieval paradigm on this subject. We have also emphasized that this difference was clearly demonstrated during the contemporary theological renewal. Vatican II clearly opted for the patristic and medieval tradition by explicitly having recourse to St. Augustine in *Lumen gentium* 14, §2: one exists in the Church "in body and/or in soul (*or* in heart)"; one does not belong to the body and/or soul of the Church. This is a very important clarification.

Conclusion

The recurring difficulty, both before and after Vatican II, remains to give an account of the unity of the various constitutive elements of the mystery of the Church, of the inseparability of her body and soul, so to speak. This is an altogether relevant difficulty, whatever the fluctuations in terminology may be, and one must admit that it has very clear practical consequences:

- Before Vatican II the emphasis was placed on sociological membership, and the paradigm of "structure," authority, and obedience was more prominent.
- After Vatican II the emphasis has been placed, in contrast, on internal membership, and the paradigm of "life," grace, and involvement in good works has gained prominence.

---

49. Constitution *Lumen gentium* 48.

But every time one minimizes the other aspect, one runs the risk of separating the different elements. This risk is important and all too often materializes. That is why the Extraordinary Synod in 1985 thought it opportune to formulate several very clear reminders, explicitly regretting that in the concrete ecclesial behavior of some clerics and some laypeople the separation of the different elements is lived, and that this disjunction sometimes finds a conceptual tool in a largely implicit philosophy of dialectical opposition. The danger is serious: if one of the elements of the mystery is removed, the whole mystery is prone to vanish, since the mystery is profoundly one.

The Synod in 1985 recalls that Vatican II proposed to search for a theological explanation of the constitutive unity of the ecclesial mystery along the lines of sacramentality. But at present we are at the beginning of this research. That does not mean that there are no other possible approaches. Charles Journet, for example, wanted to preserve the distinction between body and soul of the Church on the basis of the patristic and Thomistic tradition, and not according to the view of St. Robert Bellarmine. That is quite legitimate. We however will not take that approach for three reasons:

- The first is that an academic course does not claim to say everything!
- The second is that Vatican II indisputably wanted to give priority to sacramentality.
- The third, finally, is that from an ecumenical perspective sacramentality offers more advantages.

To conclude, we note one particular point: Vatican II did not repeat a distinction that had come to light in the early 1950s, which we have not yet mentioned because it had not yet become part of the theological currency before the Council: we mean the distinction between *institution* and *event*. A Protestant author, Jean-Louis Leuba, was the one who promoted it based on his dissertation.[50] This distinction cannot be compared at all to the distinction *society-community* or *structure-life*. It mainly comes down to this: God's work in salvation history is accomplished in two complementary modes that call for one another:

50. Jean-Louis Leuba, *L'Institution et l'événement* (Neuchâtel and Paris: 1950).

- An institutional mode: Jesus is the son of David; this is an institutional title that underscores a continuity.
- A new event-ual mode: Jesus is the Son of man; this is a title that underscores the constant, sovereign, unexpected intervention of the Spirit of God.

Thus in the life of the Church there is the institutional aspect and the eventual aspect: for example, the hierarchical institution and the conciliar event. This distinction seems to us to be quite pertinent, provided that we are careful to understand it as two conjoined modes of the one life of the ecclesial mystery and not as a structural separation within the mystery. If it is understood correctly, it is very judicious and enlightening, but it has no bearing on the speculative question that concerns us here.

It seems to us that this distinction does not express the nature of the Church, but rather allows us to understand two remarks in Scripture concerning Christ's work. The Savior presents his action in two ways that may seem contradictory:

- "Do not think that I have come to abolish the law and the prophets; I have come not to abolish them but to fulfil them." (Mt 5:17)
- "Neither is new wine put into old wineskins ... but new wine is put into fresh wineskins." (Mt 9:17)

We have here, on the one hand, a paradigm of continuity (not to abolish, but to fulfill), and on the other hand a paradigm of newness. The continuity concerns the teaching of Christ: after the announcements and preparations comes the fulfillment. Here we are on the order of knowledge. The newness is relative to that which is known [and experienced]: the grace given by Christ. Here we are dealing with a real order. So it is in the life of the Church: continuity of knowledge and newness of the gift of God at the origin of the Church that is fruitful in every age.

Bibliography

The historical doctrinal context before the Reformation

Congar, Yves. *L'Église de S. Augustin à l'époque moderne.* Paris: 1970; particularly 339–68.

Delumeau, J. *Mille ans de bonheur.* Vol. 2, *Une histoire du paradis.* Paris: 1995; particularly 55ff.

The ecclesiological assertions of the Reformers

Calvin, J. *The Institutes of the Christian Religion.* Translated by Henry Beveridge. Chicago: Encyclopaedia Britannica, 1990.

Luther, M. "On the Papacy" (1520). In *Luther's Works,* edited by Jaroslav Pelikan. Vol. 39. St. Louis: Concordia, 1986.

Studies on Reformation thought

These studies will provide other references, in particular for Luther, whose literary output was considerable and contained many shifts in teaching; hence the current debates within Protestant Christianity.

Birmelé, A. "Église." In *Encyclopédie du Protestantisme.* Paris and Geneva: 1995. Good synthesis. One might object, however, that the author tends to present the founders of the Reformation with reference to the present state of Protestantism, and not in a more historical perspective.

Courvoisier, J. *De la Réforme au protestantisme: Essai d'ecclésiologie réformée.* Series "Théologie historique" 45. Paris: 1977. Good historical perspective, mainly about Zwingli and Calvin.

Strohl, H. *La Pensée de la Réforme.* Neuchâtel: 1951; esp. 177ff. The author is careful to stay close to the original insights of the Reformation.

The Catholic response of the Counter-Reformation

Bellarmine, St. Robert. *Disputationes de controversiis christianae fidei adversus hujus temporis hereticos* (abbreviated *De controversiis*). Vol. 2. Naples ed.: 1857; particularly chap. 2. On the diffusion of this work—and particularly of the ecclesiological part—see Yves de Montcheuil, *Mélanges théologiques,* 2nd ed. (Paris: 1951), and E. Dublanchy, "Église," in *Dictionnaire de Théologie Catholique* (*DTC*), vol. 4 (Paris: 1911), col. 2143. The only really theological critique, to our knowledge, is in Charles Journet, *L'Église du Verbe incarné,* vol. 2, esp. 2:566ff. and 2:1180–83. A decisive presentation.

Controversial literature

Dublanchy, E. "Église." In *DTC.* Vol. 4. Paris: 1911, col 2143–44.

Suarez, F. *Defensio fidei catholicae adversus anglicanae sectae errores.* Coïmbra: 1613. Critical edition by the Instituto de Estudios Politicos. Madrid: 1970; esp. 41–42.

Scholastic theology

Billuart, Charles-René. *Summa Sancti Thomas.* Atrebati: Brunet, 1866–1868. 4 vols. See esp. vol. 3, dissertatio 3: *De Ecclesia.*

John of Saint-Thomas (John Poinsot). *Cursus theologicus.* Vivès ed. Paris: 1883–1886. 8 vols. See esp. 1:442ff.

Suarez, F. *Opera omnia*. Vivès ed. Paris: 1856–1861. 26 vols. See particularly vol. 12, disputatio 9: *De Ecclesia*.

———. *Summa*. Migne ed. Paris: 1858. 2 vols.

Treatises *"De Ecclesia"*

Billot, Louis. *Tractatus de Ecclesia Christi*. 3rd ed. Prati: 1909.

Perrone, Giovanni. *Praelectiones theologicae*. 2 vols. Migne ed. Paris: 1856. See esp. 1:171ff. and 1:717ff.

Schultes, R.-M. *Praelectiones apologeticae: De Ecclesia catholica*. Paris: 1925.

Manuals

Tanquerey, A. *De vera religione, de Ecclesia, de fontibus Revelationis*. 14th ed. Paris, 1911. This is the most well-known manual; it was sometimes used into the 1950s (!). Marvelously illustrates the hardening of the Bellarminian line that made nascent ecclesiology a "hierarchology."

The contemporary theological renewal

We mention here only the authors who are cited directly to give a glimpse of the speculative difficulty that the contemporary theological renewal faced; in the following chapters additional bibliographical references will be given.

Acerbi, A. "L'ecclésiologie à la base des institutions ecclésiales postconciliaires." In *Les Églises après Vatican II: dynamisme et prospective*, Actes du colloque de Bologne 1980, edited by G. Alberigo. Coll. Théologie historique 61. Paris: 1981, 223–58.

Congar, Yves. *Divided Christendom: A Catholic Study of the Problem of Reunion*. Translated by M. A. Bousfield, OP. London: Centenary Press, 1939.

———. *The Mystery of the Church*. Rev. trans. Baltimore and Dublin: Helicon Press, 1965.

de Lubac, H. *Catholicisme: Les aspects sociaux du dogme*. US 3. Paris: 1938; 1950.

———. *Catholicism: Christ and the Common Destiny of Man*. Reprinted San Francisco: Ignatius Press, 1988.

Journet, Charles. *L'Église du Verbe incarné*. Vol. 2, *Structure interne et unité catholique*. Paris: 1951.

Kasper, Walter. *Theology and Church*. New York: Crossroad, 1989.

Leuba, J.-L. *L'Institution et l'événement*. Neuchâtel and Paris: 1950.

Mersch, Émile. *Le Corps mystique du Christ*. Vols. 1 and 2. 2nd ed. Paris: 1933. This study is still remarkable for the extent of its examination of the source materials. The scriptural part is quite outdated, but the review of the Fathers is impressive. From the viewpoint of a speculative interpretation of the data that are collected, the author marvelously illustrates how and to what degree the ecclesiological renewal began by working within the Bellarminian parameters without calling them into question. Thus his distinction between *Church* and *Mystical Body* remains in the vein of the distinction between *Body* and *soul* derived from St. Robert Bellarmine. This work should not be confused with the posthumous work published on the basis of the author's notes: Mersch, *La théologie du Corps mystique* (Paris: 1946), a more directly speculative work that was not able to incorporate the findings of the Encyclical *Mystici Corporis,* since the author had died by then.

Rahner, Karl. "Membership in the Church according to the Teaching of Pius XII's Encyclical 'Mystici Corporis Christi.'" In *Theological Investigations*. Baltimore: Helicon Press, 1963, 2:1–88.

Schnackenburg, Rudolf. *The Church in the New Testament.* Translated by W. J. O'Hara. New York: Herder and Herder, 1965.

8

General Critique

We have seen that the whole question about the nature of the Church is part of the question about the visibility of the Church raised by the Reformers. In the answer of classical Catholic theology, the visibility of the Church was centered on the question of the means of grace. We must return to this question and treat it thoroughly.

We have seen that, ever since the 1950s, there has been and is today a certain widespread "intellectual method" of accounting for the constitutive unity of the various elements that make up the ecclesial mystery. We presented this by means of "binomials" such as "society-communion," "*sacramentum-res,*" and "Church-Mystical Body." Here too we have to get to the bottom of this way of thinking so as to evaluate its pertinence.

I. THE QUESTION OF ECCLESIAL VISIBILITY

To consider this question, we start with the teaching of Vatican II. The Council did not teach this question "*ex professo,*" explicitly and for its own sake, but its references to this subject call for careful attention.[1]

---

1. We could also study first the conciliar vocabulary of visibility; see de La Soujeole, *Le Sacrement de la communion,* 154–61. This review of vocabulary shows that the Church is visible not only in her "means of grace" aspect, but also in her "reality of grace" aspect. This is precisely what we must explain here.

a. Notes from Vatican II

Many references by the Council could be considered here;[2] we will limit ourselves to one particularly central reference in which the Council notes what pertains to the "nature" of the Church. The document declares:

For it is the liturgy through which ... "the work of our redemption is accomplished," and it is through the liturgy, especially, that the faithful are enabled to express in their lives and manifest to others the mystery of Christ and the real nature of the true Church. The Church is essentially both human and divine, visible but endowed with invisible realities, zealous in action and dedicated to contemplation, present in the world, but as a pilgrim, so constituted that in her the human is *directed toward and subordinated to* the divine, the visible to the invisible, action to contemplation, and this present world to that city yet to come, the object of our quest.[3]

The essential visibility of the Church is nothing new. It is clearly emphasized here. The relation between the visible and the invisible, and also between the human and the divine, action and contemplation, the present and the eschatological future, is spelled out by the two verbs *ordinetur ad* and *subordinetur ad*. What does this mean?

What is visible in the Church is ordered to (*"ordinetur ad"*) what is invisible in the Church. The verb "to order" signifies in the Latin of classical theology "to be disposed with a view to an end or purpose." In the liturgy the perceptible signs are performed for the purpose of signifying the sanctification that is accomplished. In ecclesiology what is visible is the sign of the reality of grace. In other words, the visible aspect manifests salvation inasmuch as it is given through the mediation of realities taken from this world. The visible aspect is mentioned here "upstream" from the reality of grace. It is considered within the paradigm of the descending movement through which God's gifts come to us. This visible aspect of the Church is what classical Catholic theology emphasized in opposition to the Protestants.

The visible aspect of the Church is also subordinated to (*"subordinetur ad"*) what is invisible in the Church. Subordination connotes dependence. In this sense the visible ecclesial aspect follows—in a causal

2. For the other references, see de La Soujeole, *Le Sacrement de la communion*, 154–61.
3. *Sacrosanctum Concilium* 2.

TABLE 8-1

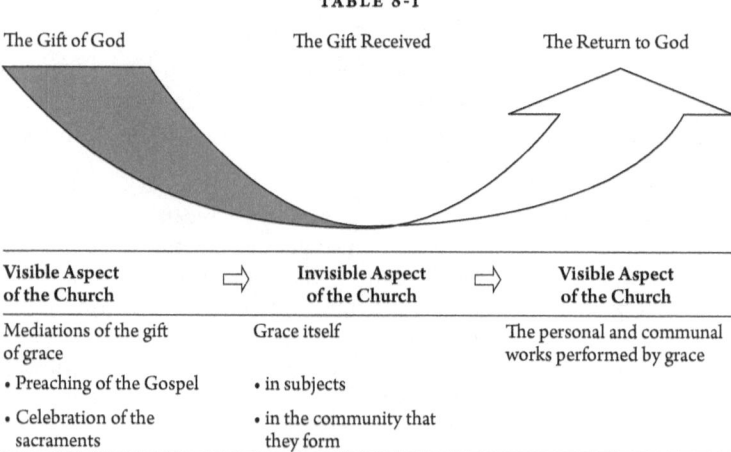

Visible Aspect of the Church	Invisible Aspect of the Church	Visible Aspect of the Church
Mediations of the gift of grace	Grace itself	The personal and communal works performed by grace
• Preaching of the Gospel	• in subjects	
• Celebration of the sacraments	• in the community that they form	

relation—the invisible ecclesial aspect. Here the visible aspect is situated "downstream" from the invisible. It expresses grace, not inasmuch as it comes from God, but inasmuch as it radiates outward through the activity of human beings once it has been received from God. This is part of the ascending movement by which men make their return to God through the gifts that he has given them.

Therefore, there is a twofold relation between the visible and the invisible aspects that shows the twofold place of ecclesial visibility: it is situated both on the side of the causes of grace and also on the side of its effects (see table 8-1).

What we must study now is the whole extent of this visible aspect of the Church.

b. The whole extent of the visible aspect of the Church

What is visible, in the proper sense, is what is perceptible to the sense of sight. What is manifest to the eye can be either the reality itself—for example, a table—or the sign of the reality. In the latter case we speak about a visible emotion: for example, when we mean that this internal feeling makes its presence in a person known by an external attitude that is perceptible to the sense (the fact that a person is weeping). Consequently, the visibility of a reality can be appreciated under two as-

General Critique

pects: the faculty that allows one to see and the reality that is actually seen. These are the two points to be considered here.

The exercise of the faculty of sight causes the *visible* object under consideration to actually become *seen*. Thus the sun during the day is only visible; it is seen only if a subject goes outdoors and looks at it. To say that something is "visible" refers to a *quality of the object*, and to say that something is "seen" depends on an *action by the subject*. Some magisterial documents describe the faculty of seeing the Church using imagery that must be understood correctly. For example:

> For this reason the Church is so often called in Holy Writ a *body*, and even the Body of Christ—"Now you are the body of Christ" (I Cor. 12:27)—and precisely because it is a body is the Church visible (*oculis cernitur*): and because it is the body of Christ is it living and energizing, because by the infusion of His power Christ guards and sustains it.... So the principle of supernatural life in the Church is clearly shown in that which is done by it.[4]

This teaching is repeated by Pius XII:

> But it is not enough that the Body of the Church should be an unbroken unity; it must also be something definite and perceptible to the senses (*concretum ac perspicibile*) as Our predecessor of happy memory, Leo XIII, in his Encyclical *Satis Cognitum* asserts, "the Church is visible because she is a body."[5]

Taken literally, these passages would lead one to think that the visibility of the Church was directed toward the eyes—in other words, that this is about the visibility of purely physical qualities. Now the citation from Leo XIII does state that what is made visible is the supernatural life of the Church. Therefore, we must think about the visibility of a sign. What is meant then, strictly speaking, when we say that the Church is visible to the eye? It is traditional in theology to speak about the eye, not in the proper sense (the physical eye), but in the figurative sense, when speaking about the eye of the intellect.[6] In the realities of salvation history, the bodily eye sees external signs in which the eye of the intellect, graced by faith, recognizes the supernatural reality itself. Thus in the case of the Eucharist, for example, what the bodily eye sees

---

4. Leo XIII, Encyclical *Satis cognitum* (June 29, 1896), par. 3 (English translation at Vatican website).

5. Pius XII, Encyclical *Mystici Corporis* (1943), no. 14 (English translation at Vatican website).

6. For example *Summa theologiae* III, q. 76, art. 7, corpus.

are the accidents that remain, but what the eye of the graced intellect sees under the sign of food is the Body of Christ. To speak of the intellect as a spiritual eye is quite common in literature, and, in the case of the knowledge of faith, it is just as common in theology. These clarifications allow us to say that the fleshly eye sees the physical qualities of the Church on the order of phenomena. The eye, then, considers a religious institution as one among many others. What the eyes of the unaided intellect can grasp are the particular characteristics of this reality called Church, its "notes" from an apologetic point of view. Finally, what the graced intellect perceives are the properties of the Church; then we are at the theological level that is based on faith. The "eyes of faith" perceive the ecclesial mystery—in other words, the signs of the supernatural life that resides in the members and is expressed by them.

These clarifications would be trivial if they had not been underestimated for too long. Recall that classical Catholic theology had come to the point where it considered the ecclesial mystery as something made up of two distinct, separable communities, one properly speaking supernatural (the soul) and the other properly speaking natural, on the sociological order. To see the latter, unaided intellect could suffice. In that case one was at best making a statement belonging to apologetics rather than to theology.

Having arrived at this point, we must consider what faith perceives—in other words, what it transfers from the realm of the simply *visible* to the category of what is actually *seen*.

The object of faith is the mystery—that is, in the first place a whole set of supernatural realities, which is by that very fact beyond the capacities of natural reason. This classical sense of the word "mystery," enshrined by the First Vatican Council,[7] was explicitly applied to the Church by Pius XII, who thus classified it among the mysteries that are accessible to reason enlightened by faith.[8] The visibility of the Church is visibility for the graced intellect. Consequently it concerns signs of realities and not the realities themselves. Faith allows one to recognize the signs as signs and through them to access the reality whose presence they announce.

We must consider next the second sense of the word "mystery," the

---

7. Constitution *Dei Filius*, chap. 4. See our previous discussion on the mystery-truth.
8. Encyclical *Mystici Corporis* 10.

General Critique 395

sacramental sense, which specifies the first sense: the Church is a "divine, transcendent, and salvific reality that is revealed and manifested by some visible means."[9] This alliance of a reality that is invisible per se with visible realities that are its sign and the means of its presence in this world was the subject of various attempts at theological explanation. In order to give an account of this complex alliance here, we call on the thought of St. Thomas Aquinas, who considered this question, not directly in an ecclesiological framework, but in relation to the New Law, in questions 106 to 108 of the *Prima Secundae* of the *Summa theologiae*.[10]

Q. 106, art. 1 is formulated as follows: Is the New Law a written law? In his answer St. Thomas sets forth the "nature" of the New Law in terms of what is written and what is not written.

"Each thing appears to be that which preponderates in it," as the Philosopher [Aristotle] states (*Ethica Nicomachea* IX, 8). Now that which is preponderant in the law of the New Testament, and whereon all its efficacy is based, is the grace of the Holy Ghost, which is given through faith in Christ. Consequently the New Law is chiefly (*principaliter*) the grace itself of the Holy Ghost, that is given to those who believe in Christ.... Nevertheless the New Law contains certain things that dispose us to receive the grace of the Holy Ghost (*quaedam sicut dispositiva*), and pertaining to the use of that grace (*et ad usum huius gratiae pertinentia*): such things are of secondary importance, so to speak (*sunt quasi-secundaria*), in the New Law.... Consequently we must say that the New Law is in the first place a law that is inscribed on our hearts, but that secondarily it is a written law.[11]

---

9. Definition of the word "mystery" in the title of chap. 1 of *Lumen gentium* (*De Ecclesiae mysterio*) by the Theological Commission of the Council, AS III/I, 170. See our discussion previously on the mystery-reality.

10. This Thomistic teaching was cited during the ecclesiological renewal. The first to have proposed it was Charles Journet, "Les protestantismes à la recherche d'une formule d'universalité," *DC* (1927): 1219–27 (esp. 1226–27); see the study by M. Cagin, "L'Église et la Loi nouvelle; note sur un apport fondamental de l'ecclésiologie de Charles Journet," *Nova et Vetera* (2001): 27f. This would be taken up by Fr. Congar, who referred to it throughout his writings. See in particular Congar, *The Mystery of the Church*, 71ff.; *Le Christ, Marie et l'Église*, 39–40 (at note 34 we read that q. 108, a. 1 is "a passage that St. Thomas would certainly have made one of the pivotal points of his treatise on the Church if he had written one."). See also Congar, *S. Thomas d'Aquin: sa vision de la théologie et de l'Église* (London: 1984), particularly "Orientations de Bonaventure et surtout de Thomas d'Aquin dans leur vision de l'Église et celle de l'État," 701.

11. In the answer to the first objection, St. Thomas explains to some extent what belongs in the *second* way to the New Law: these are written references to the Word of God that *dispose* readers or listeners to receive grace or that *organize* the acts that pro-

The New Law appears at the same time to be written and non-written. What is non-written is the *principal* thing, and what is written is *secondary*. But the New Law is one; we do not have two New Laws, one of which is non-written and the other written. The New Law is therefore a complex reality made up of a principal element, which is spiritual and invisible, and a secondary element, a this-worldly reality that is taken up (written law). One can tell the ecclesiological relevance of these references: they give a very suggestive example of the relation between various different elements within a complex whole. ST I-II, q. 108, art. 1 is as follows: Does the New Law necessarily command or forbid certain external acts? From the *corpus:*

As stated above (*ST* I-II, q. 106, art. 1–2), the New Law consists chiefly in the grace of the Holy Ghost, which is shown forth by faith that worketh through love. Now men become receivers of this grace through God's Son made man, Whose humanity grace filled first, and thence flowed forth to us.... Consequently it was becoming that the grace which flows from the incarnate Word should be given to us by means of certain external sensible objects; and that from this inward grace, whereby the flesh is subjected to the Spirit, certain external works should ensue.

Accordingly external acts may have a twofold connection with grace. In the first place, as leading in some way to grace. Such are the sacramental acts which are instituted in the New Law, e.g. Baptism, the Eucharist, and the like.

In the second place there are those external acts which ensue from the promptings of grace: and herein we must observe a difference. For there are some which are necessarily in keeping with, or in opposition, to inward grace consisting in faith that worketh through love. Such external works are prescribed or forbidden in the New Law; thus confession of faith is prescribed, and denial of faith is forbidden (Matthew 10:32–33).... On the other hand, there are works which are not necessarily opposed to, or in keeping with faith that worketh through love. Such works are not prescribed or forbidden in the New Law.

To the objection that the kingdom of heaven does not consist of external acts but only of internal acts (cf. Lk 17:21, "The Kingdom is within you"), St. Thomas replies (*ST* I-II, q. 108, art. 1, ad 1):

---

ceed from grace in a human being. The dispositive realities are specifically the preaching of the mystery of Christ in the Gospel and the exhortations concerning detachment from the world. The realities that are ordered to the proper use of grace once received are, in the Gospel, the references that invite Christians to perform virtuous works.

The kingdom of God consists *chiefly* (*principaliter*) in internal acts: but as a consequence all things that are essential to internal acts belong also to the kingdom of God.

The question of the New Law is considered in this article more broadly than in the preceding articles, in which the New Law was approached solely under the aspect of written law. But it is the same principle at work in the reply. Aquinas is actually delineating in successive steps the features in the complex nature of the New Law. The connection between the internal and the external elements—which we are studying here under the particular aspect of what is visible or invisible—can be summarized thus: the invisible, which is the chief thing, reaches us through the visible. Once it has been received, it is also the principle of human works, some of which are visible in the acting subject—for example, the confession of faith. Two reasons are brought forward: the first invokes the economy of salvation, in which grace comes to us through the humanity assumed by the Word; this is the soteriological aspect. The second is derived from the fact that man's internal acts may require the aid of external acts or may be expressed by them; this is the anthropological aspect.

This question of the exteriority of the New Law is taken up in the next article.

ST I-II, q. 108, art. 2 asks whether external acts are fittingly regulated by the New Law. In other words, is the interior reality of grace sufficiently "framed" by external realities that either transmit it or express it? St. Thomas's answer is as follows (in the article's corpus):

> Since we cannot of ourselves obtain grace, but through Christ alone, hence Christ of Himself instituted the sacraments whereby we obtain grace: viz. Baptism, Eucharist.... These are the sacraments of the New Law. The right use of grace is by means of works of charity. These, in so far as they are essential to virtue, pertain to the moral precepts, which also formed part of the Old Law (cf. the Decalogue). Hence, in this respect, the New Law had nothing to add as regards external action.

However, the questions relative to the Old Law (*ST* I-II, qq. 99–105) had explained that that Law, with its moral precepts, also included some ceremonial precepts (the organization of worship) and judicial precepts (the area of social relations in the community of salvation).

How is it under the New Law? The same article replies, again from the same perspective of external acts:

> Since these determinations are not in themselves necessarily connected with inward grace wherein the Law consists, they do not come under a precept of the New Law, but are left to the decision of man; some relating to inferiors—as when a precept is given to an individual; others, relating to superiors, temporal or spiritual, referring, namely, to the common good.

One should not conclude that ceremonial and judicial regulations are absolutely unnecessary in the New Law. St. Thomas explains the fact that they are not *determined* in the Gospel, not that they could not *exist*. They are not *written* in the Gospel because they depend on circumstances of time, place and persons, and hence are historically determined. But their existence is observable just as much as in the time of the Old Law, with this difference: their positive determination is left to human judgment.

These Thomistic findings, briefly summarized here, are important. Questions 106 through 108 set forth St. Thomas's way of conceptualizing the interiority and the exteriority of communal Christian life. By means of the necessary transpositions, this teaching has obvious ecclesiological implications, since the New Law "structures" the Church, one might say.

The major lesson of these passages, for our topic, is that they show how the external-visible-sensible element combines with the internal-invisible-spiritual element under the new regime inaugurated by Christ. In the New Law, we have a *principal* thing and a *secondary* thing. The principal thing is the internal-invisible-spiritual element, the Spirit in Person and his created gifts in the souls of the faithful, and this is served by secondary, visible-external things, that are the causes of the principal thing (in particular preaching and the sacraments), and that are human acts performed under the influence of grace (faith working through charity).

At the level of St. Thomas's vocabulary, we must note a major difference between two pairs of words that recur very often: there is the pair *principal-secondary*, which must not be confused with the pair *essential-accidental*. In the word-pair *principal-secondary* we have a statement of a substantial unity of different elements. For example, in the sacrament of holy orders, its principal element consists in the capacity to celebrate the Eucharist; preaching of the faith comes second for it, which does not mean that it is secondary or accidental: the sacrament of holy orders is one. On the contrary, when it is a question of beatitude, what is essential to it is the vision of God, and what is accidental to it is the vision of the other blessed souls.[12] This vocabulary alone already shows us that in the New Law all the elements, whether internal or external, are essential, for the New Law is one.

Moreover, the principal thing is served by the secondary thing in two ways: in its cause and in its effects. Although, from an ecclesiological perspective, the distinction between what is of the order of the causes of grace and what is of the order of the effects of grace is legitimate (the Church as means of salvation and the Church as reality of salvation), strictly speaking these two aspects are visible. The anti-Protestant dispute gave priority to the visibility of the causes and understood the effects of these causes solely as the mere possession of grace. This is very inadequate. The ultimate effect is not so much grace itself as the action of the subject under the influence of grace. In this regard the expression of St. Thomas is quite precise: "The New Law consists chiefly in *the grace of the Holy Ghost, which is shown forth by faith that worketh through love*" (*ST* I-II, q. 108, art. 1). This manifestation resides not only in internal acts, but also and necessarily in external acts.

In other words, the distinction between the Church as means of salvation and the Church as fruit of salvation does not espouse the distinction between the visible and the invisible elements in the Church, since the visible element is present in both aspects. This in no way diminishes the fact that the "heart" of the Church is grace, which as such is invisible, yet it is communicated visibly and inheres in the subject as a principle of moral action, and consequently as the source of human acts ("good works"), many of which are quite visible. This visibility prior to and subsequent to grace requires regulations (ceremonial and "judicial" precepts) that reinforce it, these regulations being a consequence of the fact that the human beings who receive grace and

---

12. About this vocabulary, especially insofar as the sacrament of holy orders is concerned, see de La Soujeole, "Les *tria munera Christi:* Contribution de S. Thomas à la recherche contemporaine," in *S. Thomas et le sacerdoce*, Actes du colloque de l'Institut Saint Thomas d'Aquin, *RT* 99 (1999): 70–72. Insofar as beatitude is concerned, see de La Soujeole, "Le débat sur le surnaturel et l'ecclésiologie contemporaine," *RT* 101 (2001): esp. 341–43.

act under its control live together. The social dimension of ecclesial life, which is part of its nature, augments this necessary visibility.

We see better now that ecclesial visibility is the visibility of grace itself, not in itself, but inasmuch as it is given in signs, and inasmuch as it renders the subject fruitful. The life of the theological virtues, as spiritual as it may be, involves essential visibility. This can be explained by the fact that grace does not exist in itself, but in order to be received in a subject for whom it is a principle of being and action. This is why the Church is visible in her members, in all her members. To clarify this point still further, this leads us to recall several fundamental points of anthropology.

c. Notes from anthropology

The concept of ecclesial visibility, as something that concerns both the means of grace and the effects of grace, presupposes a certain view of the human condition. Without entering into particular theological detail, we will limit ourselves here to general and fundamental statements of Christian anthropology as it is recalled in particular by the Constitution *Gaudium et spes*.

Man is a complex being made up of a spiritual soul and a body. The union of soul and body forms one being; it is a substantial union: "Man, though made of body and soul, is a unity. Through his very bodily condition he sums up in himself the elements of the material world. Through him they are brought to their highest perfection" (*GS* 14, §1). If man is truly one, then his corporeality, and hence his visibility, are not accidental, but essential. This is why we can say that man is *principally* spiritual, because man's soul is what is most important in him, and *secondarily* corporeal. These summary remarks already explain quite well the "nature" of the New Law. The New Law is principally internal because man is principally spiritual; it is secondarily external because man is secondarily corporeal. But in each instance the realities being contrasted are one, so that all that is external is ordered or subordinated to what is internal (*SC* 2). Strictly speaking, there is not something principal-spiritual-invisible on the one hand, and on the other hand something secondary-corporeal-visible, but rather a principal thing that manifests itself in the secondary thing, whatever it communicates, whatever it does.

This anthropology, which is per se accessible to natural wisdom, is

General Critique 401

particularly capable of explaining the theological data concerning salvation. Here we will have to look at the Christological foundations of our question.

d. Christological foundations

Another passage from St. Thomas significantly contains terminology similar to that in the questions on the New Law. We are referring to question 8, article 2, of the Third Part of the *Summa theologiae*. The question is formulated thus: Is Christ the Head of men as regards their bodies? The first objection to which St. Thomas replies is central to our topic (*ST* III, q. 8, art. 2, obj. 1).

> It would seem that Christ is not the Head of men as to their bodies. For Christ is said to be the Head of the Church inasmuch as He bestows spiritual sense and the movement of grace on the Church. But a body is not capable of this spiritual sense and movement. Therefore Christ is not the Head of men as regards their bodies.

If one concedes the objection, one must conclude that the corporeal realm eludes grace, or at least is only accidentally connected with it. In that case the Mystical Body would be essentially spiritual and would not be essentially visible per se. St. Thomas's reply in the *corpus* adduces two reasons to the contrary. The first is of an anthropological sort (the substantial unity of body and soul), and we presented it earlier. The second reason comes from Christology; it is linked to the first by reason of the assumption of a true human nature by the Savior (*ST* III, q. 8, art. 2, corpus):

> Hence the whole manhood of Christ, *i.e.* according to soul and body, influences all [human beings], both in soul and body; but *principally* the soul, and *secondarily* the body.

It is necessary to consider these matters in Christ and in the human beings whom he influences. In Christ, he is mediator according to his whole humanity. When he affects human beings it is not exclusively by the dispositions of his soul—in other words, by internal acts alone—but also by his actions and passions *in carne* [in the flesh]. Thus in the Passion it is clear that Christ suffered in his soul and in his body, and that by this set of acts Christ incorporates into himself human beings, soul and body. The influence of grace touches the soul *principally* and the body *secondarily*. This influence, which extends even to the body, is manifested in this world by virtuous acts. In the life of glory, after the resurrection of the body, this influence will be manifested also in the flesh, although in a way that is difficult to understand. We must, however, affirm this, because the substantial unity of body and soul will be reestablished.

It must be acknowledged that between Christology and the general anthropology that we have recalled there are very strong ties of fittingness that make it possible to grasp the essential visibility of the Church. Christology, ecclesiology, and anthropology are very closely related, and in our opinion this was what classical theology underestimated.

To sum up, we say consequently that the Church is necessarily visible through the human acts of her members, whether their acts cause grace in a certain way, or their acts are the expression of the grace that has been received. It is necessary now to consider some objections to the essential visibility of the Church that were made during the contemporary theological renewal. Answering them will allow us to explain in greater detail.

II. Modern objections

We have seen that the visible ecclesial element is twofold:

causes of grace—grace—*effects of grace*

In the fully formed Church, consequently, we have:

preaching of the faith, celebration of the sacraments—
grace—*works*

Since the Reformation considered only the visibility that precedes grace (rejecting works) and refused the idea of created mediation (the causes of grace), it therefore retained only the Church of grace—in other words, an invisible Church. The Catholic Counter-Reformation concentrated all ecclesial visibility in a position prior to grace, yet insisted on the created mediations of grace. The visible Church consists in the causes of grace, but since they can be supplied (by other means) or might not produce their effects in souls that are ill-disposed, theologians were led to separate it into two Churches, one visible and the other invisible. We do not share this way of looking at things: there is only one Church in which the visible element is both in the causes and in the effects of the invisible element. Let us look at possible objections.

a. The theme of *Ecclesia ab Abel*

It has been asserted that before the coming of Christ, since grace had not been given, there could be no visibility to the causes of grace. Because we speak about the Church present from the beginning, since Abel the just man, and because the visibility of the Church was being restricted to the visibility of the causes of grace, the conclusion was that the Church was not essentially visible. She has possessed a visible element from the time of Christ on, but it did not always exist. Since a thing must always have what is essential to it in order for it to exist, if the Church was alive without visibility, that tends to show that that visibility is not essential to her.

We think that the visibility of the Church is an essential feature, and consequently—since the Church existed from the time of Abel— we must look for her visible element from the very beginning of salvation history. For the sake of brevity, since the question is treated elsewhere,[13] before the coming of Christ the visibility of the Church was made up of everything that disposed mankind to the coming of Christ (prophetic preaching, prefigurative worship, kingship), the visible element prior to grace, and all the works accomplished in uprightness of heart, the visible element subsequent to grace.[14] This is valid for every age of the Church—the age of nature, the age of the promise, the age of the Law—before the coming of Christ. And this can be explained both by an anthropological reason, human nature, and also by a soteriological reason: it was a question of preparing mankind for the Savior to come who would be the Incarnate Word.

---

13. We refer the reader to our course on Catholic principles for interreligious dialogue; see in particular the ecclesiological part of the essay "Tout récapituler dans le Christ," *RT* 98 (1998): 606–23.

14. Of course here we are talking about grace disposing souls to Christ who *was to come*.

b. The transitory character of the economy of salvation

Even if one grants the essential visibility of the Church, with the qualifications just stated according to the different ages in salvation history, one may nevertheless make the following restriction: this visibility is conceivable only in this world. Indeed, the causes of grace have reasons for existing only in this world: they build up the Church, but the Church in heaven will be definitively completed. The means of grace will therefore disappear. The Church in glory is consequently an invisible reality. Now the Church on earth and the Church in heaven form one and only one Church, so that what is essential to the Church must be present in both of her states, *as something essential to each state*, and what is proper to the Church on earth is therefore accidental to the notion of Church.

This objection is strong, and it must be taken quite seriously. We must agree readily that the means of grace instituted by Christ (preaching, sacraments, pastoral ministry) will disappear when Christ returns in glory. They are not what is essential to the notion of Church; the essential thing, rather, is what they illustrate—namely, *the principle of mediation:* it is essential in the sense that God intended to proceed in that way, that the life of God comes to man through intermediaries and not immediately. Now this principle of mediation will not disappear in the Church in glory, but will be honored by the humanity of Christ. The mediation of this humanity is exercised in different ways depending on the state of the Church: through the institutions of Christ in this world, and by his glorified humanity in heaven. In other words, the Church is always formed, on earth as in heaven, by mediations. During the time of the pilgrim Church, these mediations signify and realize this mediation by Christ, but they signify also the eternal mediation of Christ in glory.[15] Hence the transitory character of earthly mediations does not make them secondary and accidental.

---

15. This statement seems to run counter to the immediacy of the beatific vision of the angels and the elect. But the eternity of Christ's priesthood must also be maintained; Ps 110:4, "You are a priest for ever"; Heb 9:11, Christ is "the high priest of the good things to come." St. Thomas resolves the question as follows (*ST* III, q. 22, art. 5): the purpose of Christ's sacrifice is so that the elect might obtain the beatific vision. Christ perfects the elect in glory by opening up for them the way to the vision of God;

There is, however, one important difference between the instituted mediations and the mediation of Christ in glory. In this world the instituted mediations are at the service of the Church's growth. In heaven the glorious mediation of Christ's humanity accomplishes not growth, but a full and permanent consummation. One property of the Church on earth is that it is something in a state of growing. That is why the instituted mediations are essential to it, although not definitive. In other words, it is essential to the Church in this world to be a living organism tending toward a fullness that is gradually attained. If, having arrived at its destination, at its full maturity, this organism ceases growing—and so it will be in the glorious Church at the end of time—that in no way diminishes the fact that it is a being that arrived gradually at its destination and that the service of the instituted mediations will have been a necessary cause of that progression.

Now, as for the visibility of the effects of grace, we note the following points: in this world the works, as we have already seen, involve most often a corporeal, visible element. In glory, since the body-soul unity will have been restored at the resurrection of the body, it must be admitted that the body will participate in its own way in beatitude. It will express, even better than here below, the dispositions of the soul, especially its joy. This is a reality that is difficult to conceptualize but about which there can be no doubt.

Conclusion

At the end of these discussions about ecclesial visibility, let us recall that when we speak about something *visible* we must distinguish it from something *seen*, because one can pass from one to the other only by faith. For example, an alms for a nonbeliever is an act of human solidarity, whereas for a believer it will be over and above that a manifes-

---

see Rv 21:23: the glory of God illumines the blessed and the Lamb is their lamp. Charles Journet summarizes this by saying, "The beatific vision and love of the angels and of the elect will plunge directly and *immediately* into the deity himself. However the power that will enable them to know God as he knows himself and to love him as he loves himself will continue to reach them *mediately*, by passing through the human nature of Christ, the eternal King of men and angels"; Journet, *L'Église du Verbe incarné*, 1:21. See also Jean-Pierre Torrell, "La vision de Dieu 'per essentiam' selon saint Thomas d'Aquin," *Micrologus* 5 (1997): 43–68 (esp. 64–66).

tation of the soul of the Church (charity) that only faith can recognize. This is what we have called the *epiphanic* status of visible Christianity.

This question of ecclesial visibility elucidates the question of ecclesial membership, and not vice versa as the Counter-Reformation thought:

- Membership is *full* when, in the members, the full visibility (of the causes as well as of the effects of grace) is connected to the invisible element (of grace). In other words, the full visibility presupposes participation in all the means of grace, and the performance of works, the effects of grace. Full membership is attainable in the community that possesses full visibility.
- There is a weakness of visibility when there is participation, but not in all the means of grace, and hence a diminished performance of the works, but in this case there can be real, albeit incomplete membership. The weakness of visibility affects primarily the means of grace in the separated Christian communities that have not preserved the Catholic fullness. But this weakness is found also in the effects of grace, because the full visibility of the effects is diminished in the communities that do not have the means of grace in their entirety. Indeed, what the good works should manifest is not only their principle, which is grace, but also the origin of this grace, which is Christ. The means of grace instituted by Christ in order to give his grace should not be considered in their effects alone but also as the sign of the cause, which is Christ in his humanity and his divinity. Thus every good work is ultimately a profession of God: "Let your light so shine before men, that they may see your good works and give glory to your Father who is in heaven" (Mt 5:16).

In order to answer objections (*Ecclesia ab Abel,* transitory economy of salvation), we have unceasingly distinguished between the visibility of the causes of grace and the visibility of the effects of grace. This distinction is important, but it should not be exaggerated. Indeed, one and the same act can express both aspects at the same time. The clearest example is pastoral activity. The multifarious work of pastors is illustrated in table 8-2.

But the fact that ordained ministers preach, celebrate, and govern

General Critique

TABLE 8-2

Pastoral Activity (as a Cause of Grace)		Temporal Relationship to Grace
• either disposes the faithful to grace (preaching)	⇒	the beginnings of grace
• or is an instrument of grace (the celebration of the sacraments)		
• or guides the life of grace that is received	⇨	what flows from grace

is an effect of the grace that they have received, especially in the sacrament of holy orders. This is their own way of expressing their faith operating by charity. Hence we see that pastoral acts are at the same time acts that cause faith in others and that express the grace received in the minister. In other words, the preaching of the faith, for example, is the primary way in which ordained ministers profess their faith. This point is important for priestly spirituality: performing their duties is for priests the genuine path by which to arrive at holiness.[16]

The same should be said about the lay faithful. The life of grace in them is externalized through acts that should aim to transmit grace by various causalities. This is the twentieth-century rediscovery of the lay apostolate. All the faithful share in the spread of the Gospel, not primarily through "delegation by the hierarchy" (the "clericalization" of the laity), but by virtue of their baptism.[17] Moreover, we must recall that the celebration of a sacrament involves two aspects: an aspect of cause, which is the sign of the grace that is given, and an aspect of effect, which is an act of religion that expresses the life of the theological virtues.[18]

Thus the cooperation of the faithful *as a whole*, laity as well as clergy, brings about ecclesial visibility. It is clear that we cannot limit our sights to hierarchical activity alone, as Bellarmine did.

16. Cf. *Lumen gentium* 41 and *Presbyterorum ordinis* 13.
17. *Apostolicam actuositatem* 3.
18. In the writings of St. Thomas these two aspects are neatly distinguished, particularly with regard to the sacraments. The cause aspect is studied in *ST* III, q. 62ff. (the sacraments as acts of Christ and of the Church) and the effect aspect in *ST* II-II, q. 89 (the sacraments as acts of religion performed by the faithful).

Bibliography

Congar, Yves. "Ecclesia ab Abel." In *Abhandlungen über Theologie und Kirche*. Festschrift für Karl Adam. Düsseldorf: 1952, 79–108.

———. *Le Christ, Marie et l'Église*. Paris: 1952, 39ff.; *Christ, Our Lady and the Church: A Study in Eirenic Theology*. London and New York: Longmans, Green, 1957, 43ff.

———. *The Mystery of the Church*. Rev. trans. Baltimore and Dublin: Helicon Press, 1965, 71ff.

de La Soujeole, Benoît-Dominique. *Le Sacrement de la communion: Essai d'ecclésiologie fondamentale*. Paris-Fribourg: 1998, esp. 162–79.

———. "Le débat sur le surnaturel et l'ecclésiologie contemporaine." *RT* 101 (2001): 329–44.

Hamer, J. *The Church Is a Communion*. New York: Sheed and Ward, 1964, 83–96.

Journet, Charles. *L'Église du Verbe incarné*. Vol. 1, *"La hiérarchie apostolique."* 3rd ed. Paris: 1962, 20ff. English edition, *The Church of the Incarnate Word*, translated by Victor Szczurek, O. Praem. San Francisco: Ignatius Press, 2004, 16ff.

9

The Intellectual Method

After our observations on the essential visibility of the Church, we can now already say that the distinction between external-visible and internal-invisible cannot be accepted as such, because there are a prior visibility and a subsequent visibility that frame the invisible element. The paradigm has three terms and not two: the invisible element is central as the end of the visible element prior to it and as the principle of the visible element that comes after it. But we must go further and inquire now in even greater depth into this "binary" way of considering the Church and bring to light the usually implicit presuppositions of this sort of presentation.

"Binomial thinking," as we suggest that it should be called, is very widespread these days. Knowing that the Church is a complex being, consequently made up of diverse elements, theologians in the twentieth century had two ways of expressing this:

- Either two elements "normally combined," but in fact separable (cf. Bellarmine and his followers). To this Vatican II replied: *one complex reality* (*LG* 8, §1).
- Or else two elements, two poles "in tension." This latter way is predominant today, and this is the one that we will analyze.

I. The common binomial method of exposition

a. The example of Fr. Congar

Fr. Congar starts from a Christological consideration:

There were things that depended on Christ as God, and others that depended on him as man, although he was both (and because he was both one *and* the other). Similarly there are things that are part of the Church inasmuch as she is already really the family of God and the community of heavenly life, and others that are part of the Church inasmuch as she is engaged in a journey and a battle far from the Lord and is being realized humanly and in a way suited to *our* world as the Church Militant.[1]

On the basis of this consideration, Fr. Congar draws up table 9-1, which divides the following elements into two distinct columns:

TABLE 9-1

1. The *simple* divine unity	1. *Complex social unity; orderly unity* of a multitude by *consensus* and organized collaboration.
2. An *organism*.	2. An *organization*.
3. *Members* of a living body animated by *faith* and *love*.	3. *Authority and subject* in a society of spiritual life involving *commands* and *obedience*.
4. *A hierarchy of holiness and virtue*; each member *has value according to what he is*; personal and moral order. What counts is the *spirit*.	4. *A strictly social hierarchy, according to functions*; each member *has value according to what he represents* and sustains of the common good. Objective order of a juridical sort. What counts is *the commission*.
5. *Christ is the only Head*, and those who cooperate in the gift that Christ makes of His life do so *instrumentally* (power of order).	5. Christ is Head, but the Church acts by herself and in a sovereign manner, not instrumentally (power of jurisdiction).
6. The Church *has neither extension nor division*; she is a living organism.	6. The Church has *quantitative extension in the world and distinct parts*.
7. The Church is a body *in the vital sense of the word*.	7. The Church is a body *in the sociological and legal sense of the word*.
8. The Church exists and *will exist eternally* because she lives with an eternal life.	8. The Church on earth is in time, for the gathering together and formation of the members of Christ. She will cease to be as such. She will give way to the Kingdom, just as prophecy and faith give way to the beatific vision.

---

1. Yves Congar, *Chrétiens désunis*, 95–96 [translated from French]; *Divided Christendom* summarizes at 75–76.

The Intellectual Method

This table has the advantage of being extremely clear. It presents the Church in terms of two poles, the first being the "divine" pole and the second the "human" pole. However, this is not very rigorous. For although the Christological model presents to us two *natures* in Christ —being God is not the same thing as being man—we cannot say the same for the Church: she has only one *nature,* human nature, *graced nature.* This manner of thinking "binomially" (structure and life, society-communion, organism-organization) developed gradually, starting in the 1920s, and little by little became "established" in the 1950s. Since Vatican II it has become a common way of presenting the subject. It has, so to speak, replaced the ecclesiology of the body and soul of the Church in the Bellarminian tradition, which is all too clearly not in conformity with the remarks in *Lumen gentium* 8, §1. We will try to show here the historical and philosophical presuppositions of this phenomenon.

b. The historical and philosophical presuppositions
1. The historical reasons

Over the course of the 1920s, the doctrine of the Mystical Body returned to the forefront in ecclesiology. Almost immediately the first binomials appeared, such as Church-Mystical Body (Fr. Mersch), organism-organization (Fr. Congar), society-communion. In order to understand this phenomenon, we must observe how the ecclesiological renewal came about. In the early 1920s, the authors gradually became aware of the fact that in the ecclesiological teaching then—especially in the manuals—they were confronting a very strong overemphasis of the societal aspect of the Church, which was understood above all as a hierarchically and juridically structured whole.[2] This was the so-called ecclesiology of the *societas perfecta inaequalis,* the history of which was painstakingly presented by Fr. Congar.[3] This doctrine had been developed very deliberately by the theologians and clearly adopted by the Magisterium.[4] The

---

2. We recommend saying "*societal* aspect," meaning a hierarchy presented juridically as separate from the faithful, which must not be confused with the *social* aspect: the people of God as a whole forming a community that is understood by way of analogy with civil society.

3. Yves Congar, "L'ecclésiologie de la Révolution française au concile du Vatican sous le signe de l'affirmation de l'autorité," in *L'Ecclésiologie au XIXe siècle,* US 34 (Paris: 1960), 77–113.

4. See the citations of Fr. Congar in the study cited in the preceding note, as well

ecclesiological renewal, reinforced by elements that it went on to rediscover through advances in exegesis and patristics in particular, then endeavored to establish a new equilibrium: although the Church is indeed a hierarchical society, she is not only that.

In itself, the undertaking was necessary and even urgent because of the birth of the ecumenical movement among the separated brethren. It was even salutary, so that ecclesiology might move on definitively from apologetics to dogmatic theology. But the reaction against this "juridico-apologetic" tendency ran the risk of being no more accurate than it had been; it was in danger of overshooting the mark and even of compromising its purpose by drifting into the idea of a purely spiritual Church. In order to avoid that, it seems that theologians generally accepted the idea that the Church is a perfect society of unequals *in the sense of public ecclesiastical law*, but in order to limit the extent of this juridical element they appealed to something more spiritual, more interior. The emphasis was then placed on something transcendent in the society, on love and life. Therefore, scholars continued to accept the idea of a juridical Church that is imposed from without: that is essentially power and authority, constraint and obedience, setting up legal frameworks in what is per se and most profoundly grace, freedom, equality.... The two aspects together form the Church, but they may not correspond exactly.[5]

To sum up, the attitude that the ecclesiological renewal took is as follows: it was about a reaction against an exaggeration. It was necessary to promote the interior-spiritual element of the Church without separating it from the external-juridical element. That gave rise to the binomials.

Yet this attitude has one major weakness: it reacts against an idea of the Church *without rethinking the Church*. There was no reform of

---

as those in another study, *Le Concile de Vatican II: Son Église: Peuple de Dieu et Corps du Christ*, coll. Théologie historique 71 (Paris: 1984), 8–14, esp. 13. It must be emphasized—something Fr. Congar omits to mention—that these magisterial citations come from *national* encyclicals or from letters addressed to particular bishops. The context is the rise of the liberal and laicist movement that disputed the Church's claim to be independent of the State. In the papal teachings addressed to the whole Church (for example, Leo XIII, Encyclicals *Satis cognitum* and *Immortale Dei*), the doctrine presented is fuller and more directly theological, especially that of the Mystical Body.

5. We have seen, in particular, how Fr. Mersch distinguished *Church* from *Mystical Body*.

The Intellectual Method 413

the Bellarminian societal concept, which remained as it was, with just some supplementary elements added to complete and rebalance it. It is striking to see that all the ecclesiological themes that were rediscovered (Mystical Body, People of God, Sacrament, Communion) were coupled with the societal vision (*society* [juridical society]—*communion* [spiritual reality], for example) or else incorporated it (*sacramentum tantum* [juridical society]—*res sacramenti* [spiritual reality], for example). This is the risk that one runs when rediscoveries and new ideas do not lead to *rethinking the whole matter:* one tries to do away with one excess, but opens the door to the opposite excess. In speaking about the Church, which is a complex entity, it is easy to emphasize one aspect to the point of losing sight of another; this is no improvement and, ultimately, the same fundamental error is being committed: no longer seeing the bond that unites the complexity.

The Encyclical *Mystici Corporis*, as dependent as it was on the status of the ecclesiological renewal at that time (1943), nevertheless had proceeded in an altogether different way. Whatever its limitations, as a matter of methodology it had intended to *rethink ecclesiology as a whole*, and this is why it does not proceed by means of any binomial, but rather takes up the theme of the Mystical Body so as to present all the aspects of the Church, from the most "external-visible" to the most "internal-invisible," thus manifesting from the outset the unity of the various aspects that make up the mystery.

Not beginning *the whole question* over again leads to false problems, such as "how to balance social constraint and individual spontaneity?" or "how to articulate what comes from above (the hierarchical element) and what comes from below (the popular element)?" This way of proceeding by add-ons, which are supposed to "rebalance" the paradigm, results in inextricably tangled thought because it does not allow one to see *the fundamental unity* of which the various elements are only aspects.

What we have just stressed is in the first place *a fact* that seems to us well established. But this fact gradually found more and more profound justifications, especially of a philosophical sort.

2. The philosophical reasons

The birth of the "sense of history"

The nineteenth and twentieth centuries were marked by the emergence of interest in the historical dimension of human realities. The progressive acquisition of a certain "sense of history" would remain one of the fundamental characteristics of the modern mind that was formed during that era. From this perspective, consideration of the fact of religion was enriched by new inquiries that were increasingly to define the way of approaching and thinking about Christianity. People began asking questions that were unheard of previously: how did Christianity arise? Here nascent exegesis found material for ever more learned studies. This question called for another: why did this religion prevail? And so we come to this question: what is the essence of Christianity? Study of the origins and development of the Christian religion was one of the great central interests in that period. This general movement, which affected both Protestant and Catholic scholars, prepared the way for the contemporary ecclesiological renewal. However "technical" they may have been, these studies, which were initially historical and exegetical, could not free themselves from more philosophic sorts of references that are always necessary in interpreting new empirical data.

The idea of "life" was at the heart of all these investigations concerning the birth, development, and persistence of Christianity. Depending on the meaning that one assigned to this notion of "life," one could add one's own concept of the knowledge that it is possible to have about that life. One's epistemology, its object and methods, necessarily contributed toward one's definition of the subject of study and one's evaluation of the findings. This is what we must explain now.

A philosophy of "life"

There are some words that are not easy to define simply, however trivially they may be used. This is certainly the case with the word "life": what is life?

The connotation traditionally accepted in the early nineteenth century was Aristotle's, as it had been adopted by St. Thomas.[6] The latter

---

6. Cf. *Summa theologiae* I, q. 18: *De vita Dei;* the prologue announces that article 2 will answer the question *Quid sit vita?* In fact article 2 is entitled *Utrum vita sit quaedam operatio?* [Whether life is an operation?].

teaches that the word "life" can be understood in the proper sense and in a derived sense. The name "life" signifies precisely:

> a *substance* to which self-movement and the application of itself to any kind of operation, belong naturally. To live, accordingly, is nothing else than to exist in this or that nature; and life signifies this, though in the abstract, just as the word "running" denotes "to run" in the abstract. Hence "living" is not an accidental but an essential predicate.

Sometimes, however, "life" is used less properly for the *operations* from which its name is taken, and thus the Philosopher says (*Ethica Nicomachea* IX, 9) that to live is principally to sense or to understand.

Therefore the word "life" designates, first of all and properly speaking, a being inasmuch as it is capable of self-movement. Pursuant to the major types of characteristic movement observed in living things, they can be classified according to their activities. In a broader sense, "life" is predicated of the operations themselves and not directly of the being that is the substrate of those operations. We therefore distinguish between "life" inasmuch as it is the self-moving being—and this points to its principle that is the soul—and "life" inasmuch as it announces its presence in a being by its acts.

Now it is significant to note that in the nineteenth century the connotation of the word "life" was restricted and expressed only the perceptible acts of the subject:

> The principal use of this term is to express generically *the whole set of phenomena that distinguish organisms from inert matter*: reproduction, nutrition, growth, decay, to which can be added still more distinctive phenomena like autonomy in motion and sensory perception.[7]

Reflection on the findings of the sciences henceforth called "biological" (the word dates from the early nineteenth century) led to a concept of life as a *dynamic phenomenon by which a subject develops according to an internal plan that implements a set of forces and organs*. This formulation is within the framework of the so-called *vitalist* or *organicist* philosophies. Whatever the specific nuances of each School may be, the idea of a certain permanence inscribed within the subject itself (the common idea of its "nature") gives way to the idea of *progression:* life is

---

7. François Duchesneau, "Vie," in *Les notions philosophiques: Dictionnaire*, ed. Sylvain Auroux, vol. 2 of *Encyclopédie philosophique universelle*, edited by André Jacob, 2: (Paris: Presses universitaires de France, 1990), 2:2730.

what develops in and of itself. We find here, in particular for the subject that we are dealing with, the whole Romantic movement, which is of the organicist type; every being is thought of after the fashion of the living organism. Thus, for example, political society is no longer considered as subsisting in the individual persons who make it up, but rather as an organism having its own reason for being, after the model of the individual. Organized social bodies acquire the attributes of individuality, such as autonomy, systematic unity and self-direction (*autotélie*, the fact of bestowing its own purpose on itself). Thus life creates for itself the organs that it needs. We have a still-relevant illustration of this perception in an exegesis of St. Paul. Some biblical scholars think that the pastoral letters (Timothy, Titus), which deal with institutions of the first Christian communities, are ipso facto necessarily later than the major letters (Corinthians, Romans), which consider the life of grace: the "organs" follow the requirements of life.[8] More precisely, the "life"—in other words, the development of the being, occurs in a certain interpenetration of contraries. The "life" of organisms shows the work of progressively giving birth to themselves, in which all the intense activity is aimed at avoiding excesses and moving always under the influence of the "vital force." Thus Johann-Adam Möhler, the great theologian from Tübingen, declares, when speaking about this particular living thing that is the Church:

> True life consists only in the penetration of that which opposes it.... A true antithesis exists only in relation to another [thesis] against which it is set in one and the same [thing], and thus unity is necessary in both.[9]

This is applied to the Church as follows:

> Catholicism is alive because, like life itself, it moves between opposed contraries. Heresy is the cause of spiritual death because it pins down one of the aspects of Christian life and separates it from the whole organism.[10]

The ecclesiological renewal was very dependent on this vitalist vision:

---

8. This dating of St. Paul's letters, however, has been criticized from the strictly exegetical point of view; see H. Ponsot, "Les pastorales seraient-elles les premières lettres de S. Paul?," *Lumière et Vie* 231 (1997): 83ff.; and *Lumière et Vie* 232 (1997): 79ff.
9. Johann-Adam Möhler, *Unity in the Church*, 196.
10. E. Vermeil, *J. A. Moehler ou l'École catholique de Tubingue*, 35.

The Intellectual Method 417

(In Möhler's writings) we touch the very foundation of the Romantic ideology. The secret of all life is the interpenetration of contraries. If the absence of diversity is the cause of monotony and stagnation, the absence of unity is the cause of anarchy. Normal life implies the reconciliation of the principles of systole and diastole. One will beware therefore of confusing "opposition" (i.e., contrariness) and "contradiction." The various elements of an organism are opposed while mutually complementing one another. The Church will unite in her bosom Christian idealism and realism, mysticism and speculation, in short all the "oppositions" possible in religious life. Only divisive heresy introduces a fatal contradiction. Any element separated from the organism devours its own substance and dies.[11]

Although Romanticism as a literary and artistic movement ceased toward the end of the nineteenth century, it nevertheless stayed very much alive in theology. Its influence was considerable, especially in Germany. Thus, for example, between the two World Wars, Arnold Rademacher discerned a veritable "vital law" of being:

The law of tension is the key to a most fruitful outlook upon earthly things. The duality of being pervades the entire organisation of the world. In the state of primal chaos there was no unity whatsoever, while at the end of the world everything will have been restored to a state of unity. In its progress from one of these termini to the other, however, the world is governed by the basic law of duality of matter and form, flesh and spirit, male and female, idea and phenomenon, and countless other realities which are related to one another. In each case the tension between the opposing terms is a principle of being and development. It is the way which leads to unity; we can see therefore that Monism contains this one element of truth. This law of polarity is the law which regulates the universe and all of human life, the law by which two things are mutually impelled towards each other and strive to become one, just as in marriage man and wife become "one flesh" (Gn 2:24), and just as, in the kingdom of God, "there is neither Jew nor Greek, slave nor free, male nor female, all are one in Christ" (Gal 3:29). The final end of all development, complete perfection, consists in the cessation of duality ceases and its giving way to unity.[12]

The author develops this paradigm without footnotes or references or justifying arguments: it goes without saying based on the observation of phenomena. The perceptions of nineteenth-century Roman-

---

11. E. Vermeil, *J. A. Moehler ou l'École catholique*, 60.
12. Arnold Rademacher, *Religion und Leben*, 2nd ed. (Freiburg-im-Breisgau: 1925), 22–23; *Religion and Life* (Westminster, Md.: Newman Press, 1962), 25–26.

ticism become here veritable "basic laws" with bearing on "earthly things" as a whole. The paradigm is therefore applied to the Church:

> There is a conflict in the Church between community and society. Originally this was scarcely adverted to at all; there was a state of equilibrium between the two, and their content and form were accommodated to each other. As the organism grew, however, conflicts arose, making it necessary for the moral precepts, dogmas and canon laws of the Church to be formulated.... The law of tension operates in the same way in respect of the mutual relations between tradition and progress, dogma and research, State and Church, authority and freedom....
>
> The ideal goal is always that of equilibrium between opposites. But in order to arrive at this goal, there must be a continual interplay between the opposing forces. The goal of all tensions is repose; but this repose lies in infinity.[13]

What was in Möhler only an intuition guided by a Romantic movement that was just starting and that indisputably fostered a *ressourcement* [return to the sources] of ecclesiology becomes here a "system" with all-encompassing claims. The central notion is that of *tension*. Tension constitutes the being itself, or rather its "life." Something that is growth, development, and progress can exist only in conflict, battle, or tension with what is static and conservative. The one calls for the other as its necessary complement in order to tend to actualize the "life" of the being. The poles that mark off "the space" in which "life" moves are clearly antinomic: living organism/juridical organization. But, it must be clearly understood, these poles do not have the same value. In a philosophy of life, development, and progress, the dynamic, innovative pole is richer, more highly valued than the static, conservative pole. This antagonism between a richer reality and a poorer reality is the very reason for the tension between the two.

However it may be with these perceptions—which are certainly new in theology—it must be emphasized that, despite the frequent assertions along these line, this is not a teaching about the unity of the constitutive elements of the being that is under consideration. For at the end of the history of the subject, at the parousia in the case of the Church, perfect life, the achievement of lasting unity will be attained *not* by bringing about harmony between the two poles, but by *suppress-*

---

13. Rademacher, *Religion und Leben*, 27; *Religion and Life*, 28–29.

The Intellectual Method 419

ing one or both of the poles: the institution will disappear so as to leave only the communion, or else faith and dogma will disappear so as to give way to vision.

This mode of exposition is still very much in use, as we already showed. Here are two more recent examples:

> The ideal of this communion is not harmony without tension. All life moves in tension, as J. A. Möhler showed;[14] where tension ends there is death. And we have no desire for a dead church. We want a living one![15]

> We must start here from the ecclesiological principle that the Church is *by its very nature* a "*complexio oppositorum*" and that tensions are *naturally* innate in it.[16]

The most important thing to remember is the concept of unity that is conveyed by this manner of exposition. Since Vatican II it has been a question of accounting for the remark in *Lumen gentium* 8, §1 ("*unam realitatem complexam*"), and so unity here is perceived not as a given characteristic of the being, but either as a sort of equilibrium to be reached between two antagonistic poles (the society is what is not the communion; the conservative element is what is not progressive), or else as a sort of overcoming of a duality of opposed elements (faith and dogma transcended in vision). However it may be, this type of unity is, so to speak, produced here below in the more or less near term in a manner that is always precarious.

This concept, which originated in the nineteenth century, is truly a novelty. One would look for it in vain in the writings of the Scholastics and in classical theology, much less in Scripture and in the Church Fathers. It suffers from a lack of clarity. At its starting point, in the writings of Möhler, we still find a perception of the harmonious unity of a complex whole, of course in a renovated form—the language of "life." The Master from Tübingen clearly distinguishes *contradictory features*, which are mutually exclusive, from *contraries*, which are in the same ge-

---

14. We would rather say "asserted," since Möhler did not justify his assertions.
15. Walter Kasper, "Church as 'Communio,'" *Communio* (English edition) 13, no. 2 (1986): 100–17. This article is a simplified version of the essay "The Church as Communion," in *Theology and Church* (New York: Crossroad, 1989), 148–65, citation at 163.
16. A. Anton, "Postconciliar Ecclesiology: Expectations, Results, and Prospects for the Future," in *Vatican II: Assessment and Perspectives; Twenty-five Years After* (1962–1987) (New York: Paulist Press, 1988), 407–38, citation at 421.

nus and can be compared, one of which is not the negation of the other, and hence the two contraries can cooperate to form the unity of the subject (complementary relation). In Möhler's writing, the relation of contrariness expresses *diversity* and not conflict. In his case there are not several realities; one remains within the framework of *a complex whole*. But after him writers move on to the idea of a *tension* between realities that *sets them against each other* in a veritable *dualism* that is not reabsorbed into unity but, at best, exists in a precarious equilibrium. This development is dependent on even more fundamental philosophical influences than that of the Romantic movement. This is very rarely pointed out and critiqued. We must consider this now.

Philosophy of knowledge, philosophy of the real

At the same time that the "vitalist" current of philosophy was developing, two philosophical influences were developing in the nineteenth century that are extremely important in understanding the modern world; we mean the influence of Kant and Hegel. What these two authors have in common is that for them the thought of an object, on the part of someone who uses his intellect, somehow makes it what it is. The idea in the mind of the thinking subject is more real and objective than the object itself. This current is called *modern idealism*. Thus a whole epistemology is at stake from the outset.

Kant's philosophy of knowledge proposes two major assertions regarding the question that we are dealing with: how do we know? And what do we know? These two points are closely connected in the following way: to know, for Kant, is to apply to a sensible datum the *a priori forms* of sensibility, to pursue this investigation by means of the principles and categories of understanding, and to arrive finally at the resolution through reason, which provides the concept. To put it more simply, to know is to project the *a priori mental forms* of reason onto the object, to apply to the object a "grid" preconceived in the intellect. "We only cognize in things *a priori* that which we ourselves place into them."[17] This way of knowing is, in this regard, the contrary of what is determined by classical realism, in which abstraction makes the object

---

17. Immanuel Kant, *Critique of Pure Reason*, preface to the second edition, translated by J. M. D. Meiklejohn (Chicago: Encyclopedia Britannica, 1990), 39:5ff. [1952, 42:5ff.].

penetrate somehow into the mind. Here the mind projects itself into the object. Kant clearly notes that knowledge cannot pretend to embrace all the aspects of the object being considered. It is appropriate therefore to distinguish in the object between the *phenomenon* (what is knowable about the object) and the *noumenon* (what remains unknowable about the object). Reality is thus divided, in each object of knowledge, between the *rational* and the *irrational*, between what reason itself can grasp and what will always elude it.

Kant maintained that reality is vaster than what one can know about it. In this respect there is still a remnant of realism in his philosophy. Hegel, though, purely and simply identifies the object thus known with the reality, and he takes this identity so strictly that he attributes to the object under consideration the *contradictions* that he admits in thought. With Hegel, logic (the rules of reasoning) is what replaces metaphysics. Once the idea is more real and objective than the object itself, all the logical "games" of which the mind is capable are games played by the object itself. Thus, for example, one can say that "what is equal is that which is not unequal." If we understand this proposition in the logical sense, which is not based on reality but on concepts, it can make sense: the definition of a state (being equal) includes the exclusion of another state (being unequal); therefore—*logically*—this excluded thing is included in the definition, since the latter negates it. Another example: what is identical is that which is not different (difference is included in what is identical): the first concept necessarily contains the second because it negates it. Thus within the object itself is set up a dialectic of contradictories: a relationship of negation is posited in the being; it is even constitutive of the being, and it engenders movement and conflict, which are its "life."[18]

Thus, as Hegelian thought spread, a form of thinking by means of the dialectic of opposition developed.[19] This did not fail to have an influence in theology. An explicit reference to Hegel is very rare in the writings of theologians, but it is not difficult to discover his influence.

---

18. For the thought of Hegel, see in particular *The Science of Logic* (London: Allen and Unwin; New York: Humanities Press, 1929) (esp. the long introduction); see also, on the point that we are emphasizing (the dialectic of contradictories), R. Verneaux, "La catégorie hégélienne de contradiction," *Sapientia* 26 (1971): 369–88.

19. Perhaps the consummate example, in political philosophy, is Marxism.

Thus, as far as the simultaneously historical and eschatological character of the Church is concerned, one frequently reads biblical scholars who say that there is here a *complexio oppositorum* in which is manifested a *tension* between the "already" and the "not yet." This can be understood in at least two ways, in the first place as a form of contradiction that Hegel calls "tendency."[20] The tendency expresses the fact that one and the same thing is at the same time itself and the lack of itself, a lack understood as the "negative of itself." In that case there is a relationship of contradiction in the object itself. But one can propose another interpretation that is not based on an internal contradiction in the object. In this case one will say that the Church possesses a perfection to a certain degree (the "already"), but that she lacks this perfection to a greater degree (the "not yet"). Here there is no relationship of contradiction, but rather a relationship of *potency to act that is gradually attained*. Specifically, one will say that the Church is the eschatological Kingdom in its pilgrim state, which is a state of *growth* toward a completed perfection that will be the end of its history. Incidentally this is how we spontaneously understand the "already" and "not yet."

For our discussion this is what must be remembered: in this way of apprehending the object, everything starts with the thought; thought apprehends its object in a dialectical way, *and consequently* the object is dialectical in itself. The *concept* of the object becomes the *reality* of the object.

We see now the discernment that must be made. In making it we will proceed in two phases; first we will see whether Vatican II adopted this view of things, and then we will propose several conclusions on this subject.

II. Conciliar data for a discernment

An ecumenical council is certainly not an academy of theology, and the magisterial assembly always claims to be free with regard to philosophical schools. Even though it has recourse to one or another finding of a school, it never canonizes any one as such. There is meanwhile

---

20. *The Science of Logic*, I, II [sect. 1], chap. 2. See *Hegel's Science of Logic*, translated by W. H. Johnston and L. G. Struthers (London: Allen and Unwin; New York: Humanities Press, 1929), 2:66–70. [Or maybe 2:128–29 (vol. I, bk. II, sect. 2, chap. 2)].

in the way of presenting the teaching a note of prudence and wisdom on which the reliability of the theological proceeding depends in some way. This is what we intend to bring to light.

a. Indications from the vocabulary of Vatican II

The form of thought that we call "binomial" uses a certain number of key words that can easily be listed. Furthermore, we must consider the subject matters that lend themselves more particularly to this vocabulary, but that we could find presented without it.

At the level of vocabulary, it is simple to verify:[21] the words *tension, to tend, dialectic, opposition, opposed, contrary, contradiction, contradict, antinomy, thesis, antithesis, synthesis* are never used by the Council in their Hegelian sense. These words are taken in their everyday sense. They never express a constitutive internal opposition of the object, but sometimes signify, in human realities, opposition of a *moral* and not ontological nature that can affect a being. In short, Vatican II thinks of things in terms of unity, harmony, complementarity; it realistically underscores the tensions that can be observed thanks to a theology of sin; it recalls the constant of "life," which is growth in terms of development.

At the level of the content taught by the Council, we can recall two subjects that are most important for our topic: the declaration of the unity of the ecclesial being and the relation between nature and grace.

In speaking about the unity of the ecclesial being, the Council does not take up any of the binomials that we have noticed in the history of the theological renewal, and those that have been used since Vatican II are not present in the conciliar teaching. The most decisive reference to this subject is the one in *Lumen gentium* 8, §1: "*unam realitatem complexam.*" The adjective *complexa* is derived from the verb *complector*, which means "to embrace, unite, join." To put it differently, the Council declares the unity of the ecclesial being by specifying that it is not a question of a "monolithic" being (i.e., one that is simple in metaphysical terms), but rather "complex"—in other words, composed of several elements, but profoundly one and not divided in itself. God and man are beings that are one, but God is simply one (no composition in

---

21. For a more extended review, see de La Soujeole, *Le Sacrement de la communion*, 211ff.

him), whereas man is one in a complex way (he is composed of a soul and a body).

b. The relationship between nature and grace

The binomials that we have noticed in contemporary ecclesiology often express a relational mode between nature and grace. To put it briefly, to say that the Church is a juridical society and a supernatural communion, for example, often means that the Church combines a fact of the natural order (society) and a fact of the supernatural order (communion). What then is the relationship between nature and grace at Vatican II?[22]

Although the Council did not directly teach any doctrine on this subject, it should be noted that many times certain discussions by the Council presuppose a view of this relation. We should recall in particular:

> The fact that it is the same God who is at once saviour and creator, Lord of human history and of the history of salvation, does not mean that the autonomy of the creature, of man in particular, is suppressed; on the contrary, in the divine order of things all this redounds to the restoration and consolidation of this autonomy. (*GS* 41)

Note the expression: *the divine order of things*. The plan of creation and the plan of redemption are not two orders, but only one, which is the plan for elevating nature by grace. One could just as well say that grace could not maintain with nature a relationship of tension in the dialectical sense; on the contrary, grace gives to nature its full dignity. Grace not only restores wounded nature, but elevates it. Grace, in other words, is a certain (restored and elevated) state of nature. Man has only one vocation: to be "deified." The Constitution *Gaudium et spes* expresses it neatly in paragraph 22: this is a matter of *the one divine vocation* of man. E. Michelin puts it this way:

> The expression *vocatio divina* performs, from man's point of view, the role that the expression *ordo divinum* plays from God's perspective: without calling the distinction between these plans into question, it underscores their unity in a concrete human being.

---

22. For further developments of this point, the reader may refer to the precise study by E. Michelin, *Vatican II et le surnaturel*; see also de La Soujeole, *Le Sacrement de la communion*, 223ff., and "Le débat sur le surnaturel et l'ecclésiologie contemporaine," *RT* 101 (2001): 329–44.

At this point the whole mystery of the economy of salvation is summed up in two statements. On the one hand it is the unity of the divine plan, which is expressed in history according to two realizations that are clearly distinguished yet never separate, the creative action and the salvific action, which both have as their origin love in its source. On the other hand, it is the uniqueness of man's vocation, a divine vocation that will be unfolded over the history of humanity, marked by original sin which, instigating division in man and among men, calls for salvation.[23]

Here we have extremely important clarifications. The relation between nature and grace is not a binomial relation in the sense that there are two realities that are interrelated, however closely. This is about one and only one reality: graced nature. If we want to distinguish within the Church the natural society and the supernatural communion, for example, we must consequently say that it is not a question of two realities in relation, but of only one complex reality.

Having arrived at this point of our critical analysis of binomial thinking, we must propose clarifications that in our view appear necessary; these will determine the very basis for our ecclesiological proposal.

III. Proposed clarifications

The clarifications that we propose here concern first of all the more philosophical bases that are indispensable to a theological presentation. Then we will complete the picture with a few theological specifications.

a. Philosophical clarifications

Pointing out a vocabulary and a certain way of presenting things should not lead to quarrels about terminology, nor does it necessarily prove a clear-cut philosophical dependence. We have to go deeper and engage the real questions. To that end, the first clarification that seems important to us is one about dialectic: when we speak about "dialectic," or when we present a "binomial in tension," what precisely does that mean?

---

23. E. Michelin, *Vatican II et le surnaturel*, 321–13.

1. Dialectic of knowledge, dialectic of the real

When we say that in ecclesiology there is a *fundamental dialectic between two poles*, what is meant by that? One example, selected from among many others, allows us to grasp the question quite precisely:

> The dynamics of the opposition between the socio-juridical, abstract and apologetic ecclesiology that was prevalent since the time of the counter-Reformation and the new ecclesiology, rooted in Scripture and the Fathers, historical and concerned with communion, which eventually prevailed in the Council, did not make the synthesis hoped for possible. We must acknowledge [that] the ecclesiology of Vatican II, as to which it would admittedly be premature to make any judgment, presents a certain *juxtaposition* of both ecclesiological trends, as can be easily seen by comparing the first two chapters of *Lumen gentium* (1 and 2) with the second two (3 and 4).[24]

However, the Council's difficult research work is the sign of a deeper duality that affects the very object that it is striving to know:

> The present relationship between the *dynamic* reality and the *social* reality of this *"koinonia"* is a continual source of *tensions* in ecclesiological doctrine and *in ecclesial life itself* (emphasis added). In ecclesiological terminology, we make a distinction between these two aspects and refer to the former favoring the term *communion,* and to the latter the term *community.* In the theology of the church, however, monistic solutions are unacceptable.[25]

These two citations, which follow each other in this precise order and in the same discussion, allow us to observe in this author two dialectics that are formally distinct, yet connected. There is, on the one hand, so to speak, a dialectic *of the knowledge* of the object and, on the other hand, a dialectic *posited in the object itself*—consequently, a dialectic of the real.

The dialectic of knowledge has a long pedigree going back to the *Topics* of Aristotle. It is the art of dialogue whereby, through a comparison of various opinions, observations, and proofs, the mind proceeds from the probable and the plausible toward the true. Above all it is about proving by disputation—in the medieval sense of the word— a given fact so as to grasp its intelligibility more profoundly. This quest is carried out, in particular, by the work of distinguishing the differ-

24. A. Anton, "Postconciliar Ecclesiology," 415.
25. Anton, "Postconciliar Ecclesiology," 417.

ent aspects of the question so as not to confuse and mix up the various points of view. The argumentation thus follows an order of division (or analysis). Once brought to its conclusion, this first phase of analysis gives way to a so-called order of composition (or synthesis) whereby the unity of the subject is reconstituted in the mind and formulated.

The conciliar debates offer a rather remarkable example of this dialectic of knowledge. The Fathers, when there was talk about starting over the schema *De Ecclesia* from scratch, undertook a whole project of analysis, which required the collaboration of all. And in fact the conciliar dialogue brought to light a major distinction between two ecclesiological paths, that of the Church-society and that of the Church-communion.[26] Did this dialectic reach its conclusion by a synthesis? It does not seem to be the case. The work of a Council is not that of a theological academy. What the Fathers did in fact was to collect a certain number of major truths of a theology of the Church, a certain set of "positive" data, leaving it to the theologians to arrive at a synthesis. We have, therefore, in speaking about the teaching of Vatican II, a dialectic of knowledge that tested a good number of the elements making up the object "Church," elements that are then transmitted to the ecclesiologists so that they can pursue this undertaking by working toward the desired ecclesiological synthesis. Here we have, quite exactly, the difference of perspectives between Magisterium and theologians. It is extremely regrettable, then, that this dialectic of knowledge—which has not yet arrived at its conclusion—has been transposed into a dialectic of the real, which places in the object itself the divisions by which the intellect gradually assimilates its object. To put it in simpler terms: because the mind that understands begins by distinguishing within the object being understood—here the Church—the human society and

---

26. Too often this dialectic of knowledge in the Council hall is interpreted as a confrontation between two staunchly defined blocks, one of which ended up conquering the other, although not without concessions; see A. Anton, "Postconciliar Ecclesiology," 415. This inaccurate view is contradicted by the testimony of participants in the Council; see in particular Yves Congar, *L'Église de Vatican II*, 8 and 55. For more detailed clarifications on this subject, see de La Soujeole, *Le Sacrement de la communion*, 227–28, and the bibliography at the end of the present chapter. The two tendencies combined to arrive *together* at a common document (with 99 percent voting *"placet"*). Besides, this is only the most constant conciliar tradition, which Vatican II recalls in *LG* 22: "the holding of councils in order to settle conjointly, in a decision rendered balanced and equitable by the advice of many, all questions of major importance."

the divine communion, that would mean that the Church *really* is society and communion. Is this inference acceptable? We propose answering this question with the two following points.

2. Integrating the moral dimension of the subject

A consideration of the life of the Church *externally*, the order of phenomena that are visible to all, shows us clearly some divisions, an occasional lack of harmony and communication. If we limit ourselves to an observation of the sociological sort, we will infer from the number and constancy of these manifestations a "law of tension" and formulate a "structural datum." A purely empirical anthropology will not fail to highlight the fallible character of human intelligence and the inconstancy of the will. A purely fact-based historiography will easily show the relativity in time of different situations within this community called "Church" and consequently the relativity of the community itself.

As for the *dogmatic* consideration, without denying any of the facts that the positive sciences bring to light, it includes another element that is proper to it, on which depends its very status as a *theological* discipline: faith, which is to say, in this case, *revealed* truths that allow for a more profound understanding of the object "Church." For the purposes of our question, we must include the major theological truth that this world and all that it contains is a world wounded by both original and personal sin. The history within which we move with all creation is a history *of salvation*—that is, a saving act communicated from God to men and women in Christ. In other words, the elements that the dialectic of knowledge distinguishes, and that observation perceives as being separable and opposable, are not *really* separable, but are sometimes *morally* separated. Only through an alteration due to sin does something that is *really one* manifest and conduct itself as something divided. For example, there is no *real* opposition between pastors and lay people, Magisterium and theologians, in the Church: they are for one another with a view to a common work. The "tensions" that no one can deny, so manifest are they, are due to the *moral* faults of one and/or the other group; their remedy is moral and by that very fact always possible (grace), whereas oppositions engrained in the entity itself would be "normal" and hence incurable.

If one considers the life of the Church—or for that matter the life of any human community—in a purely phenomenological way, and even merely at the level of unaided human intelligence, one falls into a kind of *naturalism* that ignores the truths of faith—for instance, the fact that the object being observed is a wounded reality that has begun the slow work of healing. It is therefore inevitable that one would attribute to the thing under observation the tensions that are in its very being. Now, based on a theology of creation, sin, and redemption, we say that these *moral* tensions have not ruined the very being of the subject, its ontological unity. Man is ontologically one (body and soul do not form two things; see *Gaudium et spes* 14), but morally it suffers division in the sense that the flesh struggles against the spirit. But because it has remained profoundly one, the very object of its moral life under the influence of grace is to live anew, gradually, the unity that it bears within itself, that it is: become (morally) what you are (ontologically).

3. The shortcomings of conceptualism

Once we have identified the dangers of naturalism by which one can pass from a dialectic of knowledge to a dialectic of the real, we must consider another way of passing from one to the other: "conceptualism."

We have said that the intellect that scrutinizes a real thing begins by distinguishing among its various aspects. It will thus think *concepts*, which will represent (i.e., make present) in the mind these various aspects being studied. In doing so it carries out a real abstraction in the sense that the various aspects being distinguished really exist in the object, if the abstraction is correct. But abstraction is a mental operation that leads to a *being of reason* only if the aspect being distinguished is separated from the other existing aspects. Now a being of reason does not really exist; it exists only in the mind of the one who forms it. Take, for example, a man, Peter. We can, by abstraction, consider his body and his soul, his external appearance and his interiority. This abstraction is real in the sense that Peter is indeed made up of a body and a soul; Peter is a complex being. But if we consider Peter's body *separately* from his soul, we then form a pure concept of reason that expresses nothing of the reality: what is real is the animated body or the incarnate soul. Peter, the man who really exists, is the whole. The concrete man who exists is truly one (*GS* 14)—that is, *undivided* in himself. In other words, the concepts must always maintain, in the mind in which they are, the same relations as the things that they represent have in the real object that is known. To say that man is a body and a soul is not an adequate definition, because whoever says "body" already says "soul," since a body without a soul is not a body, but a corpse.

A certain passion for abstraction developed in Western history, particularly in what could be called "Late Scholasticism." Already in the writings of Bellarmine the conceptual distinction between the body and soul of the Church expresses a separation of the two aspects, and the controversialist did not see that membership in the body of the Church alone was in reality not membership—however incomplete—but only apparent, deceptive membership, since a body without a soul is no longer a body, but a corpse. Pursuing this approach, as we have seen, a whole theological discourse developed that was based at least on an equivocation, which went so far as to think about the Church as being made up of two formally distinct and separable communities. In the contemporary period, this conceptualism has become more subtle. The distinction between *community* (*or communion*) and *society*, for example, used all the vocabulary of the "dialectical tension" to avoid the disastrous consequences of the Bellarminian perspective. But the objection that can be raised against it is basically the same: the *communion* (like the *society*) as such does not exist. What does exist is a social communion or a communional society, and if one wishes one can grasp the *real* relation between these two concepts through the comparison of the body and the soul.

Once minds were imbued, consciously or unconsciously, with the change of perspective inaugurated by Kant, thinkers were tempted to posit in reality the distinctions that our mind makes, and Hegel took this option to its ultimate conclusions. If concepts are no longer mental representations of what is real, but are the reality itself, then the oppositions that are possible between concepts—at the logical level—become real oppositions. At the logical level, as we pointed out earlier, one can in fact reason that "what is equal is what is not unequal," and thereby perceive in the concept of equality its own negation. One can then develop a whole logic of internal opposition, with the temptation to transpose this opposition into reality. The social ecclesial aspect then becomes whatever *is not* the communional ecclesial aspect, and the communional ecclesial aspect becomes what *is not* the social ecclesial aspect, the two being in a dialectical relation. In doing this, the mental abstraction that produced these concepts has separated them from the real thing. Recall that the concept of equality does not necessarily include the concept of inequality. One can perfectly well reason—and incidentally we do this spontaneously—that equality is identity of quantity, and inequality is diversity of quantity. By referring these two concepts to the reality from which they were derived, we see that one and the same genus unites them (quantity) and distinguishes them (they are contrary and not contradictory). Similarly, in ecclesiology, the concept of society is not necessarily that which is not communional, and one can very well maintain that the social aspect is one of the possible expressions of the communional. Moreover, this is how reality presents itself: we can arrive at this conceptual distinction society/communion only by starting from a *common human fact of life* in which we distinguish what unites the members *externally* (the society) and what unites them *internally* (the communion), but the real thing is the whole thing.[27] It is easy to prove this: remove one of the aspects, and the whole thing disappears.

In other words, the first phase by which a dialectic of knowledge distinguishes within the object several elements (the analysis) must always give way to the second phase (the synthesis) whereby the unity of the object is reconstituted in the mind. Consequently the necessarily distinct concepts by which one apprehends the complex object must maintain within the mind that forms them *the same relations* as the complex real object that they represent possesses in reality. We can indeed distinguish in Peter his corporeality and his "animality," but these two concepts are correlative, inseparable from one another, because the real thing—Peter—is the whole. It is the same with the Church: that by which she is an external reality and the thing by which she is an internal reality are necessarily connected; one can distinguish them, of course, but one cannot separate them.

---

27. We are not taking a stand here on the validity of this distinction—the "social-external" and the "communional-internal"; we are explaining how binomials originate.

b. Clarifications of vocabulary and concepts

We can agree to speak about "polarity." Polarity implies the reciprocal action of two elements or properties that is founded, not on an antinomy, but on a difference, a diversity. Antinomy occurs when on the *moral* level sin opposes what ought to be united by complementarity—for example, the action of the hierarchy and the action of the laity. Remember: then we are observing a being that is sick or wounded by sin, and not the being in its ontological truth. Diversity distinguishes different but complementary elements (like the soul and the body). Indeed, we must not confuse *contradiction* and *contrariety*. Contradiction expresses the *incompatibility* of two terms, one of which implies the negation of the other. So it is with the *already* and the *not yet:* considered at the same time and under the same aspect, one cannot say that the Church is the Kingdom already present and not yet arrived. This is contradictory for the same reason that one cannot say that Peter has already arrived and is not yet present. Contrariety expresses the *difference* between two terms, and there can only be a difference between them because they can be compared, because they belong to one and the same genus. Two contrary terms do not exclude one another, but are both classified within a whole that is the genus to which they belong. In the Church, her "divinity" and her "humanity" are contrary, not contradictory; the one divine order (the relation nature-grace) combines them, places them in a situation in which they call for one another, just as the body and the soul call for one another. The definition for "polarity" that we propose, therefore is: reciprocal relation of diverse elements within a single whole.

This allows us to give a very illuminating meaning to the notion of "tension." In the simplest sense, the one closest to the etymology,[28] a "tension" is a *tendency*, a movement. For the Church, we have a fundamental tension that is her eschatological tendency: a progressive actualization. The idea of finality is central here: We are talking about the directed movement of the Church toward her perfection, her completion. Various interrelated realities intervene to bring about this movement. They tend toward one another to form a relation that will allow

---

28. "Tension" comes from the Latin *tensio,* which is the substantive form of the verb *tendere ad* (or *in*) + accusative = to tend toward.

them to pursue the end that is common to all. In this sense there is a tension between the Magisterium and the theologians, for example—that is, mutual relations with a view to a deeper understanding of the faith. This relation is not a relation of contradiction because it is clear that the two terms are not mutually exclusive, but rather call for one another. But this tension can become a conflict—in the moral order—through the fault of one and/or the other correlative. There are many other realities in the life of the Church that tend toward one another for a common end: active life and contemplative life, consecrated celibacy and marriage, clerics and lay people, mystical understanding and speculative understanding. This is the wealth that results from the extreme complexity of the ecclesial body, which is unified by its unity of soul and of the end pursued by the reciprocal action of all. This is analogically true of the biological body and of the social body.

Thus the life of the Church appears to us simultaneously as the result of the richest diversity and the strongest unity. It is not a question of arbitrating the relation between unity and diversity by attempting to find a sort of "equilibrium" between the two, wherein each must yield something to the other, but rather of situating each one correctly in relation to the other in an *order* that binds them together with a view to the perfection of the ecclesial being. Unity is first, diversity is second, but by no means secondary, for unity and diversity are two equally essential aspects. This perspective allows us to see how the Church gathers together many significant differences in the harmony of interdependence. Wherever this interdependence is rejected, the harmony of the complex whole gives way to the opposition of contradiction that renders these differences incompatible, or at least to the search for an equilibrium of compromise that mutilates each of the essential elements. The two virtues of this interdependence are charity and justice.

Therefore, and this is extremely important, we must consider in the Church first of all the profound unity constitutive of her very being, and then—within her bosom—the prodigious diversity of the elements of which she is composed. We must also carefully distinguish what falls under her ontological unity (the ecclesial being constituted as such in its fundamental identity: *LG* 8, §§1 and 2), and what falls under her the moral unity, the latter being more or less effectively lived out (*LG* 8, §3).

Conclusion

At the conclusion of these discussions, we propose *not* adopting the way of presenting the Church in terms of binomials, in which one of the terms is placed in a relation of opposition to the other. The notion of equilibrium is not equivalent, in our opinion, to the notion of unity. An equilibrium exists between two realities—two beings—whereas unity expresses the "composition" of one being if it is complex. Note that this means, when speaking about the Church, that one cannot be part of the ecclesial "society" unless one is also part of the ecclesial "communion," for the real Church, the one that really exists in her mystery, is the whole thing. It seems to us for this reason that binomial thinking does not sufficiently explain the references in *Lumen gentium* 8, §1, because it leads one to divide the ecclesial being into two beings, whereas it is a question of *unam realitatem complexam*.

Even if one takes binomial thinking as a possible exegesis of *Lumen gentium* 8, §1, it must be noted that, at best, this interpretation thinks about the Church in her composition (the diverse elements that make up this complex being), but not about the unity of those diverse elements. The great ecclesiological distinction between the Church as *medium salutis* [means of salvation] and the Church as *res salutis* [reality of salvation]—enlightening as it may be in a dialectic of knowledge—is unfounded if it is transposed into a dialectic of the real. To return to a binomial that illustrates this, can we say that the Church-society is really distinct from the Church-communion? We do not think so: the society is in the communion, and the communion is in the society. To remove or diminish one of the two is to abolish or mutilate the whole thing.

These clarifications are extremely important. We will show many examples of how important they are when we get to our ecclesiological proposal. The following summary presents the terms of the speculative ecclesiological question:

The ecclesial mystery, as it is revealed through Scripture and Tradition, appears as something complex. The positive datum to be explained is the following: the Church possesses various aspects that can be encapsulated in two general ones:

The Intellectual Method

- The Church is the means of salvation *and* the reality of salvation
  or the means of grace *and* the community of grace
  or signum-instrumentum [sign-instrument] *and* res [reality].
- The point of departure for speculative reflection in particular is the Reformers' assertion:

  The Church is one *or* the other aspect: the paradigm *either-or*;
  The (true) Church is the reality of salvation, *and* it alone.
- The response of Catholic theologians before Vatican II

  It was to maintain that the Church is *both* realities: the paradigm *both-and*. But this was done in such a way that it ended up being *two separable realities* and not *one complex reality* (see the different approaches, separable body and soul, society *and* communion, etc.)
- The clarification [*discernement*] by Vatican II

  See *LG* 8, §1: "(The two aspects) *non ut duae res considerandae sunt, sed unam realitatem complexam efformant.*"
- The prevalent Catholic theology after Vatican II

The problem is to keep the two elements together in such a way that they are mutually inclusive. Paradigm *yes-no* together (tension). This is the paradigm of the opposition of contradiction: the Church is society *and* communion, the society being that which *is not* communion, and the communion being that which *is not* society.

This is the status of the ecclesiological investigation, and against this backdrop we will propose our contribution.

BIBLIOGRAPHY

The Exaggerations of Nascent Ecclesiology
(late nineteenth century)

Congar, Yves. "L'ecclésiologie de la Révolution française au concile du Vatican sous le signe de l'affirmation de l'autorité." In *L'Ecclésiologie au XIXe siècle.* US 34. Paris: 1960, 77–113.

———. *Le Concile de Vatican II: Son Église; Peuple de Dieu et Corps du Christ.* Coll. Théologie historique 71. Paris: 1984, 8–14.

The "Vitalist" Philosophies

Duchesneau, François. "Vie." In *Les notions philosophiques: Dictionnaire,* edited by Sylvain Auroux, 2:2730–33; in *Encyclopédie philosophique universelle,* edited by André Jacob. Paris: Presses universitaires de France, 1990.

Möhler, Johann-Adam. *Unity in the Church, or The Principle of Catholicism, Presented in the Spirit of the Church Fathers of the First Three Centuries,* edited and translated by Peter C. Erb. Washington, D.C.: The Catholic University of America Press, 1996, 195–97.

Rademacher, Arnold. *Religion und Leben.* 2nd ed. Freiburg im Breisgau: 1925. English translation *Religion and Life.* Westminster, Md.: Newman Press, 1962.

Vermeil, E. *J. A. Moehler ou l'École catholique de Tubingue.* Paris: 1913.

The Distinction between Philosophy of Knowledge and Philosophy of the Real

Hegel, Georg Wilhelm Friedrich. *La Science de la logique.* French translation by Pierre-Jean Labarrière and Gwendoline Jarczyk. 2 vols. Paris: Aubier Montaigne, 1972–1981. With a long and very valuable introduction to vol. 1. See esp. vol. 1, book II [section 1], chap. 2, page 83. *Hegel's Science of Logic.* Translated by W. H. Johnston and L. G. Struthers. London: Allen and Unwin; New York: Humanities Press, 1929, 2:66–70.

Kant, Immanuel. *Critique of Pure Reason.* Preface to the second edition. Translated by J. M. D. Meiklejohn. Chicago: Encyclopedia Britannica, 1990, 39:5ff. [1952: 42:5ff.].

Verneaux, R. "La catégorie hégélienne de contradiction." *Sapientia* 26 (1971): 369–88.

The Presentation of Vatican II

de La Soujeole, Benoît-Dominique. *Le Sacrement de la communion: Essai d'ecclésiologie fondamentale.* Paris-Fribourg: 1998, 211–25.

Michelin, E. *Vatican II et le surnaturel.* Venasque: 1993.

The Usual Way of Reading Vatican II Today

Anton, A. "Postconciliar Ecclesiology: Expectations, Results, and Prospects for the Future." In *Vatican II: Assessment and Perspectives; Twenty-five Years After (1962–1987),* edited by René Latourelle, 407–38. New York: Paulist Press, 1988.

The Way to Read Vatican II according to Experts Who Participated

Congar, Yves. "Regards sur le concile à l'occasion du XXe anniversaire de sa convocation." In *L'Église de Vatican II: Son Église, Peuple de Dieu et Corps du Christ.* Paris: 1984, esp. 8 and 55.

Gy, P.-M. "La liturgie de l'Église, la tradition vivante et Vatican II." *Revue de l'Institut Catholique de Paris* 50 (1994): 31: "Fr. Congar informed me that, during the Council, Paul VI, when he left for a month to summer at Castel Gandolfo, brought with him the dossier of the conciliar minority on one of the major debates, to make sure that the majority had really listened to the minority and taken its arguments into account...: that is a council, that is Church-communion."

Labourdette, Marie-Michel. *RT* 66 (1966): 341; *RT* 68 (1968): 605.

Laurentin, René. *Bilan de la 3e session*. Paris: 1965, 296 and 324.

Delhaye, Philippe. "Histoire des textes de la constitution pastorale." In *L'Église dans le monde de ce temps: Constitution pastorale "Gaudium et spes."* US 65a. Paris: Cerf, 1967, 274, concerning the action by Paul VI in favor of unanimity, and 275 on the final result: "neither the victory of one camp nor the defeat of the other".

Martelet, G. *Les Idées maîtresses de Vatican II: Introduction à l'esprit du concile*. Paris: 1967, 74–75.

10

Proposed Definition

To honor the "specifications" that the data from the sources give us, we propose the following definition: the Church is the sacrament of communion.[1] Our contribution rests on the two notions: *sacrament* (so as to manifest the unity of the various aspects of the ecclesial mystery) and *communion* (so as to express the "nature" of the unity thus brought about). These two notions are encountered constantly in contemporary ecclesiological studies, but the understanding and articulation of them has not yet reached the point of a fully satisfactory formulation.

We will proceed in three phases: first, an exposition of ecclesial sacramentality, followed by an elaboration of the notion of communion. Once this clarification has been made, we will propose a way of combining these two terms, thus demonstrating the definition.

I. The Sacramentality of the Church

One major difficulty in this matter that still hinders many authors is the fact that, even though the importance of sacramentality is perceived, it is approached starting from the seven sacraments, which leads to an impasse. One of the most significant recent examples shows this:

---

[1]. The reader can find a detailed presentation of the proposal in de La Soujeole, *Le Sacrement de la communion*, 243–347.

Proposed Definition 439

If we start from this understanding of *mysterium*,[2] it may be said that the inner nature of the church is hidden; but that it reveals itself—even if shadows remain—in the concrete, visible *ecclesia catholica*....

The term sacrament is well suited to express the differentiating relationship and the distinction between the church's visible structure and its spiritual nature....

Yet in spite of this inherent connection, the visible Church is not simply identical with the thing to which it testifies. In extreme cases the outward sign and the inward salvific reality can also be sundered.[3]

When one approaches sacramentality starting from sacramental actions and in a univocal sense, one cannot avoid applying to the Church the separability between the *signum* and the *res* (which is certainly abnormal, but possible), and one cannot get out of the speculative rut in which the visible Church and the invisible Church form two realities that are normally united yet separable, instead of two elements of a being that is inalterably one—that is, *undivided* and *indivisible*. This understanding of sacramentality is inadequate, since it cannot grasp the teaching of Vatican II, as we saw earlier. In reference to the Christ-sacrament, thanks to him and constantly dependent on him, the Church that is his Body and his Bride is *inseparably* the reality of grace and the sign-means of transmitting it, the reality being *in* the sign-means, constituting together with it only one being. All that we affirm about the Church depends on her close configuration to Christ: if she is not his Body and his Bride, the Temple of his Spirit, the People of God that he gathers together, the whole ecclesial *mystery-sacrament* vanishes.

But at this point an important difficulty appears: although we must agree that the communion of life in the theological virtues—the reality of grace—is *in* the ecclesial society—this is, the sign-means of grace[4]—in the unity of one subject, we must recognize that the Church here below is a community of sinners and not a perfectly holy individu-

---

2. That is, the meaning given by the Theological Commission of the Council for the title of chapter 1 of *Lumen gentium:* "transcendent and salvific divine reality that manifests itself visibly." See *AS* 3, no. 1, 170.

3. Walter Kasper, "The Church as a Universal Sacrament of Salvation," in *Theology and Church*, 118, 122.

4. Recall that we are borrowing this vocabulary (internal communion–external society) not to approve of what it most often expresses in contemporary ecclesiological literature, but to manifest as clearly as possible where the difficulty is that hinders to this day a solution to this speculative question.

al subject as Christ is. How then can we be sure that the community of grace, the holy and sanctifying community, is infallibly *in* this community—the "concrete" community, this diocese, for example?

In order to resolve this difficulty, we propose a consideration of the particular sacramentality by which Christ engenders his ecclesial Body through his Spirit—that is to say, the sacramentality of the Eucharist. Here we are at the foundation of what could be called Eucharistic ecclesiology.

a. At the source of the Church: The Eucharist

It is a commonplace in Tradition to say that Christ builds up his Mystical Body through his Eucharistic Body: the ecclesial mystery is the *res* of the Eucharistic sacrament. But this sacrament exhibits peculiar features in relation to the six other sacraments, and these differences decisively elucidate the mystery of the Church that is sprung from it.

1. The peculiarity of the Eucharistic sacrament

The first peculiarity to be mentioned is in the "structure" of this sacrament. This sacrament involves three terms [*instances*] and not only two (the sign-means and the reality).[5] During the Eucharistic crises of the ninth through eleventh centuries in the West, one of the chief difficulties was to determine what really happened in the case of an unworthy celebration (the priest and/or the congregation were ill-disposed morally): did the presence of Christ come about under the species or not? The solution that gradually developed was to underscore that the sacramental presence of Christ was realized, but not its fruit, which is the ecclesial edification of the unworthy participants. Thus we have a paradigm with three terms: a *sign* (bread and wine and the words of consecration)—a *reality that is immediately signified* (the Eucharistic presence of Christ), which is in turn a *sign* of—the *final reality* (ecclesial presence of Christ).[6]

---

5. In fact, each of the seven sacraments has been understood within a tripartite "structure," but this is clearly apparent only for some of them (Eucharist, baptism, confirmation, holy orders), can be demonstrated well enough for another (marriage), but still remains problematic for two of them (reconciliation and the anointing of the sick).

6. See Innocent III, *Epist. ad Joannem*, in PL 214.1120–21: "Yet [whatever the truth about the presence and the sacrifice in the Eucharist may be,] '*mysterium fidei*' is men-

Proposed Definition

The second peculiarity of the Eucharist is that, before being an action, as the other six sacraments are, it is a presence. The other six sacraments confer the grace that they signify in an instrumental manner: the grace is in them as the effects are in the tool by which they are produced; it "passes" from its divine Author to the recipient solely by flowing through the sacrament. The Eucharist is different: not only does it bring about what it signifies, but it *is* what it signifies and brings about. This sacrament does contain the power of Christ, but even more, it contains Christ himself as giving himself to men so as to incorporate them into himself.

The third unique feature of the Eucharist is the fact that the "intermediate term," which is simultaneously *res* and *sacramentum*—Christ's Eucharistic presence—is in the sign so as to be communicated to the recipient and accomplished in him. It is otherwise with baptism, for example, in that the intermediate reality (the indelible character) and the final reality (the grace) are in the recipient. In the Eucharist, there are a certitude and a sacramental presence that precede and serve as the bases for the ultimate effect of grace. The object of this sacrament is first an *esse*, to bring about the Eucharistic presence, then a *fieri*, to edify the Mystical Body.

We see therefore, by considering what is unique about the Eucharist, the considerable importance of this "intermediate" reality, which is certain and visible by faith under the sign, and a pledge of the ultimate effect.

2. The Eucharist in classical sacramental theology

We will now explain the Eucharistic mystery-sacrament in classical sacramental terms:

---

tioned, since something is believed there other than what is perceived; and something is perceived other than is believed. For the species of bread and wine is perceived there, and the truth of the body and blood of Christ is believed and the power of unity and of love.... We must, however, distinguish accurately (*subtiliter*) between three things which are different (*discreta*) in this sacrament, namely, the visible form, the truth of the body, and the spiritual power. The form is of the bread and wine; the truth, of the flesh and blood; the power, of unity and of charity. The first is the 'sacrament and not reality [*res*].' The second is 'the sacrament and reality.' The third is 'the reality and not the sacrament.' But the first is the sacrament of a twofold reality. The second, however, is a sacrament of one and the reality of the other"; English translation by Roy J. Deferrari, in Henry Denzinger, *The Sources of Catholic Dogma* (Fitzwilliam, N.H.: Loreto, reprint, no date).

The *sacramentum tantum* is the reality of this world that is evident to the senses and is taken up to signify and communicate a *present* supernatural reality. In the Eucharist, this is not the bread and wine *before* the consecration (at that moment these materials signify only ordinary food and nourish only in a carnal way), but rather *after* the consecration, when these species truly signify and are the Body and Blood of our Lord, to such a degree of realism that if the species disappear—if the sign disappears—the sacred reality disappears also. The *sacramentum tantum* is the precise sacramental mode of Christ's presence.

The term *res et sacramentum* designates an intermediate reality, which is a reality with respect to the *sacramentum tantum* and a sign with respect to the ultimate effect. This is the *reality* of the Body and Blood of the Lord, invisible in itself, but manifested by the sign that is received in faith; it is also a *sign* of the ecclesial upbuilding of the participants. Because this intermediate reality is certainly present in the *signum tantum* once the celebration has been carried out correctly, it signifies the purpose for which Christ makes himself present in this way.

The *res tantum* is the ultimate reality that is signified, but does not signify something else. It is the very objective of the sacrament, for the sake of which Christ makes himself sacramentally present—namely, to assimilate to himself those who receive It and to gather in unity the members of the Body of which he is the Head. The Eucharist not only engenders but also *is* the Church.

b. The sacramentality of the Church in Eucharistic terms

We will propose here a paradigm in three terms to describe ecclesial sacramentality, starting from the ultimate reality, which, being the final cause, gives intelligibility to everything that is ordered to it.

1. The ecclesial *res tantum*

The ecclesial reality is the community of those who live from now on by the life of God communicated to them. This personal and communal union of all who know, hope in, and love God thanks to the Spirit of Christ is a reality directed toward God and hence invisible, yet manifested through its works. The Church "contains" this supernatural life, or more profoundly, she *is* this stable, permanent, constantly active community of supernatural life. This is the absolute value to which everything else that is proper to the Church *in via* [on her pilgrim way] must be related and "relativized" in the proper sense of that word. This is the whole "sense" of the Church in this world—that is, her (eschatological) orientation and her actual reason for being. This is the level at which we can speak about the unity and even the identity between the Church in heaven and the Church on earth; not about two churches, but only one in two states that are ordered one to the other. In itself this poses no difficulty.

2. The ecclesial *sacramentum tantum*

What is commonly understood by this expression is a community of a religious sort, like many others, with its rules, rites, discipline, and culture. This community is a sign for the faith. With reference to the Eucharist, we say that this sign *contains* what it signifies, gives it its mode of being, and preserves it as long as it lasts as a sign. And so we can make the following distinction: in its *signifying materiality*, the ecclesial sign is the *social fact*, the community of human beings that is distinct from all others (e.g., association, civil society); in its *proper signification*, the ecclesial community is the manifestation in sign that it belongs to the reality of salvation. It describes itself as the community gathered together by Christ, the author of salvation, the actual source of all grace, and of the glory to come. As E. Schillebeeckx says:

> The earthly Church is the visible realization of this saving reality in history. The Church is a visible communion in grace. This communion itself, consisting of members and a hierarchical leadership, is the earthly sign of the triumphant redeeming grace of Christ.... The inward communion in grace with God in Christ becomes visible in and is actualized through the outward social sign. Thus the essence of the Church consists in this, that the final goal of grace achieved by Christ becomes visibly present in the *whole* Church as a visible society.... The Church is the visible expression of Christ's grace and redemption, realized in the form of a society which is a sign (*societas signum*).[7]

Hence we recall: the community in its *entirety*, clergy and laity, is what forms the ecclesial sign; the *common life of Christians* is the signi-

---

7. Edward Schillebeeckx, *Christ, the Sacrament of the Encounter with God*, 47–48.

fying thing, before any functional distinction. So it is, too, *mutatis mutandi*, with civil society: what it signifies in matters of particular expressions of natural sociability, depending on one's culture, is the work of all who are part of it. Of course the natural social fact, which is the adopted sign, essentially includes an organic character, which means that all the members are ordered to one another by the service of some, but once again, at the level of the sign, the social body as a whole is what represents the ecclesial Body.[8]

The ecclesial social fact manifests the communion of grace. That is the first function of the ecclesial sign: to make known that this community *is* the community of salvation, manifesting itself in the world. But this reality of salvation is not the privilege of a few: the Church must signify also that she invites all men into herself—that she takes care of her own members who are carrying out the slow work of conversion. She must therefore signify that she is for that reason the means of salvation, that she has what she possesses and what makes her what she *is*, only in order to communicate it. Here we have the locus of all the *signifying activity* of the community to dispose men to grace and to transmit it to them. From the most exalted acts—because they confer grace (the sacraments)—to the lowliest and most routine acts that dispose souls to receive it and help it to produce all its effects—in particular, witness "*verbo et exemplo*" ["by word and example"]—all of this is ecclesial action, which is ordered to the communication of what the Church is. The four properties of the Church—one, holy, catholic, and apostolic—are the major characteristics of the community of salvation, the salvation that is received in order to be transmitted.[9]

---

8. This clarification is essential in order to discern what the ecclesial sign is, and it justifies what we call a social ecclesiology, but it is conceivable only if one approaches sacramentality "from above": the grace that is given and that remains visibly by taking on a human symbolism. If one approaches sacramentality "from below," the efficacious sign of grace, there is a great risk—and this has occurred—of reducing the ecclesial sign to the hierarchy; see Yves Congar and Walter Kasper: *signum tantum:* the ecclesiastical institution alone.

9. Charles Journet clearly saw the apparent paradox of these signs: they must lead to the mystery, and yet they can be received only in light of this mystery. This is why he considers these signs at two levels of intelligibility: at the first level, they are *notes*—that is, intrinsically prodigious manifestations for the human intellect; thus they can lead open minds to accept the faith and to accept it effectively. Once the faith is accepted, these signs can then be considered in terms of what they truly bear witness to (second

We have just considered the reality present and active in the sign. This means—and here we have the central point of ecclesial sacramentality from the perspective of fundamental ecclesiology—that the Church as human community in this world *is* the community of salvation, which lives by it and communicates it. This excludes the *real* duality between "human" Church and "divine" Church because, once again, the reality of grace is *in* the human reality. Here we recall in the first place the mystery of Christ in his humanity: the man Jesus is endowed with grace in order to transmit it; there are not two beings, the man and the saint. But what is easily understandable with regard to Christ because of his perfect impeccability—he is the transparent sign and ever-efficacious instrument—cannot be understood in exactly the same way with regard to the Church. The latter, as a pilgrim community here below, subsists in members who are all sinners. Therefore, we must recognize that there is not a perfect correspondence between the sign—the human ecclesial community—and the reality—the communion of saints. Does that mean we have to go back to two separated communities and thus unavoidably to the notion of an unidentifiable, invisible Church? That would ruin the whole idea of sacramentality. The problem is evident, and the question posed is formidable: since the community-sign subsists in a group of sinners, then how can the holy community-reality be said to be *in* the sign to such a degree as to form only one being together with it? Here is where we must consider in the ecclesial sacrament a *res et sacramentum* that will allow us to make the connection between two statements that seem contradictory.

3. The ecclesial *res et sacramentum*[10]

The precise question can be formulated in these terms: What reality, truly signified by the social sign and borrowing its visibility from it, is really posited in the Church so as to make her *infallibly* the reality and the means of living the life of the theological virtues as a communi-

---

level of intelligibility)—namely, the supernatural *properties* of the ecclesial community; see *L'Église du Verbe incarné* 2:1193ff. We will return to this during our study of the Church's properties.

10. Few authors today make the effort to investigate this *res et sacramentum*. For an overview of these rare attempts, see de La Soujeole, *Le Sacrement de la communion*, 264–66.

ty? In other words, what is the identifiable fundamental permanent element in the Church that allows us to be certain of her constant supernatural and salvific identity and value? From the sign out of which it has proceeded, this *res et sacramentum* will receive its social nature; from the ultimate reality to which it is an introduction, this *res et sacramentum* will have its permanent value as a sign and instrument.

We propose the following:

- The ecclesial *res et sacramentum* can be perceived only by faith. By considering the community of a social nature (*sacramentum tantum*) for what it is—that is, something having its coherence not in itself, but by reason of its relation as signifier of a supernatural communion—one can be open to this intermediate reality that we are seeking to describe. At the same time, the latter, apprehensible by faith alone, has the objective of opening upright hearts to it.[11]
- From the social sign that refers to it, the ecclesial *res et sacramentum* takes its *communal* (as opposed to individual) nature; what we are trying to describe is found in a communal reality and not in an individual manifestation (not even one brought about by several individuals). But since a community subsists in its members, this communal manifestation must be possible in each member.
- Since it is not the ultimate reality of grace (the communion of saints), the ecclesial *res et sacramentum* does not require the *actual* presence of the theological virtues in the subjects who are the *suppositum* of this communal manifestation. But it must lead to it if there are no obstacles in the individual persons, and therefore it must contain what it bears witness to and obtains. At the level of individuals, it will be of a *charismatic* order, a gift that is common and not reserved just to some according to the unforeseeable freedom of the Spirit. Therefore, in our opinion, it will have to do with the indelible characters imprinted by the sacraments of baptism, confirmation, and holy orders. At the level of the community, this ecclesial *res et sacramentum* denotes the presence of sanctifying grace insofar as it is giving itself: the community is the

11. Concerning this apparent paradox, see the observations above at note 9.

instrument that the Spirit of Christ makes use of in order to diffuse what is in the Incarnate Word—the one who, according to his humanity, is the Head.[12] It is important here to distinguish the individual level, where sanctity may be lacking but not the character (an unworthy minister, for example, a simple instrument through which grace passes), from the communal level, where the presence of sanctifying grace is assured: the community possesses unfailingly the gifts of Christ, and they are in the community so as to be communicated by the activity of its members.

Keeping these elements in mind, we propose situating the ecclesial *res et sacramentum* as follows:

- *As a reality (res)*, it is a communal manifestation through which the mystery of salvation *is signified (sacramentum)*; the truth of this mystery is thus attested with assurance, and through this mystery the grace of Christ is communicated with a sure effect. What are the easily identifiable acts that constitute this manifestation? These will be, on the one hand, the constant proclamation of the Gospel as a whole in its integrity and, on the other hand, the uninterrupted celebration of the genuine sacraments, which assuredly contain what they signify.[13] In order for these acts to be placed, they require the collaboration of all in the community. Constant, faithful witness to the faith is based both on the exercise of the magisterial responsibility entrusted to the apostolic succession and also on the witness of the faithful (*SC* 10), the whole expressing the *sensus fidei* of the community (see *LG* 12). The uninterrupted administration of the sacraments is incumbent on the whole community, which is the true subject of the liturgical celebration (see *SC* 14 and 27). Here there is no hierarchical type of relation between clergy and laity, as in the social manifestation of the *sacramentum tantum*, but rather a "synergy" in order to bring about an effect that can be attributed to the whole as

---

12. See *LG* 8, §1: "the social structure of the Church serve[s] the Spirit of Christ who vivifies it, in the building up of the Body (Eph 4:16)."

13. At the level of faith, *the object of faith (id quod creditur)* is what is proposed with certitude; at the level of the sacraments, it is the assurance of an *authentic* celebration—i.e., one in conformity with the ever-true faith of the Church ("valid" in canonical terminology).

such. Certainly this is not contrary to the responsibility proper to the apostolic college to be the judge of last resort of the expression of the faith and of the rightness of the liturgical celebration, but it does underline the fact that the very exercise of this strictly episcopal responsibility cannot detach itself from the participation of the entire body: the pastors *discern* a given fact that does not come only from themselves, and they celebrate in their own place *within* an assembly that is celebrating as a whole.

This confident constancy and certitude in doctrinal fidelity and sacramental rectitude are a gift of the Spirit of Christ *to the community*. This gift of indefectibility assures it that it cannot err in the faith and that the authentic sacraments will always be celebrated within it.[14] On the individual level, this gift is based on the characters of baptism, confirmation, and holy orders, but although the individual as such may fail at this level (he can be an instrument of sanctification without being holy himself), the community, in contrast, has received the promises of Christ; it is sanctifying because it is holy, because the Spirit is its soul.

Thus the ecclesial *res et sacramentum* appears to us as the domain of the *sancta* [neuter plural], of the sanctifying realities—the Gospel and the sacraments—and the *res tantum* appears as the domain of the *sancti* [masculine plural], the persons actually sanctified by the *sancta*. Not only do the *sancta* make it possible, in faith, to point to the community of salvation independently of the variable and ever uncertain dignity of each of its members, but they also are, *in* the Church, the very thing that allows sinners to come or to return untiringly to baptismal purity and to grow in it. These *sancta* presuppose a community that acts so as to administer them; the permanence of the community assures the permanence of the *sancta* as well as that of the *sancti*. The following table complements the one that we presented previously:

The Church is:

---

14. Indefectibility is not a fifth note and property of the Church, but a characteristic of the four notes and properties by the very fact that it affects the ecclesial *res et sacramentum*. We will return to this point at the end of Part Three, which is dedicated to the properties of the Church.

The reality < the supernatural community of God and human beings: (*res tantum*)

→ As a matter of principle in Christ: Head of the Body,
Cornerstone,
Priest, prophet and king.

→ Brought about in human beings: Body of Christ,
Temple of the Spirit,
People of God.

in the sign < which manifests itself *in* the social sign: (*signum tantum*)

→ A community on the sociological order.

through the signs that are instruments < preaching and the sacraments (*res et sacramentum*).

In the classical sacramental paradigm (the Eucharist), one would say: The *signum tantum* bears the *res et sacramentum* that engenders the *res tantum*.

c. Conclusion on sacramentality

On the level of fundamental ecclesiology, which is essentially concerned about giving an account of the unity of the ecclesial being, the notion of sacramentality offers great advantages.

To say that the Church is a sacrament is to situate her very suggestively and precisely at her place in the *nexus mysteriorum* of Revelation. Always oriented with implicit reference to Christ—the perfect sacrament and source of the others—she received from him a profound intelligibility. Placed prior to the particular sacraments—with the necessary clarifications in regard to the Eucharist—she elucidates their nature. For this reason, the question of where a treatise on the Church is to be placed in the scheme of the dogmatic understanding of Revelation receives a conclusive answer: after Christology and before the particulars of sacramental theology. This is just the order of sacramentality itself, considered from its source to its ultimate applications. Hence we realize that the notion of sacrament is attributed analogically. In order to make this attribution, we must ask ourselves the question: what, ultimately, formally constitutes the sacramentality that is found in Christ in its perfect state, and in the Church and the seven individual sacraments by participation? The investigation that we proposed with respect to ecclesial visibility allowed us to grasp, in reference to the New Law as St. Thomas presents it, some profound connections with Christology and ecclesiology. The insight of Charles Journet and Fr. Congar on this subject is very deep, even though, in our opinion, they have not drawn all the consequences of it. What is found in the various mysteries is fundamentally identical: something *spiritual-invisible-salvific* gives itself or is given to man in his *carnal-visible* condition and forms one reality with him. We have here not only a pedagogical truth that is based on an anthropology (the manner in which God chose to save)—that is already a lot—but also and above all an affirmation of the unity between nature and grace. These two things are not extrinsically related, but call for each other, one might say,[15] so as to form one reality that is, properly speaking, *redeemed man*. Among the many statements by Vatican II on this subject we can recall one in particular that is clear. In speaking about "the basic law of the Christian scheme of things," the Council declares:

For though the same God is Savior and Creator, Lord of human history as well as of salvation history, in the divine arrangement itself, the rightful autonomy of the creature, and particularly of man is not withdrawn, but is rather re-established in its own dignity and strengthened in it. (*GS* 41)

We have already pointed out, from the *moral* perspective, what this unique divine vocation means for man. We are touching here on the *ontological* perspective that is the basis for the moral level. The "law of sacramentality" expresses an important aspect of this unity between nature and the supernatural. Whatever the fragility of man as he lives this unity, the reconciliation wrought by Christ is firm and solid. The sacramental realities—the humanity of Christ, the Church, the seven sacraments—are established definitively as pledges of this reconciliation between nature and grace, as the permanent possibility for man to have access to this reconciliation or to return to it if he strays from it. At the deepest level, the sacramentality of the Church expresses the definitively accomplished character of the redemptive work. In these reali-

---

15. Expressions such as *mutual interiority* and *reciprocal inclusion* are suggestive in this regard as long as they are not understood as referring to two realities, each of which is autonomous from the other.

ties that are called "sacrament" the unity of nature and grace is inviolably and permanently granted so as to be communicated.

Having thus seen what salvation is fundamentally and how it is communicated, we must go further in our investigation. Between the salvation that is Christ and salvation as it is received by the individual human being in the seven sacraments, we must include salvation as a communal reality, precisely as ecclesial, without which the individual dimension cannot exist. In other words, what brings about grace at the communal level, in the three fundamental aspects of the Church that we have just presented? At this point of our investigation the notion of communion appears.

II. Ecclesial communion

The sacramentality of the Church that we discussed previously gives us, as it were, the genus to which the Church belongs. We know that the reality called "Church" comes to us from above under the sign of a social community in which it resides, thanks to this intermediate reality that is the social manifestation of the *sancta*. We need to go further now by specifying *of what*, precisely, the Church is the sacrament, and *how*, specifically, this sacramentality presents itself and is accomplished. This is what expresses the notion of communion.

From the perspective of doctrinal history, the notion of communion in ecclesiology traveled a complicated path at the time of the contemporary theological renewal. It entered into the debate by way of social philosophy and sociology. Therefore there were attempts to apply to the Church the binomial *society* (or institution)—*communion* (or community). We have seen the limitations of this procedure. But at the same time, in the 1930s, biblical scholars dwelt on the word *koinōnia* and gave a theological presentation, without a dogmatic perspective.[16] In the 1950s, Fr. Congar was the first, to our knowledge, to intuit that this notion could in a certain way recapitulate a whole definition of the Church.[17]

Then Vatican II took place, and it used the word *communion* more

16. See in the bibliography the landmark studies from that period by Campbell, Seesemann, and Hauck.
17. See in the bibliography the reference to *Holy Church*.

than a hundred times in the most varied contexts, thereby showing that the Council was adopting a very broad sense of the word.

Although it may be surprising today, the promotion of the idea of communion *after* Vatican II is quite recent. It was not done immediately following the Council. It was only in the late 1970s that this term took first place in the ecumenical movement and in the various Christian denominations.[18] This movement, which is therefore recent, benefits from many of the preparations and results of the contemporary renewal, but the insight into the centrality of this notion and the compiling of all the ecclesiological material around it are only at their beginnings. Consequently, it would be quite hasty to write a treatise on ecclesial communion without first proposing some clarifications at the level of vocabulary and of the concept. To do this we will process in three steps: the use of vocabulary in the sources; the data from Vatican II; and the speculative elaboration of the notion.

a. The use of the word *koinōnia* in the sources
1. The New Testament[19]

Koinōnia is a derivative from *koinos:* common, joint, shared. Words related to *koinos* do not occur very frequently in the New Testament: they are used around forty times. Here we will consider principally the noun *koinōnia*, which by itself represents almost half of the occurrences, essentially in the writings of St. Paul.

---

18. The immediate postconciliar period was marked especially, as was already mentioned, by a focus on the People of God theme. Only gradually did "communion" become part of the theological currency. The study by A. Acerbi, *Due ecclesiologie*, played a major role in this regard. The reflection by our Orthodox brethren went hand in hand with this, and the ecumenical movement showed the same development. On these phenomena, see Jean-Marie Roger Tillard, *Church of Churches*, xi–xii; A. Birmelé, "*Status quaestionis* de la théologie de la communion à travers les dialogues oecuméniques et l'évolution des différentes théologies confessionnelles," *Cristianesimo nella storia* (1995): 245–84 (particularly 257–59 for the renaissance of the idea among Catholics).

19. We will not consider the Old Testament data, especially of the LXX. The word *koinōnia* is found in it, but never to designate the relations between God and man. A heightened perception of divine transcendence militated against the concept of such a close union between God and human beings. *Koinōnia* appears therefore to express a substantially new contribution by Christian Revelation. On this point, see the study by P. C. Bori in the bibliography.

Proposed Definition 453

A reading of the texts indicates three distinct meanings:[20]

Koinōnia = contribution, invitation, sharing

The next two passages are about the collection that St. Paul took up for the Christians of Jerusalem. The third is a reminder of the need to hold all things in common that mentions the original community in Jerusalem (Acts 2:42–47).

- 2 Cor 9:13: "(The saints of Jerusalem glorify God for) the generosity of your *koinōnia* for them and for all others."
- Rom 15:26: "For Macedonia and Achaia have been pleased to make some contribution [= to have a *koinōnia*] for the poor among the saints at Jerusalem."

The immediate context is talk about a collection. The Christians are being called to donate money to their needy brethren. But the exhortation is not limited merely to material almsgiving. The passages in question indicate that the Christians being solicited are invited to be in a deep spiritual relationship with their persecuted brethren, and that the collection is a sign of this deep relationship. Indeed, it is a matter of imitating Christ who, "though he was rich, yet for your sakes he became poor, so that by his poverty you might become rich" (2 Cor 8:9).[21]

- Heb 13:16: "Do not neglect to do good and to share (*koinōnia*) what you have, for such sacrifices are pleasing to God."

In the Letter to the Hebrews, the collection, the *koinōnia* of resources, is placed in the context of worship, which makes it a sacrifice pleasing to God. Here, too, it is a matter of not limiting oneself to an exclusively philanthropic perspective.

---

20. It is quite remarkable that Campbell and Seeseman, after working separately at the same time, found that they were thoroughly in agreement about these three meanings. Their only differences concern the attribution of this or that occurrence to one or another of the three meanings that were determined. In our discussion we follow the presentation by P. C. Bori.

21. The exegesis of 2 Cor 8:9 by the Church Fathers is first of all dogmatic and focuses on the mystery of Christ: "though he was rich (= God), yet for your sakes he became poor (= man), so that by his poverty (= the role of the assumed humanity in the divinization of mankind) you might become rich (= divinization)." This perspective leads to moral consequences: to imitate Christ is to work humanly according to divine ways.

In summary, to give some of one's goods is in these passages a way of expressing a true gift of oneself in the image of the gift that Christ made of himself for the same purpose.

Koinōnia = participation, taking part

The greatest number of passages—all from St. Paul—fall into this category.

- 1 Cor 10:16: "The cup of blessing which we bless, is it not a *koinōnia* in the blood of Christ? The bread which we break, is it not a *koinōnia* in the body of Christ?"
- 1 Cor 1:9: "God is faithful, by whom you were called into the *koinōnia* of his Son."
- 2 Cor 8:4: "[The Churches of Macedonia were] begging us earnestly for the favor of taking part (*koinōnian*) in the relief of [i.e. the collection for] the saints."
- Phil 1:5: "Thankful for your partnership (*koinōnia*) in the Gospel from the first day until now."
- Phil 3:10: "that I may know him [Christ] and the power of his resurrection, and may share (*koinōnian*) his sufferings."

In these passages, *koinōnia* is understood to be in the person who is the object thereof: by receiving something from a donor, the recipient participates in what is given and thereby in the one who gives.

Koinōnia = the community

These passages are the most comprehensive and, in a sense, the most forceful. The use of *koinōnia* here is absolute—that is, without a genitive that specifies or defines it.

- Acts 2:42: "And they held steadfastly to the apostles' teaching and fellowship (*koinōnia*), to the breaking of the bread and to the prayers."
- 2 Cor 6:14: "What fellowship (*koinōnia*) has light with darkness?"
- Gal 2:9: "When they perceived the grace that was given to me, James and Cephas and John, who were reputed to be pillars, gave to me and Barnabas the right hand of fellowship (*koinōnia*)."

The comprehensive mention by St. John

Proposed Definition

- 1 Jn 1:3, 1:6–7: "That which we have seen and heard we proclaim also to you, so that you may have fellowship (*koinōnia*) with us; and our *koinōnia* is with the Father and with his Son Jesus Christ.... If we say we have *koinōnia* with him [i.e., Christ] while we walk in darkness, we lie and do not live according to the truth. But if we walk in the light ..., we have *koinōnia* with one another."

To be in community with the apostle is to be in community with God. The origin of this *koinōnia* is based on what was seen and heard by the apostle—that is, on the fact that God, in Christ, formally announced his mystery to his disciple, and that the disciple participated in that mystery. He in turn communicates it to the faithful who thus receive the divine invitation and, in responding to it, take part in that communication, thus founding the Christian community.

In the final analysis, *koinōnia* expresses three aspects of the same reality and not three different realities: the fact of sharing along with the correlative fact of taking part (receiving what is proposed) make up a reciprocal relationship that thereby engenders the communal reality. We find ourselves here at the heart of the doctrine of the Mystical Body. Christian community is not simply having individual material or spiritual resources in common, just as a biological body is not formed by the combination of the independent members. The life in which we participate and that is shared with us exists only in its dependence on its source. The theme of the Body of Christ showed us that the life of the Church is a participation in the divine life itself, as manifested in Christ and communicated by his Spirit. Likewise the *koinōnia* is entirely founded on Christ and his Spirit: the divine communication in the humanity of Christ is the key to all the rest.

2. The patristic data

The vocabulary of *koinōnia* is not found in the early Fathers (St. Ignatius, St. Polycarp). The most important author for our study is St. Irenaeus. On the one hand, he is the first to write for the purpose of making a synthesis. He intends to confront multiple heresies and to contrast them with an overall doctrine of the Christian mystery by attempting to show how its various aspects are connected with one another. On the other hand, at the level of vocabulary, everyone knows that the magnum opus entitled *Adversus haereses* [Against Heresies] has come down to us in two versions: an incomplete version in Greek, the language of St. Irenaeus, and a complete version in Latin, which critics consider almost contemporary with the Greek source. Thus we can find invaluable testimony as to both Greek and Latin theological language in the second century. For the word *koinōnia* this is important. It is a word habitually used by St. Irenaeus (more than eighty occurrences). It is translated in the Latin version by the three words *communio*, *communicatio*, and *societas*, although at first the reader cannot see any nuances of meaning among the three.

The overall teaching of St. Irenaeus is opposed to the Gnostics who, despite the great variety of currents, agree on one point: the impossibility of communication between God and creation, between eternity and time, as well as among human beings. St. Irenaeus's plan is to refute this all-encompassing vision of the world, which turns it into a universe in which everything coexists, but nothing communicates. For the bishop of Lyons, man who is fallen because of Adam's sin no longer has access to beatitude, to *koinōnia* with God. The divine plan of salvation is therefore the restoration of the community of man with God, which is brought about through Christ, the Incarnate Word.[22]

First, the fact of the Incarnation:

> For, in what way could we be partakers of the [divine] adoption of sons, unless we had received from Him through the Son that *communio* which refers to Himself, unless His Word, having been made flesh, had entered into communion (*communicasset*) with us? Wherefore also He passed through every stage of life, restoring to all [men] *communio* with God.[23]

> The Word has saved that which really was [created, viz.,] humanity which had perished, effecting by means of Himself that *koinōnia* (*communio*) which should be held with it, and seeking out its salvation.[24]

> But now, by means of *koinōnia* (*communicatio*) with Himself (in His human nature), the Lord has reconciled man to God the Father.[25]

Christ is communicated to us by the Holy Spirit:

---

22. In the following citations we have put the Latin translation of *koinōnia* in parentheses when the Greek text is available; otherwise we cite the Latin text only.

23. *Adversus Haereses* (hereafter *A.H.*) III.18.7; ANF 1:448a.

24. *A.H.* V.14.2; ANF 1:541b; (see also III.19.2).

25. *A.H.* V.14.3; ANF 1:542a.

Proposed Definition 457

(The Word) has also poured out the Spirit of the Father for the union (*adunitio—henōsis*) and *koinōnia* (*communio*) of God and man ...; bestowing upon us at His coming immortality durably and truly, by means of *koinōnia* (*communio*) with God.[26]

This communication of the one to all is done in the Eucharist:

But if this [flesh] indeed does not attain salvation, then neither did the Lord redeem us with His blood, nor is the cup of the Eucharist the *koinōnia* (*communicatio*) of His blood, nor the bread which we break the *koinōnia* (*communicatio*) of His body.[27]

For [in the Eucharist] we offer to Him His own, announcing consistently the *koinōnia* (*communicatio*) and union of the flesh and Spirit.[28]

Here we have the common basis for all Christian soteriology, which the *koinōnia* vocabulary expresses in a way that is faithful to the scriptural data: community with God is brought about thanks to a divine communication in Christ, to which a participation of men in Christ should correspond.

Starting from that, a rapid and broad extension of the *koinōnia* vocabulary would then be observed. This terminology would later be used in a way that is logically prior to the teaching of St. Irenaeus, in Trinitarian theology, and also in a way posterior for questions concerning the life of the ecclesial community. This extension manifests the very close tie that connects the mystery of God to salvation[29] and to all aspects of Christian community life to life in God, so that the life of the Christian in its totality is an ecclesial life. We will illustrate this by way of selected citations:[30]

The theology of God connected with ecclesiology: anyone who wants to be in *koinōnia* with God must be in the ecclesial *koinōnia*:

But where God is, there exists the fear of God.... Where the fear of God is, there is seriousness, an honourable and yet thoughtful diligence, ... and a safely-guarded *communicatio*, ... and a united church, and God *in* all things.[31]

---

26. *A.H.* V.1.1; ANF 1:527a. 27. *A.H.* V.2.2; ANF 1:528a.
28. *A.H.* IV.18.5; ANF 1:486a.
29. The connection between *theology* and *economy* [*of salvation*], as the Greek Fathers would say.
30. Our presentation does not follow a strictly chronological order; our main hope is to point out the breadth of the use of the *koinōnia* vocabulary, starting in the third century.
31. Tertullian, *De praescriptione* 43.5; ANF 3:264b.

Trinitarian theology connected with ecclesiology: the Spirit of *communio*:

Through what is common to the Father and to the Son, they wanted to establish *communio* both among us and with them, and to gather us together in unity through this gift..., that is, through the Holy Spirit, the gift of God.[32]

To whom in the Trinity, therefore, can this *communio societatis* be attributed, if not to the Spirit who is common to the Father and the Son?[33]

Whoever has been guilty of impenitence against the Spirit, in whom is gathered the unity and the *societas communionis* of the Church, will never be pardoned.[34]

The notion of fraternal *communicatio*:

Therefore the churches ... are all proved to be one, in (unbroken) unity, by their peaceful *communicatio*, and title of brotherhood.[35]

It is to no avail that people may beguile themselves with the illusion that whilst they are not at peace with the bishops of God they may still worm their way in and surreptitiously hold communion (*communicare se credunt*) with certain people.[36]

The life of the community: the unity of the faith:

When the faithful in Asia had gathered together [in councils] for this purpose..., then at last they [the Montanists] were expelled from the Church and were excommunicated [i.e., debarred from the *koinōnia*].[37]

Commenting on 1 Jn 1:7: "We have fellowship (Latin: *societatem*; Greek: *koinōnian*) with one another": "They (the apostles) saw; as for us, we have not seen and yet we are in communion (*socii sumus*), for we have the same faith.[38]

---

32. Augustine, *Sermo* 71.18 (PL 38.454) [translated from Latin].
33. Augustine, *Sermo* 71.29 (PL 38.451) [translated from Latin].
34. Augustine, *Sermo* 71.34 (PL 38.464) [translated from Latin].
35. Tertullian, *De praescriptione* 20.8; ANF 3:252a–b. Note also: the orthodoxy of a particular community is assured by its *communicatio* with an apostolic Church (*De praescr.* 21.7; ANF 3:252b); the latter judge by deciding whether or not to receive the communities into their *pax et communicatio* (*De praescriptione* 32.10–11; ANF 3:258b).
36. Cyprian, *Epist. ad Florentium Pupianum* 69.8 (PL 4.419) (= Letter 66, ACW 46:121).
37. Eusebius of Caesarea, *Ecclesiastical History* V.16.10; FOC 19:316.
38. Augustine, *Commentary on 1 John* I.3 [translated from Latin with reference to the French].

The unity of the sacraments: the sacraments are the sacraments of the faith; they transmit, nourish, and refresh it, and they are administered exclusively to those who confess the true faith:

Concerning 1 Cor 1:12, in which St. Paul rebukes the divided Christians of Corinth: "[Only] those had communion (*communicabant*) in the same sacraments (*sacramenta*) who did not have communion in the same vices (*in eadem vitia non communicabant*).[39]

In particular, with respect to the Eucharist, sacrament of the *communio:*

(The Eucharist) is also called communion, *koinōnia,* and truly is so, because of our having communion (*koinōnein*) through it with Christ and partaking both of His flesh and His divinity, and because through it we have communion with (*koinōnein*) and are united to one another.[40]

The expression *communio sanctorum* (*koinōnia tōn hagiōn*).

- *Sanctorum:* masculine genitive plural = holy persons.

The Church is simply the community (*congregatio*) of all the saints.... You must believe, therefore, that in this one Church you are gathered into the Communion of Saints [*communio sanctorum*]. You must know that this is the one Catholic Church established throughout the world, and with it you must remain in unshaken *communio*.[41]

For we ought ... to be sure that if we depart from them (the saints), we put ourselves also out of their fellowship (*koinōnia*).[42]

For if our "fellowship" (*societas*) is said to be "with the Father and the Son," how is it not also with "the saints"? Not only with those who "are on earth," but also with those who are "in heaven"?[43]

- *Sanctorum:* neuter genitive plural = sacred things

The communion (*communio*) of goods in the Church is what is called in the Creed *sanctorum communionem*.[44]

---

39. Augustine, *Ad donatistas post collationem* I.21.33 (PL 43.674b) [translated from Latin].
40. John Damascene, *De fide orthodoxa* IV.13 (PG 94.1154a; FOC 37:361).
41. Nicetas of Remesiana, *Explanatio symboli* 10 (PL 52.871); *Nicetas of Remesiana [et al.]: Writings* (FOC: 1949), 49–50.
42. Athanasius, *Letter to Dracontius* 4 (PG 25.528b); NPNF, 2nd series, 4:557ff., at 559.
43. Origen, *Homily on Leviticus* IV.4; FOC 83:73–74.
44. Thomas Aquinas, *In Symbolum Apostolorum expositio* 8. We cite St. Thomas here, although he is not a Father of the Church, to give a fuller insight into the various

The organization of ecclesial life

Since the matter is well known and the documentation overabundant, we limit ourselves here to recalling the major usages:[45]

- *koinōnia-communio:* in the "administrative" conciliar documents; see the expression *ius communionis* or *communicationis* (Tertullian, St. Cyprian).
- *littera communicatoria* (*grammata tou koinōniou*): document testifying to the unity between two bishops, two churches ... or allowing a pilgrim to participate in the Eucharist in a church that is not his.
- *excommunicatio* (*akoinōnia*): deprivation of the Eucharist and consequently exclusion from the community.

Having thus presented the patristic data, we propose turning now to the other end of Tradition to compare the extent of the use of the word "communion."

3. The statements of Vatican II[46]

The Church comes from the Trinitarian *koinōnia*

In speaking about the Trinity, the Council did not use the vocabulary of *koinōnia-communio*. Vatican II does not consider the immanent Trinity, but only the Divine Persons as they work in the economy of salvation (i.e., the economic Trinity). In the vocabulary concerning the divine action (especially in *LG* 2–4) the reader can find related terminology: *unitas:* "Hence the universal Church is seen to be 'a people brought into unity from the unity of the Father, the Son and the Holy Spirit'" (*LG* 4 *in fine*, citing St. Cyprian, *De Orat. Dom.* 23): *unio:* we are united to God through union with his Son (*LG* 3); *participatio:* the Father's plan is to raise men up to participate in his divine life (*LG* 2). The

---

principal meanings of *communio*. This use of *communio* taken with a neuter object seems to be less often attested during the patristic period, at least for the commentary on the Creed. In another setting we are familiar with the admonition of the deacon as he sends away the catechumens at the end of the Liturgy of the Word: "Holy things for the holy!"

45. See especially the study by G. D'Ercole, *Communio, collegialità, primato: Sollicitudo omnium ecclesiarum: Dai Vangeli a Constantino* (St. Louis: Herder: 1964).

46. Our presentation of Vatican II closely follows the one proposed by H. Donneaud (see bibliography).

word *communio* is also used in speaking about the work of the Spirit (*LG* 4) and the effect of the Eucharist (*LG* 7).

The Church journeys toward the Trinitarian *koinōnia*

In speaking about man's vocation, the Council frequently emphasizes that it is *communio cum Deo* (*GS* 19), a *communio in vita divina* (*GS* 18). This vocation is realized in the Church, which is a down-payment already given on this communion (*LG* 9: the Church as the People constituted by Christ in the communion of life, charity and truth). All of chapter 7 of *Lumen gentium* deals with the eschatological character of the Church; the vocabulary of *communio* is well attested in it, along with the related vocabulary of *unio* and *unum*.

The Church lives by the Trinitarian *koinōnia*

In her itinerant state, the Church appears in her essential features as a *communio* in the same faith (*UR* 14: two occurrences), in the same sacraments (*LG* 13, *OE* 2, *UR* 14), thanks to the pastoral ministry. With regard to the latter, several long discursive passages deal with the *communion* that binds pastors together: the *communio hierarchica*. The *communio* in this sense is not limited to the *communio* in the means of grace; it is brought about rather in the fraternal *communio* that manifests the life of grace (*Apostolicam actuositatem* 3: the Christian life in *communion* with the brethren).

The Church is a *koinōnia*

This is the place where all the preceding elements converge: the Church is the *communion of saints*. This is not only the union of the blessed already in their heavenly homeland, but also their union with human beings who are still on this earth (*LG* 49–50: the *communio* of everyone in the Mystical Body): they are described as one family (*LG* 51). The expression *communio sanctorum* in the documents of Vatican II designates first the union of persons and then, in a second and subordinate way, union in the means of grace. This is a return to the patristic plan.

Vatican II seems to us therefore to have rediscovered the fullness of meaning that the *koinōnia* vocabulary had in the writings of the Church

Fathers. This is the starting point from which we must attempt to circumscribe the notion more formally.

b. The notion of *koinōnia-communio*

At the philological level one cannot say that *communio* is the transliteration of *koinōnia*; rather, as in the case of *mystērion-sacramentum* we have a translation that involves a thorough understanding. In both cases, in Greek and in Latin, it is a question of expressing three distinct but related meanings: to communicate [*faire-part*]—to partake—to be/have in common.

1. The elements of the notion

The first element of *koinōnia-communio* that is grasped is God's plan of communicating a good that does not cease to belong to God and therefore, if it is received, will become a good shared by God and man. Therefore, there is a first sense that is active, that we can call a *communicatio*, which is the historical work of salvation entrusted to the Incarnate Word. What is this good? It is God himself who invites us to share by grace what he is by nature. At the level of operation, one might say that God offers to man a share in his life of knowledge and love. In other words, God proposes that divine beatitude itself should be held in common. Thus, the basis of the *koinōnia-communio* does not begin with the divine offer, but already exists from all eternity in God and is God himself, his eternal beatitude. Hence this good, which come to be held in common by God and man, is not a common work of God and man, but is given by God to man. To put it even more precisely, this participation offered to man is a participation in the life of Christ. The divine good that is offered so as to be held in common receives from the Incarnate Word several specifications and modalities that are proper to it. The divine offer reaches man only in Christ: grace, all grace, is Christic—that is to say, the divine communication reaches man in an economy of incarnation as part of a system of speech and signs.

The second element of the *koinōnia-communio* is the actual reception of grace by man, the partaking. Grace gives to the man who receives it the capacity to respond to the divine offer in an act that is truly his own through the theological virtues. This human life under the influence of grace is fundamentally identical and also markedly different in each human being: identical by its object, because for everyone it is a question of knowing and loving God as he knows and loves himself; different, because what is present in fullness in Christ is manifested in various ways in the members of his Body. The multiplicity of individual lives reflects what is totally present in Christ. No individual Christian, even if he were the greatest saint, could reflect the wealth of the grace of Christ. Only the whole set of human beings who have received grace can express it to some small extent. Here we are touching on a profound theological reason for the communal character of salvation: only as a group do human beings, in and through their diversities, represent a participation in the whole wealth of divine life that dwells within the Incarnate Word. Just as the whole of creation manifests to some small extent the multiform richness and power of God, so too Christians as a whole manifest to some small extent the multiform richness and power of Christ's grace.

We can then turn to the third element of the *koinōnia-communio* that results from this exchange between God and man. If the two preceding acts—communicating and partaking—establish between God and mankind a correspondence in thought, sentiments, and actions, then this situation calls for a community. It is founded upon a having-in-common of divine beatitude and of works of knowledge and love, but even more upon a common being that configuration to Christ brings about. This ontic (*entitative*) community—which is the Body of Christ—is the foundation of the active community of life. Christic grace conforms to Christ, so that it is the principle of Christian identity and action.

2. The notion properly speaking

The divine community comes first: it preexists everything and draws everything to itself; this community is what communicates itself. The precise paradigm should not be taken too rigidly and simplistically: communicate → partake → community; more subtly this is about a community that opens up its unity to additional members. The Trinitarian *koinōnia-communio* communicates itself first and foremost in the very mystery of Christ: in him, the *koinōnia-communio* that is God marvelously includes man. Since the Church is not beatitude pure and simple, but rather beatitude insofar as a creature can partake of it, the Incarnation is from this perspective the birth of the Church. Hence the mystery of Christ is what will communicate itself. The true paradigm is: divine community → Incarnation of the Word, by the Spirit → Incarnate Word communicated to human beings by the Spirit = Church. That is the paradigm of the major Greek patristic tradition for the Church, the Body of Christ.

We propose the following formulation: the ecclesiological notion of *koinōnia-communio* expresses the divine community inasmuch as man participates in it according to a Christic economy that conforms individuals to Christ. This *koinōnia-communio* is perfect in the Church in heaven. It is still characterized by pilgrimage, progress, and a fight against evil in the Church here below. Yet these different states do not form different churches, for these are different states of participating in the same reality—the one community-as-divine-beatitude—and always through the same mediation of Christ's humanity.

3. The Church—charity

This notion of *koinōnia-communio* that we have just derived corresponds in an astonishingly precise way with the vocabulary and the notion of charity. The most enlightening illustration of this is found in St. Thomas Aquinas.

Charity according to St. Thomas Aquinas

This mutual well-wishing [i.e., friendship] is founded on some kind of *communicatio*. Accordingly, since there is a *communicatio* between man and God, inasmuch as He communicates (*communicat*) His happiness to us, some kind of friendship must needs be based on this same *communicatio*, of which it is written (1 Cor 1:9): "God is faithful: by Whom you are called unto the fellowship (*societas*) of His Son." The love which is based on this *communicatio*, is charity. (*ST* II-II, q. 23, art. 1, corpus)

Charity is understood as a particular type, the most excellent sort of friendship. St. Thomas is original in proposing this. His principal source is Aristotle, in whose writings the vocabulary of friendship is precisely that of *koinōnia*.[47] "Friendship" designates the cause of unity

---

47. On the originality of St. Thomas in his time, see in the bibliography the study by G. G. Meersseman; for the vocabulary and the notion of friendship in Aristotle, the principal passage is *Nicomachean Ethics*, Book VIII.

of a community of persons that has been formed around a common good and that expresses itself by acts of mutual benevolence. Thus one can say that the Church is a communion because the unity of this community, formed around a common good (namely, the participated life of God), is charity that is expressed in relations of mutual benevolence. Hence we see that the ecclesiology of communion is the actual way by which charity has once again become the very definition of the Church: the community of love.[48] There is nothing disincarnate or invisible about this, because it is about Christic love that conforms to Christ. This is far from the vagaries of the anti-Protestant controversy.

This ecclesiology is profoundly traditional. It is the most ancient ecclesiological paradigm. We could not possibly have one that was more in common with the Orthodox. The first service performed by Vatican II was to go beyond the groping attempts of the Counter-Reformation and to rediscover it. All of chapter 5 of *Lumen gentium*, which is devoted to the one vocation of the Church, holiness, speaks in every line about charity, either as the origin of the Church (in God, specifically in Christ), as the life of the Church (the grace of Christ), or as the end of the Church (the beatitude that has begun here below). In a word, charity—both uncreated and created—is the origin, the constant vitality and the finality of ecclesial life in all its aspects.

The contemporary development

This ecclesiology also has modern emphases in Vatican II that constitute the originality, the novelty, and the progress affirmed by the Council. Here we are talking about the discovery and teaching of new demands of charity in our days. The progress is more in moral theology than in dogmatic theology, but we note this because it had many consequences that were to renew the face of the Church, especially in the institutional aspect of her life. The philosophical and sociological promotion of the idea of communion, it seems to us, was at the origin of this progress. This notion as such did not enter into ecclesiology; it

---

48. See *LG* 23: "the fellowship of an all-pervading charity." In the classical style of magisterial documents, we frequently encounter the expression "unity of faith and of communion" (*unitas fidei et communionis*), which signifies quite exactly the unity of faith and of charity. By way of example, see Vatican I, Constitution *Pastor aeternus*, Prologue: "(so that the multitude of the faithful) *in fidei et communionis unitate conservaretur.*"

was necessary to purify it—that is, to see what the concerns of charity were.

Aside from the critiques of contemporary currents of thought, it should be noted that modern propositions converge—each in its own way—in an "internal" concept of communion that makes it the very expression of human dignity. The bond of communion in a community, especially civil society, underscores the fact that man does not endure this social situation; he wants it, builds it, and lives it responsibly. The bond of communion is then distinguished from the so-called bond "of society" in that the latter expresses natural or conventional decisions that are "endured." We have already pointed out that this intuition cannot be followed when it ends up *separating* what falls under the constraint that is endured in man's communal life from what depends on the freedom that is to be protected. But one can derive from it a correct view that can be integrated into our proposal: it belongs to the dignity of a human being to be self-activating, to define oneself, to consent freely to what will make up one's life, to participate voluntarily in the life of the human group in which he is enrolled. No one can replace the subject in his responsibility for the choices by which he constructs his life, not just his initial choices, but throughout his life. And respect for this is a demand of charity, nothing less: charity by which one loves one's fellow man, and charity by which one must love oneself.

In the Church, this is where religious liberty comes in, the religious liberty *within the Church herself:*

> It is obvious that within the Church also, and inside any other religious community, the relations among members and between them and the authorities can be regulated only according to criteria and with methods that correspond to their dignity as persons, and therefore according to the criterion and with the methods of liberty.[49]

This conveys the modern idea of communion.

> The true character of the Church is being a society *through communion,* which is brought about only from within, by adherence to which the members cordially consent.[50]

---

49. P. Pavan, "Le droit à la liberté religieuse et ses éléments essentiels," 153.

50. L. Laberthonnière, "La notion chrétienne de l'autorité," in *Oeuvres de Laberthonnière,* 248.

Proposed Definition

Therefore, the moral aspect of the "partaking" in the notion of *koinōnia-communio* is what has been developed more extensively in the modern era. The conciliar document that dwelt more particularly on this question is the Declaration *Dignitatis humanae* on religious liberty. The principal subject of this teaching is religious liberty in civil society, but this liberty is founded on a modern apprehension of liberty as such. As the prologue says:

> Contemporary man is becoming increasingly conscious of the dignity of the human person; more and more people are demanding that men should exercise fully their own judgment and a responsible freedom in their actions and should not be subject to the pressure of coercion but be inspired by a sense of duty. At the same time they are demanding constitutional limitation of the powers of government to prevent excessive restriction of the rightful freedom of individuals and associations. (*Dignitatis humanae* 1).

This passage opens the door to a deepening of ecclesial life itself:

> In its true scope, religious liberty in the Church must become not a simple juridical statute, or even a dogmatic declaration, but rather, through a daily effort, a *spirituality* that increasingly imbues mentalities and attitudes.... It should be manifested, in a way that must be exemplary, within the Church itself, in the manner in which the members treat one another, and should procure for each and every one the liberty to which he has a right. Liberty does not exclude obedience; on the contrary, liberty alone gives it its value.[51]

If it is true that the whole Church is *koinōnia-communio*, then this respect for the personal, free, and therefore responsible way in which man responds to the divine offer must be found in all areas of ecclesial life:

> The religious community, too, must cultivate in its members this respect for themselves and this proud awareness of their dignity. They have to develop for themselves a personal conviction, to convince themselves that the faith of their community and the principles of the authority are well founded. The ideal Christian ideal is by no means one who is content to assimilate passively the doctrine that is proposed, without requiring a real intellectual effort of personal reflection and well-versed faith.... When new problems confront the ecclesial community, the search for valid solutions is a common task at which all have to work together under the direction of the legitimate authority.[52]

---

51. Marie-Michel Labourdette, "Chronique de théologie morale," *RT* 72 (1972): 143.
52. E.-J. de Smedt, "Les conséquences pastorales de la déclaration (*Dignitatis humanae*)," 219.

All this shows us, furthermore, that the ecclesiology of communion per se has no need of a supplemental ecclesiology of the "societal" type to balance it. In the very requirement for communion one discovers the institutional forms that are suited to allowing for the expression of the life of the Church (synodality, participation of the laity in pastoral care). The means of regulation demand the cooperation of all, the requirement of strong unity combined with the richness of diversity.

In this aspect, which is assuredly new, Vatican II is not so much a point of arrival as a point of departure. We are still at the very beginning of the incorporation of this richer understanding of *koinōnia-communio* into ecclesial life.

III. THE SACRAMENTALITY OF THE ECCLESIAL COMMUNION

We have showed the constitutive unity of the ecclesial being through an explanation of its sacramentality, and at the same time we have seen how it falls under that profound "logic" of redemption, which is to be marked with the seal of the Incarnate Word. To say that the Church is a sacrament is to specify, as it were, the larger "genus" to which she belongs. What is sacramental in the Church is her very communal being, the fact that she is a communion. This communion is what is sacramental, which is to say, threefold: there is the communion-reality of grace present in the communion-sign by means of the communion-sign/instrument. Sacramentality indicates that this is about three communions that form only one—the ecclesial communion—and there we have the mystery.[53]

We propose now to consider in turn the aspects of this threefold communion, distinguishing in each instance the acts that engender it and the common good that results from it. We will follow the order given by the primacy of the finality: first the communion-reality of grace that we will call *the communion of the theological virtues*, then the economy by which this reality comes to be—in other words, the communion-

---

53. In Latin this would be expressed by the phrase *"triplex communio,"* which would be translated "the triple communion"; this expression is in the singular, and within this complex singular reality resides the mystery that faith offers to us to believe in and to try to understand as much as possible.

sign alone that can be called *the social communion*. This second aspect bears the communion-sign/instrument that makes the connection between the supernatural and the social aspects, which we call *the diaconal communion*.

a. The reality of grace: The communion of the theological virtues

This is the reality of grace, strictly speaking: God, in Christ and through the Spirit, gives himself to be known and loved; through man who is saved in Christ and his Spirit, God is known and loved. From this admirable exchange is born the community in which the eternal beatitude of God, insofar as man participates in it, is present in a down-payment here below.

1. The genesis of the communion of the theological virtues

Here we need to consider the various acts that take place successively in order to arrive at this common good of shared beatitude.

Divine beatitude is communicated to human beings in an economy of incarnation in which the Three Divine Persons cooperate. The two major Trinitarian manifestations during the public life of Christ show this very clearly in an ecclesial perspective. The baptism of Christ (Mt 3:15ff. and parallels) shows us the Spirit descending on Jesus in the form of a dove and the Father's voice resounding. The latter is what gives the meaning: "This is my beloved Son, with whom I am well pleased." Apostolic preaching gives the first exegesis of this passage: "after the baptism which John preached ... God anointed Jesus of Nazareth with the Holy Spirit and with power; [and] he went about doing good and healing all that were oppressed by the devil" (Acts 10:37–38). His baptism marks the beginning of the Savior's public life, the beginnings of the manifestation of the divine "communication." What this baptism signifies is the fullness of the personal grace of Christ and the fact that this fullness exists in order to be communicated. Christian baptism is announced here as the gift of an ontology of grace, the gateway to all the sacraments, and the principle of good works (charity). The account of the transfiguration (Mt 17:1–13 and parallels) is the second Trinitarian manifestation in the life of Jesus. The Holy Spirit is present as a dazzling light (the cloud), and the Father's voice resounds: "This is my beloved Son...; listen to him." Here too the first apostolic preaching gives us the exegesis of this passage: "For we did not follow cleverly devised myths when we made known to you the power and coming of our Lord Jesus Christ, but we were eyewitnesses of his majesty. For when he received honor and glory from God the Father and the voice was borne to him by the Majestic Glory" (2 Pt 1:16–17). The accent here is placed on the communication that God makes to man of the knowledge of his mystery (see "listen to him"). In other words, the preaching of Christ offers to man a participation in the divine knowledge through the grace of faith.[54] Consequently, there is a twofold divine communication in Christ: the preaching of the mystery and the gift of this same mystery.

The human partaking in this offer is a free movement under the influence of grace: confronted with the divine initiative, man responds to it by his *"fiat."* This response can only be strictly personal. From it results a certain ontological conformity that is the specific effect of baptism and that the Eucharist is meant to nourish so as to accomplish it. From the gift of this being follows a certain conformity in knowledge (faith) and in love (charity). But once this strictly personal response is given, it incorporates the individual into a community, the most intimate community that there is with God and with all those who have likewise received and responded. One and the same life of knowledge and love animates the whole community. It is necessary therefore to join together the strictly personal character of the human response with the fact that this response places the respondent into the life of a community. Human beings respond in very different ways to God, not only by their initial *"fiat,"* which has many modalities (baptism of desire, sacramental baptism), but also by moral variations throughout their entire life. This variability affects the community that they form: the communion of the theological virtues is a reality that is greatly diversified according to the firmness of the adherence of its members and according to the greater or lesser conformity of their life. There is a veritable "hierarchy" of sanctity—in other words, a greater or lesser con-

---

54. In both cases, baptism and transfiguration, we have here the common basis of the patristic tradition; for a concise expression of this, see the *Summa theologiae* I, q. 43, art. 7, ad 6.

Proposed Definition

formity to Christ. But in its source, Christ in his humanity because he is God, this communion is always offered, so that the most perfect life here below is always possible. To the diminished life of the sick members appropriate remedies are unceasingly offered, and even those who are spiritually dead can be revived. This is the reason one must always situate *within* individual persons the criteria for ecclesial membership, with reference to their sharing in the life of Christ, and must not distinguish different parts in the community itself.

2. The life of the communion of the theological virtues

The life of the theological virtues is participation in the very life of God; it is the life of faith, hope, and charity. Christ carries out his mediation differently according to the different ages in salvation history, but the reality of grace is substantially the same,[55] although with varying intensity depending on the lives of the subjects. There is not a plurality of communities of salvation (remembering the *Ecclesia ab Abel*). The specific acts of this communion express the grace that has been received, fructifying the life of the faithful. They can be summed up in the notion of spiritual sacrifice. The life of the theological virtues consists of any work that expresses and carries out the offering of oneself to God (Rom 12:1–3). This sacrifice that glorifies God is in a certain way communal as well, not just carried out together, but also offered by the faithful for one another. Its principal locus is the celebration of the Eucharist. This is not only the place where grace is given, but also the place where the fruit of grace has reached maturity, one might say. This is why this sacrament is the principal manifestation of the profound life of the Church.

Communion in the theological virtues, because it is experienced in this world, has a history. Only God possesses beatitude without having to move toward it. God did not acquire beatitude; he is identical with it. But for a creature, beatitude is always an acquisition: a human

---

55. Since all grace is Christic and conforms to Christ, it necessarily follows that the graces given *before* the Incarnation of the Word were such in direct relation to the Incarnation so as to announce it and prepare for it and were granted "in view of the merits of Christ" (to borrow the formula from the dogmatic declaration of the Immaculate Conception). Hence, it is not a "change of grace" that marks the Christian era, but rather an accomplishment, a fullness.

being moves toward it by acts performed under the influence of grace. The life of man here below is an interval, the time of a journey. This progressive genesis is a history. Considered at the level of the ecclesial community, this history can be summarized in broad strokes. In the first place, the divine offer underwent a progression (the different ages of salvation). From this perspective, this history has reached its conclusion, for we are in the last times of this progression: the divine offer in Christ has attained its perfection. Recall, however, that the succession of the different ages of salvation is not just chronological. (It is so for Christians who belong to the last times.) It is also theological. Although from an initial perspective this history has already reached its conclusion—the Church fully formed since Christ—from another perspective these different ages of salvation still coexist. It is a question here of considering non-Christian religions, survivors from the ages preceding the Incarnation of the Word.[56] Second, in the community that receives the divine offer in all its Christic specifications, can we see a history? In other words, is there a *qualitative* augmentation of the life of the theological graces in the Christian era? We think that it is necessary to answer in the affirmative. What may have been lived in its totality by some *individuals* from the beginnings with regard to faith and charity (the martyrs, for example) and throughout the Christian era only emerges more slowly through reflection into the consciousness of the community as such and then arrives at a better formulation for the good of the greater number. This is the sense in which we can understand St. Paul, it seems to us, in the Letter to the Ephesians, where he appears to be trying to note this dynamic.[57] This progression does not affect the program for the reality of the grace given; there is no more grace now than before.[58] Rather, it is moral: contemplating more deeply the truths of the faith and the requirements of charity, the ecclesial community becomes conscious of and formulates with increasing precision the richness of the Gospel.[59] Communion in the theological

---

56. With one qualification: now that the Incarnation has taken place and produced its fruit, the Christic, Christ-conforming grace that sanctifies someone who has not yet encountered the preaching of the Gospel comes from the accomplished mystery, not in view of the merits of Christ, but because of the merits acquired by Christ.

57. See Eph 4:1–16 (v. 15: the Body grows toward the Head).

58. We do not expect, for example, an eighth sacrament.

59. For example, it took eighteen centuries of Christianity to arrive at a full com-

virtues is not a stasis in this world, but rather a communal work that makes progress and matures.

b. The economy of the reality of grace

The reality of grace that we have just presented comes into this world by means of an economy that is, so to speak, the resumption of the work of creation. More precisely, we are talking about the restoration of the final goal of creation and, consequently, of the means of attaining it. Now, since this goal is twofold, the "logic" that leads to it will be twofold, also.

The first, immanent end of creation is to represent, to be a manifestation of the wisdom and goodness of the Creator. The diversity of creatures and the harmony among them are, so to speak, the reflection of what is in the one and only God. Since disorder entered in through the sin of our first parents, the redemption of Christ is, as it were, the renewal of the initial work. Grace here has the aspect of *gratia sanans* [healing grace]. The Church appears in this light under her aspect of social communion, the model for all other communions of this order, both in what concerns the fundamental principles of a social group[60] and in what concerns its historical development, for its common good is to be cultivated—it is a *construct*.

The final end, which transcends creation, is the Trinitarian communion, which the human community—by its order and its movement—tends to join by participating more and more in the perfection of Christ. Grace here is *elevating*; it surpasses the demands of the first end, which it presupposes, only to extend it in ways that would be inconceivable for unaided human reason: to be, through grace-filled participation, the community that God is by nature. Although the social communion is indeed the sign of a healed human communion, to limit it to this aspect would be to secularize it radically. For the profound truth of the social communion is to designate, to be the sign of, the in-

---

munal awareness of the intrinsic malice of slavery. Already in the Letter to Philemon we see the Apostle advising a master to treat his slave as a brother (Philem 16), and it is reasonable to think that the preaching of the Gospel was not entirely unrelated to the discovery of the malice of slavery—a notion that never crossed the minds of the greatest philosophers of Antiquity. But a clear and general judgment, valid for the whole community, came about only with time.

60. I.e., the essential realities of an *ordered whole*.

strument-sign through which God in Christ through the Spirit brings about the "assumption" to which he invites humanity. This instrument-sign is the diaconal communion in which the Christic prerogatives are present and effective through the Spirit. Its common good is not a progressive construct, like that of the social communion; it is a preexisting *given* that is to be distributed (*diakonia*).

Let us examine, therefore, the two pillars of the economy through which communion in the theological virtues comes about.

1. The social communion

The ecclesial mystery is manifested first through this sign: it is *in* this social communion, whose form it assumes.

The divine communication

Our social nature is an observable fact: man does not live alone. The end of society is to assure the well-being of its members. The sum total of necessary conditions for this well-being is the common good. The latter above all has a spiritual nature, since it is about assuring the formation and moral development of the members. The unity of the group, which depends on the correct ordering of its members to the common good and the right distribution of this common good to each one, is served by certain members who are set up as authorities. Here we are at a level of natural wisdom that depends initially on philosophy.[61]

There is, moreover, a theology of this natural sociability. God, when he created the world, did not acquire a new end, and he in no way added anything to his perfection. God willed, in a purely gratuitous way, to communicate his own perfection. Thus God created a multitude of infinitely varied creatures, because no one creature—being finite by definition—can express all the perfection and goodness of the Creator. Only by their multiplicity and diversity can they reflect to some extent the infinite wisdom and goodness of God:

For goodness, which in God is simple and uniform, in creatures is manifold and divided; and hence the whole universe together participates the divine

---

61. We refer the reader to our discussions concerning the People of God for a presentation of this social doctrine, the importance of which is evident here.

goodness more perfectly, and represents it better than any single creature whatever. (*ST* I, q. 47, art. 1, corpus)

Thus the first end of creation is said to be *epiphanic* or revelatory. What failed because of original sin is resumed in the plan of redemption. The Church has been commissioned to manifest this healed natural sociability, and this is the objective of the social communion that she forms:

> For even as in the order of natural things, perfection, which in God is simple and uniform, is not to be found in the created universe except in a multiform and manifold manner, so too, the fullness of grace, which is centered in Christ as Head, flows forth to His members in various ways, for the perfecting of the Body of the Church. (*ST* II-II, q. 183, art. 2, corpus, responding to the issue, "Whether there should be different duties or states in the Church.")

The Church, through the variety of her members and the harmonious order that unites them, manifests what exists fully in the Head: a perfection in which she participates. This participation comes about through the highly appropriate form of a social sign, which is therefore epiphanic and prophetic for every other social grouping, in particular for civil society.

Man's partaking

The way in which man accepts the divine offer is in keeping with his social nature, on the one hand. On the other hand, it will decisively bear the mark of the Christian system of salvation. Here we see the whole significance of the social doctrine of the Church, which is the subject of Part Two of the Constitution *Gaudium et spes*. Thus, and for that reason, this constitution is of great ecclesiological interest. Recall one remark: charity, which in this context takes the name of *political friendship* or *solidarity*, is the formal principle of the social unit. It is the bond that unites human beings in society and that measures all social acts. In relation to the justice that it brings about, charity is the virtue of the interdependence of all for the good of the whole and of each one. Indeed, only through love of the common good—and hence through love of each member that it gathers together—does one obey or volunteer or observe the laws or, in certain cases, exercise authority.

Man's response is charity understood as a *social* virtue, and this clearly manifests the unity of the social communion with the theological communion, since there is only one charity, though it is ordered to distinct acts.

The social communion that is thus engendered

The combined effort of individual wills to realize more and more this order and harmony of the whole is the very life of the social communion. Here this communion has its ideal as a community and its perfection, which is to be acquired in the form of a healing: the good lies ahead of it as its goal, and the good is in it, immanent, as its proper possession. This life notably includes five points that we need to see from an ecclesial perspective.

A requirement of order

The established authority in the social communion presides over many sorts of exchanges, watches over various distributions ..., in short, it orders. "Order" (the term itself) does not primarily imply the exercise of a power to constrain, but rather a requirement that the social relations should serve the common good. Naturally this requirement is found in the Church also, and this office of presiding is given to those who have received the sacrament correctly called the sacrament of holy orders. The fact that this authority is also supposed to vouch for the direction of the diaconal communion, as we will see, clearly shows that these two communions are the most closely connected, since the diaconal communion is *in* the social communion to the point where they are merely two distinct aspects of one thing. This fact, however, involves the risk of confusing the specific "logic" of these two communions. We see an example of this in the present situation of the Western and Eastern Codes of Canon Law of the Catholic Church. The science of canon law has right [i.e., that which is due to individuals and groups] as its object (the virtue of justice), and it seems to us that its preferential field of activity (*terrain d'élection*) is the social communion.[62] That

---

62. Certain statements in the Apostolic Constitution *Sacrae disciplinae leges* (January 25, 1983) that promulgated the new Code of Canon Law could be interpreted in this sense. After distinguishing, within the mystery of the Church, what pertains to grace and charisms from what falls under "the ecclesial society" (the law), John Paul II notes,

is in fact its principal place today. It must be recognized, however, that the Codes currently in force—and the same was true under the authority of the preceding Pio-Benedictine Code—deal to a great extent with the two domains of the diaconal communion (the preaching of the faith and the celebration of the sacraments).[63] We are not certain that this is the best situation, since the two communions do not require the same sort of regulation. The work of codification, which began for the first time in the Church in the late nineteenth century along the lines of modern civil codifications of law, was done while ecclesiology was still in an embryonic state, not yet able to distinguish and arrange the different aspects of the mystery. In an orderly, updated fashion canonists collected a whole set of documents, decisions, customs and compilations, which were above all the product of centuries of work by the Roman Curia, without sufficiently distinguishing which element of the ecclesial mystery these documents might pertain to. Despite the obvious advances in ecclesiology, it was not possible to elucidate better the reform of the codification that led to the new Code of 1983, and so the "mixed" character of the object of canon law remains. We are not certain that this situation is altogether satisfactory.

In the social communion, justice and charity are a service with a view to the collaboration of all in the building up of the common good. Consequently, at the particular level of those who have communal responsibilities, we should find again in the Church what *Gaudium et spes* says about civil authority:

> An authority is needed to guide the energies of all towards the common good—not mechanically or despotically, but by acting above all as a moral force based on freedom and a sense of responsibility.... Political authority ... must be exercised within the limits of the moral order and directed toward the common good (understood in the dynamic sense of the term) according to the juridical order legitimately established or due to be established. Citizens, then, are bound in conscience to obey (Rom 13:5; *GS* 74).

"A Code of Canon Law is absolutely necessary for the Church. Since the Church is established in the form of a social and visible unit, it needs rules," i.e., canonical norms.

63. It is advisable to distinguish the authentic preaching of the faith and celebration of the sacraments insofar as they depend on the social communion (ordering these services socially) and these ministries insofar as they depend on the diaconal communion (safeguarding the authenticity of these acts); since this distinction is not made, the Codes establish juridical norms for the ministries as a whole.

This function of social direction is expressed in the Church through the *munus regendi* [governing office] of her pastors:

This power, which [the bishops] exercise personally in the name of Christ, is proper, ordinary and immediate, although its exercise is ultimately controlled by the supreme authority of the Church and can be confined within certain limits should the usefulness of the Church and the faithful require that. In virtue of this power bishops have a sacred right and a duty before the Lord of legislating for and of passing judgment on their subjects, as well as of regulating everything that concerns the good order of divine worship and of the apostolate. (*LG* 27)

The verb forms "legislating—passing judgment—regulating" refer to the triad in Montesquieu's separation of powers: legislative, judiciary, executive. This is about the so-called "power of governance."[64] Here we are at the level of a *social* authority. The document just cited adds the order of worship and of the apostolate. We propose here that one should distinguish within these areas what in fact falls under a social type of administration (for example, drawing parish boundaries) and is actually involved in that sort of government, from what falls under the preaching of the faith, which concerns the diaconal communion that we will consider afterward.[65] The social authority, properly speaking, presupposes all that the ecclesial community possesses by way of sociological realities that are the object of social justice in the first place, which is then accomplished by charity.

The social communion and geography

The ecclesial social communion, unlike political social communions, is not limited by any territorial boundary. This aspect is proper to religious communities that have a universal aim. However, in order to insure the services that it must provide, this ecclesial social communion necessarily undergoes a certain geographical division into what one could call "local social communions." This geographical factor is the basis of the diversity of disciplines, liturgies, theologies ... because this local division espouses cultural diversity. For this reason,

---

64. See can. 135, §1.
65. Here we have an example of what we said about the present situation in canon law, which does not distinguish between the respective logics of the two communions and thus runs the risk of confusing them.

the universal social communion is the federation of all the local social communions. We must not jump to the conclusion that the universal Church is the sum of the local churches. In the mystery of the Church, the social communion is not the only element. We will see a little further on that the diaconal communion follows a different logic. We will discuss the complex relationship of the universal Church and the particular churches under the heading of the catholicity of the Church.

The social communion and history

The study of Church history clearly shows that the way of living in the social communion is very diversified, not only in one era because of the different cultures that coexist, but also over time. There may be advances or setbacks. There is, indeed, a certain parallelism between the way in which the political social communion lives and the way in which the ecclesial social communion lives while being present within civil society. The same persons make up the two social communions. But this is not a simple parallelism that would show points of coincidence between the two social communions. There may be mutual influences: either the ecclesial social communion shows the political social communion progress that the latter should make,[66] or, vice versa, the civil social communion may devise advances that—after discernment and sometimes delays—will be integrated into the life of the ecclesial social communion:

> The Church has a visible social structure, which is a sign of its unity in Christ; as such it can be enriched, and it is being enriched, by the evolution of [civil] social life—not as if something were missing in the constitution which Christ gave the Church, but in order to understand this constitution more deeply, express it better, and adapt it more successfully to our times. (GS 44, §3)

Because the Christian community presupposes the social character of man, advances in civil social life can clarify the progress that is to be made in ecclesial social life. Even though social progress is often made through political upheavals in which good and evil are inextricably mixed, it is necessary for Christians to be able to discern in these confused and sometimes baffling events the authentic goods that are

---

66. Think, for example, of the influence that the missions had in countries with a primitive political culture.

to be accepted. For example, the French Revolution and the movement that it imprinted on nineteenth-century political life promoted a new conception of the citizen, albeit through sharply contrasting events. Whereas the king of France thought of himself as the father of his subjects, who perpetually remained minors in his sight, the republic declared that citizens had attained majority and were capable of taking in hand the destiny of the nation. Most Christians did not see it right away and even fought it, and nineteenth-century Europe bore the scars of severe confrontations. Whatever one may think of that turbulent history, in which exaggerations, wrongs, and errors were not just on one side, the modern world has promoted a supplementary and superior dimension of human dignity: political dignity and its expression, which is the democratic ideal. It is quite clear that this cannot be inconsequential in ecclesial life.

If we want to do justice to the social aspect of ecclesial communion, we cannot refuse to consider the current demand for democracy in the life of the Church. Certainly this must be sifted carefully and cannot be applied to the diaconal communion, which has a different logic, as we will see. The claim must be tested and even purged of errors that distort the democratic ideal and render it incompatible with Christian life, as well as with sound civil social life.[67] Once these qualifications and corrections have been made—and that should suffice to clear up many misunderstandings—democracy can help us to understand better the requirements of participation, dialogue, and shared responsibility in the Church today and to put them into practice. This is not at all about rethinking what is called "the divine right constitution" of the Church,[68] any more than it can be about liberating oneself from the natural law in civil society. Rather, it is about understanding better and honoring the way in which human beings participate in a responsible, adult way—in other words, freely, in the life of a social unit. Here too, ultimately, what is at stake is charity in its modern requirements. We recalled previously in this regard the modernity of the ecclesiology of communion.

Since the distinction between what is essential and what is not is

67. For example, the denial of natural law.
68. Instead of this legal terminology, we prefer to speak about the diaconal communion as it was established and instituted by Christ on the foundation of the apostolic charism.

not always easy, a critical consideration of the evolution of the civil social reality is always necessary for ecclesial life so that it may evaluate its own way of living out its social character.

The social communion and ecclesial visibility

The social communion [of the Church] is a reality of this world—natural human sociability—and hence it is visible in its physical qualities. It appears therefore as a community of a religious sort like many others: it has a heritage, a culture, rites, a history.... But if it is considered *theologically*—that is, within the ecclesial *mystery*—we recognize that it has the nature of a *sign*, and hence its "external" visibility points to a signified reality, which is precisely the diaconal communion and, through it, mediately, the communion of the theological virtues. The social communion thus makes visible *to faith* the economy of grace, in which grace does not suppress nature, but dwells within it so as to restore it first and then to elevate it.[69] Recall that salvation as participation in beatitude is not what is signified here in the first place, but rather salvation as the restoration of the epiphanic finality of creation. This leads us to the following point.

The social communion as a source of temptation

This is a moral fact that we are just mentioning, although our dogmatic proposal is able to bring it to light.

The communion of the theological virtues is in the social communion as its most profound vital principle (charity). There is a risk, however, of confusing the first sign, which is the social communion, with the ultimate reality, which is the communion of the theological virtues. In short, one might think that the administrative, juridical, and financial well-being of "the Church" is directly connected with the well-being of the communion of the theological virtues. To put it another way, does making important progress in the social communion necessarily guarantee progress in the theological communion? Is the natural perfection of the sign necessary for the perfection of the reality of grace that it contains? It seems clear to us that history proves the opposite in

---

69. These adverbs "first" and "then" designate logical moments; in other words, they establish a distinction of order in the being and not a chronology, since grace accomplishes the restoration and the elevation of the recipient in one and the same movement.

this regard: perfection in the theological virtues is at the heart of the perfection of the sign. In other words, the fervor of faith and charity incidentally and positively reflects back upon the ecclesial social ties, which can then be expressive signs (still along the lines of the specific signification of the social communion): on the one hand, a primary signification of *gratia sanans,* and on the other hand, secondary signification referring to the diaconal communion.

This is the role of consecrated life in the Church: to remind us of this order of priority and these distinctions among the various aspects. As soon as the Church experienced the temptation of worldliness (today we would say of "secularization") at the end of the persecutions by the Roman Empire, the hermits, the ascetics, the monks and consecrated persons of all kinds recalled the eschatological purpose of our life here below. This is to say that social perfection is by no means an ultimate purpose, nor is it a prerequisite in all respects for the diaconal communion and hence for the communion of the theological virtues. Indeed, a social sign that is poor, weak, and humble, yet just and charitable, better manifests this pilgrim character of the mystery.[70] Therefore, the social sign should not be cultivated for its own sake, but should be measured by some other criterion than its worldly perfection. This is where the diaconal communion comes in.

2. The diaconal communion

We keep repeating: the communion of the theological virtues is *in* the social communion to such an extent as to be one with it. This is our first finding, to give credit to the remarks in *LG* 8, §1. This is to say that the two communions subsist in the same individual persons, and that their social relations are already relations of the theological virtue of charity. But we know that the subjects in whom these two communions subsist are all sinners, so that the theological communion can vary in intensity in these persons, and, by that very fact, what the social communion ultimately signifies is always uncertain and inconstant. This is why

70. It seems to us that this is easy to prove from experience and observation: when a local social ecclesial communion is socially rich and powerful, then often its life in the theological virtues is lax. In consecrated life it is an obvious truth that the fervent and "effective" beginnings of an institute are always poor and humble, whereas its "establishment" in a "superficial" state of ease often goes hand in hand with a certain loss of its initial fervor.

we have identified, starting from the sacramentality of the Eucharist, the existence of another communion that infallibly makes the connection between the social and the theological; this additional communion guarantees in a social form God's permanent offer in and through the theological virtues, so that we might enter ever more deeply into communion with him or to return to it if sin has separated us from him. This "intermediate" communion is the diaconal communion.

The divine communication

We have already pointed out that the communion of the theological virtues was engendered by a divine communication in the Incarnate Word and the Spirit, who bring to life in the humanity of the Savior the source of all truth (the transfiguration of Christ) and of all charity (the baptism of Christ). Tradition notes the close correspondence between these two Trinitarian manifestations and the two pentecosts of which the apostles were the beneficiaries. Here we cite St. Thomas, who is a reliable witness to the patristic exegesis:

The visible mission (of the Holy Spirit) was directed to Christ at the time of His baptism by the figure of a dove, a fruitful animal, to show forth in Christ the authority of the giver of grace by spiritual regeneration; hence the Father's voice spoke, "This is My beloved Son" (Mt 3:17), that others might be regenerated to the likeness of the only-Begotten. The Transfiguration showed (the Holy Spirit) forth in the appearance of a bright cloud, to show the exuberance of doctrine; and hence it was said, "Hear ye Him" (Mt 17:5).

To the apostles the mission (of the Holy Spirit) was directed in the form of breathing to show forth the power of their ministry in the dispensation of the sacraments; and hence it was said, "Whose sins you shall forgive, they are forgiven" (Jn 20:23): and again (the Holy Spirit was sent) under the sign of fiery tongues to show forth the office of teaching; whence it is said that, "they began to speak with divers tongues" (Acts 2:4; *Summa theologiae* I, q. 43, art. 7, ad 6).

There is a close connection between the two visible missions of the Holy Spirit upon Christ and the two visible missions of the Holy Spirit upon the apostles: the era of the Church is the era in which Christ, seated at the right hand of the Father, continually pours out through his Spirit the grace of faith and charity on all mankind by the ministry of the apostles who have been chosen for that purpose. Hence we can make two main observations as follows:

Apostolic mediation

The divine communication reaches mankind through apostolic mediation. The latter is expressed by a ministry that has a twofold object. On the one hand, the preaching of the Gospel so as to give birth to faith, instruct it, and defend it; this is the *munus docendi* (office of teaching). On the other hand, the actual gift of what was proclaimed so that believers may effectively live the mystery of divine charity; this is the *munus sanctificandi* (office of sanctifying). This is where we have situated what we called the fundamental permanence that can be discerned in the Church, which enables us to be assured of her constant identity and power to save. The real, efficacious offer of God is unceasingly addressed to mankind through this sign and this instrument (in the broad sense), which is the apostolic institution within the community. A deliberate and obstinate break with the apostles, whether in a matter of faith (heresy) or with regard to charity (schism), is a break with the divine offer itself; someone who rejects the apostles in this sense rejects Christ, and whoever rejects Christ rejects also the Father who sent him (Lk 10:16).[71]

The hierarchical communion

In order for the apostolic ministry to be unified (preaching the same faith, celebrating the same sacraments), there is a communion specific to pastors that Vatican II calls the *hierarchical communion*. In the conciliar documents this expression very precisely designates the unity of pastors with one another at all degrees of the hierarchy. Faith and charity are involved here in a way that is particular to pastors. This is why we do not share the idea that one could—at least on the basis of the teaching of Vatican II—designate by this expression the whole mystery of the Church present here below.

The human partaking

The lay faithful respond by their "fiat" to the divine offer that is expressed through the acts of preaching and sacramental celebration performed by the pastors, and this is what engenders the diaconal commu-

---

71. See *LG* 14, §1 (no salvation outside the Church); and 20.

nion—in other words, a community that as a whole confesses (*verbo et exemplo*) and celebrates (*in spiritu et veritate*), thus manifesting the ultimate reality of the communion of the theological virtues. The initial acts of the "descending" apostolic mediation are followed by the multitude of acts of the whole Christian People who make up the testimony offered to God in the sight of the world, which is their witness to the universal offer of salvation and the communication of this same salvation by way of intercession. This intense diaconal life of the whole community is permanently dependent on its apostolic source, without which it can neither be inaugurated nor remain, much less grow. But the apostolic mediation does not exhaust the whole life of this communion. The latter is really what it should be only with the collaboration of the lay faithful as a whole on the basis of the "apostolicity," one might say—a second and subordinate apostolicity, to be sure, but nonetheless real—of baptism and confirmation.[72] This leads us to consider the very life of this diaconal communion.

The life of the diaconal communion

This life is not directly dependent on the life of the theological virtues. It was founded for the sake of it, as we suggested previously, upon the sacramental characters of baptism, confirmation, and holy orders. Recall briefly the doctrine of indelible character: it is conferred by certain sacraments as a sort of participation in the *tria munera Christi* [three offices of Christ]. Christians are configured to Christ by a certain spiritual capacity to place acts that depend on the priesthood of Christ. By this priesthood, the Lord placed acts by which he arranged for human beings to enter into the communion of the theological virtues (preaching), and he effectively caused this entrance (his *acta et passa in carne*—actions and sufferings in the flesh). By the sacramental characters, Christians receive the ontological ability to place the acts of Christ during the time of the Church's pilgrimage in this world (*ST* III, q. 63, art. 5, corpus). These characters distinguish those who belong to Christ in the social ecclesial sign so that they constitute the diaconal reality with a view to the

---

72. It seems to us that this could explain the resolution of the debate concerning Catholic Action by the remarks in the Decrees *Apostolicam actuositatem* 3 and *Ad gentes* 11, which prefer to base this apostolate on baptism rather than on a delegation from the hierarchical apostolicity.

communion in the theological virtues. Because the baptism of blood and the baptism of desire are received outside the social communion, they do not confer character and do not establish those who are baptized in those ways as actual members of the diaconal communion.

From the perspective of efficacy, character should be considered in terms of *ex opere operato*. If the individual subject acts by virtue of the efficacy of the character that he has received, the community itself made up of all those who bear that character can be said in a way to bear that character, because it subsists in its members. But the community supplies its own note, on the one hand because of its permanence (the individuals pass away, the community remains), and on the other hand because of the particular bond of the community as such with the Holy Spirit, its soul. Although the particular individual, even if he is an apostle, can err in the faith, for example, the community as such cannot, because of the assistance of the Spirit promised to it by Christ. This distinction of the community as such from the individuals of which it is composed will be studied in more detail in the following question concerning the personality of the Church. For the moment let us note that the community as such, whatever may be the fervor of its members, continually guarantees the permanence of the proclamation of the true faith and of the celebration of the genuine sacraments. Once again, recall that the diaconal communion does not manifest with certainty at one or another moment in history, in this or that geographical place, the presence of the communion of the theological virtues, but it always makes it possible. To put it more precisely: the diaconal communion does not manifest the communion in the theological virtues as an accomplished fact (*in facto esse*), but rather insofar as it is becoming or in renewal (*in fieri*).

This permanence of the diaconal communion is seen in two main points:

The permanence of the faith, or the *sensus fidei fidelium*[73]

The expression *sensus fidei* signifies the universal consent of the baptized (both pastors and lay people) to the truths concerning faith

---

73. "The faithful's sense of the faith." In documents we encounter the expressions *sensus fidei* [sense of the faith] or *sensus fidelium* [sense of all the faithful]; since they designate the same reality, we combine the two expressions here.

and morals (*LG* 12). This is a constant witness of the community as such, a gift of the Holy Spirit. This is why, during a liturgical gathering, for example, the faithful do not profess their personal faith, but rather the faith of the Church. The recitation of the Creed during the Eucharist is an ecclesial act and not primarily an act of religion performed by one individual. This witness to the faith of the Church is the fundamental proclamation of the community, guaranteed in its infallibility by the Holy Spirit.

The permanence of sacramental celebration

Here the sacraments are being considered as a communal manifestation that signifies with certainty the gift of grace (the connotation of "descending" mediation). The celebration is the participation of believers in Christ's priesthood through the characters of baptism, confirmation, and holy orders. In a related way, the celebration also signifies the response of the faithful to God's gift (the connotation of "ascending" mediation), but this second aspect, which is the perfection of the celebration, depends on the communion in the theological virtues, and it can be absent or diminished.

The permanence of the sacramental offering is necessary in order for the Church to be the place—both certain and constant—where Christ builds up his Mystical Body. For this purpose there is a certain order among the sacraments that culminates in the Eucharist. In the first place, there are the sacraments that make it possible to celebrate the Eucharist—in other words, the sacraments that confer a character (baptism, confirmation, holy orders). The Eucharist presupposes also that the recipients are well-disposed by the medicinal sacraments (penance and, in this regard, the anointing of the sick). The Eucharist is the only plenary manifestation of Christ building up his ecclesial Body. The Eucharist, when we consider It under the aspect of the diaconal communion (movement of the "descending" mediation), is the instrument for edifying the communion of the theological virtues. This instrument is none other than the instrument that is the sacred humanity of Christ. Hence, when *Lumen gentium* says that the Eucharist is "the source and summit of the Christian life" (*LG* 11), we must understand that it is the "source" in the diaconal communion and the "summit" in the communion of the theological virtues.

The diaconal communion in history

The irrevocable gift [*le don sans repentance*] of God in Christ that establishes the existence of the diaconal communion, and hence the possibility of the communion of the theological virtues, is the gift of the three sacramental characters of baptism, confirmation, and holy orders, with a view to the sacrament of the Eucharist. Thus the diaconal communion possesses a definitive and invariable being that remains substantially the same throughout history.

The distinction between clerics and lay people and the relation between them are constitutive features of this communion. In a community where they were lacking, one could not speak about a fully formed diaconal communion. This is the case with the Christian communities separated from the Catholic Church that have not preserved the sacrament of holy orders. Having recalled this, we must add, however, that the relation between clergy and laity can assume very different forms, depending on the era. In this regard, considering the logic of communion, it may seem that ecclesial life was richer in the Middle Ages than in our days. Indeed, the local conciliar institution (what the current Code of Canon Law for the Latin Church calls the national council or the provincial council) was put into practice better than today. The logic of a local council requires that the People of God as a whole are represented and have an opportunity to speak. Of course, the apostolic charism that belongs to the bishop is the only one that can judge matter of faith, but the preliminary deliberation that involves the community in all its components is not a mere detail. This broad participation promotes the manifestation of the *sensus fidei fidelium*. One might also say the same thing, but in reverse, about the liturgy, especially the Eucharistic liturgy: before Vatican II the liturgy seemed to be chiefly the work of the clergy; in our days, the fact that it is a work common to the whole People of God seems to be highlighted better.

Another example: as for the celebration of the sacraments, everyone knows that, although the Church cannot change their *signification* (because the latter was instituted—in the final analysis—by Christ), the *elements of signification* have varied depending on the era.[74]

---

74. The most telling example is the case of priestly ordination, in which at least two rites were performed in succession: (1) the imposition of hands and the consecratory

After all, there are historical vicissitudes, either because the ecclesial mystery takes root gradually in a place or because it regresses during persecutions. In these cases, the diaconal communion—which in this respect is also connected to the specific state of the social communion—may not be complete to start with, or may not remain so. This is noted in the Vatican II Decree on Missionary Activity when it speaks about the birth of the Church in a place:

> Although the Church possesses in itself the totality and fullness of the means of salvation, it does not always, in fact cannot, use every one of them immediately, but it has to make beginnings and work by slow stages to give effect to God's plan. (*Ad gentes* 6)

Hence the question: what is the minimum required in order for the diaconal communion to exist? In our opinion, the necessary and sufficient condition in the beginning, or for survival, is that there be a *sensus fidei fidelium*, which presupposes sacramental baptism. The Eucharist could not be absent, but it could be received only spiritually if the faithful are prevented through no fault of their own from receiving it sacramentally. This is obviously a precarious state, but it has often been seen to preserve the community as it awaits the possibility of better conditions, especially during times of persecution.

The common good of the diaconal communion

The diaconal communion is a communal reality. Consequently, it possesses a common good. It has been pointed out that the common good of the social communion was to be built up based on the realities of nature. From this perspective, the common good of the diaconal communion is quite different. It is not something to be constructed, but rather is an *initial* gift of God in Christ, through his Spirit. It exists independently of men's seeking it, for it is the most gratuitous gift of God. It is made up of all the God-given means in Christ to attain him, to enter into the communion of the theological virtues. To put it another way, the Word of God and the sacraments, which are not under

---

epiclesis and (2) the presentation of the instruments of the Eucharist and the formula of the mandate. As for the sacraments of baptism and the Eucharist, however, for which Christ instituted *both* the signification *and* the elements of signification, the Church does not consider herself authorized to modify them, out of reverence for her Lord and respect for the historical value of this institution.

man's control, constitute this common good that is destined to be distributed without ceasing to exist, so as to be fulfilled in the personal perfection of each person who is a member of the group.

The preceding remarks do not mean that this given common good had no history. Once it was given to mankind *in via* [on their pilgrim way], it necessarily became part of the temporality that is an essential feature of human life on this earth. But this time and this history are not the time and history of a substantial growth of this reality; rather, we are talking about the time and history of the process whereby believers become conscious of this treasure and formulate it as well as possible. In other words, this time and history are called Tradition, whether doctrinal or liturgical. The infallibility of this living Tradition (i.e., the Tradition that is present and active in each era) is the expression of God's fidelity to his initial gifts made in Christ and through the Spirit. This is the true link that unites the fundamental elements of the mystery.

Conclusion

The theological unification that we propose may have several original features. But these are chiefly apparent or accidental (for example, the terminology). Above all, this theological observation is extremely traditional. It intends to synthesize the recent developments of ecclesiology in one perspective that is in harmony with all of Tradition. Our proposal has the following characteristics:

a. The rejection of a dialectical presentation

We do not follow the paradigm that we have called "binomial thinking," any more than our threefold communion fits into a pattern of "trinomial thinking." The three communions that we have distinguished are three aspects of one and the same reality: in the Church, *everything* is communion in the theological virtues, *in* a social communion *through* a diaconal communion. This is the irreplaceable contribution of [the notion of] sacramentality, correctly understood in terms of its source, who is Christ. Thus the connection between the mysteries is the principal path toward theological understanding.

b. The essential visibility of the Church

Ecclesial visibility must be confirmed as essential in all the aspects of the mystery, in each of the communions. The communion in the theological virtues, as "spiritual" as it may be, is engendered very visibly through a diaconal communion that could not be more incarnate, which subsists in a social sign. Thus the communion of the theological virtues can radiate, in its entirety, works of living faith that could not be purely interior.

This visibility has its degrees, depending on the integrity and the perfection of the three communions that are the Church. The perfection of this visibility is encountered wherever the three communions are present in all their integrity. Because of her unique fullness as far as the diaconal communion is concerned, the Catholic Church rightly claims the excellence of her visibility [as a Church]. But we must not forget the other two communions.

c. The twofold perspective: Essential and historical

We showed previously that the sequence of the first two chapters of *Lumen gentium* intended to pay homage to the essentialist perspective (the Church as Body of Christ) and the historical perspective (the Church as People of God). Our proposal tried to show that this twofold perspective could be discerned in each of the three communions—in other words, in the whole ecclesial mystery as it is present in this world.

It goes without saying that there is freedom of opinion in the area of speculative research, which is our field here. The reader may share this proposal or not, may correct it or elaborate on it.... We tried to honor the "specifications" that doctrine gives to theology in this matter: the different aspects of the ecclesial mystery do not make up different realities, but *"unam realitatem complexam efformant"* (*LG* 8, §1). We welcome criticism of this attempt.

BIBLIOGRAPHY
The sacramentality of the ecclesial communion
Sacramentality
See the bibliography at the end of Part I, chapter 5.

Congar, Yves. *Un Peuple messianique: Salut et libération.* Coll. Cogitatio fidei 85. Paris: 1975, esp. 32–33 and 63–66.
de La Soujeole, Benoît-Dominique. *Le Sacrement de la communion: Essai d'ecclésiologie fondamentale.* Paris and Fribourg: 1998, 247–73.
Journet, Charles. "Le mystère de la sacramentalité." *Nova et Vetera* (1974): 161–214.
Nicolas, Jean-Hervé. *Synthèse dogmatique.* Paris and Fribourg: 1983, 632–45.
Pagé, Jean-Guy. *Qui est l'Église?* Vol. 1, *Le mystère et le sacrement du salut.* 2nd ed. Montréal: 1982, 240–57.

The idea of communion
Biblical theology
Bori, P. C. *Koinonia: L'idea della comunione nell'ecclesiologia recente e nel Nuovo Testamento.* Brescia: 1972.
Campbell, J. A. "*KOINΩNIA* and Its Cognates in the N.T." *Journal of Biblical Literature* 51 (1932): 353–80.
Hauck, F. "*Koinos.*" In *Theological Dictionary of the New Testament* ("Kittel"). Grand Rapids, Mich.: Eerdmans, 1965, 3:789–97.
MacDermott, J.-M. "The Biblical Doctrine of *Koinonia.*" *Biblische Zeitschrift* 19 (1975): 230ff.
Seesemann, H. *Der Begriff Koinonia im N.T.* Giessen: 1933.

Patristic theology
Dewailly, Louis-Marie. "*Communio-communicatio:* Brèves notes sur l'histoire d'un sémanthème." *RSPT* (1970): 45ff.
Hertling, L. "Communio und primat." In *Miscellanea Historiae Pontificiae.* Rome: 1943. Translated into Italian as *Communio: Chiesa e papato nell'antichità cristiana.* Rome: 1961.
Lebeau, P. "*Koinonia:* La signification du salut selon S. Irénée." In *Epektasis,* mélanges offerts à J. Daniélou. Paris: 1972, 121–27.
Sieben, H. J. "*Koinonia.*" In *Dictionnaire de Spiritualité.* Paris: 1976, vol. 8, col. 1750ff.

St. Thomas Aquinas
Concerning the "quarrel" among Thomists to determine the meaning of "*communicatio*" in the theology of charity
Coconier, M. T. "Ce qu'est la charité d'après S. Thomas d'Aquin." *RT* (1906): 5–30.
Gillon, L.-B. "À propos de la théorie thomiste de l'amitié." *Angelicum* (1948): 3–17.

Proposed Definition 493

Labourdette, Marie-Michel. Cours de théologie morale, *la charité* [Course in moral theology, *charity*], mimeographed course notes for student use. Studium dominicain de Toulouse, 1959–1960, 26–37.
Lavaud, M.-B. "La charité comme amitié d'après S. Thomas." *RT* (1929): 445–75.
Simonin, H.-D. Critical review of M.-B. Lavaud. In *Bull. Thom.* III (1930): 77–79.

Concerning the definition of charity as a form of friendship; the originality of St. Thomas

Meersseman, G. G. "Pourquoi le Lombard n'a-t-il pas conçu la charité comme une amitié?" *Miscellanea Lombardiana*, Novara (1956): 165–74.

On the Aristotelian origin of the idea of friendship applied to charity

Gauthier R. A., and J.-Y. Jolif., *L'Éthique à Nicomaque*. French translation of the *Nicomachean Ethics*. Vol. 1. Louvain and Paris: 1958, book VIII. Commentary, vol. II-2. Louvain and Paris, 1959 (esp. 696–97).

On the breadth of the use of "communio-communicatio" vocabulary in St. Thomas

de La Soujeole, Benoît-Dominique. "Société et communion chez S. Thomas: Étude d'ecclésiologie." *RT* 90 (1990): 587–622.

Contemporary thought

Congar, Yves. "Peut-on définir l'Église? Destin et valeur de quatre notions qui s'offrent à le faire." In *Sainte Église*. Paris: 1963, 21–44. The author makes use of findings from German sociology.
———. "Note on the words 'Confession,' 'Church' and 'Communion.'" In *Dialogue between Christians*. Westminster, Md.: Newman Press, 1966, 184–213.

On the ambiguities caused by social philosophy and sociology

de La Soujeole, Benoît-Dominique. "L'Église comme société et l'Église comme communion au deuxième concile du Vatican." *RT* 91 (1991): 219–58 (esp. 221–34).

On the uses made of this vocabulary by modern theology

Acerbi, A. *Due ecclesiologie: Ecclesiologia giuridica ed ecclesiologia di communione nella "Lumen gentium."* Bologna: 1975. Good description of the redaction of *Lumen gentium* that establishes the two ecclesiological overviews that figure in it. No speculative investigation of the idea of communion, but some very useful elements.
de La Soujeole, Benoît-Dominique. (Preceding title.)
Hamer, Jérôme. *The Church Is a Communion*. New York: Sheed and Ward, 1964, 190ff. Theological usage on the basis of serious scriptural and patristic discernment.

Tillard, Jean-Marie Roger. *Église d'Églises*. Paris: 1987. English edition: *Church of Churches: The Ecclesiology of Communion*. Collegeville, Minn.: Liturgical Press, 1992. A wide-ranging description of the life of the ecclesial *koinonia* based on its chief acts. No speculative review, though, to define the idea.

On the uses of this vocabulary in the "Catechism of the Catholic Church"

Donneaud, H. "Note sur l'Église comme communion dans le Catéchisme de l'Église catholique." *RT* 95 (1995): 665–71.

The sensus fidei fidelium

Congar, Yves. *Lay People in the Church: A Study for the Theology of the Laity*. Part 2, chapter 3, "The Laity and the Church's Prophetical Function." Westminster, Md.: Newman Press, 1957, 258–308.

———. *Tradition and the Life of the Church*. London: Burns and Oates, 1964, 75–78.

Narcisse, Gilbert. "Sensus fidei." In *Dictionnaire critique de théologie*. Paris, 1998, 1089–90.

Pié-Ninot, S. "Sensus fidei." In *Dictionary of Fundamental Theology*, edited by René Latourelle and Rino Fisichella, 992b–95a. New York: Crossroad, 1994.

Tillard, Jean-Marie Roger. "Magistère, théologie et *sensus fidelium*." In *Initiation à la pratique de la théologie*. Paris: 1982, 1:1632–82.

SECTION 2

The Personality of the Church

The question about the personality of the Church is the summit, the quintessence of speculative ecclesiology. In order to present it pedagogically, it is advisable to start with a few philosophical reminders.

11

Some Philosophical Ideas Recalled

I. THE METAPHYSICS OF BEING OR SUBSTANCE

The *real* definition manifested the *unity* of this being that is the Church and the relations among its elements (unity of the complex being).[1] The Church is not "this" plus something else in addition; she is "this." Now, as we know, "one" is a property of being, and not being itself *simpliciter*. The oneness is not the whole being. We say that it is a *transcendental*, a fundamental note, inseparable from being, like the true and the good. Wherever there is being, there will consequently be unity, truth, and goodness.

What does "one" tell us about being? Essentially that it is not divided: "*Ratio unitatis consistit in indivisione*" (*I Sent*. d. 24, q. 1, art. 2). This also expresses identity: every being is itself and not something else or something more. Identity does not necessarily mean *autonomy*—in other words, the fact of not needing anything else but itself in order

---

1. Our speculative theological effort is based on a philosophy that is a metaphysics of substance. In order to examine in greater depth the basic notions that we recall here, the reader may consult the following works: H.-D. Gardeil, *Introduction to the Philosophy of St. Thomas Aquinas*, vol. 3, *Psychology*, and vol. 4, *Metaphysics* (St. Louis: Herder, 1956ff.); R. Verneaux, *Philosophie de l'homme*, 2nd ed. (Paris: 1964), and P.-B. Grenet, *Ontologie*, 2nd ed. (Paris: 1963). For the notion of *person* as it is assumed in dogmatic theology, chiefly to present the mystery of Christ, see *Initiation théologique*, vol. 4, 3rd ed. (Paris: 1961), particularly J.-M. Manteau-Bonamy and A.-M. Henry, "Le mystère de l'Incarnation, ou le mystère de l'union des deux natures (dans le Christ)," 85–94.

to exist. There is only one absolute One, God. Apart from the case of God, oneness or undividedness is *relative*. On the one hand, every being is *contingent*—that is, it could have not existed. Consequently it takes its existence from something other than itself. On the other hand, every being is a *composite*, of matter and form for the most part, but at least of essence and existence in all cases. These unified parts do not form an aggregate of beings, but are closely united so as to form *a single being*. Thus man (matter and form = body and soul) is not formed by the combination of an angel and an animal—it is neither one nor the other—nor by a "mixture" of the two (a "*tertium quid*"). He is *man*—in other words, a whole consisting of substantial parts. The being is only in the whole composite, because only the whole possesses unity. All this is the metaphysical background to our search for the definition of the Church.

There is however "something" above the one, the metaphysical summit, which is precisely *being*. To say that a reality is one is to affirm one of its *transcendentals*. But we must ascend higher still and ask the question of being with regard to the Church: what sort of being is the Church? To put it another way, since being is the highest perfection, how does the Church possess this first perfection that is to be?

On this subject we know that every being, except God, is created. All being, therefore, *is* through participation. At the heart of the created being we distinguish [1] substantial being and [2] accidental being. The first stands [*se tient*] *per se* in the being: once placed in that being by the efficient cause (for everything that is not God is not *ab se*, from itself) and maintained as such, it perdures on its own; it does not need any other reality; it is complete. The second, while it is true being, cannot stand alone in being (it is neither *ab se* nor *per se*); it has need of a subject in which to subsist. For example, Peter stands alone in being; he possesses it on his own (although he acquired it from another). In contrast, this color blue (not the essence of blue, but the essence plus existence, *this blue*, the *fact of being blue*) subsists in being only in a specific subject (*this* pen, *this* automobile, *this* wall). *This* blue is an accidental being.

Our question with regard to the Church is now more precise: is the Church a substantial or an accidental being? To put it differently, is there in the Church "something" that formally constitutes it the subject of attribution of everything necessary for it to exist, so that it stands by itself in being? This "something" in metaphysics is called the supposit (Latin: *suppositum*), the "receptacle" of all that is necessary for it to exist "*per se*" as a substantial being. This *suppositum* in the being that is endowed with intellect and will acquires a certain nobility and autonomy; it receives the name of person. This word applies to God (*per prius*, first and foremost), and also to an angel and to a human being by analogy of attribution. Since the Church is made up of intelligent subjects with free will, the question arises of whether this profoundly unified whole of persons also achieves the perfection of being a person. When we speak about "the faith of the Church" in which every infant is baptized, can we consider the Church as a person? Can we attribute this or that act to the Church as such? The question is extremely important. We believe that the Church is infallible (the *sensus fidei* in its constancy and rightness); this is a quality of the *Church*, not of each of its members who, taken individually, can err in the faith. In the liturgy the Church is the acting subject of many actions (particularly the prayer of intercession, the sacramental actions that it performs with Christ). Would this be a metaphorical way of speaking, or does it in fact express something real? Hence the necessity of answering the question about the personality of the Church. In order to do that, we will first recall the fundamental elements of the idea of person; then we will attempt to respond for the case of the Church.

II. The idea of person

For this ecclesiological investigation, we will consider only real persons—that is, the different realities (God, an angel, a human being, and perhaps the Church) that *are* persons. This excludes from our discussion fictional persons. A fictional person is chiefly a legal fiction that allows the law to recognize a certain permanence and autonomy in human institutions. For example, in civil law, a business firm is an institution that is considered distinct from the associates of whom it is made up. This is why the debts of the firm E. I. du Pont de Nemours and Company are not the debts of Monsieur du Pont or of any of his associates. Canon law recognizes the legal personality of a diocese; it is an institution that continues to exist canonically, even without a bishop, when the ordinary dies and a successor has not yet been appointed. A fictional person exists only in the intention of the one who considers it, in this case the legislator. That is why it is a being of reason and not a real being. It is a construct of the mind, not a datum abstracted from reality. Sometimes, especially among jurists, these fictional beings are legal entities called *moral persons*; here "moral" means "on the order of intention." Let us return to the real person.

a. The three senses of the word "person"

This word has three distinct but not separate meanings, each of which expresses one precise aspect.

1. The moral sense

This is the most self-evident meaning, as when someone says that the characteristic of a person is the command of oneself. In that case we are calling a being that freely acts by itself a person. Someone who possesses intellect and will has the ability to control himself by himself; this is a person in the moral sense.

2. The psychological sense

The idea of psychological personality is also familiar to us. This being that acts freely is in the first place a subject who is conscious of being an "I" confronting the world, faced with everything that exists, particularly other persons. It is an "I" who relates everything that is not "I" to himself, who conceives of himself as a relation. This aspect of the person is what is first awakened in a child when he starts to say "I."

Psychological personality is not the same thing as moral personality. Here independence is not the main thing (a child has no independence), but rather the consciousness of self as distinct from anything else and in relation.

3. The metaphysical sense

This meaning is not self-evident, as the preceding two are. It is perceived thanks to the first two meanings, which set us on the right path, but it is arrived at only by speculative reflection, by abstraction from the more immediate data. Moral action refers to its principle (in order to act one must be), and consciousness is consciousness of "something"—namely, the "I" (it is not confused with that "something").

Thus at the root of free action and consciousness of self there is a certain being that comprehends itself and acts, because it is ontologically self-contained and self-possessed. At the metaphysical level, this "root" of self-awareness and of free action is called the person.

b. The person in the metaphysical sense

We will focus now on the metaphysical level only.

1. Vocabulary

The metaphysical reality of the person becomes apparent upon reflection as that which is at the origin of self-awareness and free action. The person, metaphysically speaking, is a reality that stands beneath the initial perceptions of free action and self-awareness. The person in the metaphysical sense is like the "basis," the "root," the "substratum" found "beneath" free action and self-awareness. In Greek this is precisely what the word *hypostasis* means. In other words, a hypostasis is what supports "something" and is the "foundation" thereof. Latin expresses the same thing by the word *substantia*. This is a question of expressing the reality as distinguished from its manifestations. The appearances belong to the domain of what is empirically observable, but the reality is more extensive than that part of itself that it manifests to the senses. It possesses—and this is decisive in order to know it—a metaphysical level. Beneath the fact of emerging and growing, there is the metaphysical principle of this act.

The Latin word *substantia* [and its derivatives in European languages] designate the metaphysical level of any reality. We speak about the substance of the air, of this stone, of this horse, of this man . . . . The technical philosophical term "suppositum" is also used, although it is generally reserved for substances that attain the dignity of a person.

To summarize, the relatively recent word *"person"* designates a *hypostasis*, a *substance*, or a *suppositum* of the highest metaphysical rank, which is to say that it has such dignity that it makes the living thing capable of the most sublime acts—namely free actions and self-awareness. In short, every person is a hypostasis or a substance or even a suppositum, but not every hypostasis, substance, or suppositum is a person.

2. The person in himself

This uniqueness of the person must now be considered for its own sake and not in relation to the acts that are rooted in it. In order to learn about the person [in general], we will consider the human person, who is the most easily knowable to us.

The human person is, according to the classic definition of Boethius, "*an individual substance of a rational nature.*"[2]

Individuality

Every individual (except God) is always a complex being—that is, one composed of matter and form, in the case of man, or at least of essence and existence, in the case of an angel, who is only form. Individuality (the fact of being undivided) also denotes the unity of the being that does not exist in its parts, but only in the whole (human being = body + soul).

An individual is a precise being distinct from every other. Paul, Adele, John are individuals; Paul is neither Adele nor John, Adele is neither Paul nor John, and so on. Individuality is contrary to universality. The Latin word for man, *homo*, designates a universal because it applies just as much to Paul as to Adele or John. In grammar we say that the individual is designated by a proper name (Paul, Adele, John), and the universal is designated by a common noun (man).

Substance

The substance causes the individual to attain to the perfection of a subsisting thing. When an individual has its principle of subsistence in itself and not in something else, we say that it is a substantial being. An individual can, in fact, be a substance or an accident. An accident is something that subsists not by itself but through something else in which it inheres. Then that other thing is the substance.

---

2. *De Persona* III, in PL 64.1343c; St. Thomas reuses this definition in treating the subject of the Incarnate Word; cf. *ST* III, q. 2, art. 3.

Rationality[3]

To speak of a "rational nature" means here the intellect not only as the faculty of knowing, but also as the light that guides the will.

The subsisting individual endowed with intellect and will is equipped with a view to acting according to the greatest dignity that there is: acting by himself because he has mastery of his acts. He can act by himself because he knows and wills. The name of "person" is reserved exclusively to this type of being. Here we are in the order of action: knowing and willing are acts. But in order to act it is first necessary to be. Hence this perfection of operative principles, which are neither animal instinct nor the natural inclination of the vegetable kingdom, points to a perfection of being: ontological self-containment and self-possession to the highest degree, which implies psychological consciousness of self and freedom of choice.

Having made these clarifications, we can now address the question of the Church.

---

3. Vocabulary note: the faculty of knowing is the *intellect*. In man, the intellect is called *reason* because it does not grasp its object, the true, at first, but only at the end of a process of reasoning. Given that clarification, we use the words "intellect" and "reason" indifferently in the case of man, but not for God or for an angel.

12

The Question about the Personality of the Church

The Church, as the nominal definition (*Ecclesia*) already says, is a community of physical persons. We have here then a peculiarity that must be noted: in this being called Church there are physical persons and there is the unity that they form among themselves. The physical persons (Peter, Frances, John) are real persons *simpliciter*, who are substances. Can the community made up of these persons also constitute a person who is real, but *secundum quid* (in a certain way)? To answer this question we must start from the typical example of human community, which is political society.

I. Elements of social metaphysics

Let us attempt to review the constitutive elements of metaphysical personality in order to see whether there is a certain realization of this perfection in the political community.

a. The criterion of substance

The first thing that distinguishes a physical person from a community of physical persons is substance. The physical person *simpliciter* (Peter, Frances, John) is a substance; the parts of which he or she is composed (soul + body) form a single substance by their unity. For this reason we call this unity a substantial unity. The substance cannot exist without the elements of which it constitutes the unity. This unity is unity par excellence, the closest and strongest unity that there is in the created thing. On the contrary, the unity of a civil community is accidental—in other words, a *superadded* unity, a unity among elements that are already substances, the real physical persons who are members of the society and remain such. Aggregation into a society does not "depersonalize" the members. Whereas the soul and body of Paul are substantial parts and not substances, the union of which truly constitutes the "substance" Paul, the meeting of Peter, Frances, John around a common good, in political friendship, thanks to a government, does indeed form a whole that is distinct from the persons of which it is composed, but not a substantial whole. It is an accidental whole made up of substances. Nevertheless, this accidental whole is not occasional, random, left entirely to the choice of human beings. It is necessarily called for by the individual physical persons because of a requirement of their nature.[1] With regard to the first element of personality, substance, it does not seem that we can attribute personality to civil society. Should it therefore be placed at the same level as the commercial company? Is it nothing more than a moral person in that sense? It seems not, since the existence of civil society is a natural given in the first place and not only a cultural artifact. This is to say that society is founded on the substantial requirements of its members.

b. The criterion of individuality

A social community is a complex reality. It possesses parts that are its members, but it is *one* in the sense that it exists only in the group formed by its members. It is a concrete whole as distinct from an abstract universal. Hence it is distinct from other social communities, as Switzerland, for example, is distinct from France.

But this unity is not a substantial unity, because the social whole, as necessary as it is because of its natural foundation, does not subsist by itself, but rather in the particular persons who are its members. One

---

[1]. Here we encounter the importance of the statement that human beings are naturally sociable, which does not run counter to the dignity of the physical persons gathered in society, because the fact of nature is taken up into a collaboration with the fact of culture.

cannot consider society *apart from* those who make it up, unless one is making an abstraction of mere reason. It is easy to see this: to do away with the members (for example, by genocide) is to cause the society to disappear, because it has no more *supposita* in which to subsist.

c. The criterion of a rational nature

Is the political community a whole with a rational nature? Required by nature and brought about by culture, its acts are acts that proceed from the intellect and will of its members as members—in other words, as parts of the whole. Considering society, then, *in terms of* its members, subsisting in them, we can point out first of all activity belonging to the group that cannot be attributed exclusively to any part. For example, one may speak about French culture, which is the culture of the whole as such and not the sum total of what is possessed by the members, even though this culture can be built up and experienced only through the activity of the members. Indeed, the radically new thing that this whole contributes, which is distinct from each of its members, is the principle of integration [*totalisation*] or unity, which consequently implies *permanence*. The social group lasts and assures a transmission from generation to generation, has a memory and plans for the future, whereas each of its members is limited in time. If this cultural activity does belong to society, it allows us to infer a certain being to which it can be attributed, a social being distinct from the beings that are its components. Thus we can consider that there is more in the whole, even though it is accidental, than in the sum of its parts, and that this whole has a certain autonomy in relation to the parts.

Political society therefore has a certain sort of personality. In its own way it fulfills the criteria:

- Individuality: united in itself and distinct from others.
- Being: although its being is *accidental,* it is *necessary* (required by nature).
- Of a rational nature: its acts proceed from the knowledge and will of its members *as members* (parts of the whole).

Hence we see that the idea of person is imperfectly actualized by political society. The great dissimilarity is that society does not subsist by itself. Therefore it cannot be a subject purely and simply (*simplici-*

The Personality of the Church

ter). It does constitute, however, a subject distinct from those who are its components, a subject to whom we attribute some acts that cannot be attributed purely and simply to the members as individual persons. Given these clarifications, let us attempt to answer the question about the Church.

II. THE PERSONALITY OF THE CHURCH

The definition of the Church enabled us, on the one hand, to explain the different elements of this complex being and, on the other hand, to account for the unity in which these elements are held as well as their mutual relations. In short, the definition of the Church demonstrated the individuality of the ecclesial being. The Church is a reality that is one, undivided, individual. The Church does fulfill the first criterion for being a person. Now we must see whether the Church subsists by itself. Depending on whether we answer this question yes or no, we will conclude whether the acts attributed to the Church are its own or not.

a. The question as to the subsistence of the Church

Like political society, the Church does not subsist by itself, but rather in its members. Therefore it has an accidental subsistence. But the question must be pressed further because of the particular *supernatural* level at which we find ourselves in the case of the Church—not at the level where grace restores nature, but rather at the one where it elevates it. There are in the Church, above and beyond the natural level (the natural sociability that is taken up into it), two supernatural ontological levels that are distinct, yet not separate. The members in whom the Church subsists are united by created grace,[2] but they are united moreover inasmuch as they are personally and communally "animated" by the Holy Spirit in Person.[3]

There is on the one hand an ontology of grace, a *created* supernatural ontology (the grace of the virtues and the gifts) that qualifies the baptized person as such, making this human being a Christian

---

2. We are talking about the *specific* unity that we pointed out in the study of the Church as Temple of the Spirit.

3. This is what we presented as *numerical* unity.

and making the community composed of Christians as a whole—the Church. There is on the other hand an *uncreated* supernatural ontology, the indwelling of the Holy Spirit in each member, [the Spirit who is] "one and unique in each and in all" (the soul of the Church), who perfects the Church by perfecting the Christian, giving him, so to speak, a common soul with his peers. The Church consequently subsists in each Christian insofar as he is graced (created grace) and possesses the indwelling of the Spirit (uncreated grace). The subjects in whom the Church subsists are, in a certain way "more than themselves," which leads us to consider a kind of subsistence in the Spirit.[4]

b. Consequences at the level of acts placed by the Church

This extremely complex ontology explains the twofold way in which the subject "Church" places the acts that can be attributed to the community as such. On the one hand, in the case of the supreme acts of its activity—the "source" acts on which the very existence of the Church depends, the acts of the diaconal communion—we must refer them ultimately to God (the Holy Spirit), since the community of Christians is in some way his *instrument*. We are talking about the continuance in the infallible preaching of the Gospel and in the uninterrupted celebration of the authentic sacraments. Here the Church subsists ultimately in Christians insofar as they possess the indwelling of the Holy Spirit. The Church subsists, not purely and simply in the Holy Spirit—there is no union of a hypostatic sort between Christians and the Holy Spirit—but rather in the persons who are communally animated by the Holy Spirit. The quality of the acts that it places as an *adjunct instrument*[5] can be attributed in the final analysis to the Holy Spirit as the soul of the Church. On the other hand, the more "ordinary" acts of the Church, such as those that fall under the care of the social communion (although they too benefit from the assistance of the Holy Spirit), can still be attributed to the Church as a distinct subject, a *secondary cause*.

---

4. We can put it as St. Paul did: "It is no longer I who live, but Christ who lives in me" (Gal 2:20). The Church subsists in believers in whom Christ lives by his Spirit, without thereby suppressing their personality.

5. We avoid saying "conjoined" so as not to liken this case to the humanity of the Incarnate Word hypostatically united to his divinity.

The Personality of the Church

In these acts the Church subsists accidentally in Christians, and the quality of its acts depends on the quality of its members.

This twofold supernatural ontological level present in the Church makes it an absolutely unique being, with nothing in creation quite like it; the idea of person is realized in this being only by way of a distant analogy. It is a so-called *mystical* person, subsisting in human beings inasmuch as they are graced (the created grace of the virtues and gifts) and insofar as they individually and communally possess the indwelling of the Holy Spirit (uncreated grace). This results in a relation that is simultaneously a very strong relation of unity (one soul), and yet also a relation of clear distinction. This mystical personality is very mysterious. It is based on a mode of union between the creature and God that is at the same time less than the hypostatic union (the Christian is not "one" with God as the son of Mary is "one" with the Word), and more than a simply moral union. Tradition calls this unique sort of union "*mystical union.*"

We find again here the two aspects of the Church-Body of Christ (one being in a certain way because the Head and the Body do not make two beings) and the Church-Bride of Christ (two distinct, but united beings).

Conclusion

The question about the personality of the Church is not a purely intellectual exercise that smacks of rationalism and is supposed to captivate minds that have a speculative bent. It aims at a better understanding of the scriptural data. When St. Paul teaches simultaneously that the Church is the Body of Christ and his Bride, he notes at the same time the profound unity of Head and Body in one being, and the distinction between the Bridegroom and the Bride who are two beings. This is the scriptural way of pointing out the mystery. Our speculative categories try to grasp the most profound unity, which is much more than the moral unity of a political society, while at the same time maintaining the distinction. This is a *mystical* unity, which is defined chiefly by distinguishing it from what it is not rather than by affirming clearly what it is.

This term, "mystical unity," directs our attention again to the mystery-sacrament, and one could just as well speak about sacramental unity. If we remember that the ecclesial sacrament is made up of three communions that are only one, we can see better how the unity of the ecclesial sacrament is distributed according to the various levels of the mystery. The social type of unity is well suited to the social communion; here we are dealing with a moral unity, the product of grace, inasmuch as the latter renews social ties. The unity found only in the Church, which is attributed to the fact that she is animated by the Holy Spirit who by means of sacramental characters guarantees the preaching of the Gospel and the celebration of the sacraments, is a real unity—namely, the unity of diaconal communion. Finally, the highest unity of the Church, the one that is the goal pursued by the two preceding types, is unity in the theological virtues, which is also attributed to the Holy Spirit who conforms believers to the holiness of Christ. Mystical unity is the generic name for these three types of unity that make up only one—namely, the unity of the mystical person of the Church.

BIBLIOGRAPHY

The question about the personality of the Church has not been studied much at all to date and is very rarely presented by theological writers. Consequently the bibliography is very sparse. Our presentation is based chiefly on the works of Charles Journet.

Bouyer, Louis. *L'Église de Dieu*. Paris: 1970, esp. 601–6. English translation by Charles Underhill Quinn: *The Church of God*. San Francisco: Ignatius Press, 2011, 529–38.

Congar, Yves. "La personne 'Église.'" *RT* 71 (1971): 613–40. A very important study of the data of the patristic, medieval, and classical tradition at the origins of the modern problem.

Daguet, François. *Théologie du dessein divin chez Thomas d'Aquin: Finis omnium Ecclesia*. Paris: 2003. A very complete, high-quality presentation of the theology of St. Thomas concerning the union of Christ and the Church; cf. 407–51.

Journet, Charles. *L'Église du Verbe incarné*. Vol. 2. Paris: 1951, esp. chap. 4, 472ff.

———. "De la personnalité de l'Église." *RT* 69 (1969): 192ff.

———. "La sainteté de l'Église: Le livre de Jacques Maritain." *Nova et Vetera* 46 (1971): 1–33. This is the final stage of the doctrine of Journet, who adopts the developments by Jacques Maritain (see the next title). Fr. Congar bluntly critiques it, however.

Maritain, Jacques. *De l'Église du Christ: La personne de l'Église et son personnel*. Paris: 1970, esp. chap. 3. A very technical study.

Nicolas, Jean-Hervé. *Les Profondeurs de la grâce*. Paris: 1969, 306–80.

———. *Synthèse dogmatique*. Paris and Fribourg: 1985, 677ff. Good presentation of the various theological essays; the solution proposed is quite critical of Maritain-Journet.

Pagé, Jean-Guy. *Qui est l'Église?* Vol. 2, *L'Église, Corps du Christ et communion*. Montréal and Paris: 1985, 105–11. A presentation closely resembling Journet's.

Saphy, D. *L'Église est sainte: Sens du péché et repentance*. Coll. Croire et savoir 33. Paris: 2000. Good presentation of the question and a good review of the authors.

von Balthasar, Hans Urs. *Qui est l'Église?* Reprinted by Parole et Silence (S. Maur), 2000.

Part Three

The Properties of the Church

Introduction

By "properties" we mean specifications of the being of the Church, her fundamental characteristics. The Creed lists them: *one, holy, catholic, and apostolic*.

Most often theologians speak about "essential properties," for they are inseparable from the very being of the subject. If the Church ceased to be holy, for example, the whole Church as such would disappear. The distinction between essence and properties is conceptual, but there is a real identity: the same being is designated each time under one or another of its fundamental aspects. Consequently, wherever we observe apostolicity, there unity, holiness, and catholicity are found also. Although identical in the reality, these properties are conceptually distinct, because the ecclesial being is too rich for us to express in a single concept.

There are four of these properties, as listed in the Niceno-Constantinopolitan Creed. To tell the truth, as we have mentioned several times, unity is more than a property; it is a fundamental specification of being (a "transcendental"): every being is one (undivided, individual), even though it may be complex.

Does the fourfold characterization suggested by the profession of faith set a limit? Some writers add a fifth property: indefectibility. This underscores the permanence of the properties. Is this really a fifth property or a characteristic common to the four? We will conclude our study with this point.

We are dealing with *theology*; the object of our study is the *mystery* of the Church. Consequently, *one, holy, catholic, and apostolic* are considered here as properties that faith alone can recognize. That is to say that we will not address unity, holiness, catholicity, or apostolicity as simple *notes* or *marks* of the Church. What does this mean?

When we speak about the four notes of the Church, we are engaging in apologetics.[1] These are characteristics of the Church that can be apprehended by reason and are the basis for an argument about her supernatural identity.[2] Charles Journet develops this aspect by correctly saying that the notes are *miraculous facts* that everyone can see (just as everyone can see a lame person walking, miraculously healed in Lourdes). These notes are therefore above all *facts* that, being *miraculous*, are *signs* of a higher reality—namely, the properties of the Church, which, for their part, are *mysterious*. Authors do not always make this distinction between notes and properties.[3]

There is a certain orderly relationship among the four properties. We must not force things, but it is rather enlightening. From an initial perspective we can say:

- *One:* formal cause (the Holy Spirit, the grace of the virtues and of the gifts).
- *Holy:* final cause (beatitude).
- *Catholic:* material cause (all of humanity).
- *Apostolic:* efficient cause (the service of the [ordained] ministers).

This presentation, enlightening as it may be, is not without limitations, however. Some point out, in particular, that catholicity is not just a "material cause"; there is a qualitative catholicity that is decisive, but then it is not clearly distinguishable from the formal unity. This is why, in a deeper way, we must understand the properties—and the order among them—in light of the mystery of Christ, from whom the Church has come. Then we say:

- *One:* the foundation of the Church is the grace of the hypostatic union. In Christ, the unity of his divinity with his humanity is

1. "Note" comes from *notus* (past participle of *nosco*), meaning "known"; it is also used as an adjective (*notus, -a, -um*). Derivatives in English are "notorious," "notable," and the verb "to notify": to make known.

2. This is the "second look" at the Church that we described during our study of the mystery-truth.

3. See, in particular, Charles Journet, *L'Église du Verbe incarné*, 2:1194ff. and 2:1254ff.; see general bibiography.

what positions the latter as the sign and instrument of the former. There is a structural parallelism with the Church, whose supernatural and "divine" life is manifested and transmitted by her "human" life.

- *Holy:* the condition of the Church. In Christ, this is the superabundance of holiness (personal grace) that comes from the grace of the hypostatic union. In the same way, all ecclesial humanity, due to its intimate connection with the "divine" aspect of that same Church, is thus rendered holy, with an essential holiness.
- *Catholic:* the diffusion of the Church. In Christ, the fullness of personal grace is meant to be communicated (capital grace). Likewise with the Church, her holiness is meant to be communicated to all mankind.
- *Apostolic:* the vicarious presence of Christ the Head after Ascension-Pentecost and until the parousia.

While studying the Church descriptively (positive theology) and then in an explanatory way (speculative theology), we have often encountered one or another of these properties. Here we will not repeat any of that, which is all presupposed. We will now discuss more thoroughly certain questions that have not been treated with enough precision, especially catholicity and apostolicity.

13

The Church Is One

The Church is one, but Christians are divided. This chapter will discuss the efforts by which Christians are attempting to reestablish their unity. This is what has been called in the last fifty years *ecumenism*.[1]

Ecumenism is the name of the movement whereby Christians aim toward their reunion so as to *manifest* fully the unity of the Church. The unity of the Church exists—it is not something to be made; it is a gift from God since the very beginnings that cannot be lost.[2] But it is a question of manifesting it more and more, in an ever better way, so that *all the sheep may have the same faith, thanks to the same sacraments and under the guidance of the same pastors*. Ecumenism must not be confused with *inter-religious dialogue*. The latter is the dialogue between *Christians and non-Christians*. Its principles are analogous to those of ecumenism.[3]

I. Different ecumenical attitudes

The objective of the ecumenical movement has existed ever since there were divisions among Christians, and that started during the lifetime of

---

[1]. Theologians settled on the terminology "ecumenism" after World War II; before then Catholics used to speak about "the reunion of Christians" and "uniates" (*"unionisme," voire "uniatisme"*).

[2]. "*Credo unam Ecclesiam*" means, "I believe that the Church is one." The statement is in the present tense.

[3]. Interreligious dialogue is the topic of a special course that addresses the ques-

The Church Is One

the apostles. We know the struggles, the dialogues, the conciliar endeavors, the "uniate" movements throughout history that have attempted to heal these divisions. There have been successes, but always partial, and none definitive.[4] We consider here only that part of this history that started with the modern developments at the end of the nineteenth century.

One frequently hears that the modern ecumenical movement was born in the Protestant world, and that the Catholic and Orthodox Churches were late in joining it (after World War II). That is not accurate. The ecumenical *concern* arose almost everywhere in the late nineteenth century, but, admittedly, the *present institutional form* of this movement, in particular the World Council of Churches, is to a large extent the result of Protestant initiatives.

A vocabulary note: the usage of the Roman Curia is to call "Church" those communities that have preserved apostolic succession within them and, through this succession, the true Eucharist; this is the case with the Catholic and Orthodox churches. It calls "Christian ecclesial communities" those that have not preserved those spiritual goods; this is the case with Protestant Christians and the Anglican Communion. This usage, however, is dying out, leaving only the term "church." This is acceptable if one means by it that there is only one Church (*unicity*), fully manifested by the Roman Catholic Church, in which the separated "churches" participate in various ways.

a. The Roman Catholic Church

The Roman Catholic Church is the community of all the faithful whose pastors are in communion with the Bishop of Rome, who is the successor of Peter and, in connection with these two titles, head of the apostolic college. The notion of *romanitas* (Roman-ness) is dogmatic here and not liturgical (as in "the Roman Rite"). This community has the *de fide* conviction that it is the only one to have preserved intact within it the fullness of the means of salvation (faith, sacraments, ministries) and that, consequently, it is constantly and unfailingly the reality of sal-

---

tion, not only of the situation of the individual non-Christian, but also of the meaning and value of the non-Christian religion with regard to the salvation of its members. The two questions touch closely on the mystery of the Church.

4. On this point, pre-nineteenth-century ecumenism, see the fine article "Oecuménisme," in the *Dictionnaire de Spiritualité* (see bibliography).

vation present in this world as Christ willed and wills it. This teaching had already been mentioned with regard to the statements in *Lumen gentium* 8, §§1 and 2.[5]

1. The Apostolic See

Toward the end of his pontificate, Leo XIII multiplied his efforts reaching out to the Orthodox Churches and the Anglican Communion, the communities closest to Catholicism (at that time).[6] Pius X and Benedict XV published little along these lines, but prepared in many ways for the pontificate of Pius XI, which was indeed marked by a concern for "the reunion of Christians," as they used to say then. For example, we might point out the creation in 1917 of a special Congregation of the Roman Curia for the Eastern Catholic churches so as to make sure their specific character is safeguarded, and the creation of the Pontifical Institute of Oriental Studies for the in-depth study of these specific characteristics.[7] Benedict XV is the one who wrote on that occasion: "The Church is neither Latin, nor Greek, nor Slavonic, but Catholic."[8] But Pius XI was the one who increased the number of proceedings, letters, discourses, and audiences and encouraged the first meetings.[9] He was the one who approved the erection of the monastery for Church unity in Chevetogne and published the Encyclical *Rerum Orientalium*. He it was also who in 1928 published the Encyclical *Mortalium animos* on the Catholic concept of unity and the means of achieving it. However, relations with the Protestant world remained on a small scale, and Pius XII was the one who, by an Instruction from the Holy Office dated December 20, 1949, authorized official relations with Protestant Christians while issuing the first prudential rules for this dialogue. Finally, as everyone knows, the ecumenical concern was one of the principal reasons for the convocation of Vatican II by John XXIII.

---

5. A teaching repeated in the Encyclical *Ut unum sint* dated May 25, 1995, nos. 10 and 86.

6. See, for example, the Letter *Praeclara*, dated June 20, 1894, and the Encyclical *Orientalium dignitas*, dated November 30, 1894.

7. It has become pejorative to speak about these churches as "uniate churches"; nowadays Roman documents, such as those of Vatican II, no longer use that expression.

8. See the references in chapter 15, "The Church Is Catholic."

9. In particular the "Malines Conversations" with the Anglicans under the aegis of Cardinal Mercier.

2. Work for the reunion of Christians

It has two chief aims:

- That Christians may become better acquainted so as to overcome mutual prejudices that paralyze everything and may make progress toward points of convergence: this is doctrinal and "cultural" ecumenism.
- That Christians may love one another in truth; in other words, that they may, on the level of the theological virtues, offer prayers to God in many forms and coordinate their efforts in works of charity: this is spiritual or charitable ecumenism.

Due proportion between these two aspects must be maintained. It would not be charity, but sterile sentimentality, to seek to minimize doctrinal differences. It would not be rigor, but narrow-mindedness and cowardliness, to minimize the elements of common doctrine and not to engage in concrete action together for the sake of the "works."[10]

From the doctrinal perspective, various dialogues had been undertaken before 1949, but that period was above all a time of charitable ecumenism. Unity will not be the result of exclusively scholarly efforts, as necessary as they may be. Instead, it will be a "miracle," a work that is divine in the first place, a grace of God that we must ask for in prayer and make fruitful already in common works.

In the Catholic Church there have always been prayers for the unity of Christians, but until the contemporary period they asked purely and simply for the return of the separated brethren to the Catholic fold. Some attitudes did not always avoid the wrongheadedness of the prodigal son's elder brother. Basically, however, this prayer remains (see the general intercessions for Good Friday), but it is completed and balanced, so to speak, by a new form that originated in Lyons in the 1930s. At the initiative of Fr. Couturier, a yearly octave of prayers for unity was instituted, a demonstration to which the separated brethren were invited. It was a matter then of asking together for the grace of reunion. So as not to betray the doctrinal convictions of anyone, they adopt-

---

10. This is a constant reminder for all participants in ecumenical matters; see, for example, H. R. Brandreth (an Anglican theologian), "L'âme et la méthode de l'oecuménisme," in *Chrétiens devant l'oecuménisme* (Lille: 1947), 11.

ed the famous formula: pray together to obtain the visible unity of all Christians, unity as the Lord wants it and by whatever means he wills. In short, they pray that all Christians might be capable of one and the same obedience to God. Hence this prayer goes beyond the single paradigm of "return to the fold" and promotes instead the mutual spiritual assistance of all. This has gradually helped people to understand what is called "the way forward" for ecumenism—in other words, the fact that the reunion of Christians will come about by the advance of all in the one truth and the one charity. This does not mean—from the Catholic perspective—that the Roman Church has a doctrine mixed with errors, but rather that through a homogeneous development of dogma she will make it more intelligible and more acceptable to the separated brethren. Therefore she has to make this progress, and for that purpose the ecumenical dialogue should help. We will return to this.

b. The Orthodox Churches

Given the terrible trials that Orthodoxy went through in the twentieth century, in particular Communism for Russian Orthodoxy and the advances of Islam for Greek Orthodoxy, there was no solid ecumenical movement in that part of Christendom before the 1950s.[11] At the initiative of several theologians, most of them laymen, some relations were entered into, notably the slavophile movement between the two world wars. Among the major names we may mention Bulgakov and Evdokimov.

As for the Orthodox hierarchy, we have a very valuable document in which several Orthodox bishops offer a very fine clarification of their concept of the Church and of ecumenism. We mean the discourse by the Greek Orthodox Metropolitan Michael of New York, given in the name of all his confreres, to the World Council of Churches at their Conference in Evanston in 1954. Ninety-five percent of this document could be signed by a Catholic.

---

11. It should be noted, however, that as early as 1920 the Patriarchate of Constantinople, in a famous encyclical, had called all the Christian churches to practical cooperation so as to face together the dangers threatening the Christian faith. For the text of the encyclical, visit http://www.scoba.us/assets/files/guide_for_orthodox.pdf, page 21. For the participation of the Greek Orthodox in the beginnings of ecumenism, see C. Patelos, ed., *The Orthodox Church in the Ecumenical Movement* (Geneva: 1978).

The Church Is One

We would not pass judgment upon those of the separated communions. However, it is our conviction that in these communions certain basic elements are lacking which constitute the reality of the fulness of the Church.... We must recognize that there have been and there are imperfections and failures within the life and witness of Christian believers, but we reject the notion that the Church herself, being the Body of Christ and the repository of revealed Truth and the "whole operation of the Holy Spirit," could be affected by human sin. Therefore, we cannot speak of the repentance of the Church which is intrinsically holy and unerring.... Her holiness is not vitiated by the sins and failures of her members. They cannot in any way lessen or exhaust the inexhaustible holiness of the divine life which from the Head of the Church is diffused throughout all the body.

In conclusion, we are bound to declare our profound conviction that the Holy Orthodox Church alone has preserved in full and intact "the faith once delivered unto the saints." It is not because of our human merit, but because it pleases God to preserve "His treasure in earthen vessels, that the excellency of the power may be of God" (2 Cor 4:7).[12]

One of the difficulties of Orthodoxy—at first internally—is *autocephaly*. This crystallized chiefly in the nineteenth century. Some particular churches form an autocephalous group inasmuch as they gather together, especially by nationalities (Central and Eastern Europe), each one having its own synod. This has diminished to the same extent the number of churches canonically affiliated with the major patriarchates (Constantinople and Moscow). These churches, thus grouped, often act as "free electrons" of Orthodoxy. Thus, for example, in the 1930s,

---

12. "Declaration of the Orthodox Delegates concerning Faith and Order," read by Archbishop Michael at the Conference in Evanston, Illinois, in 1954. See also the proposals of the Commission for the Preparation of the Pan-Orthodox Council on matters of salvific dispensation (*oikonomia*), as reported in the journal *Contacts* (1972): 24: "Our holy Orthodox Church, although it is the one, holy, catholic and apostolic Church, not only recognizes the ontological existence of these Christian Churches (and separated Confessions), but also firmly believes that all its relations with them must be based on the elucidation, as quickly and objectively as possible, of the ecclesiological problem and of their doctrine as a whole." The third preconciliar pan-Orthodox Conference (1986) repeated almost verbatim the formulation of the Preparatory Commission; see the text in *Le christianisme vis-à-vis des religions,* ed. J. Doré (Namur: Académie internationale des sciences religieuses, 1997), the 1995 session in Athens, 207 (conference by Damaskinos Papandreou, Metropolitan of Switzerland). See also, along these lines, the conclusions of the inter-Orthodox colloquium of member churches of the World Council of Churches, Chambésy (Switzerland), 12–16 September 1991, *Service Orthodoxe de Presse* 161 (1991): 20 (particularly no. 13).

the autocephalous Church of Romania decided—for reasons that were not primarily theological—to recognize the Anglican Communion! More recently, the autocephalous Church of Georgia quit the World Council of Churches, deeming that the true nature of the Church was not respected in it, which caused quite a few tensions among Orthodox groups.

It is striking to observe that Orthodoxy, which so highly esteems the conciliar nature of the Church, and rightly so, finds it impossible to meet in council, and that this has been true since the break with Rome.[13] In fact Orthodoxy has undergone an extremely serious process of fragmentation that makes dialogue with it difficult. Within Orthodoxy the disputes between the patriarchate of Moscow and that of Constantinople are numerous and can lead, for a time, even to a rupture in their communion.

c. The world resulting from the Reformation

We speak here about the "world" because Protestantism appears as a mosaic of communities that are extremely varied, not only in their usages, but also in their doctrines. The situation is of such complexity that we cannot make an exhaustive list of these communities, but only situate the major groupings.[14]

1. The three major groupings

We can begin by mentioning the two blocs of the Lutheran churches and the Reformed churches that resulted from Calvinism. But almost one third of Protestants belong to what are called free churches. These separated from the preceding communities over the course of history for either political or doctrinal reasons (particularly their concept of ministries). Some of the numerically largest groups are the Anabaptists (who originated in sixteenth-century Switzerland), who produced the

---

13. For more than thirty years now the Orthodox Churches have been trying to convene a pan-Orthodox council; the numerous difficulties that they encounter in this regard are significant.

14. According to the *International Bulletin of Missionary Research* 24 (2000): 24–25, statistics concerning the "Christian denominations" within Protestantism are as follows: in 1970 there were 211 million Protestants distributed among 8,100 denominations; in 2000 there were 342 million Protestants forming 9,000 distinct denominations.

Baptist communities of England and the United States, and the Methodists (who originated in eighteenth-century England). Then there are the more idiosyncratic splinter groups in the form of sects, which are themselves condemned by true Reformed Christians. Then, too, there is so-called liberal Protestantism, born in the nineteenth century, which is not a distinct religious community, but rather an intellectual current crossing denominational boundaries and present in already existing communities, where it forms sub-groups. This patchwork situation results, in particular, from the principle of individual interpretation [*libre examen*].

It would be perverse [*abusif*] to group the Anglican Communion purely and simply with Protestants, but it is no stranger to that world. Within the context of ecumenical dialogue, it describes itself as a "bridge-church." It claims to have preserved the Catholic and Orthodox values of liturgical tradition, sacraments, and the episcopacy and to be at the same time the heir of the Reformation by virtue of the primacy of Scripture and of spiritual freedom.

There is no disputing the fact that there are very diverse influences within Anglicanism. But it should be noted that these values do not coalesce into the unity of a synthesis. They often developed independently of one another. This explains why this denomination is not as unified as some think, and the currents within it are very numerous and sometimes plainly divergent. We see clearly that there are two major tendencies in Anglicanism. The one is very close to the Catholic Church (the "high church"), and its buildings and liturgy resemble those of the Catholics so much as to be mistaken sometimes for theirs. The other is much closer to the Protestants (the "low church"), and its buildings and liturgy and even its doctrinal options resemble those of the Calvinists so much as to be mistaken for theirs. Coexisting within the same denomination are ministers whose doctrine is quite close to Catholic doctrine (except for the papacy, of course), and also other ministers who deny the resurrection of Christ; such has been the state of affairs since the period between the two World Wars. In the twentieth century a third current developed that is aiming to gain its own autonomy; this is the liberal tendency that takes the name of "broad church," which has been known since the eighteenth century.

These contradictions are coped with in a typically English fashion:

"comprehensiveness." For the Anglicans, it is a sign of vitality and fidelity to the message of Christ and also of respect for the freedom of the each person. Nowadays the labels are as follows: Evangelicals (low church), Anglo-Catholics (high church) and liberals or modernists (broad church). These are only currents, and not well-formed communities distinct from one another. Note that since the Oxford Movement of Newman and Pusey the Anglo-Catholic tendency has not ceased to gain ground. It maintains the so-called "branch" theory, according to which the Anglican Communion is one of the legitimate branches of the *one* Church, because there is unity of faith, sacraments, and episcopal organization, even though full *union* does not yet exist. Among these Anglo-Catholics, especially among the clergy, a so-called *papalist* tendency has developed, which accepts Catholic doctrine in its entirety, but hopes for a corporate reunion rather than individual conversions. Nevertheless, since the 1960s, by way of reaction, Anglicanism has witnessed the ascent in power of the evangelicals and liberals. This can be seen in the great doctrinal freedom and in rather extreme initiatives, such as the ordination of women. Presently the Anglican Communion is going through a period of considerable turbulence that is putting "comprehensiveness" sorely to the test.

2. Ecumenical work

Tendencies toward unity have agitated the Protestant world since the late eighteenth century. They crystallized in what is conventionally called the "ecumenical movement," which is one of the major events in twentieth-century religious history. We will summarize this story in broad strokes.[15]

The ecumenical movement is a set of sentiments, ideas, works, and institutions, meetings and conferences, ceremonies and publications, the purpose of which is to prepare for the reunion of the various Christian Churches and communities already in existence. This movement originated as an initiative of Protestant Christians. Their great diversity and the principles themselves of the Reformation make it clear that their concept of unity is their own. First, as we saw during our study of the real definition of the Church, Protestant Christians do not pose the

15. For more details, see M. Villain in the bibliography.

question about the unity *of the Church* in the same terms as Catholics and Orthodox do:

> In a general way, people wish to avoid any hasty identification between the Church, the object of faith, and the Church that is a visible, empirical reality, without however separating them artificially or setting them in opposition. The question continues to be discussed.... (Some), like Karl Barth, strive to show the connections between the "visible Church" and the "invisible Church," whereas others like Paul Tillich contrast instead the "spiritual communion" and "the statutory Church," a problematic and ambiguous entity....
>
> Most Protestant traditions (think nowadays) that the visible Church is a community of human beings who, at least externally, are faithful to the Word and to the sacraments, profess their faith, and strengthen one another. It is here and now the concrete translation of the invisible Church, even though these two expressions of the complex reality of the one Church should not be confused.[16]

The doctrine of extrinsic justification (which is connected with the doctrine of the absence of mediation between God, in Christ, and mankind) prevents Protestants from distinguishing in the unity [of the Church] the aspect of the Church as means of salvation and the aspect of reality of salvation.[17] So there is no noteworthy difference for them between the unity *of the Church* and the unity *of Christians*. Moreover, the search for unity is understood in terms of two very clear postulates: on the one hand, unity cannot result from the return of groups that are considered dissidents to a Church that is considered to be the only true Church; on the other hand, the Church willed by Christ is to come about through the reunion of all the presently existing groups, all of which are deficient in some aspect.

16. A. Birmelé, "Église," in *Encyclopédie du Protestantisme*, 489.

17. Here is an interesting recent statement of the ecumenical dialogue in France: "The Church can give only because she has first received. She can reconcile only because she has first been reconciled. She is always first and foremost a passive subject of God's grace. Everything that she does can be traced back to that source, which does not belong to her and toward which she must be transparent.... The divergence between us therefore does not concern the fact of the instrumentality of the Church in the transmission of salvation, but rather *the nature of this instrumentality: is the Church sanctified in such a way as to become herself a sanctifying subject?*" See Comité mixte catholique-protestant en France [= Joint Catholic-Protestant Commission in France], *Consensus oecuménique et différence fondamentale* (Paris: 1987), no. 11. Sacramentality itself (and thus the mediation of grace) is returning as an element in the dialogue, with one difficulty: does the sacrament contain what it signifies and causes?

It can be said that the ecumenical movement began in 1910, the date of the Universal Conference of Protestant Missions held in Edinburgh. This meeting had a doctrinal aim: to reestablish unity on the basis of the same faith and the same idea of church and of its organization. Hence the name given to this movement: "Faith and Order." A second conference was held in 1925 in Stockholm. It understood the union of Christian communities differently, as beginning with unity in charitable activities, as something based on "doing" rather than on doctrine. Hence the name of this movement: "Life and Work." These two aspects are not mutually exclusive, but would go on to become the two major orientations of the ecumenical movement (doctrinal and practical). These two orientations coalesced in 1937 at the Congresses in Oxford and Edinburgh. That was when it was decided to create a World Council of Churches (WCC), the plan for which was accepted in 1939 at the Assembly of Utrecht. The definitive constitution of the WCC was adopted at the Assembly in Amsterdam in 1948. It appeared on that occasion that the ecumenical movement was divided into two major tendencies concerning the nature of the Church and, hence, of her unity:

- The "catholicizing" tendency, expressed by Orthodox, Old Catholic, High-Church Anglican, and Swedish Lutheran groups. It underscores the importance of apostolic succession, the sacraments, and the connection between Scripture and Tradition.
- The "protestantizing" tendency, represented essentially by American, German, and French Protestants. It underscores the importance of the freedom of the Spirit and in the Spirit, of individual interpretation [*libre examen*]; and the common priesthood.

The WCC marks a very important stage in the ecumenical movement. It brings together churches and communities, and not only men of good will, as did the assemblies before the war. It is permanent. It has a ninety-member Central Committee that meets at least once a year. A General Secretariat assures the day-to-day presence of the WCC in the life of the communities. The authority of this Secretariat has grown thanks to the caliber of the Secretaries General who have been appointed, particularly Pastor Visser 't Hooft. Its headquarters are in Geneva; it includes a very active and efficient administration. The WCC sponsors an Ecumenical Institute in Bossey (near Geneva), and a first-class journal, *The Ecumenical Review*. It has a very competent press office and information service that publishes a Bulletin providing a wealth of information.

The importance of the WCC has not ceased to make itself felt, and its action has been to a large extent beneficent. But there was a dark side to this development, too. Very soon Christians of the Protestant world feared that the WCC was giving birth to a "super church" that would absorb the various confessions. To offset this danger, Protestants in the United States founded the International Council of Churches in 1952. As for Orthodoxy, its members were extremely upset, because for them there is only one Church, the Orthodox Church. Nevertheless, the WCC has published as early as 1950 a very frank declaration explaining that it would never become a "super church," because it understood itself to be nothing more than a place for exchanges and news so as to overcome prejudices. On that occasion the WCC explained that no community within it is asked to recognize that all or some of the others are true Churches nor to renounce its own claim to be the one true Church; yet each member community must at least recognize some *vestigia Ecclesiae* in the others. This stance removed certain obstacles to membership for the benefit of Rome and Orthodoxy.

What was the attitude of the Catholic Church vis-à-vis the ecumenical movement? At the beginning she was very reserved, fearing dogmatic relativism most of all. Private contacts between Catholic and Anglican theologians had been permitted by Benedict XV and Pius XI. But participation in a public debate that would address points that were considered to be revealed—and therefore indisputable—was deemed unacceptable. Even the presence of mere Catholic observers at the Conferences in Stockholm and Lausanne was rejected by Pius XI so as to avoid the risk of misunderstandings, because at that time the Protestant unionists agreed in saying that the one, unique Church of Christ did not exist and would exist in the future through the reunion of all the Christian communities. The reasons for this abstention by the Roman Catholics were spelled out in the Encyclical *Mortalium animos* (January 6, 1928), which stated the Catholic concept of unity that was to be promoted. Nevertheless, the development of the ecumenical movement gave assurances that allowed it to avoid equivocation. That is why Pius XI authorized Catholic theologians to attend the Conferences of Oxford and Edinburgh in 1937 as observers in their capacity as private persons.

Meanwhile, ecumenical fervor was awakening in Germany, Belgium, and France. One of the most famous books by Fr. Congar, *Divided Christendom: A Catholic Study of the Problem of Reunion*, was first published in French in 1937. Le Centre Istina [Istina Center], with its journal, *Vers l'unité chrétienne* [*Towards Christian unity*], dates from the same time. In Belgium Dom Lambert Baudouin founded the Benedictine monastery said to be *de l'union* [of or for union] in Chevetogne with its journal, *Irénikon*. After the war, the Holy See modified its prudential position; this was the famous Instruction from the Holy Office dated December 20, 1949: *Ecclesia Catholica*.[18] This document was the first to authorize Catholics to participate at all levels (local, national, and international) in meetings of the ecumenical dialogue. To be sure, there are many passages advising caution, and they may appear rather restrictive today, and yet this document marked the moment when the Catholic Church truly embarked on the ecumenical movement. From a doctrinal perspective, a certain passage from the Instruction has been commented on extensively: the one where the document explicitly attributes to the Holy Spirit the desire for unity that is expressed among the Protestant brethren. With that, the ecumenical movement of non-Catholic origin is clearly recognized by the Catholic Church. All this led to the presence of non-Catholic observers at the Second Vatican Council, something that would have been unthinkable at Vatican I.

II. THE ECUMENICAL SITUATION SINCE VATICAN II[19]

From the first Encyclical of John XXIII, *Ad Petri cathedram* (November 1958), concern for ecumenism is presented as something that must be one of the major axes of his pontificate. As of June 5, 1960, the Secretariat for the Unity of Christians was created and entrusted to Cardinal

---

18. See *L'Osservatore Romano*, March 1, 1950.

19. For further clarifications, in particular concerning the various documents exchanged or signed within the framework of the multilateral dialogue conducted by the Catholics, the reader may refer to the article "Oecuménisme" in *Dictionnaire de Spiritualité*, Part 3, by Bernard Sesboüé.

The Church Is One 531

Bea, former Director of the Pontifical Biblical Institute and the former confessor of Pius XII.

The conciliar Decree on Ecumenism, *Unitatis redintegratio*, marks an unexpected result at the beginning of the Council. It enunciates *the Catholic principles of ecumenism*.[20] This means that there are not several ecumenisms, but only one, prompted and guided by the Holy Spirit, for which the Catholic Church, by reason of the place that she deems her own in the Christian world, asserts her own requirements. Besides doctrinal ecumenism, this Decree also recognizes the so-called ecumenism of charity, and it clearly includes the Catholic Church in this whole movement of prayers and charitable activities that are common to all the Christian communities.

Following Vatican II several reforms, many documents, and a number of meetings with the separated brethren took place. As of 1966 the Catholic Church sent official observers to the WCC. Fr. Congar was able to write in 1982 that the Catholic Church was the community that, since the Council, had made the greatest ecumenical effort: "No other community has done as much."[21]

In this multifaceted activity significant advances are regularly observed, but they are often followed by more painful setbacks, resulting sometimes in a certain irritation or discouragement. The thing is that one notices more and more, especially in relations with the Protestants, that beyond theological discourse there are presuppositions of a more philosophical sort that are not always very clear. Consequently the doctrinal agreements run the risk of being more verbal than real, because the same words are not understood to mean the same thing. The perfect example is the Anglican-Catholic agreement on the Eucharist, concerning which the Congregation for the Doctrine of the Faith expressed serious reservations, because the text could be based on an equivocation with regard to the expression "real presence."[22] It is clear too that the various doctrinal points under discussion are part of a larg-

20. The title of the first part of the Decree. Note the difference between this and the subtitle of Fr. Congar's book in French: *Divided Christians: Principles of a Catholic Ecumenism*.
21. "L'oecuménisme de Paul VI," in *Paul VI et la modernité dans l'Église*, Actes du colloque de l'École Française de Rome, 2–4 juin 1983 (Paris: 1984), 818.
22. See the Vatican site at http://www.vatican.va/roman_curia/congregations/cfaith/documents/rc_con_cfaith_doc_19820327_arcic_en.html. On this subject, see the study by Charles Morerod cited in the bibliography.

er synthesis, and when one goes back to the fundamental principles, it is necessary to acknowledge that the parties diverge already at that level. Thus, for example, the ecclesiological discussion with Protestant Christians has made it evident that the root of the disagreement was found in Christology and with regard to the general sacramentality of salvation, which also involves a particular anthropology.[23]

III. The Catholic principles of ecumenism

The fundamental Catholic principle of ecumenism insists that the Church is not divided; she is one with a unity that man cannot change because it is an imperishable gift from God. From the communal perspective, Vatican II speaks about "the unity ... which Christ bestowed on his Church from the beginning. This unity, we believe, subsists in the Catholic Church as something she can never lose, and we hope that it will continue to increase until the end of time."[24] From an individual perspective, talking about someone who separates himself from the Church, and not about someone who is born in a community that is already separated, Fr. Congar expresses as follows a teaching that goes back at least as far as Origen and St. Cyprian: "Because the unity of the Church is from above, from God, it cannot be broken.... Either one is or one is not in the unity of the Church; it remains intact for all that [i.e., even if] individuals depart from it."[25] There are elements of ecclesiality that continue to exist in the separated communities. This fundamental principle, which governs the whole matter, is the reason the ecumenical activity of the Catholic Church is specific. As we saw in the chapter concerning the real definition of the Church, she is inseparably spiritual and "corporeal." Hence her unity will have the same characteristics; she will be at the same time spiritual and corporeal. In order to understand the Catholic position in ecumenism, it is advisable

---

23. See the study by Bernard Sesboüé, *Pour une théologie oecuménique*, cited in the bibliography.

24. Decree *Unitatis redintegratio* 4, §3.

25. Yves Congar, *Divided Christendom*, 59. Congar's own words are, "on ne lui enlève rien en s'en retirant," which mean literally, "One takes nothing away from her (the Church) when one leaves her." See, at the end of the chapter on the People of God, the presentation of the adage, "No salvation outside the Church."

The Church Is One

to consider carefully the origin of the separations that are the object of the efforts for reunion. Seeing what was at stake in a separation from the Catholic Church logically leads to the specifically Catholic requirements for the movement toward reunion.

a. The fundamental notions

Separation from the Catholic Church results either from a heresy or from a schism. Either one gives rise to a dissident community.

1. Heresy

Heresy is the clear and persistent (*pertinax*) denial of a truth of faith. It should not be confused with apostasy, which is the complete abandonment of the faith. Heresy is studied per se within the context of the course on morality under the heading of faith (sins against the faith). We mention here only the ecclesial ramifications.

To be a member of the Church is to agree to be only a part of a whole. The faith of each member is not a part of the whole faith (that would be absurd), but rather is a profession of the Church's faith. Each Christian believes with a strictly personal act of faith only within the life of the whole Church, participating in the consensus on the faith. The heretic no longer professes the Church's faith; he takes his personal choice as the basis for his belief. Now, since the faith of the community comes from God himself who reveals himself (motive for faith) and pertains to God himself as he is revealed (object of faith), we see that the heretic destroys within himself the motive for faith, because his motive for believing is his personal judgment, whereas the object of faith, what he believes, is at most a distorted, mutilated truth.

Because of the primacy of faith—this is what opens the way to the whole organism of the theological virtues—ecclesial communion in its entirety is destroyed in the heretic. This is the common axiom: "Communion in the faith is at the beginning of communion in charity."[26]

---

26. St. Paul said to Timothy, "I urged you ... [to] remain at Ephesus that you may charge certain persons not to teach any different doctrine.... [T]he aim of our charge is love that issues from (literally *estin ek:* is from) ... [a] sincere faith" (1 Tim 1:3–5). St. Ignatius of Antioch addresses those same Ephesians a little later on and tells them, "Here is the beginning (*archē*) and the end (*telos*) of life: faith is the beginning, the end is love (*agape*)"; *To the Ephesians* 14, ACW 1:65. St. Thomas puts it this way: "Consensus in the

Heresy is definitely the most radical break because it necessarily results in schism.

There are other sins against faith that must not be confused with heresy. Indeed, we must be able to distinguish between the refusal to comply with Revelation (the pagans), the refusal to advance in it (the Jews), and the refusal to persevere in it (the heretics).[27]

2. Schism

Schism is the rupture of the communion of charity.[28]

Our word "schism" comes from the Greek *skhisma*, which means "separation, division" (from the verb *skhizein:* to split, separate). There is no equivalent in classical Latin, and that is why it made its way into ecclesiastical Latin through transliteration (like *mystērion* and *ekklēsia*). Schism is a rent in the Church's social fabric. St. Paul's use of the word is very illuminating. In the First Letter to the Corinthians the word designates the divisions in the turbulent community of Corinth: 1 Cor 1:10: "[let] there be no *skhismata* among you"; 1 Cor 11:18: "I hear that there are *skhismata* among you"; 1 Cor 12:25: "[so] that there may be no *skhisma* in the body." The word does not yet have the precise sense that doctrinal development will later give it. It still mainly designates divisions of all sorts that agitated the young community. But already in the writings of St. Ignatius of Antioch we find the criterion of the theological definition that will be refined in Tradition.[29] Schism is radically refusing submission to the bishop, his preaching, and the Eucharist that he principally celebrates. A schismatic is someone who sets up "altar against altar." This criterion will be repeated by the Council of Antioch (341) in the fifth canon.

Although it originates at the level of the particular church—separation from its bishop—schism immediately has universal repercussions. The same council explains this (canon 6): If someone is excommunicated by his bishop, let him not be received by any other bishop what-

---

unity of faith is the principle of communion in charity; that is why dissent in faith excludes the friendship essential to the life of a family"; see IV *Sent.* dist. 13, q. 2, art. 3, sol. 1, ad 1.

27. On this point see *ST* II-II, q. 11, art. 1.
28. See Yves Congar, "Schisme," in *DTC*, vol. 14/1, col. 1286ff.
29. See *To the Ephesians* 3.2–4.1; *To the Philadelphians* 3 and 4; *To the Smyrnians* 7 and 8.

soever. We find the same thing in the writings of St. Cyprian: schism is a rupture with the legitimate bishop *and therefore* with the undivided episcopate. With St. Augustine we move on to another stage: union with the Bishop of Rome becomes the definitive criterion that takes precedence over the local origin of the separation. The Roman See manifests the unity of the universal Church, and to break with it is to break with the whole Church, wherever she may be.

It is significant that St. Thomas considers schism in the treatise on charity (*ST* II-II, q. 39, art. 1). This is the sin of someone who deliberately and obstinately breaks with the unity that charity procures, not insofar as charity attaches one person to another, *but rather insofar as it gathers the whole Church into the unity of one and the same love.* Schism is therefore a refusal of communion with the Roman pontiff and with all those who are united with him. In itself, schism does not necessarily involve heresy. The schismatic can profess the same faith. Nevertheless, schism is an open door to heresy because faith is no longer enlivened by charity. In order to justify his own separation, the schismatic will sooner or later fall into heresy. This can be seen at the origin of the Anglican Communion. Furthermore, heresy is sometimes nothing more than an inveterate schism.

Each of the Christian faithful believes, hopes, and loves as a member of the Church. In communities that are socially distinct (the Church in Switzerland, the Church in France, the Church in Spain) there is a *convergence* in faith, hope, and charity, in the sacraments, in their teaching, and in their unity with the pastors. This convergence is a formal identity and a connectedness of one part with another in a communal whole. This is the unity of the Church against which the schismatic offends: his is a refusal to be and to act as a part, as a member of a whole, *whatever his reason for it may be.* The schismatic, whatever his motivation, is someone who wants to be *apart.* This formidable evil occurs both when one exempts oneself from apostolic authority, insofar as it is a divinely established principle of unity, and when one refuses to communicate (i.e., to be in relation) with the members of the Church. These are the two ways of starting a schism, and the second may not be visible at the beginning (see the beginnings of the Lefebvre affair). Nevertheless, the fact remains that schism is accomplished in the soul of the refractory party even if it remains hidden for a while. Schism requires no canonical sanction in order to exist. It is a sin that originates in the will of the subject, and it can exist even though appearances remain sound.

And so schism is a basic attitude: what one wants necessarily implies a refusal of communion.[30] This may only be implicit in someone who obstinately acts in ways (for example, showing disrespect for sacramental rites) that sooner or later lead to a rupture in communion.

Brief note on excommunication

Excommunication is a canonical measure that falls under the *external* forum. In and of itself it does not exclude from the communion of grace. Like any canonical penalty, it is a punitive measure aimed at a baptized person, an obstinate sinner, who is guilty particularly of heresy or schism. It deprives that person of certain *means of grace,* including absolution. This is a very serious or even extreme measure that is justified by the preservation of the ecclesial common good. Like any penalty, it also has a medicinal aspect. It has considerable ecclesial effects: for a cleric, loss of pastoral authority (in particular loss of faculties to celebrate the sacraments), for any baptized person—being deprived of the sacramentals, of the benefit of indulgences, of the fruitful reception of the sacraments. This rent in the social fabric of the Church is canonical in nature; it excludes those excommunicated from the communion of the faithful, which is protected by the canonical powers of the Church (as a means of salvation). Wrongly used,[31] it does not in and of itself break off unity in the theological virtues. The excommunicated person is a penalized member of the Church, and is not necessarily spiritually dead.

3. Dissidence

Persons who are born in a community that originated in a heresy or a schism cannot be accused personally of the sin at the origin of their community. Heresy and schism are names of *sins;* sin is always a personal reality, and it is not something presumed. Persons who are born

---

30. This is manifest in the case of Écône (a seminary, but not the headquarters, of the Society of Saint Pius X).

31. Church history has witnessed saints who were excommunicated during their lifetime.

The Church Is One

in a separated Christian community are presumed to be "in good faith."[32] They form what is called a dissident community. Therefore to speak about a "heretical" or "schismatic" community is strictly speaking improper for two reasons: sin is always personal, and culpability is not presumed. This is not to say that the faith and the charity of that community are unaffected, but they are not affected *culpably*. Nevertheless, this lack of integrity has present-day consequences in the life of that community.

The principle of unity in that community is ambivalent. It is somewhat self-contradictory, because on the one hand it is made up of the set of Catholic values (i.e., goods and resources) that it brought with it at the time of the rupture, which can lead many people toward holiness, but on the other hand those values are wounded by error (heresy) or the refusal of charity (schism) that caused the separation.[33] This internal conflict is at the heart of this dissident Christian community. Hence we have the major Catholic pragmatic principle of ecumenism: to help them to actualize those Catholic values that they brought away with them—in other words, to cause the dynamic of the Catholic values to prevail over the contrary dynamic of the errors or refusal. For the error or the refusal has its own dynamic also, which causes delay and sometimes even setbacks in the ecumenical effort. Thus we see within the dissident community various currents that are inevitably contradictory. Some are attracted to the true Church; the others distance themselves from it. The present situation of Anglicanism shows this quite clearly. This is also the case within Orthodoxy, where certain Churches accept the *communicatio in sacris* [sharing in the sacraments] with Catholics, under certain prudential conditions, while others go so far as to rebaptize Catholics who join them.

This dissident community is thus pulled in several directions internally and externally. As a community it is in the process of exploding, because the conflicts caused by the contrary movements within it are disintegrating it. Among the Christians who are members of a dissident denomination, one must always distinguish between those who

---

32. "One cannot charge with the sin of the separation those who at present are born into these communities and in them are brought up in the faith of Christ"; UR 3.

33. We adopt here the conclusions of Charles Journet, *The Church of the Incarnate Word* 1:40–43.

accept this situation of internal contradiction without being able to distinguish what is good from what is bad and those who insist on the principle of division. The former are not heretics or schismatics.[34] They are dissidents "in good faith," and within their community they are elements of progress toward communion. The latter perpetuate or even aggravate the original causes of separation. Is this necessarily in a culpable way? We think not, since sociological and psychological causes can play an important role in this sort of situation.

The dissident community is not solely a collection of individuals. It is also a communion; it has an ecclesial value because it participates in the unity of the Church based upon the values that it brought with it at the time of the rupture. It is an imperfect realization of the one, unique ecclesiality. Hence, for example, the denomination "Anglican Communion" is equivocal. For a Catholic it signifies that there is a real, but imperfect ecclesial communion with the Catholic Church, thanks to the common values present in both groups (e.g., baptism, prayers). For an Anglican, the expression signifies the federation of the dioceses of that confession.

b. Catholic fullness

All that has just been clarified allows us to grasp the teaching that the Roman Catholic Church is the only community that has preserved intact the totality and integrity of the means of salvation given by Christ (doctrine, sacraments, ministries), and that consequently she is also the reality of salvation that these means transmit (*UR* 4).

1. The key statement of *Lumen Gentium* 8

We gave an extensive commentary on this during the positive presentation of the Body of Christ theme. On the one hand, there is the *unity* of the ecclesial being (the two aspects, means of salvation and reality of salvation, form a being that is one, unified, undivided), which is the subject of *LG* paragraph 8, §1, and on the other hand, there is the *unicity* or uniqueness of the ecclesial being (there is *only one* Church), which is the subject of paragraph 8, §2. We will not return to this discussion.[35]

---

34. The *originating* sin that caused the division is not an *original* sin; it is not transmitted and cannot be imputed without personal guilt.

35. The Vatican II Decree on Ecumenism often uses the typical expression: *una et*

What must be added here, from an ecumenical perspective, is the fact that this *one, unique* Church is consequently *fully realized* in the Roman Catholic Church, and *imperfectly present* in dissident communities to various degrees, depending on the importance of the dissidence (the number and the nature of the Catholic values brought with them at the time of the rupture). Here too there must be no all-or-nothing reasoning; the point of departure is a fullness that is shared more or less. This underscores also the real, but imperfect communion that unites us to all those who have received true baptism, whatever community they belong to. This communion is not just spiritual in the sense of "invisible," but should have its visible manifestations, such as prayer in common and common works of charity. This is the basis of spiritual ecumenism, which is, so to speak, the *sine qua non* of doctrinal ecumenism.

We remind the reader that our perspective here is *dogmatic* and not moral. To say "Catholic fullness" does not mean that all Catholics actually live the fullness of grace! They are, however, the only ones to whom the fullness of the means of grace is offered permanently. They will be judged all the more severely on account of it.

2. Evaluating the rise of a dissident movement

It is appropriate here to review the conditions in the rise of a dissident movement, because that allows us to clarify in a useful way the movement toward reunion. How are we to understand the rise of a dissident movement? We take here the example of the Reformation, because it is the clearest and the one best known historically. There are two main theses explaining this phenomenon.

The thesis of Fr. Congar is as follows.[36] Within the spiritual attitude that is at the origin of a dissident movement, a distinction must be made between two moments; first, there is a very vivid perception of an absolutely Christian truth (in Luther's case, the gratuitousness of justification), and then there is a second moment in which this truth is dismembered, torn from the larger doctrinal whole of the revealed deposit of faith of which it is a part and that gives it its true meaning. This truth is then lived separately and consequently distorted; it thus

---

unica Ecclesia"; see UR 1, §1; 3, §1; 4, §4; 24, §2), as does the Constitution on the Church (*LG* 13, §1; *LG* 23, §1).

36. Congar, *Divided Christendom,* 29 and 40ff.

becomes an error. The initial insight remains true and should be preserved; this is the "Catholic" side of the dissidents.

Charles Journet critiques this way of looking at it.[37] For him, the nucleus, the original intuition of a dissident movement, is something indivisible. In the case of Luther, for example, there is not a truth (the gratuitousness of salvation) and an error (extrinsic justification), but one distorted or ambivalent truth, rather than the juxtaposition of two ideas, one correct and the other wrong. This question is important. What are we to think? To our knowledge the Magisterium has not taken a position on this point. The Decree *Unitatis redintegratio* speaks prudently about "differences ... in doctrine" (*UR* 3) and, for the Protestant brethren, "very weighty differences ... in the interpretation of revealed truth" (*UR* 19). It is possible that Charles Journet's perspective is behind these broad formulations, because Fr. Congar's distinction cannot be found in them.[38] Be that as it may, here is what we propose to say:

Fr. Congar seems to us to be right in what pertains to the progressive development of the individual, in this case Luther. There are indeed two stages: the insight into an indisputable truth (the gratuitousness of salvation), then the warping of that truth (extrinsic justification). But when it is no longer a matter of the individual, Luther, but rather of the founder of a dissident community—in other words, as soon as separation begins based on Luther's work, by definition along with the warping of the truth that had been grasped initially—then the *community itself* is founded on just one idea that forms a deviant whole: gratuitous extrinsic justification. This tenet, which is indeed singular, is so to speak the indivisible "dogma" of the separated community.

With reference to the ecumenical dialogue it is important, we think, to consider the warped truth as one thing. We will not succeed in resolving the separation by trying to separate the good grain from the weeds, but rather by addressing the problem prior to this doctrinal difficulty by going back to the specific, prior mystery that is the basis of it—in this case, to the mystery of the Savior's grace-filled humanity in which the relation between grace and nature is posited in a perfect, exemplary way. It seems to us that the recent history of the ecumenical

---

37. Journet, *The Church of the Incarnate Word*, 40–41.
38. For the subsequent debate, see Yves Congar, *True and False Reform in the Church* (Collegeville, Minn.: Liturgical Press, 2011), 205–8.

The Church Is One

dialogue illustrates this. In these exchanges there is a gradually growing awareness that the resolution of this or that precise doctrinal difficulty demands a return to the mystery at the basis of it, of which it is a particular application.

This question of the rise of a dissident movement allows us to understand better the importance of two very popular ideas in ecumenical dialogue. It is appropriate to present them now.

c. Important ideas in ecumenical dialogue

1. The *vestigia Ecclesiae*

The WCC met in Toronto in 1950 and sought to clarify the relations among Christian communities in general. Remarkably, it declared that the member churches of the WCC recognized in the other churches elements of the true Church. It explained in particular:

> It is generally taught in the different Churches that other churches have certain elements of the true Church, in some traditions called *"vestigia Ecclesiae."* Such elements are the preaching of the Word, the teaching of the Holy Scriptures and the administration of the sacraments.[39]

This idea of *vestigia Ecclesiae* should not be confused with the Calvinist idea of *signa Ecclesiae* or of *notae Ecclesiae*, which refer to the essential elements that make up the true Church—namely, for the Calvinists, the *pure* ministry of the Word and the *right* way of administering the sacraments. (These were repeated in the Augsburg Confession in Article VII.)

Since then the expression *vestigia Ecclesiae* has had great success in the ecumenical movement. In its positive sense, it seems to agree with what Calvin called the "traces" or "remnants" of the Church. In speaking about the Roman Church, he said, "there is some vestige of a Church in the Papacy, as Baptism and some other remnants."[40]

---

39. English text at http://www.oikoumene.org/en/resources/documents/central-committee/toronto-1950/toronto-statement.html.

40. *Institutes* IV.2.11. See also the *Confession of Faith*, no. 38. Calvin also thinks that, despite the infidelity of the Papists, the Lord preserved true baptism in that Church; cf. Sermon 200 on Deuteronomy, in *Corpus Reformatorum*, vol. 57, edited by G. Baum, Cunitz, and Reuss (Brunswick: 1885), col. 227: Catholics "contaminated" baptism, but "were not able to destroy it entirely." The same opinion can be found in *Institutes of the Christian Religion* IV.2.11, where Calvin uses the word "remnants."

Vestigia Ecclesiae, however, has a negative sense, too. Any recognized common value that is present in another community is necessarily affected by the absence of communion. Thus *vestigia* suggests the idea of ruins: by the very fact of disunity, the common element is wrecked and deformed in the dissident community. This is what is recognized from the Catholic perspective.

In fact, the expression *vestigia Ecclesiae* covers two sorts of realities that must not be confused. It is a question either of holy realities in common, such as the Eucharist celebrated by our Orthodox brethren, which is authentic, or else of mere images of the reality, such as the Lord's Supper of the Calvinists, which is not the Eucharist. It goes without saying that only the first sense of the expression is intended by the WCC, although it cannot always be admitted by the Catholic and Orthodox Churches. One must be careful therefore about equivocation.[41]

2. The hierarchy of truths (*UR* 11)

The Decree *Unitatis redintegratio* declares:

When comparing doctrines with one another [in their dialogue with the separated brethren, Catholic theologians] should remember that in Catholic doctrine there exists an order or "hierarchy" of truths, since they vary in their relation to the foundation of the Christian faith.

What does this mean? Let us dismiss at the outset an absurd (which is not to say rare) interpretation: this does not mean that there are more and less important truths, or that alongside the full truths there are some half-truths that one could attenuate.

The Theological Commission of the Council presented the text of the Decree to the Fathers as this paragraph was being incorporated during the conciliar debates:

It seems, in fact, to be of the utmost importance for the ecumenical dialogue that both the truths on which Christians agree and those about which they differ should be weighed rather than enumerated. Although, no doubt, all revealed truths must be held with the same divine faith, their importance and their weight differ by reason of their connection with salvation history and the mystery of Christ."[42]

---

41. On this idea of *vestigia Ecclesiae*, see the article by J. Hamer cited in the bibliography.

42. *AS* III/7, 419.

The Church Is One

This amounts to saying that one must distinguish between the truths that concern the reality of salvation and those that concern the means of salvation given by Christ for the time of the pilgrim Church. This is the distinction between the order of the end, where there is little divergence of Christian opinion, and the order of the means to the end, where the most important divergences are found. In order to understand this question, let us highlight a point that falls under the theology of faith. Faith has for its motive the authority of God who reveals. To reject this authority for a single revealed point is to challenge the authority of God as such and thereby to replace it with one's own. Consequently, what is being rejected is all truth *inasmuch as it is revealed*. This nullifies the very motive of faith (God's authority). For if one holds other truths, one does so no longer on God's authority, but rather by personal choice. This is the very definition of heresy. This is one of the most common teachings that Luther himself preached. Comparing dogmas to the links of a chain, he affirmed that when you remove a link, the chain itself disappears. Or else, he said, if a bell is cracked in only one place, the whole bell no longer tolls correctly. Consequently, speaking about a "hierarchy of truths" cannot imply any distinction whatsoever within the obligation to believe all revealed truths.

Several documents, having different degrees of authority, were drawn up after Vatican II:

It is true that there exists an order and as it were a hierarchy of the Church's dogmas, as a result of their varying relationship to the foundation of the faith. This hierarchy means that some dogmas are founded on other dogmas which are the principal ones, and are illuminated by these latter. But all dogmas, since they are revealed, must be believed with the same divine faith.[43]

The document does state that there is, so to speak, a dogmatic synthesis, which means, as in any synthesis, that an order of intelligibility exists among the various dogmas. This is the famous *nexus mysteriorum* of Vatican I (*Dei Filius*, chapter 1).

The conciliar Decree (*UR*) does not consider truths of the faith to be more or less necessary for salvation; nor does it suggest degrees in our obligation to believe all that God has revealed. When a person responds fully by faith to God's self-revelation, he accepts this revelation as a whole. It is not a mat-

---

43. Congregation for the Doctrine of the Faith, Declaration *Mysterium Ecclesiae* (June 24, 1973).

ter of selecting or choosing from among the things that God has revealed.... Consequently there are no degrees in the obligation to believe all that God has revealed.[44]

This ecumenical declaration proposes an interpretation of the conciliar Decree that appears faithful to us, but it illustrates this hierarchy of truths more than it explains it. For example, it says a little further on in the text that there is an order between the Old and the New Testaments; that among the councils the first seven have a certain preeminence; that the Niceno-Constantinopolitan Creed and the Apostles' Creed have a particular excellence with regard to professing the faith; that baptism and the Eucharist have a primacy among the seven sacraments; that the liturgical year is centered on Easter. All this seems incontestable. "Hierarchy" signifies a certain order originating in the center of the revealed mystery: Christ and salvation history.

The document *The Interpretation of Dogmas* by the International Theological Commission goes a little further in explaining the dogmatic synthesis:

Dogmas are only intelligible through their mutual relationship to one another (*nexus mysteriorum*) (DS 3016) and in their overall structure. In this regard special attention should be given to the order or "hierarchy of truths" in Catholic teaching; this order results from the different ways in which dogmas are related to the Christological foundation of Christian faith (*Unitatis Redintegratio* 11). Although all revealed truths are surely to be accepted with the same divine faith, their meaning and importance differ depending on their relation to the mystery of Christ.[45]

The first foundation of dogma as a whole is the profession that the Word appeared in concrete, historical form, in all its fullness, in Jesus Christ. Starting from that, each one of the dogmas is integrated into the whole.

The *Catechism of the Catholic Church* adopts all the preceding discussion:

The Church's Magisterium exercises the authority it holds from Christ to the fullest extent when it defines dogmas, that is, when it proposes truths con-

---

44. Joint Declaration of delegates from the WCC and from the Pontifical Counsel for Christian Unity, 1990 (translated from the French).
45. International Theological Commission, *On the Interpretation of Dogma* (1990). English translation in *Origins* 20, no. 1 (May 17, 1990): 1–14, citation at 9.

The Church Is One

tained in divine Revelation or having a necessary connection with them, in a form obliging the Christian people to an irrevocable adherence of faith. (88)

The mutual connections between dogmas, and their coherence, can be found in the whole of the Revelation of the mystery of Christ. "In Catholic doctrine there exists an order or 'hierarchy' of truths, since they vary in their relation to the foundation of the Christian faith." (90)

Thus far the different documents state two main things, while explaining them somewhat: the hierarchy or order of truths, which implies differences among them, and the equally important obligation to believe them all. We must explain the *connection* between these two statements, whereas these documents do not. In the final analysis, this question is relevant to the course on faith. We summarize here the principle of the solution:

- The faith includes the very mystery of God and of his decrees; it does not stop at the formulations, but extends to the reality itself that is expressed. The faith pertains *ad rem.*
- The faith is expressed—not because of its object, since God himself is infinitely simple, but because of us—in terms suited to our created and therefore finite intellect. It is spelled out in various *articles of faith* (listed in the Creed). Our intellect discerns among them various aspects of the mystery of what God is in himself and what he wills for our life and our salvation.
- This ordered statement serves in the first place to present each particular mystery for our assent of faith for the same motive: God who reveals. This should not be confused with the ordered presentation that theology proposes, which is aimed at the understanding of the faith. Theology is achieved not by an act of faith, but by an act of understanding. That is why it is not up to theology to distinguish and to formulate articles of faith. That is done by God himself as he reveals, and the articles are explained by a divinely instituted and aided Magisterium. For theology, each article of faith is simultaneously a point of departure—it is the datum to be understood—and a point of arrival, an ultimate criterion for verifying theological conclusions.
- The idea of an article of faith is therefore derived from limitations proper to the human mind. To this we must add the conditions that pertain to the fact that the faith is the faith *of a community.*

And in this new respect, the faith must be formulated *publicly* for everyone according to constraints that depend no longer on the nature of the human mind alone, but also on social and historical conditions. Then, too, there is *dogmatic development*. This is not about new truths cropping up, nor about a change in the original meaning of a truth, but about an explanation that is the work of the *sensus fidei*, which is a living reality.

With the help of these reminders we can now attempt to explain this notion of the hierarchy of truths.

- We repeat that "hierarchy" does not mean "graded." There are no great or full truths and small or half-truths. That would be absurd; a statement is or is not true. Hierarchy here signifies *order*. There are first truths and second (not secondary) truths.
- What order are we talking about? It is an order of *intelligibility*. Obviously, if someone declares Mary "Mother of God," this presupposes on the level of intelligibility a previous declaration of the Incarnation of the Word, since God has no mother. These two statements are equally true; they come from the same faith. Hence a first conclusion: in ecumenical dialogue we must dwell primarily on the *first* truths. This does not mean that one must necessarily begin with them, but one must always tend toward them. From this perspective the Catholic-Protestant dialogue in France is exemplary. The dialogues began with the mystery of the Church, but the debate clearly is oriented toward the mystery of Christ, because Christology is where it appears that the keys to the ecclesiological divergence are found.[46]
- Besides these first truths and second truths, we must mention truths that one could call "third truths"; these pertain to the concrete, historical economy of salvation that has unfolded. Within the whole set of truths that are revealed and affirmed by God, there are, because of the very circumstances in which this revelation was made and the whole pedagogy that this revelation included, some statements with a different import and religious value. On the first level there is what can be called the essential

---

46. On this point the reader may benefit from consulting the study by Bernard Sesboüé in *Pour une théologie oecuménique* (see bibliography).

kernel of the faith, to which all the rest is ordered: the mystery of God who leads us to himself so as to be our beatitude. This is the mystery of God himself and of our participation in this mystery (first and second truths). But this is contained within a revelation that contains a host of other truths. For example, Abraham had two sons; David committed an act of adultery. These truths (if they are truly taught by Scripture) demand the assent of divine faith no less than the first, but clearly they do not have the same importance. Articles of faith or dogmas concern only the first and the second sorts of truths, which state who God is and what his work of salvation is. It would be another thing entirely to deny that Abraham had two sons on the grounds that Scripture is not the Word of God. In that case one would be talking about the denial of Revelation itself and therefore of a first truth. But we think that it is tenable to say, for example, that this Word is not expressed solely by reporting historical facts, but also by using metaphors and parables (the Book of Tobit is generally considered one big parable), which could be the case with Abraham's progeny, provided that this does not nullify the historicity of salvation in itself.

- The faith pertains first to him whom we hope to contemplate one day in heaven, and second to the means of arriving there. Faith is the inauguration here below of the supernatural knowledge that will reach fulfillment in the beatific vision. But it pertains also to the concrete, historical economy of this salvation. If it is truly taught that Abraham had two sons (and we are not certain of that), this fact would be no less certain than the existence of three Persons in God, and to deny it obstinately would suffice to destroy faith as a whole. If, as we think in this case, the number of Abraham's progeny is a metaphorical way of speaking, faith does not pertain to that, but instead to the first or second truth that is thereby suggested.
- This distinction between first truths and second truths is important for ecumenical dialogue. It enables us to see always an *order* among the truths, an order that faith itself follows. It would be futile to begin by dialoguing about second truths; they appear as such only in the light of the first truths. As for what we call "third" truths, the ecumenical effort has no direct bearing on them.

The expression "order or hierarchy of truths" consequently indicates a *method* of ecumenical dialogue, a method that should bear very useful fruits.

d. The methods of ecumenism

Keeping in mind all that has been said until now, we will underscore here several *practical* consequences that result from it. Let us turn now to a few rapid historical notes and several clarifications concerning the present Catholic concept of the future of ecumenism.

1. Ecumenism from a historical perspective

Historically, we note the succession of three stages in the relations between the Catholic Church and the communities that separate themselves from her.

Judgment

In the past one would have said "condemnation." That sounds repressive … and indeed it was a matter of pronouncing a penalty of excommunication affecting the originator of a separation and those who followed him. The most important thing to be emphasized here is the judgment—in other words, the statement of the reality of the separation and the doctrinal reasons for it. It is quite clear that if one community—we are not at the level of mere individuals—separates from another, it is not out of moodiness, but because both parties think that there is a real and serious matter about which they differ. If the separation lasts and the separated community becomes entrenched in its dissidence by creating its own institutions that set up something like a parallel church, it is indeed because they think that serious matters are at stake. Before embarking on relations with a separated community, it is therefore necessary that the separation be quite clear: this is to respect the positions of both sides, to honor a demanding concept of truth, without which relations between the two communities would have no genuine object.[47]

---

47. To see how the Catholic Church passes this judgment in the present day, the reader can refer to the Declaration *Ecclesia Dei adflicta*, dated July 2, 1988, concerning the separation brought about by Archbishop Lefebvre.

Controversy

Once the moment of separation is past, relations between the two communities most often adopt the mode of controversy. We showed what this was when we presented the ecclesiological debate with the Protestant Christians in the sixteenth century. Controversy is a mode of theological discussion that takes up disputed questions one by one and attempts to resolve them individually. This is not a confrontation pure and simple, the opposition of two incompatible theses, but a genuine exchange in which the arguments of the one side are weighed and discussed by the other. The typical feature of this method, however, is the absence of the broad perspective. Each controversial point is discussed for its own sake without connection to the others. This allows the parties to sort out the merely apparent conflicts, which quickly fall by the wayside, from the genuinely fundamental oppositions. This stage is a stage of clarification. But it cannot suffice. For example, a discussion with Protestant Christians about the nature of the Church cannot ignore one's view of the relation between nature and grace. But the controversy does not go that far.

Dialogue

This is the third, indispensable phase, which comes about more or less quickly. At this moment the contradictory parties go beyond the particular points of the controversy to consider as a whole the doctrines under consideration. Thanks to this more unified view, they are able to point out the fundamental "differences that separate" them; resolving these will then allow them to reconsider their doctrine as a whole. The agreement reached at this stage truly inaugurates the moment of reconciliation. The fact of having arrived at this stage is what inaugurated the ecumenical movement and, in particular, the involvement of the Catholic Church. The dialogue phase can be very long; nevertheless, it is still the one closest to the conclusion of ecumenism.

It should be noted that these three major stages can coexist. This means that when two communities have arrived at the dialogue stage, if a new point of disagreement comes up,[48] the three stages are to be re-

---

48. For example, recently with Anglicanism, with the ordination of women.

peated in regard to it: first a judgment that is as clear as possible, then a controversy, and finally the integration of this new difference into the broader perspective of the dialogue.

2. Ecumenism and the development of dogma

Among Protestant Christians, and to a certain extent among the Orthodox, people thought for a long time that the key to reconciliation could be found purely and simply in a return to the state of doctrine as it was on the eve of the separation. This is what was called "retrospective ecumenism" ["*l'oecuménisme en arrière*"]. Indeed, at that time there was a common doctrine. But for the Catholic Church this is impossible to accept for two reasons. First, concerning separations that are not schisms, this would necessarily lead to denying the assistance of the Spirit of truth who leads toward the whole truth. One cannot deny the fact and the doctrine of the development of dogma without thereby getting rid of the assistance of the Spirit to the diaconal communion—in other words, denying it as such. The second reason, concerning communities that separated over dissension affecting the faith, is that the step backward is not possible because there never was a time when the two communities were united in faith. This is why some promote a view of ecumenism that can be called "the way forward for ecumenism":

We must search in the future and in further formulations that, without losing anything of what was once defined and remains so forever, may by their own progress become more comprehensive and less partial. It is rather clear, in my view, that the formulations of Trent on original sin, while repeating entirely those of Orange, are much more acceptable for the Greek tradition, because they include an order of truths that the battle against Pelagius had brought out less than the battle against Luther. It is not by misunderstanding or disregarding Trent and Vatican I that we will effectively reunite with the Christians who are separated from Rome; one would reunite with them only based on earlier formulas that can be interpreted differently and in a sense different from Catholic truth. The historical study of these formulations and of the circumstances that surrounded the major crises, the rise of schisms and heresies, is something extremely necessary, not to take us back to the past, but on the contrary to allow us to go further into the future and to make possible, through a more exact knowledge of the different doctrines, new dogmatic advances in formulations that will be acceptable to the separated Christians, not that they would be minimalist or involve a step back-

The Church Is One

ward, but, on the contrary, because they are more complete and explicit enough to sweep away the multitude of false problems that have accumulated around what was a genuine divergence.[49]

It seems to us, in particular, that the future of the ecumenical dialogue with the Orthodox depends primarily on the ability of Catholics—with the help of the Orthodox—to express better the truth enunciated by the First Vatican Council concerning the Roman pontiff's primacy of jurisdiction. This formulation used conceptual tools that were in force at the time, especially the distinction between *order* and *jurisdiction* in the dogmatic theology of the priesthood. Now, clearly, Vatican II did not base its teaching about the ministerial priesthood on this distinction, but rather on the *tria munera* [threefold office]. How, then, can papal primacy be expressed with this new approach? Does it concern the *munera docendi et regendi* [teaching and governing offices] *in the same way*—in other words, does it apply identically in the social communion and in the diaconal communion? We are at the very beginning of research into this subject.

Conclusion

The ecumenical movement is surely one of the great spiritual events of our era. Any study of it presupposes a whole vision of the unity and unicity of the Church. Moreover, to say that the Church is indefectibly one and that Christians are divided requires a metaphysics so as not to be contradictory, for a community subsists in its members. A reality can exist fully or imperfectly without this implying that there are various Churches, one full and entire and the others diminished. To keep *together* the one, unique Church present in the Catholic Church (see *LG* 8) and the ecclesial reality of the separated communities (see *LG* 8; *UR* 3 and 4) is the "job description" for the Catholic Church (and to a great extent for the Orthodox Churches) in the ecumenical dialogue. This dialogue should help Catholics to grasp better the mystery that they believe and thus to manifest it so that it is perceived better by the separated brethren. The fruits of the ecumenical movement will thus be for the benefit of all.

49. Marie-Michel Labourdette, *Cours de théologie morale: La Charité* (Toulouse: 1959), 187.

Bibliography

The Ecumenical Question
Contemporary History

Aubert, R. *Le Saint Siège et l'union des Églises*. Brussels: 1947.

———. *Problèmes de l'unité chrétienne*. 2nd ed. Namur: 1959.

Thils, G. *Histoire doctrinale du mouvement oecuménique*. 2nd ed. Paris: 1962. With a good bibliography.

Catholic Theology of Ecumenism

Baum, Gregory. "The Ecclesial Reality of the Other Churches." *Concilium* 4 (1965): 63ff.

Congar, Yves. *Chrétiens désunis: Principes d'un oecuménisme catholique*. US 1. Paris: 1937. English translation by M. A. Bousfield, O.P.: *Divided Christendom: A Catholic Study of the Problem of Reunion*. London: Centenary Press, 1939.

Congar, Y. *Vraie et fausse réforme dans l'Église*. Paris: 1953. English translation: *True and False Reform in the Church*. Collegeville, Minn.: Liturgical Press, 2011.

———. *Dialogue between Christians: Catholic Contributions to Ecumenism*. Westminster, Md.: Newman Press, 1966.

Dumont, C.-J. *Les Voies de l'unité chrétienne*. Paris: 1954.

Küng, Hans. *The Church*. Translated by Ray Ockenden and Rosaleen Ockenden. New York: Sheed and Ward, 1968. With a good bibliography.

Lamirande, Émilien. "La signification ecclésiologique des chrétientés dissidentes." *Istina* (1964): 25–58.

Various authors. *Un nouvel âge oecuménique*. Paris: 1966.

The Vatican II Decree *Unitatis redintegratio*

Jaeger, L. *Le Décret de Vatican II sur l'oecuménisme*. Tournai: 1965.

Thils, G. *Le Décret sur l'oecuménisme du deuxième concile du Vatican*. Louvain: 1965.

Villain, M. *Vatican II et le dialogue oecuménique*. Paris and Tournai: 1967.

On the Reception of this Teaching by the Separated Brethren

Evdokimov, P., O. Cullmann, and H. Roux. *DC* (1965): cols. 1111–18.

Orthodoxy

Clement, O. *L'Église orthodoxe*. Paris: 2002.

Dumont, P., F. Mercenier, and C. Lialine. *Qu'est-ce que l'Orthodoxie?* Brussels: 1954.

Evdokimov, P. *Orthodoxie*. Neuchâtel and Paris: 1959. English translation: *Orthodoxy*. Hyle Park, N.Y.: New City Press, 2011.

Meyendorff, J. *Orthodoxy and Catholicity*. New York: Sheed and Ward, 1966.

———. *The Orthodox Church: Its Past and Its Role in the World Today*. Translated by John Chapin. Crestwood, N.Y.: St. Vladimir's Seminary Press, 1981.

Rousseau, O. "L'Orthodoxie occidentale." *Irénikon* (1958): 326ff.

The Church Is One 553

See also pertinent passages from the preceding titles, esp. Yves Congar, *Divided Christendom* and *Dialogue between Christians*, and the anthology *Un nouvel âge oecuménique*.

The World of Protestant Christians

Bertrand, A.-N. *Protestantisme*. Paris: 1938.
Birmelé, A. "Église." In *Encyclopédie du protestantisme*. Geneva and Paris: 1998.
Bouyer, Louis. *The Spirit and Forms of Protestantism*. Princeton, N.J.: Scepter, 2001. French edition 1954.
Saatman, J. W. *Le Protestantisme américain*. Louvain: 1952.
Tavard, G. *Le protestantisme*. Paris: 1958.

See also pertinent passages in the preceding titles, esp. Yves Congar, *Divided Christendom*, *True and False Reform in the Church*, and *Dialogue between Christians*, and the anthology *Un nouvel âge oecuménique*.

State of the Ecumenical Dialogue after Vatican II

Congar, Yves. "L'oecuménisme de Paul VI." In *Paul VI et la modernité dans l'Église*. Coll. de l'École Française de Rome. Paris: 1984, 807ff.
Grootaers, Jan. *Rome et Genève à la croisée des chemins (1968–1972): Un ordre du jour inachevé*. Paris and Geneva: 2005. History and reflection on the situation of the Catholic Church vis-à-vis the World Council of Churches.
Leroy, Marie-Vincent. "Note sur l'unité de l'Église catholique et orthodoxe." *RT* (1971): 528–44. An extremely precise, fine, and rigorous study on the subject of Louis Bouyer's book *The Church of God*, which concludes that there is already a profound unity between the two Churches.
Maffeis, A. *Teologie della Riforma: Il Vangelo, la Chiesa et i sacramenti della fede*. Brescia: 2004. Good presentation of the history of the developments in the reception of the teachings of Luther and Calvin by the communities that resulted from the Reformation. The presentation of the ecclesiological developments is well done.
Sesboüé, Bernard. *Pour une théologie oecuménique*. Paris: 1990. In particular assesses the Catholic-Protestant dialogue in France; very enlightening.
———. *La Patience et l'utopie: Jalons oecuméniques*. Paris: 2006. An anthology of miscellaneous conferences and articles by the author as well as new essays concerning the present situation of the ecumenical movement, chiefly in the Catholic-Protestant dialogue. Useful for a more accurate appreciation of what some people consider "stalled talks."
Thils, G. *L'Église et les Églises: Perspectives nouvelles en oecuménisme*. Louvain: 1967.
Wicks, J. "Ecclesiological Issues in the Lutheran-Catholic Dialogue (1965–1985)." In *Vatican II: Assessment and Perspectives*. New York: Paulist Press, 1988, 2:305–46.

The reader may consult ecumenical journals, especially *Istina* and *Irénikon*, which regularly offer evaluations on the status of the dialogues.

The indices of *Documentation Catholique*, especially under the headings "Oecuménisme," "Unité des Chrétitens," "Secrétariat pour l'unité des Chrétiens," list the principal documents of the multilateral dialogue since the Council.

One invaluable bibliographic resource is published by the journal *Centro pro Unione* (Rome) in regular supplements: the most recent was in vol. 69 (Spring 2006): 20–41.

Fundamental Notions

Congar, Yves. "Schisme." In *DTC* vol. 14/1. Paris: 1938, cols. 1286ff. Excellent contribution.

———. *L'Église, une, sainte, catholique et apostolique.* Coll. Mysterium salutis 15. Paris: 1970. See the chapter "Les ruptures de l'unité," 65ff.

Hamer, Jérôme. "Le Baptême et l'Église, à propos des *vestigia Ecclesiae*." *Irénikon* (1952): 142ff.

Morerod, Charles. "Le sens et la portée de la hiérarchie des vérités à Vatican II et chez S. Thomas d'Aquin." In *Nova et Vetera*. Swiss ed. (1996): 15ff.

———. "L'importance de la philosophie dans le dialogue oecuménique." *Freiburger Zeitschrift für Theologie und Philosophie* (1997), 4:324ff. To be read especially with regard to the ARCIC dialogue.

Anthologies

Enchiridion oecumenicum. Vol. 1, *Dialoghi internazionali* (1931–1984); vol. 2, *Dialoghi locali* (1965–1987); vol. 3, *Dialoghi internazionali* (1985–1994); vol. 4, *Dialoghi locali* (1988–1994). Bologna: Dehoniane, 1986ff. These anthologies are extremely well done and practically complete. Good indices and tables of contents. An invaluable resource.

Tomos agapis (*Le Livre de la charité* [*The Book of charity*]). Paris: 1972. Essential excerpts from the dialogue between Paul VI and Patriarch Athenagoras.

For General Study

Although it is an encyclopedia entry, the excellent, extensive article "Oecuménisme" in the *Dictionnaire de Spiritualité*, vol. 11 (1983), cols. 631–81, is noteworthy. It is divided into two major parts: (1) History of ecumenism, in two sections: (A) until the end of the eighteenth century (cols. 631–37); many judicious remarks on the attitude of the Fathers and above all on the controversy resulting from the Reformation; (B) from the nineteenth century to Vatican II (cols. 637–64); a precise, detailed presentation, with an important bibliography; and (2) Ecumenical activity today. Doctrinal elements of the dialogue and its status as of 1982, by B. Sesboüé. Extremely well documented. The doctrinal reflection of the author, however, seems to us inadequate, particularly as far as "the way forward" for ecumenism and the perception of the unity *of the Church* are concerned.

14

The Church Is Holy

The Church is holy; this is one of the most ancient tenets of Tradition, based on Eph 5:27: "that he [Christ] might present the Church to himself in splendor, without spot or wrinkle or any such thing, that she might be holy and without blemish." On the other hand, there is no disputing the fact that the Church subsists in her members, who here below are all sinners. Moreover, among these members there are some who are qualified to lead [*engager*] the community as such, the ministers, and these members too are sinners whose service is marred by sin. The problem therefore appears as follows: the Church, made up of sinners, is holy.[1] How then can we avoid contradiction?

Let us agree first on our understanding of holiness. We take it here in the most common sense of the word: *conformity to Christ*. This *conformitas* should not be understood in a minimizing sense—merely at the level of action in conformity to certain rules. Rather, it is on the order of being itself: *conformitas* signifies "possessing in common an essential reality" (unity in *form*). To be holy is to be by grace-filled participation what God is by nature. This supernatural ontology is manifested in the acts of which it is the principle: acts of knowledge (faith) and of will (charity, hope).

The Church comes from Israel and stands out in contrast to the People that announced and prefigured her. Israel was often unfaithful.

---

1. This is the formula of St. Ambrose: "(*Ecclesia*) *ex maculatis immaculata*," in *Commentary on Luke* 1:17 (CCSL 14:15).

The Church comes also from the Gentiles who are by definition idolaters, and she stands out even more in contrast to them. The Fathers of the Church often repeat the idea that Christ chose the Church as his Bride, even though she was a prostitute. He accepted her, impure as she was, and loved her out of sheer mercy. He purified her by faith and baptism, making her his virginal Bride. The Fathers consequently keep together the two sides of the problem: the Church is indefectibly holy; sin does not affect her in herself, but her members here below are all sinners.[2] This is precisely what we must explain. Before entering into the thick of the matter, and to set us on the path toward the answer, we now present the article from the Creed on the communion of saints.

I. The Communion of Saints

As already mentioned, the Latin expression *communio sanctorum* can be understood in two ways: *sanctorum* is the genitive plural either of *sancti* (holy persons) or of *sancta* (holy things). We will see later what *communio* signifies in this context.

a. The "*sancta*" and the "*sancti*"[3]

By *sancta* we mean those holy realities that include above all *sana doctrina* [sound doctrine], or the faithful preaching of revealed truth, and the authentic sacraments that effectively give that which right preaching makes known. To communicate in the *sancta*—to adhere to the truth and to receive the sacraments—is a sort of a description of the Church: the Church is the community formed by those who converge on the *sancta* so as to become *sancti*. At this level we will say that the Church is made up of the totality of those who profess the true faith and participate in the authentic sacraments.

By *sancti* we mean the persons who receive the *sancta*. These holy realities are sanctifying. Here the Church is the totality of those who, having received the *sancta*, live upright lives by means of them. This is the community of those who live by faith, hope, and charity.

---

2. For an exact presentation of the patristic tradition on this point, see Yves Congar, *True and False Reform in the Church*, 76–82.

3. The scriptural basis is Wis 6:10: "For they will be made holy who observe holy things in holiness."

It is the genius of the Latin language to be able to express by a single genitive (*sanctorum*) two distinct and closely related realities. It is by sharing in the *sancta* that human beings become *sancti*, and the more they progress in this holiness, the more they participate in the *sancta*. There is a reciprocal relation between these two terms: the *sancta* engender the *sancti*, and the growth of the *sancti* requires the reception of the *sancta*.

b. The *communio*

We have studied this notion at length. It is clear that the primary thing is the divine communication of the *sancta*. Man takes part and accepts this offer, and as a result a reality becomes common to God and to man and to men among themselves. We will not return to this discussion. Here we will highlight one aspect that is to a greater extent moral than dogmatic; it is important to be aware of this aspect so as to be able to interpret and appreciate correctly the life of the Church and thereby to understand her holiness and the need for reform that is felt in every era among her members.

Salvation, as has already been noted many times, is the restoration of unity with God (vertical unity) and among men (horizontal unity).[4] The same principle of unity is realized in both directions. The doctrine of the communion of saints allows us to advance in our understanding of the accomplishment of this twofold unity that ultimately is only one. More particularly, it is a question of seeing the share that every human being can and must have in the salvation of his neighbor. Man is not only someone saved; he is called to be also—in Christ—a savior.

Salvation is a divine offer to which man ought to respond. In this sense it is initially an individual reality. Paul cannot have faith, hope, and charity on behalf of Frances. These theological virtues are born in a person's heart through a free response to the divine offer that comes to him from Christ the Head. Yet Christ associates human beings with his headship. On the one hand, this is a matter of the ministers who are ordained to preach and to celebrate the sacraments. This is the first, permanent, and indispensable association with Christ's headship (the *vicarious* presence of Christ the Head) because its effect is assured (the

---

4. This is the very objective of the ecclesial sacrament; see *LG* 1.

assistance of the Spirit of Christ for preaching, which can go as far as infallibility, and *instrumental* causality in the case of the sacraments). There is, on the other hand, an association of *every believer* who is united to Christ. The priestly quality common to all the faithful comes into play at this second point.[5] The general idea is as follows: every act performed for the sake of charity unites us to Christ, and from this proximity results a participation in his headship. This is the doctrine of *merit*, which states that our acts of charity have value in the sight of Christ. Then there is the so-called doctrine of the *transferability of merits*, which states that Claire's merits can benefit John. The holier we are, the closer we are to Christ, the more influence we have on the communication of grace. Hence our merits can benefit someone else, not by making him believe, hope, and love despite himself, but by facilitating for him the acceptance of the grace of conversion, of forgiveness, of this or that spiritual progress.... Here a *moral* causality is at work: to his friends Christ grants—in response to their prayers—that one grace or another will be offered to this or that person. The key spiritual attitude here is *intercession*. Thus St. Thérèse of Lisieux prayed intensely for the conversion of the criminal Pranzini, and in her cloister she walked on behalf of a missionary despite her illness.... We are touching here upon the most intimate part of the everyday life of the Mystical Body, those multiple, vital relations among the members thanks to the Head who is Christ. Since I can merit for others, the holiness of my neighbor depends also on me.

This doctrine of the communication of merits is the foundation of the doctrine of indulgences. The latter was renewed by Paul VI.[6] It is necessary to know it and to understand it correctly because, stripped of the excesses and distortions that it underwent, it is part of the Christian mystery.

All these elements that make up the doctrine of the communion of saints show us precisely what the holy life of the Church consists of, in its causes, in its subjects, and in its effects. Anything that diminishes this holiness *in*—and not *of*—the Church must be situated within this context.

---

5. We take priesthood here in the *broad* sense that includes the *tria munera Christi* [threefold office of Christ].

6. In the Instruction *Indultiarum doctrina*, 1967.

II. The problem of faults and reforms in the Church

Although sin is a strictly personal reality, nevertheless, because of its importance and the accumulation of sinful acts, it has effects on the entire community. The communion of saints has its counterpart—in a certain way—in a communion of evil. Moreover, it was still possible for some historical situations that were not sinful in themselves—for example, the medieval Christendom that resulted from successful apostolic work—to lead to cases of serious negligence, the net effect of which was to make the Church worldly. The ecclesial community regularly feels the need to reform itself, and all ecumenical councils are reform councils at the same time that they are doctrinal. In this regard Vatican II also must be interpreted in terms of its reforming intentions.

a. The nature of an ecclesial reform

The word "reform" runs the risk of being equivocal. In the case of civil society it indicates that something new is going to be done: we say "tax reform" to signify that a new, supposedly more efficient system of taxation will replace the old one. "Reform" therefore means here the appearance of a novelty thought to be better than the old reality. This aspect exists in the case of the Church because she has a *social* dimension, as we have seen, but it is not the most important aspect. It is not the *theological* aspect of the reform affecting the communion in the theological virtues. For the Church, "reform" means first and foremost a *return to the sources*. The perfection of the Church is total in her Head who is Christ; this is an "initial" perfection to which we must ceaselessly return. This perfection can be seen in the famous summaries in the Acts of the Apostles (especially Acts 2:42ff.). This will always remain the point of reference. So too, and analogously, the reform of a religious order will always be a return to the founding charism that was expressed forcefully during the first two or three generations.[7]

b. The object of an ecclesial reform

From what must the community purify itself untiringly, and in some eras even more energetically? It will always be chiefly a matter of get-

---

7. See the Decree *Perfectae caritatis* 2.

ting rid of *worldly characteristics*. The ecclesial community is *in* the world, but not *of* the world (Jn 17:14ff.; see also Mt 13:22). It does not come *from* the world, but *from* God; it does not lead *to* the world (it surpasses the figure of *this* world, 1 Cor 7:31), but rather to God. And yet it lives *in* and *for* the world. Evidently reform affects the daily life of the community, its *conformitas*, inasmuch as it is *lived*. It could not possibly affect what the Church is essentially, but rather the concrete way in which her members live the good things that God unceasingly gives them. To be precise we will say then that there is reform *in* the Church (the life of Christians) and not *of* the Church. Catholic (and Orthodox) tradition *never* says that the Church is sinful,[8] although she is made up of sinners.

The faith, hope, and charity in the hearts of Christians are the criteria for all authentic reform. This fervor of the theological virtues is seen in the spirit of unity among the faithful. It is not just a question of avoiding the sins of schism or heresy (abandoning the community, such as it is, in order to form another supposedly purer one), but also to guard in all things against a partisan or cliquish spirit that rejects differences while trying to fit everything into the same paradigm. Diversity, however, cannot be put into practice without the risk of disintegration unless it proceeds from a profound communion in the *sancta*.

III. Resolution of the Speculative Difficulty

The faith of the Church requires believers to maintain simultaneously and without contradiction that the Church is holy and is made up of sinners. This faith needs to be explained. The contradiction appears because the Church subsists in her members. In order to remove it, Protestants advanced the theory of two Churches: one that is holy and spotless, subsisting in the predestined just, and the other that is sinful, subsisting in the reprobates. This is untenable, because it simultaneously endangers the unity and the unicity of the Church. Moreover, in Lutheran thought, in which man is *simul peccator et justus* [simultaneously

---

8. Recently Vatican II again refused to do so despite a motion by an influential group of Council Fathers; cf. *LG* 8, §3. They settled on the following formulation: "The Church, embracing sinners in her bosom, is at the same time holy and always in need of being purified [in her sinful members]."

a sinner and just], the Church would be at the same time a virgin and a prostitute. This is contradictory unless one holds the thesis of extrinsic justification, which is unacceptable in Catholic and Orthodox teaching.

In order to account for this datum of the Christian faith, we must go back to the question of the personality of the Church and, in particular, to her twofold supernatural ontological character. The Church subsists in the Holy Spirit (by appropriation) in all the most decisive acts of her existence here below: fidelity in the faith and the authentic sacraments. The holiness of the Church here is an indefectible holiness that ensures that the community will always preserve the means of salvation; this is the indefectibility of the *diaconal* communion. Whatever the moral caliber of her members may be, she will always be sanctifying, because she will always be holy in the Holy Spirit. The Church subsists also in her members. Within her there will always be saints who will be, in the communion of saints (the communion *of the theological virtues*), the effective leaven of authentic fidelity that is not only individual, but also part of the community as such. The Church subsists also in the other members, to the extent that they are on the path of conversion—that is, still integrally ordered to the fullness of Christian life, although this subsistence is more precarious and less fruitful, depending solely on the extent to which they are ordered to the fullness of life.[9] These are the members in whom reform is necessary, because in them there is the need to be purified. The faults so sadly attested in history come from them. But these faults must not be attributed without qualification to the *Church*. This is why, in magisterial documents, these are said to be the faults *of Christians* and not of the *Church*.

Conclusion

It is easy to understand that there is nothing triumphalist or vainglorious about the proclamation of the Church's holiness. It is a profession of the Lord's fidelity to his Church (the gates of hell will not prevail against her; see Mt 16:19) and at the same time an invitation to conversion. The latter is always made possible, thanks precisely to the inde-

9. Charles Journet illustrates this as follows: the borderline between the good grain and the weeds runs right through the middle of our hearts; by virtue of all that is good in us, we are ecclesial, and by virtue of all that is sin in us, we are "unecclesial," cf. *L'Église du Verbe incarné* 2:1103.

fectible holiness of the means of grace that the community constantly offers. Hence the profession of ecclesial holiness becomes one of the most powerful reasons for Christian hope.

BIBLIOGRAPHY

Congar, Yves. "L'Église est sainte." In *Angelicum* 42 (1965): 273–98.
———. *Vraie et fausse réforme dans l'Église*. 2nd ed. Paris: 1969. English translation, *True and False Reform in the Church*. Collegeville, Minn.: Liturgical Press, 2011. Very fine study, with a wealth of spiritual implications and historically very precise. Provides a vast supplementary bibliography.
———. *L'Église, une, sainte, catholique et apostolique*. Coll. Mysterium salutis 15. Paris: 1970, 123ff. A condensation of the preceding title.
de Laubier, P. "Sociologie des saints." *RT* (1991): 34–67. The essential argument is found already in *Visage de l'Église* (Fribourg: 1989), "Sociologie des saints canonisés et béatifiés," 275ff. A very interesting study that helps to put into the proper perspective the idea in the past that only clergy and religious should be raised to the honors of the altars. This essay helps the reader to understand the "politics" of canonizations, which is all the more interesting since it is not the result of a deliberate program.
Journet, Charles. *L'Église du Verbe incarné*. Vol. 2, esp. 893–934. Fine overall presentation within the context of the renewed understanding of the soul and body of the Church; see also 1115–29. See Congar's remarks in *Sainte Église* (Paris: 1963), 144–47 and 667.
———. "La sainteté de l'Église: Le livre de J. Maritain." In *Nova et Vetera* (Swiss ed.) 46 (1971): 1–33. Concerning the apparent paradox of the holy Church made up of sinners.
Labourdette, Marie-Michel. "La sainteté, vocation de tous les membres de l'Église." In *L'Église de Vatican II*. US 51c. Paris: 1966, 1105–17. Good presentation of holiness.
Maritain, J. *De l'Église du Christ: La personne de l'Église et son personnel*. Paris: 1970. See particularly—because of the current relevance of the question—chapters 11–15 on the historical sins of "the Church."
Nicolas, Jean-Hervé. *Synthèse dogmatique*. Fribourg and Paris: 1985, "Sainteté et fautes de l'Église," 688–705. Very rigorous presentation, one of the best essays on the subject.
Pagé, Jean-Guy. *Qui est l'Église?* Vol. 2. Montreal and Paris: 1979, 221–37.
Saphy, D. *L'Église est sainte: Sens du péché et repentance*. St. Maur: Parole et Silence, 2000. Very precise and valuable study that is profoundly speculative in terms of the Church's personality.
Theological Dictionary of the New Testament. "Hagios." Very good biblical presentation of the idea of holiness.

15

The Church Is Catholic

The word "catholic" is not found in Scripture, but it appears as early as the first post-apostolic generation, in the writings of St. Ignatius of Antioch: "Where the bishop appears, there let the people be, just as where Jesus Christ is, there is the Catholic Church."[1] This is the first mention known to Tradition.

The profane meaning of the Greek word would mean (linguists are cautious) "connected with the whole, according to the whole." Greek dictionaries give its meaning: "general, universal." This is the sense in which Aristotle says that the first principles of speculative or practical reason are "catholic."[2] In the writings of the first Christian authors, the meaning "universal" is the one that is applied to the Church.[3] The general idea is one of fullness. How are we to understand it?

---

1. See *To the Smyrnaeans*, chapter 8.2, in *Epistles of St. Ignatius of Antioch*, Ancient Christian Writers (Westminster, Md.: Newman), 1:93.

2. See Henricus Stephanus, "καθολικὸς," in *Thesaurus graecae linguae*, edited by C. B. Hase, G. Dindorf, and L. Dindorf (repr. Graz, Austria: Akademische Druck- u. Verlagsanstalt, 1954), 5:794–95.

3. See Clement of Alexandria, "The Universal or Catholic Church" (PG 9.548 = *Stromata* VII.17.46; ANF 2:554b).

I. The two fundamental meanings of "Catholic"

This is a matter of distinguishing a *qualitative* connotation and a *quantitative* connotation. Tradition thus develops six meanings that are divided along these two lines.[4]

a. The qualitative meaning, or *intensive* catholicity

"Catholic" first of all is a title [of great honor]: a man is a Catholic. It indicates a fullness in a subject. In this sense the Church is already catholic from her origins, starting on the morning of Pentecost. This fullness or universality is twofold:

1. Doctrinal catholicity

The Church received Revelation in its fulfillment in Jesus Christ. This is the perfection of the public Revelation ordered to the salvation of the human race. Truths can indeed exist in places other than this Church—whether they are specifically Christian truths (baptism among the Protestants, for example) or truths that are present outside the visible boundaries of Christianity (the uniqueness of God in a monotheistic religion). Nevertheless, revealed truths, along with the connections that unite them, are found in their *entirety* only in the Catholic Church. This is her first catholicity, the fullness of faith.

2. Sacramental catholicity

The Church received the seven sacraments instituted by Christ in order to imbue with grace all aspects of human life and to remedy all the weaknesses of sin. This universality underscores the fact that all of human life is indeed renewed by the gift of God, in Christ, through his Spirit.

This intensive or qualitative catholicity is the essential catholicity, in the sense that it indicates the original perfection of the diaconal com-

---

4. For a significant example, see James of Viterbo, *De regimine christiano* (circa 1301), edited by F.-X. Arquillière under the title *Le plus ancien traité de l'Église* (Paris: 1926), 122–28; see the recent English translation by R. W. Dyson (Leiden: Brill, 2009). The principal source for James of Viterbo is St. Isidore of Seville, *De origine officiorum* I (PL 83.739–40).

The Church Is Catholic

munion on which depends, to some degree, the ecclesial mystery itself in its indivisibility and perfection. Since this is the primary sense, it is in danger of being lost if one translates the Latin word *catholica* from the Creed as "universal," because nowadays the adjective "universal" is understood more in the quantitative sense that we will now present.

b. The quantitative sense, or *extensive* catholicity

There are four major connotations of this catholicity, which underscore the fact that the Church has the vocation to become more and more catholic. Her catholicity in this respect is a divine intention and a human vocation.

1. Geographical catholicity

The Church has spread or is called to be spread throughout the world so as to touch all peoples. Unlike the Synagogue that is found only among the Jews and the dissident communities that one encounters only in some regions, the true, fully constituted Church is oriented toward the whole world.

To tell the truth, this very patristic sort of apologetic argument has lost much of its force because of the great surge in Protestant missions during the nineteenth century and the great diaspora of Orthodox Christians whom the persecutions of the twentieth century drove from their traditional homelands.

This Catholic vocation[5] has always been the heart, so to speak, of the missionary movement, which from the start has been directed toward all known territories. Christianity is essentially missionary. This characteristic, which seems trivial to a Christian, is not so much so when one considers the other great world religions that, with the exception of Islam, have often remained regional religions.

2. "Human" catholicity

The Church addresses all human beings, excluding absolutely no one. Whether Jew or pagan (religious perspective), whether Greek or barbarian (cultural perspective), whether slave or free (social perspective), whether man or woman, whether rich or poor, whether noble or com-

---

5. See the conclusions of the Gospels according to St. Matthew and St. Mark.

moner, whether intelligent or uncouth ...: God is not a respecter of persons (Acts 10:34). Just as God is creator of all mankind, he is the redeemer of all mankind. "All men are called to belong to the new People of God" (*LG* 13).

Here we ought to elaborate more on the perception of this fact through the history of Christianity. Sometimes it was hobbled by a certain Augustinianism that had a restrictive idea of the predestination of all mankind to salvation. But even in that case, it was believed that in every human "category" there must be some who are saved. Although some Christians may have strayed from the central message, the fact of the broad missionary activity of the Church counts more here than one theory or another.

3. Temporal catholicity

This is a very rich subject in patristic writings. We already addressed it several times with regard to the theological history of salvation: the whole age of redemption that starts immediately after Adam's sin is the age of the Church. This is the classic theme of the *Ecclesia ab Abel* (*LG* 2). All of the just form only one Body, the Body of Christ, according to the well-known expression: the Church is simultaneously ancient and perpetual.

4. Catholicity according to state in life

The Church is made up of all those who are *comprehensores* (those who possess the beatific vision, (that is, the blessed, including the angels) and the *viatores* (those who are still "on the way"—that is, the souls in purgatory, those making their pilgrimage in this world). The Christian community includes all who have Christ as their Head.

II. CONNECTION BETWEEN INTENSIVE AND EXTENSIVE CATHOLICITY

This simple presentation of catholicity poses no particular problem. The idea of fullness is rather self-evident here. There is an essential fullness that is called to be communicated everywhere and to all. The connection between intensive catholicity and extensive catholicity, however, poses a formidable question.

a. The problem

The property of *catholicity* indicates the idea of fullness, one that is not solely quantitative ("Go into all the world"),[6] but also and essentially qualitative.[7] The two aspects are connected: the qualitative fullness is for everyone. This worldwide destination of God's gifts is not brought about, however, in a sort of totalitarianism, as though the whole world had to abandon its local peculiarities. But there is one speculative difficulty to be resolved.

Salvation and the means of salvation go beyond all human peculiarities, without compromising them. Everything must tend toward salvation, even those human realities that are only human (in particular, culture in all its forms). These cultural realities, which are different depending on the place, the time, and the persons, are not compromised per se by Catholicism, but are called to be enlivened and elevated by it. Grace does not abolish nature, but rather restores and elevates it. So we can understand that the Church "is neither Latin, nor Greek, nor Slavonic, but Catholic,"[8] but this catholicity is realized concretely among the Latins, the Greeks, the Slavs ... who nevertheless do not cease to be Latins, Greeks, or Slavs.

The precise question to be considered is the question about the distinction between the universal and the particular and about the relation between them. Let us look first at this relation at the natural level where we distinguish between nature and culture.

1. The analogous relation: Nature and culture

Vatican II explains it as follows in the Constitution *Gaudium et spes*:

Man comes to a true and full humanity only through culture, that is, through the cultivation of the goods and values of nature. Wherever human life is involved, therefore, nature and culture are quite intimately connected one with the other....

Thus the customs handed down to it form the patrimony proper to each human community. It is also in this way that there is formed the definite,

---

6. In this respect, the Church *tends to become* catholic.
7. In this other respect, the Church *is* catholic and has been since the fulfillment of Christ's promises (Pentecost).
8. Benedict XV, Motu proprio *Dei providentis*, dated May 1, 1917, creating the Congregation for the Oriental Churches, *AAS* 9:530.

historical milieu which enfolds the man of every nation and age and from which he draws the values which permit him to promote civilization. (*GS* 53)

The reader will note that this passage holds (universal) nature and (particular) culture together. This teaching intends to observe the golden mean between two extremes. The first consists in appreciating what is particular, while losing sight of the universal; this results in a sort of cultural "tribalism" that hinders communications and hence access to universal values.[9] The second, conversely, is an appreciation of the universal aspect, while losing sight of the fact that it is found only in the particular. In doing so one "crushes" the distinctive cultural features so as to bring about a totality that is characterized in fact by the predominance of only one particular model. This is a form of "imperialism"—in other words, a particular that takes itself as a universal, which frequently happens in history.[10] But there is also the attempt to capture the universal by "distilling" it from the particular, which is a very theoretical proceeding and at any rate is a rather paltry objective.[11] In reality, the two dimensions are not separable and must be kept in close relation to each other, without confusing them. The universal (nature) exists concretely only in the particular (culture). Every culture has a certain grasp of universal values, in its own way, and communication among particular cultures is what can enrich and at the same time correct all cultures. The example of the success of the Roman Empire, which is so exemplary in many respects, depends on the fact that this particular culture was able to allow itself to be enriched by the values that it encountered in the peoples among whom it became established by discerning what was positive and rejecting what was negative. The stroke of genius of Roman culture was to allow itself to be enriched by Greek culture and not to suppress it. In the West this resulted in Gre-

---

9. It is clear, for example, that if the Gauls had not been in communication with the Romans they would not have had access to the riches of Roman law, which contained many "values" that are universally true and good.

10. This was the tendency in the nineteenth-century French colonial movement, which in some places led to caricatures, such as teaching little African children the song "*Nos ancêtres les Gaulois*" ["Our ancestors, the Gauls"]!

11. This was the intention of some exegetes (notably Bultmann), who tried to remove from the Bible anything that smacked of a particular (especially Semite) culture, so as to derive the "essence" of written Revelation. Obviously the results that they obtained left practically nothing intact.

The Church Is Catholic

co-Latin culture, which is assuredly a great treasure both for those of Greek origin and for those of Latin origin. Let us apply this comparison to the ecclesial situation.

2. Application to the ecclesial situation[12]

In the Church, we do not speak primarily about nature and culture, although that is perfectly well taken up by grace. What belongs specifically to the Church is the relation between the universal that is the Gospel (grace) and the particular that is the culture situation of each people (nature + culture).[13] The Constitution *Gaudium et spes* addressed the question:

There are many ties between the message of salvation and human culture. For God, revealing Himself to His people to the extent of a full manifestation of Himself in His Incarnate Son, has spoken according to the culture proper to each epoch.

Likewise the Church, living in various circumstances in the course of time, has used the discoveries of different cultures so that in her preaching she might spread and explain the message of Christ to all nations, that she might examine it and more deeply understand it, that she might give it better expression in liturgical celebration and in the varied life of the community of the faithful.

But at the same time, the Church, sent to all peoples of every time and place, is not bound exclusively and indissolubly to any race or nation, any particular way of life or any customary way of life recent or ancient. Faithful to her own tradition and at the same time conscious of her universal mission, she can enter into communion with the various civilizations, to their enrichment and the enrichment of the Church herself.

The Gospel of Christ constantly renews the life and culture of fallen man; it combats and removes the errors and evils resulting from the permanent allurement of sin. It never ceases to purify and elevate the morality of peoples. By riches coming from above, it makes fruitful, as it were from within, the spiritual qualities and traditions of every people of every age. It

---

12. A good bibliographic reference on this subject: Michel Sales, *Le Corps de l'Église*, Collection Communio (Paris: 1989); see chap. 2, "Le christianisme, la culture et les cultures," 145ff.

13. This manner of speaking, "nature + culture," is acceptable because nature is distinct from culture. One should not conclude from it, however, that the relation is extrinsic. It is *natural* for man to be *cultural*, in the sense that culture is based simultaneously on the faculties of intellect and will and on the inclination to social life, all of which are natural in man.

strengthens, perfects and restores them in Christ. Thus the Church, in the very fulfillment of her own function, stimulates and advances human and civic culture; by her action, also by her liturgy, she leads them toward interior liberty. (*GS* 58)

This discussion adds, first of all, the observation that all cultures are wounded by original sin, that they all need the Gospel in order to be healed and elevated. All cultures that receive the Gospel have to be reformed in relation to it. This began with Semitic culture, then Greek culture, then Latin culture.

We must realize that the relation between universal (Gospel) and particular (culture) is indeed found within the Church: the Gospel exists concretely only in particular cultures. First received through and in the Semitic culture, the Gospel then moved rapidly into Greek and then Greco-Latin culture. Since the most missionary church was the church of Greco-Latin culture, the Gospel was then passed on to the Germanic peoples, to Africa, America, the Far East, to cite only the chief missionary currents in history. What was communicated was not a "pure" universal, but always the universal in a particular. Hence evangelization can never be anything other than the encounter of two particulars (the missionary and the indigenous person), the former bearing within his particularity the evangelical universal, with the obligation of "translating" this universal-particular, so that the same Gospel (universal) might be among the evangelized people who are encountered, in their particularity.

This situation is in itself the normal one, yet it poses a formidable problem: neither of the terms, universal or particular, should be privileged, since the universal never exists apart from a particular. But this respect for both the universality of the Gospel and the particularity of each culture must go hand in hand—in the Church—with the necessity of preserving the signs of Catholic unity.[14] The difficulty is as follows: although there is a legitimate diversity of customs, rites, prayers, liturgies, and theological formulations—because catholicity is not identified with a particular (cultural) form of its actualization—nevertheless catholicity must be manifested visibly by means of an expres-

---

14. Since catholicity is a property of the Church, it has the same characteristics as the Church; in other words, with respect to our present discussion, this catholicity must be visible, tangible, externally recognizable.

sion that inevitably will belong to a given culture. The problem is precisely this: local and temporal diversity is legitimate in itself, and the visible, tangible manifestation of Catholic unity is also quite legitimate. Now this manifestation of catholicity, of universality, cannot help using the means of a time and a place—in other words, of a particular culture.

We are touching here on a complex question that is posed already at the level of Sacred Scripture: when God spoke to men, he did so in a time and in a place—in other words, within a precise culture. Now this same Word is called to be catholic; it is addressed to all mankind, in all times and in all places.

b. The beginning of a solution
1. Starting from the observation of the Church's life

It is inevitable that manifestations of catholicity should be situated in time and space—that is, within a certain culture. The proper role of the apostolic ministry with regard to the doctrine of the faith and the liturgy of the faith is to ensure that only one formulation of the faith is professed and celebrated, a unique formulation toward which all cultures must converge. And so each culture must go beyond its own framework—which is always limited—so as to communicate with the other cultures in the same expression of the faith. If we absolutize what is particular to a culture, we lose the universal. Clearly, when the Gospel was preached to the Gauls or to the Germanic tribes, it required of those cultures an effort to go beyond themselves.

Yet this catholic formulation of the faith is made with the help of the resources of a specific culture. The expression *consubstantial* in the Creed first came from the Greek culture. All dogmatic formulations are elaborated in terms of a culture, until now the Greco-Latin culture, *but they must be accepted as catholic.* In acting thus, the Church is not canonizing a particular culture. Rather, she found in this particular culture, at first Greek, then Greco-Latin, through the circumstances of the birth and development of the Christian community, a wealth of resources through which this particular culture was open, in turn, to the universal. It is clear that—from the perspective of the speculative intellect—the Greek culture offered resources that the Semitic culture could not provide. And it is an obvious historical fact that the Greek culture furnished the indispensable tool to the first seven ecumenical councils, whose dogmatic contribution is fundamental. Again, Greek culture as such is not thereby canonized, yet this specific culture, because of certain aspects of its primarily philosophical wisdom, touched a universal that lent itself particularly well to the understanding of Scripture and the expression of Tradition. That culture was far from perfect, and Christian efforts developed it noticeably,[15] but it was particularly open to the specifically Christian effort of elaboration.

The historical fact is this: the Catholic expression and celebration of the faith are enormously indebted to these Greco-Latin origins, even today. This does not mean that the achievement is unsurpassable. Dogmatic development within the Catholic Church encounters other cultures, whether they be the various non-European cultures or even the modern developments of European culture. All this provides additional conceptual resources. They will certainly be incorporated into the future development to the extent that these new propositions are able to enter into the heritage that is already established, so as to enrich it. And this will not happen without serious corrections. This is an extremely difficult, but necessary task.

This question must not be confused with the issue of inculturation. The latter is not, per se, a development of the Church's understanding of her faith, even though it may also be the occasion for that. Rather, inculturation is the *translation* of the particular cultural terms that convey the universal Gospel into the particular cultural terms of those who receive this Gospel. The first difficulty in inculturation is precisely that of a faithful translation. In order to find the right word (for example, *person* for the statement of the mystery of the Trinity and of the Incarnate Word), one must search for, and if possible find, within the target language a word that suitably expresses the concept of person. Sometimes the absence of the word is a sign that the culture being encountered has not yet arrived at that bit of wisdom; therefore, it will be necessary to give it that wisdom and consequently to provide also the adequate terminology. The history of the missions amply testifies

---

15. The clearest example is the elaboration of conceptual tools with which to articulate fundamental Christological dogma: one *person* (from *prosōpon*) in two *natures* (from *physis*). Greek philosophy had these concepts, but the Church Fathers refined or corrected them to a considerable extent.

The Church Is Catholic 573

to this cultural effort of the missionaries that accompanies the proclamation of the faith. Moreover, this effort must be made not only on the level of the speculative intellect; it likewise concerns the liturgical expression of the faith. Along with speculative language, the liturgy uses other sorts of languages (metaphorical and symbolic) that must also be inculturated, while always safeguarding the expression of catholicity.[16] This is not such an easy thing, since the same basic difficulty presents itself in the case of metaphoric and symbolic language as in the case of speculative language.

2. The question of the historicity of Christianity[17]

Safeguarding the catholicity of the faith in the multiplicity of cultures is a matter of *translating* a particular that expresses the universal into another particular that receives the universal. What is at stake here is therefore the safeguarding of the correct meaning of these different languages. But if one sticks to this key aspect, one could say that, as long as the meaning is preserved, we can change the signifiers at our leisure. The clearest example is language. Whether one says "God is one" (English) or *"Dieu est un"* (French) or *"Buh je jeden"* (Czech), it is the same meaning with different signifiers (the language). Could not this same rule be applied for metaphorical and symbolic language? To a certain extent, we think that one can answer in the affirmative. This, incidentally, is how the various liturgical rites were established. What is this "certain extent"? It seems to us that it is characterized by two main points. The first, which is easier to understand, is the preservation of the basic structure of the celebration. For example, in speaking about the Eucharist, we must preserve the two parts of the Mass (liturgy of the Word, liturgy of the Eucharist: the *duplex mensa* [twofold table]), so as to be able to recognize the sacrament that is being celebrated, whatever the rite may be. The second point is even more important: it concerns the *historicity* of Christianity. Christianity is not a way of thinking, a philosophy, a value system, it is *a person*, Christ, God in the flesh, the Incarnate Word. The mystery of the Incarnation situ-

---

16. It is quite clear that if someone from Switzerland traveled to Japan, he should recognize there the Eucharist in which he participated at home.

17. Here we are only situating this question within the outline, since we treat it in detail in our course on the Eucharist.

ates God in history. Here we have the historical realism of the Christian religion, which is the result [*aboutissement*] of the historical realism of the Jewish religion.[18]

Now for *his* supreme acts through which he sanctifies men (baptism, Eucharist, etc.), Christ instituted not only the signification that must be preserved (purification by washing, food taken in a communal meal), but also the elements of signification (*the water* of baptism and the words; *the bread and wine* of the Eucharist and the words). Out of respect for what Christ did, but also in order to manifest clearly and concretely this link with history that expresses the mystery of the Incarnation, the Church does not allow anyone to change—to translate—the elements of signification when these have been chosen by Christ. This causes no problem in the case of baptismal water, because this element—water—is common to all mankind, and its use in washing is universal. But it does cause a problem in the case of the Eucharist, because wheat bread and grape wine are staples produced by certain cultures and not by others. But precisely for this reason these signs are precious expressions of the historicity of Christianity. It comes from early first-century Palestine—in other words, from the time and place where God became man.[19] Here the very center of the Christian faith is involved. In cases where our Lord did not establish signifying elements (for example, the sign of priestly ordination), the Church allows herself a bit more freedom, but always taking care not to change everything so as not to compromise the expression of catholicity. There was a time when—even within the Catholic Church—the essential rite of ordaining a priest was different in the Latin Patriarchate (*porrectio* or presentation of the instruments + words: symbolism that came from the Germans) and in the Eastern Patriarchates (the imposition of hands + words: Semitic symbolism). This caused no problem, since the meaning of the whole celebration, to which all the sacramentals contributed, remained the same. But even so, Pius XII deemed it more appropriate to return to one essential rite.[20]

18. Following in the footsteps of the Jews, we maintain that God reveals and gives himself in the history that he directs (e.g., the Passover from Egypt).

19. To say that God became man means that, like all human beings, God entered a particular culture, in a definite place and time.

20. The reason that Pius XII had for doing this was chiefly ecumenical: to return to the most ancient rite, which is shared with the Orthodox.

c. Conclusion

The question of safeguarding intensive catholicity in extensive catholicity is extremely important these days. The globalization of the communications media allows the Gospel to be presented absolutely everywhere—in other words, to take a giant step toward full extensive catholicity. But we must not lose "in depth" what we may gain "in breadth." The decisive principle in posing the question appropriately and in seeking also to answer it is the principle that affirms the presence of the universal in the particular. The intellectual tool that allows us to picture things analogically is the relation between universal nature and particular culture. The universal exists in and therefore in terms of the particular. To abstract it, to detach it from the particular notes that it acquires through its insertion into the particular, is a legitimate mental operation. This process, however, should not lead to "hypostatizing" or reifying something that exists really only in the particular. On this basis, theological reflection includes the facts of faith concerning the universal Gospel that reached us through and in the culture assumed by Christ.

III. THE UNIVERSAL CHURCH AND THE LOCAL CHURCHES[21]

This question, which is very relevant in the ecumenical dialogue with our Orthodox brethren, is rather sensitive and difficult to grasp. Nowadays one frequently expresses the universal dimension of the Church in terms of a "communion of local churches."[22] What does this mean?

a. Statement of the question

It is appropriate to start with the rather quick reference in *Lumen gentium* 23, which did not provoke discussion during the conciliar debates.[23]

---

21. Here we use the expressions "local churches" and "particular churches" as synonyms.
22. One of the chief descriptive essays on this subject is the work by Jean-Marie Roger Tillard, *Church of Churches*.
23. For the redaction of the document, see AS I/4, 26–27 (first schema); AS II/1, 236 (second schema); AS III/1, 217; and AS III/4 81–82 (second schema corrected). See also the related reference in the Decree *Christus Dominus* 11.

This collegial union is apparent also in the mutual relations of the individual bishops with particular churches and with the universal Church. The Roman Pontiff, as the successor of Peter, is the perpetual and visible principle and foundation of unity of both the bishops and of the faithful. The individual bishops, however, are the visible principle and foundation of unity in their particular churches, fashioned after the model of the universal Church, in and from which churches (*"in quibus et ex quibus"*) comes into being the one and only Catholic Church. For this reason the individual bishops represent each his own church, but all of them together and with the Pope represent the entire Church in the bond of peace, love and unity.

Taken literally, the statement concerning the relation between the universal Church and the local churches appears to be contradictory. It can be outlined as follows:

The universal Church *engenders* → the local churches, which *as a group form* → the universal Church.

One and the same reality, the universal Church, cannot be at the same time and in the same respect prior and posterior to another reality, the local churches. It is as though someone were to say, "Paul is simultaneously older and younger than John." In order to resolve the contradiction, it is necessary to distinguish between relations.

b. Several proposed solutions

Before presenting our findings, we will review several proposed solutions that will help us to frame the problem better, even though we consider them inadequate.[24]

1. The "federal" paradigm

This is the simplest, not to say simplistic explanation, which maintains that the universal Church is formed by the aggregate of the local churches. This respects only the second part of the proposition. In this case, the universal Church would be a reality of a quantitative sort, the sum total of the particular churches. This paradigm was the presupposition of the conciliarist faction that tried to prevail at the Council of

---

24. We will not expatiate on the proposed solutions that are based on "a dialectic of realities in tension"; we have treated that subject sufficiently.

The Church Is Catholic 577

Basel. It was also implied by Gallicanism and Febronianism. One of the consequences of this view is that the highest expression of the totality of the local churches, in other words of the universal Church, is the general council which is *ipso facto* above the pope.

Whereas the universal Church is not a federation of particular churches, like a sum resulting from the addition of several terms, the converse is also true: neither are the particular churches parcels of a divided whole that is the universal Church. That would be in keeping only with the first part of the proposition.

This view, federation or subdivision, remains quantitative. Presently no one seriously defends it. This perspective, moreover, is completely unknown to the Church Fathers. But we will have to investigate it so as to determine whether there is not something right about it that can be salvaged.

2. The simultaneity of the universal and the local[25]

This proposed solution intends to respect both clauses in the statement in *LG* 23 by pointing out first the two extremes to be avoided:

[We must] go beyond the opposition between a universalist ecclesiology that would see in the local church only a "part" of the universal Church, and an ecclesiology of the local church for which it alone would be the whole reality.

We can only agree with these "specifications" for the research. The same document continues:

There is no priority, neither historical nor ontological, of the universal Church in relation to the local church, or vice versa. The universal and the local are necessarily simultaneous, and both necessarily have a concrete existence.[26]

How are we to understand this simultaneity? The document does not seem to explain it clearly. Another author, Fr. Tillard, has tried to do so as follows:

---

25. As an illustration of this proposition, we cite the document by the Joint Catholic-Orthodox Commission in France, *La primauté romaine dans la communion des Églises* [The Roman Primacy in the Communion of Churches] (Paris: 1991).

26. Joint Catholic-Orthodox Commission in France, *La primauté romaine dans la communion des Églises*, 115.

The Spirit makes the (one, unique) Church that God has planned from all eternity: in the particular churches and starting from each one of them, he causes the *catholica* to exist. He does not make it exist by the addition of all the *particular* churches (later on we will talk about *local* churches). He makes it present in each one of them, according to its true *catholic* nature. But as a result of this presence in all of them, the Church exists concretely in the world through them, in this *catholicity*. Since in this context *particular* churches is synonymous with *local* churches, let us use the latter adjective exclusively. Then we affirm, on the one hand, that each *local* church exists in order for the *catholica* willed by God in his eternal plan to assume concrete shape (along with the *universality* of salvation that this plan entails), and, on the other hand, that once these *local* churches come about, the *catholica* is in fact found in them and through them, in other words, it exists concretely in real, human flesh. From this we must deduce that this Church *comes into being as catholic and local inseparably*.[27]

If we understand these passages correctly, they seem to propose two things. On the one hand, in God's plan there is a universal Church, *prima in intentione* [first in intention], actualized in this world in particular churches, in terms of which it exists. On the other hand, and this is the consequence, during the age of this world, the local and the universal are simultaneous: a local church is not truly itself unless the universal is present within it. The universal really exists in this world only in the particular. The priority of the universal is therefore in a certain way ontological—the gifts that God intends to give—but not historical. The universal here, however, is not strictly *ecclesial;* we are talking about God's *plan*, which, in being put into action, does engender the Church, but as the local church. This seems to us insufficient to make a universal *Church* truly exist, in whose image the particular churches would then be formed.

3. The mutual inclusion of the universal and the local[28]

This approach intends to emphasize an "essential" identity between the universal Church and the local church by pointing out that the particu-

---

27. Jean-Marie Roger Tillard, "Église catholique ou Église universelle?" in *Cristianesimo nella storia* 16, no. 2 (1995): 356–57 (emphasis added in the final phrase).
28. See, for example, Yves Congar, *La Collégialité de l'épiscopat: Histoire et théologie;* Henri de Lubac, *Les Églises particulières,* esp. 50; *Motherhood of the Church,* 169ff.

lar church includes the universal Church by the identity of their faith, sacraments, and ministry. The converse leads us to say that the universal Church includes the local churches. So as not to understand this in a "federal" sense, we must acknowledge a distinct and prior existence of the universal Church. The latter is formed by the "deposit" of the one sacrifice of Christ entrusted to the apostolic college, with Peter as the head, so as to be made present in all places and in all times. The apostolic institution is not just the "hierarchy" in the modern sense of the word, but first, in its etymological sense, the "sacred origin" (i.e., Christic origin) whereby the Twelve represent the New Israel.

We have here an intuition that seems productive to us, and that we will meet again by another route that we prefer, because it seems clearer to us.

c. Magisterial directions

Concerning the question under discussion, we have two recent documents. The first is the Address of John Paul II to the Roman Curia dated December 20, 1990, and the second is the letter from the Congregation for the Doctrine of the Faith dated June 15–16, 1992. The Address to the Curia is a text composed for an occasion, and, by its very form, it is certainly a minor document. Its contents, however, are worth noting. In contrast, the letter of the Congregation for the Doctrine of the Faith is a formal act, the doctrinal authority of which should not be underestimated.

1. The Address to the Roman Curia[29]

After noting the "mutual interiority" between [= "mutual inclusion" of] the universal Church and the particular churches, the Pope succinctly mentions the reciprocity whereby:

Through this unity the universal Church can feel that she is enriched by the treasures of the particular Churches, and the particular Churches can boast that they belong to the universal Church, which, indeed, is truly present and acts in them (*CD* 11).

---

29. *Acta Apostolicae Sedis* 83 (1991): 740–49; citations at 745–46; translated from the Italian.

Immediately afterward, this reciprocal relation is described in greater depth as follows:

> This sort of reciprocity, while it expresses and preserves their respective dignities, suitably elucidates the character of the one and universal Church, which at the same time finds in the particular Churches her own image and a locus of her expression, since the particular Churches are formed "after the model of the universal Church, in and from which Churches comes into being the one and only Catholic Church" (*LG* 23). The particular Churches are, in turn, *ex et in Ecclesia universali* [from and in the universal Church]. Indeed, they have their ecclesial character from this Catholic Church and in her. The particular Church is "Church" precisely because it is a particular presence of the universal Church. Thus, on the one hand, the universal Church finds her concrete existence in every particular Church in which she is present and active, and, on the other hand, the particular Church does not exhaust the totality of the mystery of the Church, given that some of her constituent elements cannot be deduced solely from the analysis of the particular Church itself. These elements are the office of the successor of Peter and the Episcopal College itself.

The text reinforces the correlation spelled out in *LG* 23: while the universal Church is *in et ex* [in and from] the particular churches, the latter too are *in et ex* the universal Church, because they are formed in her image. A reciprocal relation cannot be more clearly enunciated. The whole question comes down to which element can prevent contradiction. This element is specified: it is the office of the successor of Peter and the episcopal college. Moreover, the statement that the universal Church finds in the particular churches *both her own image and her own expression* seems to indicate a twofold consideration: one ontological (the image), and the other epistemological (the expression).

2. The Letter of the Congregation for the Doctrine of the Faith[30]

The document *Communionis notio* attempts to clarify somewhat this *mutual interiority* that is not always very clear:

---

30. *DC* (1992): 729–33 (esp. 730–31). This document intervenes in a theological debate in order to guide it, not to suppress it (see no. 2). It does not articulate thoroughly worked-out conclusions, but rather indicates a certain number of theological constraints essential to Catholic theology. As to its form, the *Letter* was approved by the pope *in forma communi*.

The Church Is Catholic 581

[The universal Church] is not the result of the communion of the [particular] Churches, but in its essential mystery it is a reality *ontologically and temporally* prior to every *individual* particular Church.

Indeed, according to the Fathers, *ontologically*, the Church-mystery, the Church that is one and unique, precedes creation, and gives birth to the particular Churches as her daughters. She expresses herself in them; she is the mother and not the offspring of the particular Churches. Furthermore, the Church is manifested, *temporally*, on the day of Pentecost in the community of the one hundred and twenty gathered around Mary and the twelve Apostles, the representatives of the one unique Church and the founders-to-be of the local Churches, who have a mission directed to the world: from the first the Church *speaks all languages*....

Arising *within* and *out of* the universal Church, [the local Churches] have their ecclesiality in it and from it. Hence the formula of the Second Vatican Council: "The Church in and formed out of the Churches" ("*Ecclesia in et ex Ecclesiis*," *LG* 23), is inseparable from this other formula: "The Churches in and formed out of the Church" ("*Ecclesiae in et ex Ecclesia*") (John Paul II, Address to the Roman Curia)....

Every member of the faithful, through faith and Baptism, is inserted into the one, holy, catholic and apostolic Church. He does not belong to the universal Church in a *mediate* way, *through* belonging to a particular Church, but in an *immediate* way, even though entry into and life within the universal Church are necessarily brought about *in* a particular Church.[31]

The principal statement asserts the *ontological and chronological* priority of the universal Church over the particular churches. The *catholica*, however, is not a Platonic idea. It exists and is manifested on the day of Pentecost when the Twelve are present as representatives of the one Church. The comparison of the mother who brings forth daughters allows us to imagine things somewhat. In fact, the mother is part of the family by being the mother—that is, *principle*—of the family: not only the mother of each child personally and distinctly, but also mother of this specific communion that the family is.[32]

Now that these basic points have been noted, we now propose our solution.

---

31. Letter *Communionis notio*, nos. 9 and 10, *Acta Apostolicae Sedis* 85 (1993): 464–71; English translation at http://www.doctrinafidei.va, May 28, 1992.
32. See de La Soujeole, "À propos de l'Église comme communion," *RT* (1993): 114.

d. Proposed solution

Any solution of the question of the reciprocal relation of the universal Church and the local churches must take the three following points into account:

- An exclusively quantitative and cumulative universality (federal paradigm) is insufficient. The solution must describe a qualitative and essential universality.
- The simultaneity between the universal Church and the local church is the expression of the essential reciprocity of the two aspects of ecclesiality, but it is insufficient to manifest the concrete presence of the universal Church in the local church.
- The question is situated at the level of the Church considered as the means of salvation, and not as the reality of salvation; still, these two aspects should not be separated.

Our proposal is based on two considerations. The first is derived from ecclesial sacramentality, which will allow us to clarify certain points. The second emerges from a "genetic" or historical observation concerning the birth of a local church.

1. Clarification through ecclesial sacramentality

In discussing the Church as a means of salvation, we have a twofold communion, social and diaconal. In the first place, the federal paradigm applies quite well to the social communion. The whole Church is, in this world, divided into various dioceses because of sociological constraints assumed by the mystery of the Church in this world. There is nothing surprising about this: in order for salvation to be proposed effectively *humano modo* [in a human manner] to each person, the effective exercise of apostolic mediation must be wedded to the sociological distribution of the population to which it is sent. History clearly shows this fact, and in Antiquity the ecclesiastical vocabulary designating this distribution often had a purely socio-political origin.[33] Al-

---

33. The most obvious example is the name *diocese*, which comes from the Greek *dia oikos*: domestic administration. A diocese was in Greek, then in Roman, governance a part of a province; then it became a group of provinces. The current ecclesiastical meaning is attested in late fourth-century Africa: a territory entrusted to a bishop. This meaning would gradually be adopted by the entire Latin Church.

The Church Is Catholic 583

though the federal paradigm is untenable for a general explanation, it should not be rejected with regard to the sociological dimension. This is an initial point—not the main point, but it must be noted. The social totality of the local churches constitutes quantitative or extensive catholicity, the Church that aims toward a universality in time, place, and persons.

Present and subsisting within the social communion, however, is the diaconal communion. The latter first appears to be geographically subdivided according to the sociological realities, but it is not governed by the same principles of unity and of life. In order to show the different logic of this *diakonia*, it is advisable to look at the birth of a local church.

2. Genetic-historical observation

Every local church was born as a result of a communication that came from a previous local church. We will explain this by means of the following historical example:[34]

The local church of Narbonne (France) seems to have been founded by its first bishop, Paulus, around the mid-third century. The founder was a missionary from Rome (*"missus a romanis episcopis,"* tradition says). The local church of Rome had been founded in the mid-first century by Christians who came from Alexandria. The local church of Alexandria had been founded by Christians from Jerusalem. One cannot go back any farther. Hence we make two observations:

- The birth of a local church

This birth presupposes some external communication that founds the church in that precise place, which is most often defined by the local socio-political circumstances. The communicating church of origin—a previous particular church—does not communicate first or foremost what makes it a local church (its customs, its law), but rather what makes it a church, in other words, the faith and the sacraments of the faith. This founding local church—Rome in our example that started with Narbonne—was itself founded by a previous local church (Alexandria) that transmitted to it the faith and the sacraments of the

---

34. We do not vouch for the complete veracity of all the specifically historical features of this example.

faith, and so one until the first origin. Everything goes back to the first *local* church, which is Jerusalem, from which all other local churches were propagated by "planting cuttings from the main shoot."[35] But what was the foundation of the local church of Jerusalem?

• The first source of every local church

This first origin is found in Jerusalem on the day of Pentecost: the apostolic college received at that moment the *depositum fidei* and the *mysteria*—in other words, the essential elements that would engender the diaconal communion subsisting in a social communion so as to lead to the communion of the theological virtues. So the first thing, the ontological precondition for every local church, is the group of the Twelve, headed by Peter. This apostolic group is the *source and rule* of the diaconal communion, a *sine qua non* of the connection between the social communion and the communion in the theological virtues. This group of Twelve continues in the episcopal college, headed by the bishop of the local church of Rome. Here we see the *apostolic* property of the Church, not only of each local church, and not just of these churches taken together, but as the constant *source and rule* of the diaconal communion. In this sense, both the birth of the Church, in the first local community of Jerusalem, and its growth and permanence throughout the world, depend on the constancy of this source and this rule. They are prior to the existence of every local church, in the sense that each local church exists and survives only in dependence on them. We have here, in the apostolic college, an ecclesiality that is *prior* to any local ecclesiality because it engenders and maintains the local ecclesiality by its unique role in the diaconal communion. We can call it the universal Church because of its vocation to be communicated to all, in all ages and in all places, and because of its permanence and its identity in all the local realizations of ecclesiality.

3. Understanding the diaconal communion

Thus we refine our understanding of the diaconal communion. We have shown by our study of ecclesial sacramentality that the diacon-

---

35. This expression is used by Louis Bouyer, *The Church of God,* 297. Tertullien correctly describes this generation as "tradition"; see *De Praescriptione* XX and XXXII (ANF 3:252a, 258a).

The Church Is Catholic

al communion is at the same time the source-rule and the constancy of the connection between the social and supernatural communions. Here we specify further: as the *source and rule*, this diaconal communion subsists in the apostolic college and precedes the social communion. Therefore it does not *yet* subsist in the social communion; it resides in the group of the Twelve. As something present and developing, this diaconal communion resides in the social communion and concerns *all* the baptized who participate in its life; this is the *sensus fidei* and the liturgical celebration, especially of the sacraments.

It may not be the best nomenclature to call this source and this rule of the diaconal communion "the universal Church engendering the local church." For anyone who says "Church" is speaking about the three communions together, and certainly the apostolic college lacks the social dimension—that is to say, the quality of leader who governs a given community. The apostles and their successors, in the diaconal communion, give birth to the community and do not just govern it. This is the duty of the apostles, and of their successors, to be vicars of Christ. But one could defend this nomenclature by pointing out that the apostles and their successors represent the one Church according to the symbolic biblical manner: the Twelve represent the Twelve tribes of the New Israel. In this sense it symbolizes that all ecclesiality has its source and takes it rule from them, because they and they alone are vicars of Christ.

If we keep these clarifications in mind, we can say that the expression "universal Church" does not designate exactly the same reality when considered before or after the local church. As an antecedent, the universal Church is its apostolicity as the source and rule of every church. As something subsequent, it is its apostolicity as it is effectively received and lived, that is, in all its communal fruitfulness.

- Local churches are *in and from* the universal-source-Church with respect to their foundation and regulation.
- Local churches united by the identity of their source and regulation *are* the universal-effect-Church that comes about through them and from them.

The sacramental paradigm situates the universal Church both at the beginning and at the end of ecclesiality, but not under the same aspect. There is a constant, fruitful source: the apostolic ministry that is charged with re-presenting (in the sense of "making present") Christ who is building up his Body by the gift of himself (grace and truth). Moreover, there is the totality of the members of his ecclesial Body, which lives by what it has received. There are two sorts of ecclesial universality: a universality of *cause* (the universal Church made present by the apostolic ministry that engenders and maintains in being), and a universality of *effect* (the universal Church of the saved, which exists and acts). The *causal* universality brings about *effective* universality in two ways: first, by being received in the local particular[ity]—this is universality "*in*"; and second, by working on the basis of the local particular[ity] for the accomplishment of salvation *ad intra* (pastoral work) and *ad extra* (missionary work)—this is universality "*ex*."

This sacramental explanation certainly valorizes the universal Church,[36] yet it does not seem to us to diminish the dignity of the local church, as one might fear at first glance. Its universality as cause underscores the primary and irreplaceable character of the apostolic ministry, making present Christ the Head who builds up his Body. This ministry is not a "structure," but rather signifies that the Church is engendered, vicariously, in and from the *persons* of the apostles and of their successors. The universal Church understood as an effect underscores the ecclesial fullness (Head and members).

The local church is the necessary link between the cause and its effect. It is appreciated by its *irreplaceable* character. Its existence is due to the fact that God assumed natural sociability in order to save the world. All the particularities that give it its concrete countenance are lifted up so as to signify and serve the communion of the theological virtues, which is per se universal, in that place where it effectively contacts human beings.[37] Its communion with all the other local churches, in particular the church of Rome, signifies and brings about the necessary transcendence of the local so as to preserve the causal universality and thus to arrive at the final universality.

36. Note that when we say the "universal-source" Church we do not mean the church of Rome, which is a local church, but rather the Church in its source here below, which is the episcopal college headed by the pope.
37. The study by H. Legrand, "La réalisation de l'Église en un lieu," is particularly interesting; it shows everything in the order of signification and of *diakonia* that is necessary at the local level, and thereby at the universal level, in order to touch human beings *effectively*.

The Church Is Catholic

The preceding discussion, it seems to us, explains the fact that, when assembled in an ecumenical council or dispersed throughout the world, but "concurring," the episcopal college does not represent first and foremost the sum total of the local churches. Each bishop does not primarily represent "his" church as a deputy represents his constituents in a national parliament; rather, each bishop is understood to be in the hierarchical communion belonging to the successors of the apostles, so as to signify first the universal Church as a *cause* and then as an *effect*. This explains why each bishop is successor *of the* apostles; he is the bishop of a diocese only insofar as he is a member of the college-cause, so as to bring about diaconal universality in that place, through and in the social-local reality, with a view to perfection in the theological virtues, which is inseparably both local and universal. History seems to confirm this.

As history shows, when a particular Church has sought to become self-sufficient and has weakened its real communion with the universal Church and with its living and visible center, its internal unity suffers too, and it finds itself in danger of losing its own freedom in the face of the various forces of enslavement and exploitation.[38]

Indeed, once a local church no longer understands itself as being enriched by a reality constantly received from Christ through the apostolic college, it cuts itself off from the diaconal reality, thus breaking the bond between its social communion and the communion in the theological virtues, and consequently it can no longer possess communion in the final effect either.

Conclusion

The property of catholicity presupposes the properties of unity and holiness. It shows how the constitutive unity of the ecclesial mystery is effectively present in the Christic economy of salvation, the ongoing Pentecost that makes the Church, and how the holiness of Christ gushes like an ever-flowing spring through the apostolic ministry for the purpose of irrigating humanity as a whole. The Church's qualitative

---

38. Congregation for the Doctrine of the Faith, Letter to the Bishops of the Catholic Church: *Some Aspects of the Church Understood as Communion*, June 15, 1992 [May 28, 1992], no. 8.

or intensive catholicity is the efficient cause of her quantitative or extensive catholicity.

We should restate how this question about the relation between the universal Church and the particular churches has furthered our knowledge of the diaconal communion. We had presented the latter within the framework of our study of sacramentality as a communal reality including the whole People of God, based on the characters of baptism, confirmation, and holy orders. Here we add the following clarification: the diaconal communion was born, two thousand years ago, from the vicarial ministry of the apostles that was manifested on Pentecost, and it remains faithful to the true faith and the authentic sacraments received from the apostles through the work of the whole community, thanks to the ordered collaboration of all its members. Baptized and confirmed Christians witness to the true faith with a view to handing it on, and they participate in the celebration of the sacraments. Each one of them, according to the gifts he has received, has a part in the progress that is always to be hoped for in understanding the life of the Church and in the ever-urgent development of the works by which the Gospel is to influence all mankind. The successors of the apostles participate in this life of the ecclesial whole first by authenticating the true faith (a function of discernment belonging to them alone), then by celebrating the sacraments according to their station.

This brings us to the fourth property of the Church: the fact that she is apostolic.

Bibliography

Congar, Yves. *L'Église, une, sainte, catholique et apostolique.* Coll. Mysterium salutis 15, 149–89. Good patristic overview.
Congar, Yves, Henri de Lubac, et al. "Catholique = universel?" *DC* (1971): 80. A rather forceful open letter to the bishops, composed at the time when the French-speaking commission for liturgical translation was planning to render the word *catholicam* in the Creed as "universal." This report allegedly caused advocates of this equivalence to retreat. Worth noting because the question comes up regularly.
Journet, Charles. *L'Église du Verbe incarné,* vol. 2. Paris: 1951. In particular chap. 9, page 1197ff. Thorough presentation that extends to the principles of missiology.
Lossky, Vladimir. "Le troisième attribut de l'Église." *Dieu Vivant* 10 (1948): 79–89.

The Church Is Catholic

Pagé, Jean-Guy. *Qui est l'Église?* Montreal and Paris: 1979, 2:149–80. Good general study with the main references.

Sales, Michel. *Le Corps de l'Église.* Coll. Communio. Paris: 1989. See chap. 2, "Le christianisme, la culture et les cultures," 145ff.

On the Question about the Relation of Universal Church to Local Church

Bouyer, Louis. *The Church of God.* San Francisco: Ignatius Press, 297 and 422ff.

Congregation for the Doctrine of the Faith. *Letter to the Bishops of the Catholic Church on Certain Aspects of the Church as Communion,* May 28, 1992. Particularly paragraphs 7–10. English text at EWTN online archives.

de Lubac, Henri. *Les Églises particulières dans l'Église universelle.* Paris: 1971. Good patristic overview. See the critical review by Marie-Vincent Leroy in *RT* (1972): 295–96. English translation: *The Motherhood of the Church.* San Francisco: Ignatius Press, 1982.

John Paul II. *Address to the Roman Curia* (December 20, 1990). *Acta Apostolicae Sedis* 83 (1991): 740–49, esp. no. 9.

Lanne, Emmanuel. "L'Église locale et l'Église universelle." *Irénikon* 43 (1970): 481–511.

Legrand, H. "La réalisation de l'Église en un lieu." In *Initiation à la pratique de la théologie.* Vol. 3, Dogmatique II. Paris: 1983, 143–45.

Neunheuser, B. "Église universelle et Église locale." In *L'Église de Vatican II.* US 51b. Paris: 1966, 607–38.

Sesboüé, Bernard. *Pour une théologie oecuménique.* Paris: 1990. Particularly chap. 8, "Ecclésiologie de communion et voie vers l'unité," esp. 137–41. See review in *RT* (1993): 645ff.

Tillard, Jean-Marie Roger. "Église catholique ou Église universelle?" *Cristianesimo nella storia* 16, no. 2 (1995): 356ff.

16

The Church Is Apostolic

In this chapter, as in the three preceding chapters dealing with the properties of the *being* of the Church, we consider apostolicity only at this level (rather than at the level of the *action* of the Church). The question about the complex relation between the universal Church and the particular churches already introduced us to this aspect. We will go into more detail so as to show the precise economy chosen by Christ.

One fact is extremely important in order to grasp from the outset the apostolic nature of the Church. Let us start with the Old Testament: David sees the end of his days approaching, and he gives his final recommendations to his son Solomon. He regulates the affairs of the kingdom for the sake of continuity (1 Kgs 2). Jesus, too, before leaving this world, transmits to his disciples some words, wisdom, and authority (Mt 28). Nevertheless, and this must be understood clearly, the disciples *do not succeed Christ*. This is quite unlike the case of David and Solomon. The Twelve will represent the Lord as signs of his presence, for he is always there. *He is the one who will continue to teach, sanctify, and govern the faithful through them.* The constant presence of Christ is the golden rule of the apostle; if he intends to succeed Christ, he is lost.

The Church Is Apostolic

I. APOSTOLICITY

a. The adjective "apostolic"

The meaning of the adjective "apostolic" is fairly clear: referring to the apostles. An apostolic man is a Christian living as the apostles did, and, in the case of apostolic religious, the "apostolic life" is the imitation of the apostles, whose contemplation of the mysteries overflowed in their preaching. In each case the reference is to a *being*. We note two particular usages of the adjective "apostolic":

1. The apostolic Traditions

We also say "unwritten Tradition." This designates a certain way in which some teachings of Christ came down to us. We cite here the Council of Trent:

the unwritten traditions, which have been received by the apostles from the mouth of Christ Himself, or from the apostles themselves, at the dictations of the Holy Spirit, have come down even to us, transmitted as it were from hand to hand.[1]

What we call Revelation is therefore a complex whole including Scripture and Tradition. Tradition is subdivided into apostolic Traditions (in the sense just described) and post-apostolic Tradition (Tradition in the usual sense: *interpretative* Tradition).

2. The apostolic churches

We speak about apostolic churches to designate the particular churches founded by the apostles.[2]

In each case, "apostolic" refers to *the apostles personally*; therefore, this is the level at which we must consider the matter.

b. The apostles

The words "apostle" and "apostolic" come from the Greek verb *apostellein:* to send. An apostle is someone who is sent. In the New Tes-

---

1. Session IV, decree dated April 8, 1546; repeated by Vatican I in the Constitution *Dei Filius,* chap. 2, and by Vatican II, Constitution *Dei Verbum* 7, §1, and 10, §2. There we find the expression "the Word of God, whether in its written form *or* in the form of Tradition."
2. This usage is attested in Tertullian, *De Praescriptione* 20.6–8 (CCSL 1:202).

tament, a particular group made up of certain disciples had been sent by Christ to spread his Word, to perform his saving acts, and to govern the community that would spring from that activity. The conclusion of Matthew's Gospel is explicit: "All authority (*exousia*) in heaven and on earth has been given to me. Go therefore" (Mt 28:18–19). The parallel passage in Mark's Gospel is identical: "Go into all the world" (Mk 16:15). St. John adds an important clarification: "As the Father has sent me, even so I send you" (Jn 20:21). In Acts an additional element concerning this group is given in connection with the replacement of Judas. St. Peter arranges for his replacement and to that end makes several decisive statements that help us understand the title of "apostle." There is talk about replacing Judas, who "was numbered among us, and was allotted his share in this ministry" (Acts 1:17); it is a service. The mention of *diakonia* is clearly repeated in Acts 1:25 in the expression "ministry and apostleship." The basic requirement for an apostle is twofold: he must have accompanied the Twelve during the whole time of the public life of Jesus until his resurrection and be a personal witness of the resurrection (because Christ did not appear in public). St. Matthias is elected and admitted into the apostolic group; all together they form the Twelve. We see clearly that the apostolic mission is not separated from apostolic being; it is a question of having been with Jesus and, by implication, of staying with him (see Jn 15:1–8 and Mt 28:20: "I am with you always, to the close of the age"). These men, the Twelve, symbolic of the twelve tribes, represent all Israel according to the Spirit (Rev 21:12–14).

St. Paul gives what has become the classic formulation of the apostle. He is first of all the *personal* witness of the Risen Lord; this is a special relation with Jesus who chose to appear to him. Subsequently it is a precise mission: to preach, above all, and then to celebrate and govern. Here is the description of the apostle in the strict sense, since the word can designate a broader reality in the letters of St. Paul.[3] We should note, furthermore, several points:

- The apostolic ministry is the first of Christ's gifts to his Church (Eph 4:11), the first of the charisms of the Spirit (1 Cor 12:28); this is what builds up the Church (Eph 2:20; 1 Cor 3:9–11).

3. For a good scriptural overview, see Jean-Guy Pagé, *Qui est l'Église?* (Montreal and Paris, 1982), 2:187ff.

The Church Is Apostolic

- First does not mean only; the apostle is first as the stock, the root, the foundation through which all Christians are joined to Christ.
- First also means chief; the apostle, and he alone, leads the new People of God decisively. This does not mean that he enlists no one for aid and counsel, but the major decisions are up to him.

c. The idea of apostolicity

From the earliest times the Church could recognize from experience the need for this very particular *diakonia*. The first divisions, the first splits began during the apostles' lifetime.

Tradition has a great wealth of testimonies to the idea of apostolicity.[4] As early as Tertullian and St. Irenaeus we find the fundamental affirmations, and in later writers it would be a commonplace. There are two essential points: the true and only doctrine is the one preached by the apostles; it is preserved by the apostolic succession. These two points are connected.[5] Therefore there is something called *the apostolicity of faith*—in other words, the fact that we take our faith from the witness of the apostles (see 1 Jn 1:1–3). This is so-called *formal* apostolicity. And then there is the fact that this true faith is preserved thanks to the apostolic succession, for which it is the decisive criterion: the pastor is subject to what he must preserve in order to transmit it. How can the pastor's fidelity be judged? The successor is not automatically faithful in his transmission of the faith.... The criterion was at first the pastor's agreement with the other pastors and then agreement with the successor of the first of the apostles, the bishop of Rome. We will return to this in connection with the primacy of the Roman pontiff.

This idea of apostolicity in no way diminishes the apostolicity of *the whole Church*, but rather shows that the latter operates through the service of apostolicity rendered by some of her members. To put it another way, the property of the whole presupposes a particular quality in some of the parts. Here we find a carefully ordered convergence.[6] This is a fundamental element that we share with our Orthodox brethren. But some Eastern theologians, like some Eastern traditions, add

---

4. A good overview is provided by Pagé (see preceding note), 194ff.
5. See the lists of bishops drawn up by St. Irenaeus, Tertullian, and St. Eusebius of Caesarea.
6. See *LG* 13 and *Dei verbum* 10.

the idea of *sobornost*—that is, the notion that the episcopate is subject to the judgment of the community. This idea of *reception* is not recognized by Catholic tradition.

To sum up, we must clearly distinguish the apostolicity of the faith from the apostolicity of the ministry in the service thereof. The apostolicity of ministry is the topic studied in ecclesiology. This apostolicity of ministry is studied in two major parts: apostolic succession by the bishops (the theme of *collegiality*) and the succession of one specific apostle, Peter, by one specific bishop, the bishop of Rome (the theme of the Roman primacy). These two points are very closely connected. The main affirmation of this is found in LG 22, §1 (and the parallel passage in the Constitution's *Nota explicativa praevia*, no. 1, §3):

> Just as, in accordance with the Lord's decree, St. Peter and the rest of the apostles constitute a unique apostolic college, so in like fashion the Roman Pontiff, Peter's successor, and the bishops, the successors of the apostles, are related with and united to one another [i.e., in a unique college].

The correspondence "Peter is to the apostles as the pope is to the bishops" is *proportional* and not identical. The relations are not strictly the same, because the successors of the apostles, like the successor of Peter, do not succeed in every respect; the charism of inspiration was given only to the apostles and ended with the death of the last of them. The proportionality results from the fact that Peter and the other apostles are not equals, just as equality does not exist between the successor of Peter and the successors of the apostles. This leads us to consider now the notion of succession.

d. The notion of succession

There is one question that we will not address, because it seems that the ecumenical dialogue in our times has gone beyond it. This is the question about the very principle of a succession, which was denied by liberal Protestants in the late nineteenth and early twentieth centuries.[7] We present here the very notion of succession.[8] The latter consists of

---

7. For this bygone debate, see chapter 4 of Yves Congar, *La Tradition et les traditions*, vol. 1 (Paris: 1962); English translation: *Tradition and Traditions* (London: Burns and Oates, 1966).

8. See the bibliography by A. M. Javierre Ortas, "Successione apostolica." The author defended and published a thesis that garnered attention: *El tema literario de la suce-*

The Church Is Apostolic

three elements, whether we are speaking about the succession of a civil or a religious authority:

- A personal element: succession in the sense of a relation between two persons.
- A real element: what is transmitted from one to the other (some knowledge, power, honor).
- A formal element: assuring the continuity over time of the real element.

Thus we can define succession as *the transmission from one person to another of a reality so that it continues*. This expression, already common in profane Greek, was used to designate the runners who passed the torch: *Paradosis kata diadochēn*.[9] There is a discrete act in the service of a continuous action. What is truly formal is the element of duration in time. To transmit something by the communication of information, for example, does not imply the idea of duration, but to transmit by a succession of persons implies duration. There are two things in the Church to be considered within this framework: on the one hand, the content of the faith and the sacraments of the faith—in other words, the means of salvation instituted by Christ; this is the apostolicity of the faith and the sacraments. On the other hand, the manner of transmitting through personal succession; this is personal or ministerial apostolicity, which is the guarantee of the previous sort of apostolicity.

Doctrinal and sacramental apostolicity is the rule of ministerial apostolicity, and ministerial apostolicity is the guarantee of doctrinal and sacramental apostolicity. This is so by the will of Christ, who instituted the apostles as *vicars* so that his presence might continue sacramentally. Consequently, there will be successors to the apostles, a so-called apostolic succession. Protestants generally do not admit this.[10] In Catholic and Orthodox doctrine there must be an uninterrupted apostolic succession; this is of capital importance. It is uninterrupted not as to place, since a particular diocese can disappear, but rather over

---

sion: *prolegomenos para el estudio de la sucesion apostolica* (Zürich: 1963). Our discussion is directly inspired by these two studies.

9. Literally, "tradition-transmission by succession-relay." The expression is from St. Irenaeus, *Adv. Haer.* III.3.1.

10. On this point, see Yves Congar, *L'Eglise une, sainte, catholique et apostolique*, Mysterium salutis 15 (Paris: 1970), 214–15.

time: one and the same apostolic college remains, the stem or the root of which is the group of the Twelve. This is what we must consider in ecclesiology: how this ministerial apostolicity is permanently assured in the Church.

II. The Succession of the Apostles

Scripture shows that Jesus did not choose the Twelve as individuals only, but also assembled them into a group, which as such receives the authority necessary for their mission. It is by being part of this group that each one receives his authority for the ecclesial mission.[11] The Twelve were succeeded by those who were very soon called the *episkopoi*. As early as St. Ignatius of Antioch the three degrees of the sacrament of holy orders are well attested, and only the highest degree is the sacrament in its fullness. The episcopate owes this fullness precisely to the fact that it assures this succession of the apostles. If each bishop is set over a particular church, the whole Church is entrusted to all the bishops. We saw during our study of catholicity the twofold role of the college of bishops: to assure catholicity-as-a-cause and to watch over catholicity-as-an-effect.[12] As Church history from the second century on shows, on the occasion of heresies or schisms (and this is already found to some extent in the Acts of the Apostles), the bishops gathered in council are the ones who remedy these troubles: together they collaborate for the integrity of the faith. This, basically, is the idea of collegiality, although the word is not scriptural.

a. The notion of collegiality

The bishop's office is to be the vicar of Christ in and for a particular church. This is a local function. But there is another function that is inseparable from it: to assure the unity of the universal Church. He is Christ's vicar for this purpose also. The bishop is the bishop of a place only if he is a bishop for the whole Church and vice versa. Communion with his brothers in the episcopate is necessary for him to assure the communion within his particular church. We emphasized this during

---

11. On the scriptural data, see Pagé, *Qui est l'Église?* 2:411ff.
12. See the relation between the universal-cause-Church that *precedes* the universal-effect-Church in our discussions of the catholicity of the Church.

The Church Is Apostolic

our study of catholicity. To be precise, one should not say "the bishop of Paris," but "the bishop of the Catholic Church that is in Paris." This relation of the bishop with his brothers in the episcopate was expressed liturgically at a very early date. The ordination of a new bishop must be celebrated by at least three bishops.[13] This is also the reason for the title given to bishops: successors of the apostles [plural].

In the nineteenth and early twentieth centuries this collegiality had lost some forms of its expression that Vatican II helped to recover.[14] Think in particular about the institution of the bishops' conference. It is often forgotten, however, that the current Code of Canon Law (can. 439ff.) provides for the institution of provincial and plenary councils.[15] This conciliar institution is par excellence the institution of "regional" collegiality. But it is not put into practice, which is really a shame, since the bishops' conference is not supposed to replace local councils.[16]

The whole Church is entrusted to all the bishops and to each bishop, who consequently must collaborate. This is the immediate consequence of collegiality. The highest point of the expression of collegiality is the ecumenical council (also called the general or universal council). The Catholic Church—and she alone—has been manifested and has acted in that assuredly very solemn form at every important moment in her history. In it the Church expresses something essential about her being: her apostolicity. The ecumenical council is the full manifestation of collegiality.

This college includes all the bishops—all those who have received the sacrament of holy orders in the highest degree—with the bishop of Rome at the head. There is no true collegiality except *cum et sub Petro* [with and under Peter]. There are derivative, imperfect forms of collegiality when the bishops gather on a smaller scale (plenary coun-

---

13. Council of Nicaea (325), canon 4.

14. One expression became popular among theologians to describe this situation: they say that before Vatican II there were many bishops, but no episcopate.

15. The plenary council assembles all the members of the same bishops' conference.

16. This situation makes some bishops apprehensive that we have gone from one extreme to the other. If before Vatican II there were bishops, but no episcopate, it could happen today that there might be an episcopate, but no more bishops, since the latter may be "fused" into an administrative-type structure. On this point see the very instructive essay by Cardinal Gouyon, "Les relations entre le diocèse et la Conférence épiscopale," *L'Année canonique* 22 (1978): 1–23 (esp. 18–22). See also the Apostolic Letter by John Paul II, *Apostolos suos*, 1998.

cil, bishops' conference), but that will be a form of collegiality only if that meeting takes place *cum et sub Petro*.[17] What makes collegiality is not the number; many ecumenical councils in history assembled only a fraction of the episcopate.[18] What matters is the *cum et sub Petro:* a body cannot exist without the head. The connection with the successor of Peter is what makes the college and its acts collegial.

b. Manifestations of collegiality

We will review this topic rapidly, because in its details the question falls under canon law.

One should note, as was already mentioned, the universal council, which is the highest manifestation. Then comes the Roman synod, which is held every five years, gathering around the pope the presidents of the bishops' conferences with the bishops delegated by those conferences. This synod has only an advisory capacity; as things currently stand it is not a decision-making organ. Then comes the Papal Curia. This includes many diocesan bishops who travel to Rome regularly to meet in the Congregations of which they are members.

In the broader sense, collegiality is exercised in the plenary or provincial councils, and in a more restricted way in the bishops' conferences. The fact that local councils do not function results in a development of the bishops' conferences that poses a serious problem at the present time.[19] The latter allegedly tend to exercise in fact a certain magisterium that has not been vested in them, but is normally the competence of councils. This is not an idle question. The bishops' conference is made up exclusively of bishops, whereas local councils are ecclesial in composition—in other words, broader, more representative of the ecclesial community. The bishops are, quite obviously, the only teachers of the faith, and they alone decide in the councils, but after all the participants have had a chance to express themselves. This

---

17. Peter may be present in person, through a legate, or by reserving to himself the final approval of the acts (the *recognitio*).

18. The classic example is the Second Provincial Synod of Orange (529), with Caesarius of Arles presiding. Its definitions on grace and original sin (in response to the semi-Pelagian crisis) were confirmed by Pope Boniface II. Thus it became the Second Council of Orange and was normative for the whole Church. (On the basis of its teachings, Trent later taught its doctrine of grace against Luther.)

19. The question is being studied seriously in several bishops' conferences.

The Church Is Apostolic

is more ecclesial than an exclusively ecclesiastical (i.e., clerical) institution. Moreover, for questions within its competence, faith, and morals, a council decides by majority vote, taking care to obtain the broadest unanimity possible, and it involves all the bishops, even those who voted against a decision. The bishops' conference, on the other hand, can take normative action only by a unanimous vote. Questions about the ecclesial status and the competence of the bishops' conference are being widely debated today. It seems to us that until the authority of the local council is revived, the confusion will remain.[20]

III. St. Peter and his successors

This question of what is called primacy is extremely complex from the historical and dogmatic perspectives. The Catholic Church's present understanding of the particular ministry of the pope resulted from a very long and very slow dogmatic development. Recall that it is not the *reality* that evolves, but rather our *understanding* of it. In turn, this understanding, as it is enriched, has an influence on the practical exercise of this ministry. It is advisable also to specify clearly what separates us from our Orthodox brethren on this point. In the Catholic dialogue with them there are on the one hand many erroneous oversimplifications made in the name of a false irenicism.[21] On the other hand, one must sort out those topics in the debate that are only historical and not dogmatic. Here we will focus on the essentials.

a. The apostle St. Peter

St. Peter is the apostle about whom the New Testament speaks the most by far.[22] Hence we can get to know him well: his characteristics, his faults, his actions, his place within the Twelve. Plainly Scripture is quite insistent with regard to him. Let us examine several aspects of his portrait.

---

20. On the current status of this question, see the anthology *Les Conférences épiscopales*, Actes du colloque de Salamanque 3–8 janvier 1988, coll. "Cogitatio fidei" 149 (Paris: 1988); reviewed in *RT* 90 (1990): 134–39.

21. To say, for example, that papal primacy is the result of an incursion of "Roman juridical" thought that is incomprehensible to "Eastern mysticism" is unserious and can even be insulting to our Eastern Catholic brethren.

22. He is mentioned 114 times in the Gospels, 57 times in the other books. His name occurs most often—46 times!—in the Gospel of St. John "the mystic."

St. Luke presents St. Peter as the faithful steward (*oikonomos:* Lk 12:42), as the very model of a missionary (Lk 5:1–11), as the one for whom Christ prayed especially that his faith might not fail so that he could strengthen his brethren (Lk 22:32–34). In Acts, St. Peter is plainly the leader of the nascent Church, and he truly presides over the missions to the pagans. He is the key man who assures both continuity with Israel and openness to the Gentiles (esp. Acts 15).

St. Matthew specifies that St. Peter is the first among the Twelve (Mt 10:2). Above all, however, the central text, Mt 16:16–19, must be noted: in this text the connection between St. Peter's confession of faith and his particular ministry is established. We will come back to this passage, which permits us to say that St. Peter is the foundation of the new Temple.

St. John emphasizes in his own way the unique place of St. Peter. The race to the empty tomb nicely illustrates the deference that the beloved disciple had for St. Peter (Jn 20:5). St. Peter alone is the one who brings onshore the net full of fish without breaking it (Jn 21:11). Again, he alone is invested with pastoral responsibility for the entire flock (Jn 21:15–17). Finally, like Christ the Good Shepherd, St. Peter concluded his life by giving his life for his sheep (Jn 10:11; 21:19).

As an initial approach to this scriptural data, we can say that St. Peter received in a special way the apostolic commission, a commission that was entrusted to the other eleven also. St. Peter's specific mission is related to the mission of the other apostles, whom he must strengthen, but also to the mission of the whole Church of which he is the pastor and rock on which she is built. This equivalence between the whole (the Twelve, the Church) and the one (St. Peter) shows the fundamental structure of the service of unity in the Church. The jurisdiction [*compétence*] that the Twelve receive together with St. Peter as one of the members is the same jurisdiction that St. Peter receives as pastor of the whole Church and as head of the college.

The two letters attributed to St. Peter are in reality pseudoepigraphs by a later author. The first is said to date from the 80s and to have been written in Rome by a priest of that church (see 1 Pt 5:1 and 13). It is addressed to the churches of the diaspora; now there is no diaspora except in relation to a center, in this case the church of Rome. The second letter attributed to St. Peter is said to be the latest document in the

The Church Is Apostolic 601

New Testament. It is a magisterial document that intends to confront the rise of heresies (2 Pt 3:15–17). The fact that is it attributed to St. Peter clearly shows the intention to highlight his office of guaranteeing the integrity of the faith.

It is advisable to examine the most important text: Mt 16:16–19 (*Tu es Petrus*). Whether it records an event before or after the resurrection, the authenticity of the passage is not disputed today. Some remarks:

- The authority that St. Peter receives is not due to his personal merits, but solely to the gratuitous revelation by the Father.
- The theme of the stone (literally the rock: *kephā'* in Aramaic) is a well-known biblical theme. Reference is made here to Is 28:16 ("Behold, I am laying in Zion for a foundation a stone, a tested stone, a precious cornerstone, of a sure foundation"). The first foundation of the Church is Christ (see 1 Cor 3:10–11) and—in a secondary and subordinate way—the apostles. Within that group, St. Peter receives in a special way the commission common to the Twelve to be vicar of Christ—in other words, to manifest visibly this first foundation that is Christ. This is the well-known exegesis of the Church Fathers: when Jesus gives to Simon the name "Peter," he gives him *his own name*, because the rock is Christ.[23]
- The keys of the Kingdom are given to St. Peter alone,[24] but the power to *bind* and *loose* is conferred on St. Peter in Mt 16:19 and likewise to the eleven others later on (Mt 18:18). Hence there are two possible types of interpretation: either the keys are the symbol of a power proper to St. Peter, or else everything that is given to St. Peter is later given to the eleven others. Whatever may be said in exegetical debate, the preeminence of St. Peter is clearly underscored.[25]

23. Based on 1 Cor 10:4 in particular. This exegesis is well attested, for example, in the writings of St. Leo the Great, *Homily for the anniversary of his episcopal ordination* 4.2–3 (PL 54.149–51); St. Augustine, *Commentary on St. John* 12.4–5 (CCSL 36, 684–85). St. Thomas Aquinas is a good witness to this tradition; see *In Matt*. c. 16, lect. 3, Marietti no. 1374 and 1382.

24. A reference to Isaiah 22:15–25, the institution of the "prime minister" in Israel, the *claviger* (Latin for key-bearer).

25. For the main studies on this subject, see R. E. Brown, et al., eds., *Peter in the New Testament: A Collaborative Assessment by Protestant and Roman Catholic Scholars* (Minneapolis: Augsburg, 1973), and Rudolf Pesch, et al., *Die biblischen Grundlagen des Primats*, Quaestiones Disputatae 187, 2nd ed. (Herder: 2002).

Another question has arisen also: since the primacy of St. Peter in the New Testament is difficult to dispute, some claim that this commission was non-transmittable.[26] To this one might object: what does "non-transmittable commission" mean? Quite simply that it was necessary at the beginning, during the lifetime of the holder of the title, but not afterward. This is in fact the case with the charism of inspiration belonging to the Twelve, which is not transmittable because it is ordained to the establishment of the Church, not to her everyday life over the course of the centuries. But as far as the pastoral commission is concerned (preach, sanctify, govern), by definition it must be assured as long as there is a community to serve—in other words, until Christ comes again in glory. The limit of the transmittable character of this commission is Christ's return; there, it is true, the commission will cease, with all the sacraments and Scripture itself. Finally, Scripture and Tradition elucidate each other: from the second century on, the church of Rome and her bishop have been recognized as the heir of the mission of St. Peter, and it is the only church that has claimed that heritage. There is indeed a reciprocal elucidation of Scripture and Tradition concerning this question. Christ's statement, "*Tu es Petrus,*" is elucidated by the chair of St. Peter in Rome, which is the application thereof, and conversely the fact of the chair of Peter in Rome has a sufficient cause in the promise made to St. Peter.

b. The succession of St. Peter in Tradition[27]

We have solid documentation of the primacy claimed and exercised by the bishops of Rome, the successors of St. Peter, a primacy recognized by the whole Church. The church of Rome is never separated from its bishop. As early as the beginning of the second century, St. Ignatius of

---

26. A position taken frequently by Protestant authors. For a presentation of this line of thought, see Oscar Cullman, *Saint Pierre, disciple, apôtre, martyr: Histoire et théologie* (Neuchâtel: 1952); important review by Pierre Benoit in *Revue biblique* 60 (1953): 565–79; a clearly articulated reaction by Charles Journet, *La Primauté de Pierre dans la perspective protestante et dans la perspective catholique* (Paris: 1953). A significant advance among the Protestants was made by J.-J. von Allmen, *La primauté de Pierre et de Paul* (Fribourg and Paris, 1977), in particular 71–79 on whether the Petrine ministry is transmittable; important review by J. Budillon in *Istina* 25 (1980): 365–87.

27. A good overview of the most ancient testimonies to this primacy handed down to the bishop of Rome can be found in K. Schatz, *La Primauté du pape: Son histoire des origines à nos jours* (Paris: 1992), esp. 26–37.

The Church Is Apostolic 603

Antioch leaves us his famous salutation to the church of Rome "presiding in love." Learned studies have shown that *agapē* in this context should be understood to mean *church*, so that St. Ignatius's remark can be paraphrased: "The (particular) church (of Rome) that presides over the (universal) Church."[28] In a well-known passage St. Irenaeus mentions the church of Rome "with which the whole world must agree." This text presents a problem in translation that would allow a minimalist reading, but the Sources Chrétiennes edition justifies at length the translation that most favors the primacy of Rome.[29]

What is certain about this history is that the primacy, excellence, and authority of the church of Rome and of its bishop have always been recognized. There are countless examples of recourse to Rome in cases of serious doctrinal difficulties, notably during the Arian crisis with the appeals of St. Athanasius to Julius I. The Councils, in particular those of Nicaea and Constantinople I, recognize this.

How then can the Orthodox East, which shares this Tradition with us, deny this preeminence? At first the conflict with Byzantium pertained to the way in which this primacy was exercised rather than to the primacy itself. But the questions are connected. The conflict later was poisoned by a quarrel that can be described as "political." By political we must understand the important place that the Eastern Church has always assigned to the civil authority, and in particular to the emperor at the time of the Roman Empire. Since the latter had transferred his seat to Constantinople, the East thought that the center of catholicity too should be changed, or at least shared between the Old and the New Rome. This is the famous principle of *accommodation*, according to which the importance of an ecclesial see corresponds to the importance of the civil seat of government. This "secular" principle was rejected by St. Leo the Great at Chalcedon by his refusal to recognize canon 28: the excellence of the see of Rome is due to the fact that it received all the prerogatives of the see of Jerusalem. Since the Gospel had been rejected by the Jews, it was preached to the pagans. St. Peter transplanted Jerusalem to Rome, so to speak, where he sealed his testimony with his blood, as did St. Paul.

---

28. See the painstaking study by O. Perler, "Patristique et Vatican II," in *Sapientia et caritas* (Fribourg: 1990), 219ff.

29. St. Irenaeus, *Adversus Haereses* III.3.2 (SC no. 210, introduction). For an interesting patristic overview, see Pagé, *Qui est l'Église?*, 3:418ff.

After the split between East and West (eleventh century), theories were developed in the East to provide a more theological rationale for what originally was a political reaction (in the sense described earlier). One must add that there were obvious blunders in the exercise of the Roman primacy. But all that is not an adequate justification. Hence the East has always made itself the champion for the Church's conciliar character. This is correct as far as it goes, but it does not nullify the primacy. Rather, since the split, history has made it apparent that the primacy is the organ necessary for conciliarity. In fact, one must observe that the Roman Catholic Church has kept the tradition of universal councils alive, whereas the Orthodox Churches, for lack of a "center," have enormous difficulties in assembling.

The Catholic concept of the Roman primacy is, basically, of a sacramental nature (sacramentality in the *broad* sense). The successor of St. Peter is the *sign and means* of unity. The Orthodox readily concede that he is the *sign*, so that a lack of communion with him clearly testifies to wounded unity. But they refuse to acknowledge that he is also the *means* of unity. This is the concept of the so-called *primacy of honor*. This is inadequate in Catholic theology. Indeed, although the bishop of Rome is *primus inter pares* [first among equals], a bishop among many bishops, we add that the first *among* the others is not the first *like* the others, precisely by reason of what makes him first. To summarize, he is the *efficient criterion* of unity.

L. Hertling sets the matter forth very exactly.[30] He poses the following question: what is the sure criterion for determining whether a particular bishop belongs to the communion that is the universal Church? Historically we can observe the rapid succession of several solutions. First, Christians said that it was necessary for that particular bishop to be in communion with any other particular church that itself belongs to the universal communion. But how can we tell whether that reference church also belongs to the universal communion? This is the question of the criterion. It was at first a quantitative criterion: the particular bishop must be in communion with a large number of bish-

30. In L. Hertling's foundational essay, "Communio und Primat," in *Miscellanea Historiae Pontificiae*, vol. 7 (Rome: 1943), a study that was revised and expanded when it was translated into Italian and published under the title *Communio: Chiesa e Papato nell'antichità cristiana* (Rome: 1961); we follow the latter edition.

The Church Is Apostolic 605

ops. What difference does it make, then, if one or two particular bishops refused him communion, if he himself is in communion with all the others? Very quickly this criterion was refined in a more qualitative sense: to be in communion with the most venerable particular churches, those founded by the apostles themselves. This criterion was applied especially in Africa during the Donatist crisis, but it was already clearly enunciated by St. Irenaeus (*Adv. Haereses* III.4.1) and Tertullian (*De Praes.* 21). But this criterion could not always suffice. Alexandria, for example, fell into the Arian heresy. Then people appealed to communion with Rome; this was the final recourse. Communion with the bishop of Rome has always been decisive: someone who is in communion with the successor of St. Peter is by that very fact in communion with the whole Church, since Rome has "the sovereignty [*principatus*] of the apostolic chair [*cathedrae*]."[31]

IV. The Catholic doctrine of the Roman primacy

a. The theological justification

In the historical data that have been presented previously, we can point out a movement of *"reductio ad unum"* [tending to reduce to one]. This shows a high degree of fittingness of a philosophical sort at first (social philosophy): a society always has one leader. But this cannot suffice; there must be a theological justification. Here we encounter sacramentality again: the pope is the sign of unity—that is clear to everyone—but what is still more important is the very *reality* of unity. Now we always go from the *sign* to the *reality* through the *means;* the sign is a sign *of an efficiency*, according to various causalities. We find not only pure signs; they exist in order to designate a certain realization of grace that is brought about in some way by them. Fr. Congar puts it as follows:

If the general system of the People of God is that of a union of the heavenly and the earthly that is simultaneously the translation of the heavenly in the earthly and the service of the heavenly by the earthly, in short, a system in which the earthly is "symbol," "icon," "sacrament" of the heavenly, are we not then authorized to look for an icon, a *"vice gerens"* of (i.e., one acting in place

---

31. St. Augustine, *Letter* 43.7; translated from Latin.

of) the Shepherd of the one flock in a supreme bishop who is steward and major-domo and therefore *claviger* [key-bearer] of the whole house of God?[32]

This clearly does not specify right away the different causalities that the sign manifests, and the Church has unceasingly progressed in her understanding of this reality. Nevertheless, as far as the Roman primacy is concerned, the bishops of Rome and, even in the case of *sede vacante* [vacancy in the see due to death or resignation], the church of Rome itself have always manifested their identity as the "sign-means" of unity; they have always *acted* on behalf of unity. The fact that Rome received such a primacy is not explained by its political importance or the development within it of a sprawling administration.[33] Nor can we attribute it to any particular prestige of its bishops. The popes before St. Leo the Great cannot compete with St. Ignatius of Antioch, St. Polycarp of Smyrna, St. Irenaeus of Lyons, St. Cyprian of Carthage, St. Athanasius of Alexandria, St. Basil of Caesarea, St. John Chrysostom.... The only reason for the preeminence of the bishop of Rome is the fact that he succeeds St. Peter on the *Cathedra* of Rome so as to be the rock. That is the only possible theological reason that takes into account the historical practice that has been observed and the authority that is claimed. One could object that the dogma of papal primacy appeared only later in history, but the argument would be in vain; this only shows that the understanding of the faith comes later, but Christians have lived out and witnessed to this faith since the beginning. All the elements of this primacy can be documented from the earliest times, but they are experiential rather than theoretical.[34]

Generally speaking, the history of the dogma is as follows:

- At first the Church examined the mystery of Christ and, in correlation with that, the Trinitarian mystery: the first four centuries.
- Then Christians pondered the way in which the divine mysteries affect man: original sin, redemption (mode, efficacy), and grace (the whole debate with the Pelagians in the fourth to seventh centuries).
- Then came the ministerial activity by which Christ touches us—

32. Yves Congar, "De la communion des Églises à une ecclésiologie de l'Église universelle," in *L'Épiscopat et l'Église universelle*, US 39 (Paris: 1962), 258.

33. Until the sixth century there was no curia for the universal Church in Rome, but only for the diocese.

34. See L. Hertling, "Communio und Primat," 51.

The Church Is Apostolic 607

namely, the sacraments, and especially the first among them, which is in some way the source of the sacramentality of the six others: the Eucharist. It is quite clear that the words, "This is my Body ... my Blood" were understood in a fully realist sense from the beginning, but it is also clear that the dogmatic elaboration of transubstantiation appears only in the eleventh and twelfth centuries (Lateran IV).
- Finally, the mystery of the Church, which presupposes that all the preceding has been speculatively clarified. What is the Church in its essence? What are the nature and extent of the magisterial office? How does that office verify at its level the sacramentality of salvation? These questions arise gradually starting in the fourteenth century. The Council of Trent gives several important benchmarks, but the Church would have to wait until Vatican I for dogmatic definitions concerning the primacy of the successor of St. Peter and the originality of its magisterial responsibility. The mystery of the Church has been examined with speculative acuity only for a very short time, about a century, and, as we have already noted, we have not yet arrived at definitive results. This same mystery has been described gradually in Tradition, and several clarifications have been made over the centuries. Again according to L. Hertling, the progress of the theological manifestation of the mystery of the Church has been as follows, in its main lines:

- There is only one Church (unicity), outside of which there is no salvation (see Cyprian and Origen).
- The sign of this one true Church is the unity of communion.
- Through Christ's institution, St. Peter is the head of the apostles, and this communion has its source and its criterion in him.
- The deposit of faith is preserved intact in the churches founded by the apostles, especially the church of Rome.
- The present bishop of Rome is the successor of St. Peter.
- Communion with Rome is decisive for membership in the Church.
- This primacy was first manifested historically and juridically.
- The primacy was defined dogmatically (Vatican I).

Now we must examine this final step.

608   The Properties of the Church

**b. The dogmatic formulation of the
Roman primacy**

1. The teaching of Vatican I

The First Vatican Council is a classic council in the sense that it was convened to respond to certain errors that were threatening the faith. These errors were of two sorts:

- Concerning the faith itself, especially Revelation. It followed logically that the question about the knowledge that we can have of God was also involved. This is the subject of the Constitution *Dei Filius*.
- Concerning the Church. The dogmatic question about the Church began to be posed in connection with the development of the concept of political society. This was the difficulty resulting from the application of eighteenth-century social theories to the Church. The Council intended to respond above all to various concepts of civil social authority that threatened the correct understanding of apostolic authority in the Church. A Constitution *De Ecclesia* was planned that would have had to consist of two principal parts: one on the Roman pontiff and the other on the apostolic college. When the Council was suspended because of unforeseen circumstances,[35] only the first chapter of the Constitution had been deliberated and voted on; the chapter concerning the bishops, although brought forward, could not be put to a vote. Pope Pius IX promulgated this first chapter, which became the Constitution *Pastor aeternus*. The Church would have to wait until Vatican II to have a thorough dogmatic exposition on the episcopate; therefore, *Pastor aeternus* is the text that we present here.[36]

---

35. The city of Rome and the Papal States were threatened by the troops of the liberal Italian party, which were only waiting for an opportunity to invade them. The armies of Napoleon III were protecting Rome. The Franco-Prussian War of 1870 led France to withdraw its soldiers from Rome. The Italian troops then occupied the city and made it the capital of the new Italian state. Pope Pius IX, thinking that the liberty of the Council Fathers was not longer assured, adjourned the Council *sine die* [without designating a future date on which it would resume].

36. See a good commentary by Jean-Pierre Torrell, "L'ecclésiologie de Vatican I," in *Visages de l'Église* (Fribourg: 1989), 25ff.

The Church Is Apostolic

The prologue of *Pastor aeternus*

This prologue is quite extensive. It is based on the most authentic ecclesiology of communion.[37] The long, well-balanced key sentence is written in the purest style of the Latin Fathers of the Church:

> But, that the episcopacy itself might be one and undivided, and that the entire multitude of the faithful through bishops closely connected with one another might be preserved in the unity of faith and communion, placing the blessed Peter over the other apostles He [Christ] established in him the perpetual principle and visible foundation of both unities. (Translation by Roy J. Deferrari, *The Sources of Catholic Dogma*)

This means first of all that the pope has no privilege in the usual sense of the word; that is not the basis of his office. He possesses a ministry, a service, the ministry of the unity of faith and charity. From this title we see already that the pope is the *means* and not the *end*. He is measured by something other than himself, something higher than himself. This (diaconal) end is the unity of the entire ecclesial Body through the unity of the bishops. There is no room here for the papolatry that considers the pope as an end and not as a means.

Given this general perspective, the following paragraphs of the Constitution spell out in a rigorous order a certain number of points that are of capital importance.

Chapter one: The primacy of St. Peter the apostle

Very carefully, the Council first approaches the question of St. Peter the apostle. He received the primacy over the other apostles, and this primacy is a gift bestowed directly and immediately by Christ. This is the traditional exegesis of Mt 16:16–18 that is common to Catholics and Orthodox. This restatement also aims at rejecting the Gallican and Febronian interpretations, which claimed that St. Peter had received his authority through delegation by the Church, specifically by the other apostles. The Council's response is clear:

> So We teach and declare that according to the testimonies of the Gospel the primacy of jurisdiction over the entire Church of God was promised and was conferred immediately and directly upon the blessed Apostle Peter by Christ the Lord.

37. See Marie-Vincent Leroy, Chronique d'ecclésiologie, *RT* 86 (1986): 133.

Chapter two: The transmission of this primacy

After recalling the case of St. Peter, the Council goes on to say that the primacy was transmitted to the successor of St. Peter, who is the bishop of Rome. The key argument is drawn from the idea of succession: if the primacy of St. Peter was instituted by Christ for salvation and the perpetual good of the Church, it must therefore last as long as the government of the Church on earth lasts. Furthermore, Vatican I recalls the principal elements of the Tradition shared with the Orthodox—namely and especially the Council of Ephesus (431) in which this primacy had been acknowledged by all, and several important Fathers of the Church (St. Irenaeus, St. Leo the Great, St. Ambrose).

Moreover, what the Chief of pastors and the Great Pastor of sheep, the Lord Jesus, established in the blessed Apostle Peter for the perpetual salvation and perennial good of the Church, this by the same Author must endure always in the Church which was founded upon a rock and will endure firm until the end of the ages.... Therefore, whoever succeeds Peter in this chair, he according to the institution of Christ himself holds the primacy of Peter over the whole Church.

Chapter three: The primacy of *jurisdiction*

This is the dogmatic formulation itself, every word of which was weighed carefully:

Furthermore We teach and declare that the Roman Church, by the disposition of the Lord, holds the sovereignty of ordinary power over all others, and that this power of jurisdiction on the part of the Roman Pontiff, which is truly episcopal, is immediate; and with respect to this the pastors and the faithful of whatever rite and dignity, both as separate individuals and all together, are bound by the duty of hierarchical subordination and true obedience, not only in things which pertain to faith and morals, but also in those which pertain to the discipline and government of the Church [which is] spread over the whole world, so that the Church of Christ, protected not only by the Roman Pontiff but by the unity of communion as well as of the profession of the same faith, is one flock under the one highest shepherd [Jn 10:16]. This is the doctrine of Catholic truth from which no one can deviate and keep his faith and salvation.

The authority in question is a full and sovereign power of jurisdiction over the whole Church, not only in matters of faith and mor-

The Church Is Apostolic

als, but also concerning the discipline and government of the Church spread throughout the world. This supreme jurisdiction is ordinary and immediate over each and every one of the particular churches, as well as over each and every one of the pastors and faithful.

We will comment briefly on this definition; then we will add several remarks on the subject of the teaching of Vatican II and will make several proposals.

This formulation may appear very broad. But an attentive reading should reveal the exact extent of it. In the first place, this jurisdiction concerns the Christian community, and by no means the order of civil society. This clarification was very useful in an era when the pope also retained temporal sovereignty (the Papal States). In the second place, the two areas for the exercise of this jurisdiction are clearly specified. On the one hand, there are matters of faith and morals. This primacy must not be confused with the charism of infallibility, which applies to the same area; here it is a question of jurisdiction, which is expressed by a teaching that is not necessarily infallible. On the other hand, "discipline" means the area of liturgical regulations and, more generally, the concrete way of guaranteeing the sacramental ministry. "Government" means the well-known field of canon law—in other words, the management of the social group of the Church. The totality of these rules forms a whole that is extremely variable according to the place and time.

This jurisdiction is qualified by several adjectives that have a very precise meaning:

- *Ordinary:* this means "pertaining to the office as such," as opposed to a *delegated* jurisdiction. It should not be understood in the trivial sense of "everyday" or "everywhere." Because it is "ordinary," papal jurisdiction is not necessarily exercised always and everywhere. That possibility is not excluded, of course, but it would not be justified per se because of the existence of the diocesan bishop, except in the case of the latter's failure, and for the duration of that failure.
- *Immediate:* in other words, it can be exercised without any obligatory intermediary, in particular the diocesan bishop. In this sense the pope can exercise anywhere the *tria munera Christi* directly. Thus, in order to deal with a bishop, the pope is not required to go

through the bishops' conference, much less through the civil government of the country, and such a stipulation cannot be part of a concordat.

- *Truly episcopal:* this does not mean that the pope is the only true bishop and that the diocesan bishops are his prefects or vicars. "Episcopal" here means that the *content* of this jurisdiction is *pastoral:* it is a matter of exercising the *tria munera Christi* and no temporal authority whatsoever.

This jurisdiction, with those qualifications, is possessed by the pope, the Council adds, as a *full and supreme* power (final canon of Chapter 3). This means that it cannot be limited by any human authority because no human authority is superior to it. Only natural law and the divine law limit it, but that is already a considerable limitation.[38]

Whatever the extent of it may be—and it is quite vast in scope—this authority is a *ministry,* a *diakonia.* It is measured by that which it must serve. Therefore, it is not without limits, since it is *relative* to a given object. It is not arbitrary, in the strict sense of the word. Yet, it is true, there is no course of redress in the case of a failing pope (e.g., for senility or heresy), and the miracle of the papacy is precisely that it has never fallen into such infirmity that it would have ruined the Church. Cajetan says that the only remedy in the case of a heretical pope is to pray and to have others pray that he will die!

During the debates at Vatican I, many feared that the authority of diocesan bishops would be weakened. That is why that same chapter 3 adds:

This power of the Supreme Pontiff is so far from interfering with that power of ordinary and immediate episcopal jurisdiction by which the bishops, who, "placed by the Holy Spirit" [see Acts 20:28], have succeeded to the places of the apostles, as true shepherds individually feed and rule the individual flocks assigned to them, that the same (power) is asserted, confirmed, and vindicated by the supreme and universal shepherd.

It must be noted here that the adjectives *episcopal, ordinary,* and *immediate* are used for the bishops, but their authority is neither full nor supreme.

38. The authorities of present-day civil societies in the West do not recognize that limitation. Therefore they consider themselves to be much more important per se and in their scope.

The Church Is Apostolic 613

Right after the Council, on March 1, 1875, Pius IX clearly affirmed the authority of each bishop in a dispatch addressed to the German episcopate, commending it for not having accepted Bismarck's theory that reduced them to being nothing but prefects of the pope.[39]

2. The teaching of Vatican II

The teaching of Vatican I concerning the papal primacy was repeated by Vatican II, but the insertion of this teaching into a new context that broadly includes the episcopate in its entirety (*Lumen gentium*, chapter 3) allows us to correlate better the primacy and the college. Vatican II indeed underscores how the primacy's role is to strengthen the episcopate and not to replace it. Conversely, the Council also notes extensively that the episcopate helps the primacy with its responsibilities, especially by its close collaboration in the Roman Curia. Thus the head and the body are not disconnected, and their mutual relations are indispensable for the life of all.

One refinement of vocabulary should be pointed out. Vatican II decided not to present the pastoral office by way of the classic distinction between order and jurisdiction. It preferred the more biblical and patristic threefold terminology of the *tria munera* [three offices]. Above all we must recall one thing that is decisive for our discussion: the *tria munera* are inseparable. They manifest *the unity* of the pastoral office. The distinction between holy orders and jurisdiction had evolved historically in such a way as to make the two realities separable: one could have holy orders without jurisdiction and, vice versa, have a jurisdiction without being invested with holy orders. Although the vocabulary of "jurisdiction" is used a few times by Vatican II with reference to the bishops, it is never within the framework of the distinction between holy orders and jurisdiction. This vocabulary is *never* used with reference to the pope. Consequently this invites us to reconsider the so-called primacy "of jurisdiction." We are only at the beginning of this new reflection, which is of obvious ecumenical interest. Catholics are invited to make sure that there is a dogmatic development of the teaching of Vatican I so as to define more clearly the papal primacy and thus to make it more acceptable, at least to the Orthodox.

---

39. See the texts cited in the essay by O. Rousseau, "La vraie valeur de l'épiscopat d'après d'importants documents de 1875," in *L'Épiscopat et l'Église universelle*, 709–36.

3. Proposal

In the context of the sacramental ecclesiology that we are proposing, we distinguish three aspects within the one and only ecclesial reality: the communion of the theological virtues, which subsists in the social communion, which bears the diaconal communion. The papal primacy is a ministry that serves as a means to the theological end of faith, hope, and charity. Consequently it has its place in the social communion and in the diaconal communion. It does not have to be exercised in the same way in both cases, since the logic of one differs from that of the other. In the social communion this primacy is political, in the precise sense that the term has in social philosophy. It is a governmental function, and the way in which it is exercised will vary depending on the cultural circumstances of each particular church and of each era. The principle of subsidiarity will be honored in a wide variety of ways. In the diaconal communion this service is a service rendered to the faith and the sacraments of the faith. Here is it a matter of a specifically ecclesial authority, the means of which will be altogether particular (e.g., ecumenical or local council, Roman Synod). The one expression "primacy of *jurisdiction*" unfortunately puts in the same category two specifically distinct types of authority, while appealing conceptually to an idea that is initially derived from juridical language and thus political. There are in fact, we think, two primacies that should not be confused with regard to their object and consequently with regard to the manner in which they are exercised. It seems to us that the primacy in the social communion could be very flexible with the Orthodox, and this could overcome their great apprehension about a monolithic monarchical authority. The primacy in the diaconal communion could be exercised more in connection with the apostolic college than before, and thus collegiality could be honored better. In the long millennial tradition that we have in common with Orthodoxy, it seems that the primacy in the social communion was not exercised very directly with the Christian East, whereas the primacy in the diaconal communion *was*, in a way that was quite acceptable to all sides. It is necessary to reconnect today with this common heritage.

It goes without saying that this distinction of the two ways of exercising primacy is of interest also for the missions. In cultures that pres-

The Church Is Apostolic   615

ent major obstacles to evangelization, in particular in the Far East, it is advisable not to confuse the social communion and the diaconal communion. The failure or foiling of a Western social model must not result in the failure or foiling of the transmission of the faith and the sacraments. The same is true with continents such as Africa and South America that—after a period of a rather Latinizing approach—intend to live out Christianity in a way more closely connected with their own culture.

c. The dogma of the personal infallibility of the pope[40]

This is one way, among others, of exercising the supreme office of the successor of St. Peter. It must be understood correctly, since the issue is so confused today in many minds.[41] Here we are in the context of the *munus docendi* [teaching office] at its highest expression: teaching with *full* authority—that is, teaching that is *absolutely* guaranteed.

The Council first recalls the centuries-old practice of the Apostolic See. The latter has always been conscious of holding a special authority in matters of teaching. It has implemented it in many ways, however: by convening ecumenical councils, by approving particular councils, by sounding out the opinions of the local churches.... This doctrinal responsibility has therefore always been exercised in connection with the whole Church. We are not talking about issuing new doctrines, but rather about preserving the *depositum fidei* intact and always expounding it faithfully. Consequently there will be no new revelations; that is unthinkable since the death of the last apostle; what is at hand is rather the special *assistance* of the Spirit of truth to guard the deposit of faith *by explaining it*. This charism of the Roman pontiff is not a charism of

---

40. Chapter 4 of *Pastor aeternus*.
41. The main documents on this subject and on the subject of the ordinary magisterium: Vatican I, Const. *Dei Filius;* Vatican I, Const. *Pastor aeternus;* Pius XII, Encyclical *Humani generis;* Vatican II, Const. *Lumen gentium* 25; Code of Canon Law, can. 749–52; Instruction *Donum veritatis* by the Congregation for the Doctrine of the Faith "On the Ecclesial Vocation of the Theologian," May 24, 1990, no. 23; the *Catechism of the Catholic Church*, nos. 890–91. On the category "ordinary magisterium" and the infallibility belonging to it, see J.-M. Garrigues, "Le magistère ordinaire," in *Nova et Vetera* (1997). An attempt to determine criteria for the various magisteria was made by M. Larivé in *Nova et Vetera* (1995). For a survey of the difficulties in understanding the personal infallibility of the pope after Vatican II, see C. Barthe, *L'Infaillibilité du pape après Vatican II: Charisme de Pierre et collège des évêques* (Paris: 1993).

inspiration, but rather of assistance: to explain [*expliciter*] means to formulate the faith anew, giving to the whole People of God an additional light of understanding, with the guarantee that the new formulation is faithful to the truth already known and believed by the whole Church. This assistance is given to each bishop, but there is a preeminence of the successor of St. Peter, whose see has always remained free from all error (see Lk 22:32). To put it differently, the office of St. Peter and of his successors includes the authority necessary to assure that the whole Church continues in the true profession of faith.

1. The dogmatic definition

It is enunciated as follows:

The Roman Pontiff, when he speaks *ex cathedra,* that is, when carrying out the duty of the pastor and teacher of all Christians in accord with his supreme apostolic authority he explains a doctrine of faith or morals to be held by the universal Church, through the divine assistance promised him in blessed Peter, operates with that infallibility with which the divine Redeemer wished that His Church be instructed in defining doctrine on faith and morals; and so such definitions of the Roman Pontiff are of themselves, and not by the consent of the Church, irreformable.

This is a long sentence interrupted by incidental clauses; this is the hallmark of a "well-cast" passage in which each word counts, in itself and in the place that it occupies. We must recall that this is a dogmatic *definition*—in other words, the expression of a truth that involves our *theological virtue of faith* as in the case of the primacy. This passage is preceded or followed by reasons, explanations, and grounds of all sorts that are themselves not covered by infallibility. Only the definition itself enjoys that guarantee. That is why we must understand the words themselves of this definition. We can clarify it in light of an objection that was made at that time: only God is absolutely infallible. This is true, and this is why papal infallibility is relative or, if one prefers, limited. It is limited in three ways:

- As to the person. The definition speaks about the pope as the *universal teacher* who is making use of his supreme apostolic authority. This excludes the pope as a private person (or teacher), as bishop of the diocese of Rome, as metropolitan archbishop of Latium, as primate of Italy.

- As to the act. What is required is a *definition,* which means a *solemn judgment addressed to the universal Church.* This is a conclusive, *definitive and direct* act—in other words, there must be no doubt about the intention to define.[42]
- As to the object. It can only apply to a matter of faith and morals. In other words, the object must be within the strictly religious sphere. It cannot concern the secular sphere, including philosophy. Philosophical wisdom often supplies reasons and conceptual instruments that are adopted in theology, but that wisdom cannot be the object of a definition to which one adheres in faith. Therefore we say that the conclusion (*what is said*) is *de fide* [a matter of faith], but not the grounds (*how it is justified*). Thus, for example, the dogma of transubstantiation articulates a *de fide* truth concerning the Eucharistic transformation of bread into the Body of Christ and wine into the Blood of Christ, but this in no way canonizes the philosophy that provides the distinction between substance and accident. While this philosophy is only particularly convenient for the theological understanding of what we believe, it does not enter the sphere of the theological virtue of faith.

These various clarifications are therefore quite important if we are to situate the charism of infallibility properly in its recipient [*titulaire*], the manner of its expression, and its object. To conclude, we should recall that the infallibility of the pope is the selfsame infallibility that the whole Church enjoys at the level of its certitude, yet is subordinate to the Church's infallibility as to its finality. In other words, the whole Church enjoys the infallibility of the *sensus fidei,* and to serve it, there is the infallibility both of the apostolic college united with the pope (council) and the infallibility of the pope alone (personal infallibility). Classically a distinction is made between these two sorts of infallibility as follows: there is the infallibility of the People of God *in credendo* [in believing], and the infallibility of their ministers *in docendo* [in teaching].

We should add one clarification on the conclusion of the definition, because much ink has been spilled on the subject. It declares, "Such definitions of the Roman Pontiff are of themselves, and not by the consent of the Church, irreformable." This must be understood correctly.

---

42. Generally one finds the expression, "We declare and define."

Vatican I intends here to reject an old Gallican theory that made the council the supreme doctrinal authority in the Church. According to that theory—which applied the federal paradigm to the whole Church without distinguishing among her aspects—in order for the acts of the pope, in particular his magisterium, to be binding, they had to receive the approval of the whole episcopate, whether prior or subsequent, tacit or explicit. That is a "conciliarist" thesis. Vatican I likewise rejects the idea of reception. Finally, there is a rejection of the democratic idea; the pope's authority does not come to him from the grass roots by delegation, but rather is an *ordinary* authority. This does not mean, however, that the pope would set himself apart from the consensus of the Church in the faith, because his charism is at the service of that consensus. Rather, it means that this consensus is not a positive act required in order to validate the pope's act. This consensus is *the very thing* that the pope expresses in the definition that he declares; one can even say that it is a prior fact that the pope's act does not so much bring about as manifest.[43] In the final analysis the most comprehensive notion is that of the *sensus fidei* (or *sensus Ecclesiae*), of which the pope is one of the organs of expression by virtue of his proper charism of personal infallibility. This *sensus* is expressed in many ways, as we have already seen.

2. The teaching of Vatican II

We have already pointed out what Vatican II assumed as far as the primacy of the pope is concerned. Similarly, Vatican II assumes the teaching of Vatican I concerning infallibility. In the latter case, the dogmatic definition is repeated literally in *Lumen gentium* 25, §3. But the context is different, as we already said, inasmuch as the developments of Vatican II incorporate the teaching of Vatican I into the teaching on the collegiality of the bishops.

The immediate context

In the case of the primacy, the immediate context is found in *Lumen gentium* 22: the college of bishops and its head. The primacy of the

---

43. See the happy formula of Newman: "It is a simple fact to say, that Catholics have not come to believe it [the doctrine of the Immaculate Conception] because it is defined, but that it was defined because they believed it"; in *Apologia pro vita sua* (New York: Longmans, Green, 1907), 281.

The Church Is Apostolic

bishop of Rome is clearly underscored, not in terms of jurisdiction, as we saw, but *always* as the head of a college. The primacy is inseparable from the college as the head is inseparable from the members. This is logically consistent, since primacy is a relative term; it is conceivable only within a group.

In the case of infallibility, the immediate context is in *Lumen gentium* 25: the teaching office of the bishops. The infallibility of *the Church* is recalled, as well as its expression by the college of bishops, and in a singular way by the pope: it is the same infallibility.

The broader context

These two dogmas are recalled in Chapter III of *Lumen gentium* on the episcopate. The pope is not cut off from the bishops, since he is *in* the college as its head. Still more broadly, when these two dogmas are incorporated into the conciliar teaching as a whole, they can acquire a new and deeper intelligibility from that whole. We have already noted this in the case of the primacy. The same goes for infallibility, it seems. This charism is not comparable to the charism of tongues or of healing.... It is a charism of a special ministry.

Western thought since the late Middle Ages has gradually concentrated on the *functioning* [*efficacité*] of one institution or another, with the well-known risk of associating too closely with juridical logic,[44] if not with legalism.... Now the sacramental approach, in general and with regard to the Church in particular, is based above all on the theological argument of *sign*. The sacrament sign designates first and foremost *the cause* (Christ), and in the second place *the effect* (the specific action of Christ). To consider only the effect is to run the risk of limiting oneself to purely functional considerations, especially of a canonical sort. Since the cause is Christ himself and the final reality (effect) is an action of Christ within the subject, we suggest speaking about the matter as follows:

- The sacramentality of the primacy makes the pope the sign-means of the constant personal presence of Christ, the one Shepherd of

---

44. Using the terminology of the speculative solution that we proposed to the question about the unity of the ecclesial being, we would say that the risk is of reducing the diaconal communion to a sort of social communion.

the flock. This is more precise than to say "vicar," which is chiefly a canonical term.
- The sacramentality of personal infallibility makes the pope the sign-means of the constant and personal presence of Christ, who is Truth (Jn 14:6).

d. The question of the supreme authority in the Church

The pope is in the college, since he is a bishop; as its head, he is the primate thereof. There is no college without a head and no head without a college. Traditionally it is said that the supreme authority in the Church belongs to the pope alone, and also to the apostolic college of which the pope is the head (*LG* 22). Hence three explanations are acceptable in theology, since Vatican II did not intend to settle the issue. Either one can say that the supreme power has two subjects that are incompletely distinct, the pope and the college,[45] or one can say that there is only one full-fledged subject, the pope, or else one can say that there are two distinct subjects, the pope and the college, the latter meaning the groups of bishops as distinct from the pope.

With the help of the notion of sacramentality, we propose saying: in the Church there is only one truly full and supreme authority, Christ in Person. Through the institution of Christ himself, this authority is exercised sacramentally in two distinct ways during the time of his physical absence from earth: either the pope alone, or the apostolic college *cum et sub Petro*. The *same authority* is engaged in either case, but in a different way. There is no distinction as to powers, since they are strictly the same, but the form of expression is different. There is the primatial manifestation and the collegial manifestation. It is true that ultimately the pope chooses which form of expression to use. He ultimately decides or approves the form in which Christ's authority will be manifested in the case of one question or another. But even in making this judgment, the pope owes it to himself to respect and therefore to honor the two forms willed by Christ; to support one exclusive-

---

45. An incomplete distinction [*distinction inadéquate*] is a distinction in which the same term is found in both parts of the distinction. For example, the distinction "body-soul," because the soul is found in the idea of body (otherwise one would have to say "corpse"). Here the pope is found in the idea of "college" because as its head he is a member thereof.

ly to the detriment of the other is not acceptable; neither in fact nor in law can the pope suppress one of them.

CONCLUSION

The Church is apostolic. This is first of all a property of her being before it describes her activity. It is important to consider this property last, not because it has any less value, but because it presupposes the other three properties. This property is, so to speak, at the confluence of the others, which call for it, establish it, and explain it. It is so important that a Christian community that has not preserved apostolic succession cannot be called "church," according to the usage of the Roman Curia.

BIBLIOGRAPHY

Apostolicity in General

Congar, Yves. "Apostolicité." In the encyclopedia *Catholicisme*, vol. 1 (1948), col. 728–30. Reprinted in the volume *Sainte Église*. Paris: 1963.

———. *L'Église est une, sainte, catholique et apostolique*. Coll. Mysterium salutis 15. Paris: 1970. Rather rapid, but very clear overview of "formal" apostolicity.

———. "Apostolicité de ministère et apostolicité de doctrine." In *Ministères et communion ecclésiale*. Paris: 1971, 51–94.

International Theological Commission. "Catholic Teaching on Apostolic Succession" (1973). In *Texts and Documents, 1969–1985*. San Francisco: Ignatius Press, 1989, 93–104. Covers the essentials. The context of this document is the need to respond to the views of Hans Küng.

Javierre Ortas, A. M. "Successione apostolica e successione primaziale." In the anthology *Il primato del vescovo di Roma nel primo millennio*. The Vatican: 1991, 53ff. An extremely penetrating study of the general notion of succession and its application to apostolic succession.

Journet, Charles. *The Church of the Word Incarnate*. New York: Sheed and Ward, 1955. Also volume 2 of the same work, *L'Église du Verbe incarné*. Paris: 1951, 678–724. The most satisfactory presentation.

Pagé, Jean-Guy. *Qui est l'Église?* Paris and Montreal: 1979, 2:181ff., with a good bibliography. A discussion of ministerial apostolicity is found in vol. 3 (Paris and Montreal, 1981), 407ff.

Various authors. *L'épiscopat et l'Église universelle*. US 39. Paris: 1962. A very rich anthology, including in particular the fine essay by Fr. Congar, "De la communion des Églises à une ecclésiologie de l'Église universelle," and the important study by O. Rousseau about Pius IX's interpretation of Roman primacy vis-à-vis the *Kulturkampf,* "La vraie valeur de l'épiscopat d'après d'importants documents de 1875," 709–36.

Concerning One Particular Question

In the early 1970s Hans Küng had suggested the idea that upon the death of the apostles they were not succeeded by bishops, but rather by "charismatic" laymen. Thus, in his view, episcopal succession came about only somewhat later and was a sign of the clericalization of the Church. (See the preceding title by the International Theological Commission.) This is a familiar binomial: charism/institution. This idea cropped up again among some exegetes. In order to establish it exegetically, one has to reject many passages in Acts (as being "inauthentic") and dismiss the letters of James, Titus, and Timothy as later writings after the apostolic age. One of the clearest authors on this subject is H. Hauser, *L'Église à l'âge apostolique* (Paris: 1996). See the essays by P. Rolland, "Le ministère pastoral, ambassade au nom du Christ," *NRTh* (1983): 161–78; *Les Ambassadeurs du Christ* (Paris: 1991); and, on the Letter of James, "La date de l'épître de Jacques," *NRTh* (1996): 839–55. As a group, these essays prepared the way for the following book by Rolland: *La Succession apostolique dans le Nouveau Testament* (Paris: 1997). On this debate see also P. Grelot, *La Tradition apostolique* (Paris: 1995), esp. Part 1. Besides the exegetical debate, it is good to be acquainted with magisterial preaching on the subject. The Apostolic Exhortation *Pastores dabo vobis* (March 25, 1992) is based on the Letters to Titus and Timothy with regard to the question of succession.

The Roman Primacy

Benoit, Pierre. "La primauté de Pierre selon le Nouveau Testament." In *Exégèse et théologie.* Paris: 1961, 2:250ff.
Brown, Raymond, ed. *Peter in the New Testament.* Minneapolis: Augsburg, 1973.
Grelot, Pierre. "L'origine de Mt 16:16–19." In *À cause de l'Évangile.* Mélanges offerts à J. Dupont. Lectio divina 123. Paris: 1983, 91–105.
―――. "Sur cette pierre je bâtirai mon Église." *NRTh* (1987): 641–59.
Refoulé, F. "La primauté de Pierre dans les Évangiles." *Revue des Sciences Religieuses* (1964): 1–41.
Rigaux, B. "Saint Peter in Contemporary Exegesis." *Concilium.* English ed. 7, no. 3 (Sept. 1967): 72–87. Nicely shows the various trends and their sometimes implicit presuppositions.
van Cangh, J.-M., and M. van Esbroeck. "La primauté de Pierre (Mt. 16:16–19) et son contexte judaïque." *Rev. de Théol. de Louvain* (1980): 310–24.

For the testimony of Tradition, the reader may consult in general the articles on "Primacy" or "The Church" in dictionaries and encyclopedias. The article "Primauté" in the encyclopedia *Catholicisme* is the most recent. The following titles indicate the classic studies on this subject.

Bevenot, M. "Episcopat et primauté chez S. Cyprien." *Eph. Théol. Lov.* (1966): 176–95.

Bodin, Y. S. *Jérôme et l'Église*. Paris: 1966.
Bonino, Serge-Thomas. "La place du pape dans l'Église selon S. Thomas d'Aquin." *RT* (1986): 392–421.
Camelot, Pierre-Thomas. "Saint Cyprien et la primauté." *Istina* (1957): 421–34.
Falbo, G. *Il primato della chiesa di Roma alla luce dei primi quattro secoli*. Rome: 1989.
Journet, Charles. *The Church of the Word Incarnate*, 387ff. The most thorough and rigorous treatment. Needs to be supplemented by the contribution of Vatican II.
La Bonnardière, A.-M. "*Tu es Petrus:* La péricope de Mt 16:13–23 dans l'oeuvre de S. Augustin." *Irénikon* (1961): 451–99.
Maccarrone, M. *Vicarius Christi: Storia del titolo papale*. Rome: 1952.
Maccarrone, M., et al. *Il Primato del vescovo di Roma nel primo millennio*. Vatican City: 1991. Anthology containing several excellent essays, esp. R. Minnerath, "La position de l'Église de Rome aux trois premiers siècles," 139ff.; V. Saxer, "Autonomie africaine et primauté romaine de Tertullien à Augustin," 173ff.; D. Stiernon, "Interprétations, résistances et oppositions en Orient," 661ff.
Minnerath, R. *De Jérusalem à Rome: Pierre et l'unité de l'Église apostolique*. Théologie historique 101. Paris: 1994. A painstaking historical perspective. Abundant source material from the earliest patristic period.
Pagé, Jean-Guy. *Qui est l'Église?* Montreal and Paris: 1981, 3:475ff. with the main bibliography.
Various authors. *Visages de l'Église*. Fribourg: 1989. In particular the essay by Jean-Pierre Torrell, "L'ecclésiologie de Vatican I," 25–40. Clear and rigorous presentation of the papal prerogatives (primacy of jurisdiction and infallibility); with bibliography, 46–47.

Ecumenical Perspectives

Cullman, Oscar. *Peter*. Philadelphia: Westminster Press, 1962. Important book (original French edition, 1952) that marked the beginning of a reexamination by Protestants of their traditional theses. See the review by Pierre Benoit in *Revue Biblique* (1953): 565–79, which surveys the whole exegetical dialogue with Protestant Christians to that date.
Dejaifvre, Georges. "La papauté, problème oecuménique." *NRTh* (1980): 235–47.
Journet, Charles. *La Primauté de Pierre dans la perspective protestante et dans la perspective catholique*. Paris: 1953. A study published as a response to O. Cullman (preceding title). Outdated from a strictly ecumenical perspective, but useful for a basic understanding of the two approaches.
Lutheran-Catholic Dialogue (USA). *Differing Attitudes Toward Papal Primacy*. Round V, 1973. Copy online at http://usccb.org.
von Allmen, J.-J. *La Primauté de Pierre et de Paul: Remarques d'un protestant*. Fribourg and Paris: 1977. Good review in *Istina* (1980): 365–87.
Various authors. *Petrine Ministry and the Unity of the Church: "Toward a Patient and Fraternal Dialogue."* Acts of the Symposium celebrating the 100th anniversary of the foundation of the Society of the Atonement, Rome, December 4–6,

1997. Collegeville: Minn.: Liturgical Press, 1997. Contributions from authors of different denominations; generally good studies; note in particular the one by G. Zizioulas, "Primacy in the Church: An Orthodox Approach," and the one by Nicolas Lossky, "Conciliarity-Primacy in a Russian Orthodox Perspective," which help the reader to appreciate correctly the present-day Orthodox attitude.

Magisterium

Congregation for the Doctrine of the Faith. *The Primacy of the Successor of Peter in the Mystery of the Church* (October 1998). *L'Osservatore Romano*, weekly edition in English (November 18, 1998): 5–6. Should be read so as to be able to distinguish between what is *de fide* and what remains a matter for theological speculation.

17

The Question of the Church's Indefectibility

We will limit ourselves here to a simple explanatory note.
Indefectibility is not mentioned in the Creed. Is it a distinct property to be counted along with the other four? The Catholic and Orthodox answer has always been clear: indefectibility should not be counted along with the four properties, but rather qualifies them all. The Church is indefectibly one, indefectibly holy, indefectibly catholic, and indefectibly apostolic. Just as the Church is at the same time human and "divine," visible and invisible with regard to each of the four properties, so too she is indefectible with regard to these four properties. This is why—despite the divisions, the sins in (and not of) the Church, the limits of her quantitative universality, and the unpredictable quality of the successors of the apostles—indefectibility was never added as the fifth property. This is her constant teaching, whereby indefectibility implies continuity in time, based on her infallibility on the doctrinal level and the continual celebration of her authentic sacraments.

Karl Barth proposed a different understanding of indefectibility that would justify making it a fifth property.[1] He maintains that the Church can fall, but that she has the assurance that Christ will lift her

1. For a discussion of Barth's *discontinuity*, see Charles Journet, *L'Église du Verbe incarné*, 2:1143ff.; see general bibliography.

up again each time. In this case, unity, holiness, catholicity, and apostolicity might be lacking in some moments of crisis, but those crises would always be of limited duration and would be overcome. The objection to this thesis is that this would not be indefectibility strictly speaking, because of the lack of one and the same being. There would be a rupture between the Church before the fall and the restored Church, so that the new Church could not be called *the same Church* as the old one. At best it would be *similar*.

The continuity of apostolic succession, as history displays it, as theology understands it, and as dogma affirms it, is the *sign* of this unicity of the Church and the proximate foundation of the Church's indefectibility in the Catholic and Orthodox sense. But we have already seen it manifest itself with each of the properties. Unity is a sort of indefectibility pertaining to the fact that the principle of the Church's unity is divine—the Holy Spirit by appropriation—and, therefore, beyond the power of human beings to impair. Holiness is a sort of indefectibility, the permanence of the *sancta* [holy things]. Qualitative catholicity is indefectible for the same reason as holiness. What is defectible *in* the Church is the life of the theological virtues led by her members. Here, indeed, we observe that one and the same subject can, because of his sins, break away from the Church, in her three aspects (social, diaconal, theological), then be readmitted through Christ's faithful mercy. Considered individually, there is indeed a subject whose fidelity is inconstant, but this characteristic of each member of the community cannot be transposed and attributed to the community as such. And this leads us again to the mystery of the personality of the Church.

General Conclusion

We have just completed a dogmatic course. To conclude, it is advisable to draw attention to the fact that this discipline is in a curious situation today. After having been one of the major themes of the twentieth-century theological renewal, after having been the central theme of Vatican II, after having been at the center of many impassioned debates during the post-conciliar era, this part of dogmatic theology has been at a sort of low ebb for some thirty years. By way of example, we can observe that in most Western teaching centers, the treatise *De Ecclesia* is no longer one of the four major dogmatic treatises that once used to structure the four years leading to a licentiate in theology. That situation, however, was a recent conquest, for the inclusion of the treatise on the Church in dogmatic theology had been one of the great successes of the contemporary renewal in theology. Formerly the Church had been treated either from a canonical perspective—the famous "hierarchology"—or else as part of apologetics. Today the ecclesial mystery is most often the object of a one-semester course for two credit hours, whereas it used to rank as a year-long course for three to four credits. To this demotion is added a shift of interest: often the Church is no longer studied for her own sake, but is first of all enlisted within the framework of the theology of interreligious dialogue. Now practically all the statements enhancing the value of non-Christian communities and arguing for the salvation of their members are based on the idea that these communities and these persons are outside the Church. The last reference work on the saying "No salvation outside the Church"[1] is significant in this respect.

1. Bernard Sesboüé, *Hors de l'Église pas de salut: Histoire d'une formule et problèmes d'interprétation* (Paris: 2004).

The Church is studied in order to see how she is no longer central; other themes replace her, such as the Kingdom or even the World. This paradigm shift can have weighty consequences, the chief of which is that it tends toward a veritable break with Tradition. We must not underestimate the danger that this situation poses for the future of ecumenism, especially with the Orthodox Churches. The development in their understanding of the faith is perhaps not as "bold" as the progress made by the Catholic Church, but they do have a profound and decisive comprehension of the unity and continuity of Tradition, which seems to us to be weakened in many theological propositions made by some Catholics.

In the course in ecclesiology that we have presented, our intention has been to bear witness to the fact that being strongly rooted in the doctrinal heritage already possessed by the Christian community is no obstacle to the developments that are needed in every era if Tradition is to stay alive. It is, on the contrary, the first prerequisite for a correct development, because it guarantees the fidelity thereof. It goes without saying that we do not claim to have provided a definitive answer to every question that was treated; we only hope to collaborate in the research that a magisterial teaching will be able to rely on [*assumer*] when it deems it sufficiently mature. This maturity plainly has not yet been achieved. The clearest sign of this, in our opinion, is the absence of an encyclical on the mystery of the Church in the nonetheless vast magisterial production that followed the Council, and despite the urgency of a unified teaching, which the Roman Synod, convened for the twentieth anniversary of Vatican II, noted. To put it without any particular stylistic precautions: today we have a major and pressing need for a definition concerning the mystery of the Church similar to the one that the Council of Chalcedon (431) expounded concerning the mystery of Christ. Our faith in the "physical" Christ now urgently requires a similar light on the "mystical" Christ. If this need is real, and we are convinced that it is, then one can fearlessly declare that the Lord will certainly attend to it. We only hope that the prayers of the humble and little ones who support the work of scholars might hasten the day when this gift is granted and might facilitate the fruitful reception thereof.

Priory of St. Albert the Great
Fribourg, Switzerland
Pentecost 2006

General Bibliography

We mention here only general works for beginners in theology. The bibliography referring to particular questions is listed at the end of each chapter.

DICTIONARIES

Dictionary articles are invaluable when beginning to study a question. Generally they give a good foundation in positive theology and present the positions of the various Schools. Moreover, they provide an initial bibliography on the subject. Many articles, however, are old (sometimes very old: the article "Église" in the *Dictionnaire de théologie catholique* is from 1911!), and hence dependent on outdated theology. This is quite clear in the case of ecclesiology, which underwent a thoroughgoing renewal starting in 1920. These articles therefore should not be read uncritically. Among the principal works we can cite:

Catholicisme: Hier, aujourd'hui, demain: Encyclopédie. Edited by G. Jacquemet, G. Mathon et al. 15 vols. Paris: Letouzey et Ané, 1948–2000. The purpose of this encyclopedia, which was compiled right after World War II, was to offer articles on subjects treated insufficiently or not at all in the existing dictionaries. The contributions related to ecclesiology are generally good and recent (particularly the article "Primauté" from 1988).

Dictionnaire apologétique de la foi catholique. 4th ed. Edited by A. d'Alès. Paris: Beauchesne, 1922. This is the oldest reference work. Generally very erudite (especially on historical matters), but rather outmoded in exegesis and theology.

Dictionnaire de théologie catholique (*DTC*). Edited by Alfred Vacant, E. Mangenot, and Emile Amann. 15 vols. Paris: Letouzey et Ané, 1903–50. Generally of good quality. The initial volumes are as old as the *Dictionnaire apologétique* and have likewise decreased in value. The more recent volumes are useful to consult.

Theological Dictionary of the New Testament (*TDNT*). Edited by Gerhard Kittel. Translated by Geoffrey W. Bromiley. 10 vols. Grand Rapids, Mich.: Eerdmans, 1964–76. The original edition was edited by a Protestant theologian. Includes an excellent article, "*Ekklēsia*," written by Karl Ludwig Schmidt (found in 3:501–36).

Vocabulaire de théologie biblique. Edited by Xavier Léon-Dufour. 5th ed. Paris: Cerf, 1981. The 2nd edition was translated under the direction of P. Joseph Cahill and E. M. Stewart as *Dictionary of Biblical Theology* (New York: Seabury Press, 1973). The reader should attempt to use the 1981 French edition, which has a wealth of material that does not appear in the preceding editions. A serious work capable of providing a good basis in positive theology.

BIBLICAL THEOLOGY

Cerfaux, Lucien. *La Théologie de l'Église suivant saint Paul.* 2nd ed. Paris: Cerf, 1965. This book has gone through two editions (the first was in 1948); the second is greatly expanded. The first edition was translated by Geoffrey Webb and Adrian Walker as *The Church in the Theology of Saint Paul* (New York: Herder, 1959).

Guillet, Jacques. *Entre Jésus et l'Église.* Paris: Éd. du Seuil, 1985. The exegetical findings of this study are interesting. The work attempts to answer a modern question in ecclesiology: What is the connection between Jesus and the community that succeeds him?

Schnackenburg, Rudolf. *The Church in the New Testament.* Translated by W. J. O'Hara. New York: Herder and Herder, 1965. A study that is still a good reference work.

PATRISTIC THEOLOGY

Bardy, Gustave. *La Théologie de l'Église de saint Clément à saint Irénée.* Paris: Cerf, 1945.

———. *La Théologie de l'Église de saint Irénée au concile di Nicée.* Paris: Cerf, 1947. Serious scholarly work, still important.

Kelly, J. N. D. *Early Christian Doctrines.* 5th ed. San Francisco: Harper, 1978. Good bibliography.

Mersch, Émile. *Le Corps mystique du Christ.* 2nd ed. 2 vols. Paris: Desclée de Brouwer, 1936. A classic that is remarkable for the breadth of its patristic research. The author's *speculative* presuppositions are debatable, but the *positive* basis is excellent. Not to be confused with another volume: *La Théologie du Corps mystique.* Paris: Desclée de Brouwer, 1953, a posthumous work that is not as interesting; translated by Cyril Vollert as *The Theology of the Mystical Body* (St. Louis: Herder, 1951).

ST. THOMAS AQUINAS

Because there is no ecclesiology, in the modern sense, in the works of St. Thomas, we have no overall scholarly studies. The presentation of Émile Mersch (*Le Corps mystique du Christ*, vol. 2) is good in reference to the doctrine of the Mystical Body (based on *ST* III, q. 8); see also Jérôme Hamer, *The Church Is a Communion* (New York: Sheed and Ward, 1965).

General Bibliography 631

TREATISES ON THE CHURCH

These works deal with the demands of positive and speculative theology with varying success. The main works by French-speaking authors are:

Bouyer, Louis. *L'Église de Dieu.* Paris: Cerf, 1970. First American edition: *The Church of God.* Chicago: Franciscan Herald Press, 1982. Reprint, San Francisco: Ignatius Press, 2011. A solid, erudite work.

Journet, Charles. *L'Église du Verbe incarné.* 3 vols. Paris: Desclée de Brouwer, 1943, 1951, and 1969. Republished in five volumes: Saint-Maurice (Switzerland): Éditions Saint-Augustin, 1998–2005. Partial English edition: *The Theology of the Church.* Translated by Victor Szczurek, O. Praem. San Francisco: Ignatius Press, 2004. Journet's work is the most important modern study. The positive research is very wide-ranging, and the speculative development is powerful. Since Vatican II these three big volumes can no longer be considered an adequate treatise, because parts of it are dated. But the reader will always profit from consulting the wealth of material in this work concerning one or another particular question.

Pagé, Jean-Guy. *Qui est l'Église?* 3 vols. Montreal: Les Éds. Bellarmin, 1977–79. To our knowledge this is the only recent ecclesiological summa. A work of considerable breadth, conducted with rigor and precision. The speculative development is, to our way of thinking, insufficient, but it has a good selected bibliography. Worth consulting.

Nicolas, Jean-Hervé. *Synthèse dogmatique.* Fribourg: Éditions Universitaires Fribourg Suisse, 1985. See especially 531–790 for ecclesiology. The study of positive theology is broad and well-structured; the speculative evaluation is incisive. Worth consulting.

HISTORY OF ECCLESIOLOGY

Congar, Yves. *L'Église: De saint Augustin à l'époque moderne.* Paris: Cerf, 1970. A very important study, with an extensive bibliography. Unfortunately it treats the contemporary era too rapidly. Worth reading.

Jaki, Stanley. *Les tendances nouvelles de l'ecclésiologie.* Rome: Herder, 1957. A survey of the major speculative themes running through the twentieth-century ecclesiological renewal.

Menard, Étienne. *L'Ecclésiologie hier et aujourd'hui.* Paris: Desclée de Brouwer, 1966. A well-written little book that nicely complements Congar for the contemporary period.

GENERAL WORKS ON VATICAN II

Baraúna, Guilherme, and Yves Congar. *L'Église de Vatican II.* US 51a–c. Paris: Cerf, 1966. A collection of very valuable essays on *Lumen gentium.*

Philips, Gérard. *L'Église en son mystère au IIe concile du Vatican.* 2 vols. Paris: Desclée, 1967–68. Commentary on *Lumen gentium* by its principal author. A precise, easy-to-read presentation. A reference work. But caution: the whole ecclesiology of Vatican II is not found in *Lumen gentium.*

Index of Names

Acerbi, A., 452n18
Aesop, 69–70
Albert the Great, St., 299
Ambrose, St., 221n34, 257, 298, 307, 368n13, 555n1, 610
Anselm, St., 6, 100
Aquinas. *See* Thomas Aquinas, St.
Aristotle, 99, 227–28, 232, 237, 239, 395, 414, 426, 464, 563
Athanasius, St., 84–86, 90, 96, 603, 606
Augustine, St., 6, 92–95, 101n68, 107n76, 116, 168–70, 175, 219, 220–21, 225, 249, 256, 258, 290, 294, 298, 299n17, 307–8, 312, 362, 365, 368n13, 372–73, 384, 535

Bacon, R., 312n43
Barnabas, St. (Letter of), 218
Basil of Caesarea, St., 165–66, 219, 606
Batiffol, P., 353
Benedict XV, 520, 529
Berengar of Tours, 64
Billot, L., 371
Billuart, R., 34, 370
Boethius, 502
Boniface II, 598n18
Boniface VIII, 15, 28, 258n110
Bossuet, J.-B., 361
Bultmann, R., 328n79, 568n11

Cajetan (Thomas de Vio), 182–84, 612
Calvin, J., 30, 102, 312, 359, 360, 365, 541
Campbell, J. A., 453n20
Cerfaux, L., 353
Clement of Alexandria, St., 82, 159–60, 257
Clement of Rome, St., 28, 80, 158–59
Congar, Y., 15, 153–54, 235, 242n67, 274–75, 316, 376n32, 380n40, 410–11, 412n4, 450, 451, 530, 531, 532, 539–40, 605–6
Couturier, P., 521
Cyprian, St., 86–87, 162n40, 188, 256, 307, 460, 532, 535, 606, 607

Daguet, Fr., 108n77
De Groot, V., 370–71
De Lubac, H., xxvi, 17, 63–64, 322n71
De Sales, F., St., 361
Duns Scotus, 109

Emery, G., 301
Epiphanius of Salamis, St., 351
Eusebius of Caesarea, St., 220

Feeney, L., 263

Gouyau, Ch., 324n75
Guardini, R., 35

Not included in this index are the names of authors cited in the chapter bibliographies or, generally, in the footnotes.

Harnack, A. von, 353
Harpagon, 141
Hegel, Fr., 420–22, 430
Hertling, L., 604, 607
Hilary, St., 79, 87–88, 89, 90, 96, 221, 307
Hippolytus of Rome, St., 162–63
Hugh of St. Victor, 373
Huss, J., 34

Ignatius of Antioch, St., 80–81, 87, 255, 294n7, 455, 534, 563, 596, 602–3, 606
Innocent III, 440n6
Innocent IV, 15
Irenaeus, St., 79, 82–84, 146, 161, 218, 219n29, 255, 373, 455–57, 593, 595n9, 603, 605, 606, 610

Jerome, St., 256, 349
Joachim of Fiore, 143–44
John Chrysostom, St., 89, 100, 166–68, 220, 221, 224, 258, 307n30, 606
John XXIII, St., 520, 530
John Paul II, St., 55–56, 129n100, 130, 476n62, 579, 581
Journet, Ch., xxviii, 128, 182, 269n119, 270, 373, 385, 444n9, 450, 516, 540, 561n9, Justin, St., 257

Kant, E., 420–21, 430

La Potterie, I. de, 274
Labourdette, M.-M., xxviii
Lactantius, 256
Lanfranc of Caen, 64
Legrand, H., 586n37
Leo the Great, St., 219, 603, 606, 610
Leo XIII, 32, 112, 120–21, 186, 235, 380, 393, 412n4, 520
Leroy, M.-V., xxviii
Leuba, J.-L., 385
Loisy, A., 49
Luther, M., 30–31, 57n25, 312, 359–60, 365, 539–40, 543, 550, 560, 598n18

Maritain, J., 250, 261n114, 264–65
Maurras, Ch., 304n24
Menenius Agrippa, 69–70

Mersch, E., 374, 411, 412n5
Michelin, E., 424
Möhler, J.-A., 35–36, 39, 185, 377, 416–17, 418, 419–20
Molière, J.-B., 141
Mounier, E., 236, 238n65

Newman, J. H., 312n46, 526, 618n43

Occam, W. of, 312n42
Origen, 160–61, 256, 532, 607

Passaglia, Ch., 36
Pastor of Hermas. See Shepherd of Hermas
Paul, St., 2, 13, 16, 27, 35n23, 36–37, 48, 50n11, 50n13, 61, 64, 65–78, 81, 82, 88, 89, 91, 93–94, 97, 99, 101, 105, 109, 110, 111–12, 117, 122, 148, 149, 151–57, 165–67, 174, 175, 178, 203, 215, 218, 221n34, 254, 258, 290, 293–94, 305–8, 328, 351–54, 374, 416, 452–54, 459, 472, 508n4, 509, 533n26, 534, 592, 603
Paul VI, 33, 242, 558
Paulus, St., 583
Perrone, J., 34, 370
Philip, St., 151
Philip IV, 15, 28
Pius IX, Bl., 259–60, 267, 608, 613
Pius X, St., 520
Pius XI, 268n118, 520, 529
Pius XII, Ven., 8, 31, 118, 121, 124n93, 186, 260, 380n40, 393, 394, 520, 531, 574
Polycarp, St., 80, 455, 606

Rademacher, A., 417
Rahner, K., 317, 376
Robert Bellarmine, St., 31, 34, 116, 184–85, 361–64, 366–76, 380, 384, 385, 407, 409, 411, 413, 430
Rousseau, J.-J., 239

Scheeben, M. J., 185, 313–14, 315
Scheler, M., 236
Schillebeeckx, Ed., 318, 323, 443
Schnackenburg, R., 148
Schrader, Kl., 36

Index of Names

Scotus. *See* Duns Scotus
Seeseman, H., 453n20
Sesboüé, B., 254n94
Shepherd of Hermas, 23n16, 80, 146
Suarez, Fr., 34

Tertullian, 163–65, 219, 307n32, 310, 458n35, 460, 584n35, 593, 605
Thérèse of the Child Jesus, St., 14, 558
Thomas Aquinas, St., xxiv, xxvi–xxvii, 10, 12, 13, 14, 21, 34, 96, 98–100, 102–3, 105, 107, 108n77, 109–11, 119, 131n104, 173, 175–77, 179n81, 180–81, 185, 186, 200n2, 222–23, 225–34, 237, 239, 242n67, 258, 265, 295, 299, 301, 309–12, 316–17, 361, 365–66, 395–99, 401, 404n15, 407, 414, 450, 459n44, 464, 483, 502, 533n26, 535, 601n23
Tillard, J.-M. R., 577
Torrell, J.-P., xxviii

Viterbo, J. of, 16

Wycliffe, J., 34

Subject Index

ages of salvation, 107–10, 131, 143–45, 150–51, 199–200, 212–13, 216, 252, 403–5
angels, 108–10
Anglicanism, 519, 525–26, 531, 537
apostasy, 13
apostles, 591–93
apostolic college. *See* collegiality
apostolic succession, 83, 587, 594–96
apostolicity, of the Church, 484–85, 515–17, 590–621
appropriation, 141–43, 188, 193

baptism, 13, 45, 68, 71, 78, 95, 96, 126, 156, 257, 264–66, 267–68, 271–72, 407, 489
"binomial thinking," 376–79, 409–25, 434, 490
bishop of Rome. *See* papacy
bishops, 80–81, 86, 587, 594–99, 612–13
Body of Christ, 61–133, 491; in the Church Fathers, 78–96; in Pius XII, 118–22; in St. Paul, 65–78; in St. Thomas Aquinas, 96–111; in Vatican I, 36, 112–17; in Vatican II, 122–31
Bride of Christ, 48, 75–77
building, the Church as, 47–48

Calvinism, 360–61, 524, 541
capital grace. *See* Jesus Christ

catholicity, of the Church, 29, 354–55, 478–79, 515–17, 563–88
charism(s), 14, 66, 69–70, 71, 73, 156
charity, virtue of, 14, 36, 81, 464–65, 534–36
Christ. *See* Jesus Christ
citizenship, 217, 246
clergy, 268–78. *See also* bishops; deacons; priests
collegiality, 587, 596–99
communion: Church as, 33, 355, 376, 382–83, 430–31, 434, 438, 443–45, 451–91, 582–83; diaconal, 469, 482–90, 614; of saints, 446, 556–58; social, 468–69, 474–82, 614; of the theological virtues, 468–73, 614
controversy, theological, 549
council and conciliarism, 29, 576–77, 598–99
Counter-Reformation, 30–31, 33–35, 361–64
creed, 296–301
conferences of bishops, national, 598–99
covenant, 207–8, 212

De Ecclesia, as separate treatise of theology, 13–19, 33–35, 627
deacons, 81, 126

Not included in this index are the author's *excursus* and remarks in the chapter bibliographies.

development of dogma, 550–51
dialectic, 425–28
dialogue, theological, 549–50
Didache, 80, 294n7
dissidence, 536–38, 539–41
Dominus Iesus (declaration of the Congregation of the Doctrine of the Faith), 55, 56–57
Donatism, 92–93

Eastern Orthodox Churches. *See* Orthodox Churches
Ecclesia ab Abel, 37, 200, 403, 471
ecumenical movement, history of, 526–32
ecumenism, 128–29, 518–51, 628. *See also* pluralism, religious
Ekklēsia, 147, 211, 345, 349–55
election, 207, 210–11, 212
episcopacy. *See* bishops
eschatology, 12, 18, 51–52, 53–54, 56, 58, 108, 150, 213
Eucharist, 13, 64–65, 68, 71, 78, 79, 80, 81, 86, 89, 90–91, 95, 96, 104–5, 132–33, 156, 191–93, 271–72, 440–42, 459, 487
evangelical counsels. *See* religious profession
excommunication, 536

faith, virtue of, 4–7, 10–11, 13, 19, 26–27, 73, 96, 257, 261–66, 296–301, 339–42, 458, 533–34, 535, 545–47, 593
family, the Church as, 48
Febronianism, 577, 609
field, the Church as, 47
flock, the Church as, 47

Gallicanism, 577, 609, 618
Gaudium et spes, 240–41
grace, 14, 75, 77–78, 94, 117, 177–78, 181, 182, 364, 395–400, 424–25, 473–74

heresy, 13, 533–34, 535, 536–38
hierarchy: Church, 14, 24, 107, 268–71, 484; of truths, 542–48
history, 414
holiness, of the Church, 130–31, 324–25, 448, 515–17, 555–62

holy orders, sacrament of, 126, 271–72, 275–78, 406–7
Holy Spirit, 80, 84, 119–20, 140–41, 145–46, 153–55, 157–58, 173–75. *See also* Temple of the Spirit

inculturation, 567–75
indefectibility, 515, 625–26
infallibility, 499, 615–20
interreligious dialogue, 54n18, 250–51, 267, 518
invisible church, Protestant notion of, 30, 359–64
invisibility, of the church, 120–21, 160, 184–85, 249, 370–72, 391–92. *See also* visibility, of the Church

Jesus Christ: capital grace of, 14, 71–75, 78, 82, 94, 96, 98–102, 106, 109–10, 111, 176–77, 222, 401–2, 517; humanity as instrument of the divinity, 24, 62n2, 82, 87, 90, 103–5, 123; hypostatic union, 96, 98, 101–2, 516–17; personal grace of, 98, 99, 101–2, 517
Judaism, 26, 243–45, 250–51, 267
judgment, theological, 548
jurisdiction, 610–13

kingship, 208–9, 214–16, 220, 221
Kingdom of God, 49–59; in the New Testament, 50–51, 52–53; in the Old Testament, 51–52
kingdom of heaven, 49, 52n14. *See also* Kingdom of God
koinōnia, 452–62

laos, 201–3, 219
laity, 268–78
law, 395–99, 476–77
local church, 29, 354–55, 478–79, 575–87. *See also* inculturation
Lumen gentium, 46, 53–54, 62–63, 122–31, 187–91, 200–201, 242–52, 319–27, 538
Lutheranism, 57n25, 359–61, 524, 539–40, 560–61

Subject Index 639

magisterium, 31
marriage, 76
Mary, Blessed Virgin, 8, 18, 79
"means of grace" (aspect of the Church), 122. *See also* "reality of grace"
ministers, 106–7, 221, 269, 406–7
munera, tria, 14, 208–9, 214–16, 220, 277, 485, 611, 612, 613
mystery, 13, 18–19, 59, 291–330, 394–95
Mystical Body, 64–65, 118–20, 374–75, 381–82. *See also* Body of Christ
Mystici Corporis Christi (encyclical of Pius XII), 35, 118–22, 260–61, 413

nature, 424–25, 567–69
"No salvation outside the Church," 54, 253–68, 627

Orthodox Churches, 29, 128, 519, 522–24, 529, 537, 550–51, 593–94, 603–4

papacy, 14, 28–29, 520, 535, 602–21
Pelagianism, 92, 93–94
"Pentecosts," 149–52
People of God, 62–63, 199–278, 491; in the modern period, 37, 225–42; in Scripture, 48, 201–17; in St. Thomas Aquinas, 225–26; in Tradition, 217–25; in Vatican II, 4, 242–52
personality, of the Church, 346, 507–10
personhood, 499–503, 504–7
Peter, St., 599–602, 609
philosophy of knowledge, 420–22
philosophy of "life," 414–20
plērōma, 73–75
pluralism, religious, 54–58. *See also* interreligious dialogue
pneumatological ecclesiology, 189–91, 193
pope. *See* papacy
priests, 208–9, 214–16, 220, 223–24, 246, 271–72, 275–78
properties of the Church, 19, 40, 515–17
prophecy and prophets, 208–9, 214–16, 220
Protestant ecclesiology, 57n25, 111–12, 359–64, 519

"reality of grace" (aspect of the Church), 122. *See also* "means of grace" (aspect of the Church)
recapitulation, 72–73, 82–83, 109
religious life, 275–78
Reformation, Protestant, 30, 57n25, 524–25, 539–40
Revelation, 7–8, 591
Roman College (Jesuit school of ecclesiology), 36, 112
Roman Catholic Church (as particular church), 586, 602–3, 606

sacrament, Church as, 33, 39, 307–30, 376, 383–84, 438–40, 442–51, 468–91, 582–83
sacraments, 13, 17–18, 45, 77, 82, 92, 105, 106, 307–30, 438–39, 459, 487, 556–58, 564–65, 574
schism, 14, 534–38
Scripture, 7, 21–22, 591
sensus fidei, 486–87, 488, 489, 499, 617–18
shepherd, 47
sin and sinfulness, 93–94, 130–31, 324–25, 559–61
society, 15, 36, 115, 216, 225–42, 366–67, 376, 382–83, 411–13, 430–31, 434, 504–7
subsistit in, 57n23, 123–29
synod of bishops. *See* council and conciliarism

Temple of the Spirit, 62–63, 140–94
Temple of the Spirit: anthropological basis, 171–73, 175–77, 181–82; in the Church Fathers, 157–75; in the Counter-Reformation, 184–85; in the modern period, 185–87; in Scripture, 48, 146–57; in St. Thomas Aquinas, 175–84; in Vatican II, 187–91
theological virtues, 469–73
Tradition, 7, 490, 591
Tübingen, School of, 35–36, 112, 416–19

unicity of the Church, 20–25, 123–29
unity of the Church, 86–87, 122–23, 182–84, 515–51
universal Church. *See* catholicity, of the Church; local church

Vatican Council I, 32, 36, 112–17, 380–81, 543, 608–13, 616–18
Vatican Council II, 33, 38–39, 122–31, 187–91, 242–52, 266–68, 319–27, 384–86, 390–92, 423–24, 460–62, 538, 613, 618–20. *See also Gaudium et spes*; *Lumen gentium*
vestigia Ecclesiae, 541–42

visibility, of the Church, 57, 120–21, 184–85, 249, 359–64, 367–72, 390–407, 481, 491. *See also* invisibility, of the Church
vocation, 207, 212

World Council of Churches, 519, 528–29, 531, 541–42

Introduction to the Mystery of the Church was designed in Arno and composed by
Kachergis Book Design of Pittsboro, North Carolina. It was printed on 50-pound
House Natural Smooth and bound by Sheridan Books of Ann Arbor, Michigan.

www.ingramcontent.com/pod-product-compliance
Lightning Source LLC
Chambersburg PA
CBHW032020290426
44110CB00012B/610